CONSUMER
BEHAVIOUR

ASKHAM BRYAN COLLEGE

YORK

JIM BLYTHE

CONSUMER
BEHAVIOUR

2nd
EDITION

SAGE

Los Angeles | London | New Delhi
Singapore | Washington DC

Los Angeles | London | New Delhi
Singapore | Washington DC

SAGE Publications Ltd
1 Oliver's Yard
55 City Road
London EC1Y 1SP

SAGE Publications Inc.
2455 Teller Road
Thousand Oaks, California 91320

SAGE Publications India Pvt Ltd
B 1/I 1 Mohan Cooperative Industrial Area
Mathura Road
New Delhi 110 044

SAGE Publications Asia-Pacific Pte Ltd
3 Church Street
#10-04 Samsung Hub
Singapore 049483

Editor: Matthew Waters
Development editor: Amy Jarrold
Editorial assistant: Nina Smith
Production editor: Nicola Marshall
Copyeditor: Elaine Leek
Proofreader: Sharon Cawood
Digital content assistant: Tanushri Shukla
Indexer: Martin Hargreaves
Marketing manager: Alison Borg
Cover design: Francis Kenney
Typeset by: C&M Digitals (P) Ltd, Chennai, India
Printed and bound in Great Britain by Ashford
Colour Press Ltd

Library of Congress Control Number: 2012947425

British Library Cataloguing in Publication data

A catalogue record for this book is available from
the British Library

ISBN 978-1-4462-6644-1
ISBN 978-1-4462-6645-8 (pbk)

Brief contents

Contents

Part One
Introduction to consumer behaviour

1 The importance of understanding consumer behaviour

Part Two
Psychological issues in consumer behaviour

2 Drive, motivation and hedonism

3 Goals, risk and uncertainty

4 Personality and self-concept

5 Perception

Part Three

Sociological issues in consumer behaviour

Part Four

Decisions and their aftermath

List of figures

List of tables

About the author

Jim Blythe has been a Merchant Navy officer, a ladies' hairdresser, a business consultant, a rock musician, a truck driver, a company director, and an award-winning playwright before becoming an academic – he always planned on having a varied life, and likes learning new skills. Currently he is trying to learn to grow vegetables, with limited success, but he has a pilot's licence and has learned to play drums in a samba band, so the beat goes on. His next venture is to study for a degree in modern languages – having left school at 16 he thinks it's time to get the education he missed out on.

Jim has written 18 books and over 50 journal articles and has contributed chapters to eight other books. He has also written open-learning packs for international training organisations, has been a senior examiner for the Chartered Institute of Marketing, holds four real degrees and one fake one, and therefore feels somewhat irritated that he is mainly known for winning the Cardiff heat of Come Dine With Me. Perhaps this latest edition of *Consumer Behaviour* will redress the balance a bit.

Acknowledgements

The publishers would like to extend their warmest thanks to the following individuals for their invaluable feedback on the first edition and the shaping of the second edition.

Dr Andreas B. Eisingerich, Imperial College Business School
Dr Kathy Hamilton, University of Strathclyde, Glasgow
Dr Kemefasu Ifie, Swansea University
Dr Ruth Marciniak, Glasgow Caledonian University, London
Julie McKeown, Aberystwyth University
Susan Moulding, Manchester Metropolitan University
Zubin Sethna, University of Bedfordshire Business School
Dr Jaywant Singh, Kingston Business School
Dr Helen Watts, University of Worcester

Preface to the
second edition

All of us consume, even those who lead a relatively monastic existence: this is what makes the study of consumer behaviour so interesting. For marketers, consumer behaviour goes to the heart of the marketing concept. Without customers, there is no business, and since everything is driven by the ultimate consumers their needs and wants become paramount. Perhaps more importantly, people have needs and wants for which businesses can supply solutions – business can be seen as the system by which we, as a species, divide up the tasks which need to be done and the wealth which we create.

This edition has been some time in the making, and has been completely revised from the first edition almost to the extent of being an entirely new book. This is not so much because there has been anything wildly different in the way people behave, but rather because there are new emphases and insights in the literature. Given that consumer behaviour is not only a core aspect of marketing (and therefore business) but is also really interesting to study, there has been a great deal written on the subject. There are many academic journals to trawl through, and even more books, ranging from texts such as this one through to detailed academic tomes on single areas of behaviour. Academic disciplines other than marketing have made tremendous contributions – psychology, sociology, economics and anthropology form the scientific base on which consumer behaviour stands as an academic subject. I have tried, in this book, to provide a concise and fairly comprehensive overview of the main aspects of consumer behaviour, but inevitably there are omissions, so at the end of each chapter I have offered some further reading if there is some aspect you find particularly fascinating.

No book is the creation of one person. I would like to thank Jennifer Pegg, who commissioned the first edition and started the whole thing rolling, plus Matt Waters, Amy Jarrold and Mark Kavanagh at SAGE who are responsible for this edition. My wife, Sue, provided many of the examples I have used (not always deliberately) and colleagues at University of Glamorgan, Westminster Business School and Plymouth Business School all helped in clarifying my thinking. Perhaps most importantly, my students should be thanked for making me think: some by asking me awkward questions, some by handing in thought-provoking coursework, some by making me laugh, and some by needing a deeper explanation than I was really ready to give. Any errors, omissions and misconceptions are of course my own.

Jim Blythe
The Alpujarras

Guided Tour

Learning objectives Highlights everything you should know or understand by the end of the chapter.

Case study An up-to-date example to get you thinking about what will be covered in this chapter.

How to impress your examiner Jim's own advice for standing out from the crowd and proving you know your stuff!

Challenging the status quo Designed to develop your critical thinking skills, these short chatty asides offer you reflective challenges.

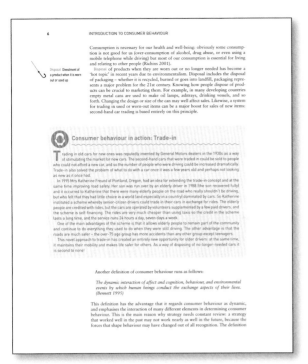

Consumer behaviour in action Additional examples to high-light what actually goes on in the real world.

Definitions To help you spot the important terms you will need for revision purposes, each new concept appears in coloured text and is defined in the margin.

Summary Covers all the essential information from each chapter and puts in context of consumer behaviour as a whole.

Key points Recaps the key topics for review at the end of each chapter.

Review questions Help test your understanding of what you have just read.

Case study revisited A look back at the case study from the start of the chapter to see how it relates to the topic at hand.

Case study and questions Offer a detailed look at real life examples and help you apply your knowledge by working through the questions.

Further reading Suggested titles for further reading to enhance your background knowledge.

Companion website

To access a variety of additional web resources to accompany this book please visit:
www.sagepub.co.uk/blythe

For students:

- Multiple choice questions – To test your understanding of each of the chapters
- Glossary of terms – A complete list of the book's glossary
- Website exercises – Web-based exercises to get you thinking!
- Video examples – Clips related to all the case studies so you can see them in action.

For lecturers:

- Instructors' manual – A chapter-by-chapter guide to the textbook with additional material
- PowerPoint(TM) slides – All the key figures and diagrams from the textbook extracted and ready to drop into your own lecture slides

Part One

Introduction to consumer behaviour

Ultimately, all business depends on someone buying something. People buy things in order to meet their physical and mental needs: business exists to create wealth, and to distribute it in ways that enable people to create worthwhile lives for themselves.

If businesses are to succeed in this, they need to understand what it is that people need and want, and to ensure that it is available in the right place, at the right time and at a price consumers are willing to pay. This is the entire foundation of all marketing – even businesses that sell only to other businesses rely, ultimately, on consumers buying products.

Apart from the obvious importance of understanding how people buy and consume, consumer behaviour is inherently interesting because it is about people (and we are all consumers, of course). This part of the book, although it consists of only one chapter, sets the scene for the more detailed chapters that follow.

CHAPTER ①

The importance of understanding consumer behaviour

CHAPTER CONTENTS

LEARNING OBJECTIVES

After reading this chapter you should be able to:

- Explain how the study of consumer behaviour has evolved.

- Show how consumer behaviour relates to marketing decision-making.

- Explain why relationships are harder to establish in business-to-consumer situations than in business-to-business situations.

- Describe the scope and nature of psychology and sociology.

- Describe the scope and nature of anthropology.

- Describe the relationship of economics with the study of consumer behaviour.

- Explain the role of exchange in improving people's welfare.

- Explain how the terms 'luxury' and 'necessity' relate to consumer behaviour.

Introduction

Every day we buy things. We exchange our money for goods and services, for our own use and for the use of our families: we choose things we think will meet our needs on a day-to-day basis, and we occasionally make buying decisions which will affect our lives for years to come. At the same time, we make decisions about disposing of worn-out or used-up possessions. All these decisions and exchanges have implications for ourselves, our families, our friends, the environment, the businesses we buy from, the employees of those businesses, and so on.

The key concept of marketing is customer centrality: we cannot ignore customer decision-making. Understanding the processes involved in making those decisions is central to establishing policy.

Consumer behaviour, and industrial buyer behaviour, have been studied by marketers since the time before marketing itself became

Customer Someone who makes the decision to buy a product

an academic subject. The academic subjects that preceded marketing include economics (the study of supply and demand), sociology (the study of group behaviour), psychology (the study of thought processes), neurology (the study of brain function) and anthropology (the study of what makes us human). Each of these disciplines has looked at the problem from a different angle, and each will be discussed in greater detail throughout the book. The study of consumer behaviour combines elements from all these disciplines: as marketers.

Case study: Pizza

Pizza was originally invented in Naples in the 16th century as a cheap, filling food for the poor. During the latter half of the 20th century, pizza spread throughout the world, with many regional variations: in Australia the basic tomato and cheese topping is garnished with bacon and eggs, in Pakistan the spicy chicken and hot sausage varieties are popular, in Sweden local cheese is used instead of mozzarella, and so forth.

The UK market is dominated by two American firms, Domino's and Pizza Hut. Domino's is entirely devoted to home deliveries of pizzas, whereas Pizza Hut has both restaurants and home delivery. Between them, these two firms have more than half the number of pizza outlets in the UK: there are some small local pizza places, and of course most Italian restaurants offer pizza as a choice on the menu, but for most people having a pizza delivered means calling Domino's or Pizza Hut.

The overall market is very substantial indeed. Although it is difficult to calculate exactly how substantial (because Italian restaurants don't keep records of exactly who ordered the pizza and who ordered the spaghetti), the market is estimated at over £1.5 billion per annum. The UK market for all take-away food is estimated at £8.5 billion (the largest in Europe), so pizza has a substantial share, and one that is probably growing.

Pizza is not on anybody's diet sheet, of course. A chunk of carbohydrate covered in melted fat, with no fresh vegetables and rather a high salt content, would not be exactly what your nutritionist would recommend. There have been links to cancer among frequent pizza eaters, due to the high salt content and predominance of processed foods such as pepperoni and ham. Yet pizza continues to be popular with most people – it is easy to eat, easy to share, and tastes good, as well as being a reasonably cheap alternative for those who don't feel like cooking or want a treat.

How to impress your examiner

Relate your answers to the real world. Use examples – this shows that you understand the theory, and can put it into a business context. While you are reading the book, try to think of examples of your own – everybody else will know the examples from the book, the examiner included!

Defining consumer behaviour

All of us are consumers: all of us behave. This does not mean that all of our behaviour can be defined as consumer behaviour, of course. Specific consumer behaviour has been defined as follows:

Consumer behaviour is the activities people undertake when obtaining, consuming and disposing of products and services. (Blackwell et al. 2001)

Consumer Someone who enjoys the benefit of a product

Product A bundle of benefits

This definition is widely used, but it still leaves some questions to answer. First, what do we mean by 'obtaining'? This presumably includes all the activities that lead up to making a purchase, including searching for information about products and services, and evaluating the alternatives. 'Obtaining' may not involve an actual purchase, but most consumer behaviour researchers and writers ignore this angle: a child who promises to keep his room tidy in exchange for a new video game is clearly obtaining a product, but this is not usually regarded as part of a study of consumer behaviour. Likewise, theft is usually ignored as an aspect of consumer behaviour, for ethical reasons.

Challenging the status quo

From a manufacturer's viewpoint, shoplifting can only be a good thing. If the product is attractive to shoplifters, more of it will leave the retailer's premises, and since the retailer has already paid the manufacturer for the goods, the manufacturer doesn't care whether the goods are bought or stolen from the retailer. Leaving ethical considerations aside (and who doesn't, from time to time?) wouldn't it be in manufacturers' best interests to make their products as easy to swipe as possible?

On the other hand, would retailers continue to stock products that were easy to steal? For the manufacturer, the retailer is the customer, not the consumer, so the manufacturer needs to focus on industrial buyer behaviour rather than consumer behaviour! Or, better still, consider the needs of both.

Other issues in the 'obtaining' category might include the ways in which people pay for the products (cash, credit card, bank loan, hire purchase, interest-free credit, and so forth), whether the product is for themselves or is a gift, how the new owner takes the purchases home, and how the decisions are affected by branding, and by social elements such as the respect of friends.

Consuming refers to the ways in which people use the products they buy. This includes where the product is consumed, when (in terms of on what occasions the product might be used) and how the product is used. In some cases people use products in ways that were not intended by the manufacturer: this is called re-invention. For example, a biologist might buy a turkey-basting syringe to use for taking water samples from a river, or a gardener might buy a china serving dish to use as a plant pot.

Consumption is necessary for our health and well-being: obviously some consumption is not good for us (over-consumption of alcohol, drug abuse, or even using a mobile telephone while driving) but most of our consumption is essential for living and relating to other people (Richins 2001).

Disposal of products when they are worn out or no longer needed has become a 'hot topic' in recent years due to environmentalism. Disposal includes the disposal of packaging – whether it is recycled, burned or goes into landfill, packaging represents a major problem for the 21st century. Knowing how people dispose of products can be crucial to marketing them. For example, in many developing countries empty metal cans are used to make oil lamps, ashtrays, drinking vessels, and so forth. Changing the design or size of the can may well affect sales. Likewise, a system for trading in used or worn-out items can be a major boost for sales of new items: second-hand car trading is based entirely on this principle.

Disposal Divestment of a product when it is worn out or used up

Consumer behaviour in action: Trade-in

Trading in old cars for new ones was reputedly invented by General Motors dealers in the 1930s as a way of stimulating the market for new cars. The second-hand cars that were traded in could be sold to people who could not afford a new car, and so the number of people who were driving could be increased dramatically. Trade-in also solved the problem of what to do with a car once it was a few years old and perhaps not looking as new as it once had.

In 1995 Mrs Katherine Freund of Portland, Oregon, had an idea for extending the trade-in concept and at the same time improving road safety. Her son was run over by an elderly driver in 1988 (the son recovered fully) and it occurred to Katherine that there were many elderly people on the road who really shouldn't be driving, but who felt that they had little choice in a world (and especially in a country) dominated by cars. So Katherine instituted a scheme whereby senior-citizen drivers could trade in their cars in exchange for rides. The elderly people are credited with rides, but the cars are operated by volunteers supplemented by a few paid drivers, and the scheme is self-financing. The rides are very much cheaper than using taxis so the credit in the scheme lasts a long time, and the service runs 24 hours a day, seven days a week.

One of the main advantages of the scheme is that it allows elderly people to remain part of the community and continue to do everything they used to do when they were still driving. The other advantage is that the roads are much safer – the over-75 age group has more accidents than any other group except teenagers.

This novel approach to trade-in has created an entirely new opportunity for older drivers: at the same time, it maintains their mobility and makes life safer for others. As a way of disposing of no-longer-needed cars it is second to none!

Another definition of consumer behaviour runs as follows:

The dynamic interaction of affect and cognition, behaviour, and environmental events by which human beings conduct the exchange aspects of their lives. (Bennett 1995)

This definition has the advantage that it regards consumer behaviour as dynamic, and emphasises the interaction of many different elements in determining consumer behaviour. This is the main reason why strategy needs constant review: a strategy that worked well in the past may not work nearly as well in the future, because the forces that shape behaviour may have changed out of all recognition. The definition

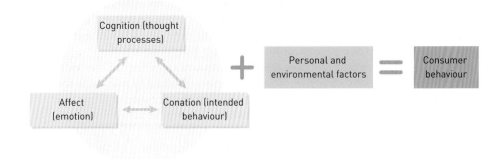

Figure 1.1　Consumer behaviour dynamics

also includes the concept of marketing as the management of exchange, which is not accepted by all marketers: few people would argue, for example, that a mother who promises a child a treat in exchange for good behaviour is engaging in a marketing process. On the other hand, the marketing-as-management-of-exchange idea has a lot to recommend it when considering not-for-profit marketing activities such as anti-smoking campaigns or political election campaigns.

The general model of consumer behaviour shown in Figure 1.1 shows that basic attitudes (formed of thought, emotion and intended behaviour) are influenced by personal and environmental factors to create actual behaviour. Marketers are able to influence this process at several points – they can influence thought processes by providing relevant information at the right time, they can influence emotion by using appealing communication and imagery, and they can provide suitable environmental stimuli (for example, pleasant shops or user-friendly websites) to stimulate purchase. On a more subtle level, marketers can even encourage greater consumption of the product – good marketing does not stop at the point of sale.

From the viewpoint of academic researchers, consumer behaviour might be considered as the field of study that concentrates on consumption activities. In the past the study of consumer behaviour has mainly focused on why people buy. More recently, the focus has moved to include looking at consumption behaviour – in other words, how and why people consume.

Studying consumer behaviour is clearly of interest to marketers, but it is an interesting study in itself, even for non-marketers, because we are all consumers. Ultimately, consumers hold all the power in the business world – as Sam Walton, founder of Wal*Mart, famously said, 'There is only one boss – the customer. And he can fire everyone in the company, from the chairman on down, simply by spending his money somewhere else.' Walton always regarded himself as an agent for his customers, finding them the best value for money: this simple philosophy moved Wal*Mart from one small store in Arkansas to being the world's largest retailer within Walton's lifetime.

Consumer behaviour in context

The fundamental basis for marketing thinking is that the customer (or consumer) should be at the centre of everything the firm does. While there may be some dissent about whether the marketing concept always applies, for marketers, customers are the key concern. This means that an understanding of how and why people make purchasing decisions is crucial to formulating a marketing plan.

Segmentation The act of dividing up a market into groups of people with similar needs

Geographic segmentation Dividing a market into smaller groups based on location

Psychographic segmentation Dividing a market according to the psychological profiles of potential customers

Behavioural segmentation Dividing up a potential market according to the behaviour of its members

Demographic segmentation Dividing up a market according to people's age, income and social standing

Service dominant logic The view that all value is co-created by the consumer and the supplier, and thus that all value can be considered as a service

In the first instance, purchasing behaviour relates strongly to segmenting the market. The whole purpose of segmentation is to determine which potential buyers are most likely to behave favourably towards our company and its products: most segmentation methods bear at least some relationship to consumer behaviour issues.

First, geographic segmentation breaks the market down according to the location in which the potential customers live. Where someone chooses to live, or is forced to live, is either an example of decision-making or dictates decision-making. Someone living in a cold climate is compelled to buy warm clothing, heating equipment, insulation products for the home, and so forth.

Psychographic segmentation and behavioural segmentation clearly relate very directly to consumer characteristics and behaviour. Psychographic segmentation is based on people's thought processes and attitudes – clearly the starting-points for behaviour. Behavioural segmentation is based on what people do – what hobbies they have, what foods they eat, how they travel, work and spend their spare time. Demographic segmentation is based on consumers' wealth, age, gender and education levels (among other things), each of which relate directly to purchasing decisions. There is more on psychological factors in Chapters 2 to 6, and more on attitude in Chapter 7.

Recently the idea has been proposed that consumers are not simply users of value (and, by extension, destroyers of value as they use up products) but should instead be considered as co-creators of value (Vargo and Lusch 2004). The thinking is that goods and services only have value when they are used – an electric drill has no value if it simply stays on the retailer's shelf, but it does create value when someone buys it and uses it. This perspective, known as service dominant logic (SDL), supposes that in fact all products are service products, since consumers are not buying a drill, nor are they buying holes, but are in fact buying a hole-drilling service for which they will provide some of the effort and therefore create some of the value. SDL has a strong appeal – after all, someone who needs to drill a hole could (presumably) hire someone to come and drill the hole for them, or could buy (or hire) a drill and do it themselves. The value created is much the same in each case, but the relative contribution by the consumer and the supplier is very different. Chapter 14 has more on services.

There are a great many conceptual implications involved in service dominant logic, and academics are still debating the practical implications for companies. However, there is certainly research supporting the idea that modern consumers are not prepared simply to accept what manufacturers provide for them, but instead seek to reinvent, add value and communicate new ideas to each other entirely independently of producers (Hewer and Brownlie 2010).

Consumer behaviour and the marketing mix

Marketing mix The combination of activities which creates an overall approach to the market

Marketing management is usually considered to consist of controlling the marketing mix. Table 1.1 shows how consumer behaviour relates to the seven Ps (7P) model of the marketing mix developed by Booms and Bitner (1981).

Although the marketing mix has been widely criticised by academics because it tends to imply things being done *to* consumers rather than things being done *for* consumers, it is still widely taught because it offers a relatively simply way to understand what marketers do. Putting each element of the mix into a separate 'silo' is one way of simplifying the real world, but looked at from the consumer's viewpoint the distinctions between the elements may not be valid at all. For example, price is regarded as a cost from the consumer's viewpoint, but might also be regarded as a promotion – a money-off special offer could be regarded as a major incentive to buy now rather than postpone the purchase. In other words, the 7P

Table 1.1 Consumer behaviour and the seven Ps

Product	The bundle of benefits consumers acquire is the basis of their decision-making. Deciding which benefits are essential, which are desirable, which do not matter and which are actually not benefits at all but drawbacks is the starting point for all rational decisions.
Price	The cost of a product goes beyond the price tag in most cases. If the product is complex, there will be a learning cost attached to figuring out how to use it: if the product is dangerous, there may be a cost attached to consequent injury. If the product is visible to others, there may be an embarrassment cost. Some products require more effort to use – an electric can opener is easier to use than a hand-operated one, but costs more money. In some cases, these extra costs may exceed the price tag – consumers will take account of them, and will weigh them in the decision, but producers will only be able to obtain the price on the tag.
Place	Convenient locations for making purchases are essential; in fact it would not be too much to say that the easier marketers make it for consumers to find the product, the more product will be sold. Like price, the location can affect the decision in ways which do not benefit the producer – equally, producers can sometimes charge a premium for delivering location benefits. Corner shops (convenience stores) are a good example: although they are invariably more expensive than supermarkets, being within easy reach of home offers a clear advantage that is worth paying for.
Promotion	Promotion is not something that is done to consumers, it is something they consume. People buy magazines, watch TV shows, go to the cinema and ride on public transport. Although they do not usually do these things in order to be exposed to advertisements, they usually pay at least some attention to them and frequently they enjoy the experience. Furthermore, people often use media such as classified advertisements and directories in an active search for information about goods they might like to buy.
People	Business is not about money, it is about people. The people who run businesses and deal with the public need to understand how other people react in purchasing situations. In some cases, the product is the person: people become loyal to the same hairdresser, the same doctor, the same restaurant chef. The people who work with the customers tend to be the most customer-orientated – and proximity to the customer is a more important factor in this than is the attitude and behaviour of senior management (Hui and Subramony 2008). In other words, senior management may or may not be customer-orientated, but working with customers will in itself tend to focus people on customer need.
Process	The way services are delivered affects the circumstances in which people buy as well as their propensity to buy. A meal out might be a ten-minute lunch stop at a fast-food outlet, or it might be a romantic dinner for two in an upmarket restaurant. The process is completely different in each case, and so is the price: in the first case, the consumer may only go through a limited problem-solving process; in the second case, the process may well be longer because the need to get it right is greater. This is called **involvement**.
Physical Evidence	Physical aspects of the service experience often relate to the pleasure one feels from receiving the service rather than the practical aspects. The surroundings in a restaurant, the food itself and the quality of the menus all affect people's perception of the service.

Involvement The degree to which an individual is attracted to, and defined by, a product or brand

model may be fine for the marketers to understand, but may not be appropriate from the consumer's viewpoint.

Chapter 16 explores the practical issues around consumer behaviour within the marketing mix.

Consumers and relationship marketing

Relationship marketing seeks to establish long-term relationships with customers rather than focusing on the single transaction. The differences between relationship marketing and transactional marketing are shown in Table 1.2.

Establishing a relationship in a business-to-business (B2B) context turns out to be a great deal easier than establishing a relationship in a business-to-consumer (B2C) context (see Chapter 15 for more on organisational buyer behaviour). The reasons for this are currently obscure, but may include the following:

1 Businesses change their needs less often than do consumers.
2 There are fewer suppliers and customers in B2B markets.
3 B2B transactions almost always involve the personal relationships between salespeople and buyers, whereas B2C relationships are often impersonal, since people often buy goods on-line or in self-service stores.
4 The possibilities for mutual advantage in establishing a relationship are often much greater in a B2B context.

Relationship marketing is rooted in the idea that it is cheaper to retain an existing customer than to recruit a new one. There is a certain appeal to this idea: acquiring new customers is a difficult business, whereas keeping someone on board should only be a matter of making sure their needs are met.

In consumer markets, this is a great deal harder than it sounds. As shown in Figure 1.2, consumer needs change relatively rapidly: the needs of someone aged 18 are likely to change dramatically by the time he or she is 25. Likewise, a childless couple's needs will change should they have a baby together, quite apart from the probable change in their financial circumstances. Second, there is a great deal more

Relationship marketing Marketing in such a way as to generate a long-term partnership with customers

Transactional marketing Marketing in which the marketer focuses on the individual sale, not on the long-term relationship with the customer

B2B Business to business

B2C Business to consumer

Table 1.2 Transactional marketing vs. Relationship marketing

Transactional marketing	Relationship marketing
Focus on single sale	Focus on customer retention
Orientation on product features	Orientation on product benefits
Short timescale	Long timescale
Little emphasis on customer service	High emphasis on customer service
Limited customer commitment	High customer commitment
Moderate customer contact	High customer contact
Quality is the concern of the production department	Quality is the concern of all

Source: M. Christopher, D. Ballantyne and A. Payne (1991) *Relationship Marketing* (Oxford: Butterworth–Heinemann)

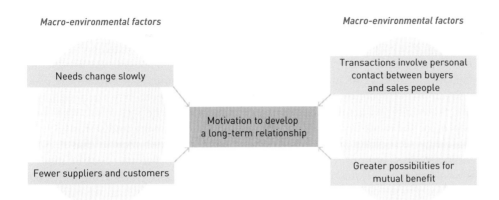

Figure 1.2 Businesses and relationship marketing

choice of supplier in consumer markets, and a great many more ways to spend one's money. People can easily be tempted away from an existing supplier and towards a new supplier. Third, there is little incentive for most consumers to remain loyal to a given supplier when there are so many tempting offers around and little to keep them on board: extra-nice service is really not enough.

Another factor is that people have become much more aware of marketing and marketers. There is a much greater understanding of marketing techniques than formerly, and consequently a greater distrust of marketers. There is evidence that this alienation of consumers is linked to the use of new technology – the Internet allows consumers to take control of the exchange process in a way that has been impossible in the past, and thus they are able to take over some of the role of marketers in managing exchange (Mady 2011).

Relationship marketing has become closely associated with direct marketing, simply because the best way to establish a relationship with a customer is to have direct dealings. Unfortunately, direct marketing has also become associated with direct mail and direct telephone marketing, both of which are extremely unpopular with the public in general; this is probably another reason why relationship marketing is less successful with consumers than with industrial buyers.

Understanding how people create and maintain relationships in their personal lives is obviously useful when considering how people create and maintain business relationships. Businesses are not about profits: they are about people.

Challenging the status quo

If businesses are about people, why is it that companies consistently report their successes and failures in financial terms? Why not report on how pleased our customers were, or on how loyal they were? Why not report on how many customers recommended us to their friends?

Or would it be too difficult to do these things? How do we know whether people are recommending us anyway? The market researchers should be able to find out – but it's obviously easier just to count up the money!

Consumers and marketing planning

Marketing planning has often been considered in terms of managing the product portfolio, developing new products, launching products, managing the product life cycle, and so forth. This involves planning communications that explain the product features and benefits, and seek to persuade consumers to buy the products. It involves deciding which distributors the products should be sold from, what price will provide the company with a good return on its investment, and so forth.

This way of looking at marketing suffers from a serious flaw in that it is not customer-centric. Suppose we were to act in a completely customer-centred manner. We would then be seeking to manage the customer portfolio, considering which customers (or groups of customers) we can serve profitably and which we cannot. We would consider which marketing communications would appeal most to the groups we want to keep, and which would be off-putting to the groups we want to lose. We might consider the customer's life cycle (see Consumers and relationship marketing above) rather than the product's life cycle, and consider price in terms of what consumers will think is fair.

Challenging the status quo

Can we really let consumers run the business? After all, if we ask people what they are willing to pay for a product, they are likely to pitch the price as low as they think they can get away with. The same applies to service – everybody wants a lot, but is only prepared to pay a little!

Not to mention the competitive arms race. As one company offers one level of service, everyone else has to match it at least, and exceed it at best. Before long we get to the point where we are grovelling to the customers!

For example, in France one would never argue with the chef. If one likes one's steak well done, the waiter will suggest the idea to the chef, but after muttering something about '*Les sales anglais!*' the chef will produce a steak which looks as if it needs a sticking plaster. Contrast with America, where the customer tells the chef exactly what to put in and leave out of the food: 'No salt, hold the mayo, just a little tabasco' and so forth. No doubt the American chef is much more customer-centred, but aren't we, as the customers, paying for his expertise? What's the point of going to a restaurant where we have a trained chef with years of experience, and then second-guessing the guy? Can we really trust the customer to know what is best for them? After all, doctors and lawyers don't expect people to know what is best for their health or legal well-being.

So where is customer centrality really located? In France, or in America?

Marketing strategies should therefore not only seek to influence consumers, they should also be influenced by them. Planning for a customer-led future means putting consumer behaviour at the centre of the firm's thinking. In the 21st century, consumers hold the power: there is evidence that people consider their spending power to be a form of voting, a way of expressing approval for what the supplier is offering

(Shaw et al. 2006). People are aware that they have choice: at first, when choice became widespread, people might have found this confusing and daunting, but as time has gone on people have found it empowering, and they do not hesitate to use their power (Davies and Elliott 2006).

For example, consumer research might show that a specific group of our customers is more profitable than another simply because they are more loyal. This means that we do not need to recruit new customers to replace those who drop out, which is of course substantially cheaper. We might therefore seek (a) to ensure that we continue to retain these customers and (b) try to find more like them. Their loyalty comes from their purchase behaviour – their propensity to repeat purchases on a regular basis – which in itself may be a function of their personalities, their degree of involvement with the products, and so forth.

Loyalty The degree to which an individual will repeat purchase of a product

Involvement The degree to which an individual is attracted to, and defined by, a product or brand

Antecedents of consumer behaviour

The study of consumer behaviour is, like marketing itself, a combination of other disciplines. As a study, it draws from economics, sociology, psychology and anthropology (and, more recently, neuroscience) for its basic theories and research approaches. Academics aim to develop a body of specifically consumer-based research, but the influence of the other disciplines will always be at the forefront of the theory that develops, as shown in Figure 1.3.

All of these areas will be discussed in much greater detail throughout the book, but a quick overview of the basic contributions of each discipline should be helpful in understanding how consumer behaviour has developed as an academic study.

Economics is the study of demand. Economists study demand in the individual transaction, at the level of the firm and its customers, and also the overall level of demand in the economy. The former study is called microeconomics, the latter is called macroeconomics. Although microeconomics appears at first sight to explain consumer behaviour, in fact it only really explains *rational* behaviour. Economists consider such concepts as utility, value for money and economic choice, not such nebulous ideas as whether one's friends will admire one's new outfit.

Economics The study of demand

Economic choice The choice made when one is unable to afford to buy both alternatives

Economics has provided consumer behaviour theorists with a number of useful concepts that help to explain the rational side of consumer behaviour.

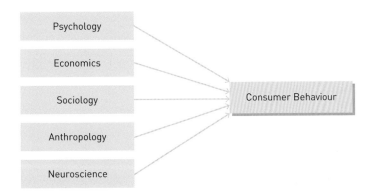

Figure 1.3 Antecedents of studying consumer behaviour

THE ECONOMIC CHOICE

This simply means that someone cannot spend money on something if he or she already spent the money somewhere else. This implies that all companies are competing with all other companies for the consumer's money: people have only a certain amount of money they can spend, or commit to borrowing. In fact economic choice is somewhat blurred by the existence of credit. People can easily be persuaded to borrow the money to buy whatever they want, which means that other factors than money might come into the equation. The theory still holds true, though, if we consider the economic choice of how we spend our time, or how we use other resources such as our cars or our homes. The theory really talks about use of limited resources in aiming to satisfy one's needs.

Marketers have certainly taken on board the concept of the economic choice, broadening out the spectrum of competitors to include anyone who aims to satisfy similar needs in consumers. This means that cinema owners recognise theatres, restaurants, bowling-alleys and other entertainment places as competitors, and in recent years have developed complexes where all leisure activities can take place under one roof: this is not just an example of taking over competitors, it is also an example of how a firm can help people make the best use of limited leisure time. With time as the constraining variable, such complexes can make best use of economic choice theory.

INDIFFERENCE CURVES

People typically own portfolios of products. Some people like to have large numbers of some products (for example, some people have several TV sets) and few of something else. Indifference theory says that people might have a 'trade-off' in their minds about how much of a given product they consider is equivalent to a quantity of another product.

Figure 1.4 shows an indifference curve comparing money and turkeys. Someone who has no turkeys but plenty of money might decide to buy a turkey: if he or she is a particular lover of roast turkey, the temptation might arise to buy one or two extras for the freezer. As the freezer fills, though, there will come a point where the turkeys would have to be a real bargain to be worth buying, and of course eventually the individual will reach the point where he or she would not buy any more no matter how good a deal the marketer offered. Likewise, someone who is desperate to buy a turkey might be prepared to spend more money than usual on one. At one end of the curve we have a mood of 'What's the use of having all this money if I can't enjoy a turkey?' and at the other end of the curve the mood would be 'How many turkeys does one person need?'

Indifference curve
The graph that shows the points at which one product will be regarded as a suitable substitute for another

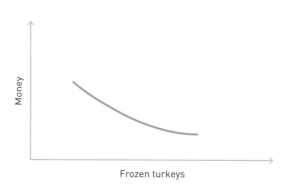

Figure 1.4   Indifference curve

For example, if one is in a pub and a friend goes to the bar, one might want a pint of beer and two packets of sandwiches. If the friend mixes up the order and brings back two pints of beer and one packet of sandwiches this may not matter to you, but if he brings backs no beer and three packets of sandwiches (or vice versa) this might not be acceptable. In those circumstances, you would have moved beyond the limits of your indifference curve: one way of returning to a satisfactory arrangement would be to swap some of your sandwiches for someone else's beer, in other words to trade.

Indifference curve theory leads on to the Edgeworth Box, which tells us that trade always makes people better off because both parties move onto a higher indifference curve.

In Figure 1.5, we have a situation where two roast turkey lovers meet and decide to trade. Each has some turkeys and some money: the axes of the box show the total amount of each that the two people have between them. Each person would be quite happy with any combination of turkeys and money along the line of the indifference curve, but obviously would be even happier with more of both. If the people concerned then trade, they will each end up with a turkey–money combination situated somewhere along the contract line; where each person ends up is a matter for negotiation.

The idea that trade is always good is actually fairly obvious: if both parties were not better off, one or other would not be prepared to make the trade. The degree to which each party is better off depends largely on negotiation skills: some people are better negotiators or are in stronger negotiating positions than others.

ELASTICITY OF DEMAND

Although a rise in prices generally means a reduction in demand (there are some exceptions), there is a question about the degree to which demand is affected by price. In some cases, a rise in price appears to make very little difference to demand – salt is the example usually given for this, because salt is extremely cheap and is rarely purchased, so even a doubling of the price would probably go unnoticed. On the other hand, some products seem to be dramatically affected by even small changes in price: this usually happens if there is a close substitute available, for example if the price of beef rose relative to the price of pork or lamb. In these circumstances, price calculations need to be carried out extremely carefully as a mistake could result in a dramatic loss of business.

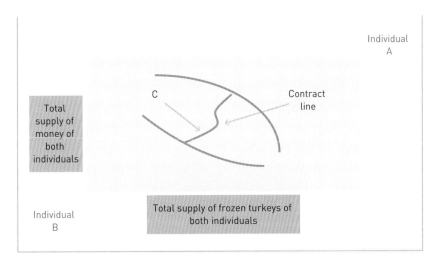

Figure 1.5 Edgeworth Box

Figure 1.6   Inelastic demand curve

Figure 1.6 shows a product that sustains much the same demand whatever happens to the price. As the price rises, demand does fall slightly but overall demand remains fairly constant.

There are elasticities other than price. For example, income elasticity of demand tells us that some products are affected by increases in the individual's spending money. In some cases, this will produce an increase in demand – as people become richer, they are likely to buy more clothes and more entertainment products, for example. In other cases, the demand for an individual product might reduce as people become wealthier: a higher income might lead someone to buy a BMW car rather than a Ford. In some cases, a general rise in income reduces demand fairly dramatically, and bread is an example. As people become richer, they tend to buy less bread, and eat more meat and vegetables instead. In recent years, rising standards of living in China and India have led to steep rises in the worldwide cost of many foods as people in those countries are able to afford more meat and vegetables, and thus do not rely as much on cheap foods such as rice and bread.

Figure 1.7 shows an elastic demand curve. Here the demand for the product is affected greatly by the price – even a small increase in price has a fairly profound effect on the demand for the product.

One point that arises from the elasticity concept is that there is no product which has a completely inelastic demand curve. In other words, there is no product which

Elasticity The degree to which demand is affected by other factors, for example price changes

Figure 1.7   Elastic demand curve

has a demand curve that is entirely unaffected by price. This means that there is no product which is an absolute necessity of life – if this were the case, the producer could charge anything at all for the product and people would have no choice but to pay, since the alternative would be death. This is an important issue for marketers, because it shows us that there is no theoretical basis for considering some products as necessities and other products as luxuries. The difference exists only in the minds of consumers. To some people, a car would be a luxury; to others it is a necessity. Likewise, water might be considered as a necessity of life, yet some people rarely (if ever) drink just plain water: they drink tea, beer, orange juice, cola, or any one of many different products containing water, all of which are substitutes for plain old tap water.

Neuroscience

Neuroscience is the study of the ways in which the human brain works. A sub-branch of the discipline, neuroeconomics, seeks to explain some economic behaviour in terms of the brain's physiology.

Neuroscientists, and especially evolutionary neuroscientists, see the brain as the result of a long series of evolutionary adaptations leading to a set of domain-specific computational systems. These systems have evolved to solve recurring problems – originally these problems were characterised by survival problems (finding food, evading predators, cooperating with tribe members, and so forth) and reproduction problems (finding a suitable mate, protection and feeding of children, and so forth). These problem-solving systems act to adapt behaviour in order to improve the individual's chances of surviving, prospering and reproducing. In the modern world, the same systems are applied to apparently new problems – career progression, financial management, learning to operate a smartphone, and many other tasks that did not exist when our ancestors evolved on the African savannah.

> **Adaptation** The process by which goals are influenced by contextual issues

Evolution is, in general, a very slow process, and in the case of human beings it has been further hindered by our dominance of the environment: people are less likely to make fatal mistakes and thus remove themselves from the gene pool.

Neuroeconomics seeks to map brain activity onto economic behaviour. In this way, neuroscientists hope to explain consumer behaviour in terms of evolutionary and survival factors. As yet, the discipline is in its infancy, but neuroscientists have already identified some of the mechanisms by which people are affected by packaging (Stoll et al. 2008), and have identified a dedicated response to celebrity-based advertising (Gakhal and Senior 2008). It seems likely that further practical insights will emerge as research continues (Garcia and Saad 2008).

Psychology

Psychology is the study of mental processes. Psychologists study the ways people think, which is of course basic to understanding how people think about the products they buy. This includes learning about products, developing an overall perception of products and brands and fitting it into one's overall perception of the world, and the basic drives that encourage people to seek solutions for their needs.

> **Psychology** The science of the mind

Each of the contributions made by psychologists (as shown in Figure 1.8) will be covered in more detail in Part Two of this book, but for the time being here is a brief overview of the main issues.

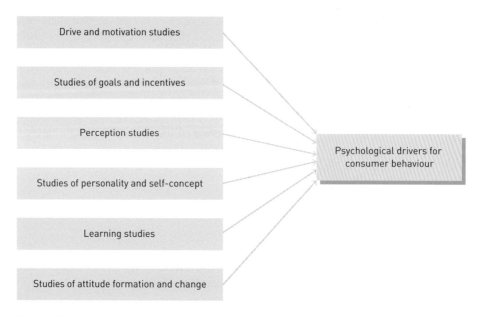

Figure 1.8   Contributions from psychology

DRIVE AND MOTIVATION

Drive The basic force of motivation, which arises when the individual's actual state diverges from the desired state

Motivation The internal force which encourages people to act in specific ways

Drives are the basic forces that make us want to do things (see Chapter 2). A drive is created when the desired state of the individual is different from the actual state: the greater the difference, the stronger the drive. A drive that has a definite target becomes a **motivation**. Part of the marketer's job is to encourage drives to develop by encouraging shifts in the desired state (it is pretty much impossible to develop shifts in the actual state). The other part of the marketer's job is to direct drives towards a specific target. For example, a marketer might encourage a shift in the desired state by saying, 'Isn't it about time you bought yourself a better car?' and follow this by saying, 'Why not treat yourself to a new Jaguar?'

GOALS AND INCENTIVES

Goals Specific targets towards which consumption behaviour is directed

Incentives Reasons for action

A **goal** is the rational element of motivation (see Chapter 3). Motives are largely emotional: goals are the rationalisation of a motivation. For example, someone might decide that they really want to learn to fly (a largely emotional motivation, based on reading adventure stories or on an unspecified emotion). The goals that derive from this might be concerned with finding an appropriate flying school, saving up the money to pay for lessons, and freeing up the time to learn. The **incentive** for achieving these various goals is the satisfaction of the need.

PERSONALITY AND SELF-CONCEPT

Personality Those factors which make up the individual's mental processes

Self-concept The belief one has about oneself

Personality is a combination of the various traits that determine who we are (see Chapter 4). The type of person we are dictates what we like and what we dislike, our preferred ways of dealing with our consumption problems, our preferred lifestyles, and so forth. **Self-concept** is about how we see ourselves – this includes how we see ourselves in terms of consumption patterns, branding and other consumption-based aspects. For example, each of us has favourite brands, which we feel express our personalities. Some of us are Ford drivers, for some of us it's BMW; some of us are Nike wearers, others Adidas; and so forth. What we buy and wear expresses who we are.

PERCEPTION

Perception is about the way we make sense of the world (see Chapter 5). Each of us has a particular view of the world, a perceptual map, which enables us to make sense of what is happening around us. We assemble this map by taking in information through our senses and using it to develop an understanding of how the world works and where different things fit into it. Psychologists study the ways in which people filter out unnecessary information, group information together in useable 'chunks' and arrange the information to create the perceptual map. Marketers are interested in these processes in order to ensure that their brand is mapped into the most effective place in the consumers' perceptions.

The word perception is often used to mean 'untrue' but in fact this is not the case. The only truth we have is what we hold in our minds, so a person's perceptual map is the truth for that person. Even though we each have different perceptual maps, they are near enough to each other for us to be able to communicate and cooperate.

> **Perception** The process of creating a mental 'map' of reality

LEARNING

Learning is the behavioural changes that result from experience (see Chapter 6). How we learn is critical to marketing communications, because marketers want people to remember the messages and act upon them in ways that are favourable to the organisation.

> **Learning** Changes in behaviour that come about through experience

ATTITUDE FORMATION AND CHANGE

Attitudes consist of knowledge, feelings and proposed behaviour (see Chapter 7). An attitude is a tendency to behave in a consistent manner towards a given stimulus: in other words, people tend to react the same way every time towards something about which they have an attitude. For marketers, understanding how attitudes are formed and are changed is useful in creating appropriate attitudes towards brands and products: sometimes attitudes need to be demolished and rebuilt if the brand is to continue.

> **Attitudes** A propensity to respond in a consistent manner to a given stimulus of object

Psychology is not the only behavioural science, however. It is mainly concerned with the individual, but human beings are herd animals: we operate in groups. In prehistoric times, being part of a group meant the difference between surviving and not surviving: even today, people who do not fit in with one or more groups usually lead unhappy lives, and there is medical evidence to suggest that they do not live as long as other people either. The behaviour of people in groups is the province of sociology.

Sociology

Group behaviour is crucial to human beings, and therefore is crucial to understanding what motivates people to buy specific brands. Buying the wrong brand can be embarrassing: we are all aware of how, in our early teens, we have to have the right brand of trainers, play the right video games, see the right films and enjoy the right music to fit in with the desired group. Even adolescent rebellion is actually a drive to join a group. The contributions from sociology are shown in Figure 1.9 and described below: the following topics will be covered in much greater detail in Part Three of the book.

REFERENCE GROUPS

People identify groups they would like to join, and also groups they would prefer not to be associated with (see Chapter 9). Almost all such groups involve some type of

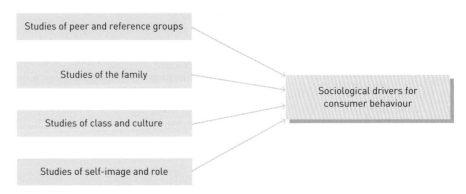

Figure 1.9   Contributions from sociology

consumption: clothing to wear, things to use in the group activities, or shared consumption of group-owned items. Most of us define ourselves at least in part by the groups we belong to, whether it is our work group, our group of friends, our family group, our religious group, or our group hobbies.

FAMILY

Family A group of people who exhibit shared consumption and who are bound by ties of genetic relationship or adoption

The family is probably the most important reference group because it exerts the most influence on us (see Chapter 10). Families share consumption of many items (food, housing, energy, etc.) and our upbringing also influences our behaviour in later years.

CLASS AND CULTURE

Culture The set of beliefs, behaviour, customs and attitudes that are common to a large group of people

The study of culture and class is part of the study of anthropology. Anthropology is a wide-ranging discipline, covering everything that makes us human: anthropologists consider archaeology as part of their discipline as well as cultural anthropology. Culture is the set of beliefs and behaviours that distinguishes one large group of people from another, and it includes such issues as religious beliefs, language, customs, class distinctions and accepted norms of behaviour. For marketers, culture is one of the driving forces of behaviour including consumption behaviour, but perhaps more importantly it is a minefield in which communications and brands can cause offence to people from other cultural backgrounds. In particular, religious beliefs can create problems for marketers since people are often inflexible about religious taboos or restrictions. Cognitive anthropology has been used to study the problem-solving behaviour of green consumers (Wagner-Tsukamoto and Tadajewski, 2006).

SELF-IMAGE AND ROLE

Role The place one has within a group

The images we form of ourselves are almost entirely derived from feedback from other people (see Chapter 4). This feedback is derived in turn from the images we project as part of our role in life. In fact, we each perform many roles in our dealings with others: as friends, work colleagues, children, fathers, mothers, professionals, and so forth: we judge ourselves as being good at each of these roles by the feedback of the people we deal with every day. The only way one can know if one is a good work colleague is by the feedback from fellow-workers.

People often define themselves, at least in part, by the products they consume. Possessions become an extension of the individual – an extended self – and thus project who the person is to others (Mittal 2006). Indeed, many acts of consumption are tribal and role-supporting, even when they do not define the self (Ryan et al. 2006).

Consumer decision-making is therefore not isolated from all other human behaviour. People try to behave in ways that enable them to enjoy their lives, to relate to their friends and families, and to contribute to society at large. In almost all cases this behaviour is likely to involve consumption of products and services produced by other people: this is the province of consumer behaviour.

Summary

Consumer behaviour studies derive from many different academic disciplines, as well as from direct studies by marketing academics. As a field of study, it has an appeal to most of us because it is, after all, about people. For marketing practitioners, understanding the ways in which people make decisions about their purchasing behaviour is clearly of crucial importance in planning almost every aspect of managing the exchange process.

 **Key points**

- The study of consumer behaviour is largely derived from other disciplines.
- Consumer behaviour is at the centre of all marketing decision-making.
- Relationships are harder to establish in business-to-consumer situations than in business-to-business situations.
- Psychology is about internal thought processes: sociology is about behaviour within groups.
- Anthropology is the study of what makes us human.
- Economics is the study of demand.
- Exchange always makes both parties better off.
- 'Luxury' and 'necessity' are subjective terms: they have no objective reality.

Review questions

1. How might marketers use knowledge of indifference curves to affect consumer choices?
2. Would you expect salt to have an inelastic demand curve, or an elastic demand curve? Why?
3. If a product has an inelastic demand curve, what does that imply for marketers?
4. If a product has an elastic demand curve, what are the implications for marketers?
5. How might group behaviour affect purchasing behaviour?
6. Why does exchange always make both parties better off?
7. What is the importance of the concept of perception to marketers?
8. Why is learning important to marketers?
9. Why are customers more important to a firm than, say, employees?

Case study revisited: Pizza

So what is it about pizza that creates its eternal appeal? In some cases, no doubt it is the convenience of the product – having someone prepare your dinner for you and deliver it to the door is convenient in itself, but pizza is also easy to eat. Probably most people eat it straight from the delivery box, so there is no washing-up either.

Then again, it is a really easy product to share. One or two pizzas will feed a family, and everyone can eat as much or as little as they want: for children, pizza is hard to beat because they can eat it with their fingers without having to deal with adult-size cutlery, tables and plates. It's an easy meal to eat in front of the TV as well.

Maybe pizza also appeals because of its cultural connotations. We see images of people ordering pizza deliveries in films and TV shows, and it has a certain American appeal about it (despite being Italian in origin). Most advertising for pizza (in the UK at least) emphasises the American aspects of the product – Chicago pizzas, New York pizzas and just plain old American pizzas are emphasised.

On the other hand, Pizza Hut have reported a £22 million pound loss for 2011–12. Despite the fact that the market is predicted to grow by 22% between 2012 and 2016, Pizza Hut's business has shrunk considerably. Some of this appears to be due to a downturn in the restaurant part of the business: people simply aren't eating out in pizza places as much as they did, and if they do they tend to go to restaurants offering a wider variety of food on the menu, or places with a rather more pleasant ambience than Pizza Hut provides.

Helen Spicer, a senior food analyst at market research company Mintel, says that Pizza Hut have failed to keep pace with changes in the eating out market, and are now seen as outdated. Perhaps closer attention to the consumers, and their behaviour, might have helped.

Case study: Center Parcs

Center Parcs started in Holland over 40 years ago, and revolutionised the holiday industry there. The company provides family accommodation in purpose-built villages in forested areas, and specialises in short breaks (i.e. visits of less than one week). The company has scored a remarkable success since entering the UK market in 1987 with its flagship village in Sherwood Forest – it now has four locations, strategically placed around England so that a Center Parc is within a short drive of most places. Center Parcs claim to have achieved 95% occupancy of their resorts – no mean feat in an industry which regards 70% as good – and also claim to be the market leader in short breaks.

The resorts themselves are entirely self-contained, with restaurants and activities on-site, but visitors can explore the local forest on bikes supplied by Center Parcs. Within the resort itself there is a dizzying range of activities on offer – everything from watercolour painting to scuba diving lessons. Many activities happen indoors, and each resort has a 'Subtropical Swimming Paradise' in which the temperature is maintained at 29 °C: it is free to all residents, and it would be entirely possible to spend the whole day in there since it has a cafe and a bar. Residents can even rent a 'cabana' for the day, in which there is a TV, comfortable chairs, free soft drinks and towels and a true tropical ambience. In view of the British climate, this little taste of the tropics must be very welcome for residents.

Restaurants and cafes on-site are run by nationally known chains: in the Sherwood Forest Center Parc residents can find Cafe Rouge (for French food), Huck's (American fast food), Forester's Inn (a gastro-pub), The Pancake House, Rajinda Pradesh (Indian food), Zilli's (Italian), Strada (also Italian), Starbucks (coffee), and Sports Cafe (casual dining overlooking the sports area). Accommodation is luxurious and has a kitchen, so that residents can cook their own food if they prefer (or if they have specific dietary needs). There is, of course, a well-stocked supermarket on-site.

Because there are so many activities for children on-site, parents are able to have some time to themselves if they want to. Apart from swimming and cycling, children can have real adventures, zipping through the trees on high wires or learning falconry. The Center Parcs approach goes well beyond simply supplying a child-minder dressed as a clown to supervise the play area – children can learn new skills such as archery, can build nesting boxes for wildlife, can learn tennis or rollerskating, and any one of dozens of skills (even including survival skills). Parents are encouraged to join in – the whole Center Parcs ethos is built around families sharing experiences.

Perhaps one of the biggest selling-points of Center Parcs is that there is always something to do, whatever happens to the weather. For most British people, holidays mean going out of the country, simply because the weather is so unpredictable (and is often rainy). Center Parcs can guarantee a sub-tropical experience, even if it is artificially created, and if the weather is bad one can always go for a sauna or a spa treatment, or the children can try something new indoors. For those who remember wet holidays in a seaside caravan park, this is a major plus. Of course, Center Parcs are not cheap: most activities have to be paid for, and the accommodation is upmarket. A long weekend (arriving Friday and leaving Monday) in peak season will cost anywhere between £600 and £1900 for four people staying three nights: this is approximately what bed and breakfast in a three-star hotel would cost. A family of four should budget at least £800 for a weekend at Center Parcs, even if they plan on self-catering.

Having said that, for a family Center Parcs offers a truly memorable experience. Families have the opportunity to spend time together and share new experiences in a way that is not often available in normal, day-to-day life in the 21st century.

Questions

1 Why the emphasis on short breaks?
2 Why have the on-site catering run by chain restaurants and cafes?
3 Why do Center Parcs have so many adventure activities for children?
4 What factors might figure in the choice to have a weekend at Center Parcs rather than go abroad?
5 Who might be most likely to take a break at Center Parcs?

Further reading

Economics by Richard Lipsey and Alec Chrystal (Oxford: OUP, 2011) is a comprehensive text covering all aspects of economics. It is written in a clear, straightforward style and covers the ground well.

Anthropology: The Basics by Peter Metcalf is a fascinating introduction to the subject. There are plenty of examples, some of which you can try yourself, and some excellent in-depth looks at cultural issues.

Sociology by Anthony Giddens (Cambridge: Polity Press, 2009) is now in its 6th edition. The latest version includes a chapter on war and terrorism, and it is jargon-free and comprehensive.

Games People Play: The Psychology of Human Relationships by Eric Berne (Harmondsworth: Penguin Books, 2010) is a humorous way of looking at the ways in which people relate to each other. Berne describes the various interactions in terms of games, with winners and losers and rules. This is not a serious textbook, but it is a fun read and it offers some entertaining insights into human interaction.

Freakonomics: A Rogue Economist Explores the Hidden Side of Everything by Steven D. Levitt and Stephen J. Dubner (Ontario: Harper Perennial, 2005) is another popular-science book.

It's very much a light read, and the academic rigour is definitely questionable – but what the authors are looking to do is to shake up some traditional thinking, and examine some economic behaviour from a different angle (for example, they show that New York drug dealers would earn more working in minimum-wage jobs). Not to be taken too seriously, but good fun nonetheless.

References

Bennett, P.D. (1995) *Dictionary of Marketing Terms.* Chicago IL: American Marketing Association.

Blackwell, R.D., Miniard, P.W. and Engel, J.F. (2001) *Consumer Behaviour*, 9th edition. Mason,OH: Southwestern.

Booms, B.H. and Bitner, M.J. (1981) Marketing strategies and organisational structures for service firms. In J.H. Donnelly and W.R. George (eds), *Marketing of Services.* Chicago, IL: American Marketing Association. pp. 47–52.

Davies, A. and Elliott, R. (2006) The evolution of the empowered consumer. *European Journal of Marketing* 40 (9/10): 1106–21.

Gakhal, B. and Senior, C. (2008) Examining the influence of fame in the presence of beauty: an electrodermal neuromarketing study. *Journal of Consumer Behaviour* 7 (4/5): 331–41.

Garcia, J.R. and Saad, G. (2008) Evolutionary neuromarketing: Darwinizing the neuroimaging paradigm for consumer behaviour. *Journal of Consumer Behaviour* 7 (4/5): 397–414.

Hewer, P. and Brownlie, D. (2010) On market forces and adjustments: acknowledging customer creativity through the aesthetics of debadging. *Journal of Marketing Management* 26 (5&6): 428–40.

Hui, L. and Subramony, M. (2008) Employee customer orientation in manufacturing organisations: joint influences of customer proximity and the senior leadership team. *Journal of Applied Psychology* 93 (2): 317–28.

Mady, T.T. (2011) Sentiment toward marketing: should we care about consumer alienation and readiness to use technology? *Journal of Consumer Behaviour* 10 (4): 192–204.

Mittal, B. (2006) I, me, and mine: how products become consumers' extended selves. *Journal of Consumer Behaviour* 5: 550–62.

Richins, M. (2001) Consumer behaviour as a social science. *Advances in Consumer Research* 28: 1–5.

Ryan, C., McLoughlin, D. and Keating, A. (2006) Tribespotting: a semiotic analysis of the role of consumption in the tribes of Trainspotting. *Journal of Consumer Behaviour* 5 (Sept–Oct): 431–41.

Shaw, D., Newholme, T. and Dickson, R. (2006) Consumption as voting: an exploration of consumer empowerment. *European Journal of Marketing* 40 (9/10): 1049–67.

Stoll, M., Baecke, S. and Kenning, P. (2008) What they see is what they get? An fMRI-study on neural correlates of attractive packaging. *Journal of Consumer Behaviour* 7 (4/5): 342–59.

Vargo, S.L. and Lusch, R.F. (2004) Evolving to a new dominant logic for marketing. *Journal of Marketing* 68 (Jan): 1–17.

Wagner-Tsukamoto, S. and Tadajewski, M. (2006) Cognitive anthropology and the problem-solving behaviour of green consumers. *Journal of Consumer Behaviour* 5 (May–Jun): 235–44.

More online

To gain free access to additional online resources to support this chapter please visit: **www.sagepub.co.uk/blythe**

Part Two

Psychological issues in consumer behaviour

Psychology is the study of human thought processes. Psychologists have made a great many contributions to our understanding of how people make consumption decisions, not least in the areas of perception and learning.

Chapter 2 is about the basic urges that make people want to change their circumstances. Many of these urges centre around seeking pleasure, so marketers will usually try to make the buying and consuming processes as pleasurable as possible. This holds true even for such mundane, practical products as commercial vehicles and tools. Chapter 3 examines the ways in which people make appropriate decisions, establishing goals, minimising risks and dealing with the uncertainty that is a factor of any decision-making. Chapter 4 is about personality – what it is that makes us who we are. These differences between one person's mental make-up and that of another create the differences in choices and choice behaviour which drive marketing.

For many people, marketing communication is mainly about establishing the brand in consumers' mental map, so an understanding of perception has a clear importance for them. Chapter 5 therefore looks at perception. For others, marketing's main aim should be to ensure that customers have a good experience of the products and come back to buy more – in which case the learning process becomes of great interest. This is the subject matter of Chapter 6.

Finally, Chapter 7 looks at the ways in which attitudes are formed and changed. Understanding how people develop their attitudes to brands, and how marketers might seek to change those attitudes, is an obvious area of interest. Equally important is understanding how people's attitudes towards one's brands might be changed by other forces (such as competitors). Maintaining a positive brand attitude is therefore equally important.

Psychology always centres around the individual, and marketers would do well to remember that each of us is an individual, with our own particular traits, talents and failings. It is all too common for businessmen and women to refer to 'the consumer' as if all people were the same. Psychologists offer the antidote to this type of thinking.

CHAPTER ②
Drive, motivation and hedonism

LEARNING OBJECTIVES

After reading this chapter you should be able to:

- Explain the role of the subconscious in motivation.
- Understand the difference between needs and wants.
- Explain how drives are generated.
- Explain the role of needs and wants in marketing.
- Explain the relationship between motivation and behaviour.
- Critique the concept of hierarchy of need.
- Explain how motivations change with changes in wealth.
- Explain the role of hedonism in purchasing behaviour.

Introduction

Dissatisfaction is the beginning of all behaviour. If we were not dissatisfied, we would simply stick with what we have – there would be no need to change what we do. The gap between where we are now and where we want to be is what drives us to make changes in our lives, and of course this is what makes us change the products we own and the services we consume.

Understanding what motivates people has clear implications for marketers. If we know what drives people to buy particular products and services we are in a much better position to ensure that our products have the features and benefits that people want. If we understand how the pressure to buy develops, we can communicate better with people to show how we can meet their needs (before the need actually arises, in some cases). If we know how people rank their needs, we know when they are likely to be ready to buy our products. Of course, marketing practitioners do not yet have all the answers, so we are a long way from being able to predict consumption behaviour with anything like real accuracy.

Much of what drives us as individuals is the desire for pleasure. In the wealthier countries of the world, our basic survival needs have long been taken care of. We no longer simply eat to survive, for example: we eat more than enough simply for pleasure, so that few of us have ever experienced real hunger. The same applies to our housing, our clothing, our heating and so forth. We therefore look to satisfy our emotional, aesthetic needs – in other words, we look for things that are pleasurable or fun.

This chapter examines the forces that drive behaviour. Beginning with drive (the basis of all motivation) the chapter goes on to look at different studies of motivation, and the role of pleasure-seeking in consumer behaviour.

Case study: Harley-Davidson

In 1901 William Harley, then aged 21, completed the design for an internal combustion engine designed to fit on a bicycle. With his friend Arthur Davidson, he built the first prototype motorcycle in a wooden shed: not only did the shed survive the experience, but so did the motorbike. It was bought by an old school friend, Henry Meyer, and in 1904 the first dealership opened up in Chicago.

The partners' enthusiasm and design skills resulted in a Harley-Davidson winning a 15-mile race on July 4, 1905, achieving an average speed of almost 50 miles per hour over the course. By the time the United States entered the First World War in 1917, Harley-Davidson was a well-established company with a reputation for reliability: the company was already selling motorcycles to police forces, but the US Army placed an order for half the firm's output, boosting the firm into the big league. The first American to enter Germany in 1918 was riding one of the 20,000 Harley-Davidsons produced for the Army during the war.

The Second World War produced an even bigger boost to the company's fortunes, this time based on soldiers' experience of riding Harleys while in uniform. Over 90,000 motorcycles were produced for the Army: many never came back to the United States (there are persistent stories about brand-new Harleys being buried on US bases at the end of the war). During the post-war economic boom in the United States, many returned soldiers were able to buy Harleys for transportation or for fun. The Harley was certainly the motorcycle of choice – the company's main competitor, Hendee (manufacturers of the Indian motorbike), went out of business in 1953.

In the wave of patriotism engendered during the Cold War, Harley-Davidson became the stuff of legends. Elvis Presley was photographed astride one in 1956, helping to create the idea that motorbikes were for the rebel, the free spirit. The 1953 movie *The Wild One* (starring a youthful Marlon Brando) helped the image, although the bike Brando rode for the movie was actually a British-made Triumph.

Harley are well aware of the myth-like status of the motorbikes. Japanese-built motorcycles are cheaper and often perform better, but there is nothing quite like a Harley!

You are very likely to be asked a question about motivation. Having a clear understanding not only of the models, but also of their weaknesses, will help you to gain extra marks – for example, most motivation models derive from personnel management studies rather than consumer behaviour studies, so something is likely to have been lost in translation. Second, consider whether the models really stack up in practice – is Maslow's hierarchy really a hierarchy? Are people really not motivated by money, as Herzberg suggests? Third, the models usually operate on a 'one size fits all' basis, which clearly does not fit well with reality – people are different from each other, and have different motivations.

Drive

Drive is the force that makes a person respond to a need. It is an internal stimulus caused by a gap between someone's actual state and their desired state. In other words, drive is created when the position someone is in at that moment differs from the position they would like to be in. A typical example would be someone becoming thirsty. The actual state is 'thirsty', the desired state is 'not thirsty', so a drive to go for something to drink is created. Other more subtle drives are apparent in human beings, of course: if the actual state is 'not accepted by your work colleagues' and the desired state is 'to be accepted by work colleagues', the drive might be even more powerful than that of thirst.

Actual state The condition in which the person happens to be at a given time

Desired state The condition in which the individual would like to be

As shown in Figure 2.1, the greater the gap between the actual state and the desired state, the greater the drive to do something about it. Once the gap between actual and desired states has closed, the drive disappears: our thirsty person, having had a drink, now no longer feels any pressure to look for a drink. The energy formerly devoted to finding something to drink can now be channelled elsewhere. In some

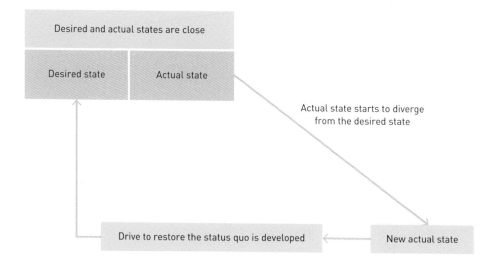

Figure 2.1   Creating a drive

cases, achieving the desired state may lead the individual to raise his or her sights and aim for something even better. For example, someone who has saved for years to buy a BMW may finally buy the car, but immediately start saving for an even more expensive car.

Marketers cannot usually do very much about the actual state. We cannot make somebody thirsty, or hungry, or remove their possessions: what we can sometimes do is encourage people to revise their desired state, in other words encourage people to aspire to something new. Most of the effort marketers put into generating drives is directed at changing the desired state, in other words encouraging people to feel that they deserve something better than whatever they currently possess. Marketers can also remind people about their actual or desired states in order to encourage them to move a purchasing decision forward.

If the drive state is at a high level (i.e. the gap between the actual and desired states is large) the individual is more open to the idea of trying a new way of satisfying the need. This is fairly obvious: if a thirsty person finds that his or her favourite brand of soft drink is out of stock at the corner shop, there are two choices available. Either the person can buy a different brand, or he or she can go to a different shop. If the person is not feeling especially thirsty, he or she might be prepared to make the trip to the next shop, but if the thirst is very strong the individual will be much more likely to buy the new brand. Most people are familiar with the problem of food shopping when hungry – most of us tend to overbuy when we are in that position because our drive level is high.

If the drive state is at a low level, a reminder might stimulate the individual to take action. For example, it is common to see signs saying 'Teas, Coffees, Sandwiches, Burgers 150 Yards' when driving. These signs are placed at the right distance from the vendor so that passing drivers have time to be reminded that they are growing hungry or thirsty before they pass the vendor.

The owner of the burger van is unlikely to have studied consumer behaviour or the psychology of drive, but will have found out by trial and error that the sign needs to be 150 yards (or 250, or 350) away from the van in order to give drivers enough time to think, discuss with a passenger, and pull over safely. Reminding people that they may have a need is called *activating the need*. Although the motorist is not actively looking for a cup of coffee or a snack, the sign acts as a reminder that a cup of coffee is enjoyable, and helps to strengthen a low-intensity drive by moving the desired state further from the actual state. Motorists whose drive state is at zero (perhaps because they just had lunch) will simply drive straight past.

Challenging the status quo

Marketers are constantly telling us about how customer-orientated they are. To hear most of them talk, you would think they are engaged in some kind of charity work – meeting the customers' needs, listening to the customers, helping consumers achieve a lifestyle and so forth.

So what's all this about 'activating' a need? Either the need is there or it isn't – and if it isn't, should we really be trying our best to put it there? Should we be messing around with people's drive states, trying to raise them and make them dissatisfied with life? In short, are we in the business of creating a need, then (just by chance) happening to have the solution to hand?

Allowing the drive to become stronger can make the consumption experience more enjoyable. Delayed gratification increases the pleasure of satisfying the need – although it is not always the case that this is worth the wait (Nowlis et al. 2003). Most of us enjoy a meal much more if we are really hungry, and even saving up for a special treat increases the pleasure when the goal is finally attained. Each of us has a level at which the drive provides a pleasant stimulus without being uncomfortable or threatening: this is called the optimum stimulation level, or OSL. If the drive goes above the OSL, the individual will seek to make an immediate adjustment by satisfying the need. If stimulation falls below the OSL, the individual is likely to allow the drive to strengthen before acting on it. In fact people often enjoy the anticipation more than they do the actual consumption (Raghunathan and Mukherji 2003).

OSL is subjective, that is to say it varies from one individual to another. Research has shown that people with high OSLs like novelty and risk-taking, whereas those with low OSLs prefer the tried and tested. People with high OSLs also tend to be younger (Raju 1980).

Drive acts as the basic component for motivation: motivation is drive directed at a specific objective. If we consider drive as a general feeling that things are not as they should be, we can see that motivation is a drive that has crystallised into a definite decision to do something about the problem. Marketers are able to help people (or direct people) towards specific ways of satisfying the drive by giving them a specific solution which they might be motivated to adopt.

Optimum stimulation level (OSL) The point at which a need has become strong, but before it has become unpleasantly so

Motivation

Motives can be classified according to the list shown in Table 2.1. Although it is difficult to separate out people's motivations for making a particular purchase, emotional and dormant motives often take precedence over rational and conscious motives.

Table 2.1 Classification of consumer motives

Primary motives	The reasons that lead to the purchase of a product class. For example, an individual might look for a new car to replace one that is becoming old and unreliable
Secondary motives	These are the reasons behind buying a particular brand. Our prospective car buyer might have reasons for buying a Toyota rather than a Ford, or a Ford rather than a BMW
Rational motives	These motives are based on reasoning, or a logical assessment of the person's current situation. The car purchaser may need a car that will carry four children and a large amount of camping equipment, for example
Emotional motives	Motives having to do with feelings about the brand. Sometimes emotions get the better of us – our prospective car buyer may end up with a sports car, despite having four children and a tent to accommodate!
Conscious motives	These are the motives of which we are aware. Because our car buyer knows he needs a new car, this element of his motivation is conscious
Dormant motives	These motives operate below the conscious level. The car buyer's desire to buy a sports car may be linked to his approaching middle age, but he may not be aware of this

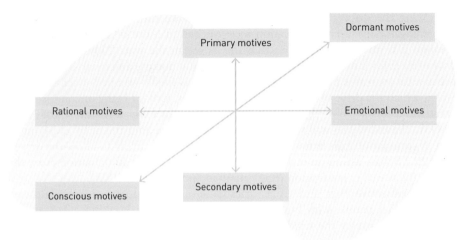

Figure 2.2   Dimensions of motives

Motives should be distinguished from instincts, which are automatic responses to external stimuli. A motive is simply a reason for carrying out a particular behaviour: instincts are pre-programmed responses which are inborn in the individual, and are involuntary. Although behaviour may result from an instinctive source (for example, ducking when a helicopter appears to fly out of a cinema screen), virtually all consumer behaviour is non-instinctive, or volitional.

Figure 2.2 shows the dimensions of motives. Motives can be classified across three dimensions, with the rational/conscious/primary ends relating to each other, as do the dormant/emotional/secondary ends. Any given motivation can be placed within the three-dimensional space represented by the diagram.

Classifying needs

There have been many psychological studies of motivation, and several that have focused on consumer behaviour issues. Needs are the basis of all motivation, so it may be worth remembering that needs are a perceived lack of something, whereas wants are specific satisfiers. In order for someone to recognise a need, the individual not only should be without something, but should also perceive this as something that would make life more pleasant or convenient. Unless the individual understands how the proposed product will make a positive difference to his or her lifestyle, the product will not be perceived as filling a need and the individual will not want it.

Need A perceived lack of something

Want A specific satisfier for a need

Perceiving a need: The Yamana tribe

Tierra del Fuego lies at the southernmost tip of South America. It is buffeted by gales from the Antarctic, and is so far south that much of the land is covered in snow throughout the harsh winters. It is inhabited largely by penguins, and by a small number of hardy farmers who use the short summers to grow their crops, then batten down the hatches to survive the winter.

The Yamana tribe inhabited this harsh country for thousands of years, but lacked something that most cold-country people discovered very early on: clothes. The Yamana never invented clothing, apart from tiny loincloths

and a few strips of cloth worn for decorative purposes. They spent their days canoeing in the icy waters, hunting penguins (which formed a large part of their diet) and fishing. They had, however, invented fire, so when the weather got really bad they would cluster round large bonfires to keep warm. It was the light of these fires that caused the early European explorers to call the country Land of Fire – Tierra del Fuego.

There is some evidence that the Yamana underwent a biological adaptation to the conditions. European explorers (including Captain Cook) reported that Yamana tribes people would often be sweating in conditions which the Europeans found cold even when fully dressed in winter clothing. Even so, following on from contact with Europeans the Yamana began to wear clothes, and within a relatively short period of time they went the way of most aborigines – disease, deliberate murder by settlers, and the disappearance of the penguins on which they depended for their diet combined to kill them.

For thousands of years the Yamana had felt no need whatsoever for clothes. Standing round their fires cooking penguins in the winter they had perfectly comfortable and happy conditions for living: although this may seem strange to us, their early contacts with Europeans must have seemed even stranger to them. Once the concept of clothing was explained, they suddenly recognised the need for clothing, and when the last pure-blooded Yamana died in the late 1990s they were certainly fully clothed and indistinguishable from any other Argentinians. Their traditional way of life, however, represented an extreme example of not recognising something as a need until a solution is presented.

There have been many attempts on the part of psychologists to develop lists of needs. Some of these lists run into the dozens: Murray (1938) listed twenty separate need categories, for example. These are as follows: succourance, nurturance, sentience, deference, abasement, defendence, infavoidance, harmavoidance, achievement, counteraction, dominance, aggression, affiliation, autonomy, order, rejection, sex, understanding, exhibition and play. Murray developed this list from his extensive clinical experience rather than from a programme of organised research, so much of the evidence for the list is anecdotal.

Virtually all these needs have marketing implications. The need for rejection is used by brand owners when they exhort consumers to reject own-label products, and the need for nurturance is emphasised in advertisements for cold cures and soup. The need for sentience is appealed to by cable stations such as the Discovery Channel and the History Channel. Murray's list is long, but probably not definitive – there are probably many other needs which are not included in the list. Also, some needs on the list conflict with each other, for example dominance and deference.

Marketing in practice: Sky TV

Sky TV, as the name suggests, had its beginnings in the satellite TV business. In 1989 Sky Television began broadcasting via the Astra satellite direct to homes in the UK and Western Europe: at that time, viewers needed a satellite dish mounted on their houses to receive the signal. The following year, Sky merged with rival British Satellite Broadcasting (BSB) to form BSkyB. Currently the company offers over 140 channels of television.

(Continued)

(Continued)

In recent years, the service has been delivered mainly by fibre-optic cable, and packaged with computer and telephone broadband services.

So who needs 140 channels of TV? Answer: Nobody. However, a large number of people have common interests in packages selected from the 140 channels. Sky offers a Children's Mix, which includes channels such as Nickelodeon, Boomerang and Jetix: it offers a Knowledge Mix, which includes Discovery, National Geographic and Animal Planet: a News and Events Mix, including Sky News, Eurosport and Bloomberg. Each mix includes many other channels, and there is even a Variety Mix which has an across-the-board selection.

Subscribers can also pay for premium channels such as movies and major sports channels. Although television stations appear to be meeting a need solely for entertainment, Sky offers solutions for a wide variety of subdivisions of need.

Because human beings are complex creatures with strong social bonds, we tend to have a wider range of needs than animals, and we also have many needs that go beyond mere survival: some commentators divide needs into primary needs, which are concerned with biological functions and survival, and secondary needs, which are concerned with everything else. In some cases, researchers have concentrated heavily on the idea that most needs are biologically determined. Internal genetic stimuli are driven by homeostasis, which is the tendency for any living entity to try to maintain a state of equilibrium: in the natural world, change is death. The drives that maintain homeostasis are involuntary, as is the behaviour that results from it. If one becomes too hot, for example, one begins sweating, and if one becomes too cold one develops goose pimples and one may even begin shivering. A sudden shock will result in adrenaline entering the bloodstream, which may be exciting (a positive outcome, which is often generated by white-knuckle rides at theme parks) or may be merely frightening (a negative outcome, which may be generated by a near-accident or a threatening situation such as a street robbery).

 ## Challenging the status quo

Humans are born with a fear of falling, yet we often go to theme parks and fun fairs, and even go bungee-jumping. Falling off a bridge with lengths of elastic round your ankles might be thrilling, but isn't it also pretty stupid? And if we like to be thrilled by such things, why isn't it fun if someone pushes you off a cliff?

Sometimes, of course, it *is* fun. If your friend playfully pushes you into a swimming pool, the correct response is to laugh – but if a complete stranger did it, or an aggressive bully, you'd probably call the police.

So where do we draw the line? How do we decide what is fun, and what is frightening? Why do we put our lives in danger (threatening our survival needs) just for esteem or self-actualisation needs?

Hunger and thirst are obviously biologically generated, but most eating and drinking happens as a result of social or aesthetic demands. Socially motivated eating might include dinner parties, meeting friends for a meal, business lunches and picnics. Curiosity is often supposed to be socially generated, and there is certainly evidence that exploration of the world has a connection with particular countries and cultures, but we also know that some curiosity is biological. Most carnivorous animals display an innate tendency to explore and investigate their environment: cats, dogs and humans all display this behaviour, and bears in zoos are generally happier if their food is hidden from them so that they have to explore and find it.

The best-known biological motivator is, of course, sex. Marketers have used mild sexual imagery in advertising throughout its history, and at various times there have been advertisements that have overstepped the boundaries of good taste and have been attacked or withdrawn. There is certainly evidence that Valentine's day gift-giving is associated with power relationships between the genders (Rugimbana et al. 2003).

The arousal theory of motivation (Zuckerman 2000) proposes that people need to be aroused if they are to become motivated (see Figure 2.3). People seek to maintain an optimum level of arousal: too little and they become bored, too much and they become stressed. Zuckerman developed a 'hierarchy' of stimulation, as follows:

1 Thrills, adventure-seeking, risk-taking through extreme sports, or adventure travel. The highest level of arousal.
2 Experience-seeking through travel, walking, the arts, books. The second highest level.
3 Disinhibition (removing the internal inhibitors that control behaviour). Social stimulation, parties, drinking alcohol, etc.
4 Boredom. The need to change things around, perhaps to buy new products, try new things, etc.

Disinhibition Removal of the internal inhibitors which constrain behaviour

At the lowest end of the hierarchy – boredom – the individual has a risk-free but also stimulation-free existence: at the highest level – thrill-seeking – the individual has an exciting but dangerous life. Most people establish a balance between the quiet life and the stimulating life, at some point on the continuum which is specific to themselves.

Probably the best-known motivation theory is Maslow's Hierarchy of Need (Maslow 1954) which sought to show that people are motivated to fulfil different needs in a specific order, beginning with survival needs (as the most pressing needs to satisfy) and ending with self-actualisation needs (the need to fulfil a long-held ambition, or to act independently of the pressures and opinions of other people, or to act for action's sake). The reasoning behind the model is that needs cannot always be met all at once. Sometimes one need must be fulfilled at the expense of another, creating motivational conflict.

Self-actualisation The need to become the ideal self

Figure 2.3   Zuckerman's hierarchy of stimulation

At the lowest level of the hierarchy, survival needs, marketers offer houses, clothes and food. However, in most cases these are not sold as survival items – more commonly the marketing communications emphasise other aspects of the products such as their appearance, flavour or location. Relatively few products are offered purely on the basis of survival, and most of these are in the category of safety equipment for sports such as aviation or boating.

At the security level, people buy insurance policies, savings plans, burglar alarms and car breakdown memberships. In recent years, we have developed new safety needs: we need to secure our computers against fraudsters and malicious viruses, and we need to be careful about our personal information on social networking sites. This has led to the development of whole new industries, developing software to combat such dangers. People also spend money safeguarding their health, hence the huge sales of products designed to help people lose weight or give up smoking. The popularity of such products in the period immediately following the New Year celebrations indicates the degree to which people believe they should safeguard their health (but not yet). Survival needs might also be satisfied through healthcare products or even slimming products.

At the belonging level, people buy a wide range of products: fashion clothing, club memberships, sports equipment and so forth. In order to be accepted at the golf club, members not only need to pay their membership fees, green fees and so forth, they also need to buy the right set of clubs, the right clothing and the right magazines. Belonging needs are therefore of considerable interest to marketers.

Esteem needs include anything that someone buys as a status symbol (see Chapter 10). Products that make a statement about oneself include fashion, cars, expensive hobbies such as flying, holidays and houses. Almost any product might have an esteem value in the right quarters, and there are even circumstances in which a lack of consumption generates esteem – backpackers may have more respect for someone who has managed to cross Asia for less money than anyone else, for example. Esteem needs may also play a part in seemingly altruistic behaviour – people who buy *The Big Issue* (the UK magazine devoted to helping homeless people) do so not so much for the actual magazine content, but because there is a dimension of helping others in the purchase (Hibbert et al. 2005). This may be coupled to the fact that the magazine is a visible purchase, whereas a contribution to a charity would not be.

Aesthetic needs can be met in many ways. In the main, such needs are traditionally associated with the arts: paintings, sculptures, books, theatre, film and music being the main ways aesthetic needs have been met. However, a hiking holiday in an area of outstanding natural beauty is also a way of meeting aesthetic needs, as is a microlight aircraft or a yacht.

At the self-actualisation level, needs might be fulfilled in a great many ways. In some cases, self-actualisation needs are met by reducing consumption, for example if the individual decides that a 'green' lifestyle should be adopted. Someone who has worked in a city for many years might, for example, buy a smallholding in the country and grow his or her own food, use solar power for electricity and run a wood-burning stove for heat. Self-actualisation might include the concept of freedom: the ability to make choices as a consumer is an expression of freedom, and is derived in part from having the necessary wealth to buy whatever one wants or needs, and in part from a lack of legal restrictions on purchases (Mick and Humphreys 2008).

Maslow's hierarchy (see Figure 2.4) has been widely criticised for being too simplistic, and for ignoring the many exceptions that can easily be seen in everyday life. For example, an artist starving in a garret is clearly placing aesthetic or self-actualisation needs ahead of survival needs, and someone who gives up a good career in order to work with poor people in developing countries is giving up security in favour of esteem self-actualisation needs. Such anomalies are commonplace. Another criticism

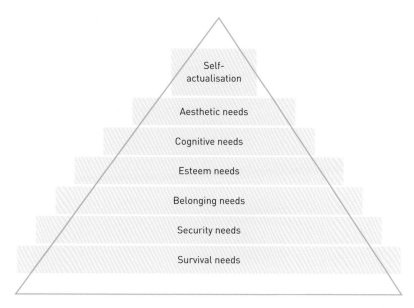

Figure 2.4 Maslow's Hierarchy of Need

of the hierarchy is that it is largely irrelevant to the vast majority of people in the wealthy countries of Europe and North America because they already have their survival and security needs taken care of, and indeed many of them are operating at the self-actualisation level already (McNulty 1985).

A further criticism is that an individual may move to different parts of the hierarchy even within a single day: for example, being primarily concerned with esteem needs during the working day, with aesthetic needs when enjoying an evening meal at a good restaurant, and with belonging needs when meeting friends for a drink afterwards.

These criticisms notwithstanding, Maslow's model is widely taught and widely referred to: there is little doubt that the needs themselves exist and can be categorised in this way, but whether they truly operate as a hierarchy is open to question. There may be evidence that the hierarchy operates for large groups of people, so that there will be a prevailing social paradigm in which some needs are brought to the forefront. Research by McNulty (1985) showed that an increasing number of people in the UK were operating at the self-actualisation level, presumably as a result of rising living standards. In the intervening thirty years, it would appear to the casual observer that this trend has not reversed, and has (if anything) accelerated. Another use of the Maslow hierarchy has been the VALS (values and lifestyles) model (Mitchell 1983), which describes nine different lifestyles, as shown in Figure 2.5.

The model supposes that people at the lower levels (which correspond with Maslow's survival and security needs) are controlled by their basic needs for food, shelter and a measure of security. After these very basic needs have been met, there is a divergence: some people become inner-directed (driven by internal motives) while others become outer-directed (motivated by the opinions of others). Inner-directed people may become selfish and uncaring of other people's well-being, they may become interested in new experiences, or they may fulfil a burning ambition to change the world for the better despite opposition. Outer-directed people may seek to copy other people whom they regard as successful, or may seek to impress other people by achieving or by conspicuous consumption. Finally, Mitchell postulates that people may adopt an integrated position, where concern and respect for others is combined with knowledge of their own needs and desires.

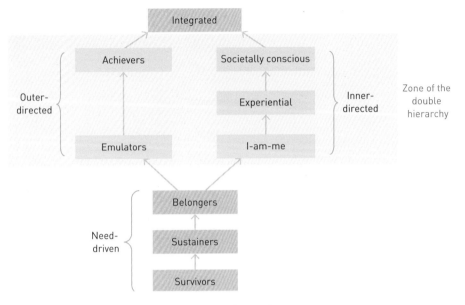

Figure 2.5   The values and lifestyles (VALS) model

Mitchell's model has been used for market segmentation purposes, and the lifestyle types have been identified both in the United States and in Europe. As wealth increases, more people operate at the higher levels: we might reasonably expect that, as countries become wealthier, levels of consumption increase but so do levels of social concern, and levels of crime increase as more people become inner-directed. This may account for crimes committed by people who are already wealthy.

Challenging the status quo

Mitchell's categorisations are all very well for segmentation, but what happens when we are dealing with people at the self-actualisation level? By definition, these people might do *anything*! They are professional individualists.

Also, how clear are the boundaries? To say that someone is outer-directed means that they care about the opinions of other people – but do they care about the opinions of everyone else, or just a few people? Are they attracted to or repelled by the opinions of the other people in question?

Finally, if someone acts rebelliously, is this because they don't care what other people think – or because they care very deeply? Being a rebel is a statement made to impress other people, is it not?

The basic problem here is that people consistently refuse to be categorised!

Motivational factors

An alternative approach to considering motivation was that advanced by Herzberg (1966). Herzberg was a medical researcher who developed the idea that some factors in life are motivational, while others are simply expected as a matter of course: the absence of these factors would be demotivating, but more of the same would not be motivational. Herzberg called the first group of factors motivators, and the second group, hygiene factors (he was a medical researcher, remember). The hygiene factors needed to be present in order to prevent the 'disease' of demotivation. Herzberg's findings were considered revolutionary at the time of their publication because he claimed that salary is not a motivator – people expect a fair rate of pay for the work they are expected to do, so it is a hygiene factor, and only affects motivation if it is seen to be unfair in some way. For marketers, Herzberg's work is interesting in that it explains product differentiation. For example, anyone buying a car expects that it will have wheels, an engine, an enclosed space to sit in and space for luggage. Nowadays, people would expect it to have a radio and a CD player as well, and possibly air conditioning. These are hygiene factors, the basic core product features that any car would have. Lack of any of these would demotivate the customer. To generate motivation to buy, though, the vehicle manufacturer would need to add features as motivators: a CD changer, smarter upholstery, an in-car refrigerator, etc.

Hygiene factors Those aspects of a product which consumers would expect as a basic feature of any product in the category

Differentiation Providing a product with features that distinguish it from competing products

Marketing in practice: Differentiation

The history of the automobile has been one of continuous adaptation, additional features and added inducements to buy. The basic need is for transportation: ever since the first human being jumped on the back of a horse we have wanted to travel further, faster and more comfortably, and although the earliest cars were less reliable (and sometimes slower) than horses, they at least had the convenience of starting fairly quickly (without the need for saddling and bridling) and of going pretty much where the driver wanted them to go rather than setting off into a field with the other horses.

Starting with Daimler and Benz's first practical automobile in 1885, manufacturers have added optional extras on a regular basis ever since. For example, in 1890 Canadian Thomas Ahearn invented the car heater. In 1901 disc brakes were added (invented by Lanchester). In 1911 Charles Kettering invented the starter motor, which eliminated the need for hand cranking the engine to start it (Kettering also invented Freon, the gas which has been identified as a major cause of holes in the ozone layer). In 1929 Paul Galvin invented the car radio, although it had to be bought as an optional extra: car manufacturers did not fit radios as standard until the 1970s. Galvin called his new radio the Motorola. Daimler introduced electric windows in 1948, and in 1966 British engineers developed electronic fuel injection.

Not all the inventors were men, incidentally. Mary Anderson invented windscreen wipers (hand-operated at first), and Helen Blair Bartlett, a geologist, invented alumina ceramic insulators for sparkplugs in 1930.

Why all this innovation? Simple. Any car manufacturer could meet the basic hygiene factor of transportation. In order to motivate people to buy a specific model, manufacturers had to add extras, making the car more comfortable, safer, more reliable, or more fun than the competitors' vehicles. Every so often someone will go back to basics and produce a car with 'no frills' for a low price, but the optional extras soon cease to be optional because price is not a good motivator – it is a hygiene factor!

Herzberg's theories are also applied to personnel management, which is outside the scope of this book. As a way of categorising needs, Herzberg's theory is undoubtedly useful, but part of the problem in applying the theory is that people have differing views on what should be a hygiene factor. Once again, it is difficult to make generalisations about people because we all have different priorities.

In Figure 2.6, the motivation line rises somewhat as the individual recognises that the hygiene factors are improving, but this is really a reduction in demotivation. Motivation as such does not start until the motivators begin to arrive, but even so

Innovation A new product of service: the act of adopting a new product or service

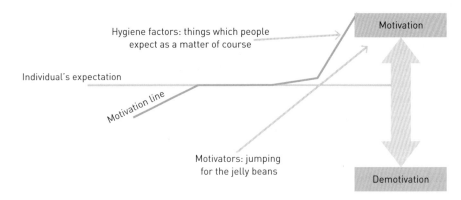

Figure 2.6 Dual-factor theory

there is no sharp rise until the motivators go beyond expectations. At this point, further increases in hygiene factors have no real effect.

Individual factors

A third approach to analysing motivation is Vroom's Expectancy Theory (Vroom 1999). Vroom suggested that motivation is the result of rational calculations made by individuals, taking into account the value of the reward itself, the expected likelihood of being able to obtain the reward, and the effort needed to achieve the reward. The trade-offs between these factors are the subject of the calculation, and if the reward is not adequate compared to the effort needed to win it, the individual will simply not bother to try for it. Equally, if the likelihood of gaining the reward is perceived as being small, the individual will not be motivated to try. Vroom's theory has much to offer – it is more comprehensive in its approach than other theories, and it takes much greater account of individual differences than do either Maslow's or Herzberg's models. As we saw already, individuals may believe that aesthetic needs are more important than survival needs, and (in terms of Herzberg) individuals may have different ideas of what constitute motivators and hygiene factors.

David McClelland suggested that people have three categories of social need in terms of motivation: achievement (the need to excel at something), affiliation (the need to be part of a group) and power (the ability to control outcomes). Different people place different levels of emphasis on these needs, but people who are achievers need constant feedback and praise, people who have a high need for affiliation will tend to want to fit in with their immediate social group, and people who seek power will try to dominate those around them (McClelland 1955). McClelland's work has mainly been used in personnel management, but there are implications for consumer behaviour as well: a person with a high need for affiliation will buy things that make them popular and respected, a person with a high need for power will want to be in control of spending, and so forth.

An aspect of motivation that is not considered in either of the above models is the idea of pain avoidance. Although needs are the basis of all motivation, there is a difference between the need to avoid bad consequences and the need to acquire a benefit. In most cases, someone who wishes to obtain a positive benefit from a purchase has only one way to obtain the benefits, whereas there are many ways to avoid a negative outcome. This was demonstrated by Skinner in his famous experiments with rats, in which rats were taught to push buttons in complex sequences in order to

Experiment A controlled activity in which a given stimulus is offered to respondents in order to discover their reactions

obtain food and avoid electric shocks: the rats became very inventive in the ways they avoided the shocks, but were unable to find any other way to obtain food (Skinner 1953). Human beings are, of course, not rats: we are probably better able to understand the longer-term consequences of our behaviour than a rat would be, so we may be more susceptible to pain-avoidance messages. On the other hand, we may be even more inventive in avoiding the pain.

For example, cautionary-tale advertising in which the negative consequences of an action are shown may result in someone behaving in the desired manner, or it may (and perhaps is more likely to) result in the individual avoiding the advertisement. This may be part of the reason why government campaigns against smoking or drinking often fail – shocking people by telling them about the diseases their habit might cause simply results in people not reading the warnings.

One way in which marketers can use pain avoidance in motivating consumers is by modelling. This is a process whereby people are shown the negative consequences of a given action through an actor who demonstrates the behaviour, and suffers the consequences. For example, an advertisement might show a commuter who has been prosecuted for fare dodging, complete with a detailed account of the consequences of the action ('It was the embarrassment of having to stand up in court and admit fiddling a £2 fare. And I lost my job, because I now have a criminal conviction.') Another example might be a housewife who 'can't shift those greasy stains'. In each case the consumer is invited to see the potential negative consequences of fiddling the fare, or using the wrong washing powder. Modelling can also be used for positive reinforcement, of course (see Table 2.2).

Models should be as similar as possible to the target audience, but at the same time need to be seen as attractive: this may appear to be a contradiction in some cases, but models show ourselves as we wish we were, rather than as we actually are.

For human beings, and especially human beings living in the wealthier countries of the world, most physical needs have been met long ago. We are therefore driven much more by social, aesthetic or psychological needs than by physical needs. This manifests itself most clearly in our eating habits. We eat for pleasure (the flavour and texture of the food), for social purposes (going for a meal with friends, sharing a

Cautionary-tale A story intended to illustrate the possible negative outcomes of a particular course of action

Modelling The act of demonstrating by example behaviour which the marketer would like the target audience to imitate

Table 2.2 Using modelling for positive reinforcement

Modelling employed	Desired response
Instructor, expert, salesperson using the product (in an advertisement or at the point of purchase)	Use product in the correct, technically competent way
Models in advertisements asking questions at the point of purchase	Ask questions at the point of purchase that highlight product advantages
Models in advertisements receiving positive reinforcement or punishment for performing undesired behaviours	Extinction or decrease of undesired behaviours
Individual (or group) similar to the target audience using the product in a novel, enjoyable way	Use the product in new ways

Source: Walter R. Nord and J. Paul Peter (1980) A behaviour modification perspective on marketing. *Journal of Marketing* 44 (Spring): 36–47

snack, going to a dinner party), and even as a means of self-expression (cooking a special meal for friends or family). These needs sometimes override our need to live a healthy lifestyle: we become obese or develop hardening of the arteries, bad teeth and many other diseases caused by eating the wrong things.

Motivational conflict

When needs conflict, motivational conflict occurs. This can take one of three basic forms, as follows:

1 Approach–approach conflict. This happens when the individual is faced with two or more desirable alternatives. For example, the person might have been invited to a party on a weekend when his or her football team is playing a match 300 miles away. Approach–approach conflicts are common, since most people have limited financial resources and often have to choose between spending money on one item, or spending it on a different item.
2 Avoidance–avoidance conflict. This occurs when the individual is faced with two or more equally unappealing choices. For example, someone might be faced with the choice of either buying new shoes to replace an old, comfortable pair, or continuing to wear the old pair despite the fact they are now letting in water and coming apart at the seams.
3 Approach–avoidance conflict. This occurs when the course of action has both positive and negative consequences. For example, some drugs have dangerous side-effects. Most purchases have an element of approach–avoidance conflict since they involve spending money or giving up something else: many purchases of new products involve a switching cost, i.e. the effort and sometimes cash expenditure involved in moving from the old product to the new one. Anyone who has bought a new BluRay player to replace their old DVD player knows about switching costs, and researchers have found that people are reluctant to spend large-denomination banknotes, since 'breaking a 50' involves a sense of loss about the entire amount (Mishra et al. 2008).

The relationship between these motivational conflicts is shown in Figure 2.7.

In many cases, the situation is far more complex than a simple dichotomy. This is because we are usually faced with several possible courses of action, each of which

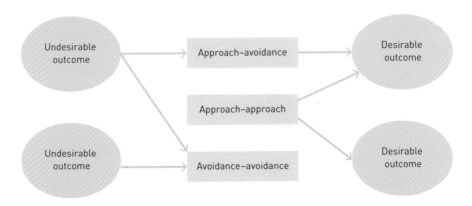

Figure 2.7   Motivation conflict

has both positive and negative consequences. If the motivational conflict is to be resolved, the individual needs to prioritise his or her needs. This is largely a matter for the individual concerned: even though Maslow tried to produce a general model for this, we have already seen that the model is far from perfect.

The intensity of the motivation is sometimes strong enough to override all other considerations, whereas at other times it may be much weaker. Sometimes motivational intensity is high due to a high level of drive (a thirteen-year-old who is being teased at school for wearing the wrong kind of trainers will be highly motivated to obtain the right kind, for example), and sometimes motivational intensity is high due to personal involvement with the product category. Involvement means that the individual places a high importance on having exactly the right product: for example, a pilot would place great importance on obtaining exactly the right spares, fuel and oil for the aircraft, since this affects the safety of the plane (and, of course, the pilot). Similarly, a musician might be very concerned to obtain the right instrument, a film star would be concerned to wear the right clothes, and so forth. Having to put some effort into the consumption experience will often increase the satisfaction the consumer has with the product – this is obviously the case with sports equipment, but may even be the case for such mundane items as self-assembly furniture (Wadhwa and Trudel 2010). Each of us has at least some products with which we are highly involved.

From the viewpoint of marketing, generating involvement is clearly crucial to establishing loyal customers. The greater the involvement, the greater the degree to which consumers make an effort to satisfy the need, and the greater the propensity to remain loyal in future. In some cases firms are able to run loyalty programmes to keep customers involved: supermarket loyalty cards and airline frequent flyer programmes are the usual examples. In other cases involvement is generated by the way the products are promoted, or by celebrity endorsement. There is more on involvement in Chapter 14.

Motivations can be divided into positive and negative. People may act to obtain a reward, or may act to avoid an unwanted outcome. For example, someone may buy aspirin in order to treat a headache (obtain a positive outcome) or to take one aspirin per day to prevent a heart attack (negative motivation). Other commentators divide motivation into internal motivations, which are those originating inside the individual, and external motivations, which are those resulting from an external stimulus or reward. An internal motivation may arise from a self-actualisation need (such as the desire to learn a new language), whereas an external motivation might arise from social needs or physical needs (such as a need to be accepted by a new group of people, or to move to a larger house).

Alternatively, motives might be divided into rational, emotional and instinctive motives. Rational motives are those resulting from a conscious thought process; emotional motives are those resulting from an irrational source such as anger, love, pride, jealousy and so forth. Instinctive motives arise from deeper drives, and may result in obsessive behaviour: in most cases, though, instinctive motives simply drive the occasional impulse purchase.

Hedonism

Hedonism is the cult of pleasure. In consumer behaviour, it refers to the pleasurable aspects of consumption: the flavour of food rather than its nutritional value, the comfort of a car rather than its performance, the appearance of clothing rather than its ability to keep out the cold (Holbrook and Hirschmann 1982). Hedonic purchases

Hedonism The cult of pleasure

are sometimes about a need for being cheered up, and can be triggered by feeling unhappy as well as by a normal day-to-day desire for comfort and pleasure. There is even evidence that a near-death experience can encourage greater pleasure-seeking behaviour, as well as encouraging people to change their lifestyles (perhaps by dieting, or sometimes by stopping a diet) (Shiv et al. 2004).

Marketers put a great deal of effort into designing products that not only work well, but also give pleasure to their owners. This is an important way to differentiate the product from those of competitors, and for some products hedonic content is virtually the entire product: fashion wear, cosmetics, holiday travel, and many service industries such as restaurants and hairdressing rely heavily on hedonism to sell their products.

Marketing in practice: The Ford Transit

Think of hedonism and probably the last thing you would think of is the light commercial vehicle. At first sight, a vehicle for delivering groceries, building materials and furniture has to be as utilitarian as it gets – and for sixty or seventy years that was what manufacturers thought as well.

Then in 1965 the industry was revolutionised by the Ford Transit. The Transit handled like a car, had comfortable seats, was relatively quiet, and had good heating and ventilation systems. It was easy to load and a real pleasure to drive.

Within a few years Ford had captured 30% of the UK light van market. The Transit became known as the People's Van: it was owned by small businesses, by budding rock bands, by hippies who slept in the back, by builders, by couriers, and even by private citizens. Camper van versions, minibus versions, open truck versions and high-roof versions were all produced by Ford for the burgeoning market. The comfort and ease of handling made it ideal for drivers who were non-professionals, i.e. drivers who delivered goods as part of their normal business rather than drivers who delivered for a living.

Even delivery companies switched to Transits as they found that their drivers performed better when they were comfortable and not tired out by wrestling with heavy steering, or trying to coax some power out of a commercial engine. Transits were fast and manoeuvrable – so much so that some police authorities had to upgrade their own vehicles to be able to catch them. Quickly the police adopted Transits as well, to use as Black Marias, as dog-carrying vehicles, or as scene-of-crime vehicles. In September 1985 stunt man Steve Mathews jumped a Transit over 15 vehicles as a fundraiser for cancer research.

Throughout its 50-year life the Transit has been the market leader. It still retains its core values: it is the People's Van because it is designed for people, not for companies. The Transit, more than any other van before it, caters to people's hedonic needs.

Utilitarianism The cult of practicality

Hedonism is sometimes regarded as the opposite of utilitarianism, which is the cult of practicality. In marketing, most products have utilitarian aspects, and some are almost entirely utilitarian: most business-to-business products are utilitarian (there is little hedonic value in a bag of cement, although what a builder builds with it might be extremely hedonic). The relationship between hedonism, utilitarianism, needs and products is shown in Figure 2.8. Utilitarian consumer products might include

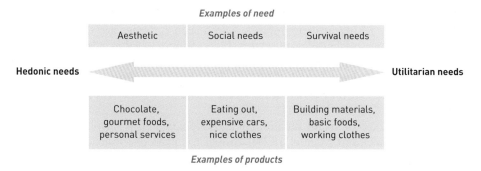

Figure 2.8   Hedonism vs. utilitarianism

cleaning products, energy (electricity and gas), basic foods and most municipal services such as street cleaning and sewage removal.

In most cases, products have both hedonic and utilitarian features. Even a basic, cheap car has comfortable seats, a radio, a heater and so forth. This is because such comforts have become regarded as hygiene factors by most people. This means that manufacturers are in a constant race to add even more hedonic features to their products in order to stay ahead of the competition. Periodically, a company may produce a 'no frills' version of the product at a much-reduced price, and the process starts again. An example of this is low-cost airlines, some of whom now offer extra services such as rapid check-in or choice of seats as a competitive measure.

Adding utilitarian features to hedonic products tends to generate negative feelings about the product, however. This may because the 'pure pleasure' aspect is no longer pure – whereas adding hedonic features to a utilitarian product tends to lead to positive feelings about the product (Saldanha and Williams 2008).

 Challenging the status quo

Is it realistic to make a distinction between hedonic needs and utilitarian needs? After all, what is a pleasure to some people is a necessity to others. For example, take sport: for many people, playing a sport such as squash or tennis is a fun thing to do, a real pleasure, whereas for others it is simply sweaty activity that they don't have to do. But supposing somebody had been told by the doctor to exercise more or risk heart failure? Such a person might take up squash as the 'least worst' alternative, in other words exercise rather than die, but in fact hate every minute of it.

Equally, for most people driving a car is a necessity, purely a means of getting from one place to another conveniently. For others, it might be a real delight – and certainly car manufacturers plug the hedonic aspects of driving far more than they talk about the utilitarian aspects.

Maybe the old saying about one man's meat being another man's poison has some truth in it!

Hedonism also includes experiential needs. People need to have stimulating experiences: we have this in common with most other mammals, especially carnivorous ones. The need to learn by trying new things, the need to have something new to think about, and the need for excitement all stem from the need for new experiences.

Experiential needs are met by playing sport (especially unusual or dangerous sports), by travel and by taking up new hobbies. Often such activities are in conflict with utilitarian and functional needs – there is really no utilitarian value in bungee-jumping or crossing India on a Royal Enfield motorcycle, but both fulfil an experiential need for someone. McAlexander et al. (2002) suggest that competitive advantage can be gained by marketers if they concentrate on the consumers' experience of owning the product.

Hedonism also accounts for the utopian marketplace. This is the place where people dream (Manuel and Manuel 1979). Utopia has been deconstructed as follows (McLaran and Brown 2002):

- Sensory No-Place: This brings feelings of a world apart from the consumer experience.
- Creating Playspace: This provides the open-ended playful nature of the utopian text contained within it.
- Performing Art: This evokes the active life of people in the creation of utopian meanings.

Our dreams and fantasies do not, of course, always turn into reality, and in many cases people prefer to keep a fantasy as just that – remaining within Utopia. This does not prevent marketers from feeding the fantasies – custom car magazines frequently have average readerships aged below the minimum age to have a driving licence, for example.

Interestingly, people sometimes use guilt as a way of controlling their own behaviour. For example, someone who is trying to lose weight might deliberately make themselves feel guilty for eating a chocolate bar, in an attempt to avoid the behaviour in future (Dai et al. 2008). In some cases, people might use 'virtuous' behaviour (such as having salad for lunch rather than sausages and chips) as a guilt-reduction strategy for enjoying a chocolate bar later (Khan et al. 2009). It has even been found that simply having a healthy choice available may lead some people to choose the less-healthy (but more attractive) alternative (Wilcox et al. 2010). This is less likely to happen if the individuals use a rejection strategy in decision-making, that is to say they operate by rejecting alternatives until there is only the healthy option left (Machin and Park 2010). Resisting temptation may lead to an angry (or at least irritated) mood afterwards – researchers found that people who resisted the temptation of a chocolate bar were more likely to choose to see an anger-related film afterwards (Gal and Liu 2010).

In general, hedonic needs account for a large proportion of consumer spending. The current trend towards service industries (as opposed to manufacturing industries) is largely fuelled by hedonic needs, as people travel more, eat out more, and enjoy services such as hairdressing, beauty therapy, cinema, theatre, music concerts and sports facilities. Hedonism is a major component in consumerism, which is the cult of consumption: people derive great pleasure from shopping and consuming. The concept of the consumer society has been around for some time now, and refers to the way in which most human activity in the developed world centres around consumption. We define ourselves by what we consume rather than by what we produce, we spend a large amount of our time consuming things or learning about things to consume (which is itself a form of consumption) and it is impossible for us to have a social life without at the same time being a consumer. Even such activities as finding a life partner cannot come about without elaborate dating rituals and consequent consumption – it would be hard to imagine someone successfully acquiring a girlfriend or boyfriend without first going on a date, eating at a restaurant, buying nice clothes and perfume (or aftershave), or even going to a dating service.

All of this consumption activity is hedonic because it helps us to feel secure in who we are and what we do: although much of it has no practical purpose whatever, it does enable us to enjoy our lives more.

Understanding motivation

One of the difficulties with understanding consumer motivation is that people are often unable to be specific about what has driven them to a specific action. In some cases this is because the motivation operates below the subconscious level, and in other cases it is because the person is not willing to admit to a particular motivation. This is easily observable in everyday life: people often lie about their reasons for taking, or not taking, a particular action since it would involve admitting to something they would prefer to keep to themselves. For example, someone may turn down the opportunity to go to a concert on the grounds of being unwell, when in fact the individual is afraid of meeting up with an ex-girlfriend who likes the same band. This might be embarrassing to admit to. In some cases, people are motivated by some need that is illegal or immoral, so would be extremely unlikely to admit to being motivated by the need. Equally, someone might be genuinely unaware, at a conscious level, of their real motivation – a reluctance to go to a concert might be a fear of crowds, but the individual might believe that actually he or she is too tired to go and would prefer a quiet night in.

In general, people are not so much rational as rationalising. A middle-aged man who is thinking about buying a sports car might actually want it because he wants to recapture his lost youth, but might rationalise the decision by talking about the car's fuel economy and good looks. 'I need a decent car to impress my clients' is a common rationalisation.

In the 1950s and early 1960s there was considerable interest in motivational research. Motivational researchers thought that they had discovered underlying reasons for consumer behaviour, and many of their propositions were seized on by marketers. Unfortunately, some of the propositions were so peculiar they could not reasonably be used – the idea that housewives were symbolically washing away their sins when they did the laundry, or were symbolically giving birth when they baked a cake were among the less credible ideas of the motivational researchers.

A further complication is that any given action is likely to be the result of several different motivations, some of which may even conflict with each other. Some actions are the result of a decision to take the 'least worst' alternative, or may be rationalised in some way in order to maintain an attitude. Sometimes people make wrong decisions, and rationalise their motives afterwards rather than admit their mistake.

Overall, then, it is difficult to penetrate the layers of motivations to find the nugget of true motivation within.

Research into motivation

Identifying consumer motivation is clearly far from simple. Finding out the true motivation for someone's behaviour is similar to finding out a hidden attitude (see Chapter 7). Projective techniques in which respondents are asked to explain the motivation of a fictitious third party will often draw out the individual's real reason for behaving in a specific way: the respondent might be asked to fill in speech bubbles in a cartoon, or be asked what the 'typical' person might think, and so forth. This method was used to research children's motivations for smoking, an activity which (clearly) they would not want to discuss openly (Brucks et al. 2010).

A classic study carried out in the 1950s sought to establish the reasons for poor sales of instant coffee. Housewives were shown two shopping lists which were identical except that one list had instant coffee on it, while the other list had ground coffee. The respondents were asked to describe the type of housewife who would have drawn up each list: the instant coffee list was seen to belong to a woman who is lazy, badly organised and not a good housewife (Haire 1950).

Means–end chain analysis (laddering) involves asking people to explain what each benefit of the product means to them (Gutman 1982: Reynolds and Gutman 1988). The respondent works through a series of 'so what?' questions to arrive at the underlying motivation. For example, someone might be asked about the motivation for buying a bottle of wine, with the questioning going as follows:

'Why did you buy that bottle of wine?'

'Because it's a good Rioja.'

'What does that mean to you?'

'It will taste good.'

'Why is that important?'

'I'm cooking dinner for my girlfriend.'

'Why is the wine important?'

'I want to impress her, and I want her to enjoy the evening.'

'Why is that important?'

'I want her to be in a good mood.'

'Why?'

'Because I'm going to ask her to marry me.'

The questioning could, of course, carry on if we wanted to know why the wine-purchaser wants to marry this specific person, but for most marketers (apart, perhaps, from those running dating agencies) this would not be especially important.

In Figure 2.9, the purchase of a single-malt whisky might be explained superficially by the purchaser as being about the quality of the whisky and its flavour.

Values	Live longer	End
Consequences	Less liver damage	
	Don't get drunk	
	Drink less	
Product attributes	Strong flavour	
	Single-malt whisky	Means

Figure 2.9 Means–end chain

Further investigation shows that the individual finds that he or she drinks less of the product because the flavour is much stronger than that of a blended whisky, which means that he or she is less likely to get drunk quickly and therefore is less likely to suffer liver damage. This enables the individual to achieve a core value, that of living a longer (and presumably healthier) life. The product attributes (quality and flavour) lead to consequences that address core values.

Summary

This chapter has considered the forces that encourage people to buy. Needs are the basic generators of drive, and consequently of motivation, so it might be true to say that need is the basis of virtually all behaviour. Drives develop when there is a gap between where we are and where we want to be – motivation develops when we can see a possible solution (or solutions) to the need problem. Some motivation relates to our physical, utilitarian needs, but as human beings we also have powerful social, aesthetic and pleasure needs, so much of our buying behaviour relates to hedonism.

 **Key points**

- Many motives are irrational or unconscious.
- Need is a perceived lack: want is a specific satisfier.
- Drive is caused by the gap between actual and desired states.
- Most marketing is about activating needs and directing wants.
- Motivation is complex, and cannot always be inferred from behaviour.
- Needs can be ranked, but there is considerable overlap.
- As wealth increases, motivations change.
- Many, even most, purchases are motivated at least in part by hedonic needs.

Review questions

1 Why do some people have higher OSLs than others?
2 What is the difference between primary and secondary motivations?
3 What are the main difficulties in categorising needs?
4 What are the main criticisms of Maslow's Hierarchy of Need?
5 Why is punishment a poorer motivator than reward?
6 What is the purpose of modelling?
7 What is meant by approach–approach conflict?
8 Why is hedonism an important factor for marketers?
9 How might marketers find out which factors are regarded as hygiene factors in a product, and which are motivators?
10 In which areas of marketing would Vroom's Expectancy Theory have most relevance?

Case study revisited: Harley-Davidson

In the early days, Harleys were used purely as economical transportation. During the war years, they were used more like mechanical horses – able to go where motor cars could not, able to travel over rough terrain, but also able to cover long distances by road much faster than a horse could. After the Second World War, motorcycles in general, and Harleys in particular, began to take on a very different set of roles.

First, motorcyclists rode for pleasure. Nothing beats a motorbike for the sensation of travelling – the wind in one's face, the feel of the road, the ability to hear and see much better than is possible from the cocoon of a car, all combine to create an exhilarating ride. Riding a big bike like a Harley-Davidson also provides a sense of power – motorbikes accelerate faster than cars, are much more manoeuvrable, and are often much faster overall.

Second, Harleys have acquired a mythology of their own, taking over from the cowboy's horse as a symbol of freedom to roam the wide-open spaces. Movies such as *Easy Rider*, in which two hippies cross America on customised Harleys, have embedded the bikes in the minds of the **Baby Boomers**, who now represent Harley's main group of customers. Outside the United States, Harleys represent the American dream, and conjure up images of small-town diners, superhighways and spectacular scenery.

Third, Harleys help middle-aged men recall their lost youth. Men who have spent their lives working to pay the mortgage, bring up the family and build a career suddenly find themselves in their 50s with money to spare and time to spend it: their wives might want a new kitchen or a swimming pool, but the man wants a Harley. The main competition for Harley-Davidson is not other motorbike manufacturers – it's home improvement companies.

Fourth, Harley owners belong together. They often organise trips together, they have a newsletter, they offer each other advice, they help each other with problems with the bikes. The Harley Owners' Group (HOG) is extremely active, in fact.

All in all, a Harley-Davidson is much more than a means of transport. It's a whole way of life.

Baby Boomer An individual born between 1945 and 1965, a period of exceptionally high birth rates in Europe and the United States

Case study: Singapore Airlines

The airline business is a tough one, and getting tougher by the day. Environmental taxes, higher costs, more crowded skies, cut-throat price competition from low-cost carriers and deregulation have all taken their toll. Some national carriers have even gone bankrupt – somewhat embarrassing for the countries concerned, but international trade rules restrict or even ban government subsidies for national flag carriers, so they are forced to compete or die.

Aircraft manufacturers are faced with a form of arms race as well. The competition is on for the most environmentally friendly (i.e. quiet and fuel-efficient) aircraft, but at the same time it needs to be comfortable for passengers and crew, and safe and cheap to run. In fact, the ability to take off, fly somewhere and land at the other end has almost become secondary.

Singapore is a small country, having only 5.2 million residents, but it is extremely wealthy: one in six households has over $1 million US in disposable wealth. Its national airline, Singapore Airlines, punches well above its weight in world terms, and was the first airline to place an order for the A380 Airbus. The A380 is a superjumbo – theoretically, it could carry 850 passengers (although no airline has ordered it in that configuration, which would be entirely economy class), and it is the world's largest airliner (the wingspan is longer than the first powered flight by the Wright Brothers).

Singapore Airlines did not buy A380s for the purpose of flying a lot of people, though. The A380's main advantage is the wide open spaces inside. Most airlines have ordered it with the traditional three classes – economy, business and first – but Singapore Airlines have what they call 'a class above first'. People prepared to pay enough for the luxury can have their own suite on board the aircraft.

The suites contain an armchair (hand-stitched by an Italian craftsman), a full-length bed and a separate padded seat for visitors. The suite has sliding doors with blinds so that the passenger can be completely private, and there is a 23-inch LCD TV set offering the latest movie releases, TV shows and news bulletins. There is, of course, a telephone and a 110-volt power supply which accepts US, Australian, Japanese and European plugs. USB connectors allow passengers to play their own music or movies if they prefer.

Bathroom facilities are shared, but the spaces are luxurious with Hollywood-style mirrors and leather upholstery. Passengers are given complimentary toiletries, nightwear and slippers, and of course alcoholic drinks are free and unlimited. The cuisine is, well, first-class: menus have been developed by a panel of world-class chefs.

Of course, none of this comes cheap. Fares are at least 10 times those paid by the passengers in Economy, and Singapore Airlines is not the cheapest way of getting from one place to another in any case. Undoubtedly, if you have £12,000 to spend on getting from London to Singapore and back, having your own suite is a wonderful thing to do – but for most of us, raising the money to fly Economy is enough of a challenge.

Of course, nothing stands still in the airline business. Emirates (the airline of Dubai) now offers on-board showers on its A380s, as well as a first-class bar and lounge area on the upper deck. Although Emirates don't have separate beds (your suite's seat has to be converted to a flat bed) they do have a personal mini-bar in each suite. The A380 offers so much space, it can only be a matter of time before an airline puts a gym on board, with a personal trainer.

Meanwhile, Singapore Airlines has its suites fully booked on many flights. Clearly there are plenty of people out there prepared to pay a lot for a bit more comfort.

Questions

1 Why might someone be prepared to pay upwards of £500 an hour for this level of comfort?
2 What factors other than comfort cause people to fly first class?
3 How might the knowledge that there are suites on board affect the feelings of people in Economy?
4 Why is the price so much higher for a suite than for Economy?
5 What basic needs are being met by having a suite?

Further reading

Classical Motivation Theories – Similarities and Differences Between Them by Stephanie Hoffman is that rare thing, a commercially published undergraduate dissertation. Stephanie is German, and the thesis is published by GRIN Verlag oHG. It provides a very useful and thoughtful set of comparisons between several classical motivation theorists (some of which have not been included in this chapter, for various reasons). Incidentally, the thesis got a B+.

For a psychologist's viewpoint on expectancy models, Henning V., Hennig-Thurau, T. and Feiereisen, S. (2012) Giving the expectancy-value model a heart. *Psychology and Marketing* 29 (10): 765–781, gives an interesting insight into motivation.

Christmas is, of course, a time for hedonistic behaviour. For a useful overview of how people create meaning for their hedonistic consumption, take a look at: Tynan, C. and McKechnie, S.(2009) Hedonic meaning through Christmas consumption: a review and model. *Journal of Customer Behaviour* 8 (3): 237–55.

Caroline Tynan and Sally McKechnie also collaborated on a paper about the co-creation of value in hedonic consumption. This takes a somewhat non-traditional view of hedonism. The paper is: Tynan, C., McKechnie, S. and Chhuon, C. (2010) Co-creating value for luxury brands. *Journal of Business Research* 63 (11): 1156–263.

There is, of course, a downside to hedonic consumption. Not everything that feels good is good for us – and this applies especially to alcohol. Students are famous for enjoying a drink – but maybe this next paper will provide some food for thought! Banister E.N. and Piacentini, Maria (2006) Binge drinking – do they mean us? Living life to the full in students' own words. *Advances in Consumer Research* 33: 390–8.

References

Brucks, M., Connell, P.M. and Freeman, D. (2010) Children's ascribed motivations for smoking elicited by projective questioning. *Advances in Consumer Research* 37: 139, 140.

Dai, X., Wertenbroch, K. and Brendl, M. (2008) Strategic motivation maintenance: the case of guilt-seeking. *Advances in Consumer Research* 35: 141.

Gal, D. and Liu, W. (2010) What movie would you watch with your salad? The implicit emotional consequences of exerting self-control. *Advances in Consumer Research* 37: 123.

Gutman, J. (1982) A means–end chain model based on consumer categorisation processes. *Journal of Marketing* 46: 60–72.

Haire, M. (1950) Projective techniques in marketing research. *Journal of Marketing* 14: 649–56.

Herzberg, F. (1966) *Work and the Nature of Man*. London: Collins.

Hibbert, S.A., Hogg, G. and Quinn, T. (2005) Social entrepreneurship: understanding consumer motives for buying *The Big Issue*. *Journal of Consumer Behaviour* 4 (3): 159–72.

Holbrook, M.P. and Hirschmann, E.C. (1982) The experiential aspects of consumption: consumer fantasies, feelings and fun. *Journal of Consumer Research* 9 (Sept): 132–40.

Khan, U., Dhar, R. and Fishbach, A. (2009) Guilt as motivation: the role of guilt in choice justification. *Advances in Consumer Research* 36: 27–8.

Machin, J. and Park, Y.W. (2010) Rejection is good for your health: the influence of decision strategy on food and drink choices. *Advances in Consumer Research* 37: 75.

Manuel, F.E. and Manuel, F.P. (1979) *Utopian Thought in the Western World*. Oxford: Blackwell.

Maslow, A. (1954) *Motivation and Personality*. New York: Harper and Row.

McAlexander, J.H., Schouten, J.W. and Koenig, H.F. (2002) Building brand community. *Journal of Marketing* 66 (1): 38–55.

McClelland, D.C. (1955) *Studies in Motivation*. New York: Appleton.

McLaran, P. and Brown, S. (2002) Experiencing the Utopian marketplace. *Advances in Consumer Research* 29: 1.

McNulty, W. K. (1985) UK social change through a wide-angle lens. *Futures*, Aug.

Mick, D.G. and Humphreys, A. (2008) Consumer freedom from consumer culture theory perspectives. *Advances in Consumer Research* 35: 18–19.

Mishra, H., Mishra, A. and Nayakankuppam, D. (2008) Money, product and individual: the influence of affective interactions on purchase intention. *Advances in Consumer Research* 35: 21–2.

Mitchell, A. (1983) *The Nine American Lifestyles.* New York: Macmillan.

Murray, H.A. (1938) *An Exploration in Personality: A Clinical Experimental Study of Fifty Men of College Age.* London: Oxford University Press.

Nowlis, S.M., McCabe, D.B. and Mandel, N. (2003) The effect of a forced delay after choice on consumption enjoyment. *Advances in Consumer Research* 30: 502–10.

Raghunathan, R. and Mukherji, A. (2003) Is hope to enjoy more enjoyed than hope enjoyed? *Advances in Consumer Research* 30: 85–6.

Raju, P.S. (1980) Optimum stimulation level: its relationship to personality, demographics and exploratory behaviour. *Journal of Consumer Research* 7 (3) (Dec): 272–82.

Reynolds T.J. and Gutman, J. (1988) Laddering theory, method, analysis, and interpretation. *Journal of Advertising Research* Feb/Mar: 11–31.

Rugimbana, R., Donahay, B., Neal, C. and Polonsky, M.J. (2003) The role of social power relations in gift giving on St. Valentine's Day. *Journal of Consumer Behaviour* 3 (1): 63–73.

Saldanha, N. and Williams, P. (2008) Mixed indulgences: when removing sin may backfire. *Advances in Consumer Research* 35: 140.

Shiv, B., Ferraro, R. and Bettman, J.R. (2004) Let us eat and drink for tomorrow we shall die. Mortality salience and hedonic choice. *Advances in Consumer Research* 31: 118 –21.

Skinner, B.F. (1953) *Science and Human Behaviour.* New York: Macmillan.

Vroom, V.H. (1999) *Management and Motivation.* Harmondsworth: Penguin Business.

Wadhwa, M. and Trudel, R. (2010) The fruit of labour effect. *Advances in Consumer Research* 37: 79.

Wilcox, K., Vallen, B., Block, L.G. and Fitzsimons, G. (2010) Vicarious goal fulfilment: when the mere presence of a healthy option leads to an ironically indulgent decision. *Advances in Consumer Research* 37: 73, 74.

Zuckerman, M. (2000) Are you a risk-taker? *Psychology Today* Nov/Dec: 54–87.

 More online

To gain free access to additional online resources to support this chapter please visit: **www.sagepub.co.uk/blythe**

CHAPTER ③
Goals, risk and uncertainty

CHAPTER CONTENTS

LEARNING OBJECTIVES

After reading this chapter you should be able to:

- Explain the relationship between drives and goals.

- Describe the various ways in which goals adopt hierarchies.

- Explain risk avoidance behaviour.

- Understand what is meant by heuristics, and explain how they help reduce risk.

- Explain the role of interrupts in problem-solving.

- Explain how dissonance arises.

- Understand complaining behaviour.

Introduction

As we saw in Chapter 2, behaviour is driven by needs. Needs develop drives, and drives are focused into motivation, but motivation achieves nothing unless it is backed up by action. The process of converting a motivation into concrete action is one of developing goals. A goal is a concrete objective, one that dictates a specific plan of action, and one that carries with it its own decision-making, risks and rewards.

Any plan of action carries with it a degree of risk. Individuals will usually try to reduce the risks to an acceptable level, sometimes by developing rules of behaviour which have proved to be successful in the past. This type of decision-making is important to marketers because it enables practitioners to put risk-reducing measures in place. The lower the risk to consumers, the more likely they are to buy the product and the less likely they are to complain afterwards.

Case study: Selling insurance

When Frank Bettger was a young man, he wanted to be a baseball star. He achieved this ambition – he played for the St Louis Cardinals – but an arm injury cut his career short, and he had to look elsewhere. At that time, players were not paid the kind of money they get nowadays, and his money quickly ran out: still in his early 20s he was penniless, jobless and unable to see a way forward. After a short period collecting hire purchase repayments (riding around Philadelphia on a bicycle) he became an insurance salesman for Fidelity Life.

After 10 months he was making absolutely no progress, and no sales. Then he remembered what his baseball coach had told him – that his lack of success on the playing field was due to lack of enthusiasm. Bettger began to present much more enthusiastically – and began making sales. Throughout his sales career he set goals for himself: he would decide how much insurance he needed to sell, then work backwards to decide how many sales he would have to close on average, therefore how many presentations he would need to make, and therefore how many people he would need to contact to persuade them to hear a presentation. To make one sale would require around 30 cold calls, because of course not everybody would want to hear a presentation, and not everyone would buy when they did.

Perhaps more importantly, Bettger addressed other people's goals. He tells the story that he sold a policy to a regular customer, a businessman who needed insurance to support his business in the event of his death. Bettger delivered the policy, then immediately began to sell him yet another policy. 'You only just delivered the last one!' the businessman said. 'I know,' said Bettger, 'and that means you're insured for $900,000. You know you won't be happy until you're insured for a million.' Needless to say, Bettger got the sale.

Bettger was, of course, in the risk management business. People buy insurance as a way of mitigating risk – maybe the risk will never materialise, but we need to be on the safe side and cover ourselves for the downside of life.

How to impress your examiner

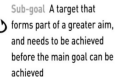

Sub-goal A target that forms part of a greater aim, and needs to be achieved before the main goal can be achieved

Heuristic A decision-making rule

Candidates sometimes forget that goals go in hierarchies, both in terms of which goals are more important than others and in terms of which **sub-goals** need to be achieved if the main goal is to come to fruition. If you can remember Huffman's model, it will certainly help you avoid this error. A further common error is to forget the role of **heuristics** in enabling people both to set goals and to achieve them – so make it a rule never to forget about heuristics!

Table 3.1　Goal choices

Goal	Possible sub-goals	Action
Go to the cinema	Which film?	Look in the evening paper, make a choice
Visit friends	Which friends to see?	Phone around to see who is available
Watch TV	Which channel?	Look in the TV guide
Rent a DVD	Which DVD?	Visit the DVD rental shop
Read a book	Which book?	Choose a book from the shelf

Goals

A goal is an external object towards which a motive is directed (Onkvisit and Shaw 1994). Goals differ from drives in that the goal is external, and pulls the person in a given direction: a drive is internal and pushes the individual. In this way the goal acts as an incentive to take a course of action (or refrain from taking a course of action, as the case may be). Having goals improves task performance: people are more risk-seeking when they have a specific, challenging goal (Larrick et al. 2001). If someone has a drive that needs to be addressed there may be several possible goals that would satisfy the drive. For example, if an individual feels the need for entertainment, this may lead to a drive to find something to do, which in turn causes the person to set some goals that would lead to some kind of entertainment. In these circumstances, several possible alternatives exist, and marketers clearly need to remember that consumers have a choice. Some examples are shown in Table 3.1.

The basic consequences, needs or values that consumers want to achieve are called end goals. These end goals can be concrete or abstract. Concrete end goals derive directly from the product purchase, whereas abstract end goals derive indirectly from the purchase.

For example, someone might buy a bottle of wine in order to go to a party. The party is the end goal, not drinking the wine (which is probably why so much cheap wine arrives at parties). The goal is abstract: it is intangible, and relates to hedonic and even irrational motives. Abstract goals need not be irrational or hedonic: someone buying a new suit to achieve the end goal of getting through a job interview has a practical purpose in mind.

Buying a new car because of a need for transport to get to work is a concrete goal: buying a car to impress the neighbours is an abstract goal. In most cases, abstract goals can be achieved in many different ways – the neighbours might be equally impressed by a new swimming-pool, or by an expensive holiday.

Goals develop for various reasons. There is clearly a relationship between consumer values and means–end chains (Pieters et al. 1995; Reynolds and Gutman 1988); in other words, the individual's basic values will translate into systems for obtaining an end result by specific methods. Research in this area has tended to assume that the goal structures are static, which is unlikely to be the case since people's needs evolve. Means–end theory also does not explain how the gap between higher-level ('being') goals and lower-level ('having') goals can be bridged.

Social identity theory (see Chapter 10) is based on two main concepts. First, we assume that people take actions (and buy products) in order to enact roles

Challenging the status quo

How easy is it to categorise goals this way? How do we know where the end of the line is with goals? For instance, take the person who buys a bottle of wine in order to go to a party. Perhaps the party is an end goal, but why do we go to parties in the first place? To have a good time? To meet a potential new girlfriend/boyfriend? To network, and thus improve our career prospects? To make new friends? To show off our nice new clothes?

Even then the goal hierarchy may not stop. Why do we want a new boyfriend/girlfriend? Perhaps with a view to marrying, settling down and having children, enjoying a happy domestic life and eventually some grandchildren, setting ourselves up for a happy and fulfilling retirement, perhaps living longer than we otherwise might (there is research evidence on this), and having a long and meaningful trip through this vale of tears.

And we get all this from buying a bottle of wine?

within society and for their own self-image (Klein and Kunda 1993; Sirgy 1982). Second, social identity theory states that people do not have a single identity, but in fact have separate identities for each social situation they find themselves in (for example, as friend, employee, volunteer worker and so forth). Again, this body of research does not tell us how the higher-order abstract goals translate into lower-order concrete goals.

Behavioural decision theory may help to resolve this problem. This body of theory suggests that choice processes and outcomes relate to the context in which the behaviour occurs, for example to the number of choice alternatives available, and task factors such as available time (Bettman et al. 1998).

Combining these theoretical approaches, Huffman et al. (2000) produced two models showing how goals relate, and how they are determined. Figure 3.1 shows the first of these.

In Figure 3.1, the individual's goals begin with life themes and values. These are concerned with the kind of person we want to be, or the kind of person we are, and are unlikely to change very greatly in the course of our lives. At the doing level, we have immediate concerns, which lead to consumption intentions. Finally, at the having level, we would be concerned with specific benefits from products, which in turn leads to a search for specific features in the products we consume. For example, an individual might have a life theme of being a world traveller. This might translate into a life project to visit every continent in the world. In the process, current concerns (such as earning a living in a profession that allows plenty of time off for travel) might provide a set of goals: the consumption intention might be to have at least one long-haul trip each year. Finally, the individual would be looking for specific benefits from each trip (the possibility to learn about the local culture, for example), which would require specific features when planning each trip.

This model shows a clear sequence from the general needs of the individual through to the final purchase goals for each individual product (in this case, each trip). There are likely to be many products and many sub-goals involved in leading a life that is dedicated to travel: the same would apply to someone whose life is based around being surrounded by artworks, or around having a large family, or having a high-powered working career.

The model shows the sequence of events that occurs, and also the relationship between the goals, but it does not illustrate the actual processes involved. These are shown in Figure 3.2.

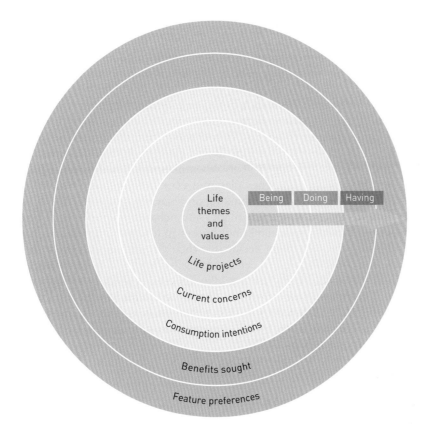

Figure 3.1 A hierarchical model of consumer goals

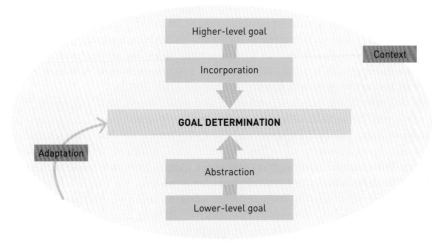

Figure 3.2 A model of goal-determination processes

In Figure 3.2, incorporation refers to the top-down process whereby higher-level goals shape goals at lower levels. Incorporation helps the individual to ensure that all the goals fit together in a logical and sensible way, and also it enables the individual to translate a set of ill-defined and possibly subconscious needs into a coherent set of choice problems.

Abstraction refers to the bottom-up process whereby lower-level goals help to determine what the higher-level goals must be if there is to be consistency between the various goals.

Adaptation is the process by which goals are influenced by contextual issues such as the cultural and social environment, current concerns and consumption intentions. Contextual factors appear to operate in two ways: first, the context may activate a pre-existing set of sub-goals in the individual's memory. Different contexts generate different goals, for example one's goals when planning a visit to one's parents are very different from one's goals when planning a friend's stag night. Second, the context may influence the individual's thinking on what is actually possible. If someone does not believe, for example, that there is any chance whatsoever of being promoted at work, then he or she might not bother to 'dress to impress'. In the case of being-level goals, someone might decide that their circumstances prevent them from ever becoming a particular type of person. At the having level, someone might decide that, much as they would enjoy driving a Porsche, this is unlikely to happen because of financial constraints. Research shows that people with low incomes tend to set very stringent goals, and thus do not achieve their goals as often – consequently, they often feel less successful in life, and do not enjoy the consumption experiences they do achieve (Scott and Nowlis 2010).

Problems with goals

Some end goals are too general for the individual to make any real decisions. For example, someone who says 'I just want to be happy' may not have any idea how to achieve this. On a more concrete level, saying 'I want to buy a better computer' is not much help to the salesperson who is trying to find a machine that will meet the customer's needs. In this case, the customer clearly does not know enough about the technical aspects of computers to be able to make an informed decision alone. 'I want to be respected' is also a difficult goal for which to develop a strategy.

Sometimes goals will conflict. In these circumstances, the strongly-active goal will inhibit competing goals until the stronger goal has been achieved, at which point the weaker or less active goal will re-emerge (Brendl et al. 2002).

Table 3.2 gives some purchase end goals and motivations, with examples. In practice, marketers have little influence over consumers' main goals, since these often derive from basic values. Marketers can try to influence the less abstract end goals, such as the desired functional or psychosocial consequences, through promotional strategies. For example, although it may be difficult to persuade someone that he or she ought to dress well in order to impress other people, we can much more easily influence those who already believe in dressing to impress, perhaps encouraging them to shop at a specific retailer or buy specific clothing brands. Thus these factors act as drivers for end goals, as shown in Figure 3.3.

Examples of this are common, as the following list shows:

- *If you want to get ahead, get a hat.* This slogan was thought of in the 1930s when the wearing of hats by men was going out of fashion. In fact the slogan was not very successful: hats still went out of fashion, and it was not until the 1990s that they returned to the fashion scene.
- http://www.howtolookgood.com/askcaryn_2_feb.html. This website offers fashion advice and hyperlinks to on-line fashion and cosmetics retailers.

- http://www.net-a-porter.com/About-Us/Our-Company. This is another fashion website, but this time at the top end of the market. It provides an information service for people with anything up to £3000 or more to spend on a new dress.
- *Just do it!* This slogan for Nike nudges people towards making a decision on the spot, although it appears to be about taking a determined approach to sports participation. Nike athletic shoes are primarily a fashion item – only a small proportion of the shoes are worn for actually playing sports.

Table 3.2   Examples of purchase end goals

Dominant end goal	Basic purchase motivation	Examples
Optimise satisfaction	Seek maximum positive consequences	Buy dinner at the best restaurant in town rather than risking a cheap diner
Prevention	Avoid potential unpleasant consequences	Buy weatherproofing for a house so as to maintain the good appearance of the house, and protect its value
Resolve conflict	See satisfactory balance of positive and negative consequences	Buy a moderately expensive car of very good quality so as to avoid high maintenance costs and unreliability, while still keeping within a reasonable expenditure
Escape	Reduce or escape from current aversive circumstances	Buy an anti-dandruff shampoo, in order to avoid embarrassment
Maintenance (satisfice)	Maintain satisfaction of a basic need with minimal effort	Buy bread at a local shop. This satisfies the need for bread without having to go to the out-of-town hypermarket where you do your main weekly shopping

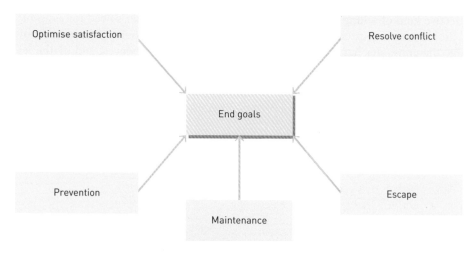

Figure 3.3   Drivers for end goals

It is not always feasible for an individual to go straight for an end goal. In fact, it is far more common for people to establish a series of subsidiary goals that will lead, eventually, to the end goal. Goal hierarchies are series of sub-goals that provide a structure for decision-making. In other words, people set priorities. If the individual has previous experience this will help, because consumers without previous experience will have more trouble establishing goal hierarchies and are likely to go by trial and error. For example, someone who has never bought a car before will not really know what to look for because he or she will not have been able to prioritise needs or form a hierarchy of goals. A simple goal hierarchy for buying a car might run as follows:

1   Find out which car would best suit your needs.
2   Find out which is the cheapest way of funding the purchase.
3   Find out who has the right type of car for you.
4   Do the deal and buy the car.

To translate this into an action plan, the person will have to establish a series of activities to meet each sub-goal. Here is an example of the buying process for the second-hand car:

1   Buy a used-car guide.
2   Decide which car looks like the make and year that would best suit your needs.
3   Decide what price range is affordable.
4   Telephone banks and loan companies to obtain the best terms for a loan.
5   Buy the local paper as soon as it hits the news stands.
6   Telephone car dealers (or private sellers) who seem to have the right kind of car, go to see the car, and make the purchase.

In Figure 3.4, the end goal is created by the need, but the path to meeting the need is not direct. Sub-goals are created, and even sub-sub-goals, and these sub-goals must be achieved on the way to achieving the final goal.

The experienced consumer – for example, someone who buys second-hand cars regularly, or who is a real car enthusiast – will already understand the process and will establish the goal hierarchy and action plan immediately. Inexperienced consumers have to establish the goal hierarchy from scratch, often by trial-and-error approaches, and develop a decision plan for each sub-goal. Marketers, and especially salespeople, can help here because they can guide individuals through the process. This is the most effective kind of selling activity since it addresses the consumer's need for assistance.

Problem-solving processes are greatly affected by the amount of product knowledge the consumer has already acquired through past experiences, and by the level

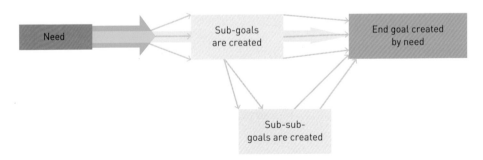

Figure 3.4   Creation of sub-goals

of involvement with the product (and indeed with the choice process itself). In other words, if the individual has a great deal of knowledge about the product category, or has a strong interest in the product category, the process of finding a suitable product or brand will proceed along very different lines. The inexperienced car buyer might follow a plan such as this:

1 Decide to buy a car.
2 Ask around among family and friends to find out which car might be most suitable. This might involve some discussion to decide what the individual's needs are: an experienced car buyer might be aware of needs which the inexperienced buyer would not think of. The financing of the purchase might also be discussed at this point.
3 Go to used-car showrooms to examine the different makes and models.
4 Find a helpful salesperson who appears honest and trustworthy.
5 Tell the salesperson what the needs are.
6 Listen to the salesperson's advice about the particular models in stock. Again, the financing of the purchase might also be discussed at this stage.
7 Make the decision based on the closeness of fit between the salesperson's description of the car and the needs that have been identified.
8 Buy the car.

Consumers' relevant knowledge about the product category (or, if you prefer, the problem category) is obviously important in problem solving (Crosby and Taylor 1981), so inexperienced purchasers are likely to take a knowledgeable friend with them when they go to make a major purchase such as a car. Sometimes relevant knowledge is brought forward from the individual's memory, and some knowledge is acquired during the purchasing process (Biehal and Chakravarty 1983). Any brands that have simply been remembered are part of the **evoked set** and for regular purchases or familiar product categories these may be the only brands that are considered. The result of the information search process is to create choice alternatives, which are further refined into a **consideration set**. The consideration set is the group of products that will be actively considered.

In Figure 3.5, the many brands in the evoked set, and the even more numerous brands that might be brought to the individual's attention, are filtered and refined to create the consideration set, which may only comprise a few brands. The individual will then usually select one or possibly two brands to feed into the goal hierarchy as being the desirable brands for solving the need problem.

Evoked set The group of brands a consumer can remember spontaneously

Consideration set The group of brands which a consumer believes will meet his or her need, and which are therefore seriously being considered for purchase

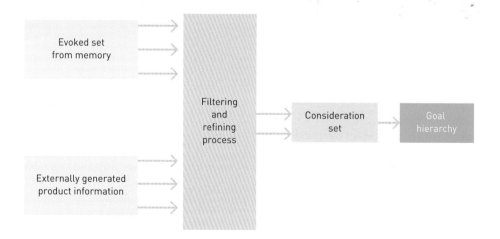

Figure 3.5   Developing goals

From the viewpoint of marketing, ensuring that one's brand is in the evoked set, and more especially is part of the consideration set, is an important objective of marketing communications activities. If the brand is not going to be evaluated, it is impossible for it to be purchased: if it is already in the evoked set, it is likely to become part of the consideration set. The potential for a brand to be included in the consideration set is called its 'top of mind awareness', and this is influenced by several factors: first, past experience of the brand in terms of previous purchase and use; second, the level of marketing communications devoted to the brand – the amount of advertising out there (Baker et al. 1986); third, the distribution strategy of the brand – if the brand has been seen in a large number of places, it is more likely to be purchased, especially since some estimates state that 65% of purchase decisions are made in the shop; fourth, package design will influence both the consideration set (due to its impact on the individual's consciousness) and the probability of the brand entering the consideration set. Packaging also provides important information about the formulation of the product, its use and its probable effectiveness for the purpose for which the consumer wants to use it.

 ## Challenging the status quo

There is an old joke about someone who has a lot of debts, and who writes to a particularly persistent creditor to say that each month all the bills are put in a pile, three are drawn out at random and paid, and the rest have to wait. 'If you continue to threaten me,' wrote the debtor, 'your bill will not go into next month's pile.'

It would appear that marketers are operating on the same basis. We try to get our product into the pile of products in the consideration set, otherwise there is no chance of it being purchased.

Does this analogy stack up, though? What if the creditor were simply to send hundreds of bills, so that most of the bills in the pile are his, and therefore (statistically) his bill is more likely to be paid? Is this what marketers do when they saturate the media with advertising? Do people simply throw away the excess information, in the same way as the debtor would throw away the red reminders?

The probability that existing knowledge about the brand will be used in the evaluation process is influenced by the means–end relevance of the knowledge to the goal involved (Grunert 1986). People will try to predict what the outcomes of purchase will be (i.e. will try to predict whether the purchase will meet the goals) but we cannot always do this directly, unless it is possible to test the product beforehand as one does when test-driving a car. For example, it is not usually possible (at least in the UK) to taste fruit and vegetables before buying them, so people use other criteria such as the colour, shape and texture of the fruit to judge what it will taste like. Likewise, items such as cleaning products can only be judged from the packaging, smell and consistency of the product.

Achieving each sub-goal in the purchase process may not always be straightforward: finding a suitable time to visit car showrooms (for example) might be difficult, establishing which salespeople are reasonably trustworthy and which are not may take considerable judgement, and identifying one's needs correctly can be a major task in itself.

Interrupts

Sometimes the goal hierarchy cannot be followed exactly because events occur that force the individual to re-think the situation. These events are called interrupts, and they fall into four categories:

Interrupt Something that diverts an individual away from a goal, usually temporarily

1 Unexpected information that is inconsistent with established beliefs. For example, if the shop that the consumer had expected to buy from has changed hands or closed, the consumer has to rearrange the goals to encompass finding a new supplier.
2 Prominent environmental stimuli. An in-store display might offer an alternative to the original purchase (perhaps by offering a large price discount on a similar product). This may divert the consumer away from his or her usual brand choice, or at the very least cause the consumer to consider switching.
3 Affective states. Hunger, boredom or tiredness during a shopping trip might lead to a change in goal. This may be a change away from looking for a new suit, and towards looking for the coffee shop.
4 Conflicts. These are the motivational conflicts discussed in Chapter 2. If an individual is confronted with an approach–approach conflict, or an approach–avoidance conflict, there will be a temporary cessation of goal attainment while new goals are formulated and the conflict resolved.

The effect of interrupts will depend on how consumers interpret the interrupting event. On the one hand, the interrupt may activate new end goals (as when the shopping trip turns into a search for a cup of coffee). On the other hand, a choice heuristic might be activated – for example, if the unexpected information is a friend recommending a brand, this may activate a heuristic about acting on friends' recommendations. Sometimes the interrupt is severe enough that the individual shelves the problem-solving behaviour indefinitely (for example, if the unexpected information is that the person has lost his or her job, or if a prominent environmental stimulus such as an anti-fur protest is taking place outside the fur emporium). (See Figure 3.6).

Challenging the status quo

In recent years we have been hearing a lot from politicians about increasing people's choice: choice of schools, choice of hospitals, choice of public services in general have all come into the realm of politics. But how true is it that people actually want more choices? Surely the more choices we have, the more difficult it is to make decisions?

The more ways there are of achieving our goals, the more possibilities for conflict there will be. Wouldn't it be more accurate to say that what people actually want is products and services that work and are not too expensive? And doesn't this apply as much to public services as it does to things we buy in shops?

Or perhaps people need choice because each of us has different needs and therefore we need to be able to select the solution that best suits our own situation?

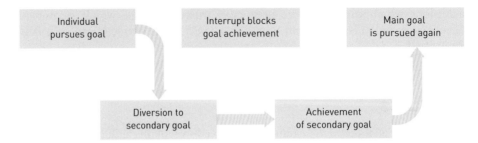

Figure 3.6   Temporary effects of an interrupt

The strength of the interrupt is also important (see Figure 3.7). If the goal is a strong one, and the interrupt weak (for example, consider a husband who has forgotten his wife's birthday, and who is shopping in the last ten minutes before the store closes – he is unlikely to take a break for a sandwich, no matter how hungry he is). A weak goal and a strong interrupt will clearly result in a break in the problem-solving behaviour (for example, the intention to check the prices on GPS units for a possible purchase when one's bonus comes through is unlikely to take precedence over a desperate need for the toilet). A weak goal and a weak interrupt may or may not result in a divergence from the planned behaviour, and a strong interrupt and a strong goal are likely to lead to considerable stress on the individual.

In most cases people tend to resume an interrupted task fairly quickly. Even though a marketer might be able to distract somebody away from their shopping to have a cup of coffee or a snack, the shopping task will be resumed fairly quickly afterwards. Once a goal hierarchy is established, it usually takes some effort to dissuade an individual from following it.

	Strong goal	*Weak goal*
Strong interrupt	Powerful stress set up in the individual	Goal will be ignored or abandoned and a secondary goal will be established
Weak interrupt	Goal will continue to be pursued	Goal may be interrupted or abandoned or interrupt may be ignored

Figure 3.7   Goal and interrupt strengths

Risk and uncertainty

In the case of the inexperienced buyer, there is a greater risk attached to making the purchase. Inexperienced buyers have, by definition, less knowledge of the product category they are trying to buy into. Most consumers will try to reduce risk in this situation, and of course this is part of the reason for establishing goal hierarchies. By doing so, individuals can break down the task into manageable portions that can each take a share of the risk. People are more prepared to take risks with later goals if the earlier goals in the sequence were accomplished successfully (Dhar and Novemsky 2002). Risk can be categorised in different ways, as shown in Table 3.3.

Table 3.3 Categories of risk

Type of risk	Explanation	Examples
Physical risk	The risk of injury from using the product	Buying a car which is faulty, or perhaps buying a medicine with unpleasant side-effects
Financial risk	The risk of losing or wasting money	Buying a car that depreciates quickly, or buying a computer and finding that the price drops dramatically when a new model comes out
Functional risk	The risk of finding that the product is not fit for purpose	Buying a product that breaks down regularly, or buying a painkiller that does not stop a headache
Psychosocial risk	The fear of looking foolish	Buying clothes that your friends think look weird on you, or buying a make of car with a poor reputation

The amount of risk an individual perceives depends on two factors: first, how serious the downside is. If the possible negative consequences of buying the product will have a strong effect on the individual's well-being, the risk is high. Second, risk will be perceived as higher if the negative outcomes are thought to be highly likely. For example, someone buying a light aircraft knows that faults with the airframe would be extremely serious, but also knows that such faults are fairly unlikely. On the other hand, someone buying a lottery ticket knows that the chances of losing the purchase price are extremely high, but the loss of the money is not serious compared with the possible gain. It is the balance between the two that determines how seriously the individual regards the risk.

Between individuals, a further factor is the degree to which the individual is risk-averse – clearly some people are quite happy to take risks in life, where others are more cautious. This can be a crucial factor in some marketing situations: for example, financial advisers in Britain are required by law to assess the individual's degree of risk-aversion before making recommendations for investments or borrowing. In recent years, there have been several scandals concerning the mis-selling of financial products, in particular high-risk high-return products sold to people who are in fact risk-averse and did not realise that there was a risk of losing part (or even all) of their investment. People tend to become more risk-averse as they grow older, since it would be more difficult to recover from any loss.

It may also be the case that people perceive risk differently: in particular, someone who can see a way of mitigating any losses is likely to perceive the risk as lower than someone who can only see the loss itself. This may be one of several factors that account for people's differing responses to risky situations: someone who is confident of being able to find the way home is less likely to be afraid of getting lost in a desert, whereas someone with no experience or knowledge of navigation might well be fearful of going on such an expedition. In a consumer behaviour context, someone who is a competent mechanic will perceive less risk in buying a second-hand car in an auction, as compared with someone who knows nothing about the workings of cars, simply because he or she would feel able to fix any problems should the car prove to have mechanical faults.

Risk reduction strategies are shown in Figure 3.8. The main tactic for reducing risk is to increase one's knowledge about the product category. Our prospective

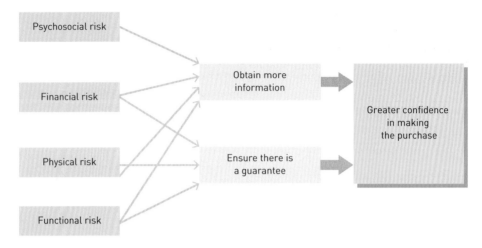

Figure 3.8   Reducing risk

aircraft purchaser is likely to seek a great deal of advice from a great many sources, and is likely to have the aircraft thoroughly inspected by a qualified engineer. If the risk is still perceived to be high the consumer will simply not make the purchase. This is why most retailers offer money-back guarantees or no-quibble return policies: such guarantees reduce risk for the consumer, so making purchase more likely. Since most purchases work out reasonably well (at least they do if the manufacturers have done their work properly) products seldom need to be returned.

People often spend considerable time shopping around, increasing their knowledge of the product categories in order to reduce risk. This has been compared to the hunter–gatherer behaviour of our ancestors, and may account for the fact that the vast majority of retail purchases are still made in high street shops rather than through mail order or the Internet. The need to inspect products personally as a way of reducing risk has been identified as a barrier to Internet purchase (Dailey 2003). On the other hand, some aspects of Internet purchase appear to reduce people's aversion to risk: on-line investing has been shown to lead to greater risks being taken: the theory is that the on-line experience is less 'real' than a live experience of dealing with a live stockbroker, so people are prepared to take more risks (Zwick 2004).

People will frequently choose the middle-ranked or mid-priced brand as a compromise between buying the worst alternative on the one hand, and risking spending too much by buying the 'best' brand on the other. This means that, in a two-choice situation, a brand's chances of being bought are helped if a third brand is available which places it in the middle range (Sheng et al. 2003). Presumably this implies that a company that finds itself in second place to a major brand should consider introducing a third, cheaper, brand into the market in order to boost sales of its existing brand.

Other tactics for reducing risk might include seeking help from a competent friend, or taking out insurance against the risk, or hedging the risk by setting aside resources (typically money) to cover against anything going wrong.

Mood can have an effect on risk-taking behaviour: people tend to buy more lottery tickets if the weather is bad, but whether this is a way of making life more exciting in dull weather or whether it is a way of cheering oneself up with the prospect of a big win is debatable (Bruyneel et al. 2006). Most people like to take a risk in some circumstances – people like to buy lottery tickets, or to do adventurous things like free-fall parachuting or white-water rafting, but usually these risks are taken in fairly carefully controlled circumstances.

Heuristics

Another way of reducing risk and simplifying the decision-making process is to establish rules for buying. These are called heuristics, and they consist of simple 'if … then' decision-making rules, which can be established before the search procedure begins. Heuristics are also subject to alteration in the light of new knowledge, so sometimes they are established as the search procedure continues. Heuristics can be divided into three groups, as follows:

1　Search heuristics. These are rules for finding out information. For example, someone might establish a rule to the effect that they will always ask advice from a friend when making a major purchase.
2　Evaluation heuristics. These are rules for judging products. For example, someone might have a rule that they never buy products made in a country where child labour is widely used.
3　Choice heuristics. These are procedures for comparing evaluations of alternatives. For example, someone might have a rule of never buying the cheapest (or never buying the most expensive). In fact, most people do tend to go for the middle-priced product when offered a choice of three products at different price levels.

Some examples of these heuristics are given in Table 3.4.

Kahneman and Tversky (1979) went so far as to suggest that people go through a fairly complex process of using heuristics to assess (and probably reduce) risk. They proposed that people will identify possible outcomes and group ones that are seen as being essentially identical: those outcomes that would realise a more favourable result would be considered as gains, while those that would realise a less favourable outcome would be considered as losses. Following on from this, the individual would assess the likelihood of each outcome actually happening, and would be able to calculate which course of action to take in order to balance risk and reward. Kahneman and Tversky took the view that people would vary in their attitude towards risk-taking: some would be risk-averse, and would take the options they considered to be least likely to lead to loss, whereas others who are happier to take risks might prefer an option that would lead to the greatest gain. The theory is called prospect theory, because it purports to explain how people weigh up the prospects of their decisions.

Downside risk is, of course, part of the equation. This might be calculated as the value of the potential loss, calculated against the likelihood of it happening. Someone who buys a lottery scratchcard for £1 is well aware that the chances of winning anything are slight, and the chance of winning the jackpot is negligible, but the loss is limited to £1 so the risk is worth taking. Someone buying a second-hand car for £15,000 from a total stranger is taking a much greater risk: on the one hand, there might be a saving of £2000 over buying from a dealer, but on the other hand there might be a loss of £15,000. Someone who is a risk-taker might reason that the loss is unlikely to be the

Table 3.4 Examples of heuristics

Search heuristics	Examples
Store selection	If you are buying meat, always go to the butcher across the street
Source credibility	If a magazine accepts advertising from products it tests and reports on, the tests may be biased in favour of the advertiser
Evaluation heuristics	**Examples**
Key criteria	If comparing processed foods, examine the sugar content
Negative criteria	If a salient consequence is negative (for example, high sugar content) give this choice criterion extra weight in the integration process
Significant differences	If the alternative is similar on a salient consequence (for example, all the alternatives are low sugar) ignore that choice criterion
Choice heuristics for familiar, frequently purchased products	**If choosing among familiar products ...**
Works best	Choose the product that you think works best – the one that provides the best level of performance on the most relevant functional consequences
Affect referral	Choose the alternative you like best (in other words, select the alternative with the most favourable attitude)
Bought last	Select the alternative you bought last time (assuming it proved satisfactory)
Important person	Choose the alternative that an 'important person' such as a spouse, friend or child likes
Price-based rule	Buy the least expensive alternative, or perhaps the most expensive alternative, depending on your beliefs about the relationship between price and quality
Promotion rule	Choose the alternative for which you have a special-offer coupon, or that you can buy at a reduced price (due to a sale or special offer)
Choice heuristics for new, unfamiliar products	**If choosing among unfamiliar products ...**
Wait and see	Do not buy a new product until someone you know has used it for a while and recommends it. In the case of electronic products, wait until the next year or year after its introduction, when the price is likely to have reduced considerably
Expert consultant	Find an expert or more knowledgeable person, have them evaluate the alternatives in terms of your goals, then buy the alternative that the expert suggests

whole value of the car, but would probably be restricted to a few hundred for repairing something that the buyer has concealed. People use heuristics for this.

Although Kahneman and Tversky offer a fairly complex formula to explain the calculation process, in fact people rarely sit down with a pen and paper and work out the odds. Normally, we use heuristics to simplify the process – the risk-averse don't often buy lottery tickets, and they buy their cars from dealers.

Heuristics are used to simplify decision-making. They may be stored in memory, or constructed on the spot based on information received, but in either case they allow the individual to reach rapid decisions without over-stretching their cognitive capacity (or brainpower). In the extreme, the use of heuristics leads to habitual behaviour. For example, someone might go to the same pub every Friday night and order the same drinks and sit at the same table each time. Routinised choice behaviour such as this is comforting and relaxing since it does not involve any decision-making at all. In fact, most people find it disturbing if their routines cannot be carried out for whatever reason.

What happens if it goes wrong?

In the event of the downside risk happening, people may simply accept the situation; they may try to do something to recover, or they may complain (i.e. expect someone else to help in recovering the situation). In the consumer behaviour context, there are many possibilities for complaint behaviour, because most firms would prefer that people come back and say if they have a problem, rather than complain to other people and damage the firm's reputation.

Complaining behaviour and other post-purchase behaviour is covered more fully in Chapter 13, but for people who decide to live with the consequences of the risk there are three main outcomes.

First, the individual might suffer a degree of lost self-esteem, through having made a mistaken judgement. Second, there may be corrective action needed – someone may need to buy another, better product or might have to make new financial arrangements. Third, and more positively, the individual will learn from the mistake and will almost certainly adapt future heuristics to avoid making similar losses in future.

Summary

Goal-setting is often a subconscious activity that arises from our deepest feelings about who we want to be, what we want to do and what we want to own. In the course of meeting our goals, we may find obstacles in our path: the goals may not be possible, we may need to achieve other goals before we are in a position to achieve the main goal, or we may be interrupted in the task by more pressing matters. Part of the problem in achieving goals is the fact that life is uncertain. We try to mitigate the problem by assessing the risks and taking measures to minimise them, often by following decision rules. When things go wrong, we become dissatisfied and this in turn leads to complaining behaviour.

 **Key points**

- Goals are external: drives are internal.
- Goals operate in hierarchies.
- Choice processes and outcomes relate to the context in which the behaviour occurs.
- Themes relate to being: life projects and current concerns relate to doing: features and benefits relate to having.

(Continued)

(Continued)

- Brands need to be in the evoked set, and subsequently in the consideration set, to have any chance of being bought.
- People usually act in ways that minimise risk.
- Perceived risk depends on the seriousness of the negative outcome as well as on the likelihood of the negative outcome happening.
- Heuristics are decision rules intended to reduce cognitive effort and risk.
- Interrupts usually only delay problem-solving behaviour, but the delay depends on the strength of the interrupt and the strength of the goal.

Review questions

1 How might a marketer seek to make an interrupt more effective?
2 How are drives converted to goals?
3 What is the difference between the evoked set and the consideration set?
4 What mechanisms are available for reducing risk?
5 How might heuristics help someone who is buying a product he or she has no experience of?
6 How might someone assess the risk of buying a new car?
7 How do life goals derive from life themes?
8 How does context affect choice in, say, the travel industry?
9 How might a marketer try to ensure that a brand is in the consideration set?
10 In terms of consumer goals, what are the key features of 'having' as opposed to 'life themes'?

Case study revisited: Selling insurance

Frank Bettger had some set phrases: for example, at that time, most insurance companies required clients to have a medical examination if they were taking out a large policy, and Bettger would say, 'If you look as good on the inside as you do on the outside, there won't be any problem.' Or if someone said that they would like to talk to other insurers, Bettger would say 'That's a fine company, and I'm sure they would do a good job for you. But I'm in a position to do something for you today that no one else in the world can do. I can get your medical examination carried out immediately.' He would go on to point out what a tragedy it would be if the client were to meet with an accident while waiting for other insurers to quote.

His great strength, though, lay in telling stories, 'cautionary tales', which illustrated the risks of not having insurance. He had one story about a little girl he knew who, once every month, would go to the bank with her mother to pay in a cheque 'from her Daddy'. Her Daddy had died, and of course the cheque was from his insurance company. For men with children, the implication was clear – wouldn't any loving father like to think that he could send money to his family, from beyond the grave? He also told a tale about a man who had a successful business, but when he died unexpectedly his business partners had a terrible time buying out the various beneficiaries of his will, who of course wanted their money right now and no arguments. In the end the company was bankrupted, and the business he and his partners had built up over the years was gone. Which company founder would not want to protect his partners and business? Key-man insurance is now big business.

Life insurance purchase is one of the strangest purchases, at first sight. The individual is committing to paying for something for which he or she will never see any tangible benefit at all. It is entirely about managing downside risk for other people – family, business partners, even lenders. Yet trillions of pounds, dollars, yen and euros are devoted to buying it. Partly it is about risk mitigation, partly it is about goals and vanity – and perhaps part of it is about believing that the perversity of the universe means that those with insurance live forever, while those without die young.

Case study: White-knuckle rides

Human beings are born with three instinctive fears: loud noises, sudden approaches and falling. Gradually these instincts are overcome by intellect, but the basic shock factor remains – try bursting a balloon behind someone and see what happens. Normally, of course, the person jumps and then looks round, sees that the noise was harmless and laughs (although some people might be annoyed at being frightened). People naturally laugh at danger past, and also will laugh at their own foolish reaction to something harmless. Perhaps it is this reaction, laughter, that has led to the resurgence of roller-coaster rides.

When the roller-coaster was first invented in 1885, the rides were thrilling but not all that frightening – riders were taken up and down a series of slopes in small trains. Although the motion of the vehicles was unfamiliar, the ride was relatively sedate compared with the roller-coasters seen nowadays. Anyone visiting Melbourne (or of course resident there) can visit Luna Park, home to the world's oldest functioning roller-coaster ride, and make the comparison for themselves: the Luna Park ride is almost a sight-seeing trip, with nice views over the sea and the city, rather than something frightening.

During the Depression amusement parks fell into decline, and the roller-coaster did not revive in popularity until the 1970s, when the first white-knuckle roller-coasters were built. Disneyland's **invention** of tubular-steel tracks (rather than the wooden tracks of earlier roller-coasters) enabled designers to bend the tracks into any shape. Now the trains could be twisted through loops, turned upside down, be sent around sharp curves, and generally hurtled about in an alarming manner. This rather more stimulating type of roller-coaster caused its passengers to grip the handrail in front of their seats in such a manner that their knuckles turned white – hence the term 'white-knuckle ride'.

Since the 1970s, the challenge has been on to produce a faster, higher, more scary roller-coaster than ever before. Roller-coasters have been built more than 450 feet high (the equivalent of a 45-storey skyscraper), some have double or triple loops, and the world's fastest reaches 150 mph (it is at Ferrari World in Abu Dhabi, itself the world's largest indoor theme park – although the roller-coaster is outside, mainly). The steepest is at Fujiyoshida in Japan, with a maximum angle of 121 degrees.

Roller-coaster enthusiasts have formed clubs so that people can swap stories, travel together to ride new roller-coasters and even host fellow enthusiasts who are visiting local theme parks. Riding roller-coasters leads to people developing challenges all of their own – supermarket worker Ian Jones of Cheltenham, UK, has had over 10,000 rides on a total of 298 roller-coasters throughout Europe and the United States. In 2010 he rode the Nemesis roller-coaster at Alton Towers in the nude, as a charity fundraising stunt. He holds the Guinness Book of Records record for the nude roller-coaster ride he made in 2004, with 112 other fans,

Invention A new product, usually developed by an individual

at Alton Towers' Nemesis ride. Ian rides the Megaphobia ride at Oakwood, South Wales, every year for 8 hours, as a charity stunt – but for that one he wears clothes (too cold otherwise).

Ian's achievements pale into insignificance next to those of B. Derek Shaw of York, Pennsylvania. Shaw has ridden 1200 roller-coasters in 19 countries on three continents. He is the past vice president of American Coaster Enthusiasts, and is often called upon to rate new roller-coasters and advise roller-coaster builders. He is Manager of Special Projects for the American Lung Association, and looks like any other American executive in his late 50s, but he is clearly a collector – he is also famous for his record collection and writes for music-industry publications.

There are of course many other types of white-knuckle ride. People pay to be swung upside-down, dropped from a great height, hurtled towards each other and anything else solid, and generally engage in anything with a thrill attached. Is it the adrenalin rush they get from it that makes them do it? Or the need for an element of risk in an otherwise stable life? Or simply the urge to collect, whether it be records or roller-coasters? Whatever the reasons, the race to build ever larger, ever more frightening roller-coasters seems to be continuing forever.

Questions

1 What would a theme park call a roller-coaster Megaphobia?
2 What is the purpose of joining a roller-coaster enthusiast's club?
3 How might a roller-coaster enthusiast establish a consideration set?
4 How does roller-coaster riding equate with minimising risk?
5 How does being a roller-coaster enthusiast relate to goal-setting?

Further reading

How I Raised Myself from Failure to Success in Selling, by Frank Bettger (New York: Simon Schuster, 1992; first published by Prentice Hall, 1947) is the anecdotes and advice of a veteran insurance salesman. His practical understanding of people's goals and risk-management needs is exemplary – yet he never went to college. It's also an engaging, jolly book to read.

http://www.medicinenet.com/script/main/art.asp?articlekey=51891 provides a somewhat disturbing article about the extremes people will go to in order to experience the next thrill. These include being paid to be kidnapped at a random moment, blindfolded and kept in a cellar.

http://www.mindtools.com/page6.html is a webpage that offers career advice. This particular page leads you through your personal goal-setting (for a better, more successful life).

Jonathan Fields' *Uncertainty: Turning Fear and Doubt into Fuel for Brilliance* (New York: Portfolio Hardcover, 2011) is another self-help book. This time the author talks about ways of reducing the fear that arises from uncertainty – and he certainly experienced the downside of uncertainty, having opened a new business in Manhattan the day before the 11th September terrorist attacks. Who could have foreseen that?

References

Baker W., Hutchinson, J.W., Moore, D. and Nedunadi, P. (1986) Brand familiarity and advertising: effects on the evoked set and brand preference. *Advances in Consumer Research* 13: 637–642.

Bettman, J.R., Luce, M.F. and Payne, J.W. (1998) Constructive consumer choice processes. *Journal of Consumer Research* 25 (Dec): 187–217.

Biehal, G. and Chakravarty, D. (1983) Information accessibility as a moderator of consumer choice. *Journal of Consumer Research* (June): 1–14.

Brendl, M., Markman, A. and Irwin, J.R. (2002) Suppression and activation of competing goals. *Advances in Consumer Research* 29: 5.

Bruyneel, S., DeWitte, S., Franses, P.H., DeKimpe, M. and Arnik G. (2006) Why consumers buy lottery tickets when the sun goes down on them. The depleted nature of weather-induced bad moods. *Advances in Consumer Research* 33: 46–50.

Crosby, L.A. and Taylor, J.R. (1981) Effects of consumer information and education in cognition and choice. *Journal of Consumer Research* (June): 43–56.

Dailey, L. (2003) Understanding consumers' need to personally inspect products prior to purchase. *Advances in Consumer Research* 30: 146–7.

Day, R.L., Brabicke, K., Schaetzle, T. and Staubach, F. (1981) The hidden agenda of consumer complaining. *Journal of Retailing* 57 (Fall): 86–106.

Dhar, R. and Novemsky, N. (2002) The effects of goal fulfilment on risk preference in sequential choice. *Advances in Consumer Research* 29: 6–7.

Grunert, K.G. (1986) Cognitive determinants of attribute information usage. *Journal of Economic Psychology* 7: 95–125.

Huffman, C., Atneshwar, S. and Mick, D.G. (2000) Consumer goal structures and goal-determining processes: an integrative framework. In S. Ratneshwar, David Glen Mick and Cynthia Huffman (eds), *The Why of Consumption*. London: Routledge.

Kahneman, D. and Tversky, A. (1979) Prospect theory: an analysis of decision under risk. *Econometrica*, 47 (2) (March): 263–92.

Klein, W.M. and Kunda, Z. (1993) Maintaining self-serving social comparisons: biased reconstruction of one's past behaviors. *Personality and Social Psychology Bulletin* 19, 732–9.

Larrick, R.P., Heath, C. and Wu, G. (2001) Goal-induced risk taking in strategy choice. *Advances in Consumer Research* 29.

Onkvisit, S. and Shaw, J.J. (1994) *Consumer Behaviour: Strategy and Analysis*. New York: Macmillan.

Pieters, R., Baumgartner, H. and Allen, D. (1995) A means–end chain approach to consumer goal structures. *International Journal of Research in Marketing* 12 (3): 227–44.

Reynolds, T.J. and Gutman, J. (1988) Laddering theory, method analysis and interpretation. *Journal of Advertising Research* (Feb/March): 11–31.

Scott, M. and Nowlis, S. (2010) The effect of goal-setting on consumption and consumer well-being. *Advances in Consumer Research* 37: 124.

Sheng, S., Parker, A.M. and Nakamoto, K. (2003) Decision uncertainty, expected loss minimisation, and the compromise effect. *Advances in Consumer Behaviour* 30: 47.

Sirgy, J.M. (1982) Self-concept in consumer behaviour: a critical review. *Journal of Consumer Research* 9 (Dec): 287–300.

Zwick, D. (2004) Online investing: derealization and the experience of risk. *Advances in Consumer Research* 31: 58.

More online

To gain free access to additional online resources to support this chapter please visit: **www.sagepub.co.uk/blythe**

CHAPTER ④

Personality and self-concept

CHAPTER CONTENTS

LEARNING OBJECTIVES

After reading this chapter you should be able to:

- Describe the various ways in which personality is studied.
- Define personality.
- Explain the role and purpose of self-concept.
- Describe the derivation of self-concept.
- Explain the mechanisms of inner and outer direction.
- Explain the reasons for an increase in inner-directedness.
- Explain self-monitoring.

Introduction

This chapter is about some of the factors that make up the individual person. People are complex and individual – our mental make-up affects what we buy, how we respond to marketing communications and how we plan our future lives. From a marketing viewpoint, understanding personality is useful in segmenting markets and also in planning marketing communications.

Case study: Mobile telephones

The mobile telephone is a relatively recent phenomenon. The first cellular systems began in the 1980s, using what was then extremely sophisticated technology: the science of physics had, until then, believed that mobile telephones would be impossible, since they would require too much bandwidth and far too much power to be crammed into something that would be light enough to carry around. Engineers seem to view the word 'impossible' as a challenge, however, so the difficulties were overcome: nowadays, mobile telephones are ubiquitous. Everybody has one, but the range of types, features, styles and of course prices is tremendous.

Mobile telephone capability splits into two sections – the network and the telephone itself. Network services might be offered on a pay-as-you-go basis, by which people buy credit, or on a contract basis, by which people pay a monthly fee that includes some free calls, paying extra for any use over and above the included minutes. Contracts frequently include a telephone: the actual cost of the handset is therefore buried somewhere in the other charges, but from a consumer's viewpoint it is effectively free.

Naturally, people have differing ideas about what they want from a mobile telephone. Telephone calls, of course – but modern mobile telephones can do so much more. Silicon chips can hold vast amounts of data and can accommodate a very wide range of functions – so why not take advantage of this? Short message service (SMS, or texting) is one such function, and of course a clock – which leads to a calendar and diary, and the capability to let the telephone organise your life. Then there are games, and a camera: there is the capacity to connect two cameras, so that video calls via Skype can be set up (another feature that physicists thought was impossible forty years ago).

The culmination of all these add-ons is the smartphone, which embodies everything anyone could want, all in one device. The iPad takes this even further, by including a notebook computer in the package.

Of course, not everybody wants all these features – some people just want to be able to call home to say they are on the train, and will be home in fifteen minutes. For marketers, the iPhone and iPad raise an interesting conceptual question, of course – we have been telling people for years not to use the product concept, yet here is a hugely popular product which does just that.

How to impress your examiner

You may be asked to compare the various type approaches to classifying personalities. Note that these type theories are not necessarily mutually exclusive: it would be perfectly possible to classify people across each of the types, because the typologies are based on combinations of traits, and the same traits might be combined in different ways in order to create a typology.

Personality

Personality is the collection of individual characteristics that make a person unique, and which control an individual's responses and relationship with the external environment. It is a composite of subordinate processes, for example attitude, motivation and perception. It is the whole of the person, and is the system that governs behaviour rather than the behaviour itself.

The elements that make up personality are called traits. Considerable research effort has been put towards linking individual personality traits to buying behaviour, but with limited success. This is despite the apparent logic that people would buy products that reflect their personality traits (for example, outgoing flamboyant people might be expected to buy more colourful clothing). In fact, there is some evidence that personality relates to new product purchasing behaviour, and there is more on this in Chapter 12; there is also some evidence that the degree to which someone is influenced by what other people think affects some buying behaviour. Overall, though, it is the total personality that dictates buying behaviour rather than each individual trait.

Trait A component of personality

Personality has the following features:

1 It is *integrated*. That is to say, all the factors making up the personality act on each other to produce an integrated whole.
2 It is *self-serving*. The characteristics of personality facilitate the attainment of needs and goals. In other words, the personality exists to meet its own needs.
3 Personal characteristics are *individualistic* and unique, in degree and intensity as well as presence. Although many personal characteristics are shared with other people, the possible number of combinations of traits is huge, and therefore each individual is different. This is what makes each person a separate and unique being.
4 Personality is *overt*. External behaviour is affected by personality. In other words, the personality can be observed (albeit indirectly) and deduced from the person's behaviour.
5 Personality is *consistent*. Once a person's basic personality has been established, it will change only slowly and with some difficulty; for practical purposes, an individual consumer's personality will stay constant throughout the buying process.

Because people are individuals it is difficult for marketers to take a standardised approach, yet the exigencies of the business world require standardisation. For this reason, many attempts have been made to establish groupings of personality types, which can be approached with a standardised offering. This is one of the bases of segmentation (the process of dividing the market into target groups of customers with similar needs). For this reason, and of course for the purposes of treating abnormal personalities, there is a long history of studying personality.

Approaches to studying personality

There are four basic approaches:

1 The *psychoanalytic* approach. Here the emphasis is on psychoanalysis, or studying the processes and events that have led to the development of personality

traits. The focus is on the individual. This approach is typified by Freudian psychiatry, which seeks to help patients to confront the life events that have shaped their personalities.

2 *Typology*. Here the individuals are grouped according to recognised personality types.

3 *Trait and factor theories*. The individual traits of personality can be examined as factors making up the whole person, and each trait can be categorised.

4 *Psychographics*. Consumers are measured using their behavioural tendencies in order to infer personality traits.

These four basic approaches deserve a more comprehensive explanation.

The Freudian approach is very much centred on the individual. Here the researcher (or, more usually, psychologist) asks the patient or subject to talk about anything regardless of logic, courtesy, self-defence, etc. A Freudian would analyse these statements in terms of id, ego and superego.

Id The unconscious part of the mind responsible for basic desires

According to Freud, the **id** is the underlying drive of the psyche. It is the source of the most basic, instinctive forces that cause people to behave in particular ways, and operates below the conscious level: it may be responsible for the compulsive behaviour exhibited by some individuals. There is some evidence to show that compulsive behaviour such as buying lottery tickets and scratchcards is linked to other compulsive behaviour such as smoking, and negatively linked to agreeableness and intellectual dimensions of personality (Balabanis 2002). The **ego** is the conscious self, the part of the mind that makes the day-to-day decisions that lead to the satisfaction of the id; the **superego** is an internalised parent, the conscience that holds us back from selfish gratification of the id's needs. The superego also operates mostly below the conscious level, and is the 'brake' on behaviour; in a sense, the ego is constantly making compromises between the id's demands and the superego's restraints. This is shown in Figure 4.1.

Ego The conscious self

Superego The component of mind that acts as a restraint on behaviour

In simple terms, the id acts like a spoilt child, demanding instant gratification regardless of consequences; the superego acts like a stern parent, urging self-restraint and devotion to duty, and the ego acts like a good lawyer, arranging compromises and settlements between the two parties which will not lead to bankruptcy. Hedonic needs (see Chapter 2) largely derive from the id, so advertising with a hedonic appeal is intended to strengthen the id's demands and encourage the ego to find in favour of the id. Some advertising also weakens the effects of the superego – marketers might suggest that life is too short to listen to your conscience all the time, for example.

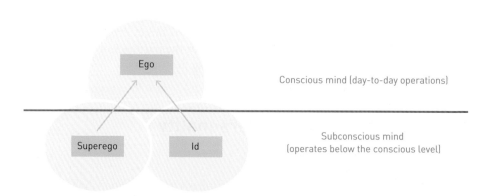

Figure 4.1   The id, the ego and the superego

Challenging the status quo

How much of what we think and do is really unconscious? Are we really so easily swayed by things that happened in our childhood? After all, we have the largest brain (relative to our size) of any known animal, so we ought to be able to think a bit, surely!

Or maybe we are not so much rational, as rationalising. Perhaps we make our decisions on gut instinct, then justify them afterwards. In other words, perhaps we put our big brains to use to persuade ourselves that we are doing some real thinking!

The Freudian approach led to motivation research, which purported to explain the underlying reasons for buying. Motivation research was at its most popular in the 1950s and was, for a time, believed to be able to predict consumer behaviour in terms of basic drives that supposedly came from the id. Some of the claims made for motivational research now seem fairly ridiculous; for example, it was claimed that crunching cornflakes appealed to the killer instinct because it sounds like crunching animal bones, and that baking a cake is a substitute for giving birth. Convertible cars were thought to be a substitute for a girlfriend, and so forth. Motivational research became somewhat discredited because of the extravagant claims made, but still has something to say to marketers. Finding out what people really think, as opposed to what they say they are thinking, enables marketers to address people's underlying needs and wants much more accurately.

The depth (or guided) interview is an example of a motivational research method that is still widely used. A small number of respondents (50 or less) is interviewed without the use of a formal list of questions. Interviewees are encouraged to express their innermost thoughts and feelings about the object of the research (perhaps a new product). The interviewer needs considerable skill to keep the interview on course without leading the interviewee into expressing beliefs that are not his or her actual beliefs: it is easy to give the interviewee the impression that there is a 'right' answer.

A variation on this is the focus group, in which a group of ten or so respondents is invited to discuss their feelings and motivations collectively. The advantage of this method is that the respondents will tend to stimulate each other, and therefore there is less risk of the interviewer introducing bias into the results: the problem is that people may be reluctant to express attitudes that are embarrassing or might put them in a bad light.

Projective tests are widely used in psychological counselling and psychiatry, and occasionally have applications in market research. They are based on the assumption that the individual may sometimes have difficulty in answering questions directly, either because the answers would be embarrassing or because the answers do not readily come to mind. In effect, a projective technique requires the respondent to say what somebody else might think about a given topic. Sometimes this is done by showing the respondent a cartoon strip of people in a relevant situation: sometimes the respondent is asked to complete a sentence, sometimes the respondent will be asked to draw a picture describing his or her feelings about the attitudinal object. In all cases the intention of the research is to allow the respondents to convey their innermost feelings in a non-personal way.

In Figure 4.2, the person on the left is expressing an opinion that may be controversial: the respondent in the research is asked to fill in what the person on the right

Depth (guided) interview Open-ended interviews conducted with a small sample of respondents in order to assess their innermost thoughts and feelings

Focus groups A group of people assembled for the purpose of gathering their collective views about a given issue

Bias The factor which affects the processing of information as a result of the pre-existing mindset

Projective test A research technique whereby respondents are asked to give an opinion of what they think someone else's attitude or feelings might be on a given topic

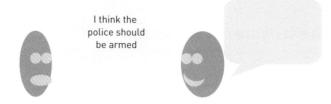

Figure 4.2   Cartoon projective technique

might say in response. In theory, the respondent will fill in his or her own opinion, but without the social risk of expressing the opinion openly. This method is particularly useful for uncovering hidden attitudes, perhaps where the individual has an attitude that might be regarded as antisocial or offensive.

Motivational researchers tend to be interested in the id, claiming that this dictates the individual's basic drives. The assumption is that knowledge of the id's demands will enable marketers to shape arguments for the ego to use in overcoming the super-ego's restraining influence.

From a marketing viewpoint, research of this nature allows firms to determine people's real attitudes to topics such as excessive drinking, cosmetic surgery, or sexual imagery in advertising. All these topics have caused people to feel embarrassed and to avoid answering truthfully – but marketers need to get to the truth if they are to address people's real needs without causing offence.

Type approach

Freud was the earliest of the scientific psychologists. In subsequent years, additional beliefs to Freud's grew up. The followers of Jung categorise people (in addition to Freudian belief) as introverts (preoccupied with themselves and the internal world) or extroverts (preoccupied with others and the outside world). This was an early attempt to classify people into broad types, and this process has continued ever since, with different researchers discovering different ways of grouping people according to personality types.

The mother and daughter team of Kathryn Briggs and Isabel Myers developed the Myers-Briggs Type Indicator, shown in Figure 4.3 (Briggs and Myers 1962), with four personality dimensions:

> Introvert Someone who is withdrawn from other people
>
> Extrovert Someone who demonstrates his or her personality traits in a strongly overt or obvious manner to other people

1 Extrovert/introvert
2 Sensing/intuitive
3 Thinking/feeling
4 Judging/perceptive.

The combinations can define people into 16 different types; for example, an extrovert-sensing-feeling-judging person is warm-hearted, talkative, popular and likes harmonious relationships. An introvert-intuitive-thinking-judging person is likely to be quiet, intelligent, cerebral and reclusive.

Note that most of us are on a continuum in terms of the Myers-Briggs dimensions. Relatively few people would be at the extremes of any of the dimensions, but the model does provide us with a means of categorising people broadly.

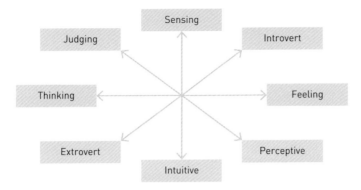

Figure 4.3 Myers-Briggs Type Indicator

Karen Horney defined people across three dimensions (Horney 1945):

1 *Compliant.* Moves towards people, has goodness, sympathy, love, unselfishness and humility. Tends to be overapologetic, oversensitive, overgrateful, overgenerous, and overconsiderate in seeking love and affection.
2 *Aggressive.* Usually moves against people. Controls fears and emotions in a quest for success, prestige and admiration. Needs power, exploits others.
3 *Detached.* Moves away from people. Conformity is repugnant to the detached person. Distrustful of others, these people are self-sufficient and independent, and value intelligence and reasoning.

There is empirical evidence to show that these categorisations have some effect on people's buying behaviour. For example, it has been shown that compliant people use more mouthwash and toilet soap, and prefer branded products; aggressive people use more cologne and after-shave. Detached people show low interest in branding (Cohen 1967). It seems likely that compliant people will be very eager to please, and reluctant to offend, which is likely to mean that they will be suitable subjects for campaigns emphasising gift-giving or caring behaviour. The problem, as always, lies in identifying these individuals.

Reisman (1953) categorised people against three characteristics, in terms of the sources of their basic drives:

1 *Inner-directed* people are essentially driven from within, and are not too concerned with what other people think.
2 *Other-directed* people get their motivation and take their cues from other people.
3 *Tradition-directed* people get their cues and motivations from the past, from traditional beliefs and sources. These people are nowadays in a very tiny minority.

Reisman's categories (see Figure 4.4) have been used in the past for marketing purposes. Inner-directeds, for example, were shown to be innovators for cars and foodstuffs (Donnelly 1970), whereas outer-directeds have tended to be fashion victims (Zinkhan and Shermohamad 1986). There appears to be a change in the social paradigm, however, which is turning these views in a different direction. Broadly speaking, it would appear that more and more people are becoming inner-directed; according to some researchers, the current figure is around 40% of the population (Evans and Blythe 1994; McNulty 1985). This has led to a shift in the prevailing social paradigm away from the basically conformist attitude of the Victorian era towards a more individualistic, free-thinking society.

Innovators People who are the first to try a new product

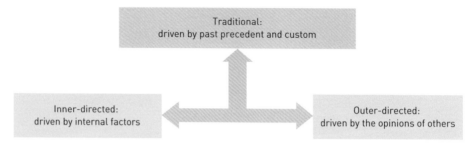

Figure 4.4   Reisman's typologies

As with all the other classifications, most people are on a continuum. To some extent we are all driven by all three factors: Reisman's model is intended to show that some people may lean more towards one type of influence than towards others.

This shift in the social paradigm is having several effects: first, the fashion market has fragmented and almost anything goes (Evans and Blythe 1994). Second, there is a declining respect for authority and an increase in the crime rate. Third, and more positively, there is an increase in the tendency for people to espouse causes and work towards altruistic goals, even in the face of opposition from the Establishment. The shift in the social paradigm is coming about as a result of increased wealth and security in the Western world; as consumers move up Maslow's Hierarchy of Need (see Chapter 2) more of them are operating at the self-actualising level (McNulty 1985).

The movement towards a more inner-directed population has given rise to the VALS typology described in Chapter 2.

Overall, the type approach has much to offer marketers. There is little doubt that personality type affects buying behaviour, and since such types are easily identified and are easy to appeal to through marketing communications, it is not difficult to approach these groups, typically by using models.

Traits and factors

Personality is composed of traits, or individual 'atoms' of personality. These individual predispositional attributes exert influences on behaviour, so the traits must be identified before people can be typed or classified.

Traits tend to be enduring facets of personality. In other words, traits tend not to change much over time, and even when they do change they tend to do so rather slowly. Those that might tend to change with age are: anxiety level (which tends to go down as the individual gets older), friendliness (which can change either way) and eagerness for novelty (which tends to go down) (Goleman 1987). A few traits may vary throughout life, but studies show that adult personalities do not vary significantly as a person ages. This is not to say that behaviour and attitudes never change; merely that the underlying personality tends to stay very much the same. Changing roles, responsibilities and circumstances have much more effect on behavioural changes.

The psychologist Raymond Cattell developed a sixteen-factor trait analysis which has proved useful in defining personality types. Each factor has a high and low range, so that people can be ascribed a position along the continuum between low and high across each factor. Table 4.1 shows the factors and the typical features of someone at either extreme (Cattell 1946; Cattell and Mead 2008).

Table 4.1 16PF trait analysis

Low range descriptors	Primary factor	High range descriptors
Impersonal, reserved, detached, distant, cool, formal, aloof	Warmth	Warm, easy-going, participating, likes people, outgoing, attentive to others, kindly
Concrete thinking, less intelligent, lower general mental capacity, unable to handle abstract problems	Reasoning	Abstract-thinking, more intelligent, bright, higher general mental capacity, fast learner
Reactive emotionally, changeable, affected by feelings, emotionally less stable, easily upset	Emotional stability	Emotionally stable, adaptive, mature, faces reality calmly
Deferential, cooperative, avoids conflict, submissive, humble, obedient, easily led, docile, accommodating	Dominance	Dominant, forceful, assertive, aggressive, competitive, stubborn, bossy
Serious, restrained, prudent, taciturn, introspective, silent	Liveliness	Lively, animated, spontaneous, enthusiastic, happy-go-lucky, cheerful, expressive, impulsive
Expedient, nonconforming, disregards rules, self-indulgent	Rule consciousness	Rule-conscious, dutiful, conscientious, conforming, moralistic, staid, rule-bound
Shy, threat-sensitive, timid, hesitant, intimidated	Social boldness	Socially bold, venturesome, thick-skinned, uninhibited
Utilitarian, objective, unsentimental, tough minded, self-reliant, no-nonsense, rough	Sensitivity	Sensitive, aesthetic, sentimental, tender-minded, intuitive, refined
Trusting, unsuspecting, accepting, unconditional, easy	Vigilance	Vigilant, suspicious, skeptical, distrustful, oppositional
Grounded, practical, prosaic, solution-oriented, steady, conventional	Abstractedness	Abstract, imaginative, absent-minded, impractical, absorbed in ideas
Forthright, genuine, artless, open, guileless, naive, unpretentious, involved	Privateness	Private, discreet, nondisclosing, shrewd, polished, worldly, astute, diplomatic
Self-assured, unworried, complacent, secure, free of guilt, confident, self-satisfied	Apprehension	Apprehensive, self-doubting, worried, guilt-prone, insecure, worrying, self-blaming
Traditional, attached to familiar, conservative, respecting traditional ideas	Openness to change	Open to change, experimental, liberal, analytical, critical, free-thinking, flexible
Group-oriented, affiliative, a joiner and follower, dependent on others	Self-reliance	Self-reliant, solitary, resourceful, individualistic, self-sufficient
Tolerates disorder, unexacting, flexible, undisciplined, lax, self-conflict, impulsive, careless of social rules, uncontrolled	Perfectionism	Perfectionistic, organized, compulsive, self-disciplined, socially precise, exacting will power, control, self-sentimental
Relaxed, placid, tranquil, torpid, patient, composed, low drive	Tension	Tense, high energy, impatient, driven, frustrated, over-wrought, time-driven

The study of individual traits as they relate to buying behaviour seems unlikely to produce concrete results. This is probably because personality is interdependent; studying a few traits in isolation gives an insufficiently complete view of the whole person (*Marketing News* 1985). However, a combination of hierarchically-arranged traits has been linked to the propensity to undergo cosmetic surgery or to use tanning studios (Mowen et al. 2009).

Traits are clearly interrelated, but given the number of traits that have been identified (several thousand, according to some authors) the interrelationships are likely to be complex, especially as people exhibit the different traits to a greater or lesser degree.

Psychographics

Psychographics Using behavioural tendencies to infer personality traits

Psychographics is sometimes known as lifestyle studies, since it is concerned with people's values and approaches to life. Essentially, it is a quantitative study of consumer lifestyles for the purpose of relating those lifestyles to the consumers' purchase behaviour. For example, somebody who has a 'green' set of values is likely to have an eco-friendly lifestyle, which in turn means that the individual will be more likely to buy a bike than a car, be more likely to be a vegetarian than eat red meat, and so forth. These ethical values can be powerful forces in decision-making (Fraj and Martinez 2006; Shaw et al. 2005). By knowing what a person's basic lifestyle is we can make a fair prediction as to their purchasing behaviour, and the kind of products and promotions that will most appeal to that individual.

The psychographic approach to personality study combines the strengths of motivation research on the one hand with those of trait and factor theories. The assessment of lifestyle often involves very lengthy and involved studies of large samples of the population; the Target Group Index annual research programme, which is run by BMRB, asks people to respond to 246 lifestyle statements. From this survey different lifestyles can be identified and consequently different purchasing patterns can be predicted.

An example of this approach is the VALS breakdown referred to in Chapter 2. A UK equivalent was developed by Taylor Nelson, as shown in Table 4.2. The relative

Table 4.2 Lifestyle Types

	Lifestyle type	Characteristics	% of population
	Belonger	People who believe in the establishment, traditional family values and patriotism. Averse to change	19%
Sustenance-driven groups; motivated by the need for security	Survivor	People who are fighting a 'holding action'; accept authority, hard-working, quiet, traditional. Strong class consciousness	16%
	Aimless	Two main categories: young unemployed whose main motivation is short-term 'kicks', and the very old, whose motivation is simply day-to-day existence	5%
Outer-directed group	Conspicuous consumer	Interested in material possessions, taking cues from reference groups (friends, family). Followers of fashion	18%
Inner-directed groups; motivated by self-actualisation	Social resister	Caring group, motivated by ideals of fairness and a good quality of life at the societal level. Altruistic, concerned with social issues like ecology and nuclear disarmament	11%
	Experimentalist	Materialistic and pro-technology, individualistic and interested in novelty	14%
	Self-explorer	Motivated by self-expression and self-realisation. Tolerant, able to think big and look for global, holistic solutions.	16%

Source: Adapted from McNulty 1985.

percentages of each group are likely to have changed in the intervening thirty years, of course – as noted earlier, there is a trend towards greater inner-directedness.

Psychographics approaches have in common that they all try to predict behaviour from knowledge of lifestyle and attitudes. The drawback with this approach is that the necessary research is complex, time-consuming and ultimately relies heavily on the judgement of the researchers to decide which factors are appropriate to a particular lifestyle.

Challenging the status quo

Trying to infer personality types from behaviour seems to be fraught with risk. Someone who describes themselves as environmentally friendly might still drive a car, for example – running your car on biodiesel might be greener than running it on mineral diesel, but does that make you environmentally friendly? Someone might be a humanitarian, but still join the Army because being a soldier might be seen as a way of fighting for the greater good of humanity.

The list goes on. People behave in all sorts of funny ways, so aren't we pushing our necks out by trying to guess *why* they behave the way they do? Maybe we can predict behaviour from knowledge of personality traits, and maybe we can analyse personality traits by observing behaviour, but isn't it just as likely that personality and behaviour have no connection whatever? Or maybe what we are talking about is not something that is absolute, but rather something that is subjective!

The psychographics approach appears to have strong potential to tell us about what people will buy, since clearly most purchases are related to a chosen lifestyle. The problem is therefore not conceptual, but rather one of definition.

Self-concept

Of all the personality concepts which have been applied to marketing, self-concept has probably provided the most consistent results and the greatest promise of application to the needs of business firms. (Foxall 1980)

Self-concept is the person's ideas and feelings about him- or herself. It has an important role to play in understanding consumer behaviour, since people will buy products that contribute to the self-concept. For example, a woman who thinks of herself as a 'femme fatale' will choose chic clothes to enhance that image; or a man who thinks of himself as a handyman will equip himself with the most sophisticated tools.

Essentially, people project a role and this is confirmed (or denied) by the people around. In order for the role to be confirmed, the person will try to develop all the exterior accoutrements appropriate to the role. In this sense, the person becomes a work of art; a sensory stimulus to other people, which is intended to generate affective responses. The person may well use all five senses to generate the affective response: sight (by dressing appropriately, wearing make-up, etc.), hearing (by speaking with the right accent, or using the voice well), smell (by wearing perfume or deodorant), touch (by looking after the skin, perhaps by wearing clothes that feel good) and even taste (by using flavoured lipstick, mouthwashes).

Some of these sensory stimuli will, of course, only be available to the individual's closest friends, and often only available to lovers, but most people at some time or

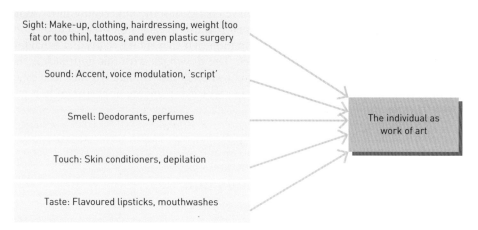

Figure 4.5   The person as artwork

another will consciously set out to create a work of art of themselves in order to 'make a good impression' on somebody. The extent to which people do this depends on the following factors:

1 The degree of importance attached to impressing the other person (or people).
2 The degree to which the individual anticipates that the 'target audience' can be impressed.
3 The cost in time and money of creating the desired image.

Clearly, though, the fact that people do create these works of art has led to the invention of whole industries to cater for the need – the cosmetics industry and fashion industry, to name but two. The forces involved can be very strong indeed: even in Nazi concentration camps people were prepared to trade food for clothing and cosmetics, thus placing their survival at risk for the purpose of maintaining their dignity (Klein 2003). In some cases fashion items also represent personality determinants and even rite-of-passage symbols. Research by Russell Belk showed that shoes can represent a  rite of passage (a girl's first high heels, for example) and that people often define themselves by their footwear (brands of trainer, for example) (Belk 2003). African Americans sometimes wear African clothing as a way of identifying themselves with their roots (deBerry-Spence and Izberk-Bilgin 2006).

Rite of passage An event or action which marks a change in an individual's life circumstances

Challenging the status quo

Re-inventing ourselves is a common event. We change our hair, or our clothes, and effectively become someone else. But are we justified in considering this to be a work of art? Art is supposed to make people re-think the world around them – does this really happen when someone gets a haircut?

Or perhaps the person-as-artwork idea only applies at the extremes, where someone undergoes radical cosmetic surgery to give themselves a cat-like face (for example) or a body shape which is so extreme as to be a caricature?

Also, who is the artist here? The individual, or the cosmetic surgeon, hairdresser or beautician who carries out the work?

Self-concept is a learned construct. Children tend to look for role models to imitate; these may not always be the same people, and the child may try several different role models before settling on one that is appropriate. Children can be crushed by a denial of the role being projected, for example if people laugh while the child is copying the behaviour of a favourite auntie or uncle. During the teenage years a further refinement occurs as the individual tries to develop an adult role, and again the role models may shift, typically away from the family members towards a hero (pop star or sporting personality) or sometimes to an individual within a peer group (a school friend, for example). Usually the role model will be an adult a few years older.

Peer group Those people who are near to being one's equals

 ## Consumer behaviour in action: The Divine Image

The Divine Image is a consultancy with a strong foothold in a growing market – that of personal image.

Managing director Camelia Fredericks is a former lawyer, now turned image consultant. She is a member of the Federation of Image Consultants, and has built The Divine Image on a foundation of sleek, upmarket chic (to quote the corporate website).

The Divine Image will, under the direction of Camelia and her staff, carry out a personal analysis of what colours the client should wear, what style of clothes, and what hairstyle and cosmetics are appropriate. What the consultancy does goes further

than the TV makeover cliché – The Divine Image will advise on correct body language and 'personal branding' to project the right image. The company is quite up front about what they are aiming to do for clients: they aim to develop confidence, develop dress sense and style, improve self-esteem and, overall, improve self-image.

The service does not stop with advice, either. Consultants will go shopping with clients and help them find the right clothes, and will even precede this with a visit to the client's wardrobe to see what is already suitable and (more importantly) what is not. Consultants are available to advise on dating – everything from making the first approach to making a good impression on the night, and making the other person fall head over heels in love. Heaven on earth, for only £50 an hour for a consultation.

The service is not, as one might imagine, confined to women. Exactly the same service is available to men, and The Divine Image has a great many male clients.

Why do people use services like The Divine Image? Simple – most of us know that we would do better in our careers, in our love lives and in our social lives if we could only project the right image. Few of us are experts in this, and we envy people who seem always to wear the right clothes, say the right things and influence the right people. Any money invested in image consultancy will come back tenfold in improved job prospects and less time and money wasted on unsuitable clothing and dating. After all, the investment is in something that can never be lost, repossessed or taken away – yourself.

Self includes gender, and there are many studies on how the individual's perception of gender affects purchasing behaviour. People typically form a view on the gender-appropriateness of brands: there is evidence that men are more concerned

Table 4.3   Components of self-concept

Component	Explanation
Real self	This is the actual, objective self, as others see us. There is a problem with this definition, since other people never know the whole story. This means that the 'real' self may be something other than the face shown to the world
Self-image	This is the subjective self, as we see ourselves. Self-image is likely to differ radically from the real self, but to an extent this is modified over time because of feedback from others. We modify our self-image in the light of the reactions of others
Ideal self	How we wish we were; this connects to the self-actualisation need that Maslow identified. This self is often the one that provokes the most extravagant spending, as the individual tries to make up the gap between self-image and ideal self
Looking-glass self	The social self, or the way we think other people see us. This does not always coincide with the way people actually see us, since we are not able to read minds. Feedback from others will be constrained by politeness or by a desire to project a self-image on the part of the respondent, so we are not always aware of what other people really think we are like
Possible selves	These are the selves we might become, or the selves we wish we could become

about this than women, being less prepared to adopt a brand extension that they perceive as coming from a 'feminine' brand (Jung and Lee 2006). Men also tend to define masculinity in part through advertisements they see (although they may interpret what masculinity means in different ways). Extensions from a 'male' brand are much more likely to be adopted (Tuncay 2006).

Self-concept has four attributes, as follows:

1 It is learned, not innate.
2 It is stable and consistent. Self-perception may change; self-concept does not. This accounts for brand loyalty, since self-concept involves an opinion about which products will 'fit the image'.
3 It is purposeful; in other words, there is a reason and a purpose behind it. Essentially, self-concept is there to protect and enhance a person's ego. It is therefore advisable not to attack a person's beliefs directly; people often become angry or at least defensive when this happens.
4 The self-concept is unique to the individual, and promotes individualism.

Self-concept breaks down into different components, or dimensions (Walker 1992). These are shown in Table 4.3.

There is some overlap, but the differences are quite marked between the dimensions. Each dimension has some relevance for marketers, and the implications are as shown in Table 4.4 below.

Table 4.4   Relevance of self-image

Dimension	Relevance to marketers	Examples
Real self	As the face that is shown to the world, this is the one that people most wish to influence	Conspicuous consumption of cars, houses, etc. Cosmetics, fashion and hairdressing
Self-image	Useful in two ways; first, the negative aspects of self-image influence the ideal self, and second the positive aspects influence purchases which reinforce the self-image	Somebody whose self-image is 'cool' will not want to jeopardise that, and will buy appropriate products to match that image. Somebody whose self-image is poor will want to correct discrepancies
Ideal self	The aspect that leads to the greatest purchases of self-improvement products	Correspondence courses, cosmetics, cosmetic surgery, musical instruments and any number of other products that lead to self-development
Looking-glass self	The way we *think* others see us; this influences us in making changes to those views, or reinforcing views that are perceived as positive	A man who thinks his friends see him as being staid or boring might be prompted to buy a sports car in order to correct the image. Conversely, somebody more outer-directed might deliberately buy a car to fit in with the image he thinks he has with his friends; perhaps to buy a Ford Focus or Volkswagen Golf because his friends see him as a solid, down-to-earth person
Possible selves	The selves we might become, or the selves we wish to become, are not necessarily the same. We may fear what we might become (for example, being afraid of becoming overweight, or of contracting a serious disease, or of becoming an alcoholic)	In some cases marketers have a role in helping people to formulate and fulfil their dreams – education and training courses are an example. In other cases marketing techniques are used to enable people to avoid becoming what they fear being: social marketing campaigns encourage people to eat healthily, take exercise, cut down on smoking and over-eating, and control their alcohol intake

For marketers, the differences are useful. Ideal self predicts attempts at upward mobility: purchases of training courses, self-improvement classes, upmarket products, cosmetic surgery, etc. Looking-glass self is relevant for other-directed people.

In Figure 4.6, self-concept is generated partly by internal factors such as looking-glass self, ideal self and self-image, but these are modified (particularly through looking-glass self) by the real self. This is because those around us give us feedback on how we are coming across, either by showing approval of what we do or by showing disapproval. These forces are so powerful that they even extend to on-line identities: researchers have found that similar-looking avatars tend to congregate together in virtual reality, and are less friendly and welcoming than are groups of different-looking avatars. Even owning the right set of virtual possessions is important in cyberspace (Wood et al. 2009).

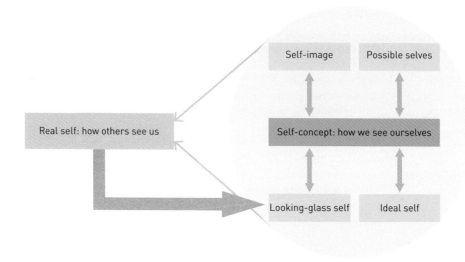

Figure 4.6   Relationship between components of self-concept

Market maven Someone who is a self-appointed expert about a particular product category or market

In recent years, the concept of the market maven has developed. Market mavens are people who define themselves as knowledgeable about the market for a particular product type: the word 'maven' derives from a Yiddish word for 'wise'. Such people enjoy sharing their knowledge with others, and enjoy the self-concept of being an expert: this improves their self-confidence as well (Clark et al. 2008). Obviously mavens are important to marketers (especially those in high-tech industries), since they influence purchase decisions of others very strongly. Mavens differ from opinion leaders: opinion leaders tend to have high levels of emotional involvement with product categories, while mavens have a more intellectual, knowledge-based stance. Mavens also show a higher need for variety in their lives than do opinion leaders – in other words, they may well switch brands if they discover information that means the new brand is better (Stokburger-Sauer and Hoyer 2009).

Self can also be categorised as actual self, ideal self and worst self (Banister and Hogg 2003). This is a simpler model, but it includes the concept of the worst self – the self we are ashamed of. For marketers, products can be promoted as being good for avoiding the worst self, or can be promoted as being good for appeasing the worst self.

Self-image is relevant to what we think we deserve; what is the 'right' product for us. Teenagers use music consumption as a way of building social capital, creating boundaries and defining who is excluded or included in the social group (Nuttall 2009). People are swayed by what is promoted as being 'just right for people like you' – children can be told they are having 'the special children's meal'; students can be swayed by a 'special student discount'; elderly people by the special 'senior citizen's service'. Sometimes this type of promotion can backfire – there may be fears about the quality of the service or product, for instance, and (especially in the case of older people) the self-image of the person might differ from the image the marketer has of their group. This is why advertising aimed at elderly people often uses actors in their fifties and sixties rather than actors in their seventies or eighties. An interesting piece of research showed that people tend to relate more strongly to brands that contain letters from their

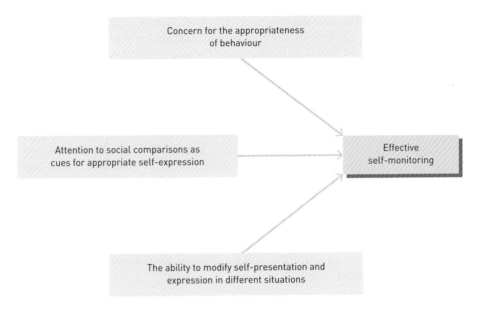

Figure 4.7 Self-monitoring

own names: this is probably a subconscious association with the brand (Brendl et al. 2003).

Real self is not known to the consumer, although it is one of the greatest motivators in consumer behaviour. In the words of Burns, 'To see ourselves as others see us' is not in our gift – and this may be just as well.

Achieving the ideal self is very much about getting appropriate applause and critical acclaim, so that we know whether we are getting it right; but perhaps more importantly there is the element of learning the lines and getting the production right in terms of costume, make-up and script. People therefore modify their behaviour according to the feedback obtained; this is called self-monitoring (Snyder 1974). As shown in Figure 4.7, self-monitoring has three forms of expression: concern for the appropriateness of behaviour, attention to social comparison as cues for appropriate self-expression, and the ability to modify self-presentation and expression across situations (Nantel and Strahle 1986). Another example is people's attitude to credit: people with strong self-monitoring mechanisms, and people with low price-consciousness, are less likely to rely on credit cards than are people with low self-control or high price sensitivity (Perry 2001). Such self-monitoring mechanisms only have a limited amount of mental resources backing them up: often people who normally exhibit great self-control will sometimes 'snap' and buy something entirely on impulse (Vohs and Faber 2003).

In other words, people ensure that their behaviour is appropriate for the occasion by observing what others are doing and by acting in harmony with that behaviour. Rather like the inexperienced diner who watches others to see which knife and fork to use for each course, people take cues from those around them in order to ensure polite behaviour. Low self-monitors are more likely to behave according to some inner drive, and may even prefer to be seen as being different from the rest of humanity; high self-monitors are more likely to conform with those around them, and are therefore more susceptible to appeals to be fashionable.

Self-monitoring The regulatory mechanism which controls behaviour, without outside intercession

Some products are transformational, in other words they allow people to change who they are. For example, cosmetic surgery, correspondence courses and self-improvement books all offer people the opportunity to change their self-concept. Identity-related perceptions form the basis for choosing such products and for evaluating their success (or otherwise). People will also decide whether or not their self-concept can accommodate the changes (Kleine et al. 2009). For example, someone who is considering doing a correspondence course will evaluate the course on the basis of perceived weaknesses in his or her self-concept, but will also consider whether doing the course will result in a self-concept that is equally less than ideal. Perhaps the individual recognises a need to take a course in computer science (for self-actualising reasons) but does not want to be thought of as a 'nerd'.

People's decisions to undergo drastic transformations (for example, cosmetic surgery) are also influenced in different ways by the people around them. For example, in the case of teenage girls contemplating cosmetic surgery, support from family tends to reduce the need for the surgery, whereas support from friends tends to increase it (Pentina et al. 2009).

Summary

In this chapter we have looked at what constitutes people's personalities and self-concept. We have also looked at role-playing, and have looked at some of the ways these elements affect consumers' buying behaviour. Car manufacturers still sell on personality; perfumiers such as Jean-Paul Gaultier and Calvin Klein, and even pet food advertisements, also rely on personality. The Kit-E-Kat cat is lively, inquisitive, a little mischievous and always affectionate to its human owner. The implication is that feeding the cat Kit-E-Kat will make it into this type of cat, even if it starts out as a less-than-perfect house pet.

 **Key points**

- Personality is made up of traits; so far several thousand possible traits have been identified.
- Personality is a self-serving, individualistic, unique, overt and consistent gestalt.
- Self-concept is concerned with one's feelings about oneself.
- Self-concept is learned, stable, purposeful and unique.
- As wealth increases, more people are becoming inner-directed.
- High self-monitors take their cues from others; low self-monitors take their cues from an inner drive.

Review questions

1 Why are personality traits an important concept for marketers?
2 Why is self-concept such a useful way of segmenting markets?
3 What might be the impact of increased inner direction on fashion in the future?
4 How might high self-monitors respond to an increase in inner direction in the rest of the population?
5 How might the Myers-Briggs type dimensions be used by marketers for a perfume company?
6 What are the marketing implications of the possible self?
7 What are the marketing implications of the gender perception of brands?

Case study revisited: Mobile telephones

So how does someone's personality affect their choice of mobile phone?

Presumably owning one at all indicates someone who likes to be well-connected. Of course, this may be a result of work needs rather than social needs, but the preponderance of mobile telephone ownership in wealthy countries indicates that many people use their telephones for managing their social lives.

Having a telephone with all the features on might be an indication of someone with a very practical orientation: having one device that does everything is clearly more efficient than having many different devices to carry around. Equally, it might denote someone whose self-image is one of technical expertise, the maven who knows all about the latest technology.

Case study: The National Society of Allotment and Leisure Gardeners

Most of us have toyed with the idea of growing our own food at one time or another. Having a little patch of ground to grow our own vegetables perhaps takes us back to our beginnings as human beings: we have been cultivating our own food for 10,000 years or more, and it's maybe hard to break the habit.

In the UK, the Allotment Act of 1908 requires local councils to provide an 'adequate' number of plots of land for city dwellers to grow their own. Usually allotments are of sufficient size to grow enough vegetables for a family of six: the intention was to ensure that poor people would be able to eat fresh vegetables on a regular basis, and would have some time in the fresh air, away from the factory bench.

The allotment movement had a major boost during the Second World War, when the U-boat blockade in the North Atlantic threatened to starve the country into submission. The 'Dig for Victory' campaign encouraged people to turn any open space into a food farm: municipal parks, golf courses, spare land around airfields and waste ground were all brought under cultivation as people supplemented the official rations with fresh vegetables. The war years have been said to be the healthiest period (in terms of diet) that the UK has ever seen, and after the war many people continued with the habit, having got used to the better quality (not to mention lower price) of home-grown veg.

Later, allotments fell out of fashion. During the 1970s and 1980s allotments were regarded as the domain of old men in flat caps, as cheap supermarket food became available and people's working lives became more demanding. However, since the beginning of the century allotments have come back into vogue. Concerns about the additives and preservatives used in supermarket food, coupled with the need to find a less stressful way of living, have prompted people from all age groups and backgrounds to apply for an allotment. There is now, typically, a waiting list of several years for plots in popular areas, and no shortage of people applying for them.

The National Society of Allotment and Leisure Gardeners is now over 100 years old. It was formed to represent the interests of allotment holders throughout the UK, and also has an international section representing a total of 3.5 million gardeners. The Association operates as an Industrial and Provident Society rather than as a charity, and members pay a membership fee of £20 a year (or £300 for a life membership) in exchange for which they are allocated a share in the society. Members are entitled to discounts on seeds, free legal advice if their allotment is under threat from developers, discounted insurance, an allotment management service (aimed at allotment clubs) and a free monthly magazine. Perhaps most importantly, the Society enables allotmenteers to contact each other for advice, best practice, exchange of seeds and plants, and tips on cooking the veggies.

One of the problems allotmenteers face is the loss of their site due to redevelopment. Although local councils are required to provide an 'adequate' supply of allotments, there is no definition in law as to what exactly 'adequate' means. Since many allotments were established on waste ground in inner-city areas, the land often acquires great value for building development: local authorities often see this as a way of raising money fairly quickly and easily without annoying the taxpayers. For this reason, the Society has a full-time lawyer on the staff, charged with the task of defending allotments in court if necessary.

Having an allotment is not necessarily a big money-saver: by the time the eager gardener has costed out buying seeds, fertiliser, slug pellets and site rental there isn't a great saving to be made (the figures work out even worse if time is taken into account). Yet having an allotment is still very rewarding: the fun of seeing the plants grow and produce food, the friendliness of one's fellow allotmenteers, and of course the knowledge that what you have grown yourself will be healthier for you (and will taste better) than commercially produced vegetables more than make up for the time and effort.

Questions

1 What personality traits might an allotment holder have?
2 How might one's self-image be affected by having an allotment?
3 What type of person would join the National Society of Allotment and Leisure Gardeners?
4 What has shifted in the collective consciousness to allow allotment-keeping to become desirable to young people?
5 How might a marketer identify suitable allotment holders for the purpose of selling organic seeds?

Further reading

For an interesting insight into the issues discussed in the chapter case study, see Hein, W., O'Donohoe, S. and Ryan, A. (2011) Mobile phones as an extension of the participant observer's self: Reflections on the emergent role of an emergent technology. *Qualitative Market Research* 14 (3): 258–73.

Concepts of the Self by Anthony Elliott (Cambridge: Polity Press, 2007) gives an overview of the key arguments in self-concept. It's a straightforward, lively account, which gives the counter-arguments as well as the theories, so that the various thinkers are linked together well.

Otto Kroeger and Janet M. Theussen's book *Type Talk: The 16 Personality Types* (New York: Bantam Doubleday Dell, 10th edn, 1989) gives a lot of applied examples of the Myers-Briggs Type Indicator. This is a very useful book in understanding why people behave the way they do.

References

Balabanis, G. (2002) The relationship between lottery ticket and scratchcard buying behaviour, personality and other compulsive behaviours. *Journal of Consumer Behaviour* 2 (1): 7–22.

Banister, E.N. and Hogg, M.K. (2003) Possible selves? Identifying dimensions for exploring the dialectic between positive and negative selves in consumer behaviour. *Advances in Consumer Research* 30: 149–50.

Belk, R. (2003) Shoes and self. *Advances in Consumer Research* 30: 27–33.

Brendl, C.M., Chattopadhyay, A., Pelham, B.W., Carvalho, M. and Prichard, E.T. (2003) Are brands containing name letters preferred? *Advances in Consumer Research* 30 (1): 151–2.

Briggs, K. and Myers, I. (1962) *Manual: The Myers-Briggs Type Indicator*. Princeton, NJ: Educational Testing Service.

Cattell, H.E.P. and Mead, A.D. (2008) The sixteen personality factor questionnaire (16PF). In G. Boyle, G. Matthews and D.H. Saklofske (eds), *The Sage Handbook of Personality Theory and Assessment, Vol. 2. Personality Measurement and Testing*. Los Angeles, CA: Sage. pp. 135–78.

Cattell, R.B. (1946) *The Description and Measurement of Personality*. New York: World Books.

Clark, R.A., Goldsmith, R.E. and Goldsmith, E.B. (2008) Market mavenism and consumer self-confidence. *Journal of Consumer Behaviour* 7 (3): 239–48.

Cohen, J.B. (1967) An interpersonal orientation to the study of consumer behaviour. *Journal of Marketing Research* 6 (August): 270–8.

Conn, S.R. and Rieke, M.L. (1994) *The 16PF Fifth Edition Technical Manual*. Champaign, IL: Institute for Personality and Ability Testing, Inc.

deBerry-Spence, B. and Izberk-Bilgin, E. (2006) Wearing identity: the symbolic uses of native African clothing by African Americans. *Advances in Consumer Research* 33: 193.

Donnelly, J.H. Jr. (1970) Social character and the acceptance of new products. *Journal of Marketing Research* 7 (February): 111–13.

Evans, M. and Blythe, J. (1994) Fashion: a new paradigm of consumer behaviour. *Journal of Consumer Studies and Home Economics* 18: 229–37.

Foxall, G. (1980) *Consumer Behaviour: A Practical Guide.* London: Routledge.

Fraj, E. and Martinez, E. (2006) Influence of personality on ecological consumer behaviour. *Journal of Consumer Behaviour* 5 (May–June): 167–81.

Goleman, Daniel (1987) Basic personality traits don't change, studies say. *New York Times*, 18 June.

Horney, K. (1945) *Our Inner Conflict.* New York: WW Norton.

Jung, K. and Lee, W. (2006) Cross-gender brand extensions: effects of gender of the brand, gender of the consumer, and product type on cross-gender extensions. *Advances in Consumer Research* 33: 67–74.

Klein, J.G. (2003) Calories for dignity: fashion in the concentration camp. *Advances in Consumer Research* 30: 34–7.

Kleine, R.E., III, K., Schultz, S. and Brunswick, G.J. (2009) Transformational consumption choices: building an understanding by integrating social identity and multi-attribute attitude theories. *Journal of Consumer Behaviour* 8 (1): 54–70.

Marketing News (1985) 13 September, p. 56.

McNulty, W.K. (1985) UK social change through a wide-angle lens. *Futures*, August.

Mowen, J.C., Longoria, A. and Sallee, A. (2009) Burning and cutting: identifying the traits of individuals with an enduring propensity to tan and to undergo cosmetic surgery. *Journal of Consumer Behaviour* 8 (5): 238–51.

Nantel, J. and Strahle, W. (1986) The self-monitoring concept: a consumer perspective. *Advances in Consumer Research* 13: 83–7.

Nuttall, P. (2009) Insiders, regulars and tourists: exploring selves and music consumption in adolescence. *Journal of Consumer Behaviour* (Jul/Aug), 8 (4): 211–24.

Pentina, I., Taylor, D.G. and Voelker, T.A. (2009) The roles of self-discrepancy and social support in young females' decisions to undergo cosmetic procedures. *Journal of Consumer Behaviour* 8 (4): 149–65.

Perry, V.G. (2001) Antecedents of consumer financing decisions: a mental accounting model of revolving credit usage. *Advances in Consumer Research* 28: 13.

Reisman, D. (1953) *The Lonely Crowd.* New York: Doubleday.

Shaw, D., Grehan, E., Shiu, E., Hassan, L. and Thomson, J. (2005) An exploration of values in ethical consumer decision-making. *Journal of Consumer Behaviour* 4 (3): 185–200.

Snyder, M. (1974) Self-monitoring of expressive behaviour. *Journal of Personality and Social Psychology*, 34: 526–37.

Stokburger-Sauer, N.E. and Hoyer, W.D. (2009) Consumer advisers revisited: what drives those with market mavenism and opinion leadership tendencies and why? *Journal of Consumer Behaviour* 7 (3): 100–15.

Tuncay, L. (2006) Men's responses to depictions of idea masculinity in advertising. *Advances in Consumer Research* 33: 64.

Vohs, K. and Faber, R. (2003) Self-regulation and impulsive spending patterns. *Advances in Consumer Research* 30: 125–6.

Walker, B.A. (1992) New perspectives for self-research. *Advances in Consumer Research* 19: 417–23.

Wood, Natalie, Chaplin, Lan Nguyen and Solomon, Michael (2009) Virtually me: youth consumers and their online identities. *Advances in Consumer Research* 36: 23–4.
Zinkhan, George M. and Shermohamad, Ali (1986) Is other-directedness on the increase? An empirical test of Reisman's theory of social character. *Journal of Consumer Research* 13 (June): 127–30.

More online

To gain free access to additional online resources to support this chapter please visit: **www.sagepub.co.uk/blythe**

CHAPTER ⑤
Perception

CHAPTER CONTENTS

LEARNING OBJECTIVES

After reading this chapter you should be able to:

- Explain the role of analysis and synthesis in perception.

- Explain the role of synergy in creating a perceptual impression.

- Understand the problem created for marketers by selectivity.

- Explain how past experience affects perception.

- Describe Weber's Law.

- Describe the relationship between perception and reality.

- Explain the conscious and unconscious aspects of perception.

- Explain the difference between internal and overt perceptual responses.

- Discuss subliminal advertising.

- Explain the role of colour in perception.

Introduction

How we analyse the environment around us and develop a picture of the world is of great interest to marketers. Ensuring that the company's brands become part of the world-view of the potential consumers is the main purpose of marketing communications: understanding perception processes is what puts the product there.

Perception is the keystone of building knowledge, not just about products but about everything else in the world. Although it is common to refer to perception as if it were somehow different from the truth, this is not the case: perceptions may differ between individuals, but for each person their own perception is the whole truth. This is sometimes difficult to remember – but in fact, our whole experience of the world happens inside our heads, filtered by our senses and moderated by our previous experiences.

Case study: First Impressions

First Impressions is an international consultancy dedicated to helping people create a favourable first impression on others. Founded in 1985, the company has consultants in the UK, France, Switzerland, Singapore, Ireland, Turkey and Hong Kong. As well as advising people on their appearance, body language and speech, First Impressions trains other people to become image consultants – perhaps strange, considering that the firm is thus creating competitors for itself, but an indication of the level of demand there is for this service.

Making a good first impression is a subtle thing, but important. Whatever happens later will be judged in the light of the first impression – if people get the idea that you are a freak or a loser, it is very hard to recover, whereas if people feel you are person worth knowing they will forgive a great deal later on. Lack of self-confidence is far more common than most people think – which is of course where a consultancy like First Impressions comes in.

First Impressions consultants are dotted around the country, so there is no need to go to the head office in Warwickshire to obtain advice. Consultants advise clients on what to wear, how to wear one's hair, which colours best suit the individual, and behaviour (deportment). Some offer a shopping service – the consultant will either accompany the client on clothes shopping expeditions, or will (if necessary) simply buy the clothes and deliver them to the client. Clients pay £75 an hour or more to image consultants, with top consultants commanding fees that lawyers and financial advisers can only dream of.

The economic crisis gave a huge boost to the image consultancy industry. People who had lost their jobs, often in high-powered positions, needed help in creating a good first impression with prospective employers. Sales people and other business development executives needed to try harder if they were to secure business, and company officials needed to impress shareholders and others. The Association of Image Consultants International has 1300 members worldwide with more joining every day: becoming an image consultant is an appealing way of finding work when times are hard.

Image consultancy is a young industry. It started in the 1980s, grew rapidly in the 1990s and is now showing another spurt of growth. Managing perceptions is obviously becoming big business.

How to impress your examiner

You may be asked to explain the process of developing a world-view. You should be very clear about the synthetic aspects of perception as well as the analytic aspects: perception is not about misunderstanding the world, it is about creating a useable working model of the world on which to base decisions. There is a very strong link between perception and learning, and this should also be understood. As always, real-life examples help to show that you understand the theory.

Elements of perception

Perception is a process of converting sensory input into an understanding of how the world works. Because the process involves combining many different sensory inputs, the overall result is complex to analyse; for example, people often judge fabrics by touch, but memory and confidence in the evaluation is improved if the 'touch' input is reinforced with verbal information (d'Astous and Kamau 2010). Human beings have considerably more than five senses. Apart from the basic five (touch, taste, smell, sight, hearing) there are senses of direction, sense of balance, a clear knowledge of which way is down and so forth. Each sense is feeding information to the brain constantly, and the

Table 5.1 Conventions about perception

Convention	Explanation
Perception is about more than the substantive part of the message	Messages may be expressed directly in words, but the observer 'reads between the lines' and creates new meanings from what is seen or read
The law of similarity says that we interpret new information in a similar way to information we already hold	If we read a newspaper report in a paper we trust to be accurate, we will tend to assume that the news report is also accurate. If we see packaging (for example a brown coffee jar) we will associate this with similar brown packaging on other brands of coffee
Expectations	If we expect a particular sequence of events, or a particular message, then we tend to see that message and interpret accordingly
'Figure–ground' relationships influence interpretation	An individual will interpret a printed message differently according to which part of the image is interpreted as the message and which part as the background
The Law of Closure	This means that people can only obtain the whole message if they have all the components of the message. This particularly applies in advertisements that are intended to intrigue consumers: an advertisement that contains a puzzle or a visual joke will not be understood by the observers unless they are in possession of enough information to infer the punch line
The Law of Continuity	Gestalt perception is based on the idea that the elements of the overall message form a continuum rather than a set of separate elements. In other words, even when a particular stimulus (for example an advertisement) is composed of music, speech, pictures and moving images the person watching it will still form an overall impression. Of course, someone who is asked to analyse an advertisement will be able to separate out the various elements, but in normal behaviour few people would do this
The whole is greater than the sum of its parts	When the message consists of a number of elements, the elements often combine to create a stronger message
Colour influences perception	Because human beings have a well-developed colour sense, colours are often influential in creating an overall image of a product. This may be due to the need, in prehistoric times, for hunter–gatherers to assess the ripeness or nutritional value of fruit

amount of information being collected would seriously overload the system if one took it all in. The brain therefore selects from the surroundings and cuts out anything that seems irrelevant.

In effect, the brain makes automatic decisions as to what is relevant and what is not. Even though there may be many things happening around you, you are unaware of most of them; for example, experiments have shown that some information is filtered out by the optic nerve even before it gets to the brain. People quickly learn to ignore extraneous noises; for example, as a visitor to someone else's home you may be sharply aware of the noise from the dishwasher, whereas your host may be entirely used to it and unaware of it except when making a conscious effort to check that the machine is still cycling.

There are eight main conventions regarding perception, as shown in Table 5.1.

Perception is, in part, a process of analysis in which the outside world is filtered and only the most important (as defined by the individual) or interesting (as defined by the individual) items come through. Therefore, the information entering the brain does not provide a complete view of the world.

In Figure 5.1, most of the stimuli surrounding the individual are filtered out. The remaining stimuli are combined and interpreted, then included with memory and imagination to create an overall perception.

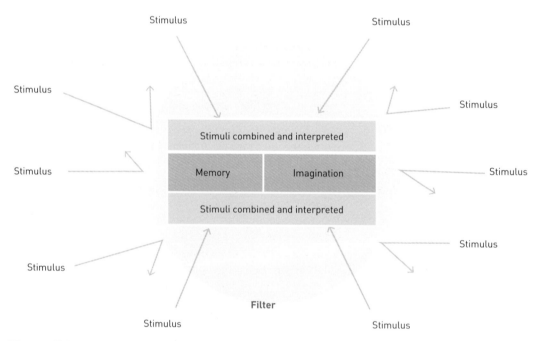

Figure 5.1　Selectivity and synthesis

Challenging the status quo

It looks as if we are all just making this up as we go along. If perception is reality, and we are imagining most of the world, why don't we imagine somewhere a great deal pleasanter?

We could imagine an earthly paradise, with free beer and sandwiches for all, if we just filter out the bad parts and keep the good bits. So why not do this? After all, there are plenty of lunatics about who seem to be perpetually cheerful and optimistic.

Or perhaps we need to let some of the threatening aspects of life enter in order to defend against them?

Creating a world-view

The perception process is a social-psychological phenomenon. It involves cue selection and cue interpretation, and combining these cues to create an overall impression. There are six components of perception, as follows (Warr and Knapper 1968):

1 Stimulus.
2 Input selector.
3 Processing centre.
4 Consumer's current state.
5 Consumer's stable characteristics.
6 Response.

The stimulus is the object that is being perceived. In this sense, the object could be a person, a product, an event, a situation, a communication or anything that catches the individual's attention. For marketers, the stimulus on offer is likely to be a brand, a product, a retail shop or a marketing communication.

When the individual constructs a world-view, he or she assembles information to map what is happening in the outside world. Any gaps (and there will, of course, be plenty of these) will be filled in with imagination and experience. The cognitive map is therefore not a 'photograph'; it is (at least in part) a construct of the imagination. This mapping will be affected by the following factors:

1 Subjectivity. This is the existing world-view within the individual, and is unique to that individual. People have differing views of the world – this is what makes being a human being so much fun, because we argue a lot – and this means that we interpret any incoming stimuli differently according to who we are.

2 Categorisation. This is the 'pigeonholing' of information, and the prejudging of events and products. This can happen through a process known as chunking whereby the individual organises information into chunks of related items (Miller 1956). For example, a picture seen while a particular piece of music is playing might be chunked as one item in the memory, so that sight of the picture evokes the music and vice versa.

3 Selectivity is the degree to which the brain is selecting from the environment. It is a function of how much is going on around the individual, and also of how selective (concentrated) the individual is on the current task. Selectivity is also subjective; some people are a great deal more selective than others. Research shows that people judge the authenticity of Irish themed pubs by the behaviour of the employees and the patrons rather than from the decor, showing that people are being selective in the factors they use to judge the pub (Munoz et al. 2006).

4 Expectations lead individuals to interpret later information in a specific way. For example, look at this series of numbers and letters:

A 13 C D E F G H I
10 11 12 13 14 15 16

In fact, the number 13 appears in both series, but in the first series it may well be interpreted as a B because that is what the brain is being led to expect.

5 Past experience leads us to interpret later experience in the light of what we already know. This is called the Law of Primacy by psychologists. For example, adverts shown early in ad breaks generate greater brand recall than those in later slots (Li 2010). Sometimes sights, smells or sounds from our past will trigger off inappropriate responses; the smell of bread baking may recall a village bakery from twenty years ago, but in fact the smell could have been artificially generated by an aerosol spray near the supermarket bread counter.

Subjectivity Judging everything from a personal viewpoint

Categorisation The pigeonholing of information in order to prejudge events and products

Chunking The learning process by which items of information are grouped by the brain

Selectivity The part of perception that deals with rejecting unnecessary stimuli

Expectation The existing information and attitudes that cause people to interpret later information in a specific way

Law of primacy First experiences affect the interpretation of later experiences

An example of cognitive mapping as applied to perception of product quality might run as follows. The individual uses the input selector to select clues and assign values to them. For quality, the cues are typically price, brand name and retailer name. Most of us tend to assume that a higher-priced product will be better quality, and also that a well-known brand name will be better than a generic product; although the retailer name is less significant, it still carries some weight. For example, many consumers would feel confident that a major department store such as Harrod's would sell higher-quality items than the local corner shop, but might be less able to distinguish between rival supermarket chains such as Sainsbury's and Tesco.

The input selector is the mechanism by which the individual selects cues from the stimulus and assigns a meaning to each one. The input selector takes the various environmental factors and processes them one at a time: the processing centre has the task of integrating the cues to generate an overall perception. The input selector and the processing centre are not actually separate functions: they almost certainly operate at the same time, because the cues are delivered simultaneously or at least very closely after one another. For example, someone seeing an advertisement for a car might remember the shape of the car but not the make, or might remember the background detail of the advertisement (the scenery against which the car is filmed, perhaps) and remember nothing about the vehicle itself. It has been shown that people perceive a task as being more difficult if the instructions on how to do it are written in a hard-to-read font (Song and Schwarz 2009).

This is a perennial problem in marketing communications. Knowing which cues people most often select is clearly of great interest, especially if we are considering a specific factor such as quality. In some cases people judge quality on the basis of price, in other cases on the physical attributes of the product, but the current view is that the use of an extrinsic cue such as price and intrinsic cues such as physical and performance attributes depend on prior knowledge (Rao and Monroe 1988). As consumers become more familiar with the product's intrinsic attributes, price becomes less important as a surrogate for judging quality. In some cases, products are consumed almost entirely for their symbolic value: in some emerging economies such as China, products are often bought simply because they are Western brands, symbolising a desirable lifestyle. These brands are sometimes desired even when the consumer has never seen the actual product (Clark et al. 2002).

The processing centre is likely to be influenced by the individual's current state. The current state includes factors such as mood, motivation, goals and the physical state of the individual at the time the cues come along.

A mood is transitory: it will pass, no matter how strongly it is felt at the time. When we are in a good mood we tend to feel favourably towards more cues, whereas if we are in a bad mood we tend to be negative about cues. This is partly responsible for the halo effect (or horns effect) in which we tend to think that, if one thing is bad about something, everything is bad about it. If people feel a momentary disgust with a company or a product this will carry over into future decisions, changing the status quo (Han and Lerner 2008).

Positive moods tend to create less elaboration (i.e. people think less when they are in a good mood) and decisions are often made much more automatically than would normally be the case (Batra and Stayman 1990). There is evidence that marketing messages that express positive outcomes are much more effective than those that stress negative outcomes, presumably because the former create good moods whereas the latter create fearful or worried moods (Zhao and Pechmann 2006). On the other hand, sad expressions on the faces of victims generate greater charitable donations, perhaps because donors feel the need to change the unpleasant feelings that arise from seeing the charity's advertisements (Small and Verrochi 2008).

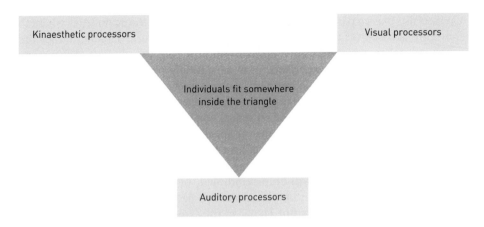

Figure 5.2 Information processing types

Individuals process information in individual ways, of course: neuro-linguistic programming theory tells us that some people prefer to process visual information, some prefer auditory information and yet others prefer tactile or kinaesthetic processing. Most of us are on a continuum on which we absorb and process cues from all three areas: it is simply that we prefer one route over another.

Visual processors are likely to respond better to advertising with strong graphics or visual content. Auditory processors prefer the spoken word, or music. Kinaesthetic processors prefer to touch or try out products, so would be most likely to respond to advertising that offers a trial or free sample. As shown in Figure 5.2, most people fit somewhere inside a triangle formed by the three processing methods, favouring one or other but still able to process information in all three ways.

There are five main influences on perceptual mapping, as shown in Figure 5.3.

The information is subjective in that people base decisions on the selected information. Each of us selects differently from the environment, and each of us has differing views. In the case of distinguishing between rival supermarket chains, each individual will have a slightly different view of the supermarkets concerned. If this were not so, we would rapidly develop a situation in which only one supermarket chain existed. The individual's previous experience also has a bearing – for example, research shows that adolescents who live in areas where there are high levels of drug use and sexual promiscuity over-estimate their own knowledge of these things (Parker et al. 2006).

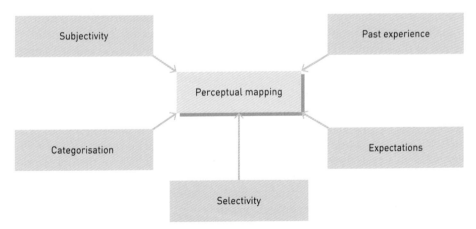

Figure 5.3 Influences on perceptual mapping

Culture also plays a part in perception – people who come from countries where the architecture is based on circles and cylinders (for example rural Zambia) rather than squares and boxes sometimes have difficulty interpreting two-dimensional pictures, because they have had less experience in understanding perspective. Equally, culture affects the ways in which people interpret gestures, pictures, tones of voice and many other signals – for example, in many Indian languages a question is indicated by the use of a falling tone at the end of the sentence, whereas in English it is indicated by a rising tone. For an English speaker, someone speaking with a falling tone at the end of a sentence would sound as if they are making a flat statement, which in some contexts may sound strange or even offensive, leading to a false perception of the speaker.

Information about quality will be pigeonholed, or **categorised**, so that products from different categories might be placed next to each other in the cognitive map. For example, an individual may put Jaguar in the same category as BMW, but might also include Sony or Grundig in the same grouping. It is common to hear people refer to a product as 'the Rolls Royce of …' whichever product category is under consideration.

Selectivity will depend on how much is going on in the environment, on the individual's interest and motivation regarding the subject area, and on the degree of concentration the individual has on the task in hand. People with a highly developed ability to concentrate select less from the environment, because they are able to 'shut out' the world much more.

Expectations of quality play a huge part: if the individual is expecting a high-quality item, he or she will select evidence that supports that view and tend to ignore evidence that doesn't.

Past experience will also play a part in quality judgement. If the consumer has had bad experiences of Japanese products, this might lead to a general perception that Japanese products are poor quality.

Price has a strong effect on people's assessment of products. Researchers have shown that people's confidence in guessing the 'right' price for an article varies according to how many zeroes there are in the stated price – the more zeroes, the greater the confidence in the guess (Thomas et al. 2010). Also, there is a general belief that the higher the price, the better the quality in some way; often this view will be justified, of course. People tend to think that a bargain is a better bargain if they also think that the marketers have made a mistake, in other words if people think the product has been accidentally marked at the wrong price they will tend to see it as a better bargain than if the marketers are explicit about the offer (Bardhi and Eckhardt 2010).

The downside from a marketer's viewpoint is that price has a negative effect on perceived value and on willingness to buy. The problem therefore lies in knowing how big a price reduction will increase sales without leading to a negative perception of quality. Weber's Law states that the size of the least detectable change depends on the size of the stimulus. This means that a very intense stimulus will require a bigger change if the change is to be perceived by the consumer. For example, 20 pence off the price of a chocolate snack is a substantial discount, and would attract attention in advertising; 20 pence off the price of a BMW would go unnoticed. Clearly at this level of intensity (a price of a few pence compared with a price of thousands of pounds) Weber's Law may not work very precisely but in the middle range of prices the Law appears to work well. Incidentally, reducing the price from £10 to £9.99 is very noticeable even though the actual reduction is only 0.01% of the initial price. The important element here is that the reduction be noticeable.

Weber's Law also applies to product differentiation. The Law can be applied to determine how much better the product has to be for the difference to be noticeable, or conversely to determine how similar the product needs to be to be indistinguishable from the leading brand.

Weber's Law The size of the least detectable change will depend on the size of the stimulus

Perception and the brand

Branding is all about perception. The marketer's aim is to develop the most favourable perception possible of the brand through working with its strengths, whether the brand's strength lies in its quality, its price competitiveness, or any other area. Developing a suitable brand personality means encouraging people to imbue the brand with human characteristics – which means assembling a range of stimuli to create an overall image.

Using senses which (at first sight) appear to be unrelated to the primary senses to which the product relates can be extremely powerful: for example, the 'snap, crackle and pop' of Rice Krispies relates sound to the brand, whereas one would normally expect a food product to be primarily concerned with flavour and (perhaps) texture. People are prepared to pay more for food that is well-presented – up to 140% more in some cases (Payne and Wansink 2010).

Some experiments have been conducted in the use of multisensory brands. Nike found that people who tried out their trainers in a floral-scented room preferred them to the same trainers when they tried them in a non-scented room (Lindstrom 2005). Obviously if the fragrance is an inherent part of the product (for example, soap) any changes in the fragrance will have a profound effect on perception of the brand, even when the primary function of the brand is unaffected (Milotic 2003).

Perception and store atmospherics

There are three factors in the information processing of store atmospherics: proxemics, kinesics and paralanguage (see Figure 5.4).

Proxemics refers to the use of physical space in conveying a perceptual stimulus. In a retail environment, for example, a shop assistant might stand too far away (which might be interpreted as dislike for the customer) or too close (suggesting a threatening invasion of personal space). Kinesics is about body language, eye contact and gesture: greater eye contact between buyers and sellers would indicate positive feelings between them.

Paralanguage refers to the way words are used. Use of 'here' and 'this' is more positive than using 'there' and 'that'. Some other sound cues such as yawning, speaking too loudly or too softly, or speaking too quickly or too slowly also convey messages about how the individual feels about the product.

Atmospherics The factors that create the overall ambience in a retail environment

Proxemics The use of physical space to convey a perceptual stimulus

Kinesics The interpretation of non-verbal communications related to body movement

Paralanguage Communication carried out in a manner other than through words

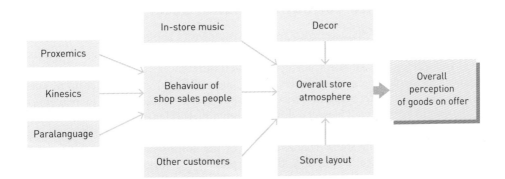

Figure 5.4   Perception and store atmospherics

Challenging the status quo

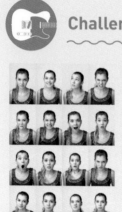

We are all aware that body language makes a great deal of difference to communications. Gestures and subtleties of facial expression can completely change the meaning of words used. Yet most of this happens without us even being aware of it. We operate on gut feeling – we get a sense of when someone is lying, for example, without necessarily being able to say what particular facial expression or gesture gave the game away.

So how can we possibly expect to train shop assistants to behave in a particular way? Aren't we liable to make poor play-actors out of them, and thus give customers the impression that we are lying to them?

Or maybe we should just hire nice people to begin with?

Another example is the way in which store atmospherics are manipulated to generate perceptions about the products on offer – music played in-store will tend to increase purchases of hedonic products (Lee and Thomas 2010).

Moods can be manipulated to an extent by store atmospherics, which in turn affect purchasing behaviour – moods also affect processing of information from advertising (Bakamitsos and Siomkos 2004). Brand extensions are received more favourably if the individual is in a good mood (Greifeneder et al. 2007), and even the way the message is framed can affect perception: researchers found that smokers who read that almost 1000 people die of smoking every day found the message more powerful than saying that 440,000 people a year die of smoking. This is apparently because the shorter time-frame means that the message has more immediacy (Chandran and Menon 2003).

Time-frames may have other effects – positive cues are often overrated when considering a future event because people broaden the range of factors they take into account when considering the future (Grant and Tybout 2003). Dates are regarded as abstract, whereas time intervals are concrete: in other words, 'six months' interest-free credit' sounds a great deal better than 'interest-free credit until 30th November' (LeBoeuf 2006).

Perception and consumers' characteristics

A consumer's stable characteristics are the basic factors about an individual that do not change, or change only slowly. Gender, personality, social class, age, educational level and intelligence all affect perception. Such differences can and do produce differences in the accuracy of interpretation of cues, and also in the selection of cues. Therefore, wide differences in processing ability, and consequently in perception itself, should be expected between different individuals (Henry 1980).

Some demographic variables may be responsible for the misunderstanding of cues; however, although the stable characteristics of the consumer might be expected to have a strong effect on perception, the interplay of the various factors is such that researching the effect of each one proves difficult. So far, therefore, research has been somewhat inconclusive on this issue.

Consumer behaviour in action: Wolff Olins and Orange

When mobile telephones first appeared in the 1980s they were heavy, expensive and unreliable, but like all new technologies they quickly became more refined and sophisticated. The UK market for mobile telephones was seen in the industry as one of the more lucrative ones – a country with a relatively small geographical area, and a densely packed wealthy population, offered advantages both technically and economically.

The Hong Kong conglomerate Hutchison Whampoa had not failed to see the implications, and had tried to enter the UK market with a brand called Rabbit. This disappeared without trace; a second attempt, in 1994, used branding consultants Wolff Olins to manage the brand. The consultants came up with a concept that changed marketing history – the Orange brand.

The aim of the brand was to move mobile telephones away from being the preserve of business people and yuppies and move them into the mainstream of everyday life. The brand was conceived as being warm and friendly, energetic and optimistic. The philosophy behind the Orange brand was that landlines only connect one place to another – mobile telephones connect people with people.

Using the strap line 'The Future's Bright – The Future's Orange', the consultants developed a series of eye-catching advertisements. Using the colour orange meant that marketing communications became even more powerful and memorable – within two weeks of the launch the brand had achieved an unprecedented 45% awareness with the British public, and within two years awareness was over 70% (considerably higher than its rivals, Vodafone and Cellnet).

Wolff Olins managed the Orange brand from 1994 until 2000 (when the brand was sold to Mannesmann). At that time, the brand sold for the equivalent of £5000 per customer, which perhaps shows that perception of brands affects more than just consumers.

Perception and behaviour

Responses are not necessarily overt or external. In terms of perception, a response can just as easily be internal and non-behavioural. The perceptual response has three components: attribution, expectancy and affection (see Figure 5.5).

Attribution is about applying a certain characteristic to an object. For example, someone who is scowling might be perceived as being angry. It is possible that the person is actually deep in thought about a problem that has just arisen, but the observer has attributed the characteristic of anger based on the cue of the facial expression. The same process happens when people are confronted with a product or brand: they attribute characteristics to it, based on the cues received.

Expectancy is about what the individual thinks the object will do. In the case of the scowling person, the observer might expect that the person will shout or even become violent. In marketing, expectancy is what leads people to believe that a well-known brand is better than the generic brand, even though the formulation is the same. One of the best-known examples of this is analgesics (pain killers). Branded aspirin actually works better than generic aspirin, even though the active ingredient (acetylsalicylic acid) is identical in each case.

Affection is about emotional responses. In ordinary language, affection implies a positive response, but in psychology affection merely describes any emotional effect,

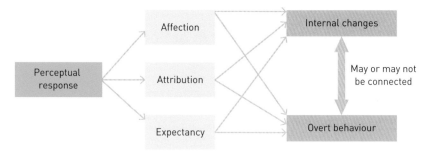

Figure 5.5   Perceptual responses

whether positive or negative. Such responses to a given stimulus might be liking, sympathy, fear, respect, disapproval, disgust and so forth. An affective response is what we refer to when we talk about gut feeling or instinct: it is not a rational response, but that does not necessarily mean that it is wrong or ill-conceived.

Combining factors

The processing centre combines the various cues to create an overall impression. This is likely to include attribution, expectation and affection components, but there are three basic models which seek to explain how this happens in practice. These are as follows:

Inference Extra detail added to a message by a recipient, based on meta-analysis of the message

1   The linear additive model (Figure 5.6). This states that the inferences from each clue will build towards an overall perception. This means that the implications that attach to a particular characteristic will become stronger with the addition of each cue, regardless of how intense each cue is. A strong cue will not be weakened by a subsequent weak cue, in other words.

2   The linear averaging model (Figure 5.7). This is a refinement on the previous model, since it assumes that the implication of a particular characteristic will be strengthened or weakened by subsequent cues, according to their strength. This means that the quality of the information may be more important than the quantity of the information, so that marketers who try to provide people with very large amounts of positive information may find that the effect is weakened if people regard some of the information as being of less interest than other information. Salespeople generally understand this phenomenon well: they are trained to find out first what the customer is interested in about the product, then to talk only about those aspects. There is also some (rather old) research evidence to show that the linear averaging model fits the facts better than the linear additive model (Anderson 1965).

3   The configural model (Figure 5.8). Linear models have the underlying assumption that the meaning of each cue remains the same when other facts are revealed. This is not necessarily the case: as cues are brought together, the meanings of previous cues are likely to be revised in the light of the new information. The configural model is intended to address this issue. The problem with this model is, of course, that it is virtually impossible to calculate what may or may not happen in a particular individual's mind as a result of being presented with a number of cues, and it is even difficult to know what will happen across a target audience of potential customers, which makes advertising difficult.

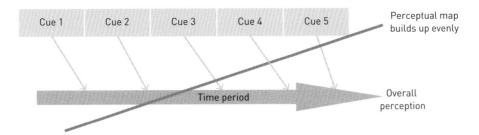

Figure 5.6 Linear additive model

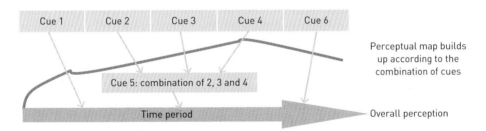

Figure 5.7 Linear averaging model

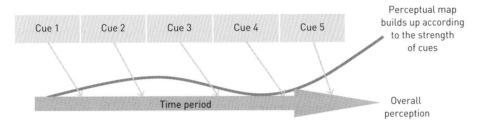

Figure 5.8 The configural model

As with any models, all three of the above are simplifications of reality, and therefore do not tell the whole story. It seems likely that people perceive the whole of a given object, rather than breaking it down into individual cues, but this (naturally) varies according to circumstances. Someone choosing a new car might well want to consider every aspect individually – the comfort of the seats, the sound of the door closing, the quality of the interior finish, the space in the back seats and in the boot, the shape of the steering wheel, the layout of the various controls, and so forth. The motive for including the car in the consideration set in the first place might be an overall impression offered by the firm's advertising, however.

Of course, we rarely have complete information about anything. Our brains are proactive in filling in the gaps – neuroscience has demonstrated that we continuously generate predictions about what to expect in the environment around us (Bar and Neta 2008).

Equally, the purchase of a brand of biscuits is unlikely to involve the same level of analysis. Few people would trouble to read the list of ingredients and the nutritional information on the packet, or ask a friend's advice, or go on-line and investigate the company's history and manufacturing methods.

An interesting area of research, therefore, is to try to find out which rules people use at particular times. Sometimes people will use a linear rule, at other times they might use a configural method, and at still other times people might use a combination of rules to form an overall opinion. Research carried out by Meyer in 1987 seemed to indicate that people tend to use configural methods, but later on in the process the decisions move towards additive rules (Meyer 1987).

It may be that the more utilitarian aspects of the product are judged against a linear set of rules, whereas the hedonic or affective aspects are judged against the configural model (Holbrook and Moore 1981).

Subliminal perception

Perception is not necessarily a conscious process. Much of what happens in our minds happens below the conscious level (see Chapter 4), and we know that often people have a 'gut feeling' about something without being able to define why. Most of us have had the experience of falling in love at first sight – with people or with products. This happens without our having any real facts to go on, and without our having any way of analysing the reasons.

Subliminal perception has a controversial history in marketing. During the 1950s it was claimed that subliminal advertising, as it was called, could make people do things they otherwise would not do. The theory was that brief exposure to a message (for example, flashing 'Drink Cola' onto a cinema screen during a film) would cause people to experience a sudden mysterious desire to drink cola. The theory was that the message would appear and disappear much too quickly for the input selector mechanism to operate, so the message would bypass the normal perceptual safeguards and enter the person's consciousness unedited (see Figure 5.9). These claims were so powerful that subliminal advertising was banned in some countries and was regulated in others; in fact, the general air of paranoia in the 1950s may have contributed to the scare, since there is little evidence to support the claims made for subliminal advertising. One widely publicised 'experiment' in 1957 was later found to have been faked by the researcher, but the story still circulates about the effectiveness of flashing messages onto cinema screens.

Wilson Key has published several books on the subject of subliminal perception in advertising (Key 1973, 1976, 1980, 1989) in which he claims that advertisers have airbrushed in words such as 'U Buy' into the shadows around a bottle of rum, and various sexual images in advertisements for cigarettes and even cake mix. In 1957, Vance Packard published a book called *The Hidden Persuaders* in which he analysed

Subliminal perception
Perception that occurs below the conscious level

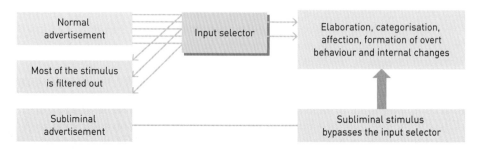

Figure 5.9 Subliminal advertising

the various ways in which the media industry manipulates opinion: he included subliminal advertising in his analysis (Packard 1957). However, in both cases the authors have been criticised for failing to produce solid evidence, and for making too many assumptions and suppositions.

The evidence for and against subliminal perception, at least as far as marketing goes, is mixed to say the least. There is some evidence that drive and behaviour may be influenced (Hawkins 1970), and there is also some evidence that flashing brand names onto cinema screens has impact when the stimulus is related to right-brain processing (Cuperfain and Clarke 1985). Other studies have failed to find any evidence for subliminal perception (Beatty and Hawkins 1989; Gable et al. 1987; Kelly 1979).

Subliminal perception, and from that subliminal advertising, is supposed to work in the same way as self-hypnosis tapes. Such tapes are often sold as a means of losing weight, giving up smoking and so forth, yet there is no evidence that they have any effect whatsoever (Anon 1991). People's attitudes towards subliminal perception are ambivalent – on the one hand, people tend to fear it, since they are afraid that marketers (and others) might use it to manipulate them unfairly, and on the other hand people often hope that it does work when they buy self-hypnosis recordings (Spencer et al. 2003).

 Challenging the status quo

Subliminal advertising has been dismissed as a figment of the imagination, a product of Cold War paranoia and people's general mistrust of marketing. But of course marketers would say that, wouldn't they?

We know that a lot of our impressions of the world come from deep below the conscious level, from cues we are not really aware of, so why wouldn't this be true of advertising? If self-help hypnosis tapes don't work, why do people keep buying them? Is it simply that there is a widespread belief that they will work (and therefore people subconsciously act on the belief but not on the tape) or is it more likely that the tapes do have some effect on the individual's thought processes?

Even worse – are marketers for faceless corporations using subliminal advertising to make us into robots?

Even if subliminal advertising were shown to work, it seems probable that it would be ineffective. First, different people have different perception thresholds, so some people might be aware that the message has flashed onto the screen. Second, there is a very high risk of misunderstanding; after all, people frequently misunderstand or misinterpret advertising which is in plain language, so the potential for missing the point in an advertisement which is flashed onto a cinema screen for a fraction of a second must be very much greater. Finally, the selective nature of perception means that most stimuli are ignored or rejected by the input selector, even when the stimulus is strong. The fleeting nature of subliminal messages is likely to mean that they never register with the observer. This view accords with Weber's Law (explained earlier in the chapter).

Colour

Colours are used to attract attention, but they also convey particular emotions and meanings. These meanings are culturally specific: for example, in Japan white is the colour of funerals, whereas in the United States and most of Europe it is black; in China, bright colours symbolise high quality, whereas in the UK they are often associated with low price, low quality articles. A study by Madden et al. (2000) found that red is perceived as hot, active and vibrant across all cultures, while black and brown are perceived as sad and stale. Black and brown are also perceived as formal in Brazil, Colombia, China and Taiwan, and as masculine in Austria, Hong Kong and the United States.

Table 5.2 shows some common colour perceptions, particularly as they relate to packaging and advertising.

Colours have a strong effect on perception. Research conducted in the 1960s showed that people believed that coffee from a dark brown container was stronger than coffee from a blue container, and that coffee from a yellow container was weak in both flavour and aroma (Dichter 1964). In fact, the coffee in each container was identical.

Table 5.2 Colour perceptions

Colour	Perceived meaning
Yellow	A strong attention-grabber, yellow often symbolises summer. It works well as a background colour for black print, because it makes the print stand out, but it can sometimes be perceived as 'cheap and cheerful'. Some people associate yellow with warmth, novelty or caution
Orange	Orange is a sociable colour, but in packaging it is mainly used for products (such as orange juice) which actually contain oranges. Some products (and many billboard posters) use dayglo orange as an attention-grabber; in the UK, this was successfully used in billboard advertising for the washing powder Radion. Unfortunately, the product itself did not fulfil its early promise and has now been withdrawn – but the bright orange colour is still used by low-cost airline easyJet
Red	This is a strong attention-grabber because it can stand for most human emotions. It is often regarded as hot, exciting, passionate and strong
Purple	Purple was formerly associated with royalty, and it has retained its upmarket image. Because it is the most expensive colour to reproduce, and has poor resistance to fading, its use in packaging is limited
Blue	Blue is rarely associated with food packaging, because very few foods are blue. It is commonly used to denote coolness or cleanliness, and it is often perceived as having authority and commanding respect. This is why many countries use blue as the colour for police uniforms
Green	The rise of environmentalism has increased the use of green for packaging and advertising. It carries connotations of naturalness, security and calmness. For some people, green can denote Irishness since green is the national colour of Ireland: for many Americans, green is the colour of money, since all American banknotes are green on one side
Pink or magenta	Pink has always been regarded as a feminine colour, so it has been widely used on cosmetics, but in recent years it has been used for baby products and some categories of household goods. It has also become associated with the gay movement
White	In most European countries and the United States, white is the colour of purity and cleanliness. In Japan it is the colour of mourning, however
Brown	In food packaging, brown usually denotes strong flavours such as pickles and sauces, or coffee and chocolate. For gardening products, it conveys a rich earthiness
Black	Black is usually associated with death, but combined with gold it can denote exclusivity and premium prices
Grey	Grey can symbolise sadness, transition, compromise, depression, boredom and monotony, but in recent years it has become a fashionable colour for high-tech products and modern design

This research is not generalisable across cultures, and it also suffers from the major weakness that (not unnaturally) respondents will try to find a difference between the coffees if they are asked to do so. Having said that, the differences that Dichter found were remarkably consistent between the respondents, with 87% of them agreeing that the coffee from the yellow container was too weak. Had people been inventing differences simply to please the researcher, the differences would have been much less consistent. In packaging colour often has a profound effect on people's perceptions of the actual product: for example, Heinz use turquoise for their baked bean cans (even though most other Heinz cans have different colours) as turquoise makes the beans look brighter orange when the can is opened.

These perceptions may not, of course, translate into other countries or cultures. In some cases, colour may be a fashion statement – Goths wear black, for example. Each year has its 'fashionable' colours – for 2006 it seemed to be white and gold, but in 2011 Pantone reported that the top three colours were honeysuckle, coral rose and peapod (Pantone 2011).

Colour also has a dramatic effect on search times for products (see Figure 5.10). Bright colours and contrasting colours make a product stand out, but people also use colour as a way of identifying brands rapidly (Jansson et al. 2004). Companies often therefore adopt a corporate colour, or a colour denoting specific brands in the range. Coca Cola uses red and white, Heinz uses red for its range of soups, and so forth. In the UK, firms have (in recent years) been able to include corporate colours in their trade mark registration, so that, for example, the shade of green used by BP on its forecourts is now protected by law. This does not mean that other people cannot use the same shade of green, but it would mean that other oil companies would not be able to use it as part of their forecourts if the result might be to confuse the public into thinking that they were actually buying from BP. So far, there has been very little litigation based on infringements of corporate colours, although Orange and easy-Group have disputed the use of the colour orange for mobile telephone networks and the low-cost airline respectively.

Deliberate attempts to confuse consumers are called 'passing off', because one company is trying to pass off its products as being from the other company. This is illegal in most countries, since it is obviously against consumer interests as well as against the interests of the brand owner.

The naming of colours is a crucial factor in the marketing of products such as paint and fabrics. Names such as midnight blue, dawn pink, apple green or corn yellow have a positive effect on consumer perception because there is an underlying assumption that the information must be useful in some way, which leads people to put a positive 'spin' on the colour name (Miller and Khan 2003).

Figure 5.10   Colour in marketing

Summary

From a marketing viewpoint, the fact that perception is so nebulous and individual a thing is probably helpful in the long run. People's views of products and services rely heavily on perceived attributes, some of which have no objective reality; the difficulty for marketers lies in knowing what will be the general perception of the members of the market segments with whom we are attempting to do business.

Perception is, if nothing else, an individual thing. The way one person selects and interprets information will be very different from the way someone else selects and interprets the same basic cues. This chapter has dealt with the processes that lead up to the formation of a view of the world: the selection, processing and interpretation of information and the subsequent keying-in of new information to existing knowledge is what enables us to understand our surroundings and deal with problems.

Key points

- Perception is both synthetic and analytic.
- Stimuli combine synergistically to create the whole impression.
- Selectivity is a key issue in perception, and is a key problem for marketers.
- Past experience contributes to the way new stimuli are interpreted as well as to the overall impression.
- Changes in the stimulus will go undetected if the stimulus is a large one.
- Perception and reality are not intrinsically different.
- Most perception happens below the conscious level.
- Perceptual responses may be internal or overt.
- Subliminal advertising is unlikely to be effective.
- Colour speeds search times, as well as attracting attention.

Review questions

1. What effect does selectivity have on an integrated marketing communications campaign?
2. How might colour perceptions be complicated in a global market?
3. Why is subjectivity a problem for marketers?
4. How do internal responses create problems for marketers?
5. What is the difference between the linear additive model and the linear averaging model?
6. Explain Weber's Law.
7. What is the difference between kinaesthetic processing and visual processing?
8. What is the Law of Primacy?
9. What is the role of expectancy in branding?
10. What are the arguments for the effectiveness of subliminal advertising? What are the arguments against?

Case study revisited: First impressions

The initial perception of an individual comes from a number of different elements, not all of which appear to be very logical – but then, perception isn't about logic. According to various experts in the field, the following are the main elements in coming across well on first meeting.

- Look confident. Shake hands – contact is essential.
- Stand up straight. Slouching makes you look like someone who is defeated, or tired.
- Don't fidget. Displacement behaviour such as tapping pencils, crumpling napkins or twisting your hair make you look insecure and nervous.
- Relax and be yourself. Don't appear too rigid, or too eager to impress.
- Make eye contact, and take an interest in what the other person is saying.
- Dress appropriately – if it's a formal occasion, dress formally; if it's a casual occasion, dress 'smart casual'.
- Be careful about personal hygiene, and don't go too heavy on the perfume or aftershave.
- Stay positive – don't disparage other people or companies; this gives the impression that the person you are talking to might be next.

None of this is exactly rocket science, yet many people fail to make that first impression count. That's why there is a need for image consultants!

Case study: Politics and spin

In 2010 the UK held what turned out to be a crucial general election. At the time, the country was in the grip of a serious economic crisis – the sub-prime mortgage lending crisis in the United States had led to a dramatic series of collapses and near-collapses of banks in the UK, including a run on Northern Rock, in which depositors tried to get their money out, thus effectively wrecking the bank. To add to the seriousness of the election, there had been a major scandal exposed in the *Daily Telegraph* newspaper during the summer of 2009. The *Telegraph* had obtained details of expense claims made by MPs, and exposed what was clearly widespread abuse of the system by senior members of Parliament across all  parties. Public fury led to 148 MPs deciding not to fight the election, but instead to stand down and retire into private life.

With public perception of MPs at its lowest ebb, Labour leader Gordon Brown (who had been Chancellor of the Exchequer under the previous Prime Minister) was defending his ruling government. His personal popularity was a great deal lower than that of his predecessor, Tony Blair, but he had taken over when Blair stepped down in 2007. In effect, Brown had not been elected as Prime Minister – the previous election had been fought with Blair in charge. Feeling in the country was running high against Labour, but equally people were fearful of what a Conservative government might do to tackle the economic crisis, and at the same time a number of marginal parties were coming to the forefront (for example the UK Independence Party (UKIP), which had an agenda for taking Britain out of the European Union).

Since this election would be closely fought, parties went to a great deal of trouble to manage their images. David Cameron, the Conservative Party leader, presented himself as a nice family man, concerned for the environment, but tough enough to deal with the crisis. His party portrayed Labour as being the party of waste and over-borrowing, the party that had led the country into its economic woes. On the Labour side, Gordon Brown was portrayed as the steady hand at the wheel, the elder statesman who would not panic in the face of adversity, and who would protect government services and the lower-paid in society. For a brief period the National Health Service (a political sacred cow in Britain) was used as an issue: Labour claimed that the Conservatives would cut expenditure on health, and the Conservatives had to rush out posters showing Cameron saying that the NHS was safe in his hands.

The campaign began to get nasty, as is often the case: Cameron was filmed cycling to work (and thus showing his green credentials) but Labour then pointed out that he also had a limousine following him with his briefcase and security people on board. Labour frequently used Cameron's moneyed background against him. Meanwhile, Gordon Brown was recorded calling a Labour supporter a 'bigot' and asking why the meeting with her had been set up: his testy remarks had been picked up by a Sky News microphone which he had forgotten he was wearing, and of course were broadcast on every news service within minutes. This gaffe seriously affected his credibility with the public, especially since he was seen in a TV interview holding his head in his hands while he tried to explain his statement.

Meanwhile, other parties were coming to the forefront – the Liberal Democrats were making gains in the opinion polls (despite having no members with experience of government) and UKIP were also making gains, as people began to blame foreigners for the country's ills. A lot of small parties, often with purely local agendas, also began to appear in what was expected to be an election with an exceptionally large turn-out of voters. Labour candidates began to worry about losing their seats due to vote-splitting: traditional Labour voters might vote for a minority party instead (for example Plaid Cymru, the Welsh nationalist party), and thus allow the Conservatives to win even if the Conservative vote remained the same.

Because of the UK's 'first past the post' system, the candidate with more votes than any other candidate wins the seat, and the party with the most seats forms the government. This means that votes for any other than the winning party are effectively wasted; it also means that it is rare for a party to need a majority of the votes cast in order to win power. Politicians are usually careful not to offend people – so they tend to talk in obscure platitudes rather than state their real beliefs. The result is that elections become popularity contests in which style takes precedence over substance. The Conservatives have acquired the reputation of being 'the nasty party' because they typically are the party that cuts expenditure on public services and welfare; Labour has a reputation for overspending, over-borrowing and supporting fashionable causes rather than focusing on the economy.

In the end, the election produced a hung Parliament, with no party having an overall majority. Gordon Brown tried to cling on for a few days, looking to make deals with smaller parties, but in the end he had to step down because the Liberal Democrats and Conservatives agreed to work together to form a coalition government. This meant that the new government had a further problem managing perceptions – traditional Conservative voters were against involving the centrist LibDems, while traditional LibDem supporters saw the coalition as a sell-out by their leader, Nick Clegg. Overall, all parties had something of a mountain to climb in keeping the electorate sweet.

Questions

1 How might public perception of the expenses scandal have affected people's voting?
2 Why are personalities more important than issues in election campaigns?
3 Why do the supporters of specific parties not like the idea of a coalition?
4 Explain voting behaviour in terms of attribute, expectancy and affection.
5 Why did Gordon Brown's 'bigot' comment have such a strong effect on his campaign?

Further reading

For a paper on brand perceptions, read Salciuviene, L., Ghauri, P., Streder, P. and De Mattos, C. (2010) Do brand names in a foreign language lead to different brand perceptions? *Journal of Marketing Management* 26 (11–12): 1037–56.

For more on political marketing and in particular the management of perceptions, see Dermody, J. and Hanmer-Lloyd, S. (2005) Promoting distrust? A chronicle of the 2005 British General Election advertising campaigns. *Journal of Marketing Management* 21(9–10): 1021–47. (Special edition: The Marketing Campaign: The 2005 British General Election). There are, of course, more papers on political marketing in that special edition: one that provides more insight into the use of emotion to overcome reason is Dean, D. (2005) Fear, negative campaigning and loathing: the case of the UK election campaign. *Journal of Marketing Management* 21: 1067–78.

The perception of the ideal woman in advertising has been a somewhat controversial topic in recent years. The following paper may help to pick out the issues. Feiereisen, S., Broderick, A.J. and Douglas, S.P. (2009) The effect and moderation of gender identity congruity: utilizing 'real women' advertising images. *Psychology & Marketing* 26 (9): 813–43.

If you're interested in the perception processes concerned with vision, a very clear and easy-to-read book on the subject is *Basic Vision: An Introduction to Visual Perception* by Robert Snowden, Peter Thompson and Tom Trosciano (Oxford: OUP, 2012).

For a clear, well-written, basic overview of perception theory you might like *Perception: Theory, Development and Organisation* by Paul Rookes and Jane Willson (London: Routledge, 2000). The book is actually intended for A-level psychology students, but it covers the major theories well and is very readable.

References

Anderson, N.H. (1965) Averaging versus adding as a stimulus combination rule in impression formation. *Journal of Experimental Psychology* 70: 394–400.

Anon (1991) Self-help tapes are worthless, study says. *San Jose Mercury News*, 25 September.

Bakamitsos, G. and Siomkos, G. (2004) Context effects in marketing practice: the case of mood. *Journal of Consumer Behaviour* 3 (4): 304–14.

Bar, M. and Neta, M. (2008) The proactive brain: using rudimentary information to make predictive judgements. *Journal of Consumer Behaviour* 7 (4/5): 319–30.

Bardhi, F. and Eckhardt, G.M. (2010) Market-mediated collaborative consumption in the context of car sharing. *Advances in Consumer Research* 37: 66–7.

Batra, R. and Stayman, D.M. (1990) The role of mood in advertising effectiveness. *Journal of Consumer Research* 17 (Sep): 203–14.

Beatty, S.E. and Hawkins, D. (1989) Subliminal stimulation: some new data and interpretation. *Journal of Advertising* 18 (3): 4–8.

Chandran, S. and Menon, G. (2003) When am I at risk? Now, or now? The effects of temporal framing on perceptions of health risk. *Advances in Consumer Research* 30: 106–8.

Clark, I., III, Micken, K.S. and Hart, H.S. (2002) Symbols for sale – at least for now: symbolic consumption in transition economies. *Advances in Consumer Research* 29: 25–30.

Cuperfain, R. and Clarke, T.K. (1985) A new perspective of subliminal perception. *Journal of Advertising* 14 (1): 36–41.

d'Astous, A. and Kamau, E. (2010) Consumer product evaluation based on tactile sensory information. *Journal of Consumer Behaviour* 9 (3): 206–13.

Dichter, E. (1964) *Handbook of Consumer Motivations: The Psychology of the World of Objects.* New York: McGraw-Hill.

Gable, M., Wilkens, H.T., Harris, L. and Feinberg, R. (1987) An evaluation of subliminally embedded sexual stimuli in graphics. *Journal of Advertising* 16 (1): 26–31.

Grant, S.J. and Tybout, A.M. (2003) The effects of temporal framing on new product evaluation. *Advances in Consumer Research* 30: 1.

Greifeneder, R., Bless, H. and Kuschmann, T. (2007) Extending the brand image on new products: the facilitative effect of happy mood states. *Journal of Consumer Behaviour* 6 (Jan–Feb): 19–31.

Han, S. and Lerner, J. (2008) When the status quo turns sour: robust effects of incidental disgust in economic transactions. *Advances in Consumer Research*, 35: 153.

Hawkins, D. (1970) The effects of subliminal stimulation on drive level and brand preference. *Journal of Market Research* 7 (Aug): 322–6.

Henry, W.A. (1980) The effect of information processing ability on processing accuracy. *Journal of Consumer Research* 7 (June): 42–8.

Holbrook, M.P. and Moore, W.I. (1981) Feature interactions in consumer judgement of verbal versus pictorial presentations. *Journal of Consumer Research* 8 (June): 103–13.

Jansson, C., Marlow, N. and Bristow, M. (2004) The influence of colour on visual search times in cluttered environments. *Journal of Marketing Communications* 10 (Sep): 183–93.

Kelly, J.S. (1979) Subliminal imbeds in printing advertising: a challenge to advertising ethics. *Journal of Advertising* 8 (Summer): 43–6.

Key, W.B. (1973) *Subliminal Seduction.* Englewood Cliffs, NJ: Signet.

Key, W.B. (1976) *Media Sexploitation.* Englewood Cliffs, NJ: Prentice-Hall.

Key, W.B. (1980) *The Clam-Plate Orgy and Other Subliminals the Media Use to Manipulate Your Behaviour.* Englewood Cliffs, NJ: Prentice-Hall.

Key, W.B. (1989) *The Age of Manipulation: The Con in Confidence, the Sin in Sincere.* New York: Henry Holt & Co.

LeBoeuf, R.A. (2006) Discount rates for time versus dates: the sensitivity of discounting to time-interval description. *Advances in Consumer Research* 33: 138–9.

Lee, L. and Thomas, M. (2010) Music and consummatory focus: how background music changes preferences. Being revised for third review at *Journal of Consumer Research*.

Li, C. (2010) Primacy effect or recency effect? A long-term memory test of Super Bowl commercials. *Journal of Consumer Behaviour* (Jan/Feb), 9 (1): 32–44.

Lindstrom, M. (2005) Sensing and opportunity: sensory appeal. *The Marketer* No. 10 (Feb): 6–11.

Madden, T.J., Hewett, K. and Roth, M.S. (2000) Managing images in different cultures: a cross-national study of colour meanings and preferences. *Journal of International Marketing* 8 (4): 90–107.

Meyer, R.J. (1987) The learning of multiattribute judgement policies. *Journal of Consumer Research* 14 (2): 155–73.

Miller, G.A. (1956) The magical number seven, plus or minus two: some limits in our capacity for processing information. *Psychological Review* 63: 81–97.

Miller, S.G. and Khan, B. (2003) Shades of meaning: the effects of novel colour names on consumer preferences. *Advances in Consumer Research* 30: 11–13.

Milotic, D. (2003) The impact of fragrance on consumer choice. *Journal of Consumer Behaviour* 3 (2): 179–91.

Munoz, C.L., Wood, N.T. and Solomon, M.R. (2006) Real or blarney? A cross-cultural investigation of the perceived authenticity of Irish pubs. *Journal of Consumer Behaviour* 5 (May–June): 222–34.

Packard, V. (1957) *The Hidden Persuaders.* New York: Pocket Books (reissued Ig Publishing, 2007).

Pantone (2011) Top 10 PANTONE colors for women's fashion chosen by New York designers for spring 2011. http://www.pantone.com/pages/Pantone/Pantone.aspx?pg=20752&ca=4 (accessed October 2012).

Parker, A.M., Fischhof, B. and deBruin, W.B. (2006) Who thinks they know more – but actually knows less? Adolescent confidence in their HIV/AIDS and general knowledge. *Advances in Consumer Research* 33: 12–13.

Payne, C. and Wansink, B. (2010) What is beautiful tastes good: visual cues, taste and willingness to pay. *Advances in Consumer Research* 37: 49–50.

Rao, A.R. and Monroe, K.B. (1988) The moderating effect of price knowledge on cue utilization in product evaluations. *Journal of Consumer Research* 15 (Sep): 253–64.

Small, D.A. and Verrochi, N.M. (2008) The face of need: reactions to victims' emotion expressions. *Advances in Consumer Research* 35: 135.

Song, H. and Schwarz, N. (2009) Safe and easy or risky and burdensome? Fluency effects on risk perception and effort prediction. *Advances in Consumer Research* 36: 10–11.

Spencer, S.J., Strahan, E.J. and Zanna, M.P. (2003) Subliminal priming and choice. *Advances in Consumer Research* 30: 151–3.

Thomas, M., Morwitz, V. and Pyone, J.S. (2010) The precision effect in numbers: how processing fluency of numbers influence response confidence. *Advances in Consumer Research* 37: 151–2.

Warr, P. B. and Knapper, C. (1968) *The Perception of People and Events.* London: Wiley.

Zhao, G. and Pechmann, C. (2006) Regulatory focus, feature positive effect, and message framing. *Advances in Consumer Research* 33: 100.

More online

To gain free access to additional online resources to support this chapter please visit: **www.sagepub.co.uk/blythe**

CHAPTER ⑥
Learning

LEARNING OBJECTIVES

After reading this chapter you should be able to:

- Explain what constitutes learning and what does not.

- Explain the role of classical conditioning.

- Describe how operant conditioning works.

- Describe how cognitive learning can be used by marketers.

- Understand the role of motivation in learning.

- Show how experiential learning is more effective than vicarious learning.

- Describe the various components of consumer knowledge and their importance to marketers.

Introduction

Learning is not only about classroom-type learning. Most behaviour is learned as a result of external experiences; most of what people know (and almost certainly many of the things they are most proud of knowing) they learned outside school. People learn things partly through a formalised structure of teaching (or of self-teaching, perhaps by correspondence course) and partly through an unconscious process of learning by experience.

Consumption habits particularly are learned. British people were not born with a liking for fish and chips, any more than a Bangladeshi is born with a liking for curries or a Frenchman for horsemeat. Learning is highly relevant to marketing, since consumers are affected by the things they learn, and much consumer behaviour is actually based on the learning process.

Persuading consumers to remember the information they see in advertisements is a major problem for marketers; for example, some years ago a series of humorous advertisements were produced for Cinzano vermouth. The ads starred Leonard Rossiter and Joan Collins, and were widely screened throughout the UK, yet they were ineffective in increasing sales of the product. The reason for this was made clear when market research discovered that most consumers thought the ads were for Martini vermouth, Cinzano's main competitor. The underlying reason, however, is that humour in advertising appears to impair memory for products but enhance memory for the advertisement itself (Hansen et al. 2009).

This chapter is about the ways in which the brain orders and stores information.

Case study: Gurgle.com

UK-based store chain Mothercare specialises in everything for new parents, from pregnancy clothing through to baby toys. The store has been a tremendous success story, because it is a one-stop shop for everything a new mother and her baby could possibly need – including advice.

As people have become more mobile, young people are often cut off from traditional sources of advice about pregnancy and child-rearing. There was a time when a young mother could talk to her own mother, aunt or grandmother and get good advice, but as society has become more fragmented (and **birth rates** have fallen) there are relatively fewer people to turn to. Mothercare staff have always been able to offer plenty of advice about the products the store sells, but for many women it just isn't enough, and of course getting advice means travelling to the store and buying something.

Also, some advice is outside the store's remit – finding out what to do about a baby who can't sleep at night, or who develops a mysterious rash, may be something that staff at the store can't (or are reluctant to) offer advice about. Advice on trying for a baby is also a difficult area – it's perhaps not a subject one would wish to discuss with family either, so women trying to become pregnant have to rely on advice from friends, some of whom may have no experience of pregnancy either.

Learning about becoming, and being, a parent is an obvious use for the Internet, and that is exactly what Mothercare realised when they set up advice website Gurgle.com.

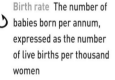

Birth rate The number of babies born per annum, expressed as the number of live births per thousand women

How to impress your examiner

You are likely to be asked to compare theories of learning and how they relate to advertising. If you can provide real examples of repetitive advertising (classical learning), interactive websites (operant learning) and viral advertising in which a game is played or something similarly active (cognitive learning), you will show that you understand the theory and can apply it in practice.

Defining learning

Learning is defined as 'the behavioural changes that occur over time relative to an external stimulus condition' (Onkvisit and Shaw 1994). According to this definition, activities are changed or originated through a reaction to an encountered situation. We can therefore say that someone has learned something if, as a result, their behaviour changes in some way. The factors involved in learning are shown diagrammatically in Figure 6.1: existing behaviour is modified by events, information and stimuli, and new behaviour results in future.

The main conditions that arise from the definition are as follows:

1 There must be a change in behaviour (response tendencies).
2 This must result from an external stimulus.

Learning has not taken place under the following circumstances:

1 *Species response tendencies.* These are instincts, or reflexes; for example, the response of ducking when a stone is thrown at you does not rely on your having learned that stones are hard and hurt the skin.
2 *Maturation.* Behavioural changes often occur in adolescence due to hormonal changes (for example), but again these or not a result of learning.
3 *Temporary states of the organism.* Whilst behaviour can be, and often is, affected by tiredness, hunger, drunkenness, etc. these factors do not constitute part of a larger learning process (even though learning may result from those states; the drunk may well learn to drink less in future).
4 *Damage to the brain.* Changes in behaviour due to surgery, disease or injury are also not a result of learning.

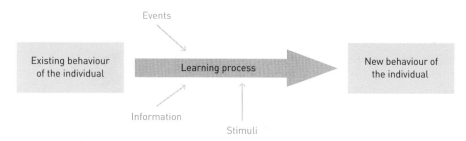

Figure 6.1 Learning

Studying learning

Regarding the study of learning there are two main schools of thought: first, the stimulus–response approach which further subdivides into classical and operant conditioning, and second, cognitive theories where the conscious thought of the individual enters into the equation.

CLASSICAL LEARNING THEORY

The classical theory of learning was developed by, among others, the Russian researcher Pavlov (1927). Pavlov's famous experiments with dogs demonstrated that

Unconditioned stimulus
A stimulus that occurs without the intervention of an experimenter

Unconditioned response A natural response to stimulus

Classical conditioning
The learning process characterised by repeating a stimulus at about the same time as a given behaviour occurs, with the aim of creating a permanent association between the stimulus and the behaviour

automatic responses (reflexes) could be learned. What Pavlov did was present a dog with an unconditioned stimulus (in this case, meat powder) knowing that this would lead to an unconditioned response (salivation). At the same time Pavlov would ring a bell (the conditioned stimulus). After a while the dog would associate the ringing of the bell with the meat, and would salivate whenever it heard the bell, without actually seeing any meat. This mechanism is shown in Figure 6.2.

Classical conditioning like this occurs with humans: many smokers associate having a cup of coffee with having a cigarette, and find it difficult to give up smoking without also giving up coffee. Likewise, the use of popular music in advertisements is an example of classical conditioning. Repeated exposure to the advertisement leads the individual to associate the music with the product. This leads to two results: first, if the consumer likes the music, that extends to liking the product, and second the consumer will tend to think of the product whenever she or he hears the music. Assuming the song used actually becomes (or is already) a hit, the company will obtain some free exposure whenever the song is played on the radio. Likewise, Christmas music played in retail shops during December tends to create a mood in which consumers are more likely to buy presents and seasonal items.

Challenging the status quo

This all sounds rather depressing. We are apparently very easily led – our buttons can be pushed by the ringing of a doorbell, or the clink of a coffee cup. Does this really happen quite so automatically?

One product that might give us the answer is the Tinkle Toonz Musical Potty. An American product which has been available since 1986, this is an aid to toilet training: if the child pees in the potty, he or she is rewarded with a tinny rendition of 'Old Macdonald Had a Farm'. If Pavlov was right, then adults who were trained on the Tinkle Toonz Musical Potty would presumably be conditioned to pee every time they hear 'Old Macdonald Had a Farm'. Since those original babies are now in their mid-20s, just the age for practical jokes, one can envisage all sorts of fun.

So does it happen? Do we have lawyers, army recruits, warehouse staff, supermarket managers, taxi drivers, doctors and young people in general avoiding 'Old Macdonald Had a Farm'? Or worse, *not* avoiding it? Or are human beings capable of overcoming their conditioning?

Try whistling 'Old Macdonald Had a Farm' and find out!

Conditioned response The behaviour that results from classical conditioning

For this to work it is usually necessary to repeat the stimulus a number of times in order for the conditioned response to become established. The number of times the process needs to be repeated will depend on the strength of the stimulus and the receptiveness (motivation) of the individual. Research has shown that, although conditioning has been reported for a single conditioning event (Gorn 1982), perhaps as many as 30 pairings may be required before conditioning is maximised (Kroeber-Riel 1984).

Before conditioning, the unconditioned stimulus feeding into the brain causes the unconditioned response. During the conditioning both the conditioned stimulus and

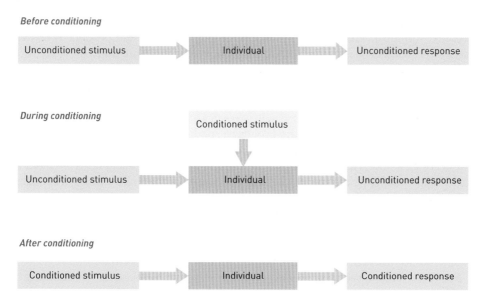

Figure 6.2   Classical conditioning

the unconditioned stimulus are presented, so that after conditioning the conditioned stimulus alone will produce the response.

Behaviours influenced by classical conditioning are thought to be involuntary. If the doorbell rings, it is automatic for most people to look up, without consciously thinking about whether somebody is at the door. Most people are familiar with the start of recognition that sometimes occurs if a similar doorbell is rung during a TV drama. Classical conditioning also operates on the emotions; playing Christmas music will elicit memories of childhood Christmases, and advertisements evoking nostalgic feelings will generate warmth towards the product.

Another factor in the effectiveness of classical conditioning is the order in which the conditioned stimulus and the unconditioned stimulus are presented (see Figure 6.3). In forward conditioning the conditioned stimulus (CS) comes before the unconditioned stimulus (US). This would mean that the product would be shown before the music is played.

Forward conditioning A circumstance where the conditioned stimulus comes before the unconditioned stimulus

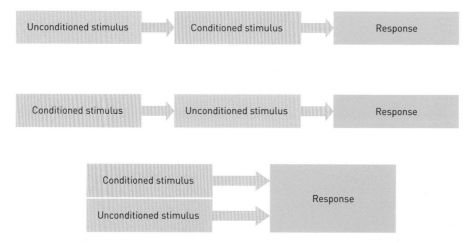

Figure 6.3   Ordering of stimuli

Backward conditioning A situation in which the unconditioned stimulus is presented before the conditioned stimulus

In backward conditioning the US (unconditioned stimulus) comes before the CS (conditioned stimulus). Here the music would be played before the product is shown. Simultaneous conditioning requires both to be presented at the same time.

It appears that forward conditioning and simultaneous conditioning work best in advertising (McSweeney and Bierley 1984). This means that it is usually better to present the product before playing the popular tune, or play both together; the responses from this approach are usually stronger and longer-lasting. If classical conditioning is being used, clearly the broadcast media will be better-suited since it is easier to control the order in which the stimuli are presented; with print media this is not necessarily the case. For example, not everybody reads newspapers from front to back. Many people would start with the sports pages (at the back) and work forward, or perhaps read the headlines on the front pages then go straight to the TV pages before coming back to the local news. Even if the conditioned stimulus and unconditioned stimulus are placed in the same ad on the same page, it is still possible that the reader's eye will be drawn to each stimulus in the wrong order; in other words, people do not necessarily read each page from top to bottom, either.

Simultaneous conditioning In classical conditioning, a state of affairs whereby the conditioned stimulus and the unconditioned stimulus are presented at the same time

For these reasons the print media are not as effective for classical conditioning as are the broadcast media such as radio and TV, where the order of presentation of the stimuli is controllable.

Extinction The process of forgetting a conditioned reflex

Extinction occurs when the conditioned stimulus no longer evokes the conditioned response. This occurs in the ways shown in Table 6.1.

Generalisation happens when a stimulus that is close to the existing one evokes the same response. Pavlov found that a sound similar to the bell he used could also stimulate salivation, and it is often the case that a similar brand name can evoke a purchase response. A very common tactic in marketing is to produce similar packaging to that of one's competitor in order to take advantage of the generalisation effect. For an example of this, observe the similarity in packaging between Tesco Premium coffee and Nescafé Gold Blend.

Generalisation The tendency for a conditioned stimulus to lead to a wider than intended set of conditioned reflexes

Discrimination is the process by which we learn to distinguish between stimuli, and only respond to the appropriate one. Consumers quite quickly learn to distinguish between brands, even when the design of the packaging is similar. Advertisers will

Discrimination The process by which people distinguish between stimuli

Table 6.1 Extinction

Reason for extinction	Example	Explanation	Techniques to avoid extinction
The conditioned stimulus is encountered without the unconditioned stimulus	The product is shown without the background music	Seeing the product without the music tends to reduce the association of the music with the product; other stimuli will replace the music	Ensure that all the advertising uses the same music, or imagery associated with the music
The unconditioned stimulus is encountered without the conditioned stimulus	The background music is heard without the product being present	In this case, other stimuli may be evoked by the music; it will become associated with something other than the product	Either ensure that the music is not played anywhere other than when the product is being shown, or ensure that the product is available when the music is played. For example, if the product is a drink to be sold in clubs, ensure that the clubs have an ample supply of the drink being advertised

often encourage discrimination by pairing a positive US with their own product, but not with the competitor's product. For example, the HSBC slogan 'The world's local bank' conveys a clear image of a bank with worldwide experience coupled with familiarity with local customs and banking practice. Other banks are clearly excluded from this slogan. Even greater discrimination occurs when the competitor's product is paired with a negative US, for example by using phrases such as 'Unlike our competitors, we do not charge you a service fee'.

Classical conditioning is responsible for many repetitive advertising campaigns, and for many catchphrases which are now in common use. Some advertising fosters this, such as the 'Does exactly what it says on the tin' campaign for Ronseal, which has resulted in the slogan entering the language. In some cases these stimuli can be very long-lasting: for many years, people with the surname Hudson were nicknamed Soapy, after Hudson's Soap, which ran a series of advertising campaigns in the 19th century (one of which featured writing the brand name on a balloon, which was probably the earliest use of aerial promotion).

Classical conditioning assumes that the individual plays no active role in the learning process. Pavlov's dogs did not have to do anything in order to be 'conditioned', because the process was carried out on their involuntary reflex of salivation. Although classical conditioning does operate in human beings, people are not usually passive in the process; the individual person (like most higher animals) is able to take part in the process and cooperate with it or avoid it. This process of active role-playing is called operant conditioning.

Operant conditioning
The learning process in which the learner is rewarded for a correct action, and in which the learner plays an active role

OPERANT CONDITIONING

Here the learner will conduct trial-and-error behaviour to obtain a reward (or avoid a punishment). Burris F. Skinner (1953) developed the concept in order to explain higher-level learning than that identified by Pavlov. The difference between Pavlov's approach and the operant conditioning approach is that the learner has choice in the outcome; the modern view of classical conditioning is that it also involves a cognitive dimension. In other words, Skinner is describing a type of learning that requires the learner to do something rather than be a passive recipient of a stimulus. The modern view is that even Pavlov's dog would have thought 'Here comes dinner' when the bell rang.

The basis of operant conditioning is the concept of reinforcement. If someone buys a product and is pleased with the outcome of using it, then he or she is likely to buy the product again. This means that the activity has had a positive reinforcement, and the consumer has become 'conditioned' to buy the product next time. The greater the positive reinforcement, the greater the likelihood of repeat purchase.

Challenging the status quo

How active are people in learning? Do we really seek out knowledge and consider everything that comes our way? Or does most of it go in one ear and out the other?

How many times have you been able to answer (say) a quiz question without having any idea where that nugget of information came from? How often do you say, 'Oh, that's common knowledge'. So were you born knowing this stuff? Games such as Trivial Pursuit are based on this kind of mental fluff – useless facts that just happen to have lodged in your brain, not through repetition (classical conditioning) nor through operant conditioning, but just through some kind of alien implanting process.

So is there something missing from the theory?

If the reward works, the consumer will try to think of a way to make it even better: 'If a little will help, a lot will cure.' This can lead to over-indulgence in food or alcohol, or indeed almost any other pleasurable activity. Typically this will happen if the consumer's need cannot be totally met by the product, but will be helped; a person with a serious psychological problem may well find that alcohol helps, but doesn't cure. An increasing intake of alcohol will never result in a complete meeting of the person's psychological needs because eventually sobriety will begin to set in again.

An example of operant conditioning is the growth of loyalty cards in retail stores, for example Tesco's Clubcard. Customers who remain loyal to Tesco are sent extra discounts and offers, and also their purchasing behaviour can be traced through the electronic point-of-sale systems so that offers can be targeted to those Tesco customers who will really be interested in them.

Airline loyalty schemes have also seen huge growth in recent years. These are aimed at reinforcing the frequent flyers, whose loyalty is desirable since they are likely to be the most profitable customers. The airlines offer free flights to their most regular customers, and for many business travellers these free flights offer an attractive reason for choosing the same airline every time. Loyalty cards are especially attractive to business customers because their flights are often paid for by their firms, so they are less likely to have to shop around for cheap deals.

The problem with this type of loyalty scheme is that it is perfectly feasible for people to carry loyalty cards for several stores (or join the Frequent Flyer clubs of several airlines) and thus reap the rewards without actually having to remain loyal to any supplier. In effect, people have been taught to play the system, gaining the benefits without actually having to contribute anything.

Consumer behaviour in action: Pizzaland

Although pizza appeared on a menu dated 1934, it was virtually unknown in Britain before 1965, when the first Pizza Express restaurant opened in London. Within just a few years, pizzerias were springing up all over the UK, and in the 1970s Pizzaland made its first appearance.

Pizzaland positioned itself as a cheaper version of Pizza Hut (although at first, bizarrely, the restaurants had a Tyrolean-themed decor). The restaurants offered all-you-can-eat promotions, special two-for-one offers, and themed evenings. This aggressive approach meant that the chain grew rapidly until there were Pizzalands in every major town in the UK.

On the other hand, an over-use of incentives can lead to negative consequences for the producer. Pizzaland's discount vouchers, which were given away in newspapers, on bus tickets, and even on cans of tuna, resulted in a major re-education of customers. Many people would not eat at Pizzaland unless they had a discount voucher. In this way, the positive reinforcement backfired on the company, since there is an implied *negative* reinforcement in *not* going in with a voucher.

Of course, the company was now giving away so many pizzas that profits dropped dramatically: if the two-for-one offer stopped, people simply went elsewhere until the offer was re-instated, so Pizzaland were effectively selling all their pizzas at half price. In these circumstances, the company would hope to make up the difference by selling more desserts, beverages and starters, but since their clientele were mainly bargain hunters (some might say cheapskates) it was not unusual for people to have just the pizza, then go to the pub to buy a beer or a glass of wine afterwards.

Eventually Pizzaland disappeared altogether, a monument to the learning abilities of consumers.

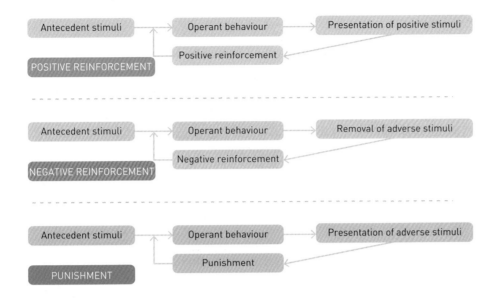

Figure 6.4 Operant conditioning

(Adapted from Stanley M. Widrick (1986) Concept of negative reinforcement has place in classroom. *Marketing News*, 20: 48–9).

Figure 6.4 charts three forms of operant conditioning.

In the first example, positive reinforcement, the individual receives a stimulus and acts upon it. This action works, and the individual gets a good result; this leads to the behaviour being repeated if the same antecedent stimulus is presented at a later date. For example, if you are in a long queue at a retailer such as the DIY store B&Q you might notice that the customer service counter is empty, and go there to make your purchases instead of the usual tills. This gets you through quicker, so if you are in B&Q again and the queue is over-long, you would try the same tactic again.

The second example in the diagram shows a negative stimulus: this time the operant behaviour relieves the problem, and again the individual has learned how to avoid bad consequences when faced with a difficulty.

The third example shows how punishment fits into the learning process. If the operant behaviour leads to a bad result, for example the customer service counter won't serve you and you lose your original place in the queue, you will not try that tactic again. The problem with punishment as a motivator is that it may lead to the individual not shopping at B&Q again. (See Chapter 2 for a discussion of pain avoidance.)

Operant conditioning does not necessarily require a product purchase; marketers will frequently give away free samples in the hope that a positive experience from using the product will encourage consumers to purchase in future. Likewise, car dealers always offer a test drive; some go even further, and allow the customer to borrow a car for 24 hours or more in order to get a very clear reinforcement of the car's merits.

Operant conditioning is helpful in explaining how people become conditioned, or form habits of purchase; however, it still does not explain how learning operates when people become active in seeking out information. To understand this aspect of learning, it is necessary to look at the cognitive learning process.

COGNITIVE LEARNING

Not all learning is an automatic response to a stimulus. People analyse purchasing situations taking into account previous experiences, and make evaluative judgements. Learning is part of this, both in terms of informing the process as a result of earlier experiences, and also in terms of the consumer's approach to learning more about the product category or brand.

When considering cognitive learning, the emphasis is not on *what* is learned (as in stimulus–response theories) but on *how* it is learned. Classical learning and operant conditioning theories suppose that learning is automatic; cognitive learning theories assume that there is a conscious process going on. For most people this is true in many cases of consumer behaviour.

The classical and operant theories assume that what goes on inside the consumer's head is a 'black box' in that we know that a given stimulus will prompt a particular response, but for most practical purposes we have no real way of knowing what is happening inside the black box. Within the cognitive learning paradigm, however, we are concerned with what happens inside the box, and we try to infer what is going on by analysing behaviour and responses from the individual. Figure 6.5 illustrates this.

The black box contains the cognitive processes; the stimulus is considered in the light of the individual's memory of what has happened in the past when presented with similar stimuli, his or her assessment of the desirable outcome and an assessment of the likely outcome of any action. Following this processing, the individual produces a response.

Cognitive learning expertise has five aspects, summarised in Figure 6.6:

- Cognitive effort
- Cognitive structure
- Analysis
- Elaboration
- Memory.

Cognitive learning
Acquiring and retaining new information through a conscious effort or thought

Cognitive effort is the degree of effort the consumer is prepared to put into thinking about the product offering. This will depend on such aspects as the complexity of the product, the consumer's involvement with it and the motivation for learning. Making a complex decision can often lead to forgetting not only what the decision was, but in some cases forgetting that a decision has been made (Norton and Chance 2008). Most of us are familiar with making a choice from the restaurant menu, then forgetting what it was we had ordered when the food arrives.

Cognitive structure is about the way the consumer thinks, and the way the information is fitted into the existing knowledge.

The *analysis* of information is first concerned with selecting the correct, relevant information from the environment, and second with interpreting the information correctly in order to obtain a clear action plan.

Elaboration is the structuring of the information within the brain, and adding to it from memory in order to form a coherent whole.

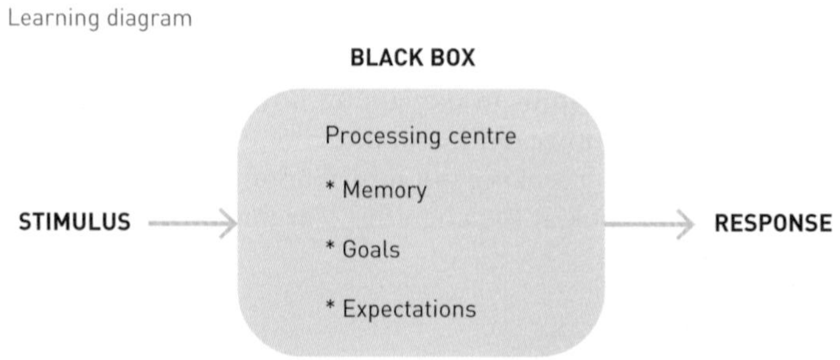

Cognitive effort The amount of work needed to consider a course of action or understand a set of issues

Cognitive structure The way the individual thinks, and the way new information is fitted into existing knowledge

Elaboration The structuring of information within the brain, relating it to existing memory

Learning diagram

BLACK BOX

Processing centre

* Memory

STIMULUS ⟶   ⟶ **RESPONSE**

* Goals

* Expectations

Figure 6.5   Cognitive learning

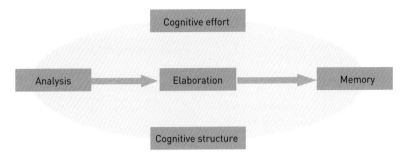

Figure 6.6   Factors in cognitive learning

Memory is the mechanism by which learned information is stored. In fact, nothing is ever truly forgotten; information will eventually become irrecoverable by the conscious mind (forgotten) but the brain still retains the information and can be stimulated to recall it, either by hypnosis or by association of ideas.

Cognitive learning processes are important to marketers since they are helpful in predicting consumer responses to advertising. Stephen J. Hoch and Young-Won Ha (1986) say that consumers view advertisements as tentative hypotheses about product performance that can be tested through product experience. Early learning about a product will affect future learning; this is called the Law of Primacy (see Chapter 5). For this reason first impressions count for a great deal.

According to Hoch and Ha, advertising will tend to be ignored if there is unambiguous objective evidence to hand; if you can test the product for yourself, advertising has only a small effect. If the evidence is ambiguous or unobtainable at first hand (as is often the case), advertising might sway you, and in fact advertising appears to have dramatic effects on consumers' perceptions of quality. For example, it is possible for somebody to visit a computer retailer to test a new laptop before making a commitment to buy. Thus, advertising plays a small part in computer purchase, only serving to alert the consumer to what is available within the current technology. Conversely, somebody spending a similar amount on a package holiday has no chance to try out the holiday before buying it, and is therefore more likely to be swayed by the advertising or other communications (brochures, salespeople, etc.). One of the main considerations for a consumer in that position is the reputation of the tour operator, since the consumer is, after all, buying a promise. Chapter 15 has more on the topic of services marketing.

Learning from experience is a four-stage process, as Table 6.2 shows.

In most cases people prefer to learn by experience, especially for major product purchases; few people would buy a car without having a test drive first, and still fewer would buy one on-line unless they were people with previous direct experience of the car. It is for this reason that on-line retailers have a no-quibble money-back guarantee; if this were not the case, few people would be prepared to buy on-line rather than visit a high street shop where they can see and feel the goods.

There are also three moderating factors in the cognitive learning process:

1 *Familiarity* with the domain. This is the degree to which the consumer has pre-existing knowledge of the product category. For example, an IT enthusiast would go through a different, and probably shorter, learning curve for buying a new laptop than would a complete novice. Familiarity with the components of a brand name make it more memorable (Lerman 2003).

Table 6.2 Learning from experience

Stage	Explanation	Example	Marketing response
Hypothesising	Developing a rough estimate as to what's happening or what's available	Getting information from a friend, or reading some advertising material; getting some brochures	Have clearly written brochures and advertising, don't use too much jargon, especially if your product is a complex one, or can be 'test-driven'
Exposure	Having a look at the product, trying one out, getting direct experience of it	Visiting a computer shop to try the product and ask questions about it	Ensure that the product is on display, and allow plenty of opportunity for hands-on testing
Encoding	Making sense of the information	Translating the jargon into something comprehensible, perhaps getting some clarification; understanding what the product is and does in terms that fit in with previous experience	Have sales people who can explain things in lay terms, and who don't frighten off the customer by using too much technical language
Integration	Fitting the new information into the existing knowledge bank	Thinking about the new information gained about computers and discarding previous misconceptions	Ensure that customers feel able to come back for further explanations if they still have problems. Make sure that customers understand everything before leaving the shop

2 *Motivation* to learn. If the purchase is an important one, or the possible effects of making a mistake would be serious, the consumer is likely to be highly motivated to obtain as much information as possible. People also appear to remember advertising better if they either love or hate the advert; neutral advertising is quickly forgotten (Kenning et al. 2009).

3 *Ambiguity* of the information environment. If the information is hard to get, contradictory or incomprehensible, this will hinder the learning process. Sometimes consumers give up on the process if this is the case.

Figure 6.7 illustrates these moderating factors in terms of classifying readiness to learn from experience.

If someone is highly motivated to learn (for example, someone who has committed to buying a holiday home in Spain might be highly motivated to learn Spanish) the learning process is most susceptible to management. The individual would probably want to follow a formal course of study (evening classes or a distance learning course) and would welcome help in managing the learning process. If the individual already speaks Spanish, but has bought a house in Catalonia, the motivation to learn Catalan might be just as strong, but familiarity with the domain (learning a foreign language) might cause the individual to form beliefs that are unrealistic.

People who are only weakly motivated to learn are obviously less likely to want their learning managed, or indeed to manage it themselves. If the person is unfamiliar with the domain, he or she is unlikely to be interested in learning at all; if, on the other hand, the domain is all too familiar, complacency sets in and the person is likely to say 'I already know all that stuff' and thus will have no interest in managing learning. Motivation has an effect on the tendency to zap TV advertisements – if the

Zapping Using the TV remote control to avoid advertisements, often by switching to another channel. Also called *flicking*

How motivated are people to learn?	What do consumers already know?	How much can experience teach?	
		Little (High ambiguity)	A lot (Low ambiguity)
Highly motivated to learn	Unfamiliar with the domain	Learning is most susceptible to management	Learning is spontaneous, rapid and difficult to manage
	Familiar with the domain	Formation of superstitious beliefs is possible. Existing beliefs inhibit suggestibility	
Weakly motivated to learn	Unfamiliar with the domain	Learning is slow to start and difficult to sustain, but is susceptible to management	Learning is difficult to initate and, once started, is difficult to manage
	Familiar with the domain	Complacency inhibits initiation of learning, so experience is unresponsive to management	

Figure 6.7 Managing the learning process

Source: Hoch, S.J. and Deighton, J. (1989) Managing what consumers learn from experience. *Journal of Marketing* 53 (April): 1–20.

advertisement is unpleasant or uninformative, the advert is more likely to be zapped, but at higher levels informativeness and pleasantness are incompatible because of a reduced motivation and ability to process information (Elpers et al. 2002).

If people are unable to learn much by experience, the situation becomes ambiguous; if learning by experience is the main way of learning, the situation is unambiguous but learning is difficult to manage. From the viewpoint of marketers, encouraging people to learn about products is easiest when the individuals are motivated to learn, and where the situation is ambiguous and therefore needs careful explanation.

Cognitive lock-in occurs when there is a high cognitive cost to obtaining information. This happens on the Internet: people tend to stick with the sites they are familiar with rather than going to the trouble of learning how to navigate a new site, especially if the initial setting up or the ongoing usage is difficult (Murray and Haubl 2002; Zauberman 2002). The result is that searches carried out on-line are (perhaps surprisingly) limited, with an average of only 1.1 book sites, 1.2 CD sites and 1.8 travel sites being visited (Johnson et al. 2002).

Incidentally, people who respond most favourably to Internet advertising are those with a high motivation to learn, high social escapism and high Internet ability due to its perceived informativeness (Zhou and Bao 2002). Evidently a desire to learn affects the ways people learn as well as their capacity for learning.

Cognitive theories recognise that consumers influence the outcome in an active manner, so the learning process is not always easy for an outsider (i.e. a marketing person) to manage. This may be some of the reason why new products fail so frequently; weak motivation to learn about new products leads to difficulty for marketers in starting the learning process.

Cognitive learning can also be viewed as having five elements, as shown in Figure 6.8.

1 **Drive.** As seen in Chapter 2, drive is the stimulus that impels action. It is strong, internal and general. The impulse to learn can be driven by a fear of making an expensive mistake, or by a desire to maximise the benefits of the purchase.

Cue An external trigger that encourages learning

Response The reaction the consumer makes to the interaction between a drive and a cause

Reinforcement The process of consolidating classical conditioning

Retention The stability of learned material over time

2 **Cue**. This is some external trigger which encourages learning. It is weaker than a drive, is external and is specific. For example, a public service such as the Health and Safety Council might exhort employers to send for a leaflet on safety in the workplace. Sometimes firms will use advertisement retrieval cues to trigger responses.

3 **Response**. This is the reaction the consumer makes to the interaction between a drive and a cue. With luck, this results in a sale; but humans learn, and will base future purchases on their concrete experience of the product rather than on the marketer's cues.

4 **Reinforcement**. Purchase response should be rewarded with a positive experience of the product. The object of reinforcement is to get consumers to associate the product with certain benefits.

5 **Retention**. This is the stability of the learned material over time, or in other words how well it is remembered. For example, advertising jingles have very high retention. People can often recall jingles that have not been broadcast for thirty years or more. This is particularly true for advertisements that were popular when the consumer was a child. (The opposite of retention is **extinction**.)

Cognitive learning usually involves some form of reasoning – people need to think about what they are seeing or hearing in order to remember the information. If the person has a low involvement with the product or brand, it will take a long time for the information to sink in, whereas if the individual has a high involvement with the product the information is processed and absorbed much more effectively, presumably because the person is thinking about the product much more (Krugman 1965).

Part of the problem for marketers is that they have little or no control over how people think about the messages they are shown. For example, an advertisement may be designed to be as interesting as possible in order to cut through that advertising clutter and attract attention, but the people who see the ad may become more interested in the cleverness of the advertising than they are in the brand (Pieters et al. 2002). This is exemplified by the Cinzano adverts mentioned earlier in the chapter – enjoyment of a clever and entertaining advertisement detracted from people's understanding of what was actually being advertised. The reasoning process is shown in Figure 6.9: the stimulus is followed by a reasoning process, which may lead either to retaining

Clutter Excessive information, especially applied to advertising; a situation in which the recipient is presented with a large number of stimuli at the same time

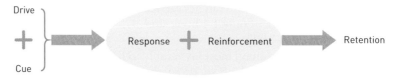

Figure 6.8   Five elements of cognitive learning

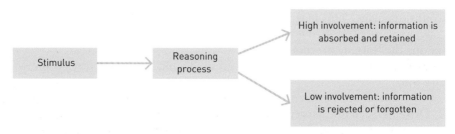

Figure 6.9   Reasoning and cognitive learning

the information or forgetting it, according to how interested the individual is in the subject matter.

A further possibility for cognitive learning is vicarious learning, in which we learn from the experiences of others. This is an extremely useful way of learning, since it requires much less effort and risk than learning directly by trial and error. It requires either direct observation (watching what happens to someone else when they buy a product or behave in a particular way) or effective communication (as when someone describes their learning experiences). Because human beings are excellent communicators compared with most other species, we are particularly good at vicarious learning. In the marketing context, advertisers use models to show how products are used, and to show (or describe) the benefits of using a specific product. Having said that, learning by doing is generally much more effective than vicarious learning – imagine how far you would get in learning to drive a car if all you were ever allowed to do was to observe other drivers and read an instruction book.

Challenging the status quo

So learning by doing is more effective than thinking about things. If that's so, why do we still sit in classrooms, read books and (eventually) get a degree or other qualification? Why don't we do all our learning at work? Whatever happened to getting oneself apprenticed at 14 and spending seven to ten years becoming a master craftsman?

I suspect most of us can remember assignments we have written a great deal better than we can remember any lectures we attended – and we can remember how to play cricket, football, netball, hockey and so forth a great deal better than we can remember Shakespeare's plays (unless we acted in them, of course). So much for schoolroom lessons!

Maybe it's just about motivation to learn, but maybe there is something wrong with the way the education system operates: perhaps sitting through an hour-long monologue delivered by someone in a beige cardigan is not the best way to learn!

Learned responses are never truly unlearned. The brain remembers (stores) everything, but rather like a computer with a faulty disk drive it may not always be able to recall (retrieve) everything. Also, the human memory is huge; the *Encyclopedia Britannica* contains around 12,500 million characters, but the brain has approximately 125,000,000 million characters in storage capacity. This is enough storage to hold 10,000 *Encyclopedia Britannica*s, which makes the human brain easily the world's most powerful computer.

The need for knowledge

The purpose of learning about products is mainly to reduce risk. The more one knows about the product and the product category, the lower the level of risk, as shown in Figure 6.10. In many cases, less knowledgeable buyers will ask a more knowledgeable friend to help in making the purchase. In some cases, people will spend considerable time researching information about the product category and individual brands (this is mainly true where there is high involvement with the product or where there is a high risk).

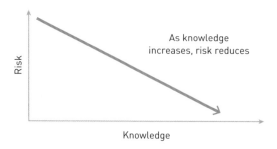

Figure 6.10   Knowledge and risk

Lack of knowledge may lead to a purchase that is inappropriate: for example, an inexperienced car buyer might miss a sign of potential engine problems, whereas more experienced and knowledgeable buyers would not. Knowledgeable people have a better understanding of what attributes to look for, and how to evaluate the product against those attributes (Alba and Hutchinson 1987).

The key point here, however, is that people understand that they need to know about the products they buy, especially when a major commitment is involved. This means that there is a motivation to learn, arising from a need for knowledge (see Chapter 2). This need is met through the same ways as any other need – goals are set, heuristics are developed and the process is as subject to interrupts and dissonance as the actual purchase itself.

 Challenging the status quo

If we have such a drive to learn, why is it that so many people dislike school? How come truancy rates are the highest they have ever been – and university classes are not always as well attended as they might be! And even more to the point, this is in a situation where attendance and learning affect one's capacity to earn money – a project dear to most people's hearts!

Perhaps it isn't so much that we don't want to learn as that we don't want to be told what to learn? Or maybe we just don't like to be taught!

This drive to extend knowledge about products accounts for the widespread sale of specialist consumer magazines. For example, a magazine aimed at private pilots will contain flight tests of new light aircraft, information about flying schools and detailed tests of auxiliary equipment such as radios and GPS units. In most cases, the products are supplied to the magazines by the producers in order to gain publicity for the products: this is clearly a marketing communications activity, but the magazine's readers are eager to learn about products that may make their flying easier, safer and more enjoyable.

Each individual has many different types of knowledge, as shown in Figure 6.11. This is far from being a comprehensive list of an individual's knowledge categories, but some knowledge in each category will relate to marketing issues. The main types of knowledge of interest from a marketing point of view are as follows:

1 *Product knowledge*. This subdivides into *product category knowledge* and *brand knowledge*. Product category knowledge is the information an individual remembers about all the possible solutions to the need problem.

2 *Purchase knowledge*. This is about how to buy, what things cost and where to buy from.

3 *Consumption* or *usage knowledge*. This is about how to use the product, how to dispose of whatever is left after use and what the risks are in using the product.

4 *Persuasion knowledge*. This is an understanding of the goals and tactics of people who might be trying to persuade us to buy – in the main, this is knowledge about marketers, but it includes knowledge about friends who might be recommending a product to us.

5 *Self-knowledge*. This is knowledge about one's own needs, including knowledge about one's own failings. For example, a novice golfer might be well aware of his or her lack of knowledge about the game, and therefore be more prepared to buy books about the game, extra coaching and equipment suitable for novices.

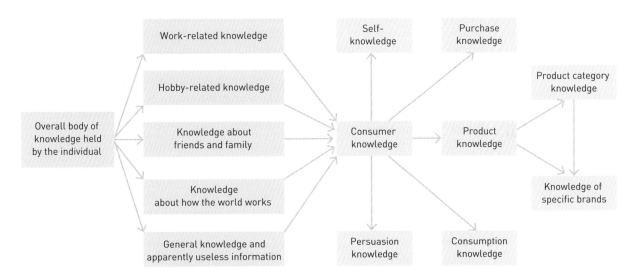

Figure 6.11   Categorising knowledge

PRODUCT CATEGORY KNOWLEDGE

This type of product knowledge is fairly general. For example, we all know what a television set is, and broadly we all know how to operate one, and know what it will do for us in terms of entertainment. Relatively fewer of us would know the difference between plasma and LCD screens, even if we know that both terms refer to flat screens. Few of us would really understand how digital TV works, even though this is the only available TV system in the UK. If we head into the technical detail of different types of microchip almost all of us would be lost. Someone who has basic product knowledge is called a product novice; someone who has a large amount of product knowledge is a product expert. Those who have large amounts of product or market knowledge and enjoy sharing this knowledge with others are called market mavens (see Chapter 4).

Knowledge about these different factors would be chunked in the individual's memory under the category of 'TV sets'. For most people, information is frequently cross-referenced, so that information about the microchips might also be contained in the category of 'things I know about electronics' or, in some cases, 'things I deal with in work'.

Novices Customers who have purchased the product for the first time within the last 90 days

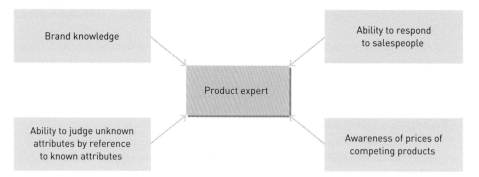

Figure 6.12   Product expert knowledge

Product expert knowledge is shown in Figure 6.12. A product expert would also have extensive knowledge of the members of a product category (the brands). A product expert would be able to judge unknown product attributes by reference to known attributes (for example, knowing that the product's components are reliable would give an indication of the longevity of the product as well as its reliability), and would influence acceptance of a price for a product since the expert would be aware of the prices of competing products. Knowledge influences responses to salespeople, which places a burden on salespeople to judge quickly and accurately how much the prospective customer already knows.

BRAND KNOWLEDGE

Brand knowledge is concerned with what people know about a specific product within the general product category. From a marketing viewpoint, the starting point of brand knowledge is whether people remember the brand at all. The next level is whether people associate the brand strongly with the product category: further increases in knowledge about the brand may follow, but without knowing that the brand exists and that it relates to a particular product there is no chance whatever that the brand will be included in the consideration set.

To test whether individuals have this level of knowledge, market researchers have two main tools. The first is a *recall test*, which tests top-of-the-mind awareness. Respondents might be asked to list all the breakfast cereals they can think of, for example, and the researcher would be able to tell first whether the brand being tested is included in the list, and second where it stands in relation to the other brands. The second method is a *recognition test*, in which people are shown a list of brand names and are asked to say which ones they recognise. The problem with this test is that people may claim to recognise brands they have never heard of rather than appear to be ignorant: sometimes researchers will include fictitious brands in the list to test for this.

The tests are used for different circumstances. A recall test might be useful for testing advertising effectiveness or to determine the product's position in consumers' perceptual maps. A recognition test might be more useful when testing merchandising success, since it is important that people recognise the brand when they see it in-store.

Both recall and recognition are enhanced when the brand has a strong symbol attached to it. The Michelin Man, the Nokia ring tone and the Volkswagen VW logo are all powerful symbols, each in a different way. Each one provokes instant recognition, and a clear image of what the product is and what it does.

Encouraging people to learn about brands is a major part of advertising, and certainly of the more information-based, cognitive approaches to advertising. Many sales promotions are aimed at increasing people's knowledge about brands, encouraging

Symbol A method of converting thought into something that can be transmitted as a message

them to learn more: for example, the tourist boards of countries sometimes run informative advertisements about their countries, linked to a competition for which the prize is a holiday in the country. In order to win the prize, participants have to complete a questionnaire about the country, which means that they need to read the advertisement to find out the answers.

Brand associations (see Figure 6.13) are the connections people make between the brand and other concepts (Blackwell et al. 2005). Brand associations include beliefs and perceptions about what the brand will do, in other words, the consumption benefits. Brand associations are important to marketers because they tend to influence the degree to which consumers will adopt the product, and also the degree to which they will accept brand extensions and recommend the product to others (Belen del Rio et al. 2001). The higher the consumer's perception of brand quality, the more likely he or she is to recommend the brand (no surprises there) and also to buy brand extensions.

In other words, brand association tends to mean that people will buy a different product, perhaps with no associated characteristics, simply on the basis that the brand is the same as another product that is tried and tested. Brand extensions may, of course, be in products that have some related production similarities, so that one might assume that a firm which is good at making the one product would also be good at making the other. Saab have played on this assumption in their advertising: since the company manufactures fighter aircraft as well as cars, it might be reasonable to assume that the engineering capabilities within the company would be high. There is absolutely no reason to suppose that Virgin would be good at running airlines, commissioning new rock bands, running an insurance company and launching spacecraft. Yet the fact that the Virgin brand appears on the products is apparently seen as a signal of quality, and people who have been happy with one Virgin product seem to accept that other Virgin products will have similar quality values.

Developing appropriate brand associations for new products is an especially challenging task (there is more on this in Chapter 13). An almost equally challenging task is that of moving an existing product into a new market, and this is precisely the problem firms have when they move to Internet trading. A brand that is well known in its home market might be entirely unknown in the rest of the world, so apart from the logistical problems of arranging physical distribution the firm faces the challenge of establishing a consistent brand image across a wide spectrum of foreign cultures.

PURCHASE KNOWLEDGE

Purchase knowledge is the information people have about buying products. This includes where the product can be bought, whether discounts apply at some times

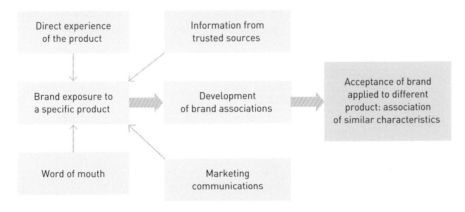

Figure 6.13 Brand association

or in some places, how much the product should cost, and what the procedure is for buying the product.

Price is an important issue, because it is the measure of what the consumer has to give in return for the product benefits. This judgement is made not only on the basis of the cost of the brand from different sources, but also on the cost of products that provide similar benefits (Rao and Sieben 1992). If one has little knowledge of the pricing within the product category, one might assume that a reasonable price is far too high (or be delighted to find that the actual price is lower than expected). In some cases, marketers (and especially salespeople) will try to give an impression that the price will be higher than it actually is, in order to delight the customer with the real price. This is called price conditioning. For example, a salesperson selling fitted kitchens might, at an early stage of the presentation, suggest that the new kitchen might cost £10,000 or more. When the actual price turns out to be only £8500 the customer is delighted, but if the customer had been expecting a price of £6000 the delight would have been replaced by an entirely different feeling.

It is useful if marketers have knowledge of what people think is a reasonable price for a product. This will be a combination of what people believe is reasonable when they see the actual product, and what people already know about the price of competing products (see Figure 6.14). Relative price knowledge is what people know about one price relative to another (Barone et al. 2004). For example, one American study found that people thought that buying books on-line was about 3% cheaper than buying them from a bricks-and-mortar retailer, whereas in fact the price difference was an average 10% (Tedeschi 2005). This is clearly bad news for the on-line retailers, who are apparently cutting their profit margins without effectively communicating the price savings to their customers.

Marketers may decide prices (at least in part) on how well informed they believe customers to be about competitors' prices. If the products are rarely purchased, consumers will be unlikely to have very precise knowledge of prices (although this is a major motivator for customers to learn about prices before committing to a purchase). A further factor would be the ease of finding out about prices – in the case of home improvements, for example, it might prove extremely time-consuming to obtain quotes from different contractors, even if the contractors are willing to provide quotes (which they are often unprepared to do, given that this is a time-consuming activity for them and most builders have more than enough work as it is). In this respect, the Internet represents something of a threat to marketers since price comparisons are relatively easy to make, especially in such areas as booking flights or ferries.

Knowing when to buy is also an important part of purchase knowledge. In some cases purchases are seasonal – for example, flights are cheaper at off-peak times, and so also is hotel accommodation. For those with the flexibility to travel at any time, there are considerable savings to be made. Buying in advance may also save money. The advantages of having purchase knowledge are shown in Figure 6.15 – the

Price conditioning
Managing the expectations of a potential customer regarding price

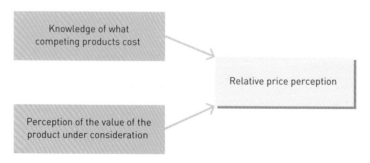

Figure 6.14 Relative price information

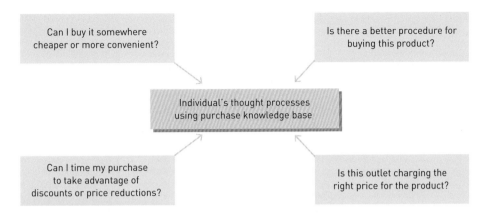

Figure 6.15 Advantages of having purchase knowledge

individual is able to make much better decisions from a basis of knowing about the purchase factors and parameters.

Another example is consumer electronics. Most people are well aware that when a new product is launched the price is high – for example, plasma-screen TV sets started off priced in the thousands of pounds, but prices dropped dramatically as the sets gained in popularity. Partly this is due to reduced manufacturing costs on longer production runs, and partly it is due to the need for manufacturers to recoup development costs, but it is also due to manufacturers knowing that some people are prepared to pay a premium price for the pleasure of being the first to own a new, exciting product.

Knowing where to buy the product is a more complex issue than it once was, due to the increasing number of possible retail outlets from which products can be purchased. Fifty years or so ago retailers were much more specific in the range of products they carried: stationers only sold stationery, chemists only sold medicines and so forth. Nowadays, products are available from a wide range of stores, and also on-line. Items such as soy sauce or spices are often cheaper from specialist Chinese or Indian grocers than they are from supermarkets, for example. In addition, someone may need a specific product and have no knowledge of where to buy it – specialist products for motor or building work might not be available from normal hardware stores, but might instead need to be bought from specialist outlets or ordered from the manufacturers. In these circumstances manufacturers need to be sure that people are aware of where the products can be bought.

CONSUMPTION KNOWLEDGE

This type of knowledge is the information consumers have about how a product's benefits can be obtained in use. Lack of such knowledge would mean that people would be unlikely to buy the product in the first place: mobile telephones suffered from this problem for some time, since people found the systems and choices confusing (many still do). Other high-tech products suffer from similar problems – many people have trouble using their DVD players properly, digital cameras are in general complex to operate and download pictures, and many people even have trouble understanding how to programme their washing machine correctly. A product that is used incorrectly is unlikely to perform to the required standard, which in turn is likely to lead to consumer dissatisfaction or even injury (Staelin 1978).

In Figure 6.16 ignorance about the correct use of the product can lead to two outcomes: either the consumer uses the product incorrectly, which leads to dissatisfaction

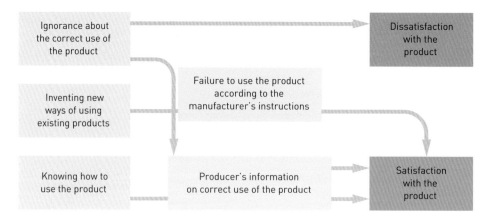

Figure 6.16 Consumption knowledge

with the product's performance, or the consumer reads the producer's information about the product (the manual) and learns how to use the product correctly. This should lead to satisfaction. In some cases, consumers effectively re-invent the product, failing to use it according to the manufacturer's instructions, but are still satisfied with the performance. The final possibility is that the consumer knows how to use the product, uses it according to the instructions, and is thus satisfied with the product.

At an obvious level, it is difficult to sell cars to people who do not have driving licences, and difficult to sell computers to people who have no idea how to use one. At a more subtle level, there may be uses for the product which are not obvious to consumers – using baking powder for deodorising fridges is a well-known example, but using bath oil to remove tar spots from cars is less obvious. Whether a manufacturer would want to promote this use for bath oil is doubtful, but consumers do invent ways of using products in novel ways and this knowledge enters the product experts' minds even when it is not put there by the producers.

PERSUASION KNOWLEDGE

Persuasion knowledge is what people know about the goals and tactics of those trying to persuade them (Friestad and Wright 1994). People are often sceptical about the motives of marketers, with good reason: marketers are not in business to do consumers a bit of good, they are in business for their own ends, and aim to manage the exchange between consumers and the firm. Since most of us resent being managed, we tend to seek out information about marketing tactics in order to strengthen our own negotiating position.

In recent years, people have become more marketing aware, and marketing jargon is commonly heard from people who are not marketers. Understanding how marketers (and perhaps especially salespeople) operate has been shown to affect consumers' opinions of marketer sincerity adversely (Brown and Krishna 2004). A study by Bearden et al. (2001) showed that people were able to make the following statements about their understanding of persuasion:

1 I know when an offer is 'too good to be true'.
2 I can tell when an offer has strings attached.
3 I have no trouble understanding the bargaining tactics used by salespeople.
4 I know when a marketer is pressuring me to buy.
5 I can see through sales gimmicks used to get consumers to buy.
6 I can separate facts from fantasy in advertising.

This clearly has implications for the marketing approach. Marketers cannot naively assume that consumers can be led around by the nose or can be easily persuaded by a glib sales patter: people are suspicious, and are able to see through many marketing ploys.

SELF-KNOWLEDGE

This area of knowledge is about the individual's understanding of his or her own mental processes (Alba and Hutchinson 2000). People who understand their own strengths and weaknesses, as well as what they like and do not like, are in a better position to make realistic purchasing decisions than people who are not in touch with their own personalities. Self-knowledge is important to market researchers, since much commercial market research is based on self-reports by consumers.

For example, knowing that one likes cream cakes and doesn't like chicken pies is a useful piece of knowledge for choosing lunch. Knowing that one cannot eat just one cream cake without going on to eat the whole box is a useful piece of self-knowledge which might prevent a dietary disaster.

Sources of consumer knowledge

People gather information about products from a large number of sources, both personal and impersonal. The sources may be controlled (or at least influenced) by marketers, or may be entirely independent.

Marketer-controlled sources include the following:

- Sales people
- Service people
- Paid product endorsers (for example, athletes who recommend sports equipment).

These would be classified as personal sources of information, since they are provided by people.

Non-personal sources that are controlled by marketers would include the following:

- The products themselves
- Point-of-purchase materials
- Advertising
- Catalogues
- Corporate websites
- Directories such as Yellow Pages.

Non-marketer influences may also be personal or impersonal. Personal sources would include family and friends, work colleagues, other shoppers, market mavens and other influential people, and Internet sources such as forums and bulletin boards. Impersonal sources would include non-corporate websites, TV and radio shows, books, government reports and the press.

In fact, even the non-marketer-controlled sources can be influenced by marketers. Product placement in films and TV programmes is common (in the UK paid product placement in TV shows became legal in February 2011, albeit with many controls).

People are naturally suspicious of marketer-controlled information sources, but will use them and will often base most of their decision-making on the rival claims of different producers. Word of mouth and impartial articles in newspapers and magazines are trusted much more, because people feel that there is no purpose to be served by the source lying to them. It is for this reason that marketers try to influence word of mouth, word of mouse and the opinions of journalists (who are, after all, powerful influentials).

The most useful source of information is, of course, consumption of the product itself. Actually using a product and forming a judgement about it is clearly far and

Personal sources Sources of involvement derived from means–end knowledge stored in the individual's memory

Word of mouse Electronically mediated personal communications about brands and products

away the best route for gaining information. Obviously this is not always possible, but for cheap, low-risk products it is often the best choice.

Sometimes a lack of knowledge can be an advantage. Research shows that giving people a surprise (i.e. providing information for which there are no antecedents) can lead to them evaluating a surprising brand higher than do people to whom the information was not a surprise (Vanhamme and Snelders 2003).

Summary

Learning is something that we all do, every day of our lives, and the bulk of what we learn comes from outside the classroom. Learning comes about in many ways: sometimes it happens subconsciously, as in the case of classical conditioning; sometimes it requires conscious effort, as in cognitive learning. We never really forget anything we have learned, however.

From a marketing viewpoint, how people find out about products and brands, and more especially what drives people to do so, is the basis of our thinking when developing communications strategies. How people store the information in memory, and where they store it, is the basis of our communications strategies. Even though people flip past advertisements, we do have a natural desire to learn, and we also have considerable pressures on us to know about the products we buy – the downside of not knowing varies from losing our money, through social embarrassment, to physical injury.

 **Key points**

- Learning is behavioural change over time relative to an external stimulus.
- Classical conditioning is largely involuntary on the part of the learner.
- Operant conditioning assumes that the learner has choice in the process: 'good' behaviour is reinforced by reward, 'bad' behaviour is reduced by punishment.
- Cognitive learning involves conscious thought and effort.
- Motivation is a key factor in all learning.
- Learning by experience is more powerful than learning vicariously.
- Consumer knowledge breaks down into product knowledge, purchase knowledge, consumption knowledge, persuasion knowledge and self-knowledge.

Review questions

1 How might a marketer use music in classical conditioning?
2 What methods of operant conditioning are available to marketers?
3 What is the role of cognitive learning in major purchases?
4 How might a marketer motivate a consumer to learn about a product?
5 How can learning by experience be used in selling high-value products such as stereo systems?
6 How might mavens be recruited for a word-of-mouth campaign?
7 What effect does persuasion knowledge have on marketing communications?
8 How can self-knowledge be enhanced by marketers?
9 How can marketers encourage people to improve their purchase knowledge?
10 What should marketers do to ensure that consumers have adequate consumption knowledge?

Case study revisited: Gurgle.com

Gurgle.com is an interactive website (and now a publishing company) owned by Mothercare. It operates as an independent company, so it isn't solely a marketing platform for Mothercare stores: it funds itself through advertising and book sales.

The site has a timeline across the top, going in stages from 'trying for a baby' through to 'toddler'. Clicking on the line at the stage the mother is currently at links to a page of information and advice for that stage of pregnancy or motherhood, plus a forum for comments from other women. There are further links to other articles – some of which are serious, informative articles and some of which are humorous or light articles (for example, there is an article listing the top five rude comments people make to pregnant women). Expectant mothers can sign up to a free e-mail service, by which they will be sent a weekly article containing advice about the particular stage of pregnancy or motherhood they find themselves in.

The forums are extremely popular – women are able to offer and receive advice from others in the same situation, without having to provide a name: most of the women posting on the site use an online alias, although no doubt some do use their real names. Posters discuss everything from labour pains to the latest novels, and there is a real atmosphere of support and self-help about them.

Advertising on the website is low-key and fairly unobtrusive, and is of course geared to its target audience. Detergent manufacturers, baby food manufacturers, toy companies and pharmaceutical companies are all more than willing to buy space on such a well-targeted and well-used website.

The essential aspect of the website is that it promotes interactive learning about the problems facing a pregnant woman. The website doesn't preach, doesn't offer gratuitous advice and doesn't tell its readers what to do: it merely allows them to learn from each other and to hear what experts in the field have to say. As a model for the learning process, it has a great deal to offer – if only school were as easy and pleasant!

Case study: Jingles

A jingle is a short song specially written to promote a product. A good jingle has a catchy tune and memorable lyrics, and often these little songs will stay in people's heads for days or years.

Jingles had their origin in the United States, where commercial radio was introduced in the 1920s. The first true jingle is thought to be the one for General Mills' breakfast cereal Wheaties. The jingle was sung live on air by a quartet of male singers (eventually they became known as the Wheaties Quartet), in the Minneapolis–St Paul area. General Mills had been thinking of withdrawing the product due to poor sales, but when sales in the area rose to the point where they accounted for over half of all production, the future of the jingle was assured.

Jingles are often the only songs people can remember all the way through: most people in their thirties and forties can still remember the jingle used to promote Libby's fruit drink, Um Bongo. This jingle first aired in the mid-1980s, predominantly on children's television, with the catchy strap line 'Um Bongo, Um Bongo, they drink it in the Congo'. In fact, the drink is not marketed in the Congo at all, but the fruits it contained were tropical in origin. Other jingles include 'You can't get better than a Kwik-Fit fitter' (again from the mid-1980s), and for over 20 years Cadbury's Fudge was promoted using the jingle 'A finger of Fudge is just enough ...', which was written by Mike D'Abo who was a member of the Manfred Mann band and wrote many hit songs (including 'Handbags and Gladrags' for Chris Farlowe).

Sometimes jingles are used in government campaigns. In Australia, a jingle was used to explain the new decimal currency: the tune was taken from a traditional Australian song, 'Click Go the Shears, Boys'. In the United States, the US Army commissioned songwriter Jake Holmes to write a recruitment jingle with the title 'Be All That You Can Be'.

As time has gone by, the specially-composed jingle has become less popular in favour of using tunes that are already well known. UK comparison site Go Compare uses George

M. Cohan's First World War song 'Over There', while rival site Confused.com uses Village People's hit 'YMCA' for their commercials. Another innovation has been the tag, or sonic logo, which consists of only a few notes: the Intel tag of five notes, the five-note MacDonald's 'I'm Lovin' It' tag, and the somewhat longer 20th Century Fox fanfare are all examples of sonic logos. Associating a brief sound with a brand has even been extended to machine noises – Harley-Davidson have registered the sound of their V-twin engine as a sonic logo.

Whatever the changes in jingles, music has the power to stick in people's minds – meaning that the brand sticks there, too.

Questions

1 Why might a company prefer to put new lyrics to an existing popular song?
2 Why do brands become more memorable if enshrined in a song?
3 Which aspects of consumer knowledge are likely to be enhanced by jingles?
4 What is the role of classical conditioning in explaining the effectiveness of jingles?
5 How might operant conditioning be relevant to jingles?

Further reading

Contemporary Theories of Learning: Learning Theorists ... In Their Own Words by Knud Illeris (ed.) (Abingdon: Routledge, 2009) is a useful book of essays in which leading learning theorists explain their ideas. If you are interested in learning about how people learn, this book provides an excellent overview.

Soap, Sex and Cigarettes: A Cultural History of American Advertising by Juliann Sivulka (Boston, MA: Wadsworth Publishing Inc., 2011) provides an entertaining view of how advertising has both created and been created by American society. The book shows how advertising has helped Americans learn how to be American – and, of course, the same processes have gone on in other countries.

Human Memory: Theory and Practice by Alan Baddeley (Hove: Psychology Press, 1997) is about the mechanisms of memory. It covers the interconnectedness of learning, knowledge and memory, and explores three different types of memory.

Advertising and the Mind of the Consumer: What Works, What Doesn't, and Why by Max Sutherland (London: Kogan Page, 2000) explains how exposure to advertising builds up in people's memories. The author uses a lot of anecdotes and real-life examples, as well as an entertaining writing style to get the point across.

References

Alba, J.A. and Hutchinson, J.W. (1987) Dimensions of consumer expertise. *Journal of Consumer Research* 13 (March): 411–54.

Alba, J.A. and Hutchinson, J.W. (2000) Knowledge calibration: what consumers know and what they think they know. *Journal of Consumer Research* 27 (September): 123–56.

Barone, M.J., Manning, K.C. and Miniard, P.W. (2004) Consumer response to practical price comparisons in retail environments. *Journal of Marketing* 68 (July): 37–47.

Bearden, W.O., Hardesty, D.M. and Rose, R.L. (2001) Consumers' self-confidence: refinements in conceptualisation and measurement. *Journal of Consumer Research* 28 (June): 121–34.

Belen del Rio, A., Vacquez, R. and Iglesias, V. (2001) The effects of brand association on consumer response. *Journal of Consumer Marketing* 18: 410–25.

Blackwell, R.D., Miniard, P.W. and Engel, J.F. (2005) *Consumer Behaviour*, 10th edn. Mason, OH: Thomson South-Western.

Brown, C.L. and Krishna, A. (2004) The skeptical shopper: a metacognitive account for the effects of default options on choice. *Journal of Consumer Research* 31 (December): 529–39.

Elpers, J. W., Wedel, M. and Pieters, R. (2002) The influence of moment-to-moment pleasantness and informativeness on zapping TV commercials: a functional data and survival analysis approach. *Advances in Consumer Research* 29: 57–8.

Friestad, M. and Wright, P. (1994) The persuasion knowledge model: how people cope with persuasion attempts. *Journal of Consumer Research* 21 (1): 1–30.

Gorn, G.J. (1982) The effects of music in advertising on choice behaviour: a classical conditioning approach. *Journal of Marketing* 46 (Winter): 94–101.

Hansen, J., Strick, M., van Baaren, R.B., Hooghuis, M. and Wigboldus, D.H. (2009) Exploring memory for product names advertised with humour. *Journal of Consumer Behaviour* 8 (2/3): 135–48.

Hoch, S.J. and Deighton, J. (1989) Managing what consumers learn from experience. *Journal of Marketing* 53 (April): 1–20.

Hoch, S.J. and Ha, Y. (1986) Consumer learning: advertising and the ambiguity of product experience. *Journal of Consumer Research* 13 (Sep): 221–33.

Johnson, E., Moe, W., Fader, P., Bellman, S. and Lohse, J. (2002) On the depth and dynamics of on-line search behaviour. *Advances in Consumer Research* 29: 8–10.

Kenning, P., Deppe, M., Schwindt, W., Kugel, H. and Plassmann, H. (2009) The good, the bad and the forgotten – an fMRI-study on ad liking and ad memory. *Advances in Consumer Research* 36: 3–4.

Kroeber-Riel, W. (1984) Emotional product differentiation by classical conditioning. *Advances in Consumer Research* 11: 538–43.

Krugman, H.E. (1965) The impact of television advertising: learning without involvement. *Public Opinion Quarterly* 29: 349–56.

Lerman, D. (2003) The effect of morphemic familiarity and exposure mode on recall and recognition of brand names. *Advances in Consumer Research* 30: 80–1.

McSweeney, F.K. and Bierley, C. (1984) Recent developments in classical conditioning. *Journal of Consumer Research* 11 (Sep): 619–37.

Murray, K.B. and Haubl, G. (2002) The fiction of no friction: a user skills approach to cognitive lock-in. *Advances in Consumer Research* 29: 11–18.

Norton, M. and Chance, Z. (2008) Decision amnesia: why taking your time leads to forgetting. *Advances in Consumer Research* 35: 55–8.

Onkvisit, S. and Shaw, J.J. (1994) *Consumer Behaviour, Strategy and Analysis*. New York: Macmillan.

Pavlov, I.P. (1927) *Conditioned Reflexes*. London: Oxford University Press.

Pieters, R., Warlop, L. and Wedel, M. (2002) Breaking through the clutter: ad originality and familiarity effects on brand attention and memory. *Advances in Consumer Research* 29: 89–90.

Rao, A.R. and Sieben, W.A. (1992) The effect of prior knowledge on price acceptability and the type of information examined. *Journal of Consumer Research* 19 (Sep): 256–70.

Skinner, B.F. (1953) *Science and Human Behaviour*. New York: Macmillan.

Staelin, R. (1978) The effects of consumer education on consumer product safety behaviour. *Journal of Consumer Research* 5 (June): 30–40.

Tedeschi, B. (2005) Cheaper than it seems. *New York Times*, 10 January.

Vanhamme, J. and Snelders, D. (2003) What if you surprise your customers – will they be more satisfied? Findings from a pilot experiment. *Advances in Consumer Research* 30: 48–56.

Zauberman, G. (2002) Lock-in over time: time preferences, prediction accuracy and the information cost structure. *Advances in Consumer Research* 29: 8–10.

Zhou, Z. and Bao, Y. (2002) Users' attitudes towards web advertising: effects of internet motivation and internet ability. *Advances in Consumer Research* 29: 71–8.

More online

To gain free access to additional online resources to support this chapter please visit: **www.sagepub.co.uk/blythe**

CHAPTER (7)

Attitude formation and change

LEARNING OBJECTIVES

After reading this chapter you should be able to:

- Describe what is meant by attitude.

- Explain how attitudes can be inferred from behaviour.

- Explain why behaviour cannot be assumed from knowing attitude.

- Describe the components of attitude.

- Explain the role of salient beliefs in forming attitudes.

- Explain the purpose of attitudes.

- Explain the relationship between attitude and behaviour.

- Describe the factors which determine the strength of attitude.

- Explain the difference between public and private attitudes.

- Show the effect of situation on attitude.

- Explain the role of changing beliefs in changing attitudes.

- Explain how emotions are important in changing attitudes.

- Describe the various complaint behaviours that arise from post-purchase dissatisfaction.

Introduction

Attitudes are what put us in the right position for behaviour. We each have attitudes towards many things – our friends, our possessions, our families, government policies, other people's behaviour and so forth. Our differing attitudes are (in part) the differentiators between us as human beings, and since attitudes are the precursor to any consumption behaviour they are of great interest to marketers, both in terms of finding out what they are and in seeking to change them.

Case study: Attitudes to smoking

Most smokers start smoking before it is legal to do so, in school. Generally speaking, campaigns aimed at school-age smokers are fairly ineffective – emphasising the long-term health risks is unlikely to have much effect on a fourteen-year-old, because the risks are so far in the future. Of course, the risks are there, and are very real – around 3000 young people in the United States start smoking every day, and about one-third of those will die of a smoking-related illness.

A high-school kid who takes up smoking would have to be from the planet Zog not to know that smoking is dangerous. Health warnings are everywhere – on the advertising, on TV, in every doctor's surgery, even on the cigarette packets themselves. Obviously, lack of knowledge and information is not the problem – so what is it that makes young people take up smoking? Could it be that it is forbidden? Could it be that a streak of adolescent rebellion makes them do it, in the face of all the advice to the contrary from grey-haired, boring adults?

Your typical teenager has a somewhat paradoxical set of attitudes – although heavily influenced by peer pressure, teenagers value the sense of being in control, and having a degree of self-determination in their lives. This is understandable in people who are emerging from childhood, where they are expected to obey a bewildering set of rules, and who have not yet got the hang of the new set of rules which govern adult behaviour. However, the adults who are responsible for health care know that natural teenage experimentation can go badly wrong if they become addicted to, and eventually killed by, cigarette smoking.

Preaching to young people about health risks was never going to work, but a reasoned campaign that addressed the underlying motivations of the teenagers themselves stood some chance of having an effect.

How to impress your examiner

You are likely to be asked how attitudes might be changed. It's very tempting just to dive into the various methods of changing attitudes without first making clear that attitudes actually are quite hard to change from the outside – more typically, attitude change comes from within, as a result of experience. You should also give a brief outline of how attitudes are formed in the first place – this will make the explanation of how to change them much easier.

Defining attitude

Attitude can be defined as 'a learned tendency to respond to an object in a consistently favourable or unfavourable way' (Onkvisit and Shaw 1994). Whether a product will be bought or not depends to a large extent on the consumer's attitude towards it, and therefore much marketing effort is expended on finding out what consumers' attitudes are to product offerings, and in seeking to change those attitudes where appropriate.

To break down the definition and make it easier to handle:

1 Attitude is learned, not instinctive.
2 It is not behaviour, it is a predisposition towards a particular behaviour.
3 It implies a relationship between a person and an object. The object of the attitude could be another person, an institution or a physical article; 'object' is used here in the sense of 'an objective'.
4 Attitudes are fairly stable; they do not change much with physical states or circumstances. For example, if someone's favourite painkiller is Panadol, that attitude remains whether or not the individual has a headache. The behaviour (actually taking the tablets) may not happen, but the attitude remains.
5 The relationship between a person and an object is not neutral. It is a vector, having both direction and intensity; if you express an attitude about something, you either like it or you do not. If you are neutral about it, or indifferent, you would say you don't have any attitude towards it.

Attitude has to be inferred from statements or behaviour; it is intangible and not directly observable. In other words, although we can observe and measure behaviour, we have to ask people about their attitudes to various things, and hope that their replies are honest ones. This can cause difficulties if we are researching a sensitive topic.

The formation of attitude is based on experience of the object, normally direct experience; driving a particular make of car, or trying a particular brand of beer, will lead to the formation of an attitude. The individual builds up a mental picture (perception) of the object, and forms an attitude accordingly. First impressions are important, since they colour our later information gathering (see Chapter 5) – this is why people behave themselves on the first date, so that the other person forms a favourable attitude.

 ## Challenging the status quo

So attitudes form through experience. And yet we often base our beliefs on very limited experience, do we not? Someone who travels by sea for the first time and is seriously seasick is unlikely to want to travel on a ship ever again – even though the seasickness might have been caused by the worst storm ever!

Are we really that stupid when it comes to developing attitudes? Is this some weakness in the human brain? Or is it, perhaps, a sign of one of our great talents – the ability to develop a working hypothesis based on limited data?

Either way, we seem to form attitudes almost spontaneously, and often with little effort to review them later!

Some experience is indirect: recommendations and the communicated experiences of friends or relatives are important when forming attitudes towards objects of which we don't have direct experience. This can sometimes lead to superstitious beliefs and prejudices due to the synthetic nature of perception. If your friends have all told you that a particular film is boring, you are likely to maintain that attitude, even if you have not seen the film yourself. Negative attitudes are often formed in this way. Advertising, and indeed marketing communications generally, can help a lot here by providing additional sources of information (public relations has a particularly important role in this, since it is an activity that deals mainly with attitude formation and change).

Synthetic That which is constructed from disparate components. In perception, an overall view derived from grouping together a set of stimuli

There is a perceptual component in attitude. The manner in which an object is perceived is affected by the consumer's stable characteristics (personality, intelligence, previous knowledge, culture, gender, etc.) and by current characteristics, such as mood, state of the organism, etc.

Dimensions of attitude

Attitude has three dimensions, as shown in Figure 7.1, and Table 7.1 explains the relationship between each of these components.

It is important to note that attitude and behaviour are separate things. Simply because an individual has a particular attitude about something does not mean that

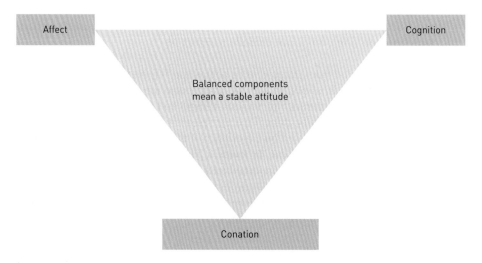

Figure 7.1   Dimensions of attitude

Table 7.1   Dimensions of attitude

Dimension	Definition	Explanation	Example
Cognition	The perceptual component of attitude	This is the individual's awareness, knowledge, beliefs and images of the attitudinal object. It is the conscious, thinking part of attitude	An individual's attitude towards a car may be composed of comparative information, e.g. the Ford Focus is cheaper to buy than the Volkswagen Golf, but the Golf holds its value better. These are the facts (or beliefs) informing the attitude
Affect	The evaluative component of attitude	These are the emotions, the feelings of like and dislike which do not always have a basis in objective fact	Drivers frequently have affective relationships with their first cars. The car is given a name, and often the driver will speak to it
Conation	Behavioural intention	Conation is about what we intend to do about the attitudinal object; whether to approach it, reject it, buy it, etc. It is not the actual behaviour; merely an intention	Having formed an attitude about a car ('I love the bodywork, it really looks great, and it does 40 to the gallon as well') the consumer forms an intention ('I'm going to take out a loan and buy one'). This intention is the conation

the individual will act on the attitude. For example, someone might hear that his bank is investing in a country with an oppressive regime. This is cognition. He may think that this is unethical; he does not like the bank doing this (affect). He therefore decides to move his account elsewhere (conation). Conation may not always lead to behaviour; our ethical bank customer may have second thoughts later and decide to leave the account where it is, perhaps on the basis that switching to another bank is just too complicated. Other factors often prevent us from taking the course of action we had originally planned.

The three elements are interrelated in a complex way. Purchase intentions relate to beliefs and brand evaluations, and likelihood of buying a brand has been shown to be influenced by attitudes towards advertising as well as attitudes towards brands (Homer and Yoon 1992).

The traditional view of attitude is that affect towards an object is mediated by cognition; in other words, emotional responses about something are controlled to a marked extent by rational evaluation. This was challenged by Zajonc and Markus (1985), who assert that affective responses do not have to be based on prior cognition. People can develop a 'gut feel' about something without conscious evaluation, and even on limited information, then rationalise the decision afterwards. This may sometimes be due to classical conditioning; for example, the individual may form a favourable attitude towards a product because the advert uses a favourite song as background music (see Chapter 6). Affect also influences information processing: there is a 'meddling-in' effect in which cognition is influenced by the way in which information is processed, which is in turn influenced by emotions (Mishra et al. 2006). In fact, forming an attitude about a product might start with any of the three components, with the others coming into play afterwards. Also, if the outcome of any action is expected to be affect-rich (pleasurable, unpleasant, emotionally moving, etc.) the individual will evaluate the action by its effect on feelings. Affect-poor outcomes trigger evaluation by calculation (Hsee and Rottenstreich 2002). In other words, putting a strong emotional bias into marketing communications is likely to lead to emotionally based decision-making.

Although it may seem illogical or dangerous to form an attitude without first finding out a lot about the attitudinal object, most people are familiar with the feeling of having 'fallen in love' with a hopelessly impractical purchase. Likewise, most people are familiar with the feeling of having taken an instant dislike to somebody without first getting to know the person. This is illustrated in Figure 7.2.

Attitude contains components of belief and opinion, but it is neither. Attitude differs from *belief* in that belief is neutral, not implying good or bad. Belief is concerned with the presence or absence of an attribute, and is usually based on a judgement of the available evidence. Attitude contains an element of affect, and evaluates whether the existence of an attribute will result in satisfaction or dissatisfaction. For example,

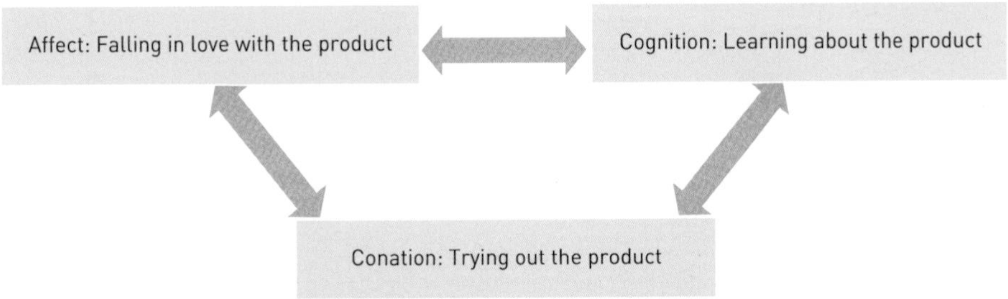

Cognition Thought processes: the element of attitude derived from conscious thought or knowledge

Affect The emotional element of attitude

Conation The behavioural intentions that arise from attitudes

Figure 7.2 Starting points for attitude formation

a consumer might believe that a Volvo is a reliable, well-engineered car but have no particular feelings about this either way. Conversely, another consumer might feel that the Volvo is a good car, or a desirable car, because it is well-engineered and reliable.

Attitude differs from *opinion* in that opinion is an overt, vocalised expression of an attitude. Attitude can also be expressed nonverbally (facial expressions, body language, etc.), or indeed may not be expressed at all. While opinions may arise from attitudes (i.e. be expressed as the result of an attitude) and attitudes may arise from hearing the opinions of others, the two are in fact separate entities.

Attitude formation

A more complete model of the formation of attitudes about brands shows that it is a somewhat complex process. Figure 7.3 gives an overview of the complete process. The diagram begins with the consumer's needs, both utilitarian (practical) and expressive (emotional). This feeds into the consumer's motivation to process information, as does advertising; motivation and exposure feed into the processing, but the consumer also needs to have the ability and the opportunity to process the information.

Within the processing 'black box' the consumer's level of processing is affected by attention and capacity for processing; in other words, by the degree of interest the consumer has, and his/her ability to process the information. The result of the processing is both cognitive and affective, feeding into the formation of attitudes about the brand.

Situational variables surrounding the brand or product will also affect the attitude formation process. For example, an unpleasant salesperson or an inconveniently located dealership may affect the way we perceive brands. Exposure to ad stimulus plays a major part in encouraging learning and the formation of attitudes, but the main drive comes (as always) from the consumer's needs (Berger and Mitchell 1989). Pre-existing attitudes may colour the formation of attitudes about a particular situation. Researchers have found that people can be categorised according to their

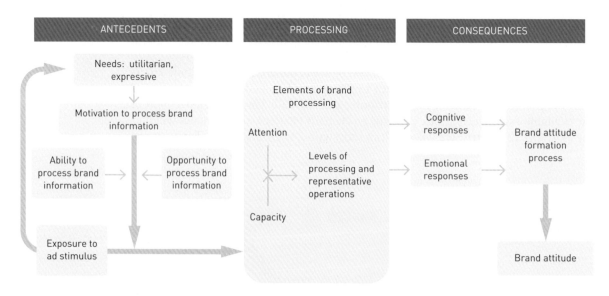

Figure 7.3   Attitude formation

Source: Deborah J. McInnis and Bernard J. Jaworski (1989) Information processing from advertisements; toward an integrative framework. *Journal of Marketing* 53 (4): 1–23.

attitudes about Christmas, for example; these attitudes are themselves formed by attitudes about religion, about gift-giving and about commercial influences (Gurau and Tinson 2003). Likewise, people who are materialistic will get into debt to fund their purchases even if their incomes are very low (Ponchio and Aranha 2008).

Consumers acquire salient beliefs about products. Because the cognitive system can only hold a relatively small number of facts in mind at once, the salient beliefs are the ones that are used by the consumer to make a judgement. Usually the salient beliefs will be those that the consumer holds most important, but they may be merely the ones that have been most recently presented (Fishbein and Ajzen 1975).

A consumer's overall attitude towards an object is a function of many attributes of the object. The attitude forms as a result of the consumer's strength of feeling, or the strength of the salient beliefs, about the attributes and also the evaluation of those beliefs. Table 7.2 shows an example of a belief set about a restaurant.

The question marks represent areas where the consumer has no knowledge, or has the knowledge but is not taking it into consideration. In other words, only the salient beliefs are taken into account.

This *multiattribute attitude model* attempts to explain how the consumer's salient beliefs help to form the final attitude. The attributes listed are integrated to form an overall attitude; in this example, the consumer will form an attitude about the restaurant as to whether it is a good restaurant or a bad one. The attitude may be qualified in some way: the restaurant may be regarded as a good one for lunch, but a bad one for dinner, or perhaps as a good one for a quick meal when one doesn't feel like cooking, but a bad one for special occasions.

Attitude formation is clearly affected by context: conation in particular may be affected by the feasibility of carrying out a particular behaviour, or the need to modify it to take account of what is happening around the individual (Bless et al. 2002).

Salient belief A belief which is key in the formation of an attitude

Attitude measurement

Measuring attitudes is clearly a subject of some interest to marketers, since attitudes play such a major role in consumer purchasing behaviour. It is obviously of importance for manufacturers to know what the consumers' attitude is to the product, but it is difficult to quantify. This is because attitude contains elements of both cognition and affect. Here are two contrasting models for attitude measurement: the Rosenberg Model and the Fishbein Model.

Table 7.2 Example of a belief set

Attribute	Strength of salient belief (out of 10)	Level of importance (out of 10)
Convenient parking	5	7
Good food	6	8
Friendly waiters	?	4
Pleasant decor	7	5
Clean cutlery	3	7
Reasonable prices	?	3
Open on Wednesdays	?	5

The *Rosenberg Model* (Rosenberg 1960) says that an individual's attitude towards an object represents the degree and direction of the attitudinal effect aroused by the object. Put more simply, attitude is composed of a *quantity* of feeling and a *direction*, and has two main components:

Perceived instrumentality The degree to which an action or product is thought to be useful in a practical way

1 Perceived instrumentality. This is the subjective capacity of the object to attain the value in question, in other words the usefulness of the object.
2 Value importance. This is the amount of satisfaction the person derives from the attainment of a particular value. More simply, this is the importance of achieving the result that the consumer is hoping to achieve by buying and using the object of the attitude.

Value importance The level of satisfaction the individual gains from the achievement of a particular value

Perceived instrumentality means the degree to which the person believes that the product will work as it is supposed to. Value importance is the degree to which getting the job done is important to the consumer.

Theoretically, perceived instrumentality and value importance are actually independent, and taken separately they don't predict responses well, but taken together they are good predictors of behaviour that is illustrative of attitude.

The *Fishbein model* (Fishbein 1980) takes a different perspective on the problem by focusing on the consumer rather than on the product. For Fishbein, attitudes can be predicted from beliefs and evaluation. Belief is the probability that the object possesses a particular attribute; evaluation is whether that attribute attracts or repels. This is not compatible with the value importance concept in the Rosenberg model.

In this model, the consumer's belief in the product's capabilities replaces the perceived instrumentality aspect. For example, it may be useful for a car to have a large boot (Rosenberg model) but whether a particular car's boot is large or not is a relative term and relies on the consumer's beliefs (Fishbein model). Furthermore, the belief that a car's boot is large does not necessarily mean that the prospective owner will like that attribute (Fishbein model). This will depend on how important the attribute is to the customer (Rosenberg model).

Combining the two models, there are three distinct aspects of the importance of attitude:

1 Perceived instrumentality.
2 Evaluative aspect (affect).
3 Value importance.

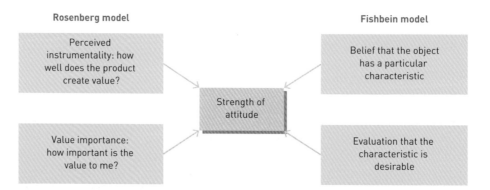

Figure 7.4 Strength of attitudes

These are illustrated in Figure 7.4. Examples of these aspects are as follows:

1   I believe the Ford Mondeo is the most comfortable car in its class.
2   I like comfort.
3   Comfort is very important to me.

Note that the second two are not identical. Someone can like something without it being very important to him or her.

Functions of attitudes

Attitudes have a function in helping consumers make decisions about their purchasing practices, and also serve other functions according to the individual's circumstances. Four main categories of function have been identified, as shown in Table 7.3 (Locander and Spivey 1978).

These functions of attitude may not all be present at the same time: a given attitude may only serve one or two of these functions, while still being valuable. The relationship between them is illustrated in Figure 7.5. In some cases, the ego-defensive function and the value-expressive function might conflict with each other. If the individual has beliefs that go against the majority, the ego-expressive function may not protect the person from attacks by others. Equally, having attitudes that accord with those of other people may conform well with the ego-defensive function.

Ego-defensive function
The function of attitude which enables the individual to maintain stability of the conscious self

Value-expressive function The factor in group behaviour that allows the members to display their own beliefs and attitudes

Table 7.3   Functions of attitudes

Function	Definition	Explanation	Example
Instrumental function	The individual uses the attitude to obtain satisfaction from the object	The individual thus aims to maximise external reward while minimising external punishment	An individual might develop an attitude towards a particular pub because his friends go there and the beer's good
Ego-defensive function	Protects against internal conflicts and external dangers	Here the attitude shields the individual from his/her own failings	Someone who is unable to understand how to use the product might have the attitude that manufacturers make products too complex
Value-expressive function	Opposite of ego-defensive; the drive for self-expression	The attitudes expressed often go against the flow of opinion	Most radical political viewpoints are examples of the value-expressive attitude in action
Knowledge function	The drive to seek clarity and order	Related to the need to understand what the object is all about. Comes from the belief that if you know what you like and dislike, decision-making is easy	Somebody who has an interest in hi-fi systems is likely to read magazines about them, to visit exhibitions, and to discuss them with friends so as to know what the latest products are

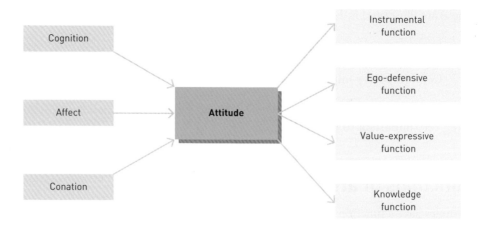

Figure 7.5   Functions of attitudes

 Consumer behaviour in action: From stage to screen

Sooner or later in a pop star's career his or her agent suggests making a movie. This is often a quick way to leverage a star's fame to generate earnings from box-office receipts – and in most cases the stars sing in the movie, which generates record sales.

In some cases it works fine – The Beatles made *Hard Day's Night* and *Help!* which were considerable successes, but went on to make *Magical Mystery Tour* and *Yellow Submarine*, both of which virtually disappeared without trace. Later outings by the individual band members were equally poorly received: John Lennon's films (with Yoko Ono) scarcely saw the light of day, and Paul McCartney's *Give My Regards to Broad Street* sank like a stone. The greatest success has probably been Ringo Starr's voice-overs for *Thomas the Tank Engine*. Others have not even achieved this limited success – Elvis Presley made a string of low-budget, tacky movies which undoubtedly tarnished his image as a controversial and innovative musician, and more recently Madonna, The Spice Girls, Britney Spears and Mariah Carey have all made films that have been listed among the Top Ten Worst Films of All Time. Newsday said of Madonna's *Swept Away*: 'New ways of describing badness need to be invented to describe exactly how bad this movie is.'

So why does this happen? No doubt these people are talented individuals, capable of holding an audience's attention, and capable of performing a role. They already have a substantial fan base, most of whom are likely to go to see the movie. They have good, capable managers, and they already know the entertainment business.

Is it, perhaps, that we have already developed an attitude towards these stars as singers and musicians, and find it hard to relate to them when they are playing a part? The Beatles' successful movies both showed them purely as a band, to some extent mocking their own success and image, whereas the flops showed them acting a part. Fans want to see their idol, not someone who looks like the idol but is actually supposed to be somebody else! The willing suspension of disbelief is essential for enjoying a night at the cinema, and somehow this is damaged if one is unable to believe in the lead character.

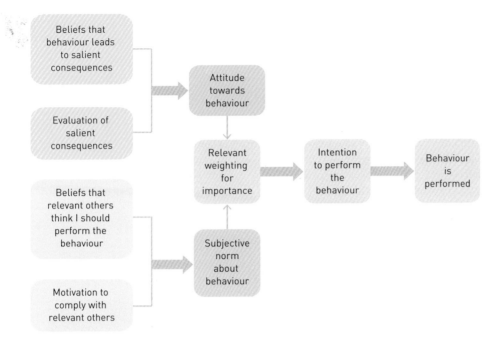

Figure 7.6   The theory of reasoned action

Source: Martin Fishbein, 'An overview of the attitude construct' in G.B. Hafer (ed.) A Look Back, A Look Ahead Chicago: *American Marketing Association*, 1980: 8.

Attitude and behaviour

The *theory of reasoned action* (Ajzen and Fishbein 1980) says that consumers consciously evaluate the consequences of alternative behaviours, and then choose the one that will lead to the most favourable consequences. Figure 7.6 shows the four main components of the theory – behaviour, intention to behave, attitude towards the behaviour and subjective norm. The subjective norm is the component that reflects the social pressures the individual may feel to perform (or avoid performing) the behaviour being contemplated.

The individual's beliefs about the behaviour and the evaluation of the possible main consequences will combine to produce an attitude about the behaviour. At the same time, the individual's beliefs about what other people might think, and the degree to which he or she cares about what other people think, go towards developing a subjective norm about the contemplated behaviour. The individual will then weight the relative importance of the attitude and the norm, and will form an intention of how to behave. This may, in turn, lead to the behaviour itself.

The theory of reasoned action assumes that consumers perform a logical evaluation procedure for making decisions about behaviour, based on attitude towards the behaviour, which in turn derives from attitudes towards the product or brand.

Logically, attitude should precede behaviour. In other words, we would expect that someone would form an attitude about something, then act on that attitude. In fact, much of the evidence points the other way. It appears in some cases that people behave first, and form attitudes afterwards (Fishbein 1972).

An extension of the theory of reasoned action is the theory of planned behaviour, shown in Figure 7.7. (Ajzen and Madden 1986; Ajzen 1988). Planned behaviour assumes that the individual also takes account of the ease or difficulty of performing

Challenging the status quo

If attitudes are formed as the result of a logical thought process, how come we often take a sudden dislike to someone or something for no apparent reason? Is the theory wrong, or is there some other mechanism at work?

Perhaps we form our attitudes below the conscious level, so that there is some kind of logical process going on without our being aware of it. Equally possible, of course, is that we rationalise a decision we made originally on gut instinct – which may or may not be a logical process.

Even if we do go through a thinking process to form our attitudes, how good a process is it? How reliable are the factors on which we base our decisions? How reliable are our brains anyway?

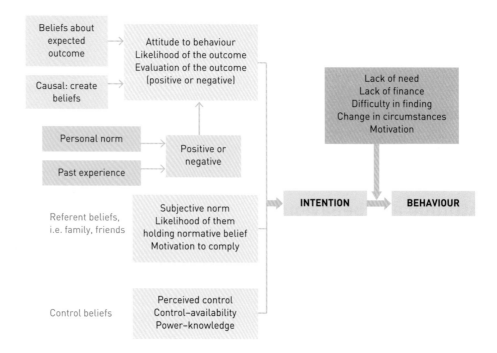

Figure 7.7 The theory of planned behaviour

the planned behaviour, in other words the degree of control the individual has over the behaviour and its outcomes. This depends in part on past experience, and in part on the anticipation of future obstacles.

Essentially, the model attempts to predict behaviour based on conation (intent to commit the behaviour). The overall attitude towards the behaviour is predicted by the salient beliefs about the behaviour and its possible outcomes, and the subjective norm is determined by the individual's beliefs about what salient others (friends and family) would think about the behaviour, coupled with the level of motivation to comply with the views of others. For example, it appears that women and men have very different attitudes towards genetically engineered foods: women tend to distrust the science (a conative factor) and also tend to have ethical views about GM (an affective factor). This is the major contributor to differences in purchase intention, with women being much less likely to buy GM products (Qin and Brown 2008).

Marketing efforts often encourage people to try products first, then form attitudes; free samples, test drives, demonstrations and coupons are all more powerful in forming attitude and behaviour consistency than are advertisements (Smith and Swinyard 1983). Attitudes formed without trial experience are probably weak and easily changed. In this context, the Pepsi Challenge represents a way of persuading people that Pepsi is better than Coca-Cola. Each summer stands are set up in shopping malls and at seaside resorts and passers-by are offered the chance to compare Pepsi with Coke in a blind taste test.

Part of the reason for this is that the two drinks do, in fact, taste very similar and without the visual cue of the packaging the consumers often cannot tell the difference between the two. Since Pepsi has a smaller market share than Coke, the company only needs half of the respondents to prefer the Pepsi in order to gain a greater market share than it currently holds. In fact, there is a slight preference for the Pepsi, since around 65% of people state that they prefer it in blind taste tests, often to their surprise.

Trial of a product is so much more powerful than advertising in forming favourable impressions that car manufacturers are prepared to give special deals to car rental companies and driving schools in the hope that hirers and learners will buy the same model at a later date.

It may not matter greatly whether attitude precedes behaviour or not. Attitude is not always followed by the proposed behaviour; most people are familiar with having proposed doing something, then doing something else instead. This may be because attitude and behaviour are not always consistent. For example, a smoker may take the attitude that smoking is unhealthy and antisocial, but may still not give up smoking. Dieting is a similar example: even though an overweight person may believe that being fat is unhealthy and unattractive, losing weight may not be the end result. Many other examples abound; in Freudian terms, the attitude may have come from the superego, but the demands of the id result in a failure to act (see Chapter 1).

In fact, it seems more likely that, at least regarding fast-moving consumer goods (FMCG), the process of attitude formation and behaviour are interwoven. Figure 7.8 illustrates this.

In this model there is a feedback loop that allows the consumer to re-evaluate and reconsider his or her attitudes. The formation of attitude is thus seen as a dynamic process, with the behaviour itself forming part of the process.

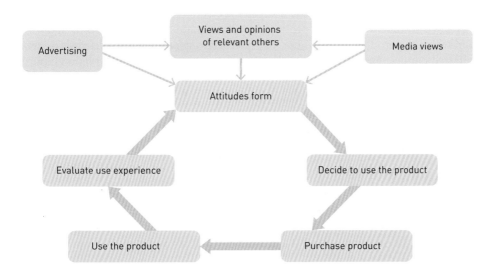

Figure 7.8   The cycle of attitude and behaviour

Private vs. public attitudes

Often people hold attitudes that they are reluctant to admit to in public. This is particularly true in recent years due to the fashion for political correctness. This makes attitude measurement difficult because respondents will give a rational or acceptable answer rather than a true one. Few people would be prepared to admit openly that they have racist attitudes, for example, yet it is undoubtedly the case that many people do have such attitudes.

In marketing terms, people are often reluctant to admit to buying products that are embarrassing (or illegal). Many people would be reluctant to admit, for instance, that they like pornography, and therefore it is easier to sell such products over the Internet than it is to sell them through retail outlets. The Internet preserves the anonymity of the customer.

Clearly there are implications for market research, since any questions that enquire into these attitudes are likely to meet with evasive answers or just plain lies. Most people will have some private attitudes and some opposing public attitudes, and therefore measurement of these private attitudes can best be carried out by using projective techniques such as sentence completion or cartoon tests. These research techniques were discussed in Chapter 4.

Often people's private attitudes do not have a logical basis, and therefore the individuals concerned are even more reluctant to admit to holding those views. Sometimes there is a reluctance to express an opinion when it has no logical basis; attitude, as we have seen, has a strong affective component.

Attitude vs. situation

During the 1930s, in a hotel in the South of France, a strange ceremony was acted out daily. One of the Romanoff princes (from the Russian royal family) would ask his chauffeur to mash up a plate of strawberries, and then eat them. This ceremony took place every day, even when the strawberries had to be specially flown in for the purpose. The reason was that the prince loved the smell of strawberries, but was allergic to them and therefore couldn't eat them. His attitude towards the 'product' therefore could not result in his consuming it, due to his situation.

In Figure 7.9, the thwarted conation feeds back information to the cognition element of attitude, which may cause a slight shift in the attitude itself.

Positive attitude towards the product may not equate to positive attitude about the *purchase* of the product. A consumer may have a strong positive attitude towards light-coloured clothes, but not buy them because she works in the city and light-coloured clothes show the dirt.

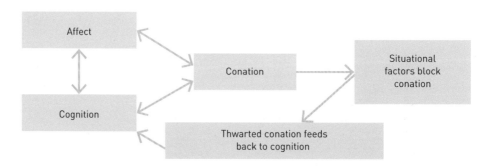

Figure 7.9   Effect of situation on attitude

Challenging the status quo

Presumably if one had an attitude that was permanently thwarted by one's situation, the attitude would have to change. For example, most of us have academic subjects we dislike – many people do not enjoy maths, as an example. Yet we often have to study something we dislike in order to be given a particular qualification, or as the precursor to studying something we do like.

Does this ever make us like the actual subject? Or do we simply like the outcome? How can we maintain an attitude in the face of its unpleasant aspects?

Fishbein suggests that the model be modified to take account of this (Fishbein 1972). The attitude to be measured should, under the extended model, be the attitude towards performing a given act (e.g. purchase or consumption) rather than an attitude towards the object itself. The evidence is that this model is a better predictor of purchasing behaviour than merely measuring attitudes towards the brands themselves, but of course there is greater complexity involved in understanding why a consumer has a particular attitude, since more variables are involved.

Attitudes can be changed due to situational changes. For example, a sudden drop in disposable income might lead somebody to think that a product is too expensive, even if it was seen as good value for money previously. Intentions can be checked against later performance by means of garbage analysis or self-report: Cote, McCullough and Reilly found that 'behaviour-intention inconsistency is partly attributable to unexpected situations' (Cote et al. 1985).

Attitude towards ads vs. attitude towards the brand

An individual may love the ads and hate the product, or vice versa. Although there is an assumption that a positive attitude towards the advertisement will lead to a positive attitude about the product, the two are actually separate hypothetical constructs (Mitchell 1986).

This is because the attitude towards the brand is affected by many more factors than the advertisement, whereas attitude towards the advertisement is only affected by the ad itself. The perception of the brand is much more likely to have a major cognitive element in it, whereas most advertising is intended to produce an affective response.

The evidence is that liking the advertisement relates to whether the product is meaningful and relevant to the consumer at the time (Biel 1990). There is some evidence that food and beverage advertisements are more likeable than non-food advertisements (Biel and Bridgwater 1990). Liking the advertisement will tend to spill over into liking the product, and the combination of the two is also likely to lead to an increase in sales (Biel 1990; Stapel 1991). This situation can be reversed in the case of some financial services products (e.g. insurance) because the advertising is often of the 'cautionary tale' type in which the advertisement shows what can go wrong if the individual does not buy the insurance. This naturally means that the advertisement is unpleasant and worrying.

Perhaps not surprisingly, people who have a high need to justify their decisions rationally (that is, people with a high need for cognition) are less likely to be swayed by their liking for the advertisement. People with a low need for cognition tend to like products that are advertised in a likeable way (Reinhard and Messner 2009).

Other factors in creating an attitude might include the way the message is framed – emphasising the cost of a better product rather than its higher quality may result in a poorer perception of the product and a lower propensity to buy it (Gamliel 2010). This may be because people experience losses more intensely than they experience gains of the same magnitude (Kahneman and Tversky 1979).

General vs. specific attitudes

It is necessary to look at specific attitudes when attempting to predict behaviour. It is possible to hold one attitude generally, but an opposing attitude in a specific case; for example, it is possible to dislike children while still loving one's own children, or to like wine in general but dislike Pinot Grigio. For marketers, the important attitude to measure is, of course, the attitude to the specific brand rather than the attitude to the product class as a whole.

Having said that, there is an issue regarding brand switching. If a consumer has a generally negative attitude about a product class, but will use a specific brand within that class, it may be possible to switch the consumer towards another brand similar to the one that is already acceptable. Consumers may already be prepared to do this in the event that the desired brand is out of stock; the difficulty lies in knowing why the individual consumer has made the decision to keep to only one brand of a class of products that he or she dislikes.

For example, a consumer may feel that, generally speaking, mayonnaise is thoroughly disgusting, with the exception of Hellmann's. It is possible that the consumer could be switched to Heinz if the Hellmann's is out of stock, but this would only happen if the consumer can be persuaded that the Heinz is just as good. If it turns out that the consumer is allergic to every other brand but Hellmann's, however, there will not be any way of achieving a brand switch.

Changing attitudes

Attitudes derive from consumer need, and from beliefs. People select salient beliefs (the beliefs that are most relevant to their individual needs) and build attitudes towards products based around those beliefs. For example, superstitious beliefs have been shown to affect attitudes towards novelty-seeking (Hernandez et al. 2008).

The model is useful to marketers in that it helps when devising strategies for changing consumer attitudes. There are four ways of changing attitudes, as follows:

1. *Add a new salient belief.* For example, a restaurant might point out that it has a strolling Gypsy violinist on Saturday nights. This would be a new fact for the consumer to take into account.
2. *Change the strength of a salient belief.* If the belief is a negative one, it can be discounted or played down; if it's a positive one, it can be given greater importance. If a restaurant customer has a low level of belief in the cleanliness of the cutlery, but a high evaluation of this attribute, then the restaurant needs to address this point specifically in its promotional messages. The restaurant might, for example, make a point of telling customers that the cutlery is specially checked before it reaches the table. In many Chinese restaurants, chopsticks are delivered to the table in paper sleeves: although the chopsticks have been used

many times, putting the sleeves on after they have been washed reassures the customers.

3 *Change the evaluation of an existing belief.* A customer may have a low evaluation of the prices in a restaurant, perhaps being more concerned about enjoying a romantic evening than about getting a cheap meal. The restaurant could increase the evaluation of this attribute by pointing out that the low prices mean that the customer can come more often, or treat friends to a meal without breaking the bank.

4 *Make an existing belief more salient.* A restaurant customer might not regard friendliness of the waiters as a salient attribute. The restaurant could therefore emphasise that it makes a big difference to the enjoyment of the evening if the waiters are pleasant.

If the three components of attitude (cognition, affect and conation) are in balance, it is difficult to change the attitude because the attitude becomes stabilised. For example, if somebody is becoming overweight, believes that this is a bad thing and therefore diets, the attitude is stable and would be difficult to change. If, on the other hand, the same person is overweight, believes that it is bad but just somehow never gets round to dieting, it is relatively easy to tempt the person to 'treat' themselves to a snack or two. In the second case, the attitude is not consistent because the conation does not match with the affect and cognition. Changing a person's beliefs can be an effective route to attitude change (see Figure 7.10).

Inconsistency between the three components of attitude may come about when a new stimulus is presented. New information might affect the cognitive or conative aspects or a bad experience might change the affective aspects. When the degree of inconsistency between the three components exceeds a certain tolerance level, the individual will be compelled to undertake some kind of mental re-adjustment to restore stability (see Figure 7.11). This can come about through three main defence mechanisms:

1 Stimulus rejection.
2 Attitude splitting.
3 Accommodation to the new attitude.

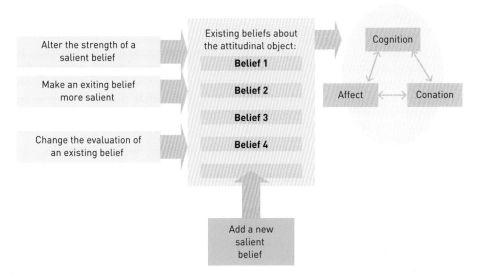

Figure 7.10 Changing beliefs

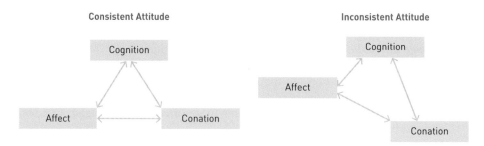

Figure 7.11   Consistent vs. inconsistent attitude

Stimulus rejection The
process of protecting
an attitude by ignoring
information that conflicts
with it

Stimulus rejection means that the individual discounts the new information. For example, an overweight person might reject advice that slim people live longer than fat people, on the grounds that the research does not examine people who used to be fat but are now slim and have kept the weight off. By rejecting the new information, the individual is able to maintain the status quo as regards the cognitive element of attitude. Sometimes stimuli are rejected simply because they come from a marketing source – there is evidence that consumers remember products which have been placed in movies and TV shows, but will often reject them because of a feeling of being manipulated (Bhatnagar and Aksoy 2004). Likewise, teenagers tend to respond better to new media such as the Internet and text messaging rather than to traditional mass media (Brennan et al. 2010). People are generally much more marketing-literate nowadays, and often know what marketers are trying to do as well as understanding how they intend to do it – marketers would do well to remember this.

Attitude splitting The
process of protecting an
attitude by accepting only
part of a new piece of
information that conflicts
with the attitude

Attitude splitting involves only accepting that part of the information that does not cause an inconsistency. Here, the individual might accept that the new information is basically true, but that his or her own circumstances are exceptional. For example, if an individual finds out that the company he or she was planning to sue has gone bankrupt, this will alter the conative element of attitude since it is impossible to sue a bankrupt company. The individual might agree that this is *generally* the case, but decide that the circumstances are such that he or she can sue the directors of the company instead.

**Accommodation to the new
attitude** Accepting new
information and using it to
re-form an existing attitude

Accommodation to the new attitude means, in effect, changing the attitude to accommodate the new information. The fat person may join a gym and start dieting, the smoker may cut down or give up altogether, the prospective litigant may just chalk it up to experience.

The three elements are so closely related to each other that a change in one element will usually cause a change in the others (Rosenberg 1960). New information causing a change in cognition will change the consumer's feelings about the product, which in turn is likely to change the consumer's intentions about the product.

Central route A route to
attitude change which relies
on reasoned argument: an
appeal to cognition, in other
words

The *elaboration likelihood model* (Petty et al. 1983) describes two routes by which attitude might be changed. The **central route** involves an appeal to the rational, cognitive element; the consumer makes a serious attempt to evaluate the new information in some logical way. The **peripheral route**, on the other hand, tends to involve the affective element by associating the product with another attitudinal object. For example, if a rock star appears in an ad for a soft drink this might cause the star's fans to change their attitudes towards the drink. This has nothing to do with the attributes

Peripheral route Using
emotional appeals in order
to change the affective
component of attitude

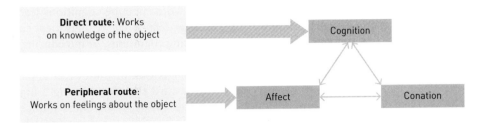

Figure 7.12   Peripheral and direct routes to attitude change

of the drink, but everything to do with the attributes of the star. Peripheral cues such as this are not relevant to a reasoned evaluation, but because of the interdependence of the components of attitude, change will occur. In effect, the affect felt towards the star 'rubs off' on the product.

Changing existing attitudes relies heavily on market research, but in particular the teasing-out of the factors that go to make up the attitude can be a demanding task. This is because of the halo effect – the tendency for attitudes about one salient belief to colour attitudes about another. For example, if a diner had a bad meal at a restaurant, this is likely to lead to a view that everything else about the restaurant was bad, too. Likewise, a favourable view of some factors often leads to respondents reporting a favourable view of other factors.

Halo effect The tendency for an individual to believe every aspect of something is good, based on a belief that some aspects are good

Challenging the status quo

Halo effect is said to be the process by which attitudes about one aspect of a product (or person) tend to colour the whole perception of the product (or person). Apparently, if we think our new car is really comfortable and cosy, we will also think its fuel consumption is good.

How about the reverse case? If we think something is really bad – perhaps the car is unreliable – do we then think its performance is bad as well? Probably so, if the theory is correct. In that case, what happens if something is brought to our attention? If the rock star we loved and admired turns out to be a paedophile, do we stop liking the music? If so, where does that leave the company that used that rock star in their advertising?

Using the peripheral route to attitude change means working on the affective component of attitude. Research has shown that emotional appeals often work a great deal more effectively than do cognitive, logical appeals; emotional appeals also appear to have a greater effect on explicit memory, so people remember the advertisement better (Williams 2003). Much depends on the group of individuals being studied. For example, studies have shown that campaigns to discourage smoking among teenagers work best on boys if they use emotional 'cosmetic' appeals (for example, telling boys that the smell of smoke on their clothing is repellent to girls) whereas long-term health appeals (a logical, cognitive approach) work better on teenage girls (Smith and Stutts 2003). Mood also has an effect on the interpretation of information: people in a good mood tend to process and remember brands better (Bakamitsos and Siomkos 2004).

Cognitive dissonance theory states that holding two competing cognitions leads to discomfort and an eventual readjustment (Festinger 1957). The readjustment can take two forms: rejecting one or other of the competing cognitions, or introducing a third idea which resolves the conflict between the other two.

The most interesting aspect of dissonance theory is that attitudes can apparently be changed more easily by offering a low reward than by offering a high reward. In a famous experiment conducted in the 1950s, researchers induced students to lie to other students about a task they were being recruited to undertake. The actual task was to place round pegs into holes, turn the pegs one-quarter turn, then remove the pegs. The students were told that this was a psychological experiment, and were then asked to recruit other students primarily by telling them how interesting and fun the task was. Since it would be difficult to imagine a more tedious task, these students obviously had to lie: the experimenters offered a recruitment reward, but some students were only offered $1 to lie, whereas others were offered $20 (a substantial sum of money in 1959). The students being paid the lower amount were found to actually believe the lie, whereas the higher-paid students simply told the lie as a lie without changing their own attitudes. The theory is that the higher-paid students justified lying on the basis that they were being well-paid for it, whereas the other students could not use this justification and therefore needed to find another reason for lying – in this case, they decided that actually what they were saying must be at least partly true (Festinger and Carlsmith 1959).

In Figure 7.13, the situation in which lying is linked to only a small reward leads to the attitude that the lie must be at least partly true, since the reward is not in itself sufficient to make lying worthwhile. In the second situation, the individual can justify lying on the basis that the reward is generous enough to justify not telling the truth, and therefore the lie remains a lie.

Cognitive dissonance is a powerful force in attitude change because the individual is, almost by definition, personally involved in the process. Reduction in dissonance always involves some kind of internal debate and (ultimately) some self-justification (Aronson et al. 1974). This happens because the individual tends to believe that the dissonance has arisen through an act or thought that is immoral or stupid. The most common manifestation of cognitive dissonance in consumer behaviour is post-purchase dissonance, in which someone who has just made an important purchase finds out that the product is not quite what was expected (see Figure 7.14). In other words, the individual has been presented with new information that contradicts his or her pre-purchase expectations. In most cases, actual experience with the product conflicts with information obtained in the

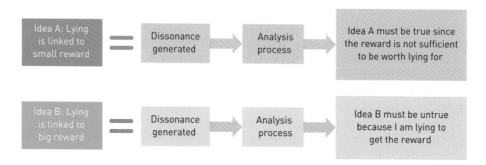

Figure 7.13 Cognitive dissonance

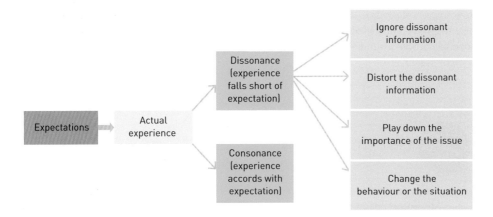

Figure 7.14 Post-purchase dissonance

pre-purchase information search. For example, someone buying a new flat-screen television set might have expected it to be wall-mountable, like a picture. On opening the packing, our new purchaser finds that the wall-mounting bracket makes the TV stand out six inches from the wall, and that this is a necessary factor because of the wiring, controls and air vents at the back of the set. At this point, the buyer has four basic choices:

1 Ignore the dissonant information and look for positive (consonant) information about the product. In the case of the TV, the buyer might just accept that the TV will stick out from the wall a bit and will instead admire the quality of the picture, the excellent stereo sound, the ease of tuning the set, and so forth.
2 Distort the dissonant information. In this case our buyer might convince himself or herself that the TV really does not stand away from the wall too much after all. With some careful lighting, no one will notice.
3 Play down the importance of the issue. Here the buyer simply says that the distance from the wall is really not that important anyway.
4 Change the behaviour or the situation. Our TV buyer might take the TV back to the shop and ask for a refund, or might decide to put the TV on a table instead, and buy a picture for the wall.

For marketers, minimising post-purchase dissonance is key to avoiding complaint behaviour. There is more on post-purchase evaluation in Chapter 13.

Summary

In this chapter we have looked at attitudes and how they are formed and maintained. We have also looked at ways of changing attitudes, and at some of the theories of attitude measurement.

Attitude is the starting point of all behaviour: people's attitudes inform their decision-making, create their motivations, and both create and are created by their consumption experiences. Marketers are always concerned with creating favourable attitudes towards both the product and the firm, and most marketing communications are aimed at developing those favourable attitudes.

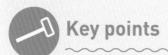

Key points

- Attitude is a learned construct that shows a person's tendency to respond to an object in a consistently favourable or unfavourable manner.
- Attitude is not neutral.
- Although attitude is not behaviour, it can be inferred from behaviour.
- Likewise, behaviour can be inferred from attitude, but the relationship is not reliable.
- Attitude is multidimensional, comprising affect, cognition and conation.
- Consumers only use salient beliefs when forming attitudes, not all the facts.
- Attitudes serve four useful purposes: instrumental, ego-defensive, value expressive and knowledge.
- Behaviour affects attitude more than attitude affects behaviour.
- Attitude has three dimensions: affect, cognition and conation.
- The strength of an attitude is determined by perceived instrumentality, evaluative aspect and value importance.
- People may also assess the difficulty of carrying out the behaviour when establishing an attitude.
- Attitudes may be public or private.
- Situations may prevent behaviour without altering attitude.
- Beliefs are the basis of cognitive change: this type of change comes about through the direct route.
- Emotions are the basis of affective change: this type of change comes about through the peripheral route.
- Post-purchase dissonance may evoke several possible complaint behaviours.

Review questions

1 What is the role of belief in forming attitudes?
2 How might marketers appeal to the cognitive element in attitude formation?
3 What is the difference between the ego-defensive role of attitude and the value-expressive role?
4 How might a marketer increase the strength of an attitude?
5 What is the purpose of measuring private attitudes?
6 How does situation affect attitude?
7 What processes might be important in forming attitudes?
8 What is the relationship between affect and the evaluative aspect of attitude strength?
9 What difficulties might exist when trying to infer attitude from behaviour?
10 How might beliefs be formed?

Case study revisited: Attitudes to smoking

In Florida, the decision was taken to carry out a counter-marketing campaign called Truth. This campaign did not seek to preach at teenagers; instead, it tapped into their underlying need for self-determination and independence.

The basis of the campaign was to show how the big tobacco companies were manipulating people into smoking. The campaign focused around the idea of a youth movement that would seek out the truth about tobacco, and would confront the tobacco companies. Billboards showed complacent-looking executives sneering at teenagers for being stupid enough to pay for their big cars and fat bonuses, and TV ads depicted teenagers confronting tobacco companies with the truth – that 1200 people a day die from smoking tobacco.

One TV advert (which went global on YouTube) showed some teenagers visiting a tobacco corporation headquarters and asking its chief executive some very pointed questions. This conversation quickly moved into a song-and-dance routine based on the line 'Let's all focus on the positives!' in which the tobacco company executives focus on the positives (such as getting something off your chest). The entire clip is surreal, but it avoids preaching, and it certainly shows teenagers controlling their own destinies.

The campaign relies heavily on attacking the adults (and especially the wealthy executives) who control the tobacco industry. Looking at the problem from a different perspective enables teenagers to resist peer pressure more easily – resisting because you don't want to be a dupe of big business is a lot easier than resisting because you're afraid you might get some disease or other.

The backers of the campaign, the American Legacy Foundation, claim that at least one million fewer teenagers now smoke as compared with the period before the campaign started. Interestingly, American Legacy Foundation was funded in large part by the tobacco companies, under an agreement that released them from obligations to compensate the Medicare programme for costs incurred by treating smokers, in exchange for funding both Medicare and American Legacy.

Final word from the Truth website:

'Heck, we love everybody. Our philosophy isn't anti-smoker or pro-smoker. It's not even about smoking. It's about the tobacco industry manipulating their products, research and advertising to secure replacements for the 1,200 customers they "lose" every day in America. You know, because they die.'

Powerful stuff.

Case study: Kindle

Kindle is an electronic device used for downloading, storing and reading books. It is available from Amazon, the on-line bookshop, and has been around since 2007.

Kindle is an unusual device because it uses a different type of display from the system used for computer screens and telephones. Rather than a lighted screen, Kindle uses electronic 'ink' to create the display. The display is in black and white (or, more accurately, black and grey) and looks very similar to a printed page. The result is a page that reads like a book, without any strain on the eyes. The Kindle device allows people to download wirelessly from anywhere in the UK and many other countries. E-books are considerably cheaper than hard copies, and indeed some books are free – books that are out of copyright, such as Samuel Pepys' Diary, can be downloaded for nothing.

As with any radical new technology, people need to be convinced that it will do what it says it will do. A Kindle represents quite an investment – the first models sold for $399 – and book readers are notoriously conservative. If Kindle was to shift people's attitudes, some work would need to be done.

First, Amazon briefed the designers to create a reading system that the reader would forget about. The aim was to make the medium (the Kindle) as forgettable in use as a paper book – in other words, the reader should very quickly become engrossed in the reading, with the device being so easy to operate the reader would not notice it at all. Operation therefore needed to be fairly intuitive – not easy to achieve in an electronic device.

Second, the device needed a very long battery life. This would prevent people from continually being disturbed in their reading by having to recharge the device. Third, the device needed to be extremely lightweight – certainly no heavier than a small book. Finally, it would need to have a large memory, capable of holding a substantial library.

The Kindle never becomes hot, unlike a notebook computer, and in effect it disappears while the reader uses it – rather like a traditional paper book.

Amazon's approach to marketing is generally very low-key. The company relies heavily on word of mouth from its customers, and on its website to generate business: in the case of the Kindle, the product itself was so revolutionary that the company's founder, Jeff Bezos, was able to give interviews to the media in order to promote the product. After that, the company basically just let nature take its course, and was able to rely on the huge amount of web traffic its sites experience to promote the product.

Word of mouth was very strong and very effective in shifting attitudes. The product itself is so exciting people couldn't resist telling friends about it: there was a small amount of low-key advertising, but typically it was linked to the books rather than to the Kindle device itself (saying that such and such a book was available on Kindle, for example) and the whole tone of the company's promotion seemed to centre around the idea that owning a Kindle was just a very normal thing, that anyone with any sense would naturally do.

The results have been dramatic. Kindles have sold in their millions worldwide, and although Amazon are a little cagey about exact numbers, in December 2011 the company announced that sales had exceeded one million units per week – obviously Kindles were a popular Christmas gift that year. More to the point, people do use Kindle. In August 2012, Amazon announced that sales of books on Kindle in the UK had, for the first time, exceeded sales of traditional paper books.

Questions

1 Which route to attitude change does Kindle appear to have used?
2 Why is it important that the Kindle should 'disappear' in use?
3 Why is word of mouth so important in this context?
4 What salient beliefs about electronic devices might have needed to be changed?
5 Why might someone feel moved to tell friends about Kindle?

Further reading

As an example of how attitude is formed in an online environment, you might enjoy
     Miller, C.H., Reardon, J., Salciuviene, L., Auruskeviciene, V., Lee, K. and Miller, K.

(2009) Need for cognition as a moderator of affective and cognitive elements in online attitude toward the brand formation. *Journal of Business and Economics Research* 7 (12): 65–72.

For an interesting study in how an unpopular or counter-social attitude can affect the way an individual fits into a culture, read Piacentini, M. and Banister, E.N. (2009) Managing anti-consumption in an excessive drinking culture. *Journal of Business Research* 62: 279–88. This paper is about the experiences of students who do not like to engage in heavy drinking.

For a good book on attitude and attitude change, try Greg Maio and Geoff Haddock's *The Psychology of Attitudes and Attitude Change* (London: Sage, 2009). In particular, this book explains clearly how attitudes can be used to predict behaviour.

A textbook that cuts through the mass of theory and jargon about attitude is Philip Erwin's *Attitudes and Persuasion* (Hove: Psychology Press, 2001). It is written in a no-nonsense, straightforward style, and gives a good road map of the subject.

References

Ajzen, I. (1988) *Attitudes, Personality and Behaviour.* Milton Keynes: Open University Press.

Ajzen, I. and Fishbein, M. (1980) *Understanding Attitudes and Predicting Social Behaviour.* Englewood Cliffs, NJ: Prentice-Hall.

Ajzen, I. and Madden, T.J. (1986) Prediction of goal-directed behaviour: attitudes, intentions and perceived behaviour control. *Journal of Experimental Social Psychology* 22 (5): 453–74.

Aronson, E., Chase, T., Helmreich, R. and Ruhnke, R. (1974) A two-factor theory of dissonance reduction: the effect of feeling stupid or feeling awful on opinion change. *International Journal of Communication Research* 3: 340–52.

Bakamitsos, G. and Siomkos, G. (2004) Context effects in marketing practice: the case of mood. *Journal of Consumer Behaviour* 3 (4): 304–14.

Berger, I.E. and Mitchell, A.A. (1989) The effect of advertising on attitude accessibility, attitude confidence, and the attitude–behaviour relationship. *Journal of Consumer Research* 16 (Dec): 269–79.

Bhatnagar, N., and Aksoy, L. (2004) Et tu, Brutus? A case for consumer skepticism and backlash against product placements. *Advances in Consumer Research* 31: 87–8.

Biel, A.L. (1990) Love the ad. Buy the product? *ADMAP* 299 (Sep): 21–5.

Biel, A.L. and Bridgwater, C.A. (1990) Attributes of likeable television commercials. *Journal of Advertising Research* 30 (3): 38–44.

Bless, H., Wanke, M. and Schwartz, N. (2002) The inclusion/exclusion model as a framework for predicting the direction and size of context effects in consumer judgments. *Advances in Consumer Research* 29: 86–7.

Brennan, R., Dahl, S. and Eagle, L. (2010) Persuading young consumers to make healthy nutrition decisions. *Journal of Marketing Management* 26 (7&8): 635–55.

Cote, J.A., McCullough, J. and Reilly, M. (1985) Effects of unexpected situations on behaviour–intention differences: a garbology analysis. *Journal of Consumer Research* 12 (2): 188–94.

Festinger, L. (1957) *A Theory of Cognitive Dissonance.* Stanford, CA: Stanford University Press.

Festinger, L. and Carlsmith, J.M. (1959) Cognitive consequences of forced compliance. *Journal of Abnormal and Social Psychology* 58: 203–10.

Fishbein, M. (1972) The search for attitudinal–behavioural consistency. In Joel E. Cohen (ed.), *Behavioural Science Foundations of Consumer Behaviour.* New York: Free Press.

Fishbein, M. (1980) An overview of the attitude construct. In G.B. Hafer (ed.), *A Look Back, A Look Ahead.* Chicago, IL: American Marketing Association.

Fishbein, M. and Ajzen, I. (1975) *Belief, Attitude, Intention and Behaviour: An Introduction to Theory and Research.* Reading, MA: Addison-Wesley.

Gamliel, E. (2010) Message framing of products causes a preference shift in consumers' choices. *Journal of Consumer Behaviour* (Jul/Aug) 9 (4): 303–15.

Gurau, C. and Tinson, J. (2003) Early evangelist or reluctant Rudolph? Attitudes towards the Christmas commercial campaign. *Journal of Consumer Behaviour* 3 (1): 48–62.

Hernandez, M.D., Wang, Y.J., Minor, M.S. and Liu, Q. (2008) Effects of superstitious beliefs on consumer novelty seeking and independent judgement making: evidence from China. *Journal of Consumer Behaviour* 7 (6): 424–35.

Homer, P.M. and Yoon, S. (1992) Message framing and the interrelationships among ad-based feelings, affect and cognition. *Journal of Advertising* 21 (March): 19–33.

Hsee, C.K. and Rottenstreich, Y. (2002) Panda, mugger and music: on the affective psychology of value. *Advances in Consumer Research* 29: 60.

Kahneman, D. and Tverksy, A. (1979) Prospect theory: an analysis of decision under risk. *Econometrica* 47 (2) (March): 263–92.

Locander, W.B. and Spivey, W.A. (1978) A functional approach to the study of attitude measurement. *Journal of Marketing Research* 15 (Nov): 576–87.

Mishra, A., Mishra, H. and Nayakankuppam, D. (2006) Meddling in of affect in information integration. *Advances in Consumer Research* 33: 48.

Mitchell, A.A. (1986) The effect of verbal and visual components of advertisements on brand attitudes and attitudes towards the advertisements. *Journal of Consumer Research* 13: 12–24.

Onkvisit, S. and Shaw, J.J.(1994) *Consumer Behaviour, Strategy and Analysis.* New York: Macmillan.

Petty, R.E., Caccioppo, J. and Schumann, D. (1983) Central and peripheral routes to advertising effectiveness. *Journal of Consumer Research* 10 (Sep): 135–46.

Ponchio, M.C. and Aranha, F. (2008) Materialism as a predictor variable of low income consumer behaviour when entering into instalment plan agreements. *Journal of Consumer Behaviour* 7 (1): 21–34.

Qin, W. and Brown, J.L. (2008) Factors explaining male/female differences in attitudes and purchase intention toward genetically engineered salmon. *Journal of Consumer Behaviour* 7 (2): 127–45.

Reinhard, M. and Messner, M. (2009) The effects of source likeability and need for cognition on advertising effectiveness under explicit persuasion. *Journal of Consumer Behaviour* 8 (4): 179–91.

Rosenberg, M.J. (1960) An analysis of affective-cognitive consistency. In Milton J. Rosenberg et al. (eds), *Attitude Organisation and Change.* New Haven, CT: Yale University Press.

Singh, J. (1988) Consumer complaint intentions and behaviour: definitions and taxonomical issues. *Journal of Marketing* 52 (Jan): 93–107.

Smith, K.H. and Stutts, M.A. (2003) Effects of short-term versus long-term health fear appeals in anti-smoking advertisements on the smoking behaviour of adolescents. *Journal of Consumer Behaviour* 3 (2): 155–77.

Smith, R.E. and Swinyard, W.R. (1983) Attitude–behaviour consistency: the impact of product trial versus advertising. *Journal of Marketing Research* 20 (3): 257–67.

Stapel, J. (1991) Like the advertisement but does it interest me? *ADMAP*, April.

Williams, P. (2003) The impact of emotional advertising appeals on implicit and explicit memory: an accessibility/diagnosticity perspective. *Advances in Consumer Research* 30 (1): 87–8.

Zajonc, R.B. and Markus, H. (1985) Must all affect be mediated by cognition? *Journal of Consumer Research* 12 (Dec): 363–4.

More online

To gain free access to additional online resources to support this chapter please visit: **www.sagepub.co.uk/blythe**

Part Three

Sociological issues in consumer behaviour

Although people are individuals, they act in groups. Human beings are herd animals, and rely heavily on each other for support, advice, practical help, entertainment and security.

Chapter 8 is about the social environment in which we live and behave. Our social class and culture are derived from the people around us, and form the basis for our social behaviour as well as our understanding of who we are as individuals. This naturally affects our purchase behaviour, since we buy things that tend to validate our status.

Chapter 9 is about the types of group of which we are members. These groups have a great influence on us as sources of information, as 'sanity checks' to ensure that we are behaving appropriately, and as support systems for us in our daily lives. Each group influences us in different ways, but each group has its own role in helping us to function effectively as human beings.

Finally, Chapter 10 is devoted to the most influential group of all – the family. It is through our families that we first learned to behave appropriately, and as we get older and have children of our own we are influenced by their needs (as well as having a role in teaching them to be effective consumers). However the family is defined, and however humanity might change the structure of what is considered to be the family, the closeness of kinship and shared consumption will always ensure that families are at the heart of what makes us what we are.

CHAPTER (8)

The environment, class and culture

LEARNING OBJECTIVES

After reading this chapter you should be able to:

- Explain how store atmospherics affect consumer behaviour.

- Understand what is meant by the functional environment.

- Explain how cultural factors colour our purchasing behaviour.

- Describe the difference between high-context cultures and low-context cultures.

- Understand the problems raised for people who move from one culture to another.

- Describe how class distinctions have changed in the last fifty years or so.

Introduction

This chapter is about the contexts within which behaviour takes place. Individual decision-making always occurs within a social, cultural, environmental or class context, since human beings interact and need to consider the responses of others. Also, the physical environment within which decisions are made can affect the outcomes dramatically: some environments are conducive to paying higher prices, or buying more of a specific type of product, whereas others encourage greater thrift.

Culture provides the social environment within which people live. This chapter also considers what happens when people change culture, or when their own culture shifts around them; it also considers the variations within a culture that are called subcultures.

Subculture A set of beliefs and attitudes which, while part of a main culture, represents a distinctly separate set

Case study: Flying for fun

There are approximately 21,000 civil aircraft registered in the UK, 96% of which are used by private pilots for pleasure flying or training. In Britain, 28,000 people hold a private pilot's licence of one sort or another, and in addition there are around 10,000 certified glider pilots. Perhaps surprisingly, many professional commercial pilots also fly light aircraft as a pastime – clearly there is a big difference between flying a Boeing 747 and a Cessna 152.

Private flying happens in a wide variety of aircraft. At the wealthier end, there are jet aircraft and helicopters – lottery winners and successful businessmen are the main pilots of these, but there are also plenty of ex-military pilots who fly occasionally to maintain their ratings, and people of modest means who put every spare penny into flying. At the more economical end, there are microlight pilots who perhaps share a small aircraft with others, flying at evenings and weekends, and maintaining (or even building) the aircraft themselves. Costs vary greatly, of course – a helicopter is likely to cost at least £250 an hour to fly, whereas a microlight might only cost £15 an hour, including fuel and maintenance.

Pilots fly from all kinds of airfields – everything from Second World War ex-RAF bases to farmers' fields, and (interestingly) there is no record of how many airfields there are in the UK. Many do not need to be licensed in any way, and landowners are allowed to use their fields as airstrips for 28 days of the year without asking for planning permission. Many parts of the country are not subject to air traffic control, especially at the low levels most light aircraft use, so there is nothing to stop a qualified pilot from buying a microlight, parking it at a local farm and flying at most weekends.

Private flying appears to be a solitary occupation – yet pilots congregate together frequently, to swap stories, seek advice and organise social events. The love of flying is the glue that holds them together.

How to impress your examiner

Questions about culture will definitely benefit from giving examples of how culture affects purchasing behaviour. You should be very wary of ethnocentrism – the belief that your own culture is the 'right' one – because this will make you sound patronising. You should be able to critique Hofstede's findings as well.

Questions about the environment will involve discussion of atmospherics. Remember that atmospherics includes other customers: also, the atmosphere, decor etc. will affect different people in different ways, so that some people will like one type of decor, whereas others will not.

Class is a shifting concept. Questions about class often assume that people remain in a particular class for their entire lives, so it is worthwhile mentioning social mobility.

Environmental influences

The environment refers to the physical surroundings in which decision-making takes place. It includes physical objects (the products themselves, the display stands in stores and even the stores themselves), spatial relationships (the location of products in stores, the amount of space available within the stores, the location of the stores) and the behaviour of other people within the environment.

For example, the shopping experience in an upmarket department store such as Harrod's in London, El Corte Ingles in Madrid or David Jones in Sydney is a great deal different from the shopping experience in markets such as Brick Lane in London, the Rastro market in Madrid or the Kirribilli market in Sydney. The actual goods on offer may even be the same in many cases, but the level of service, the behaviour of fellow shoppers and the general atmosphere will be totally different, as of course will be the prices.

Figure 8.1 shows some of the relationships between elements of the environment. The level of service, decor, presence or absence of music, and the other customers in the store all affect the store's brand image, but other factors over which the store management has little or no control will also affect the functional environment, which in turn affects the buying behaviour of the individual shoppers.

At a more subtle level, people may be influenced by factors such as music played within the store, use of colour in the store and the perceived social class of other store users. For a marketer, the difficulty lies in assessing which factors are crucial, and how those factors might affect different people; some people like to have music playing in-store, for example, whereas others are irritated by it. Likewise, some people enjoy the buzz and bustle of shopping in a street market, whereas others might find it distracting or even threatening.

Class The social and economic grouping of individuals

The concept of store atmospherics was first described by Kotler (1973). Atmospherics are all the factors that go to make up the atmosphere and general 'feel' of a retail store:

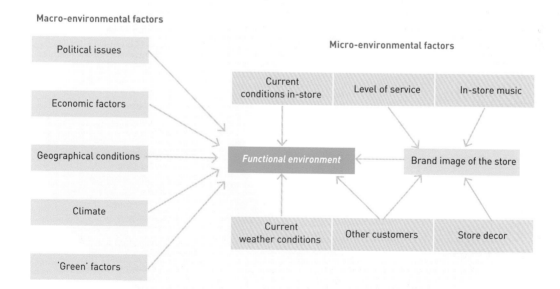

Figure 8.1 Elements in the environment

the decor, the music, the temperature and humidity, and so forth. Atmospherics go a long way towards determining whether a customer remains in the store longer, spends more (or less) money and returns at a later date. Since Kotler, researchers have taken two basic approaches to researching atmospherics. The first approach concentrates on the factors that make up store atmosphere, whereas the other approach regards atmosphere in a holistic way and concentrates instead on its effects on consumers. Under the first approach, studies have been made of colour and lighting (Bellizzi et al. 1983), social factors (Baker et al. 1992), music and lighting (Kellaris and Kent 1992), crowding (Eroglu and Harrell 1986) and point-of-purchase displays (Philips and Bradshaw 1990). There are two common findings in these studies: first, that manipulating these various elements correctly can result in outcomes favourable to the retailer, i.e. people stay in the store longer and spend more money, and second, that these elements affect people's physical and psychological states, and hence their behaviour.

The second main thrust of research, an examination of the kind of effects atmospherics have on people, has produced some interesting results. Several researchers have used the Mehrabian–Russell Environmental Psychology Model to explain some of the features of store atmospherics (Mehrabian and Russell 1974). The M–R Model says that environmental stimuli lead to emotional states (e.g. pleasure or arousal) which then lead to approach or avoidance responses. In a study of CD shops in Hong Kong, researchers were able to expand and modify the model to provide the example shown in Figure 8.2 (Tai and Fung 1997).

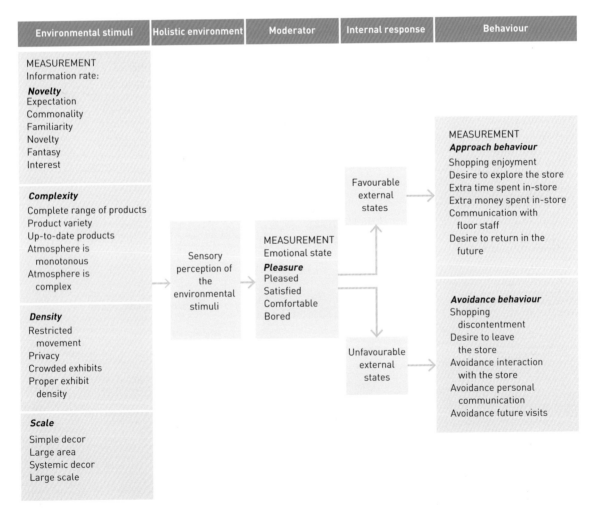

Figure 8.2   Adapted Mehrabian–Russell model

Figure 8.3 The functional environment

The left-hand box in the model refers to the information rate. This is the degree to which the shopper is exposed to novelty and surprise – the more novel the environment, the greater the information rate. Likewise, the more complex the environment the higher the information rate. Mehrabian and Russell (1974) postulate that an individual's propensity to develop approach or avoidance behaviours is a function of three elements – pleasure (or displeasure), arousal (or boredom) and dominance (or submission). In the study of CD stores, the researchers found that information rates have a marked effect on arousal, but not necessarily on pleasure: in other words customers did not necessarily like having a high information rate, even though they found it stimulating or exciting. The researchers further found that in-store behaviour contributed more to the pleasure of the experience, so from a marketer's viewpoint it would seem sensible to allow people plenty of latitude to examine goods, interact with staff and so forth.

The environment as perceived by the consumers themselves is called the functional (or perceived) environment (Block and Block 1981). The functional environment will be different for each individual, because individuals differ in their knowledge, beliefs, experience and (of course) preference. Since marketers generally deal with groups of people rather than individuals, subtle differences and idiosyncrasies are likely to be ignored in favour of creating a generally acceptable environment for the target group of customers.

Figure 8.3 shows some of the elements of the functional environment. The macro-environment affects everything else, including the store and its branding: store decor, music, service levels and other customers all affect the store's brand image, but the behaviour and number of other customers also affect the functional environment directly. The current conditions in the store (crowding, cleanliness, availability of assistants) and the current weather (whether it is hot, rainy, cold) have a direct bearing on the functional environment. There are of course many other factors that may affect the individual: situational factors such as time pressures, physical interrupts such as hunger or thirst, and so forth. Since the functional environment is subjective, the individual's personality, tastes, moods and behaviour act as moderating factors.

 Challenging the status quo

It sounds as if the functional environment is really difficult to deal with. It's subjective, it's easily affected by factors over which we have absolutely no control and it changes with every passing minute. So why do we bother? Why not just pile everything up on the counter, and hope people buy it?

Maybe that's a bit of an exaggeration, though. Maybe we should influence the bits we can influence, and live with the bits we can't influence. At least we'll be able to make SOME difference to people's perceptions!

The subjective nature of the functional environment can be problematical in an international context, because there are often marked differences between individuals in different countries; even with the European Union this is a problem, despite the relative similarities between member states in terms of wealth, aspirations and product availability (Askegaard and Madsen 1995). Because of this, it is tempting for marketers to treat each country as a separate segment, whereas in fact this can be inappropriate since new transnational segments are appearing as people travel more and the European Union converges (Brunso et al. 1996). Recent research identified four consumer styles which transcend national boundaries (McCarty et al. 2007):

1 *Price-sensitive consumers*. These are people who check prices, shop around for special offers and are not brand-loyal.
2 *Variety-seekers*. These people like to try new things and are the first to buy new products.
3 *Brand-loyal consumers*. These people buy known brands, and are likely to be brand-loyal even when this costs more; they are less likely to check prices or shop around for bargains.
4 *Information-seekers*. These people exchange information with other people, are more receptive to advertising and will try new products but tend to stick to known brands.

Other styles identified in the research differed across cultural boundaries – German consumers are less brand-loyal and more price-sensitive than consumers from some other countries, but they tend to enjoy shopping more than the French do, for example.

In the context of consumer behaviour, the environmental factors can be divided into macro-environmental factors (climate, economy, politics, geography, and so forth) and micro-environmental factors, such as the shop assistant, the store's cleanliness and decor, the current weather conditions and the other shoppers. Each of these factors is relevant: macro-economic factors will dictate what people need to buy in terms of clothing, housing, transport and so forth, as well as what they are able to buy either as a result of their wealth or as a result of legal restrictions or requirements. Micro-economic factors influence decision-making at the point of purchase: people are unlikely to linger in noisy, crowded or dirty stores, and they become frustrated if there are long queues at checkouts (Park et al. 1989).

Macro-environment
Those environmental elements that are common to all firms in a given industry

Micro-environment
Those elements of the environment that affect the individual firm

Consumer behaviour in action: Avoiding the queue

Nobody likes having to wait around in a queue, and nowhere is it worse than in supermarkets. Having found what you want, you find yourself waiting for a checkout operator to finish dealing with a slow or difficult customer, while your frozen foods melt and your fresh vegetables wilt. Research shows that 68% of shoppers will simply drop the goods and walk out if they have to wait too long – a real problem for supermarkets, who then have to replace goods on shelves or (in the case of frozen food) simply dump the products.

Tesco Stores, the giant UK supermarket chain, has an interesting approach to reducing queues at its checkouts. The aim of each store is to allow no more than one person to be ahead of each customer in the queue. Although in practice this is impossible, Tesco have managed to use computer technology to minimise the waiting time of its customers.

Every 15 minutes each till freezes and can only be unlocked by the checkout operator entering the number of people waiting in the queue. This process takes a moment, but it provides store managers with instant information. The managers can then open up more checkouts, using back-up operators, until either the queues have reduced or all the tills are open and no more can be done. At the same time, the tills send the data through to the central Tesco computer, which calculates the average number of times in the day that there is a longer queue than two people. Store managers are expected to reach their targets 95% of the time, so if there are more than two people in the queue on

more than 5% of the times the operators enter the number, the managers are asked to account for themselves. This leads them to try to anticipate potential bottlenecks and organise staff breaks and so forth accordingly – one simple method is to observe how many people enter the store, since this gives an advance warning of how many of them are likely to be at the checkouts in the near future.

This system means that Tesco have shorter queues at the checkouts than almost any other supermarket – a real benefit to customers, and one that does not cost the company anything beyond a few seconds spent by checkout operators in entering a single number. Customers like the system, and it is rare for anyone to be seen dumping goods and walking out of a Tesco store.

The social environment

The social environment includes all the behavioural inputs received from other people. In some cases, these may be direct interactions (a conversation with a salesperson, advice from a friend, an encounter with someone unpleasant) and in other cases they may be indirect (observing how a friend negotiates with a vendor, seeing an advertisement on TV, seeing how other people act in a new social situation).

The social environment can also be divided into macro- and micro-environments. The macro-environment has three components: culture, subculture and social class. Each of these has profound influences on behaviour because they have been powerful drivers in the formation of attitudes, beliefs and values. Although people from the same cultural background differ considerably among themselves, there will still be similarities. Each of these elements will be dealt with in more detail later in this chapter.

As shown in Figure 8.4, the micro social environment comprises the face-to-face social interactions we have with our friends, work colleagues, family and others in the groups of which we are members. These micro-environmental interactions will be dealt with in more detail in the next two chapters. The macro-environment comprises those factors that are common to everyone living within the same country or region; in other words, those factors that affect us all.

Culture

Culture is the set of shared beliefs, attitudes and behaviours associated with a large and distinct group of people. Culture is learned, but it is often so deeply ingrained

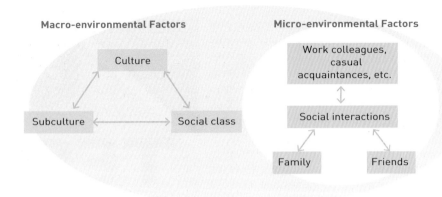

Figure 8.4   The social environment

in people that they imagine that the rules of their particular society or group have the status of natural laws. As a result, culture is one of the main drivers of behaviour and influences almost everything we do, including (of course) our consumption behaviour.

The main elements of culture, summarised in Figure 8.5, are as follows:

- *Religion*. Religious beliefs colour people's behaviour in many ways, from laying down rules about clothing to prescribing which foods are permissible and which are not. For example, for many years Roman Catholics were officially forbidden (as a fast or a penance) to eat meat on Fridays, which many interpreted as an injunction to eat fish instead. Even after the original religious injunction was relaxed (on the basis that eating lobster thermidor could hardly be considered a fast or a penance) people continued the tradition of having at least one fish meal on a Friday. The stricter restrictions on Muslims and Jews against eating pork, and the symbolic meal taken by Christians during Communion, are other examples.
- *Language*. Language clearly affects purchasing behaviour in many ways. First, the ability to understand and act on marketing communications relies not only on understanding the specific language but also on understanding specific words and sentence constructions within the language. For example, slang terms and puns might not be accessible to all the observers of the communication, and communications written in dialect might not be understood by non-native speakers of the language. Second, some products (such as books and newspapers) are clearly of no use to someone who does not understand the language in which they are written. The market for books in Welsh, for example, is confined to Wales and parts of Argentina, with few (if any) sales elsewhere. The structure and rules of languages can affect consumer perceptions: in languages where brand names acquire gender (Spanish and French, for example) this will affect consumer perception of the product as being either masculine or feminine. In languages that include a neuter gender (English and Greek are examples) this is not an issue unless the marketer deliberately uses a masculine or feminine ending on the brand name (Yorkston and deMello 2004).
- *Customs*. These are norms of behaviour handed down from the past. Some customs grow out of religious beliefs (many of the traditions associated with Christmas have come from Christian belief, although some are pagan or pre-Christian), while others come from traditions associated with climate or shared

experiences. For example, throughout most of southern Spain villages and towns celebrate the Fiesta of 'Moros y Cristianos' which refers to the overthrow of the Moorish invaders between 722 and 1492 AD. The date varies in each village, as each village overthrew its Moors on a different date, but for most it is a spectacular celebration involving fireworks (symbolising the fighting and also the traditional destruction of remaining ammunition to show that the shooting really is over) and a great deal of dancing and partying throughout the night.

- *Food.* Food is strongly linked to culture. While cheese is regarded as an essential part of any meal in France, and each region of the country produces several distinct examples, in Japan it is regarded as being as appealing as rotted milk and is a somewhat exotic food. In Britain, people will not eat insects but will happily eat prawns, while in Zambia deep-fried caterpillars are a delicacy. In Mexico, the tortilla has a cultural significance that is bound up in what it means to be a Mexican, but (paradoxically) there is an underlying belief that everything emanating from the United States is better than anything Mexican: there is evidence that even American tortillas are considered to be somehow better than Mexican ones (Gabel and Boller 2003). These differences in taste are explained by culture rather than by random differences in taste between individuals: behaviours tend to be shared by people from the same cultural background.

- Mores. Mores are customs with a strong moral incentive. In most societies, cannibalism is regarded as immoral and is not part of the cultural mores; in other societies (most of them in the past) cannibalism is not only moral but is regarded as a necessary and respectful way of dealing with dead people. Violation of mores often results in strong reactions from other members of the culture – in some cases these can be abusive or even violent, while in other cases the law becomes involved and the individual receives a formalised punishment. Mores **Elements** of a culture

- *Conventions.* These are norms regarding the conduct of everyday life. For example, in the UK a dinner guest would normally be expected to bring a bottle of wine, and many dinner guests would also bring flowers; in Hawaii people would bring small snacks called puu-puus. Some spoken phrases are conventional – someone who asks you 'How are you?' is expecting the answer, 'Fine, thanks' rather than an actual description of the other person's current circumstances. Table manners, appropriate clothing for formal occasions and rules about when it is permissible to make a noise (for example, play loud music) and when it is not are also examples of conventions.

- *Myths.* A myth is a story that contains symbolic elements expressing the shared emotions and ideals of a culture. The outcome of a myth might illustrate a particular moral pathway, and it thus serves to provide a guideline to the world. An example might be the 'urban myths' that often circulate by e-mail, to warn people of inappropriate behaviour or to provide entertainment.

- *Rituals.* A ritual is a set of symbolic behaviours that occur in a fixed sequence. For example, weddings follow a fairly well-defined path in most cases, and there are many rituals attached to sporting events such as football matches. The singing of specific songs, the consumption of specific foods or beverages (few football fans would watch the match while drinking a glass of Chardonnay – beer is the ritual drink) and the wearing of specific clothing are all ritualistic. Many people have grooming rituals (brushing one's hair 100 times each day, showering to a specific pattern, and so forth) which serve to transform the individual from the private persona to the public persona. Gift-giving is another example of a ritual – in most Western cultures, gifts should be wrapped in attractive paper and should contain an element of surprise, the price tag should be removed and the recipient has to look pleased to receive the gift. Deviation from this ritual causes discomfort for one or the other party to the transaction. In China, on the other hand, giving a gift imposes an obligation on the recipient to do the other person a favour at some time or to reciprocate; over-effusive thanks for a gift can be interpreted as an attempt to avoid this obligation.

- *Rites of passage.* A rite of passage is an event or a set of behaviours that moves an individual from one state to another. The Freshers' Ball at university is an example, as is the traditional 21st birthday party, which of course relates to the time when 21-year-olds were regarded as full adults. This has been diluted somewhat by changes in legislation, which now confers full responsibilities and rights at different stages during an individual's teenage years. In Japan, where the age of majority is 20, there is a special public holiday dedicated to those who will reach age 20 during that year. Some rites of passage are more individual in nature: marriage ceremonies or divorce proceedings are rites of passage between the single and married states, but may occur at almost any stage in the individual's adult life, or may not occur at all. Rites of passage are important to people as statements of status, and new rites are invented periodically to take account of new situations: legislation in the UK has allowed same-sex 'marriages' through the Civil Partnership rules, and at a more mundane level there are definite rituals that are observed when someone changes job.
- *Sacred consumption.* Some places are set apart as special because something of great significance happened there. In some cases these places have mystical or religious significance, for example Stonehenge or Bethlehem, while in other cases the place might have no religious significance as such but acquires sacred qualities. A prime example is the Millennium Stadium in Cardiff, UK. The actual pitch is often referred to as 'the hallowed turf' and there have been numerous attempts (some successful) to scatter the ashes of deceased Welsh rugby fans on the pitch.

These elements of culture are common to all cultures, but vary in type and importance between cultures. For some cultures, religion is almost the defining factor: Islamic states that operate under Sharia law as laid down in the Koran, and countries such as Spain where fiestas, public holidays and many aspects of daily life are conducted with reference to the Catholic church, are prime examples. For other cultures, other aspects may contribute more.

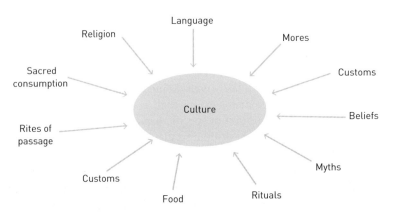

Figure 8.5   Elements of culture

Consumer behaviour in action: Football violence?

In some cultures, football seems to have acquired religious status. Feelings run high when people build their entire self-images around supporting a particular football team, and football matches worldwide have often been accompanied by riots and violent behaviour on the part of fans. Often this is thought of as a particularly British activity, but even the most violent British fans would be hard-put to keep up with Latin American fans.

The most violence ever attributed to football occurred in 1969 when Honduras and El Salvador were competing in the qualifying rounds of the World Cup. The Salvadoran team was set to play the Honduran team at the Tegucigalpa stadium in Honduras. The night before the match, the Salvadoran team was besieged in their hotel by a hostile crowd of Hondurans letting off fireworks, sounding their car horns and throwing stones at the windows. Not unnaturally, after having had a poor night's sleep, the Salvadorans lost 1–0 the following day. This might have been a minor incident had not one of the Salvadoran fans, 18-year-old Amelia Bolanios, shot herself through the heart with her father's pistol after witnessing the Honduran goal. She was accorded a state funeral with the President of the Republic among the mourners.

Unfortunately, the two teams ended up tied on points so the match had to be replayed, this time at the Flor Bancal stadium in San Salvador. The Salvadorans were ready for the Honduran team – this time the hotel windows were shattered and rotting animal carcasses thrown into the rooms. At the match, the Hondurans were delivered by armoured car and a military cordon armed with machine guns surrounded the pitch. The match organisers burned the Honduran flag in front of the players and ran a dirty dishcloth up the flagpole in its place, so the Hondurans were in no doubt as to the feelings of the Salvadorans. Honduras lost 3–0 this time, and the team was rushed away to the airport and flown home.

The Honduran fans were not so lucky. Fleeing for the border, many were caught and killed and hundreds were seriously injured. Within hours the border was sealed off. At dusk the next day a Salvadoran military aircraft bombed the Tegucigalpa stadium and the city was blacked out. Cross-border gunfire developed during the night, and border villages were shelled and destroyed. On both sides of the border nationals of the other country were rounded up and imprisoned (ironically) in football stadiums. The war only lasted five days, due to pressure from neighbouring Latin American countries, but during that period over 6000 people were killed and 15,000 seriously injured, plus thousands were left homeless.

A peace treaty between the two countries was finally signed in 1980, eleven years after the war began, but there is still ill-feeling between the countries and the occasional shot is fired across the border.

In the immortal words of Bill Shankly: *'Some people believe football is a matter of life and death. I'm very disappointed with that attitude. I can assure you it is much, much more important than that.'*

To an extent, national characteristics can be identified. The most famous (and widely taught) study of national characteristics is that of Hofstede (1980). This research reports on a study of 6000 respondents in 66 countries, all of whom worked for IBM. Hofstede initially identified four cultural dimensions, as follows:

- *Individualism vs. collectivism.* This is the degree to which the culture values *individualism and individual freedom above that of the group.*
- *Uncertainty avoidance.* This is the degree to which the culture adheres to rules and customs to avoid risk.
- *Power distance.* This is the degree to which power is centralised in the culture.
- *Masculinity–femininity.* This is the degree to which the culture exhibits 'masculine' qualities of assertiveness, achievement and wealth acquisition rather than the 'feminine' attributes of nurturing, concern for the environment and concern for the poor.

Hofstede later revisited the data and the problem, and came up with a fifth dimension. This is long-term versus short-term orientation, and is a dimension that is particularly relevant to Oriental cultures.

These categorisations, summarised in Figure 8.6, are interesting, and may be useful for planning the overall tone of a communications campaign, but it would be dangerous to make assumptions about individuals based on these broad generalisations. The average Taiwanese may be more collectivist than the average American, but the most individualistic Taiwanese is likely to be a great deal more individualistic than the most collectivist American.

Hofstede's research has been widely criticised for several reasons. First, the research was conducted with IBM employees, and since IBM has a strong corporate culture it seems likely that this will have affected the results. Second, Hofstede was concerned mainly with work-related values rather than with consumer behaviour, yet the research has often been used to justify marketing communication activities. Third, the actual survey was conducted in the late 1960s, more than forty years ago, and the world has become considerably more globalised since then – recent research shows that the opening up of China, for example, has resulted in markedly changed attitudes to cosmetic surgery, formerly the prerogative of Western societies (Lindridge and Wang 2008). Even then, though, the same research showed that participants were encouraged to undergo plastic surgery because of the interplay of traditional Chinese hierarchies of family and society.

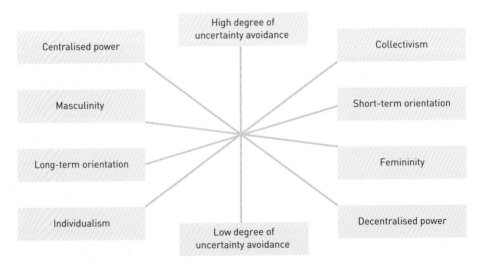

Figure 8.6   Dimensions of culture

Challenging the status quo

H ofstede might be getting a critical hammering these days, but there is little doubt that different cultures do generate different behaviours and attitudes – that's sort of the point! So why can't we identify and classify these differences? Is it a fear of being politically incorrect? Or is it just that these differences are notoriously difficult to pin down?

Maybe it's just that we are daunted by the prospect of carrying out a research project on that scale!

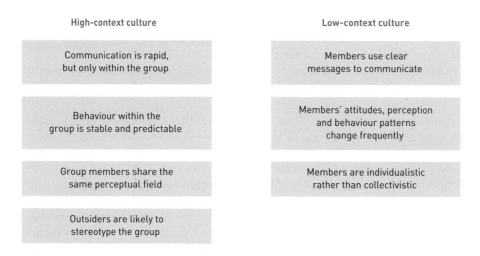

Figure 8.7   High-context vs. low-context cultures

There are three main approaches to studying culture, as follows:

1 *Taxonomies of culture*. This involves dividing cultures into different levels and/or into high-context or low-context cultures (see Figure 8.7).
2 *Lifestyle analysis*.
3 *Identification of cultural universals*. These are aspects of culture found in all societies. For example, all cultures use some form of bodily adornment (tattooing, cosmetics, jewellery, clothing, etc.). All cultures have sexual taboos (who is 'permissible' for sexual activity and who is not, and even what sexual practices are acceptable), all cultures have gift-giving rituals and all cultures have differences in status between members.

High-context cultures are those in which norms of behaviour and values are deeply embedded in the members of the culture, and thus do not need to be explained in any specific way (Hofstede 1980). Members communicate easily, because they share the same basic beliefs and reference points – there is no need to explain, so people can communicate non-verbally relatively easily. Characteristics of high-context cultures are as follows:

- Communication is rapid and efficient within the group, but rapidly breaks down with outsiders because the group members find it harder to explain matters that they think of as obvious.

- Behaviour within the group is stable and predictable.
- The nature of the group is such that outsiders are likely to stereotype the group, as the only way they have of understanding the culture.
- All parties within the group share much the same perceptual field.

High-context cultures are therefore totalitarian, orthodox and conservative. There is little room for personal expression or change, but each member has a clear (and perhaps reassuring) understanding of their role and responsibilities as well as what they can expect from the other members of the culture. Rigidity gives a degree of security in a high-context culture.

Low-context cultures are much less rigid, but require more effort of their members. They have the following features:

- They are individualistic rather than collectivistic.
- Members communicate using clearly coded messages.
- Members' values, attitudes, perceptions and patterns of behaviour are diverse and liable to change quickly.

The United States and most of Western Europe have low-context cultures, because of mass migrations and world travel, which have combined to expose the members of the cultures to many diverse cultural influences. Countries such as Japan, which have relatively few foreigners living in them, tend to have high-context cultures.

Ethnocentrism The belief that one's own culture is 'correct' and other cultures are derived from it

The degree to which people are ethnocentric affects behaviour as well. Ethnocentrism is the belief that one's own culture is the 'right' one, and others are mere copies. It has been shown that ethnocentric people are much more likely to be loyal to products from their own countries; by the same token, people who are culturally sensitive (i.e. understand and respect other cultures) are more open to buying imported products (Lu Hsu and Han-Peng 2008; Nguyen et al. 2008). If the local identity is more accessible than the global one, local products will be preferred (and vice versa). In other words, the easier it is to understand and access local products, the more likely they will be preferred over global ones (Zhang and Khare 2009).

CONSUMER CULTURE

The cult of consumerism identified in Chapter 2 has an effect on the wider culture in which it sits. It can be considered as a subculture: people who consume particular brands can be defined by the brand (for example, people who enjoy the TV series *Star Trek* sometimes define themselves as Trekkies, and people who buy Gucci handbags have a specific view of themselves).

Problems with consumer culture have been identified, however. First, consumer culture tends to erode national cultures because the culture associated with specific brands becomes more important than the 'naturally occurring' cultural identity of the individual. For example, there is strong evidence for a worldwide 'youth' culture based on consumption of music (via MTV and others) and fashion items. This culture means that young people worldwide tend to wear similar clothing and listen to similar music rather than wearing the clothing typical of their countries and listening to traditional music. Second, consumer culture creates superficial social interactions and encourages people to be competitive rather than cooperative. Third, consumerism is regarded as bad for the environment because it encourages excessive use of natural resources.

These criticisms do not in fact stand up very well (Miller 1995), since people do still take pleasure in retaining the traditions of their own region and family background. The criticisms do indicate that the consumer society is not necessarily an unmitigated force for good in the world. No doubt debate will continue on this topic.

Consumer behaviour in action: Gift-giving behaviour

Everybody likes getting a gift – but human beings seem to like giving gifts as well. Every human culture contains some kind of gift-giving behaviour, from small gifts to oil the wheels of our working lives to major gifts to family and friends on special occasions. We give gifts as a way of apologising, as a symbol of respect, as a 'thank you' or because we feel obligated to by social conventions.

Although gift-giving is common to all cultures, the connotations of some gifts can be different in different cultures. For example, in China it is common practice for someone to give a small gift to a superior, or someone in power. The gift is not intended to influence the person especially, although it is intended as an ice-breaker; if the superior then makes a decision that goes against the gift-giver, there would not be any special feeling of resentment. However, to a Westerner these gifts look suspiciously like bribes. In the West, one might offer a gift after the business has been concluded, but even this is fraught with social risks: one does not tip one's superiors. In Western cultures, it is more likely that the gifts would come from the superior to the subordinate, not the other way round.

Bribery is, of course, a horse of a different colour. A bribe is a gift given on the explicit understanding that some advantage will be conferred on the donor as a direct result. This also happens in China, but the rules are different and the outcomes are also different. This is a business transaction rather than a true gift.

In many Western cultures, the period around Christmas is the main time of year for exchanging gifts. Typically, people aim to spend about the same amount on each other (so as to avoid embarrassment) and sometimes even agree an approximate figure beforehand. For small children, parents maintain that the gifts do not in fact come from the parents at all, but from Santa Claus (also known as Papa Noel, Père Nöel, Kris Kringle, Sinter Klaas, Babbo Natale, Joulupukki, and many other names). The gifts are supposed to be a surprise, although among adults people often ask each other what would be a suitable present. Recipients of the gifts have to look surprised and pleased as they open the gifts on Christmas Day (for the UK and USA, or at Epiphany, or on Christmas Eve, or whatever date is appropriate to the local culture), even if they knew in advance what the gift was, or (worse) if it is something they do not want. All this is regarded as normal, polite behaviour.

A study by Joel Waldfogel (1993) showed that the giving of gifts at Christmas destroyed anything up to 30% of the monetary value of the gift. This was because the recipient of the gift frequently ascribed a cash value to it well below the actual price paid by the donor. What Waldfogel's research did not take into account is all the social aspects of the gift itself – the choosing, the wrapping, the performance rituals attached to the actual exchange of presents. For most people, it seems that these are far more important than the actual gift itself.

Subcultures

Subcultures are distinctive groups of people within a society who share common cultural meanings, behaviours and environmental factors. Although a subculture shares most of the mainstream culture within which it is embedded, its members have a distinct and identifiable set of behavioural norms, customs, scripts and so forth which distinguish them from the rest of the culture. In some cases, the subculture requires members to buy specific items, and members will often not buy items from outside the subculture (Richardson and Turley 2006).

Subcultures might be based on age, ethnic background, gender type or special interests. For example, Goth culture is distinct from mainstream UK culture, but has a distinct set of behaviours and beliefs. Likewise, second-generation immigrant populations often develop subcultures that are combinations of the new country's culture and elements from the parents' home country culture. Bicultural consumers often switch between the two cultures and make different judgements depending on which cultural context they happen to be 'switched' to at the time (Chattaraman et al. 2010).

Some subcultures are defined by the ways they interpret messages: these are called interpretive communities (Kates 2002). For example, a subculture of conspiracy theorists would tend to interpret all official statements as evidence of a cover-up. An anti-globalisation interpretive community would respond with deep suspicion or even hostility to any marketing messages, which makes marketing to such communities difficult; however, they are still consumers.

In Figure 8.8 the main culture's beliefs are shared by the subcultures but each subculture has beliefs and behaviours that lie outside the mainstream. Often the behaviours associated with the subculture can create problems for its members as members of the mainstream culture see them as outsiders or rebels, and therefore a threat to the mainstream.

GEOGRAPHIC SUBCULTURES

Geographic subcultures can be very significant for marketers. Most countries have geographical subcultures: Friesland in the Netherlands has a distinct language and traditions, Bavarians regard themselves as culturally different from the neighbouring 'Prussians' (and often feel closer to their Austrian neighbours in Salzburg than they do to their fellow-Germans in Stuttgart). In the UK, Wales and Scotland regard themselves as separate, and have different food, language and customs from those of England, and Ulster has (as is well known) a different culture from both the UK of which it is legally a part, and Eire of which it is historically a part. The significance for marketers lies in the possibilities for causing offence – for a Welshman, Wales is not, and never has been, part of England. There is also a positive significance in terms of recognising the differences between the subcultures, perhaps by referring to local events or using local dialects in advertising. For example, some major supermarkets in the UK offer locally sourced products in their stores and have signage in both Welsh and English in their stores in Wales.

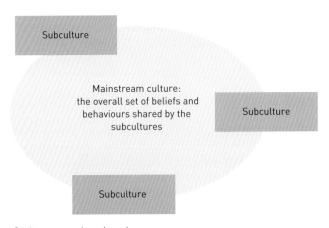

Figure 8.8 Culture and subculture

AGE SUBCULTURES

Age subcultures sometimes exist because the members have differing attitudes and values. This is often called the generation gap. In some cases people retain behaviours and attitudes that were current in their youth – this is typically the case with popular music, for example. In other cases people change their views as they age, perhaps becoming more politically right-wing as they become wealthier and less inclined towards radical changes.

Teenagers form a distinct, and often international, subculture. They are important not only because of their own spending power (which can be substantial) but also because they have a strong influence on their parents' spending. Often teenagers have at least some responsibility for the household shopping, and undoubtedly influence family choices about food brands, environmental issues and media consumption. The teen market is notoriously difficult to deal with, since brand preferences change with each year: each group of teenagers wants to have its own favourite brands, so that fourteen-year-olds are unlikely to be loyal to the same brands as their sixteen-year-old brothers and sisters. This means that producers need to be at the forefront of what is going on. Teenagers are often very communications-literate, and understand that they are being 'marketed to'.

Baby boomers are people born between 1946 and 1964. These years saw an unprecedented number of births, following on from the Second World War as soldiers returned to civilian life and began raising families. This period was also one of rising prosperity and improved health care, so that more people survived into adulthood and had greater expectations from life.

Baby boomers are now aged between 50 and 70, and are heading towards retirement: the younger of them are in their peak earning years, and the older of them often have substantial savings and pensions. They represent the largest and most affluent market in history, and will continue to have a major economic and social impact for the next 30 years at least. Since baby boomers have tended to have smaller families than did their parents, the spend per child has been much higher, and in the longer term the levels of inheritance that baby boomers' children will receive will also be higher.

A phenomenon of increasing importance within Europe, Japan and the United States is the ageing population. As life expectancies increase, there are progressively more people in the over-50 age group. This is commonly called the grey market, but it should not be assumed that it is homogeneous: it is unlikely that a 55-year-old man would have a lot in common with his 80-year-old mother, at least in terms of consumer behaviour. By 2025 it is estimated that 22% of Europe's population will be aged over 65 (compared with 15.4% in 1995), and this has dramatic implications for pensions, prosperity and of course marketing (Eurostat 2002). In Japan the situation is far more serious – the birth rate is extremely low, to the point where the population is shrinking rapidly. By the end of the century, Japan's population is forecast to shrink from its current 130 million to less than 50 million, most of whom will be very elderly (Dejevsky 2006).

The assumption has always been that these older consumers would be prime candidates for walking frames, stairlifts, hearing aids and little else. However, the rising life expectancy has been accompanied by a rise in the level of fitness of older people, due to better nutrition and health care. Obviously products such as over-the-counter medicines, hearing aids, spectacles and the like will become even bigger markets, but the grey market also consumes holidays, leisure activities such as golf or aviation, restaurant meals, recreational vehicles, education and so forth.

The market for the over-50s is extremely diverse – considering that, in the UK, it currently comprises one-third of all adults, this is not surprising (Office for National

Statistics 2012). At the younger end, most of this group are at the peak of their earning power and often have paid off their mortgages and are free of commitments to children. Their discretionary income is therefore higher than it has ever been. As we look at older members of the group, many have retired or are semi-retired and have a great deal more leisure time, while frequently enjoying generous private pensions and savings. Many older people use this time to take holidays, enjoy new hobbies, improve their education and so forth. These new activities are not necessarily those traditionally associated with elderly people: the holidays on offer in the Saga brochure are just as likely to include windsurfing, mountaineering or ski-ing as they are to include bridge playing or coach tours. Some flying schools report that the majority of their students are over 50, and Open University applications from the over-60s run into the thousands.

Equally, some other members of the segment fit the more traditional pattern, happy to dig the garden and perhaps do an evening class. This is far from being a homogeneous subculture.

Challenging the status quo

Apparently many older people are not ready for the rocking-chair and daytime TV just yet! We see plenty of people in their fifties, sixties and even seventies joining the gym, taking flying lessons, canoeing up the Amazon and generally behaving like teenagers. At the same time the rising divorce rate sees older people at the disco, or using dating services, or chatting each other up on holiday.

Is nothing sacred? Is Granny going to be out dancing and getting thrown out of nightclubs at four in the morning? Perhaps there is no such thing as an age-related product. Perhaps we should ignore age altogether in our planning!

On the other hand, Granny isn't what she used to be in many ways. Physically, older people are not going to be as fit as they were when they were young, and mentally things begin to deteriorate as well – greater experience might be a fine thing, but when you can't remember what you came upstairs for experience may not help a lot. So perhaps there will still be a few things we can sell specifically to older people – if only we can get them off the windsurfer.

ETHNIC SUBCULTURES

Ethnic subcultures are a growing group within Europe. Ethnic marketing is much more advanced in the United States, probably because the US is composed of a wide variety of cultures, whereas within Europe ethnic minorities usually account for less than 5% of the population. These groups are growing as migration continues, and tend to fall into two main groups: those who have emigrated from their country of origin, and are therefore perhaps best considered as members of their home-country culture, and those whose parents came from another country but who were born in the host country. The latter group often develops a distinct culture which is part way between their parents' national culture and the culture of the host country. Research conducted in Canada, for example, showed that Muslim women used the *hijab* (the face-covering material used by some Muslim women) as a way of indicating that they are traditional and therefore respectable when using an on-line dating service (Zwick and Chelariu 2006). This is a distinct move away from the cultural origins of the *hijab* in the Middle East, showing a willingness to comply with religious norms of conduct rather than a genuine belief in those norms.

Clearly these groups have specific purchasing behaviour: specific foods to meet religious restrictions or personal tastes, non-Christian greetings cards, clothing, cooking utensils and products from the country of origin. On the other hand, most immigrants are happy to embrace at least some aspects of the host country culture, and in some cases deliberately seek out local products as a way of expressing a desire to integrate (Bann 1996). Equally, migrant groups sometimes identify themselves around cultural factors from the country of origin – religion is especially powerful in this context. It has been shown that Sikhs in Britain use conspicuous consumption of their religion to establish their identity, while Muslims tend to reject Western cultural values of consumption while embracing British liberalism (Lindridge 2009).

How these groups should be addressed by marketers is a matter for considerable thought. At present, advertising largely ignores ethnic minorities, and attempts to include minorities (or advertise directly to them) have sometimes been interpreted as patronising or even offensive (Sudbury and Wilberforce 2006). Part of the difficulty here is that what some people regard as offensive can be regarded as totally acceptable by others: the UK Advertising Standards Authority, which responds to examples of offensive advertising, will take action even if a relatively small number of people complain. This may cause advertisers to avoid the issue by not including ethnic minorities in their advertising at all.

The degree to which individuals from ethnic minorities differ in their behaviour from the rest of society depends largely on their degree of acculturation. Acculturation refers to the degree to which people from one cultural background adapt to the meanings, values, beliefs, behaviours, rituals and lifestyles of another culture or subculture (Faber et al. 1987). For marketers, consumer acculturation is clearly of more interest: this refers to the process of becoming a skilled consumer in a different culture or subculture (Penaloza 1989).

Acculturation The process of adopting a new culture

For example, a British citizen who buys a retirement home in Spain might at first believe that everything is cheaper in Spain. Alcoholic drinks, cigarettes, meals in restaurants, petrol and many other daily items are indeed much cheaper in Spain than in the UK. Some items, however, are more expensive or unobtainable: fresh milk is almost impossible to find, and of course British food such as pork pies or brown sauce are unobtainable outside British enclaves. The new immigrant therefore has to learn how to function within the new consumer environment. Obviously these problems are multiplied if the individual moves to a consumer environment that is further removed from the UK – a British immigrant to India would find that supermarkets as they are known in Britain hardly exist at all, that toilet paper is almost unknown and that bartering is commonplace even for everyday purchases. Acquiring the skills to become an effective consumer in India would take considerable time and effort, and one would have to assume that immigrants coming the other way would face the same steep learning curve.

The degree to which someone can adapt to the new culture will depend on the level of cultural interpenetration he or she experiences. The more the individual interacts socially with members of the host culture, the more he or she is able to adapt. This does not necessarily mean giving up one's original cultural norms and beliefs; it does mean understanding and being sympathetic to the cultural norms and beliefs of the host culture (Andreasen 1990). In some cases, migrant populations use consumption as a way of integrating with the host country – buying a locally made car, eating local food, moving out of immigrant neighbourhoods and buying a house in an area populated by the host society, and so forth (Hughes 2010). This partial adoption of the host culture helps migrants to feel part of their new society.

Adoption The process of building an innovating product into one's daily life

There are four stages in acculturation, as follows (Oberg 1960):

1 *Honeymoon stage.* The individual is fascinated by the culture or subculture, but because interpenetration is shallow and superficial, there is very little acculturation. The honeymoon stage is typical of tourists traveling in another country: on their return from holiday, they may feel a desire to go and live in the country, having only seen the positive aspects of life there.
2 *Rejection stage.* After further cultural interpenetration, the individual realises that previous cultural norms are not adequate for dealing with the new culture, and that new norms and behaviours will need to be adopted. Often people become hostile to the new culture at this point, seeing the drawbacks rather than the advantages. Cultural conflicts are at a maximum in this stage.
3 *Tolerance stage.* Here the interactions have increased to the point where the individual accepts the new culture with all its drawbacks. This stage is reached by a process of cultural interpenetration, learning more about the new culture and reducing the level of cultural conflict.
4 *Integration stage.* At this stage the individual has made the necessary adjustments, valuing the new culture for its good qualities while still retaining important elements of the old culture. The new culture is seen as a perfectly viable way of life, as valid in its own way as the old culture.

In Figure 8.9, the individual's initial degree of happiness with the new culture is high in the honeymoon stage, as is motivation to learn about the culture: actual knowledge of the culture (and therefore ability to function well within it) is low. At the rejection

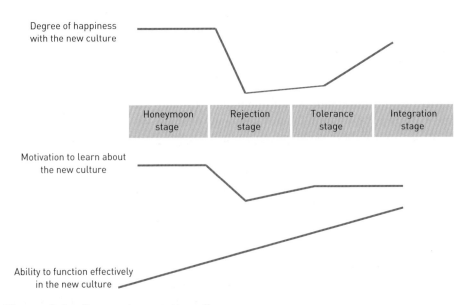

Figure 8.9   Stages in acculturation

stage, satisfaction with the culture drops dramatically, as does motivation to learn, but ability to function is still rising. With the tolerance stage comes a renewed interest in the culture, and also greater satisfaction with it. Finally, in the integration stage the individual is functioning well, knows about the culture and is consequently much happier within the culture. The initial disappointment at the rejection stage may account in part for the fact that the majority of immigrants return home within a few years.

Recent research has indicated the existence of cultural fractures caused by crossing borders (Davies and Fitchett 2004). These are as follows:

1 Emotional fracture. This can lead to feelings of loneliness and lack of a support infrastructure from friends and family left behind, or could be characterised by a willingness and ability to make new friends in the new country.

2 Symbolic fracture. This is characterised by running out of things to say in everyday conversation, not knowing what are the appropriate greetings for different people, and a difficulty in 'reading the signs' to understand what people are thinking or feeling. There is also a difficulty in understanding how people socialise in the new country.

3 Functional fracture. This is about the ease or difficulty of carrying out functional tasks such as opening a bank account, using trains and buses, or buying and preparing food.

4 Culture shock. This is how life in the new country differs from expectations.

5 Consumer behaviour. This is the gap between what one would buy at home and what one buys in the new country.

6 Demographic fracture. This is the disparity between the socio-economic structure one was part of in the old culture, and the socio-economic structure in which one finds oneself in the new culture. Sometimes immigrants move down the social scale, sometimes up, depending on the relationship between the host country and the old country.

OTHER SUBCULTURES

Gender may also be the basis for a subculture. Although there are relatively few products which are gender-specific, there has been a growing re-acceptance in recent years that men and women's consumption behaviours are different in many ways. In the post-feminist era, women have developed 'girly' activities, and 'new laddism' has grown up as an exclusively male subculture. It would be a serious mistake to stereotype either gender: most men are not 'new lads' and most women do not spend their free time on girls' nights out or marathon shopping expeditions. However, these subcultures have become acceptable and are a part of the 21st century mainstream.

Brand-based subcultures also exist – Harley-Davidson owners, football fans, World Wrestling fans and so forth have an entire set of rules, beliefs and language surrounding the products they consume (Deeter-Schmelz and Sojka 2004). Even when not linked to a specific brand, subcultures can grow up around product categories: people who enjoy sailing have a specific culture, as do private pilots (see case study).

Class

Some sociologists regard class as being one of the central concepts of the discipline, yet it is an ill-defined and ambiguous concept. For non-sociologists the concept of class is beginning to seem outmoded: at the beginning of the 20th century, around 75% of people in industrialised countries were manual workers of one sort

Emotional fracture The sense of loss of emotional support encountered when moving from one culture to another

Symbolic fracture The disparity between old and new communication paradigms encountered when moving from one culture to another

Functional fracture The disparity between old and new systems for daily living encountered when moving from one culture to another

Culture shock The discomfort that arises from being displaced from one's normal cultural milieu

Consumer behaviour Activities undertaken by people in the process of obtaining, using and disposing of goods and services for personal use

Demographic fracture The disparity between old and new socio-economic structures, encountered when moving from one culture to another

or another, quite clearly distinct in behaviour and wealth from the better-educated white-collar workers and (of course) the aristocracy. As machines have largely taken over from muscle power, education has become universal, and differential taxation has eroded differences of wealth – the differences between 'working class' and 'middle class' are almost undetectable. Even aristocrats now work for a living.

In the 1911 Census in the UK, the government decided to record socio-economic groupings for the first time. The system used is shown in Table 8.1.

Table 8.1 UK socio-economic groupings

Social grade	Social status	Head of household's occupation
A	Upper middle class	Higher managerial, administration or professional
B	Middle class	Intermediate managerial, administrative or professional
C1	Lower middle class	Supervisory or clerical, junior managerial, administrative or professional
C2	Skilled working class	Skilled manual workers
D	Working class	Semi-skilled and unskilled manual workers
E	Lowest level of subsistence	Unemployed, casual or lowest-grade workers, state pensioners

This system of classification worked fairly well for several decades, but shifts in social patterns made much of its assumptions irrelevant: the table assumes that incomes are lower further down the scale, but in the 21st century plumbers earn more than doctors (at least in much of Western Europe) and changing patterns of working life mean that today's labourer is tomorrow's film star (and vice versa). The basic lifestyles and indeed standards of living do not vary greatly between the groups – Group D individuals probably still own cars and have foreign holidays, even if Group A individuals run bigger cars and go to more exotic destinations. The classification, sometimes known as the ABC classification, is still used in a great deal of published market research. Partly this is because it is familiar to researchers, and partly it is because researchers sometimes need to make comparisons with previous studies, but it is well known that the system is seriously flawed.

In 2001 the UK government introduced an alternative classification method – the Socio-Economic Classification System. This classification system has eight categories, the first of which can be subdivided. There is a ninth category, 'Not classified', which is reserved for students and people whose occupations have not been adequately described. The categories are as shown in Table 8.2.

Although this classification system is a better reflection of 21st century society, it still suffers from a number of weaknesses common to all such classification systems. First, it does not take account of the possibility of rapid social movement: someone might change occupations very rapidly, without (presumably) changing lifestyle very much. Equally someone might change lifestyle rapidly without officially changing

Table 8.2 The Socio-Economic Classification System

1	Higher managerial and professional occupations
	1.1 Large employers and higher managerial occupations
	1.2 Higher professional occupations
2	Lower managerial and professional occupations
3	Intermediate occupations
4	Small employers and own account workers
5	Lower supervisory and technical occupations
6	Semi-routine occupations
7	Routine occupations
8	Never worked and long-term unemployed

occupation – a teacher who decides to leave an inner-city school for a less stressful life in the country would be an example. Third, the classification usually refers to the head of the household, which might have been a reasonable concept in 1911 but which has many possible interpretations now. In 1911, the head of the household would almost certainly have been the father of the family, the main (and probably only) earner. In 2008, several people in the household are likely to be earning, and decision-making is likely to be shared in many different ways.

There is, of course, more to social class than occupation. Class implies a position in the power hierarchy: the further up the class ladder an individual is, the more power and influence he or she will have. This can vary from the small powers and discretions exercised by a warehouse manager up to the hire-and-fire decisions made by a managing director. Early sociologists such as Karl Marx and Max Weber examined social class (see Figure 8.10). Marx saw class as being essentially about the power to set the prevailing intellectual climate. He said that 'The ideas of the ruling class are, in every epoch, the ruling ideas, i.e. the class which is the ruling material force of society, is at the same time its ruling intellectual force' (Marx and Engels 1848).

Weber defined class in terms of life chances (Weber 1946). For Weber, a class is a group of people who have in common a specific causal component of their life chances which is represented by possession of goods and opportunities for income, and which operates under the conditions of the commodity or labour markets. In

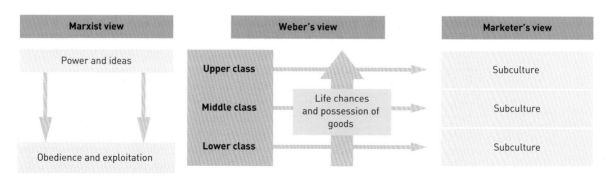

Figure 8.10 Studying social class

Challenging the status quo

Social class seems to be a bit problematic. People move up and down the social scale, they find it hard to define their own social class never mind anybody else's, and changes in the structure of society in general mean that we have trouble now identifying classes anyway.

Is it still realistic to talk about social class at all? Can we really predict someone's behaviour based on how they earn a living? And if we take more factors into account, are we really looking at social class, or are we defining people in different ways?

In short, given that people in the 21st century are not only individuals but are also individualistic, is social class a concept that still has any relevance?

other words, the individual's class is determined by the opportunities presented to that individual in terms of earning opportunities and the level of possession of goods.

Looked at in this way, it would appear that the individual's consumption pattern is as much a determining factor of social class as it is the result of social class. Those individuals who are able to accumulate possessions and improve their opportunities to earn money can move up the social scale. For example, a bricklayer would clearly be classified as working class (skilled manual worker). Yet if that same bricklayer saves some capital and sets up his own business, he could eventually become a wealthy property developer or house builder and thus be redefined as middle class (managerial) or even upper middle class (higher managerial, larger employer). His basic attitudes and values might change a little during this process, but he would probably still define himself as working class. This type of social mobility has become more common as class barriers break down, and educational opportunities increase.

From the viewpoint of marketers, social class is more a reflection of the existence of a set of subcultures based on the education level, occupational requirements and economic power of the individual members. In this context, marketers use class-related imagery in advertising in order to involve the consumer. Although the old social class distinctions are disappearing, new social classes are emerging and new ways of categorising people have appeared: the basis is still wealth, societal power, social skills, status aspirations, community participation, family history, cultural level, recreational habits, physical appearance and social acceptance (Kroeber-Riel and Weinberg 1996). Social class represents a set of subcultures because the class distinctions are generally agreed upon within the main culture, and the members of each class share most of their meanings and behaviours. The assumption is that people from one social class are less likely to mix socially with people from other social classes, preferring the company of members of their own class.

Social class is measured in two basic ways. People can be asked which social class they belong to (self-assignment), or their social class can be inferred from objective criteria. In market research, the latter approach is much more common, but in most cases respondents are only asked about their income, occupation and education level, which may not be the only determinants of social class. Certainly there is likely to be some discrepancy between a self-assignment and an objective measure in cases where there has been upward social mobility – an individual who comes from a working-class background but who has become educated, professional and wealthy might still self-assign him- or herself to the working-class category. Likewise, the same might be true of someone who has been downwardly mobile, for example someone who dropped out of university to become a train driver.

More useful measures of social class have emerged in recent years, notably geo-demographic measures such as ACORN and MOSAIC. These measures work by classifying people according to the area in which they live, which is likely to be a better indicator of social class than income or occupation data.

ACORN A Classification of Residential Neighbourhoods

Overall, social class still has some relevance to marketing activities, but increasing social mobility and a steady reduction in wealth concentration are eroding the old distinctions between classes.

The on-line environment

The virtual environment created on-line has a strong influence on consumer behaviour, not least because consumers themselves often help to create it. On-line environments break down into the following types:

- Interactive, navigable websites that provide a platform for consumers to access information about the firm and its products, purchase products and provide feedback to the firm.
- Social networking sites such as Twitter, Facebook and Linked-In which provide a forum for people to interact with each other. This environment is created in large measure by the consumers themselves.
- Virtual reality sites such as Second Life, which allow people to establish a new identity and live in a virtual world where they can meet new friends, go to cultural events, have a new career, build a house and in general establish a completely new existence in parallel with their existence in the real world.

Overall, the on-line environment is much like a marketplace or an exhibition hall: people are able to choose which 'stalls' or 'stands' they go to, and firms need to work at making their websites as attractive as possible in order to lure suitable customers. This means that companies need to establish hyperlinks with other websites, have the most appropriate key words in order to rank well in the search engines, and also be prepared to pay for insertions in the advertising sections on search engines.

Retaining customers in the virtual environment is akin to retaining customers in the real-world environment. Firms need to establish trust: traditionally, this has relied on two factors – a shared cultural and institutional background, and a knowledge of the trustee's identity. At first sight, these conditions do not apply in the on-line environment, but some authors assert that not only can these two conditions not be met on-line, they are actually not necessary (Papadopolou 2007; Vries 2006; Weckert 2005).

Nissenbaum (2001) identified four factors that create trust, as follows:

1 Publicity. This is the possibility for all actions to be made public, whether good or bad. In the on-line context, this would mean that sites such as TripAdviser which publish testimonials from customers of hotels and restaurants might be used by potential customers in order to assess the trustworthiness of the firm. The problem then, of course, is whether people trust the reference website.

2 Reward and punishment. Can the website be punished for betrayal, and can the customer be rewarded for their trust? On-line, this would clearly be difficult, but if the customer feels that the site owner has some vulnerability, this will tend to increase trust levels.

3 Promulgations of norms, both cultural and moral. Websites from one's own culture tend to be trusted more, since the customer assumes that the website owner shares the same moral code. For website owners, this places a premium

on ensuring that the website is truly multinational and multicultural, or (in the case of larger firms) there are separate websites for each country or region.

4 A set of public policies which provide redress in the case of betrayal. In many cases, this is simply not possible on the Internet, because of its global nature. However, some firms (especially those in financial services) are heavily regulated within their own countries, so a customer might feel able to trust (for example) an on-line bank which is ruled by the authorities in the customer's country.

In other respects, the on-line environment has parallels with the physical environment. The relationship between micro- and macro-environmental factors remains much the same, except that the micro-environment no longer has as many geographical factors – competitors might come from anywhere in the world, and neighbours might be any other website with which the firm has something in common. However, within the environment created by social networking sites, customers play the biggest role in creating and managing the environment.

Summary

Consumer behaviour (and indeed all behaviour) happens against a backdrop of environmental and cultural factors. These vary from place to place and from time to time, and some of these variations are greater than others, but as consumers we have to learn to operate within the environment and culture we inhabit.

The environment of consumer behaviour includes the social environment as well as the physical environment. The social environment is the sum total of the human interactions that surround us, both those we are directly involved with and those we are not. Some of these interactions involve social class as well as personal behavioural preferences.

The physical environment includes store atmospherics, climatological elements and so forth. These have a bearing on the mood of the customers – we are all affected by our physical surroundings, and clearly our moods affect our purchasing behaviour. What is difficult from a marketing viewpoint is to make accurate predictions of how the environment will affect our target group of customers.

Key points

- Atmospherics affect the degree of pleasure people obtain from the shopping experience, which in turn affects their approach–avoidance behaviour.
- The functional environment is subjective: it is affected by objective environmental factors, but the effects may not always be predictable.
- Cultural factors colour all our behaviour, not just our purchasing behaviour.
- High-context cultures have deeply embedded norms of behaviour.
- Low-context cultures are individualistic and characterised by change.
- Moving from one culture to another is almost always problematic in terms of learning to be a consumer.
- Class is as important now as it has ever been, but class distinctions are not the same as they were fifty years ago.

Review questions

1 Why is it that other customers have an effect on store atmospherics?
2 What might be the problems for someone emigrating from a low-context culture to a high-context culture?
3 What might be the problems for someone emigrating from a high-context culture to a low-context culture?
4 How might social class affect consumption behaviour?
5 Which aspects of the purchasing environment can be controlled by the store management, and which cannot?
6 What special marketing approaches might be useful at traditional gift-giving times?
7 What are the main problems with the ABC system of social classification?
8 What special difficulties might arise for a firm seeking to export products to a high-context culture?
9 What are the main criticisms of Hofstede's work?
10 How should marketers approach marketing to a subculture?

Case study revisited: Flying for fun

Needless to say pilots have developed their own culture. Flying is a great leveller – there is no snobbishness about which aircraft a pilot flies, or which airfield he or she flies from; all that matters is that all the pilots just love to get airborne. Private pilots in general are more than eager to help one another – flying with someone to collect a new aircraft or aircraft parts, advising someone about local airfield regulations, lending someone an air chart, or simply showing someone a flying technique.

Flying naturally has its own language and folklore. Apart from the technical terms – 'airprox' for a near miss, 'avgas' for aviation fuel, 'prop wash' for the stiff breeze created by a spinning propeller – there are words such as 'bimble' for an aimless flight around the local area, looking at the scenery, and 'the hundred-quid bacon sandwich' to describe a visit to another airfield (the sandwich costs £2, but it costs £100 to get there). Folklore includes pilot proverbs such as:

'There are old pilots, and bold pilots, but no old bold pilots.'

'It's better to be down here wishing you were up there, than up there wishing you were down there.'

'Airspeed, altitude, and brains – if you have two out of the three, you're safe.'

Private pilots spend a great deal of time in each others' company. Apart from anything else, the weather frequently grounds aircraft unexpectedly, so airfield clubhouses are often filled with people drinking coffee and occasionally looking out of the window to see whether the fog has lifted yet. Additionally, airfields often organise 'fly-ins' in which non-resident pilots are invited to visit. A typical fly-in will include such attractions as a barbecue, a spare-parts market, perhaps some demonstrations by aircraft manufacturers, and often some camping around the airfield. Pitching a tent under the wing of the aircraft makes a lot of sense – pilots do not necessarily want to have to take a taxi to a hotel, and in any case it's a great deal pleasanter to have an evening chatting with fellow-pilots at the airfield.

Private flying is a subculture driven by a sense of adventure, and a shared joy in being above the earth: flying feels like walking with giants. Pilots do not care what the other pilots do for a living, or how much they earn, or how they pay for their flying – just sharing the experience is enough.

Case study: The Mall of the Emirates

Dubai is part of the United Arab Emirates, and is the name given both to the emirate itself and to its capital. Dubai is one of the few Middle Eastern countries that did not become wealthy through oil exploration: for many years, the city earned its living by being the entertainment and shopping capital of the region. Although oil was discovered there in 1966, this miniature country derives its main earnings from tourism and business, with people coming from all over the world to experience its outstanding attractions.

Dubai's tourism has nothing to do with ancient monuments or spectacular scenery. It is largely a desert country, with few ancient buildings. What it does have is spectacular modern architecture, and some of the most amazing shopping malls in the world. One of these, the Mall of the Emirates, has 520 stores and over 80 restaurants, but this is only the beginning. There is a full ski resort inside, offering skiing, snowboarding, hot chocolate and even penguins. Ski Dubai has five ski runs of varying difficulty, the longest being 400 metres in length with a drop of 60 metres. The temperature inside is –4 degrees, but visitors need not bring their own ski outfits – they are supplied as part of the ticket price. Professional ski instructors are on hand, and there are two restaurants where one can enjoy après-ski hot drinks and meals.

Elsewhere in the Mall of the Emirates there is a children's play area. This is somewhat more than just a playground, though; it is spread over two levels, has white-knuckle rides and the world's only racing simulator that is open to the public, plus video games, a soft play area, an 8-metre climbing wall and professional childminders for those who want to drop the kids off while they go shopping.

Elsewhere in the mall is DUCTAC, an arts centre containing two theatres, 16 studio spaces, a music school and (of course) a café. There are fourteen cinemas in the mall, with leather reclining seats and tables for each couple.

The choice of restaurants is equally astounding. Everything from fast-food to Jamie Oliver's Italian, with every possible variety of cuisines available. There is a food court with 30 fast-food outlets, a French restaurant, several Indian restaurants and a wide variety of Middle Eastern cuisine on offer.

Everything about the Mall of the Emirates is larger than life. It is perfectly possible to spend an entire day there, from dawn to midnight, without having to repeat any experiences – in fact, it is probably possible to spend a week there, staying in one of the two luxury hotels in the complex, provided the money holds out.

Questions

1 Why would someone want to visit such an artificial environment?
2 What is the purpose of having penguins in the ski resort?
3 What is the reason for having such a wide range of restaurants?
4 Why have a ski resort in a desert country?
5 How would you analyse the functional environment of the Mall of the Emirates?

Further reading

Consumer Culture Theory, edited by Russell Belk and John Sherry Jr. (Greenwich, CT: JAI Press, 2007) is the outcome of a major conference on consumer culture theory. It contains papers from a wide range of authors, on a wide range of aspects of consumer culture. For some cutting-edge theory it's hard to beat, although it is somewhat academic in its style.

Consumer Behaviour and Culture: Consequences for Global Marketing and Advertising by Marieke de Mooij (Thousand Oaks, CA: Sage, 2003) gets right to the heart of the problem of culture and marketing. Marieke de Mooij makes the point that the theories which come from the United States do not necessarily apply elsewhere in the world – and ethnocentrism is always hovering in the wings ready to trap the unwary.

Multicultural Perspectives in Consumer Behaviour, edited by Maria G. Piacentini and Charles Cui (London: Routledge, 2012) is another edited collection of papers from a wide variety of authors. The book was originally a special edition of the *Journal of Marketing Management*, so it is a rigorous and academic book, with papers from the UK, Greece, Austria, Germany and China.

For something a little more out of the ordinary, you might like *Material Culture and Consumer Society: Dependent Colonies in Colonial Australia* by Mark Staniforth (New York: Kluwer, 2003). This is actually a book about underwater archaeology, but the author examines how material goods served to link early colonists to the home country, to distinguish themselves from the indigenous population, to help establish their own social relationships in terms of wealth and position, and to reassure the colonists about their place in the world.

References

Andreasen, A.R. (1990) Cultural interpenetration: a critical consumer research issue for the 1990s. In Marvin E. Goldberg, Gerald Gorn and Richard W. Pollay (eds), *Advances in Consumer Research*, vol. 17. Provo, UT: Association for Consumer Research. pp. 847–9.

Askegaard, S. and Madsen, T.K. (1995) European food cultures: an exploratory analysis of food related preferences and behaviour in European regions. MAPP Working Paper no. 26. Aarhus: Aarhus School of Business.

Baker, J., Levy, M. and Grewal, D. (1992) An experimental approach to making retail store environmental decisions. *Journal of Retailing* 68: 445–61.

Bann, G. (1996) Race for opportunity. *New Impact Journal* Dec 1996/Jan 1997: 8–9.

Bellizzi, J.A., Crowley, A.E. and Hasty, R.W. (1983) The effects of colour in store design. *Journal of Retailing* 59: 21–45.

Block, J. and Block, J.H. (1981) Studying situational dimensions: a grand perspective and some limited empiricism. In David Magnusson (ed.), *Toward a Psychology of Situations: An International Perspective*. Hillsdale, NJ: Lawrence Erlbaum. pp. 85–102.

Brunso, K., Grunert, K.G. and Bredahl, L. (1996) An analysis of national and cross-national consumer segments using the food-related lifestyle instrument in Denmark, France, Germany and Great Britain. MAPP Working Paper no. 35. Aarhus: Aarhus School of Business.

Chattaraman, V., Rudd, N.A. and Lennon, S.J. (2010) The malleable bicultural consumer: effects of cultural contexts on aesthetic judgements. *Journal of Consumer Behaviour* 9 (1): 18–31.

Davies, A. and Fitchett, J. (2004) Crossing culture: a multi-method enquiry into consumer behaviour and the experience of cultural transition. *Journal of Consumer Behaviour* 3 (4): 315–30.

Deeter-Schmelz, D.R. and Sojka, J.Z. (2004) Wrestling with American values: an exploratory investigation of World Wrestling Entertainment as a product-based subculture. *Journal of Consumer Behaviour* 4 (2): 132–43.

Dejevsky, M. (2006) Japan: A country in crisis? *The Independent*, 26 August.

Eroglu, S. and Harrell, G.D. (1986) Retail crowding: theoretical and strategic implications. *Journal of Retailing* 62: 346–63.

Eurostat (2002) The social situation in the European Union 2002. Luxembourg: Office for Official Publications of the European Union.

Faber, R.J., O'Guinn, T.C. and McCarty, J.A. (1987) Ethnicity, acculturation, and the importance of product attributes. *Psychology and Marketing* Summer: 121–34.

Gabel, T.G. and Boller, G.W. (2003) A preliminary look into the globalization of the tortilla in Mexico. *Advances in Consumer Research* 30: 135–41.

Hofstede, G. (1980) *Culture's Consequences*. Beverley Hills, CA: Sage.

Hughes, M.U. (2010) From resistance to integration: changing consumer acculturation practices of immigrants. *Advances in Consumer Research* 37: 13.

Kates, S. (2002) Doing brand and subcultural ethnographies: developing the interpretive community concept in consumer research. *Advances in Consumer Research* 29: 43.

Kellaris, J.J. and Kent, R.J. (1992) The influence of music on consumers' temporal perceptions: does time fly when you're having fun? *Journal of Consumer Psychology* 1: 365–76.

Kotler, P. (1973) Atmospherics as a marketing tool. *Journal of Retailing* 49 (Winter): 48–64.

Kroeber-Riel, W. and Weinberg, P. (1996) *Konsumentenverhalten*, 6th edn. Munich: Vahlen.

Lindridge, A. (2009) Acculturation, religion and consumption in normative political ideology. *Adavnces in Consumer Research* 36: 16.

Lindridge, A.M. and Wang, C. (2008) Saving 'face' in China: modernization, parental pressure, and plastic surgery. *Journal of Consumer Behaviour* 7 (6): 496–508.

Lu Hsu, J. and Han-Peng, N. (2008) Who are ethnocentric? Examining consumer ethnocentrism in Chinese societies. *Journal of Consumer Behaviour* 7 (6): 436–47.

Marx, K. and Engels, F. (1848) *The Manifesto of the Communist Party*. London: The Communist League.

McCarty, J.A., Horn, M.I. and Szenasy, M.K. (2007) An exploratory study of consumer style: country differences and international segments. *Journal of Consumer Behaviour* 6: 48–59.

Mehrabian, A. and Russell, J.A. (1974) *An Approach to Environmental Psychology*. Cambridge, MA: MIT Press.

Miller, D. (1995) Consumption as the vanguard of history. In D. Miller (ed.), *Acknowledging Consumption*. London: Routledge.

Nguyen, T.D., Nguyen, T.T.M. and Barrett, N.J. (2008) Consumer ethnocentrism, cultural sensitivity, and intention to purchase local products – evidence from Vietnam. *Journal of Consumer Behaviour* 7: 88–100.

Nissenbaum, H. (2001) Securing trust on-line: wisdom or oxymoron? *Boston University Law Review* 81 (3): 635–44.

Oberg, K. (1960) Cultural shock: adjustment to new cultural environments. *Practical Anthropologist* 7: 177–82.

Office for National Statistics (2012) Aging in the UK Datasets, 2011 Pensions Act Update (January release). Newport: ONS.

Papadopolou, P. (2007) Applying virtual reality for trust-building e-commerce environments. *Virtual Reality* 11 (2–3): 107–27.

Park, C.W., Iyer, E.S. and Smith, D.C. (1989) The effects of situational factors on in-store grocery shopping behaviour: the role of store environment and time available for shopping. *Journal of Consumer Research* March: 422–33.

Ethnicity The cultural background of the individual

Penaloza, L.N. (1989) Immigrant consumer acculturation. *Advances in Consumer Research* 16: 110–18, 121–34.

Philips, H. and Bradshaw, R. (1990) How customers actually shop: customer interaction with the point of sale. *Journal of the Market Research Society* 35: 51–62.

Richardson, B. and Turley, D. (2006) Support your local team: resistance, subculture and the desire for distinction. *Advances in Consumer Research* 33: 175–80.

Sudbury, L. and Wilberforce, F. (2006) The portrayal of black people in UK television advertising: perception and reality. *Journal of Consumer Behaviour* 5 (Sept–Oct): 465–76.

Tai, S.H.C. and Fung, A.M.C. (1997) Application of an environmental psychology model to in-store buying behaviour. *International Review of Retail, Distribution and Consumer Research* 7 (4): 311–37.

Vries, P. de (2006) Social presence as a conduit to online trust. In W. IJsselsteijn, Y. de Kort, C. Midden, B. Eggen and E. van den Hoven (eds), *Persuasive Technology*. Berlin/Heidelberg: Springer. pp. 55–9.

Waldfogel, J. (1993) The deadweight loss of Christmas. *American Economic Review* 83 (5): 1328–36.

Weber, M. (1946) Class, status, party. Published posthumously in Hans H. Gerth and C. Wright Mills (eds), *From Max Weber*. Oxford: Oxford University Press.

Weckert, J. (2005) Trust in cyberspace. In R.J. Cavalier (ed.), *The Impact of the Internet on Our Moral Lives*. Albany, NY: University of New York Press. pp. 95–120.

Yorkston, E. and deMello, G. (2004) Sex sells? The effects of gender marking on consumers' evaluations of branded products across languages. *Advances in Consumer Research* 31: 148–51.

Zhang, Y. and Khare, A. (2009) Consumers' local–global identity: measurement. *Advances in Consumer Research* 36: 43, 44.

Zwick, D. and Chelariu, C. (2006) Mobilising the hijab: Islamic identity negotiation in the context of a matchmaking website. *Journal of Consumer Behaviour* 5 (Jul–Aug): 380–95.

More online

To gain free access to additional online resources to support this chapter please visit: **www.sagepub.co.uk/blythe**

CHAPTER ⑨
Reference groups

LEARNING OBJECTIVES

After reading this chapter you should be able to:

- Explain how reference groups influence individual members.

- Explain what is meant by normative compliance.

- Describe the main drivers for normative compliance.

- Explain the role of word of mouth communication.

- Describe ways of handling complaints.

- Explain the importance of e-mail communication.

Introduction

Human beings are social animals: we form ourselves into groups, and in fact most of us are members of several different groups, formed for different purposes. In most cases we join groups because we can achieve more as part of a group than we can as an individual, but there are some groups which we belong to without ever having made a voluntary decision to join. Examples are our gender group, our ethnic or racial group and our family group. Because the family is such an important group it has a chapter to itself; this chapter deals with other groups that affect consumption.

Groups have considerable influence on our buying behaviour, either because we need to own certain items in order to join the group (there is no point in joining a golf club if one does not own a set of golf clubs, for example, although the loud check trousers are usually optional), or because we have joint consumption within the group for the purposes of saving ourselves time, money or effort. For example, members of a yacht club are able to share facilities such as berthing, a club house, maintenance facilities, and so forth.

Sociology is the study of human behaviour in groups, so much of the research into groups comes from sociologists rather than from marketing academics. Marketers are, of course, mainly interested in how group behaviour affects purchasing behaviour.

Sociology The study of human behaviour in groups

Case study: Facebook

Facebook is probably the world's biggest social networking site. It derives its name from the books of photographs handed out to new students at some American universities so that they are able to recognise other students and faculty members around the campus.

Facebook was invented by a group of students led by Mark Zuckerberg. The original intention was that the site would be available only to students at Harvard, but the founders quickly saw the potential of expanding the concept and opened it up first to students at other universities, and eventually to everyone aged over 13. The website allows people to upload a personal profile, find and contact friends, and post news about themselves; members can control which people they share the information with, and can see who their friends know. The site is even able to ask people if they know someone who is currently not a friend.

The purpose of the site is to enable people to keep in touch in a very broad manner – to share stories, photographs and even videos with a group of friends. Facebook's mission is 'to give people the power to share and make the world more open and connected'. One of the main benefits of the site is that it is global – people with friends and family in other countries can stay in touch very easily and cheaply, since use of the site is free.

Of course, if the site is free to users the running costs have to be met somehow. The chosen method, perhaps not surprisingly, is advertising. Facebook are able to target very specific segments of their 900 million members worldwide, and can offer tailored advertising. Because people provide details of their ages, work history, education, gender and interests they can be segmented automatically by computer. In addition, businesses can buy 'sponsored stories' to send to friends of their customers – if someone has posted that they have 'checked in' at a restaurant, the restaurant can buy a sponsored story to send out to the individual's friends. This type of promotion is very much an extension of word of mouth, and is thus extremely powerful.

How to impress your examiner

You are likely to be asked to compare different types of reference groups and/or explain their influence on people. You should try to use marketing examples to illustrate your answer – for instance, that peer groups sometimes pressure people into buying the 'right' product, or that dissociative groups will tend to tarnish brand values. This not only shows that you understand the theory, it also shows that you can apply it in a marketing context.

Formation of reference groups

Reference group A group of people who act as the yardstick for our behaviour

A **group** is two or more persons who share a set of norms and whose relationship makes their behaviour interdependent. A reference group is 'a person or group of people that significantly influences an individual's behaviour' (Beardon and Etzel 1982). The reference groups provide standards or norms by which consumers judge their attitudes and behaviour.

Originally, groups formed for the purpose of cooperating on survival activities. Because human beings could cooperate in such activities as hunting, food-gathering and defence from predators, we were able to increase the chances of survival for the species as a whole. Interestingly, this still appears to hold true; social researchers have reported that socially isolated people have mortality rates between 50% and 300% higher than people who are strongly integrated into groups (Koretz 1990). For all of human history we have cooperated with each other to survive and prosper, and we continue to do so for both practical and social reasons.

Most people prefer to fit in with the group (to a greater or lesser extent). This is either through politeness or through a desire not to be left out of things. Particularly with groups of friends, people will 'go along with the crowd' on a great many issues, and will tend to adopt the group norms regarding behaviour and attitudes. The process starts from an early age – children as young as 8 are aware of the importance of having the right brands of food in their lunch boxes, and this awareness becomes stronger as they grow older (Roper and La Niece 2009).

Experiments conducted by Solomon Asch in 1951 demonstrated this in a graphic manner. In the experiment, subjects were asked to judge the lengths of different lines. The lines were displayed on a large board, and each person was seated with a group of strangers who were also supposed to be making judgements about the line lengths. In fact the strangers were Asch's assistants who had been instructed to agree with each other about the length of each line, but to make errors; the experimental subjects consistently agreed with these errors, even though the errors were sometimes glaringly obvious. Respondents did not make the same mistakes when there were no other people present, however. It appears from this that the fear of seeming foolish or of being the odd one out is enough to make the individual doubt the evidence of his or her eyes, or at the very least to lie about the evidence (Asch 1951).

Responses to group pressures may, in some circumstances, be gender-specific. Fisher and Dube (2003) found that men and women respond differently to emotional advertising depending on whether other people are present. Specifically, women show the same emotional responses to advertisements whether other people are present or not, whereas men are affected by the presence of others, especially if the emotional response is regarded as gender-specific. For example, an advertisement that causes someone to shed tears would cause the same response in a woman whether or not other people are around, whereas a man would be more likely to suppress this response if others are present (even if he were to shed a tear when in private).

Perception of what is fair and what is not also seems to be influenced by social interaction with the group one happens to be in at the time (Carlson and Sally 2002). For example, when associating with a group of middle-class professionals one might perceive welfare payments as unfair, since they are paid for by hard-working taxpayers; in the company of a more left-wing group, one might perceive welfare payments as unfair because they do not provide enough money for a dignified and comfortable lifestyle.

Challenging the status quo

Do we really go along with things that easily? Is it so straightforward to lead people round by the nose? If so, how come we get into arguments with our friends? How come we have so many people who are prepared to stand up against the general flow of opinion, and disagree?

Asch's experiment might just show that students try to please their lecturers, or that people try to give the 'right' answers in situations that look a lot like exams. Or maybe the results are good, but only when we are in the company of strangers – does our natural politeness (and fear of a punch in the mouth) make us wary of arguing with someone we know nothing about?

Reference groups fall into many possible groupings; the following list is not intended to be exhaustive.

Primary groups are composed of those people we see most often: friends, family and close colleagues. A primary group is small enough to permit face-to-face interaction on a regular basis, and there is cohesiveness and mutual participation which results in similar beliefs and behaviour within the group. Because people tend to choose friends who think in similar ways, and have similar interests, the primary group is often very cohesive and long-lasting. Possibly the strongest primary group is the family, but primary groups might be close friends, colleagues in work or people with whom we share a hobby.

Secondary groups are composed of people we see occasionally, and with whom we have some shared interest. For example, a trade association or a sports club would constitute a secondary group. These groups are correspondingly less influential in shaping attitudes and controlling behaviour, but can exert influence on behaviour within the purview of the subject of mutual interest. For example, if you are a member of a cycling club, you may be persuaded to take part in a sponsored bike ride, or perhaps a protest in favour of creating more cycle lanes. Within a secondary group, primary groups will sometimes form; there will often be groups of special friends whose shared interests go beyond those of the rest of the secondary group. For example, a cycling enthusiast might have a close friend with whom he cycles regularly: the friends might be members of a cycling club, and arrange with a few other members of the club to go on an evening out. In this example, the friends are a primary group, but met through a secondary group (the cycling club) and formed a new primary group to enjoy a different shared interest (the evening out).

Aspirational groups are the groups the individual wants to join. These groups can be very powerful in influencing behaviour, because the individual will often adopt the behaviour of the aspirational group in the hope of being accepted as a member. People who feel excluded because of some kind of stigma (perhaps being heavily tattooed, or being from a poor background) will modify their consumption patterns (either buying specific products, or reducing their consumption of other products) in order to conceal or reduce the stigma (Crosby and Otnes 2010). Sometimes the aspirational group will be better off financially, or will be more powerful; the desire to join such groups is usually classed as ambition. For example, a humble office worker may dream of one day having the key to the executive washroom. Advertising commonly uses images of aspirational groups, implying that use of a particular product will move the individual a little closer to being a member of an aspirational group.

Dissociative groups, on the other hand, are those groups that the individual does not want to be associated with. Like a backpacker who does not want to look like a typical tourist, or a Marxist who would not want to be mistaken for a capitalist, the individual tries to avoid dissociative groups. This can have a negative effect on behaviour; the individual avoids certain products or behaviours rather than be taken for somebody from the dissociative group. Like aspirational groups, the definition of a group as dissociative is purely subjective; it varies from one individual to the next.

Formal groups have a known list of members, very often recorded somewhere. An example might be a professional association, or a club. Usually the rules and structure of the group are laid down in writing; there are rules for membership, and members' behaviour is constrained while they remain part of the group. However, the constraints usually only apply to fairly limited areas of behaviour; for example, the Chartered Institute of Marketing lays down a code of practice for marketers in their professional dealings, but has no interest in what its members do as private citizens. Membership of such groups may confer special privileges, such as job advancement

Primary group The group of people we see daily, and to whom we feel closest

Secondary group A group of people whom we do not necessarily see every day, and who are not our closest friends, but to which we belong nonetheless

Aspirational group A group of individuals which one wishes to join

Dissociative group A social group to which one does not wish to belong

Formal group A group of people with a known, recorded membership and a set of (usually written) rules of membership

or use of club facilities, and may lead to responsibilities in the furtherance of the group's aims.

Informal groups are less structured, and are typically based on friendship. An example would be an individual's circle of friends, which only exists for mutual moral support, company and sharing experiences. Although there can be even greater pressure to conform than would be the case with a formal group, there is no written set of rules. Often informal groups expect a more rigorous standard of behaviour across a wider range of activities than would a formal group; such circles of friends are likely to develop rules of behaviour and traditions that are more binding than written rules.

Automatic groups are those groups to which one belongs by virtue of age, gender, culture or education. These are sometimes also called category groups. Although at first sight it would appear that these groups would not exert much influence on members' behaviour, because these are groups that have not been joined voluntarily, it would appear that people are influenced by group pressure to conform. For example, when buying clothes older people are sometimes reluctant to look like 'mutton dressed as lamb'. Also, membership of some racial groups can influence behaviour because of the associated physical characteristics: some cosmetics are specifically designed for skin and hair types that are genetically determined.

Virtual groups are a recent phenomenon, brought about as a result of chatrooms on the Internet (Okleshen and Grossbart 1998). The communication is virtual rather than face-to-face, which means that people can (in effect) be whoever they say they are. Such Internet communities are based on social interactions that can often be more open and uninhibited than would be the case in a real space rather than a virtual space (Fischer et al. 1996). This allows people to express views that might be controversial, and of course since the chatrooms are not geographically based people with unusual interests (such as collecting rare whiskies or building light aircraft) are able to share information much more easily. Satisfaction with virtual communities such as chatrooms comes from interactions with the members: the organisers of chatrooms have little influence over this (Langerak et al. 2004). On the one hand, chatrooms allow individuals to discuss issues of common interest, and to share information about whatever topics interest them (however obscure). On the other hand, chatrooms open up possibilities for people to misrepresent themselves, perhaps for social purposes (for example to appear more interesting or desirable), or perhaps for criminal purposes such as fraud or paedophilia.

There are four types of virtual community, as follows (Muniz and O'Guinn 2001):

- *Brand communities*. These are groups who have a shared interest in a specific brand, for example owners of a particular motorcycle or classic car. These groups share experiences, help each other with obtaining peripherals, spare parts etc., and offer each other advice when things go wrong.
- *Communities of interest*. Typically these are hobby sites for people who share an interest such as a sport, or a professional interest.
- *Fantasy communities*. These are based on games, whether fantasy games or ordinary games, such as chess or bridge.
- *Relationship communities*. These are based on common shared problems and experience, for example support groups for people with mental illness, victims of crime, or action groups who campaign for reform.

The above categories of group are not mutually exclusive. A dissociative group could also be an informal one; a formal group can be a secondary group (and often is) and so forth. For example, one may not wish to become friends with a group of drunken

Informal group A group of people that has no recorded membership and no written rules

Automatic group A group of people to which an individual belongs by reason of race, gender or other non-changeable factor

Category group See *Automatic group*

Virtual group A social group mediated by the Internet

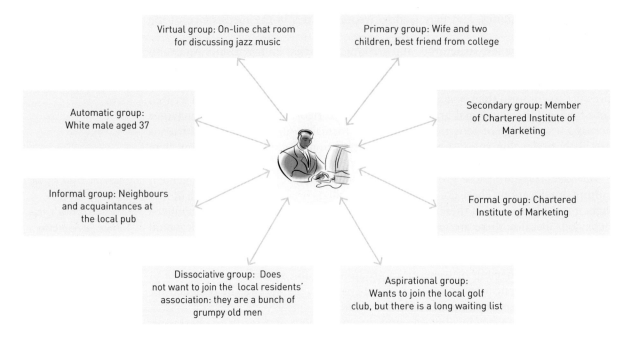

Figure 9.1   An individual and his reference groups

hooligans (who see themselves as an informal group of friends having a good time). Likewise, the golf club could be a place of refuge to which one retreats to have a quiet drink with like-minded people, as well as a place where golf is played.

Figure 9.1 shows how an individual might be a member of several groups, each one with different purposes, members and characteristics. Each group develops a set of shared knowledge and behaviours – this is called social constructivism – and therefore the individual will behave (and even think) differently when interacting with each separate group. In some cases the groups will fall into more than one classification: for this person, the Chartered Institute of Marketing is both a formal group (with a known set of members) and a secondary group (one that he relates to occasionally, because he has a professional interest). Social constructivism suggests that we are created as individuals through our social interactions with members of groups to which we belong – this contrasts somewhat with the psychological theories of personality discussed in Chapter 4.

Influence of reference groups

Socialisation The process of becoming an effective and integrated member of society

Reference groups affect people in several ways. First, groups tend to modify members' behaviour through a process of socialisation. This is a learning process for the individual, leading to an understanding of which behaviours are acceptable within the group and which are not. For example, there may be a formal set of rules laid down by a golf club regarding care of the greens, dress codes, behaviour in the clubhouse and so forth, but it is the existing members who will advise new members on which rules are essential and which are often ignored. More importantly, the existing members will advise new members on behaviour that is expected but is not in the written rules – for example, buying a round of drinks when one scores a hole in one.

Going shopping with friends is an important way of learning what is appropriate and what is not, which may be one of the reasons why adolescent females spend a lot of time shopping with friends (Haytko and Baker 2004). Shopping also provides a shared activity that develops social education, companionship and an understanding of what is safe and what is not in the adult world.

Challenging the status quo

If shopping has become a hobby, and more particularly an educational experience for young teenage girls, marketers must think they've finally struck gold! But how true is it that young girls behave in this way? Haytko and Baker's research was conducted in the United States, where 'going to the mall' is inbuilt within the culture. But does it apply in Europe, or elsewhere in the world?

Would most European shopping malls be happy for gangs of teenagers to be hanging around anyway? And is the situation in Europe different culturally? Maybe we don't rely on malls so much because there are other places for teenagers to go – but in some places we only have street corners. Maybe malls are a better way to go after all!

Second, people develop a self-concept through their interactions within groups. How we see ourselves is a result of how others see us: feedback from others is the basis of our understanding of who we are. This is particularly apparent when the group has a specific purpose, such as supporting a football team: supporters often wear uniforms to show which team they support, thus identifying with the group and also projecting their own identity, not only to the group but to any other observers. This is a way of blending one's personal identity with the culture surrounding the team (Oliver 1999). Marketers use this aspect of group behaviour to sell uniforms; it is also a feature of celebrity endorsement – by using a particular product, the individual associates him- or herself with the celebrity.

Third, groups affect people through conformity. This is a change in beliefs or actions based on group pressures. There are two types of conformity: compliance and acceptance. Compliance happens when an individual goes along with the behaviour of the group without really accepting its beliefs. For example, someone who is not a football supporter might accompany a friend to a match and cheer on the friend's team without actually having any long-term interest in the team's fortunes. Compliance is common in the workplace. Acceptance occurs when the individual not only adapts behaviour, but also adapts his or her beliefs to come into line with the group. This might happen if the non-supporter decides that the experience was so exciting, and the team played so well, that he (or she, it could be she) decides to become a supporter. Acceptance commonly occurs through religious conversions. Overall, conformity can be considered as behaviour one adopts by observing others when confronted with membership of a new group; it is most likely to occur when the costs of conforming are outweighed by the advantages. Advantages might include self-esteem, acceptance by an aspirational group, companionship, practical benefits such as the potential for earning or saving money, and so forth (Homans 1961).

Fourth, people use groups for social comparison. We evaluate ourselves by comparing our performance with others – for example, when we consider our wealth or

Conformity The social pressure to behave in similar ways to other people

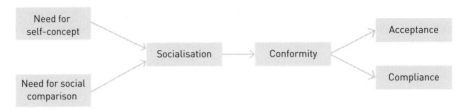

Figure 9.2   Modifying behaviour through groups

our social standing we compare ourselves with people whom we consider to be our equals in other respects. Comparisons are not necessarily made with groups with whom we have personal contact: for example, a lawyer might compare his or her salary with what other lawyers earn, or alternatively might make the comparison with other professionals such as doctors or accountants. If the groups are similar, the individual has greater confidence in the comparison (Tesser et al. 1988), but people generally value differing views when they are themselves confident in their own ability and opinions (Wheeler et al. 1969). This may explain why some people opt for cosmetic surgery (nose jobs, liposuction, breast implants, etc.) whereas other people are apparently quite happy to live with physical 'imperfections'.

In Figure 9.2 the need for social comparison and self-concept drive the socialisation process. These are the reasons why people are prepared to accept socialisation. The result of socialisation is conformity, either by acceptance or by compliance.

The mechanisms by which reference groups affect consumer behaviour are shown in Table 9.1, and diagrammatically in Figure 9.3.

Normative compliance
The force that compels people towards agreeing with the rest of the group

Of the above three influences, normative compliance is probably the most powerful. The source of normative compliance lies in **operant conditioning**; the individual finds that conforming behaviour results in group approval and esteem, whereas non-conforming behaviour results in group disapproval. Eventually the 'good' behaviour becomes automatic and natural, and it would be difficult to imagine any other way of doing things (see Chapter 6 for more on operant conditioning). For example, materialistic people are often stigmatised by groups, whereas people who enjoy experiential consumption are not. This, in time, results in behaviour modification (Van Boven et al. 2009).

The principles of good moral behaviour are not absolutes; they are the result (in most cases) of normative compliance with a reference group. Normative compliance may be less important now than it used to be for four reasons: first, the influence of the extended family (grandparents, parents, aunts and uncles) may be reducing as people move away from their home towns, and second there is strong evidence that people are becoming more inner-directed (McNulty 1985). Third, the reduction in face-to-face interaction may be leading to this move away from normative compliance; increasingly people communicate by impersonal means such as text messages and e-mail. Whether this is a cause of the paradigm shift or one of its effects is difficult to decide at present. Fourth, there is a weakening of respect for social norms, generated by a feeling of alienation from society. This is called anomie by sociologists (Durkheim 1951). Some people have little or no respect for rules made by other people, and conform grudgingly or not at all, because they do not feel that they have a position within society as a whole.

Of course, the pressure to conform will only work on someone who has a strong motivation to be accepted. If the pressure is coming from an aspirational group, this is likely to be the case; if, on the other hand, the pressure is coming from a dissociative

Table 9.1 Effects of reference groups on consumer choice

Type of Influence	Definition	Explanation	Example
Normative compliance	The pressure exerted on an individual to conform and comply	Works best when social acceptance is a strong motive, strong pressures exist from the group, and the product or service is conspicuous in its use	Street gangs require their members to wear specific jackets, or other uniform. The members want to be accepted, the pressure to wear the jacket is great, and the jacket itself is a conspicuous badge of membership
Value-expressive influence (Burnkrant and Cousineau 1975)	The pressure that comes from the need for psychological association with a group	The desired outcome is respect from others; this pressure comes from the need for esteem, rather than from the need to belong	The businessman in his pinstripe suit and the hippy in his colourful shirt, sweatband and jeans are both seeking respect from others by expressing a set of values in the way they dress
Informational influence (Calder and Burnkrant 1977)	The influence arising from a need to seek information from the reference group about the product category being considered. Small groups tend to exercise more influence (Soll et al. 2010)	People often need to get expert advice and opinion about their product choices. This can often be provided by the appropriate reference group	Many professional organisations and trade bodies offer their members free advice about useful products for their businesses. Clearly a recommendation on, say, computer software for a hairdressing business would be well-received if it came from the Hairdressers Federation

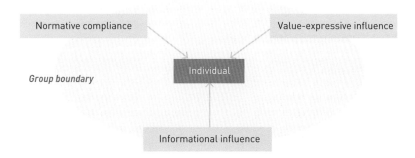

Figure 9.3 Mechanisms for controlling behaviour

group, the reverse will be the case and the individual will not feel under any pressure to conform. For example, most law-abiding citizens would comply with instructions from the police, and would usually go out of their way to help the police. Criminals, on the other hand, might avoid helping the police even in circumstances where their own crimes were not at issue.

The conspicuousness of the product or service is also crucial to the operation of normative compliance. For example, if all your friends vote Labour you might be under some pressure to do likewise, but since the ballot is secret nobody will know if you vote Conservative instead, so there is little pressure for normative compliance. Likewise, if your friends all drink Stella Artois lager you may feel under pressure to do the same, but might be happy with supermarket own-brand when you're having a beer in the back garden at home. Conspicuous behaviour carries its own downside, though – the more conspicuous the behaviour, the more embarrassing it becomes if the group does not acknowledge the signal (Han and Nunes 2010).

Advertisers often appeal to the need to belong to an aspirational group. Advertising that shows desirable groups having a good time together, all thanks to the product, are so common that they are regarded as clichés. Typically, products with a social element such as beer, entertainment and some food products are advertised in this way.

The reference group will not exert influence over every buying decision. Even in circumstances where group influence does come into play, people will be influenced by other variables such as product characteristics, standards of judgement and conflicting influences from other groups. Table 9.2 shows some of the determinants of reference group influence.

Modelling

Modelling was briefly discussed in Chapter 2, with regard to motivation and pain avoidance. The effectiveness of the role model in modelling behaviour will depend on the personal characteristics of the role model (see Figure 9.4). *Attractive* models will be imitated more than unattractive ones; *successful-looking* models are given more credence than unsuccessful-looking ones; and a model who is perceived as being *similar* to the observer is also more likely to be emulated (Baker and Churchill 1977). Somewhat more recent neuropsychological research has shown that average-looking celebrity models produce high levels of electrodermal response; in other words, they create the strongest physical effect on the observer (Gakhal and Senior 2008).

Role model An individual who acts as a reference point for judging one's own behaviour

Table 9.2   Determinants of reference group influence

Determinant	Definition	Explanation	Example
Judgement standards	The criteria used by the individual to evaluate the need to conform	Judgement standards are **objective** when the group norms are obvious and when the group approach is clearly the sensible course of action. The standards are **subjective** when it is not clear which is the most sensible course of action	Decisions of the ruling party in government are often portrayed as being unanimous; in the UK, the Conservative party is famous for presenting a united front, and individual members of the Cabinet therefore believe it is important to conform. The Labour party, on the other hand, has a tradition of public debate and therefore its shadow Cabinet is more likely to disagree in public, since members do not see a need to conform
Product characteristics	The features of the product that are salient to the group influence	The two main characteristics necessary for group influence to work are that the product should be **visible**, and that it should stand out (**non-universal ownership**)	A member of a judo club will be proud to wear the black belt, since it not only denotes a high level of expertise, but it is not available to other members unless they achieve the same level

Determinant	Definition	Explanation	Example
Member characteristics	The traits of the group member which make him or her more or less susceptible to group pressures	People vary considerably in the degree to which they are influenced by pressures from the group. Some people remain fairly independent, where others conform habitually. Personality, status and security all seem to play major roles in determining whether an individual will conform	It transpires that university students are much more likely to conform with group norms than are housewives (Manz and Sims 1981). This is possibly because the university students are young, poor and often away from home, and thus have a greater need to belong
Group characteristics	The features of the group that influence individuals to conform	The power of the group to influence the individual varies according to size, cohesiveness and leadership. Once the group is bigger than three members, the power to influence levels off. This is probably because the group has difficulty reaching a consensus. Likewise, the stronger the leadership the greater the influence, and the greater the cohesiveness the stronger the influence, because the group reaches a clear decision	Most smokers take up the habit as a result of peer group pressure when they are aged around 12 or 13. If a child's friends are strongly anti-smoking, the influence from advertisers, and even family background is likely to be much less of an influence
Role model	An individual whose influence is similar to that of a group	A role model is a hero, a star or just somebody the individual respects and admires, and wishes to imitate	Many young women seek to imitate top models by extreme dieting, to the extent that the Madrid fashion week banned all models with a body mass index below 18: Milan threatened to follow suit (BBC 2006). During the 1930s, when Clark Gable took off his shirt in a movie and showed that he was not wearing a vest, sales of vests plummeted because it became non-macho to wear one

There is also some evidence to show that observers are more likely to identify with role models who have some difficulty in completing the modelled task (Manz and Sims 1981). There has, of course, been debate about whether crime shows on TV encourage people to copy the behaviour that is shown in the programmes; according to the theory, modelled behaviour will be copied if the observer feels able to identify with the role model. Presumably, therefore, a programme showing young working-class men making a living from selling hard drugs might encourage other young working-class men to do the same. However, the saving grace of this scenario is that the role model must also be seen to be successful and attractive – and in most TV dramas and movies the criminal is shown as being, ultimately, unsuccessful.

Some recent research has shown that role models can be too good to be true – Superman turns out to be too super, so that people who compare themselves to

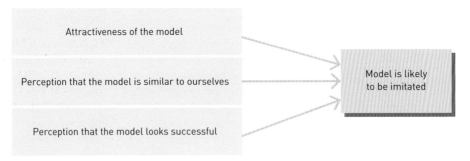

Figure 9.4   Factors in modelling

Superman are less likely to volunteer to help others, simply because they feel that they do not measure up to the role model (Nelson and Norton 2005).

Mechanisms of personal influence

Personal influence is commonly conducted via word of mouth. Word of mouth communication is informal, and is conducted between individuals, neither of whom is a marketer. Word of mouth is therefore conducted without the ulterior motive of profiting from a sale.

Groups and individuals obviously have a strong influence on people's attitudes and behaviour through word of mouth; there are three main theories regarding the mechanisms whereby this personal influence is exerted. The history of the theory is not so much one of advancing knowledge about the mechanisms involved, but is rather a history of the way society has changed in the period in which the theories were evolving.

Trickle-down theory says that lower-class people often imitate upper-class people (Veblen 1899). Influence is transmitted down from the wealthier classes to the poorer classes, as the poorer groups in society seek to 'better themselves'. In fact, trickle-down is rarely seen in industrialised, wealthy countries like the UK because new ideas are disseminated overnight by the mass media and copied by chain stores within days. This is particularly true of clothing fashions, and the Punk revolution in the mid-1970s was an example of 'trickle-up', where the fashion came up from the poorer classes. What is replacing trickle-down theory is **homophilous influence**, which refers to transmission between those of similar age, education, social class, etc. – in other words, those who already have a lot in common. The main area in which trickle-down theory can be observed is in the cult of celebrity: famous people are frequently imitated, and marketers use this to their advantage by obtaining celebrity endorsements of products. Soap operas play an important role here, because they mimic group life in the real world, so much so that people often associate themselves with the cast of a soap opera in the same way as they would with a real group of people. This can affect people's aspirational consumption patterns (Russell and Stern 2006).

Two-step flow theory says that new ideas flow from the media to 'influentials' who then pass the information on to the rest of society (Lazarsfeld et al. 1948). When this theory was first formulated in the late 1940s and early 1950s it probably had a great deal of truth in it, and there is still evidence for this view; certainly in the **diffusion** of innovative high-tech products there is strong evidence for it. However, there is a weakening of this mechanism due to the preponderance of mass media. In the 1940s most homes did not have TV and there was no commercial radio in the

Trickle-down theory The belief that innovations are adopted by wealthy, educated people first and eventually 'trickle down' to people in lower socio-economic groups

Homophilous influences The transmission of ideas between people of similar standing in the community

Diffusion The process of adoption of an innovation throughout the market

Challenging the status quo

Obviously, in the early 21st century we are well beyond the forelock-tugging attitude of our Victorian forebears, aren't we? Or are we? We may not have much respect for the opinions of the aristocracy, but there are other opinion leaders around – rock stars, TV stars, footballers and so forth. Even the subtle aristocracy of the TV chef has an influence on what we eat.

The plethora of 'I'm a Celebrity' TV shows, where C-list 'celebrities' whom nobody has heard of put themselves into embarrassing situations demonstrates that people still have an interest in what the famous have to say. Or is it simply that we like to see the once-famous come a cropper?

Trickle-down theory

Wealthy classes obtain information and adopt products

Poorer classes imitate their 'betters'

Two-step flow theory

Media generates information which reaches the 'influentials'

'Influentials' adopt the product

Remainder of the population follows the 'influentials'

Figure 9.5   Mechanisms of personal influence

UK; the availability of commercial information was therefore more restricted to the wealthy. Also, two-step flow assumes that the audience is passively waiting for the information to be presented, whereas in fact people actively seek out information about new things by asking friends and relatives and by looking for published information. A comparison of two-step flow theory and trickle-down theory is shown in Figure 9.5.

The **multistage interaction** model (see Figure 9.6) agrees that some people are more influential than others, but also recognises that the mass media affect both influentials and seekers. The influential doesn't mediate the information flow, as the two-step model suggests, but rather acts as a mechanism for emphasising or facilitating the information flow. Within the model there is a continuous dialogue between marketers, seekers and influentials, with many stages of influence before the new idea is adopted or rejected. If there are several influentials, their influence is very much stronger if they occupy a number of different positions in the network rather than being at the top of the network (Stephen and Berger 2009). This may be because the person being influenced receives the message several times, i.e. there is redundancy in the communication.

Clearly it is important for marketers to identify who the influential people are likely to be, and much research has been carried out into this area. Table 9.3 shows the main characteristics of influentials which have been identified so far. This is probably not an exhaustive list, nor will it be generally applicable to all cases.

Influentials (and market mavens – see Chapter 6) like to pass on their knowledge, and there are several reasons for doing this.

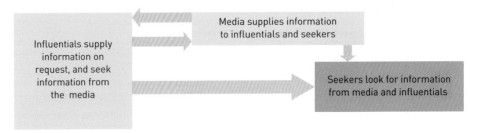

Figure 9.6   Multistage interaction model

Involvement is a major force. The influential is usually very interested in the product category, and wants to share the excitement with others; mavens also have a high need for variety (Stokburger-Sauer and Hoyer 2009). A hi-fi enthusiast who buys a new Arcam stereo will want to tell friends and colleagues all about it on Monday morning. Telling other people acts as an outlet for the pleasure of owning the equipment.

Self-enhancement is about airing one's superior knowledge. People like to appear to be 'in the know' – perhaps being able to say 'I discovered a wonderful unspoiled place for a holiday'. Appearing to be a connoisseur, whether of fine wines or works of art or classic cars, is something many influentials, and especially mavens, strive for. People often ask a friend or relative to help when choosing a gift for a third party, especially where the gift-giving might be risky (where little is known about the third party, or where a lot of importance is placed on the gift). This usually increases the social bonding between the giver and the adviser (Lowrey et al. 2004).

Concern for others often precipitates influence. The genuine desire to help a friend to reach a good decision often prompts the expert to say 'OK, I'll come with you when you go to the shop'. This factor works most strongly when there is a strong link between the individuals concerned, and when the influential has been very satisfied with the product or service concerned. People with high levels of altruism are especially likely to help (Kaikati and Ahluwalia 2010). This can have a very direct effect on consumption: there is evidence that people often feel guilty about buying themselves a treat, but if a free gift for someone else is included, the guilt is very much reduced or even disappears altogether (Lee and Corfman 2004). This implies that firms in the 'treat' or 'luxury' business would do well to offer an extra little something to 'give to a friend'. Laphroaig Whisky Distillers do this: periodically they ask established customers ('Friends of Laphroaig') to pass on the names and addresses of three friends, to whom the distillery sends a small bottle of the whisky. Naturally, people are asked to obtain permission from their friends before passing on their details, but the promotion is successful on two fronts: it rewards the loyalty of the existing customer, and it brings the whisky to the attention of the friends. People generally enjoy giving gifts to their friends and sharing good fortune – people who are given gift vouchers enjoy the vouchers more when it involves sharing with a friend (Norton et al. 2010).

Message intrigue is the factor concerned with comments about advertising messages. If an advertisement is particularly intriguing or humorous, people will discuss it; this enhances the message by repetition. Advertisements for Guinness have often used this approach – at the time of writing, Guinness have a TV advertisement that shows young drinkers regressing backwards through evolution to the status of lungfish, and expressing their disgust at the pond-water they are drinking: this implies that human evolution was driven by the need to drink something better than pond water, i.e. Guinness. This advertisement needs to be watched

Self-enhancement The practice of airing one's superior knowledge in order to create a better image

Message intrigue The element of a message which arouses the interest of a recipient

Table 9.3 Characteristics of influentials

Characteristic	Description of influential
Demographics	Wide differences according to product category. For fashion and film-going young women dominate. For self-medication, women with children are most influential. Generally, demography shows low correlation and is not a good predictor
Social activity	Influencers and opinion leaders are usually gregarious
General attitudes	Generally innovative and positive towards new products
Personality and lifestyle	Low correlation of personality with opinion leadership. Lifestyle tends to be more fashion-conscious, more socially active, more independent
Product related	Influencers are more interested in the specific product area than are others. They are active searchers and information-gatherers, especially from the mass media

carefully several times for the joke to become apparent, but since it is also eye-catching and uses exceptionally good graphics people are more likely to watch it and remember.

Dissonance *reduction* is about reducing doubts after making a major purchase. As word of mouth influence this can be good or bad; sometimes the influential will try to reassure him/herself by telling everybody about the good points of the product; more often, though, the disappointed customer will use word of mouth to complain bitterly and explain how the wicked manufacturer has cheated him/her. This is sometimes a way of passing the responsibility over to the supplier rather than admitting that the influential has made a bad decision or a bad choice.

The forces driving influentials are summarised in Figure 9.7.

Dissonance A mental state that arises when outcomes do not match with expectations

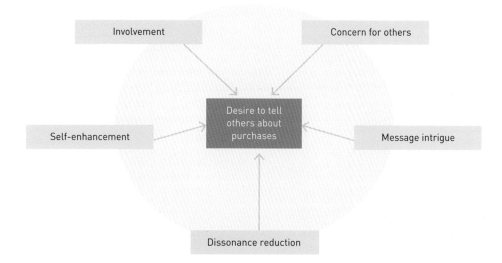

Figure 9.7 Forces driving influentials

Challenging the status quo

Interestingly, most of the reasons influentials have for passing on what they know are selfish ones. They want to show off their knowledge, pass on an interesting bit of gossip, reassure themselves that they made the right decision by persuading someone else to make the same choice, and so forth.

Only occasionally, apparently, are they motivated by concern for others – passing on a good tip to a friend, in this case. Does this tell us that people are essentially selfish? Or should we give people credit for getting their kicks by being helpful rather than destructive?

Overall, word-of-mouth influence is much stronger than advertising or other marketer-produced communications. For marketers, then, the problem lies in knowing how to use word of mouth to its best advantage. Table 9.4 offers some comparisons and strategies.

It is not usually possible to rely entirely on word of mouth, but marketers should take steps to stimulate it as a promotional tool. Advertising that provokes word of mouth about the advert itself can be very powerful – research shows that a very creative advertisement that prompts people to tell others about it leads to a much greater intention to purchase after the other people see the advertisement for themselves (Moldovan and Lehmann 2010). In other words, someone who is told about a very exciting or entertaining advertisement will be prompted to look out for the advert, and is then much more likely to buy the product. Sometimes marketers are able to encourage word of mouth by giving influential people a product sample and asking them to blog about their experiences with the product. Most people in that position

Table 9.4   Word of mouth

Strong influence	Weak influence	Tactical suggestions
Seeker initiates conversation with source	Source initiates conversation with seeker	Advertising could emphasise the idea of 'Ask the person who owns one'. Network marketers could emphasise a more advisory role for their salespeople rather than a strongly proactive approach
Negative information	Positive information	Because marketers are uniformly positive about the product, the seeker is more alert to any negatives. The essential thing for marketers to do is to ensure that any complaints are dealt with immediately and thoroughly
Verbal communication is stronger for thinking and evaluation	Visual communication is stronger for awareness and stimulation of interest	Where appropriate, marketers could encourage satisfied customers to show their friends the product; this tactic is often used for home improvement sales, where customers are paid a small reward or commission for introducing friends to the product. This is also the basis for party-plan selling, e.g. Tupperware and Anne Summers

will accept, embrace, ridicule or apologise for accepting the role as a marketing tool, and very few ignore their role by not mentioning in the blog that they were given the product (Kozinets et al. 2008).

If the company is in a position to be able to identify influentials, it is well worthwhile offering to lend them the product (or even give them it, if the cost is low enough) so that they can be stimulated into talking about it to friends. Advertising should be interesting and involving, perhaps even controversial, so that debate ensues. Although it is not true to say that any word of mouth will be good for a company, it is certainly true to say that controversy and debate will always increase brand awareness, even when it does not enhance brand image. For example, Harveytiles (a brand of Harvey Roofing Products Ltd, a South African roofing tile manufacturer) produces advertisements that are extremely controversial. The slogans use religious references ('A roof without Harveytiles is like being burnt in hell without a saviour: Only heaven is covered with Harveytiles') that have proved to be extremely offensive to the committed Christians of Zambia. The result has been that everyone in Zambia has heard of Harveytiles, but of course this does not necessarily mean that people will buy the product. Some people undoubtedly boycott the product because of the religious references.

Another way of stimulating word of mouth is to allow people to try out the product. Car manufacturers usually give exceptionally generous discounts to car hire companies,

Consumer behaviour in action: *The Da Vinci Code*

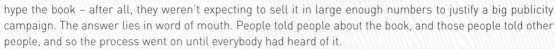

Dan Brown's climb to fame was far from meteoric. He failed at several careers before getting into writing – and even then his earlier books hardly set the world on fire. Yet everyone needs to learn their craft, and eventually Dan hit the jackpot with *The Da Vinci Code*, published in 2003.

The book, which puts forward the theory that Jesus married Mary Magdalene and had children by her, was not exactly a great work of literature, but it caught the public imagination. Initially the publishers planned only a short print run – based on the sales of Dan's other books, it seemed unlikely that the book would be a runaway best-seller. The rest, of course, is history: the book had sold 2.2 million copies by March 2005, and received another boost when the film version was released in 2006.

So how come this book sold so much better than expected? The publishers certainly didn't hype the book – after all, they weren't expecting to sell it in large enough numbers to justify a big publicity campaign. The answer lies in word of mouth. People told people about the book, and those people told other people, and so the process went on until everybody had heard of it.

Research by Nielsen Bookscan in 2005 showed that a large number of best-selling books have achieved success this way – *Captain Corelli's Mandolin*, *Eats, Shoots and Leaves* and *The Lovely Bones* were all cited as million-plus sellers that had succeeded almost entirely on personal recommendation.

As a result, the World Book Day organisers ran a campaign encouraging people to recommend a book to a friend – another resounding success!

taking the view that hirers might well be tempted to buy the same model at a later stage, and are also very likely to talk about the vehicle to others.

To prevent negative word of mouth, marketers should do more than merely satisfy any customer complaints. In 1981 a survey was carried out on behalf of the Corporate Consumer Affairs Department of the Coca-Cola Company among customers who had complained to the company. Here are the main findings (Coca-Cola Company 1981):

- More than 12% told twenty or more people about the company's response to their complaint.
- Those who were completely satisfied with the response told a median of four to five others about the experience.
- Nearly 10% of those who reported being completely satisfied increased their purchases of company products.
- Those who thought their complaint was not dealt with fairly told a median of nine to ten other people.
- Of those who thought their complaint was not dealt with fairly, nearly one-third subsequently boycotted company products entirely, and another 45% reduced their purchases.

From these figures it follows that marketers should encourage people to complain, and should go beyond the call of duty in satisfying complaints, since this will actually increase the loyalty of those who complain.

Word of mouse

In recent years word of mouth has been supplemented by e-mail communications, sometimes called word of mouse. E-mail is a fast and powerful communications medium, but more importantly it provides a semi-permanent record of what was said, so that communications can contain facts and figures that can be referred to later. Encouraging people to e-mail each other about products has become a growth area for e-marketing, and is a feature of many websites. The decision to forward a message implies that the individual endorses it: the person's involvement in the product is of course important, but the decision to forward a message seems to depend much more on the amount of e-mail traffic between the individuals concerned (Harvey et al. 2011).

Word of mouse also happens in chatrooms and on blogs. Virtual communities are extremely powerful in promoting products – they frequently ask each other for specific recommendations about products. Young consumers have been shown to develop on-line personalities, which may differ from their real personalities but which act in very similar ways in terms of group behaviour. People are often excluded from groups, bullying is used as a way of establishing group norms and boundaries, and avatars associate with other avatars whom they regard as friends (Wood et al. 2009). Social networking sites that focus around celebrities often generate a very strong sense of togetherness and belonging, amounting to a tribal situation, despite having no reality outside cyberspace (Hamilton and Hewer 2010).

On-line communities provide support and help for their members in the same way as 'real' groups. A study of a slimming website revealed that there are three main types of participant: Passive Recipients obtain high levels of informational and emotional support, but communicate passively; Active Supporters are much more proactive in communication, and obtain high levels of support; and Casual Browsers communicate passively and receive little support (Ballantine and Stephenson 2011). On-line communities on Facebook often 'nudge' each other towards buying particular products (Harris and Dennis 2011), and on-line communities can be very powerful in raising brand commitment (Kim et al. 2008).

Sometimes on-line communities can be damaging for marketers. Counter-brand and alter-brand behaviour is easily facilitated in cyberspace: users can develop dangerous opposition, or even their own products that compete directly with firms, without the need for corporate involvement.

Web forums can be used by companies to attract new customers and to provide an outlet for people's discussions about products. People use such sites as information sources, and as ways of validating their self-concept as being knowledgeable, or as 'insiders'. They can be particularly powerful for arts organisations such as orchestras, art galleries and museums (O'Sullivan 2010).

Website design has moved through a number of phases (Figure 9.8). During the late 1990s most websites were merely 'presence' sites, giving a brief outline of the company and its products and directing the interested potential customer to a telephone number or 'snail-mail' (postal) address. As the decade progressed, more and more sites became interactive, allowing customers to navigate around the site, place orders on-line and e-mail the company as appropriate for further information.

By the early 21st century, sites had gone a step further, and were offering the capability of involving visitors' friends. 'E-mail this site to a friend' buttons became commonplace, and eventually firms began to add value to the site by including games and puzzles, and even jokes, to encourage site visitors to enrol their friends onto the site. This approach helped to overcome major problem of Internet marketing – making your voice heard through the clutter of almost 5000 million websites worldwide.

A somewhat insidious development is the linking of marketing messages to self-replicating viruses. The virus operates by sending itself to everyone in the victim's address book, displaying the marketing message in the form of an e-mail. It then copies itself into all the other recipient's address books and sends itself out again. Soon it has sent the message to everyone on the planet (often several times). Although in the vast majority of cases recipients simply ignore the message and delete it, even a tiny response rate will represent a very large amount of business for the initiating firm. Some countries have enacted legislation to prosecute firms that do this, but such prosecutions are rare – an international response is essential for tackling an international problem.

There is little doubt that word of mouse will grow as access to the Internet and consequent increased use of e-mail spreads throughout the world. Future developments (notably voice e-mail and voice-over-internet protocol such as Skype) may bring us back to vocal delivery of messages (word of mouth) but web-enabled viral marketing is likely to be an increasing force for the foreseeable future.

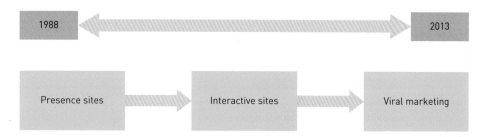

Figure 9.8   Evolution of websites

Summary

In this chapter we have looked at some of the interpersonal factors that influence purchasing behaviour. In particular, we have looked at the groups and individuals who most influence consumers, and at the ways the influence is exerted. Finally, we have looked at ways marketers can use these interpersonal factors to improve customer relations and customer loyalty.

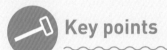

Key points

- Most people are members of several reference groups, all of which influence the individual in different ways.
- Normative compliance is probably the most powerful influence on behaviour.
- Conspicuousness is the most crucial product characteristic for normative compliance.
- Word of mouth spreads because the informant (influential) likes to talk about the products concerned.
- Complaints can be turned to the marketer's advantage by generous handling.
- Word of mouse is likely to be a growth area in marketing communications in the 21st century.

Review questions

1   How might companies encourage word of mouth?
2   What is the role of normative compliance in fashion marketing?
3   How might peer pressure encourage people to try new things?
4   Why is word of mouse becoming more popular with companies?
5   How can companies counteract negative word of mouth?
6   How might membership of an automatic group affect buying behaviour?
7   How might membership of an automatic group affect someone's propensity to join a secondary group?
8   How might a secondary group also be a formal group?
9   What are the defining characteristics of a primary group?
10 How might a marketer make use of a virtual group?

Case study revisited: Facebook

Facebook represents the ultimate in peer and reference groups. It facilitates communication between peers in a way that, in the past, has been impossible, and it allows people to separate out the different communities of which they are members.

The new Timeline system on Facebook allows people even greater capability for sharing and selecting. Timeline allows people to have a running history of what they are currently doing – which friends they have added, which movies they have seen, which books they have read, which restaurants they have visited, and so on.

Having a Facebook page is becoming almost compulsory: in 2010 it was estimated that 41% of Americans had a Facebook account, which considering that the site only accepts people over 13 years of age means that probably half the eligible US population has an account. (It should be noted that there may well be under-age Facebook members – there is really no way of knowing.)

Members join 'like' pages, which are clubs for people with an interest in a specific product or hobby. Often these pages are operated by marketers, who are able to glean useful information about their target markets.

Facebook has met with problems – it has been banned in many workplaces because employees were spending too much time relating to friends (and each other) and not enough time doing the actual work, and it has been banned in several countries because it may contain anti-Islamic or anti-Communist statements (in other words, Facebook encourages free speech, which some dictators find threatening). Overall, though, it has proved to be a hugely successful tool for facilitating group interaction – as well as a useful tool for marketers.

Case study: The George Formby Society

George Formby was a music-hall performer in the 1920s, but by the 1930s and 1940s he had developed a film career as an actor, musician and comedian. He was famous for his cheeky songs (accompanying himself on the ukulele or banjo-ukulele) and his toothy grin.

A native of Lancashire, he used his broad Northern accent to comic effect, establishing a stage persona as an amiable, accident-prone and folksy working-class man. He wrote many of his own songs, which were always humorous with a great many double-entendres, and which were set to heavily-syncopated jazz-like tunes; he is credited with inventing a new style of playing the ukulele, a very distinctive technique called the split stroke. By 1939 he was Britain's highest-earning entertainer, making what would now be the equivalent of around £5 million a year. When war broke out, he set out to entertain the troops, playing concerts to over 3 million servicemen during the next six years.

Formby lived the kind of life any successful musician nowadays might live. He drove fast cars (he was the first man to drive at over 100 miles an hour at Brooklands race track) and he owned a Norton motorbike which sold at auction for over £30,000 after his death.

Formby died of a heart attack in 1961, aged only 56, but he left behind a legacy of 21 hit films and over 230 recordings. He also left behind a legacy of loyal fans, and indeed the number of fans has grown rather than shrunk as the years have passed.

The George Formby Society was formed in 1961, six months after Formby's death. Members are not required to play the ukulele, although many do and non-playing members are encouraged to learn. Members pay a small fee (£21 for UK members, £26 for European members, £31 for the rest of the world). The Society has hundreds of members worldwide, all dedicated to the memory of George Formby. The Annual General Meeting is usually held in September at the Imperial Hotel, Blackpool, and a minimum of fifty members need to be present for the meeting to be quorate – an indication of how many members there actually are. The Society publishes a quarterly magazine, *The Vellum*, which contains articles about George Formby's life and times as well as news of the various meetings and conventions run by the Society and its branches worldwide. *The Vellum* is a 32-page, glossy, professionally produced magazine which is mailed to all members as part of their membership benefits.

There are 15 branches of the Society (including one in Perth, Western Australia) and meetings are held monthly to talk about George's life and works (and of course play his tunes). Branches welcome non-members at these meetings, no doubt with a view that they may become members in due course. Members help each other to improve their playing style, swap sheet music, help locate recordings and of course develop friendships that go beyond the Society's aims.

A statue of Formby was erected in his birthplace of Wigan in September of 2007: more than 200 Society members attended the unveiling, some playing their ukuleles, before going on to a celebration buffet at the Britannia Hotel. Of course this buffet was marked by a great deal more ukulele playing, with formal stage performances of George's songs as well as audience participation – no doubt the sound of 200 ukuleles being strummed will live on in the memories of Wiganites for many years.

Fifty and more years after Formby's death it may seem surprising that so many people are still interested in keeping his memory alive. What is perhaps more surprising is that most of the Society's members were born after Formby died – it is a society that appeals to many young people who cannot possibly ever have seen Formby perform except on film, or heard him play except on recordings made using 1940s technology. In the UK generally, Formby is half-forgotten, and nowadays often regarded as outdated, his songs unfunny (because humour shifts), and his 'cheeky chappie' style of comedy has no place alongside modern, cynical comedians. Perhaps the George Formby Society looks back to a more innocent age, when saying 'knickers' was considered to be risqué humour, and people could laugh at something as innocent as George Formby's toothy grin.

Questions

1 What type of group is the George Formby Society?
2 Why do so many members play the ukulele, or learn shortly after joining?
3 What is the purpose of *The Vellum*?
4 Why might someone from outside the UK join the Society?
5 What is the motivation for attending monthly meetings?

Further reading

For some more on gift-giving, try McKechnie, S. and Tynan, C. (2006) Social meaning in Christmas consumption: an exploratory study of UK celebrants' consumption rituals, *Journal of Consumer Behaviour* 5 (2): 130–44. Also, *The Gift of Thanks: The Roots and Rituals of Gratitude* (Boston, MA: Houghton Mifflin Harcourt, 2009) by Margaret Visser explores the other side of gift-giving – gratitude on the part of the recipient.

Ervin Goffman's *Presentation of Self in Everyday Life* is a classic read (Harmondsworth: Penguin, 1990). It explores the ways in which we present ourselves in different group situations, and it explains his 'life as theatre' analogy.

Also by Goffman, *Stigma: Notes on the Management of Spoiled Identity* (Harmondsworth: Penguin, 1990) explores another side of groups – the fate of those who are excluded. His research was carried out among people who were disfigured through birth or accident, people from racial or religious minorities, and people with mental illnesses. Goffman notes that other people tend to focus on the distinguishing feature, not on the whole personality, therefore such people become defined by their differences rather than by their similarities. This is a thought-provoking book, and often a very moving one.

For a humorous look at the fashion industry, and at our obsession with wearing the right clothes, you might like *Fashion Victim: Our Love–Hate Relationship with Dressing, Shopping and the Cost of Style* by Michelle Lee (New York: Broadway Books, 2003). The author takes a wry look at the fashion industry, and pokes fun at some of the 'rules' of fashion ('Thou Shalt Pay More to Look Poor' being one of them). This is a fun read, with some interesting ideas underneath it.

References

Asch, S.E. (1951) Effects of group pressure on the modification and distortion of judgements. In H. Guetzkow (ed.), *Groups, Leadership and Men*. Pittsburgh, PA: Carnegie Press.

Baker, M.J. and Churchill, G.A. Jr. (1977) The impact of physically attractive models on advertising evaluations. *Journal of Marketing Research* 14 (4): 538–55.

Ballantine, P.W. and Stephenson, R.J. (2011) Help me, I'm fat! Social support in online weight loss networks. *Journal of Consumer Behaviour* 10 (6): 332–7.

BBC (2006) News. Wednesday 13 September.

Beardon, W.O. and Etzel, M.J. (1982) Reference group influence on product and brand purchase decisions. *Journal of Consumer Research* 9: 184.

Burnkrant, R. and Cousineau, A. (1975) Informational and normative social influence on buyer behavior. *Journal of Consumer Research* Dec: 206–15.

Calder, B. and Burnkrant, R. (1977) Interpersonal influences on consumer behavior: an attribution theory approach. *Journal of Consumer Research* 4: 29–38.

Carlson, K.A. and Sally, D. (2002) Thoughts that count: fairness and possibilities, intentions and reactions. *Advances in Consumer Research* 29: 79–89.

Coca-Cola Company (1981) Measuring the Grapevine: Consumer Response and Word-of-Mouth. Coca-Cola Company Consumer Information Center.

Cova, B. and White, T. (2010) Counter-brand and alter-brand communities: the impact of Web 2.0 on tribal marketing approaches. *Journal of Marketing Management* 26 (3&4): 256–70.

Crosby, E. and Otnes, C. (2010) Consumption as a strategy for stigma management. *Advances in Consumer Research* 37: 28–9.

Durkheim, E. (1951) *Suicide: A Study in Sociology*. New York: Free Press.

Fischer, E., Bristor, J. and Gaynor, B. (1996) Creating or escaping community? An exploratory study of Internet consumers' behaviours. *Advances in Consumer Research* 23: 178–82.

Fisher, R.J. and Dube, L. (2003) Gender differences in responses to emotional advertising: the effect of the presence of others. *Advances in Consumer Research* 30: 15–17.

Gakhal, B. and Senior, C. (2008) Examining the influence of fame in the presence of beauty: an electrodermal 'neuromarketing' study. *Journal of Consumer Behaviour* 7 (4/5): 331–41.

Hamilton, K. and Hewer, P. (2010) Tribal mattering spaces: social networking sites, celebrity affiliations, and tribal innovations. *Journal of Marketing Management* 26 (3&4): 271–9.

Han, Y.J. and Nunes, J.C. (2010) Read the signal but don't mention it: how conspicuous consumption embarrasses the signaler. *Advances in Consumer Research* 37: 82.

Harris, L. and Dennis, C. (2011) Engaging customers on Facebook: challenge for e-retailers. *Journal of Consumer Behaviour* 10 (6): 338–46.

Harvey, C.G., Stewart, D.B. and Ewing, M.T. (2011) Forward or delete: what drives peer-to-peer message propagation across social networks? *Journal of Consumer Behaviour* 10 (6): 365–72.

Haytko, D.L. and Baker, J. (2004) It's all at the mall: exploring adolescent girls' experiences. *Journal of Retailing* 80 (1): 67.

Homans, G.C. (1961) *Social Behavior: Its Elementary Forms*. New York: Harcourt, Brace and World.

Huang, L. (2010) Social contagion effects in experiential information exchange on bulletin board systems. *Journal of Marketing Management* 26 (3&4): 197–212.

Kaikati, A.M. and Ahluwalia, R. (2010) Word of mouth communication as helping behavior. *Advances in Consumer Research* 37: 127–8.

Kim, J., Choi, J., Qualls, W. and Han, K. (2008) It takes a marketplace community to raise brand commitment: the role of online communities. *Journal of Marketing Management* 24 (3&4): 409–31.

Koretz, G. (1990) Economic trends. *Business Week*, 5 March.

Kozinets, R.V., de Valck, K., Wilner, S.J.S. and Wojnicki, A.C. (2008) Opening the black box of buzzing bloggers: understanding how consumers deal with the tension between authenticity and commercialism in seeded word-of-mouth campaigns. *Advances in Consumer Research* 35: 49–51.

Langerak, F., Verhoef, P.C. and Verleigh, P.W.J. (2004) Satisfaction and participation in virtual communities. *Advances in Consumer Research* 31: 56–7.

Lazarsfeld, P.F., Berelson, B.R. and Gaudet, H. (1948) *The People's Choice*. New York: Columbia University Press.

Lee, S.N. and Corfman, K.P. (2004) A little something for me, and maybe for you too: promotions that relieve guilt. *Advances in Consumer Research* 31: 28.

Liang, B. and Scammon, D.L. (2011) E-word of mouth on health social networking sites: an opportunity for tailored health communication. *Journal of Consumer Behaviour* 10 (6): 322–31.

Lowrey, T.M., Otnes, C.C. and Ruth, J.A. (2004) An exploration of social influence on dyadic gift-giving. *Advances in Consumer Research* 31: 112.

Manz, C.C. and Sims, H.P. (1981) Vicarious learning: the influence of modelling on organisational behaviour. *Academy of Management Review*, January.

McNulty, W.K. (1985) UK social change through a wide-angle lens. *Futures*, August.

Moldovan, S. and Lehmann, D. (2010) The effect of advertising on word of mouth. *Advances in Consumer Research* 37: 119.

Muniz, A. and O'Guinn, T. (2001) Brand community. *Journal of Consumer Research* 27 (4): 412–32.

Nelson, L.D. and Norton, M.I. (2005) From student to superhero: situational primes shape future helping. *Journal of Experimental Social Psychology* 41 (4): 423–30.

Norton, M.J., Aknin, L. and Dunn, E. (2010) Putting the 'social' in prosocial spending: interpersonal giving promotes happiness. *Advances in Consumer Research* 37: 43.

O'Sullivan, T. (2010) Dangling conversations: Web-forum use by a symphony orchestra's audience members. *Journal of Marketing Management* 26 (7&8): 656–70.

Okleshen, C. and Grossbart, S. (1998) Usenet groups, virtual community and consumer behaviours. *Advances in Consumer Research* 25 (1): 276–82.

Oliver, R.L. (1999) Whence consumer loyalty? *Journal of Marketing*, 63 (Oct) 4: 33–44.

Roper, S. and La Niece, C. (2009) The importance of brands in the lunch-box choices of low-income British school children. *Journal of Consumer Behaviour* 8 (2/3): 84–99.

Russell, C. and Stern, B. (2006) Aspirational consumption in US soap operas: the process of parasocial attachment to television soap opera characters. *Advances in Consumer Research* 33 (1): 36.

Soll, J., Larrick, R. and Mannes, A. (2010) When it comes to wisdom, smaller crowds are wiser. *Advances in Consumer Research* 37: 95.

Stephen, A. and Berger, J. (2009) Creating contagion: cascades in spatially dispersed social networks. *Advances in Consumer Research* 36: 37.

Stokburger-Sauer, N.E. and Hoyer, W.D. (2009) Consumer advisors revisited: what drives those with market mavenism and opinion leadership tendencies and why? *Journal of Consumer Behaviour* (Mar–Jun), 8 (2/3): 100–115.

Tesser, A., Miller, M. and Moore, J. (1988) Some affective consequences of social comparison and reflection processes: the pain and pleasure of being close. *Journal of Personality and Social Psychology* 54 (1): 49–61.

Van Boven, L., Campbell, M.C. and Gilovich, T. (2009) Stigmatising materialism: on stereotypes and impressions of materialistic versus experiential consumers. *Advances in Consumer Research* 36: 14–15.

Veblen, T. (1899) *The Theory of the Leisure Class*. New York: Macmillan.

Wheeler, L., Shaver, K.G., Jones, R.A., Goethals, G.R., Cooper, J., Robinson, J.E., Gruder, C.L. and Butzine, K.W. (1969) Factors determining the choice of a comparison other. *Journal of Experimental Social Psychology* 5 (Apr): 219–32.

Wood, N., Chaplin, L.N. and Solomon, M. (2009) Virtually me: youth consumers and their online identities. *Advances in Consumer Research* 36: 23–4.

More online

To gain free access to additional online resources to support this chapter please visit: **www.sagepub.co.uk/blythe**

CHAPTER ⑩
The family

LEARNING OBJECTIVES

After reading this chapter you should be able to:

- Describe the different definitions of family, and explain the influences on creating the definitions.

- Explain the role of culture in creating decision-making styles.

- Explain the roles of family members in decision-making.

- Describe ways in which conflict is generated and resolved.

- Describe the process by which children become effective consumers.

- Explain how brand loyalty is passed down through the generations.

- Critique family lifestyle models and explain the possible alternatives.

- Describe the roles family members take in the purchase and consumption process.

Introduction

Of all the reference groups, the family is probably the most powerful in influencing consumer decision-making. Almost all of us are members of families: our parents teach us how to be effective consumers from an early age, and we influence our brothers and sisters, our parents and eventually our own children in their purchasing choices.

The family has gone through many changes in structure, but still remains the most important social grouping. The reasons for this are as follows:

1 In the case of children, the parental influence is the earliest, and therefore colours the child's perception of everything that follows. In fact, the superego (see Chapter 1) is thought to be an internalised parent.

2 In the case of parents, the desire to do the best they can for their children influences their decision-making when making purchases for the family. Clear examples are the purchase of breakfast cereals and disposable nappies, where the appeal is almost invariably to do with the comfort and well-being of the baby.

3 In the case of siblings, the influence comes either as role model (where an older sibling is looked up to by a younger one) or as carer/adviser to younger siblings.

4 Because families share a large part of their consumption, decision-making is often joint, or follows formalised rules that control consumption behaviour within the group.

Because we value the opinions of our family members, we take their advice and often conform to their norms of behaviour. Even though the structure of families has undergone major changes in recent years, it is still true to say that the family is the basic unit of society.

Case study: 'Little buddhas'

The annual conference of the Association of Teachers and Lecturers is not generally known for producing controversial statements and headline stories, but the 2012 conference certainly caused some ripples. Dr Mary Boustead, the general secretary of the union, stated that some middle-class parents were bringing their children up to be 'little Buddhas', in other words, were worshipping them instead of parenting them.

Dr Boustead went on to say that children who had no boundaries at home could not be expected to respond well to having boundaries in school. She went on to ask how many parents expected their children to contribute to the running of the home.

Her comments followed on from a survey of 814 teachers, of whom more than half said that behaviour in class (and incidences of violence against teachers) had worsened in recent years. Behaviour problems were as likely to come from middle-class families as from children from disadvantaged backgrounds, and some teachers reported being victims of violence or threats of violence. Some teachers have said that the problem has worsened since corporal punishment was banned in 1986 – although none of them wanted a return to the use of physical punishment, there were many calls for disciplinary measures of equal seriousness to be brought in, and some even suggested that military-style discipline should be introduced.

A school in Manchester staffed entirely by ex-military personnel opened in September 2012, and the UK government has proposed that all secondary schools should have an active Army cadet programme in place to teach self-discipline.

Of course, most children are perfectly fine. The majority are reasonably polite, reasonably hard-working in school, and turn into reasonably-functional adults (we don't have angels to work with, just human beings). The minority, however, create disruption out of all proportion to their numbers – and that is where family life has a lot to answer for.

How to impress your examiner

You will probably be asked about decision-making patterns in families, and especially about the role of children. It will gain you extra marks if you can provide the downside of decision-making, by outlining the ways in which children are influenced by their peers and by marketers. The question also implies that you should understand that decision-making and indeed all family consumption behaviour is very much culturally driven.

Defining families

The concept of what constitutes a family varies from one culture to another. In the UK and United States, families usually consist of parents and their natural or adopted children: this is called the nuclear family. In some other cultures, families might extend to aunts, uncles, grandparents and cousins all living in the same house and sharing their consumption. These extended families are becoming rare in industrialised countries, partly because of the mobility of workers: someone who finds a job in another part of the country is unlikely to find it convenient to take a large number of extended family members along.

Even in nuclear families there will also be influences from uncles, aunts, grandparents and cousins. While these influences are often less strong in UK households than they might be in some other countries where the extended family is more common, the influences still exist to a greater or lesser extent. For statistical purposes, Eurostat has adopted the United Nations definition of a family, which is as follows:

> *The persons within a private or institutional household who are related as husband and wife or as parent and never-married child by blood or adoption.*

For the purposes of the definition, couples who live together without marrying are still regarded as a family. On the other hand, the European Community Household Panel defines a family household more broadly as a shared residence with common housekeeping arrangements.

From a marketing viewpoint, the level of demand for many products is dictated more by the number of households than by the number of families. For example, most households in affluent countries would have a washing machine, but hardly any would have two washing machines. The relevance of families to marketing is therefore much more about consumer *behaviour* than about consumer *demand levels*.

In terms of its function as a reference group, the family is defined by the following characteristics:

1 *Face-to-face contact.* Family members see each other most days, and interact as advisers, information providers and sometimes deciders. Other reference groups rarely have this level of contact.
2 *Shared consumption.* Durables such as fridges, freezers, televisions and furniture are shared, and food is collectively purchased and cooked (although there is a strong trend away from families eating together). Purchase of these items is often collective: children even participate in decision-making on such major purchases as cars and houses. Other reference groups may share some consumption (for example, members of a model railway club may hire a workshop and share tools) but families share consumption of most domestic items.
3 *Subordination of individual needs.* Because consumption is shared, some family members will find that the solution chosen is not one that fully meets their needs. Although this happens in other reference groups, the effect is more pronounced in families.
4 *Purchasing agent.* Because of the shared consumption, most families will have one member who does most, or all, of the shopping. Traditionally, this has been the mother of the family, but increasingly the purchasing agent is the older children of the family – even pre-teens are sometimes taking over this role. The reason for this is the increase in the number of working mothers – women who work outside the home – which has left less time for shopping. This has major implications for marketers, since pre-teens and young teens generally watch more TV than adults

Purchasing agent
Someone who has the task of making purchases on behalf of a group, usually the family

and are therefore more open to marketing communications. Other reference groups may well have a purchasing agent, but this is probably only for specific items rather than for all those items the group is interested in – and most informal groups would appoint a purchasing agent for occasional purposes only (for example, to send out for pizza or to book a weekend away).

In some cases products are passed on from one generation to another as a way of preserving family identity and values. Whether this means passing on great-grandmother's wedding ring or handing over the family's old car to the newly licensed eldest child, the family link is continued (Curasi 2006). The same behaviour has been found in investments, with parents passing on investments and investment advice to children (Williams 2006). Products passed on in this way can move between 'sacred' and 'profane' values (Hartman and Kiecker 2004). For example, Granny's wedding ring might be worn on a chain round the neck of a teenager: equally, Grandad's old pen-knife might be preserved as a family heirloom. The older generation often pass on these items, complete with their history and an account of their significance, in the hope that the younger generation will continue to cherish them (Curasi 2011).

Family decision-making is not as straightforward as marketers have supposed in the past. There has been an assumption that the purchasing agent (e.g. the mother) is the one who makes the decisions, and while this is often the case, this approach ignores the ways in which the purchasing decisions are arrived at.

There is a problem here with terminology. Traditionally, studies of the family have referred to the male partner as the husband, and the female partner as the wife. The increasing number of families in which the parents are not married has rendered this approach obsolete; the research reported in the next section was conducted in the 1970s, when the vast majority of parents were married. The validity and relevance of the research is not in question, since it refers to traditional roles that may or may not actually be adopted by specific families.

Role specialisation is critical in family decision-making because of the sheer number of different products that must be bought each year in order to keep the family supplied. What this means in practice is that, for example, the family member responsible for doing the cooking is also likely to take the main responsibility for shopping for food. The family member who does the most driving is likely to make the main decision about the car and its accessories, servicing, fuelling, and so forth; the family gardener buys the gardening products, and so on.

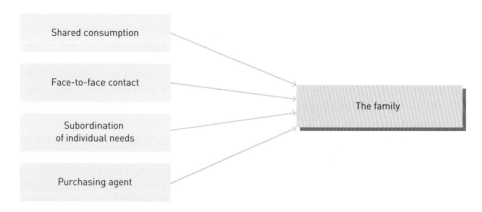

Figure 10.1   Defining characteristics of families

Four kinds of marital role specialisation have been identified: wife dominant where the wife has most say in the decision, husband dominant where the husband plays the major role, syncratic or democratic where the decision is arrived at jointly, and autonomic where the decision is made entirely independently of the partner (Filiatrault and Ritchie 1980). For example, the wife may have the biggest role in deciding on new curtains, the husband may have the lead role in choosing the family car, they may decide together on a home extension, and the husband alone might choose the fertiliser for the garden. Marketers need to identify which role specialisation type is typical of a target market in order to know where to aim the promotional activities. Some more recent research indicates that in the event of disagreement about a joint decision it is the man's decision which is likely to prevail (Ward 2006). This research was conducted exclusively in Tennessee, however, which may account for at least some of the result.

Product category affects role specialisation and decision-making systems. When an expensive purchase is being considered, it is likely that most of the family will be involved in some way, if only because major purchases affect the family budgeting for other items. At the other end of the scale, day-to-day shopping for toilet rolls and cans of beans entails very little collective decision-making. Where the product has a shared usage (a holiday or a car) the collective decision-making component is likely to increase greatly. Conversely, where the product is used predominantly by one family member, that member will dominate the decision-making even when the purchase is a major one (the family chef will make most of the decision about the new cooker, for example).

Culture has a marked effect on family decision-making styles. Religion and nationality will often affect the way decisions are made: African cultures tend to be male-dominated in decision-making, whereas European and North American cultures show a more egalitarian pattern of decision-making (Green et al. 1983). In India, gold carries very strong family significance at weddings. The bride is thought to be purified by gifted and borrowed gold – typically her new husband's family will lend jewellery to her, as a way of binding her to the new family (Fernandez and Veer 2004).

There are two issues here for the marketer: first, what is the effect on the marketing mix of the multi-ethnic society now emerging in Europe, and second what is the effect when dealing internationally? This is a somewhat sensitive area, and one that marketers are still getting to grips with. There is more on the general aspects of culture in Chapter 9.

Wife-dominant decision-making Decisions that are left to the female adult of the family

Husband-dominant decision-making A situation in which the male of the household has the most power in consumption decisions

Syncratic (democratic) decision-making In group decision-making, the type of decision that is made on the basis of consultation

Democratic decision-making See *Syncratic decision-making*

Autonomic decision-making A type of decision that is made by the individual without recourse to others

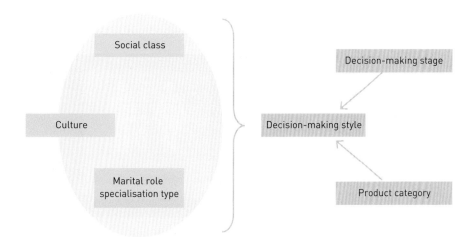

Figure 10.2   Determinants of decision-making style in families

Social class creates patterns of decision-making. Among very wealthy families there appears to be a greater tendency for the husbands to make the decisions, but at the same time the norms of purchase tend to be well-established and therefore discussion is unnecessary (Komarovsky 1961). Lower-class families, with low incomes, have traditionally been more matriarchal, with the wives often handling the financial decisions about rent, insurance, food bills and Christmas clubs without reference to the husbands. Poorer families will often divert a large proportion of their limited resources towards ensuring that the children are not stigmatised by poverty: often children of poorer parents will still wear the latest trainers and go on school trips (Hamilton and Catterall 2006). Obviously there is a stronger possibility of conflict when resources are limited, but in most lower-income families there is an emphasis on not allowing conflict to develop in the first place, rather than on conflict resolution after the event (Hamilton 2009). Middle-class families tend to show greater democratic involvement in decision-making. These social class distinctions are gradually breaking down, however, as a result of increasing wealth and mass education.

The family may well adopt different roles according to the *decision-making stage*. At the problem-recognition stage of, for example, the need for new shoes for the children, the children themselves may be the main contributors. The mother may then decide what type of shoes should be bought, and the father may be the one who takes the children to buy the shoes. It is reasonable to suppose that the main user of the product might be important in the initial stages, with perhaps joint decision-making at the final purchase.

These determinants of decision-making style are summarised in Figure 10.2.

Other determinants might include such factors as whether both parents are earning. In such families, decision-making is more likely to be joint because each has a financial stake in the outcome. Some studies seem to indicate that family decision-making is more likely to be husband-dominated when the husband is the sole earner, whereas couples who are both earning make decisions jointly (Filiatrault and Ritchie 1980). Males also tend to dominate highly technical durable products (e.g. home computers, DVD players or TV equipment). Interestingly, spendthrifts and careful savers appear to be attracted to each other – a situation that often results in conflict (Rick et al. 2010).

 ## Challenging the status quo

In recent years we have been almost morbidly preoccupied with gender equality. Yet at the same time we have seen a rise in new laddism, and in girl power. Women seem to be revelling in traditional female behaviour, and men seem to be reverting to traditional male stereotypes. So if women are getting together with their girlfriends to gossip, and men are swilling beer and going to the football, are we heading back to a traditional division along gender lines?

Are we going to see women fluttering their eyelashes and asking men to help them change a flat tyre? Are we going to see men refusing to change the baby? Or are we perhaps just observing a minor blip in our road to equality?

Gender role orientation is clearly crucial to decision-making. Husbands (and wives) with conservative views about gender roles will tend towards the assumption that most decisions about expenditure will be made by the husband. Even within this type of decision-making system, however, husbands will usually adjust their own views to take account of their wife's attitudes and needs.

Conflict resolution tends to have an increased importance in family decision-making as opposed to individual purchase behaviour. The reason for this is that, obviously, more people are involved, each with their own needs and their own internal conflicts to resolve. The conflict resolution system is as shown in Table 10.1.

Table 10.1   Conflict resolution in families

Resolution method	Explanation
Persuasion through information exchange	When a conflict occurs, each family member seeks to persuade the others of his or her point of view. This leads to discussion, and ultimately some form of compromise
Role expectation	If persuasion fails, a family member may be designated to make the decision. This is usually somebody who has the greatest expertise in the area of conflict being discussed. This method appears to be going out of fashion as greater democracy in family decision-making is appearing
Establishment of norms	Families will often adopt rules for decision-making. Sometimes this will involve taking turns over making decisions (perhaps over which restaurant the family will go to this week, or where they will go on holiday)
Power exertion	This is also known as browbeating. One family member will try to exert power to force the other members to comply; this may be a husband who refuses to sign the cheque unless he gets his own way, or a wife who refuses to cook the dinner until the family agree, or a child who throws a tantrum. The person with the most power is called the **least dependent person** because he or she is not as dependent on the other family members. Using the examples above, if the wife has her own income she won't need to ask the husband to sign the cheque; if the other family members can cook they can get their own dinner; and if the family can ignore the yelling toddler long enough, eventually the child will give up

Least dependent person The individual within a buying group who has the highest degree of autonomy

Source: Adapted from Sak Onkvisit and John J. Shaw (1994) *Consumer Behaviour: Strategy and Analysis* (New York: John Wiley).

Influence of children on buying decisions

First-born children generate more economic impact than higher-order babies. Around 40% of babies are first-born; they are photographed more, they get all new clothes (no hand-me-downs) and get more attention all round. First-born and only children have a higher achievement rate than those born second, third, etc., and since the birth rate is falling, there are more of them proportionally. More and more couples are choosing to have only one child, and families larger than two children are becoming a rarity. Childlessness is also more common now than it was thirty years ago.

Children also have a role in applying pressure on their parents to make particular purchasing decisions. The level of 'pester power' generated can be overwhelming, and parents will frequently give in to the child's demands (Ekstrom et al. 1987). Children rapidly become adept at negotiating with their parents, and are quite able to recognise the various responses parents will make (agreement, refusal, procrastination, negotiation) as well as the parents' reasons for their decisions. Children often see this as a good-natured game between themselves and the parents rather than as a source of conflict as the literature tends to suggest (Lawlor and Protheroe 2011).

Although the number of children is steadily declining, their importance as consumers is not. Apart from the direct purchases of things that children need, they influence decision-making to a marked extent. Pre-teens and young teens may have a greater influence on family shopping choices than do the parents themselves for these reasons:

1 Often they do the shopping anyway, because both parents are working and the children have the available time to go to the shops.
2 They watch more TV, so are more influenced by and more knowledgeable about products.
3 They tend to be more attuned to consumer issues, and have the time to shop around for (for example) free-range eggs or organic vegetables.

In recent years, children have become much more aware of what they eat, partly due to in-school health education programmes. Sometimes on-package health claims have a negative effect (perhaps due to a mistrust of marketer-generated information) but education programmes do have an effect in encouraging more healthy choices (Miller et al. 2011). However, children are well aware that 'children's food' often consists of cheap junk food (Elliott 2011). The problem lies in translating this knowledge into action, since children still make unhealthy choices even when they know better (Dias and Agante 2011).

When parents and children are making joint decisions about food purchase, the children will often use subtle techniques to get their own way – offering to help with the shopping reduces conflict and means they are more likely to impose their own choices, for example (Norgaard and Brunso 2011).

Children have to be taught how to be consumers, since they will (eventually) become adults and will need to manage their money and make appropriate choices in their purchasing behaviour. Children's development as consumers goes through five stages (Figure 10.3):

1 Observing
2 Making requests
3 Making selections
4 Making assisted purchases
5 Making independent purchases

In the observing stage, children see how their parents go about obtaining the things they need. At this point, the child will probably not understand that money is a finite resource, but can easily understand the basic system: things that the family needs are available in shops, and they can be bought with money if you know what to do. Observation is actually more important than teaching in children's development, especially when the family has a good quality of relationship between its members (Mittal and Royne 2010). Usually children will begin to consider ways in which they might obtain goods themselves – quite young children can grasp the idea that goods must be paid for, and they will sometimes try using 'money' (perhaps play money or tokens) to pay for things.

Pester power The ability of children to influence their parents by means of repetitive requests

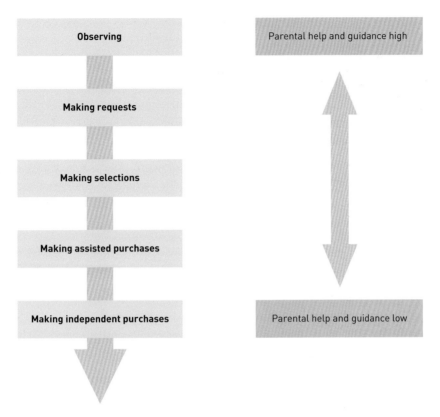

Figure 10.3 Children's stages of development as consumers

At a very early stage children learn to make requests. Even before being able to talk, children recognise brands and favourite products and are able to reach for them or point to them. As they grow older and more able to articulate requests, they can (and do) develop 'pester power'. This means that they make insistent demands for products, sometimes throwing tantrums or continually wheedling their parents to obtain what they want. At this point parental judgement may vary – some parents will give in fairly quickly and provide the child with what he or she wants, while others will refuse to buy the product (making a judgement as to its suitability for the child). In many cases the request becomes a basis for negotiation – the parent agrees to buy the product on condition that the child behaves in a certain way.

Children use a wide variety of tactics to influence their parents (Wimalasir 2004). These are shown in Table 10.2, and the relationship between them is shown in Figure 10.4

Parenting style has an obvious effect on the likely response to such requests. Broadly, there are five basic styles of parenting (Carlson and Grossbart 1988):

1 *Authoritarians*. These parents are cold and restrictive.
2 *Authoritative*. These parents are warm and restrictive.
3 *Permissives*. These parents are warm and non-restrictive.
4 *Strict-dependent*. These parents foster dependence in their children, almost to the point of not allowing them to grow up.
5 *Indulgent-dependent*. These parents foster dependence by giving their children everything they want and need, even into adult life.

These parenting styles are not necessarily universal, in fact they happen almost exclusively in collectivist cultures (Rose et al. 2002). It is easy to see that authoritarian and authoritative parents are unlikely to yield easily to pester power, strict-dependents would

Table 10.2   Tactics used by children to influence their parents

Tactic	Explanation
Pressure tactics	The child makes demands and uses threats or intimidation to persuade the parents to comply with his/her request
Upward appeal	The child seeks to persuade the parent by saying that the request was approved or is supported by an older member of the family, a teacher or even a family friend
Exchange tactics	The child makes an implicit or explicit promise to provide some sort of service such as washing the car, cleaning the house or taking care of the baby in return for a favour
Coalition tactics	The child seeks the aid of others to persuade the parents to comply with his or her request, or uses the support of others as an argument for the parents to agree with him or her
Ingratiating tactics	The child seeks to get the parent in a good mood or think favourably of him or her before asking the parent to comply with a request
Rational persuasion	The child uses logical arguments and factual evidence to persuade the parent to agree with his or her request
Inspirational appeals	The child makes an emotional appeal or proposal that arouses enthusiasm by appealing to the parent's values or ideals
Consultation tactics	The child seeks the parent's involvement in making a decision

not allow the child to pester, and permissives and indulgent-dependents are unlikely to need to be pestered – they would simply accede to the request the first time round.

In most cases, parents will agree to purchases subject to conditions being met. This is an important lesson, because the child needs to know that products are subject to exchange processes. In this case, the parent is demonstrating that, in order to obtain benefits, there will need to be concessions in terms of behaviour. Parents frequently use the promise of supplying (or withholding) products as a way of modifying the child's behaviour. There is evidence to suggest that this is culturally based in some respects: American parents apparently seek to develop autonomy in their children, making them into independent consumers, whereas Japanese parents maintain greater

 Challenging the status quo

What responsibility do marketers have for pester power? We hear all the time that wicked marketers are encouraging children to want the latest toys, games, gadgets and even fashions – so are we to blame if they then pester their parents?

On the other hand, people do have to buy things. It's the way the world works. Children have to learn to distinguish between advertising and programming – and they have to learn that they can't just demand anything they want in this life. So maybe marketers are carrying out a public service, educating the consumers of tomorrow and teaching children that they can't just have everything!

control over their children's consumption, so that the children tend to develop consumer skills at a later age (Rose 1999).

Once children reach an age when they can understand money, parents will typically provide them with pocket money so that they can learn to make their own selections. In most cases pocket money is supplied as a fixed amount: this is so that the child can learn that money is not an infinite resource, and must be spent carefully. In other cases, pocket money might be provided as a reward for specific behaviour (for example, cleaning the car or mowing the lawn) so that the child learns the concept of working for rewards. This is a further reinforcement of the exchange concept. In the early stages of having pocket money, parents will often help the child make choices, applying their own sense of value to the transaction. As time goes on, the child will be able to make choices alone, and will ultimately (perhaps during teenage years) become a fully fledged consumer by spending money earned by doing odd jobs or part-time work.

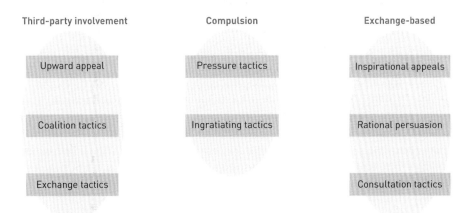

Figure 10.4 Children's persuasion tactics

At this point, the individual is more likely to look to friends or role models for ideas on acceptable consumer behaviour (John 1999). Although younger children respond best to advertising in which the spokesperson is a parental or authority figure, teenagers often buy products simply because their parents disapprove of them (Rummel et al. 2000). This is probably part of the process by which people become independent adults, and demonstrates that they are no longer children.

Socialisation continues down the generations even after the child has become a fully independent adult, however. Some research shows that brand loyalties can be passed down from one generation to another, even for three or four generations within the same family (Mandrik et al. 2004; Olsen 1993). The reason for this is that people enjoy using the brands that they remember from their childhood: specific brands of sauces, soups, marmalade or soft drinks commonly remain popular in the family for many years after the child has grown up and left home. In some respects the family identity is carried on through the generations by these means (Epp and Arnould 2006).

Consumer behaviour in action: Teenagers and technology

The communications revolution has certainly made it much harder to monitor the behaviour of teenagers – not that it was ever easy, of course. Each generation of teenagers takes great care to prevent their parents from knowing what they are really doing, but electronic communications have made the situation much easier.

Consider the case of buying illicit drugs. One teenager called Sean entered the names of some common illegal drugs into Google and came up with a lot of information telling him not to do drugs; he also came up with a lot of information saying that small amounts of drugs would make him feel great. He used the information to decide which drugs he really wanted to try and which ones he should leave alone. He became an addict by the time he was 17 – he was only 15 when he started. Another teenager, Amy, was given a mobile phone when she was 12 years old. She found the phone extremely useful for calling her drug supplier, especially when using text. She had no fear at all of being caught: 'I knew for a fact my parents didn't have a clue about it,' said Amy. 'My parents got a cell phone four months ago and my dad is still like, "How do you call?"'

Also consider the widespread use of electronic games. Teenagers (and even pre-teens) like to play the latest games, but some games are clearly labeled '18+' meaning that they are not considered suitable for younger children. Games such as *Grand Theft Auto*, which involves carnage on an unprecedented scale, is clearly not the kind of game that most parents would want their 14-year-old to play. However, it appears that (according to a 2005 survey by market researchers Modulum) most parents are concerned about the amount of time their children spend playing video games, but are less concerned about the content of the games (Hermida 2005). This may be because parents are not aware of the extent to which game graphics have moved on in the last ten years or so, from jerky cartoon characters to images that are close to live actors. Parents who would not allow their children to watch films with violent or sexual content seem to have no problem with games with the same content, even though the games are interactive (which makes them more powerful) and the unsuitable content goes on throughout the game, not just for a few minutes during an otherwise acceptable film.

Since adding the '18+' symbol increases dramatically the desirability of the game, game manufacturers are not entirely displeased; however, firms know that they must, eventually, clean up their act or legislation will be brought in. Meanwhile, children will continue to wheedle and manipulate their parents into buying the latest games, suitable or not.

Changing nature of the family

One of the changes currently occurring throughout Western Europe is the increase in the number of single-person households; in the UK, these now represent 29% of all households (Office for National Statistics 2012); there is, of course, a difference between a household and a family. A further change, coming about through the tremendous increase in the divorce rate, is the growing number of single-parent families. A third major change is the worldwide shift in attitude towards having

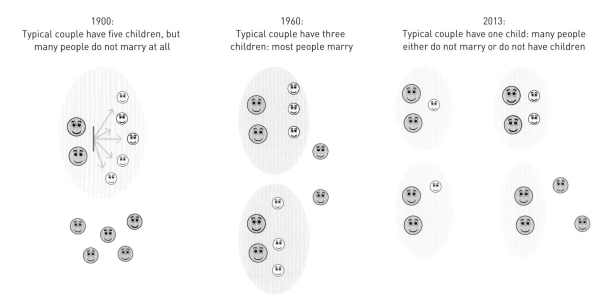

1900:
Typical couple have five children, but many people do not marry at all

1960:
Typical couple have three children: most people marry

2013:
Typical couple have one child: many people either do not marry or do not have children

Figure 10.5   Effects of falling birth rate

large families. Since the advent of mass contraception, more and more women say that they would prefer to have fewer children than was the case even ten years ago. Currently, European birth rates are below the replacement rate for the population, meaning that the population would be shrinking if it were not for immigration. One UK study predicted that one in five women born between 1960 and 1990 will never have children, and the birth rate among those women who do have children will be half that of their mothers' generation (European Union 1995).

In Figure 10.5 the 1900 family has more children, but the other five people (those outside the family circle in the figure) remained single, like many other people at that time. From the seven people in the example, only five children are born. In 1960, a more typical family size would be three children, but many more people married and had children (only two people are outside the family circles): that was an expectation of the baby boom years. Nowadays, families are smaller and many people never have children at all, so in our final example the ten people in the diagram only manage four children between them. Two of the family circles only contain one child, the other one contains none, and we have two people who remain single. It should be noted that these are examples only: the birth rate actually has not fluctuated quite that dramatically over the period.

The family is a flexible concept, and families go through life cycles. There have been various versions of the family life cycle, but most are based on the original work of Wells and Gubar (1966). Table 10.3 shows the stages of the family life cycle.

The main problem with this model is that it was originally developed in the 1960s, when couples rarely lived together without being married, there were very few single-parent families and the divorce rate was dramatically lower than it is in the 21st century. Towards the end of the life cycle (from Empty nest I onwards) it is likely that the model holds true fairly well, but it is unlikely that the earlier stages will follow the same pattern.

For example, it is now the case that single-person households represent 29.1% of UK households, whereas households comprising a married couple and their

Table 10.3   The family life cycle

Stage of life cycle	Explanation
Single stage	Single people tend to have low earnings, but also have low outgoings so have a high discretionary income. They tend to be more fashion- and recreation-orientated, spending on clothes, music, alcohol, eating out, holidays, leisure pursuits and hobbies, and 'mating game' products. Often they buy cars and items for their first residence away from home
Newly married couples	Newlyweds without children are usually dual-income households and therefore usually well-off. They still tend to spend on similar things to the singles, but also have the highest proportion of expenditure on household goods, consumer durables and appliances. They appear to be more susceptible to advertising
Full nest I	When the first child arrives, one parent usually stops working outside the home so family income drops sharply. The baby creates new needs that alter expenditure patterns: furniture and furnishings for the baby, baby food, vitamins, toys, nappies and baby food. Family savings decline, and usually couples are dissatisfied with their financial position
Full nest II	The youngest child is over 6, so often both parents will work outside the home. The employed spouse's income has risen due to career progression, and the family's total income recovers. Consumption patterns are still heavily influenced by children: bicycles, piano lessons, large-size packages of breakfast cereal, cleaning products, etc.
Full nest III	Family income improves as the children get older. Both parents are likely to be working outside the home, and both may have had some career progression; also, the children will be earning some of their own money from paper rounds, part-time jobs, etc. Family purchases might be a second car, replacement furniture, some luxury items and children's education.
Empty nest I	Children have grown up and left home. Couple are at the height of their careers and spending power, have low mortgages and very reduced living costs. They often spend on luxury travel, restaurants and theatre – so they need fashionable clothing, jewellery, diets, spas, health clubs, cosmetics and hairdressing
Empty nest II	The main breadwinner has retired, so there is some drop in income. Expenditure is more health-orientated, buying appliances for sleep and over-the-counter remedies for indigestion. The couple often buy a smaller house, or move to an apartment in a retirement area or warmer country
Solitary survivor	If still in the workforce, widows and widowers enjoy a good income. They may spend more money on holidays, as well as the items mentioned in Empty nest II
Retired solitary survivor	These people have the same general consumption pattern as above but on a smaller scale due to reduced income. The individual has special needs for love, affection and security, so may join clubs, etc.

dependent children only comprise 22.6% of households (Office for National Statistics 2012). The traditional nuclear family of two parents with their own children has become a minority of households: it is more likely that a household will consist of a mother with her children from her first marriage, a husband or partner who pays maintenance to his ex-wife for the children from his first marriage, and possibly a new child from the new partnership. Even more common is a childless home, either a single-person household or a childless couple living together: these represent more than half of all UK households (Office for National Statistics 2012).

It may be more realistic to consider the life cycle of the individual, and link this to possible family roles and responsibilities rather than consider different possible family structures. Here are some of the life stages an individual might have:

1 Living alone I. This is someone who has left home, has a job and is living alone.
2 Cohabiting, no children I. This would be a couple who are living together without being married, but have no children.
3 Cohabiting, with joint children. This couple have a child or children, but are not married.
4 Married, no children I. Similar to 'Cohabiting, no children I' but have a legal relationship as well as a romantic one.
5 Married, with joint children. Similar to cohabiting, but with the legal relationship.
6 Living alone II. This is someone who is divorced or widowed.
7 Cohabiting, no children II. This couple are divorced or separated from earlier partners, and are now living together.
8 Cohabiting, with children II. The children may be from a previous relationship, or may not live with the couple at all, but be occasional visitors at weekends or during the week.
9 Married, no children II. This couple have been married before, and may or may not intend having children together at some future time.
10 Married, with children II. This couple is second-time married, with children from earlier relationships who may or may not live with them.
11 Married or cohabiting couple with grown-up children still at home. This situation is becoming more common as single people find it harder to buy a home. These households can be extremely wealthy, since three or more adults are contributing to the overall income.

There are likely to be other, more complex, situations but each of these situations impacts on family decision-making, and (particularly in the case of cohabiting or married couples with children from previous relationships) other people who are not actually part of the family will also need to be considered (in this case, ex-partners). Working out the decision rules between the various players is likely to be difficult in these cases, and in some cases special marketing activities are in place to take account of single parents who have access rights to their children on specific days. The concept of being 'a father for half an hour in McDonald's' has become familiar, and some advertising reflects this.

The divorce–remarry cycle also means dramatic surges in income. Divorce usually means a dramatic fall in disposable income as the economies of scale in shared consumption evaporate and the individuals have to set up their own homes: this can mean a boost for businesses selling furniture, household appliances and homes, of course. Later on, though, the remarry phase often leads to a sudden sharp increase in wealth as the previously single people pool their resources. When people in their forties remarry, having finished paying out for child maintenance and (often) now owning substantial equity in their homes, when they combine their assets they can find themselves suddenly wealthy.

Gender roles

There are more women than men in the population, largely due to two factors: greater infant mortality among boys, and greater life expectancy of women. Women's role has changed greatly over the past thirty years or so; women make more (or most) of the purchasing decisions, earn around a third of the household income and make most of the decisions regarding the home and the children.

Major purchasing decisions are far more likely to be made jointly, and men are now much more likely to participate in decisions regarding the household expenditure. An American survey carried out in the 1990s showed that 35% of couples said that they were equally responsible for food shopping; 8% said the man was solely responsible; the other 57% said the woman did the food shopping (Opinion Research Corporation 1990). In another survey carried out in Scotland ten years later, 30% of men reported doing the food shopping (Ellaway and Macintyre 2000). Although it is still the case that the bulk of food shopping is done by women, the trend is for more men to do some (or all) of the shopping and some (or all) of the cooking.

The change in gender roles, summarised in Figure 10.6, comes from the following factors:

1 Technology means that most jobs do not require physical strength, so more careers are open to women.
2 Mass contraception has freed women from childbearing.
3 A more ordered society has led to greater physical security; there is less need for the defence role of the male.
4 More widespread education means that women are not satisfied to stay home and do housework.

This shift in gender roles and expectations is affecting marketers, who are now changing the appeal of their advertising to meet the new conditions. For example, Flash Wipes are advertised showing a man doing the cleaning: he is portrayed as the average man, doing the cleaning and winning praise for doing so, but revealing to the audience that in fact the cleaning is really no big task. Twenty years ago such advertisements would only have been shown for comic purposes, and even now men are frequently portrayed as being incapable of doing the housework properly.

Gender roles might also include sexual orientation, which affords another dimension to the definition of family. In the UK, civil partnerships between same-sex couples were introduced towards the end of 2005, and there was consequently a flurry of people in long-term relationships going through the ceremony. Registering a civil partnership in this way gives the couple the same legal status as if they were a heterosexual

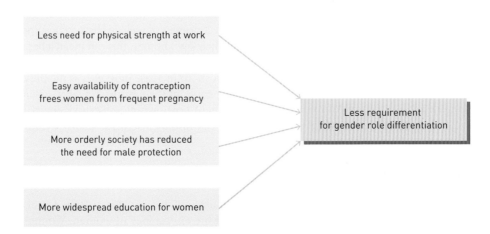

Figure 10.6   Drivers for gender role change

married couple: giving the relationship a legal status means that such partnerships have the status of being families by the definition. No doubt the people concerned already felt as if they were families, and in many cases they have even had children either from previous heterosexual marriages or by adoption.

Gay people tend to be wealthier than heterosexuals: male homosexuals earn an average 23% more than heterosexual men, have twice as many credit cards as the general population, and spend more on entertainment than average (BBC 1998). In the UK, gays' disposable income is called the Pink Pound (in the US it is called the Dorothy Dollar) and is worth around £6bn a year. This has meant that gays have been targeted by some financial institutions and by information services, clubs and even holiday companies, such as Pink Pound Travel. Since gays are estimated to account for at least 4% of the population (the exact figure is hard to determine as some gays still feel that they would face prejudice or hostility if they were open about their sexuality), they represent a substantial market.

Eventually one might expect that gender role will not be an issue in advertising at all, but since advertising (at least in part) reflects society, this may still be some way off.

Other functions of the family

Families also provide economic well-being, emotional support and suitable family lifestyles. Because families share consumption, the standard of living of the members is higher than would have been the case had they chosen to live separately. In some families, economic well-being is also generated by employment in the family business. Because the overall tasks within the family are divided between the members, some members might exchange earning their own money for taking on a larger role within the family, for example staying at home to care for small children. In most instances this is a female role, but there are more and more cases of men becoming 'house husbands' and it is certainly an option that is open when both parents have a career.

In the majority of UK families both parents work outside the home. There is considerable debate as to whether this has a detrimental or a positive effect on children, but it certainly has a positive effect on the family's finances, increasing spending

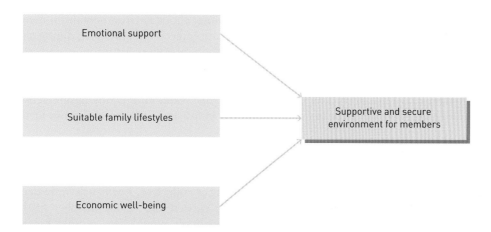

Figure 10.7   Other functions of the family

power and also (on the downside) increasing the need for labour-saving devices and behaviour, for example ready meals, childcare and children's entertainment devices, which leave the parents free to carry out other tasks.

In traditional societies children are expected to contribute to the family's finances, in particular teenage children are expected to work and contribute. In most Western families teenagers would be expected to retain any earnings, either to save towards their education or adult life in general, or at least to pay for their own entertainment and perhaps clothing items.

Challenging the status quo

In less 'advanced' societies, children are with their parents pretty much all the time. Little boys are with their fathers, building huts or digging for crops or making things, while little girls are with their mothers, collecting fruit or cooking or making clothes. In our more 'advanced' society, we go out to work and we apparently subcontract our child-rearing to nannies, childminders, childcare centres and schools.

Are we really doing ourselves any favours here? Are we raising a generation of confused kids who don't know whether the nanny is the true authority on everything, or Mummy and Daddy? Anyway, does it matter? After all, one great advantage of our way of doing things is that most children make it past five years old, most don't get eaten by predators and most don't suffer from debilitating diseases!

Economic well-being is also provided when (for example) parents pay for a child's education, or help with the deposit for a house. Sometimes the help goes in the other direction: grown-up children might pay for a care home, or for improvements to an elderly parent's home. In either case, marketers have a role in providing facilities for this to happen.

Emotional support is a core function of families. This can comprise love and affection, but also involves moral support and encouragement: this emotional support has formed the basis for the entire greeting-card industry. When families are unable to provide appropriate emotional support from within the group, it may turn to counselling or even psychiatric services to provide professional help for its members.

Finally, families also help to establish suitable lifestyles. Family members bear more than a physical resemblance to each other; they tend to have similar attitudes about the importance of education, about reading, about environmentalism, about home decor, about holidays and about appropriate entertainments (sport, dining out, etc.). Even though there is a trend towards family members acting independently rather than sharing activities, the idea of spending 'quality time' with each other has recently led to a tendency to seek out activities and experiences that can be shared. Marketers have not been slow to capitalise on this, promoting family leisure activities such as weekends away in hotels, meals out in fast-food restaurants and so forth.

Roles in family consumption

Within families, a great deal of decision-making is collective. Even such basic decisions as buying underwear might be shared or carried out by one member of the family on behalf of another. The traditional example would be a mother buying underwear for the children of the family, but many women buy underwear for their husbands, and it is far from unknown for husbands to buy underwear for their wives, often as Valentine or birthday gifts.

Table 10.4   Roles in family decision-making

Role	Explanation
Influencers	These are the family members who perhaps have no direct involvement in the purchase or consumption of the item, but who can offer help and advice
Gatekeepers	These members control the flow of information to the others. A gatekeeper may be the person who reads the brochures or watches the advertising on TV
Deciders	These members have the final say on the product being bought or consumed. In most families, the deciders would be the parents, but this is not always the case: it depends on the product being considered
Buyers	Family members who make the actual purchase are the buyers. It may be that a decision is made to book a particular holiday, and the member with the best IT skills is given the task of booking it online, for example
Preparers	These members transform the product into a form suitable for the others to consume it. The obvious example is cooking food, but the concept could equally apply to one of the children of the family programming the new TV set
Users	The family members who will consume the product
Maintainers	The family members who will ensure that the product is in good condition for the others to use it. This not only applies to someone who mends the kitchen cupboards, it also applies to someone who cleans the house and does the laundry
Disposers	Members who have the job of removing the used products and packaging or arranging for the sale or trade-in of products for which the family has no further use

Preparers A family member responsible for transforming a product into a condition suitable for other members to use it

Within families, consumption and purchase roles are often divided between family members. There are thought to be eight basic roles in family decision-making, as shown in Table 10.4.

Depending on the type of product being considered, family members may adopt different roles for each decision. In other words, deciders are not necessarily deciders for everything – they may be deciders for some categories of product (e.g. holidays) and gatekeepers for another category (e.g. home entertainment systems). Likewise, roles often overlap, or the same person occupies more than one role.

In Figure 10.8 the main arrows show where each individual has a major input. The fine arrows show where the individuals have a lesser input. Obviously the same individual may have more than one role in the purchase decision.

Children appear to have a greater role in family decision-making than in the past. As children (and of course their parents) grow older, parents begin to seek the advice of their children on some aspects, particularly where new technology is concerned or where the child has acquired specialist knowledge. Research shows that parents in lower income groups are more likely to see their children as being 'consumer savvy', especially if the child is female and at the older end of the spectrum

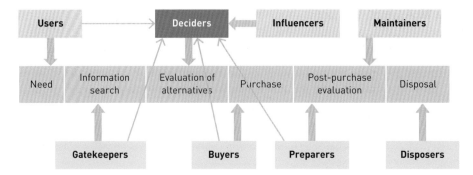

Figure 10.8   Family roles and decisions

(Nancarrow et al. 2011). Parents with a 'warm' approach to parenting are more likely to learn from their children (Grossbart et al. 2002).

Children themselves believe that they have considerable influence in many family purchase decisions, even including buying a car among these decisions (Tinson and Nancarrow 2005). The areas in which children believe themselves to be most important as decision-makers are shown in Table 10.5.

Other research carried out in Canada indicates that children there have an even greater influence on decisions: 40% of children in one study believed themselves to be the main decision-makers with respect to choice of restaurant when eating out (Labrecque and Ricard 2001). The same study showed that children underestimate their influence on the decision to go to a restaurant in the first place.

Table 10.5   How children perceive themselves to have influenced the purchase of different products

Product	Percentage Influence
Casual clothes for me	91%
Trainers for me	88%
CDs for me	84%
Sweets for me	83%
Computers for me	83%
Soft drinks for me	80%
School shoes for me	80%
A family trip to the cinema	73%
Food for me for lunch at the weekend	73%
A holiday I would go on with the family	63%
Going out for a family meal	52%
A family car	37%

There is some evidence to suggest that the family's communication pattern is also related to the child's influence on the decision-making process. Communication patterns usually fall into one or other of the following categories (Shoham et al. 2004):

1 *Pluralistic parents*. These parents encourage their children to express their ideas and preferences. Not surprisingly, these families experience the greatest influence from the children.
2 *Consensual parents*. These parents encourage their children to seek harmony, but they are influenced by the children's ideas.
3 *Protective parents*. These parents believe that 'mother knows best' and in general expect children to agree to the parents' choices.

It seems probable that children with pluralistic parents would be likely to develop consumer skills early, but they might also be the most likely to use pester power to get their own way. Children with protective parents might take longer to develop consumer skills, but would perhaps be more likely to adopt brands favoured by their parents in later life.

Some teenagers spend a great deal of time on the Internet, and consequently regard themselves as experts at researching information relating to major purchases. These teenagers, called Internet mavens, can contribute significantly to family decision-making, especially in the information search phase of the process (Belch et al. 2005). Internet mavens are usually accepted by their parents as having more knowledge and more information-gathering skills than anyone else in the family.

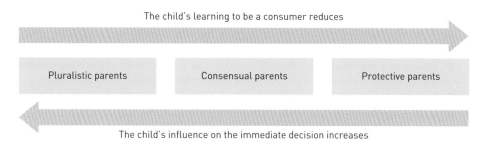

Figure 10.9 Communication pattern and children's influence

Summary

Families are often said to be the building-blocks of society. We are influenced more by our families than by anybody else: partly this is because the influence starts at a very early age, partly it is because we spend a large part of our lives living with our families, and partly it is because our family relationships (especially those with our siblings if we have them) are the longest-lasting relationships in our lives.

Because families share so much of their consumption, the ways in which they interact and make decisions are of great interest to marketers. Families share decision-making in many ways, and the views of family members are still important even when it is the parents who make the final decision.

There are many different patterns of family, but what they have in common is relationships by blood, marriage or adoption; shared consumption; face-to-face contact on a daily basis; emotional, economic and lifestyle support for their members; and finally, shared regard for each others' welfare.

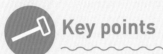

Key points

- 'Family' has several definitions, each of which is dependent on culture and circumstances.
- Culture has a marked effect on decision-making styles.
- All members of a family have some input into decision-making.
- Conflict is common in families because of shared consumption.
- Children have to be taught to be effective consumers.
- Brand loyalty can pass down through several generations.
- Family life cycle models are pluralistic in 21st century society.
- Family members often adopt specific roles in the purchase and consumption process.

Review questions

1   Why is the family powerful in influencing consumption behaviour?
2   Why is the family a culturally based concept?
3   What are the main changes in the family in recent years?
4   How might family purchase roles change in the next twenty years?
5   What are the drivers for change in family purchase roles?
6   How might the change in the ethnic structure of European society affect family decision-making?
7   How do children influence decision-making?
8   How does parenting style affect children's consumption behaviour?
9   What are the main criticisms of the family life cycle concept?
10   What are the key functions of a family?

Case study revisited: 'Little buddhas'

Social and demographic changes have undoubtedly contributed to the poor quality of parenting received by some children. The large number of single-parent families means a reduction in the parenting time available: with the best will in the world, there is only so much time available for parenting when one has to earn a living and carry out all the household tasks alone. Even when there are two parents involved, the conditions of modern life mean that (at least in middle-class, professional families) both are likely to have jobs outside the home, which again reduces available time to spend with children.

At the other end of the spectrum, disadvantaged families might have difficulty in finding enough time and energy left over from the daily grind of dealing with their circumstances. Such families often live in poor housing conditions, in high-crime areas, and thus the children are exposed to negative influences from an early age.

Some ATL members blame fashions in child-rearing: several of those questioned in the survey said that parents seemed to want to be friends with their children rather than take on a disciplinary, parental role. This was essentially the aspect targeted by Dr Boustead: that parents were not parenting, but were instead treating their children as honoured guests. Given that parents spend less time with their children than might have been the case 50 years ago, it is highly likely that they would not want to spend that time in some kind of battle or confrontation about whose turn it is to do the washing up, or whether the children have tidied their bedrooms. Other ATL members blamed the prevalence of electronic games, many of which are violent, and of television programmes that seem to show that fame and fortune can be obtained by luck rather than hard work.

The TV reality show *Supernanny* sets out to provide help and advice for parents experiencing behavioural difficulties with their children. The show's presenter, Jo Frost, is a professional nanny who advocates punishment such as 'the naughty corner' where misbehaving children are put until they apologise. She advocates regular bedtimes and mealtimes, and uses behavioural psychology to foster good behaviour. Of course, these methods may work very well in the home, but are hard to implement in schools: the Victorian method of making children wear a dunce's cap, or stand in the corner, are no longer fashionable but do have echoes in Frost's approach. The TV series has been a colossal hit, and has become established in the United States as well: the show's website contains a lot of useful advice for parents to try at home.

Whatever the causes, and whatever the outcomes, there is little doubt that family life has changed a lot in the last fifty years. Fortunately, most people do turn out to be decent adults – but there is certainly a lot of work to be done with some children while they are still of school age.

Case study: Learning Resources

Learning Resources Ltd is the sister company of Learning Resources Inc. of Illinois, USA. The company produces educational toys for the European market. Although originally aimed at teachers and other education professionals such as kindergarten operators, Learning Resources is happy to supply parents and retailers with their products.

Educational toys usually have features that encourage specific learning activities – for toddlers, a learning toy might have a range of textures to enable children to learn what things feel like, or may have a set of buttons, knobs and handles to teach manipulative skills. For older children educational toys might include construction sets or engineering sets, enabling children to learn how mechanical objects work. Learning Resources provide products such as Snap 'n Learn Shape Butterflies, which clip together to make up different shapes of butterfly. The wings are shaped as hearts, circles, squares, triangles and so forth which match up to the shapes of the heads. This toy helps children recognise shapes, and is aimed at ages 2 to 6 years.

For older children there are games to help with mathematics, games that teach the proper way to hold a pen for handwriting, games to promote literacy, and even HM Treasury-approved play money.

The European toy market is worth around €16bn, which is almost exactly a quarter of the world's total toy market. Although it is difficult to define exactly what an 'educational' toy is (since children learn by playing with almost anything), it is certainly true that putting 'educational' on the packaging will help sales. Learning Resources scores by being the brand that teachers trust – teachers like the products, and use them in the classroom, which is of course a strong commendation of the play value of the toys.

Parents also like the toys. Most parents want the best for their children, and most especially want their children to grow up able to cope successfully with the world in which they find themselves. For many parents this translates into ensuring that the child grows up to be strong and brainy enough to beat the other kids to the best jobs and houses. The pressure is on to buy educational toys rather than 'fun' toys – even when the distinction is difficult to make in practice.

Of course, many of the Learning Resources toys have a strong American flavour to them – teaching maths by learning how to divide up a pizza may seem more attuned to an American audience rather than a European one. Many of the games are produced in the United States and shipped over, but many more are developed in the UK.

Learning Resources makes full use of PR opportunities: the company sends out press releases to teaching professionals' journals such as *Teach Primary* and *Primary Teacher* and exhibits at the Education Show, as well as targeting parents through *Good Housekeeping* and *The Independent*. For the toy trade, the firm exhibits at the Nuremburg Toy Fair, the Scottish Learning Festival and Special Needs London. The toy business generally is highly seasonal; normally between 60% and 80% of toys are sold during December, as Christmas presents. Educational toys are slightly less susceptible to this level of seasonality because they are bought by schools and also by parents and relatives of younger children, for their birthdays or because the child is at a particular stage of development.

There are many manufacturers and importers who claim to offer educational toys. In a sense, any toy can be classed as educational – most parents can tell stories about buying the latest expensive toy, only to see the child play happily for hours with the box it came in. Where Learning Resources scores is that their toys are bought and used by teachers – a solid endorsement for parents seeking to help their child's development.

Questions

1 If children learn by playing with almost anything, why would parents spend so much money on educational toys?
2 Why is an endorsement by a teacher more important than the child liking the toy?
3 What might be a problem with having toys that were originally developed for the American market?
4 How does PR help sell the toys?
5 What is the role of teachers in the decision-making process?

Further reading

If you want to know more about dealing with children who misbehave, you might like *Raising Your Spirited Child: A Guide for Parents Whose Child Is More Intense, Sensitive, Perceptive, Persistent and Energetic* by Mary Sheedy Kurcinka (New York: Harper Perennial, 1992). This American book might seem a bit 'worthy' but it does have some very good advice and techniques for dealing with children who get upset easily, or who challenge their parents.

There are many anthropological texts on childrearing practices in different cultures. An example is the rather scholarly *Turkish Mothers' Attitudes to Child-Rearing Practices* by Gokce Tekin (Cambridge: Proquest/UMI Dissertation Publishing, 2011). It is in fact a PhD thesis, so can be hard going, but it shows how childrearing practices can vary greatly according to cultural differences.

For a look at the other face of marketing to children, Ed Mayo and Agnes Nairn's book *Consumer Kids: How Big Business is Grooming Our Children for Profit* (London: Constable, 2009) reveals some of the alleged tactics used by large corporations to target children. The book is maybe a little one-sided, but it certainly is thought-provoking and raises a number of ethical issues.

Another precautionary tale comes from Juliet Schor. Her book *Born to Buy: The Commercialised Child and the New Consumer Culture* (New York: Simon and Schuster, 2006) outlines some American marketing practices (many of which would be illegal in the UK and indeed in most of Europe). These include an educational TV channel available only in schools in which commercials are embedded in the teaching materials. Scary stuff – and something that certainly goes against the tenets of responsible marketing.

A comprehensive look at the theory of communication within families comes from *Communication in Family Relationships* by Patrick Noller and Mary Ann Fitzpatrick (Englewood Cliffs, NJ: Prentice Hall, 1993). A note of caution, though – although English is a universal language, there are marked differences between American culture and those of other English-speaking countries (not to mention non-English speaking countries). Since family life is very culture-specific, theories developed in the United States may not apply elsewhere – so use your own judgement as well!

References

BBC (1998) *Business: The Economy. The Pink Pound.* Available at: http://news.bbc.co.uk/1/hi/business/142998.stm (accessed December 2012).

Belch, M.A., Krentler, K.A. and Willis-Flurry, L.A. (2005) Teen Internet mavens: influence in family decision-making. *Journal of Business Research* 58: 569–75.

Carlson, L. and Grossbart, S. (1988) Parental styles and consumer socialisation of children. *Journal of Consumer Research*, 15: 77–94.

Curasi, C. (2006) Maybe it IS your father's Oldsmobile: the construction and preservation of family identity through the transfer of possessions. *Advances in Consumer Behaviour* 33: 83.

Curasi, C. (2011) Intergenerational possession transfers and identity maintenance. *Journal of Consumer Behaviour* 10 (2): 111–18.

Dias, M. and Agante, L. (2011) Can advergames boost children's healthier eating habits? A comparison between healthy and non-healthy food. *Journal of Consumer Behaviour* 10 (3): 152–60.

Ekstrom, K.M., Tansuhaj, P.S. and Foxman, E. (1987) Children's influence in family decisions and consumer socialization: a reciprocal view. *Advances in Consumer Research* 14: 283–7.

Ellaway, A. and Macintyre, S. (2000) Shopping for food in socially contrasting localities. *British Food Journal* 102 (1): 52–9.

Elliott, C. (2011) It's junk food and chicken nuggets: children's perspectives on 'kids' food' and the question of food classification. *Journal of Consumer Behaviour* 10 (3): 133–40.

Epp, A.M. and Arnould, E.J. (2006) Enacting the family legacy: how family themes influence consumption behaviour. *Advances in Consumer Research* 33: 82–6.

European Union (1995) The population of the EU on 1 January 1995. Statistics in Focus. Population and Social Conditions No 8. Luxembourg: Office for Official Publications of the European Communities.

Fernandez, K.V. and Veer, E. (2004) The gold that binds: the ritualistic use of jewellery in an Indian wedding. *Advances in Consumer Research* 31: 53.

Filiatrault, P. and Ritchie, J.R.B. (1980) Joint purchasing decisions: a comparison of influence structure in family and couple decision-making units. *Journal of Consumer Research* 7: 131–40.

Green, R.T., Leonardi, J., Chandon, J., Cunningham, I.C.M., Verhage, Bronis and Strazzieru, Alain (1983) Societal development and family purchasing roles: a cross-national study. *Journal of Consumer Research* 9 (4): 436–42.

Grossbart, S., Hughes, S., McConnell, P.S. and Yost, A. (2002) Socialisation aspects of parents, children and the Internet. *Advances in Consumer Research* 29: 66–70.

Hamilton, K. (2009) Consumer decision-making in low-income families: the case of conflict avoidance. *Journal of Consumer Behaviour* 8 (5): 252–67.

Hamilton, K. and Catterall, M. (2006) Consuming love in poor families: children's influence on consumption decisions. *Journal of Marketing Management* 22 (9/10): 1031–52.

Hartman, C.L. and Kiecker, P. (2004) Jewellery: passing along the continuum of sacred and profane meanings. *Advances in Consumer Research* 31: 53–4.

Hermida, A. (2005) Parents 'ignore game age ratings', June, BBC article. Available at: http://news.bbc.co.uk/1/hi/technology/4118270.stm (accessed December 2012).

John, D.R. (1999) Consumer socialization of children: a retrospective look at twenty-five years of research. *Journal of Consumer Research* 26 (Dec): 183–213.

Komarovsky, M. (1961) Class differences in family decision-making. In Nelson N. Foote (ed.), *Household Decision Making*. New York: New York University Press.

Labrecque, J. and Ricard, L. (2001) Children's influence on family decision-making: a restaurant study. *Journal of Business Research* 54 (Nov): 173–6.

Lawlor, M. and Prothero, A. (2011) Pester power – a battle of wills between children and their parents. *Journal of Marketing Management* 27 (5&6): 561–81.

Mandrik, C.A., Fern, E.F. and Bao, Y. (2004) Intergenerational influence in mothers and young adult daughters. *Advances in Consumer Research* 31: 697–9.

Marketing News (1983) Teenage daughters of working mothers have a big role in purchase, brand selection decisions. 18 (Feb): 20.

Miller, E.G., Seiders, K., Kenny, M. and Walsh, M.E. (2011) Children's use of on-package nutritional claim information. *Journal of Consumer Behaviour* 10 (3): 122–32.

Mittal, B. and Royne, M.B. (2010) Consuming as a family: modes of intergenerational influence on young adults. *Journal of Consumer Behaviour* 9 (4): 239–57.

Nancarrow, C., Tinson, J. and Brace, I. (2011) Profiling key purchase influencers: those perceived as consumer savvy. *Journal of Consumer Behaviour* 10 (2): 102–10.

Norgaard, M.K. and Brunso, K. (2011) Family conflicts and conflict resolution regarding food choices. *Journal of Consumer Behavior* 10 (3): 141–51.

Office for National Statistics (2012) *Families and Households 2012*. Newport: ONS.

Olsen, B. (1993) Brand loyalty and lineage: exploring new dimensions for research. *Advances in Consumer Research* 20: 575–9.

Opinion Research Corporation (1990) *Trends: 1990 Consumer Attitudes and the Supermarket*. Princeton, NJ: ORC.

Rick, S.I., Small, D.A. and Finkel, E.J. (2010) Fatal (fiscal) attraction: tightwads and spendthrifts in marriage. *Advances in Consumer Research* 37: 36.

Rose, G.M. (1999) Consumer socialization, parental style, and developmental timetables in the United States and Japan. *Journal of Marketing* 63: 105–19.

Rose, G.M., Dalakis, V., Kropp, F. and Kamineni, R. (2002) Raising young consumers: consumer socialization and parental style across cultures. *Advances in Consumer Behaviour* 29: 65.

Rummel, A., Howard, J., Swinton, J.M. and Seymour, D.B. (2000) You can't have that! A study of reactance effects and children's consumer behaviour. *Journal of Marketing Theory and Practice* (Winter): 38–45.

Shoham, A., Rose, G.M. and Bakir, A. (2004) The effect of family communication patterns on mothers' and fathers' perceived influence in family decision making. *Advances in Consumer Behaviour* 31: 692.

Timmins, N. (1995) One in five women to remain childless. *The Independent*, 4 October.

Tinson, J. and Nancarrow, C. (2005) The influence of children on purchases. *International Journal of Marketing* 47 (1): 5–27.

Ward, C.B. (2006) He wants, she wants: gender, category and disagreement in spouses' joint decisions. *Advances in Consumer Research* 33: 117–23.

Wells, W.D. and Gubar, G. (1966) The life cycle concept in marketing research. *Journal of Marketing Research* 3 (Nov): 353–63.

Williams, T.P. (2006) Money and meaning: the role of social bonds and capital in inter vivos gifting. *Advances in Consumer Research* 33: 84–5.

Wimalasir, J.S. (2004) A cross-national study on children's purchasing behaviour and parental response. *Journal of Consumer Marketing* 21 (4): 274–84.

More online

To gain free access to additional online resources to support this chapter please visit: **www.sagepub.co.uk/blythe**

Part Four

Decisions and their aftermath

This is the largest section of the book, and is devoted to examining the practical aspects of consumer behaviour. Chapter 11 is concerned with what actually happens when someone goes out to buy something. The person involved will only do so in order to correct a lack of something in his or her life: whether this lack is brought about by a new need, or by running out of something that he or she buys regularly, affects the type of decision-making process.

Chapter 12 is about one of the most important areas for marketers – innovation. Companies must always have new products coming to market if they are to stay ahead of the competition, but at the same time innovation means taking a risk. Understanding how people relate to new products is an essential component of any company's new product strategy.

Chapter 13 looks at what happens after purchase. Apart from consuming the product, people make assessments of how much they liked (or disliked) it, and also have to consider how to dispose of it when it is no longer useful. Whole industries have developed around this aspect alone. In the 21st century, service industries have become far more important than manufacturing industries on almost every measure. Services employ more people, represent a bigger chunk of gross national product, have higher turnovers and are growing more rapidly than any manufacturing industry. Chapter 14 covers the consumer behaviour aspects of this phenomenon.

Chapter 15 considers buyer behaviour in business-to-business markets. Although strictly speaking this is not consumer behaviour, industrial buyer behaviour still impacts on corporate success – especially since most marketing activity is in fact between businesses.

Finally, Chapter 16 is about the relationship between consumer behaviour and the 7Ps of marketing, in other words the marketing mix. Consumer behaviour impacts on each element of the mix, and of course the reverse is also the case – each element of the mix impacts on consumer behaviour. This chapter goes through each element in turn, explaining how it relates to consumers.

CHAPTER ⑪
New and repeat buying behaviour

CHAPTER CONTENTS

LEARNING OBJECTIVES

After you have read this chapter you should be able to:

- Describe how needs become apparent.

- Explain some of the limiting factors on information searches.

- Explain how assortment management affects problem-solving.

- Explain the role of consideration sets.

- Explain how decision rules are established and used.

- Explain the relationship between involvement and information processing.

- Show how involvement relates to end goals and values.

- Describe how dimensions of involvement can be used to segment markets.

- Explain the role of word of mouth in high-tech purchase behaviour.

- Explain what is meant by unsought goods.

Introduction

This chapter is concerned with the ways consumers approach making purchase decisions. The methods used depend on whether the purchase is a new one, or a repeat of a previous purchase; whether the product is novel or tried and tested; whether the purchase is routine or out of the ordinary. Decision-making does not end when the purchase is made: people evaluate their purchases, and use the information in the next round of decision-making.

In fact, many decisions are made without much conscious thought. Decision-making often happens below the conscious level, but this does not necessarily mean that the processes used in a more complex decision are not followed – it merely means that the consumer is not aware of them.

Case study: Confused.com

Confused.com is a UK-based comparison website that specialises mainly in insurance. The company was founded in 2002, and aims to cut through the lengthy process required to search through the many insurance companies' quotes in order to find the right one for the customer. The company is a subsidiary of Admiral Group, a major UK insurer, but operates entirely independently (in other words, Admiral's own products are not favoured over others in the country).

The company offers a wide range of choices from many, though not all, UK insurers. Some insurers such as Direct Line prefer to deal directly with the public, while others prefer to deal through brokers. What Confused.com does is enable people to fill in one insurance form, and obtain instant quotes from a wide range of companies.

Obviously this makes life a great deal easier. Rather than have to shop around, giving the same details over and over, people can minimise their search for information. This has proved so popular that imitators have appeared – Compare the Market.com, Go Compare and Moneysupermarket.com. Although each of these specialises mainly in insurance, they also offer comparisons for other financial services – credit cards, loans, pensions and so forth. Since the comparison sites tend to deal with the same group of suppliers, developing a USP is difficult and therefore companies tend to rely on some very catchy, creative advertising approaches. All the companies advertise on television, and all of them use some very wacky, off-the-wall advertisements. Currently, Confused.com uses an animated cartoon of people singing a parody of the Village People hit 'YMCA'; Go Compare has an operatic tenor singing a parody of George M. Cohan's First World War recruiting song 'Over There'; and Compare the Market.com has a computer-generated meerkat called Aleksandr Orlov promoting his fictitious website, Compare the Meerkat.com. (Incidentally, Compare the Market.com has now established a genuine Compare the Meerkat.com site, and Aleksandr Orlov has become something of a cult figure.)

In effect, comparison websites act as brokers for the financial services companies. What they achieve is cutting through the clutter of application forms and competing claims by insurers.

How to impress your examiner

You are likely to be asked to compare various decision-making models. If so, remember that they are not necessarily mutually exclusive: some are simpler than others, but the more complex ones still only add extra stages or influences to the basic models. Also bear in mind that decision-making is not necessarily linear, and it certainly isn't necessarily rational: emotions play a large part.

Decision-making models

Decision-making models are often complex and involve many stages. The John Dewey model (Dewey 1910), outlined more than 100 years ago, gives the following five stages:

1 A difficulty is felt (need identification).
2 The difficulty is located and defined.
3 Possible solutions are suggested.
4 Consequences are considered.
5 A solution is accepted.

This model of decision-making is probably excessively rational, and is certainly far more complex than most purchase situations warrant. In the vast majority of purchase situations, the individual simply buys the same brand as last time, or spends very little time in evaluating choices. Life is simply too busy to spend much time agonising over which brand of biscuit to buy.

Later, Engel, Kollat and Blackwell developed the EKB model of consumer behaviour, which later became the CDP (Consumer Decision Process) model (see Figure 11.1), and which follows seven stages (Blackwell et al. 2005). These are:

1 *Need recognition.* The individual recognises that something is missing from his or her life.
2 *Search for information.* This information search may be internal (remembering facts about products, or recalling experiences with them) or external (reading about possible products, visiting shops, etc.)
3 *Pre-purchase evaluation of alternatives.* The individual considers which of the possible alternatives might be best for fulfilling the need.
4 *Purchase.* The act of making the final selection and paying for it.
5 *Consumption.* Using the product for the purpose of fulfilling the need.
6 *Post-consumption evaluation.* Considering whether the product actually satisfied the need or not, and whether there were any problems arising from its purchase and consumption.
7 *Divestment.* Disposing of the product, or its packaging, or any residue left from consuming the product.

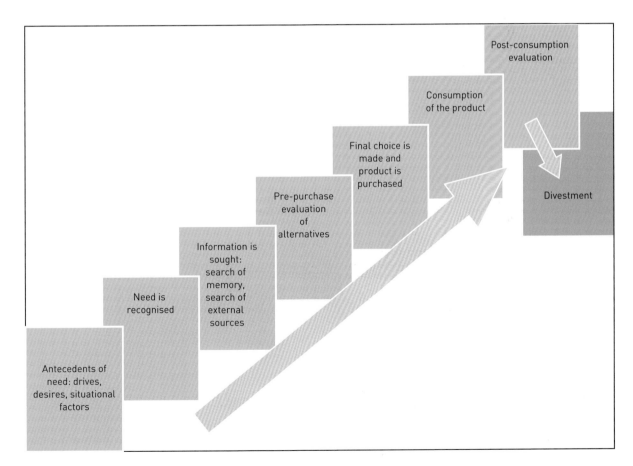

Figure 11.1 The decision-making process

The similarity between Dewey's model and the CDP model is obvious, and similar criticisms apply, but both models offer a basic outline of how people make consumption decisions. People do not buy unless they feel they have a need (see Chapter 1 for a definition of what constitutes a need). A need is felt when there is a divergence between the person's actual state and their desired state. The degree of difference between the two states is what determines the level of motivation the person feels to do something about the problem, and this will in turn depend on a number of external factors.

As explained in Chapter 1, need becomes apparent when there is a divergence of the desired and actual states. The motivation that arises from this depends on the level of disparity between the actual state and the desired state. For example, a driver who is late for an appointment may be thirsty, but not thirsty enough to stop the car at a motorway services. Likewise, a householder might have run out of one or two items, but still has enough food in the house to get by on; as the days go by more and more items are used up, and eventually a trip to the supermarket becomes essential. The disparity between the actual and desired states grows greater, in other words, and therefore the householder becomes more strongly motivated to do something about it.

There are two possible reasons for a divergence between the desired and the actual states: one is that the actual state changes, the other is that the desired state changes. In practice, it is rare for the actual states and the desired states to be the same, since this would imply that the consumer would be perfectly happy and have everything that he or she could possibly want, which is rarely the case in an imperfect world.

Causes of shift of the actual state might be taken from the following list (Onkvisit and Shaw 1994):

Assortment depletion The reduction in one's overall quantity of possessions

- Assortment depletion. Consumption, spoilage, or wear and tear on the stock of goods or products within the individual's assortment.
- Income change. This can be upwards, through a salary increase or windfall, or downwards through (say) redundancy.

Causes of shifts in the desired state are often more to do with marketing activities. This is because new information may change the individual's aspirations. If the individual sees a better car, hears a better stereo or otherwise becomes aware that there is a better solution to the problem than the one currently in use there is likely

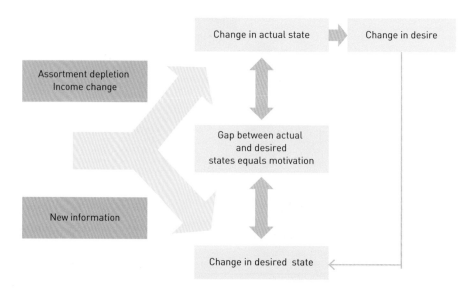

Figure 11.2 Actual and desired states

to be a shift in the desired state. From a marketing viewpoint, this approach is most effective when consumers are not satisfied with their present products.

Changing desire is often brought on by a change in actual state; getting a new job may mean moving house, for example. Sometimes a pay increase (which is a shift in the actual state) will raise the individual's aspirations and he or she will consider purchases that previously had been out of reach and therefore not even considered. For example, a lottery win might prompt an individual to book the holiday of a lifetime somewhere. The relationship between these factors is shown in Figure 11.2.

The psychology of complication says that people complicate their lives deliberately by seeking new products, even though they are fairly satisfied with the old one. (This may account in part for the high divorce rate.) The psychology of complication is the opposite of the psychology of simplification, which says that consumers try to simplify their lives by making repeat purchases of the same old brand (Hoyer and Ridgway 1984). Probably both these mechanisms act on consumers at different times.

Psychology of complication The tendency for people to make their lives more complex, and therefore more interesting

Psychology of simplification The tendency for people to make their lives less complex and therefore less stressful

Challenging the status quo

Marketers are often accused of creating needs. There is a view that somehow marketers can persuade people to want things for which they actually have no use – and of course marketers hotly deny this.

In practice, of course, marketers have very little influence over the actual state of consumers, but do they have influence over the desired state of consumers? Emphatically yes – otherwise all that advertising is just going to waste. So is it all right to seek to change people's desired state? Is it ethical? Or are we simply continuing the process that all people indulge in – advising each other about ways to make our lives more comfortable and enjoyable?

Conditions causing shifts in actual and desired states are interdependent; that is to say, a shift in the actual state (sudden redundancy, for example) will cause a shift in the desired state (instead of looking for a promotion, the individual would now be glad just to have a job at the old grade). Likewise a shift in the desired state (seeing a programme about a holiday in Sri Lanka and wanting to go there) will cause a shift in the actual state as soon as the consumer tries to save for the trip, since he or she will have to reduce expenditure elsewhere in order to accumulate savings.

Since people often make decisions on the basis of immediate gain and emotion, neurological factors often contribute to our understanding of how and why people buy (Foxall 2008).

Pre-purchase activities

Having recognised the need, the consumer will undertake a series of pre-purchase activities.

The information search comes from two sources: an internal search (from memory) and an external search (from outside sources). In both cases most of the information originates from seller-based sources, and is therefore readily available and low-cost.

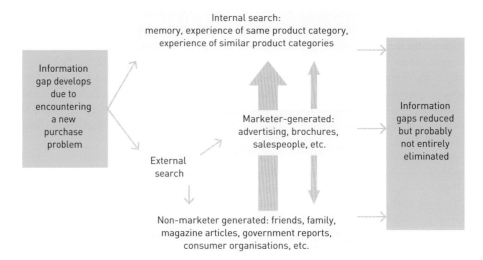

Figure 11.3   Information searching

If the internal information search is insufficient, that is to say the individual does not have enough knowledge of the product category to be able to make a choice, an external search will be undertaken.

Sources of information might be marketer-dominated (advertising, brochures, product placements in films and TV shows, websites, sales people, retail displays and so forth) or non-marketer dominated (friends, family, influential journalists, opinion leaders, consumer organisations, government and industry reports, news stories and so forth) (Figure 11.3). Most non-marketer communications use word of mouth (or e-mail, sometimes called word of mouse). Word of mouth communications are generally more powerful than any marketer-generated communications, for the following reasons:

- Word of mouth is interactive, because it involves a discussion between two or more parties. This forces those involved to think about the communication.
- It allows for feedback and confirmation of the message in a way that one-way communications like advertising do not.
- Because the source is a friend or family member who has no profit motive (unlike the marketer) the communication is more credible.

People often discuss products and services: they like to talk about their own recent purchases, to advise people about purchases and even to discuss recent controversial marketing communications. It should be noted that non-marketer generated sources are themselves influenced by marketers, and also much of the consumer's memory of the product comes from marketer-generated communications, so that even the internal search is affected by marketers.

From a marketer's viewpoint, the problem is that people will talk about products and companies whether the firm likes it or not, and may very well discuss products in negative terms. A great deal of word of mouth is negative; bad news seems to travel twice as fast as good news, and there is very little marketers can do about this.

Sometimes an individual will set out with the belief that he or she has sufficient internal information to make the purchase, but is then presented with new information at the point of purchase. For example, somebody who already owns a mobile phone but would now like to buy another might already feel familiar with the product. On entering the shop, the individual might be presented with a staggering array

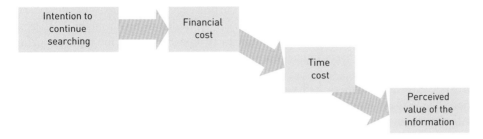

Figure 11.4 Limits on the information search

of mobile telephones with features that were not available two or three years ago, and that might even be incomprehensible. In that case the consumer may feel the need to ask the sales staff questions in order to gain enough information to make an informed decision. In other cases, people experience 'choice paralysis' brought on by having too wide a range of possible products to choose from (Shankar et al. 2006). Because choosing involves a degree of emotional effort as well as cognitive effort (people often become quite stressed when faced with a difficult choice between expensive options) the individual might well run out of self-regulatory capacity and make a hasty choice (Baumeister 2004). In other words, if the individual is finding it hard to choose, he or she might cut the decision-making process short by just grabbing the nearest product, simply to end the stress of trying to reach a decision.

Incidentally, it is common for people with limited information to base their decisions on price, simply because they lack the necessary understanding to make a judgement based on other features of the product.

Search efforts are not very extensive under most circumstances, even for major purchases like houses, because of the amount of time and effort that has to be expended. Usually consumers will continue to search until they find something that is adequate to meet the need, and will then not look any further. A US study (Formisan et al. 1982) found that almost three-quarters of purchasers of insurance policies bought from the first company they saw, for example.

The information search is often carried out on the Internet. Some searches can be time-consuming, but as users become more adept, and as website design improves, searching is becoming much more rapid (Hogue and Lohse 1999). It is possible that people will become more price-sensitive as the ease of searching becomes greater – the cost of searching is low in terms of both money and time, so it becomes easier to shop around for bargains. Limits on the search are shown in Figure 11.4.

Surfing behaviour has been classified as follows (Muylle et al. 1998):

- *Exploratory surfing.* This is characterised by low purposiveness and low specificity. The surfer is gathering information for fun, killing time or seeking amusement. It is the Net equivalent of window-shopping.
- *Window surfing.* This has medium purposiveness, and low specificity. Here the surfer follows up on interesting items – perhaps visiting a website that has details of a new sports car – without necessarily having a specific purpose in mind.
- *Evolved surfing.* Medium purposiveness, high specificity. The surfer is looking for particular categories of information, perhaps surfing travel pages or car dealerships. Even though no particular purchase is intended, the information is highly specific.
- *Bounded navigation.* High purposiveness, low specificity. The individual has determined the search boundaries in advance, and is looking for any available information about the search object.

- *Targeted navigation.* This has high purposiveness, and high specificity. For example, someone who is looking for cheap flights to Spain might go directly to the low-cost airlines' home pages to compare prices. This type of surfing obviously has a direct impact on price sensitivity.

In some cases, consumers will visit websites that carry complaints about companies. There is evidence that most Web users are not aware of these websites, but will visit them once they become aware of their existence (Bailey 2004). In order to simplify the process, online recommenders have sprung up. Online product recommendation agents gather information from consumers, then search the Web to find products that match the consumer's needs; there is evidence to show that these agents should offer more than one solution for the consumer to choose from, which of course dilutes the advantage to some extent (Aggarwal and Vaidyanathan 2003).

Information search patterns are also gender-specific (Cleveland et al. 2003). Women in general tend to use impersonal information sources (but are more wider-reaching in their information gathering) than do men, whereas men are more likely to use sales staff as an information source, and be more specific in their questioning.

Marketing in practice: McNitemares

McNitemares websites are sites that are consumer-generated and carry scurrilous (and often untrue) stories about major firms. In some cases, firms respond to these accusations on their own websites; in others they simply ignore the statements made. In some cases the allegations are serious – the websites accuse the companies of fraud, of criminal negligence and of deliberately creating dangerous products and failing to withdraw them despite overwhelming evidence.

For the companies, the problem is that they are unable to respond effectively. If they attack the websites and sue those who spread the libel, they will be accused of oppression and stifling free speech – but if they ignore the websites, the stories will continue to be spread. Most of the sites do have feedback chat rooms, in which supporters of the companies under attack can have their say – but of course they are just as promptly jumped on by the company's attackers. There is of course no way of proving the truth or otherwise of most of the statements made in the chat rooms.

Whether consumers believe the information on the McNitemares sites or not is only partly relevant. The sites form part of the information consumers are presented with, and there will inevitably be some effect, even if the accusations seem unlikely. Perhaps fortunately for the companies concerned, the McNitemares sites are not as frequently visited as the companies' own websites – although critics of major corporations might feel that this is also detrimental!

Assortment adjustment
The process of substituting some possession for others in order to improve one's overall position

Assortment adjustment is the act of entering the market to replenish or exchange the assortment of products the consumer owns. Assortment adjustment can be *programmed* (habitual) or *non-programmed* (new purchases) (see Figure 11.5). Non-programmed assortment adjustment divides into three categories. *Impulse purchases* are not based on a plan, and usually just happen as the result of a sudden confrontation with a stimulus – for example, in-store promotions might trigger an impulse purchase. People often buy as a result of lowered stimulation levels; in other words, bored shoppers might buy as a result of a stimulating promotion in-store (Sharma et al. 2010).

Such purchases are not always of familiar products; sometimes people will spend quite substantial amounts on a whim, whether it be a sudden urge to buy a particularly attractive jacket or a fancy electronic gadget. Impulse buying has been further subdivided into four categories (Hawkins 1962): pure impulse, based on the novelty of a product; reminder impulse, which relates to a product that has been left off the shopping list; suggestion impulse, which is about products that fulfil a previously unfelt need; and planned impulse, which occurs when the customer has gone out to buy a specific type of product but is prepared to be swayed by special offers.

For example, someone may set out to the supermarket to buy the week's groceries, plus something for lunch today. On the way round, he sees a jar of almond-stuffed olives and decides to buy some to try (pure impulse). Next he notices the green lasagne, which reminds him he's out of pasta (reminder impulse) and also on the shelf near it a special rack for keeping lasagne separate while it's cooking (suggestion impulse). Finally, he notices that the smoked chicken is on special offer, and decides to buy some for lunch (planned impulse). This type of scenario is familiar to most people who shop in supermarkets, and indeed supermarkets will often capitalise on this in the way the shelves are stocked and in the way the store is laid out.

The other two types of non-programmed decision-making involve either limited decision-making or extended decision-making. Of the two, limited decision-making is probably the most common.

Limited decision-making takes place when the customer is already familiar with the product class and merely wants to update his or her information or fill in a few gaps revealed by the internal search. This is typical behaviour for someone who is replacing a car; since this is usually an infrequent activity, consumers often find it necessary to check out what new models are available and renew acquaintance with the price levels being charged, even though (as a driver) the consumer will have considerable knowledge of what a car is and what it can be expected to do.

Limited decision-making also tends to occur when the consumer is not completely satisfied with the existing product and seeks a better alternative. Here the consumer is only looking for something that overcomes the perceived problem with the existing product. A trigger for this might be a change of context: someone who moves home will have the usual routines disrupted and may be open to changing his or her purchasing behaviour across a spectrum of goods (Neal et al. 2008).

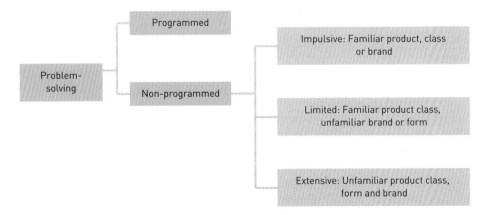

Figure 11.5   Programmed and non-programmed problem-solving. (From Onkvisit and Shaw 1994)

Extended decision-making occurs when the consumer is unfamiliar with the product class, form and brand. For example, for some people a satellite navigation device for a car would be a completely new class of product and they would have to undertake a fairly extensive information search before committing to a particular model. Extended decision-making is caused by unfamiliarity; consumers who know little about the product category, brands, etc. will tend to shop around more.

Factors affecting the external search for information

The extent and nature of the external search for information will depend on a range of factors connected with the consumer's situation, the value and availability of the information, the nature of the decision being contemplated and the nature of the individual. Figure 11.6 illustrates how these factors interrelate.

Assortment adjustment can take the form of either assortment replenishment, i.e. replacing worn-out or consumed products, or assortment extension, adding to the range of products owned. Assortment replenishment will usually require very little information searching or risk, since the product is already known. Assortment extension is more likely to lead to an extensive problem-solving pattern.

The type of problem-solving adopted will depend on the task at hand. A programmed decision pattern will lead almost immediately to purchase; these are the regular, always-buy-the-same-brand type decisions. Non-programmed decisions may still lead immediately to a purchase by impulse, but this type of decision pattern will more likely lead to limited or extensive information search patterns.

The perceived value of the information is important in terms of how extensive the information search will be. In other words, the extent of the external search depends on how valuable the information is. If there is plenty of information in the 'internal files' within the consumer's mind, the extent of external information seeking will be correspondingly less; consumers who are highly familiar with the product will search less than those who are only moderately familiar (Bettman and Park 1980).

The relevance of this information is also a factor; if it's a long time since the last purchase, the stored information may not be relevant any longer. New alternatives may have developed or the product may have improved. If the individual was satisfied with the last product (which may by now have been consumed or has worn out) the internal information will probably be regarded as relevant, and the search will be less extensive or non-existent (Kiel and Layton 1981).

Any action by a consumer produces unpredictable consequences, some of which might be unpleasant. These consequences form the perceived risk of the transaction. Financial risk is present since the consumer could lose money; for houses, cars and other major purchases the risk is great because the commitment is long-term. Because the risk is reduced as knowledge increases, greater perceived risk will tend to lead to greater information search efforts, and the benefits of such a search will be correspondingly greater. If the consumer feels certain about the decision already, there will be correspondingly less benefit in carrying out a search for information.

The fear of losing face with friends and associates is the major component of social risk. It is determined in part by product visibility; consumers who buy an inappropriate car can risk ridicule from their friends and colleagues, and might therefore carry out a more extended information search to ensure that the car will not provoke this reaction.

Assortment replenishment Replacing possessions that have been worn out or used up

Assortment extension Increasing one's overall quantity of possessions

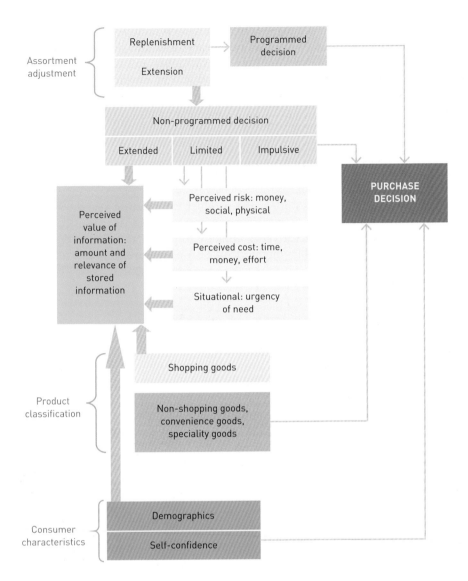

Figure 11.6 Factors affecting the external search for information

Perceived cost is the extent to which the consumer has to commit resources to the search. People will frequently cut the search down simply because it is taking too much time, money or effort. This is because the potential loss of making a wrong purchase decision is seen as being less than the cost of making a full search.

Time is a cost relating to search. It is sometimes measured in opportunity cost, or in terms of what the person could be doing instead of spending time searching. For example, highly paid people may value their time highly because they can earn more money at a desk than they save by shopping around, so they are prepared to spend money in order to save time. Poorer consumers may be more prepared to spend time shopping around in order to save money (Urbany 1986).

Money costs are the out-of-pocket expenses of searching. Clearly a consumer who wants to buy olive oil might compare different brands in Tesco but is unlikely to drive to Sainsbury's to check their prices, and would certainly not cross the Channel to check the prices in Carrefour in Calais (even though olive oil would almost certainly be cheaper in France).

The psychological costs of the information search include frustration, driving, chasing around to different shops, talking to shop assistants and generally giving a lot of thinking time to the search. Often the consumer will become overwhelmed with the quantity of information available, and will be unable to reach a decision because of information overload.

Sometimes the reverse happens and the consumer actually enjoys the shopping experience as an entertainment. Ongoing search is different from external search in that consumers go to look for product information to augment stored product knowledge, and just for the fun of it. In other words, some people go shopping just for fun and this is often a more important motivator than a genuine need to buy something (Bloch et al. 1986).

Situational factors will also affect the product information search. The search will be limited, for example, if there is an urgent need for the product. If a driver's car has broken down the driver is unlikely to phone around for the cheapest breakdown van. Other variables might include product scarcity, or lack of available credit.

Challenging the status quo

Some people really do seem to enjoy shopping. In fact, most of us do at one time or another – we go to the shops when we are on holiday, we wander round high streets trying on clothes or we wander round car showrooms looking at the cars. Browsing in bookshops, trying out new electronic equipment, even cruising the aisles of the supermarkets all provide entertainment for some people.

So where does that leave Internet shopping? How can we have a day out, when the Internet means having a day in? How can we take a friend with us for advice? How can we try on the dress, or kick the tyres convincingly when they are only on a screen?

In terms of product classification, shopping goods are those for which a new solution has to be formulated every time. Non-shopping goods are those for which the person already has a complete preference and specification, and therefore is able to buy the same brand almost all the time (Bucklin 1963). For example, tomato ketchup is usually a non-shopping product, whereas a DVD player is a shopping product.

Consumer characteristics are those features of the consumer that affect the information search. Demographics affect the search in that outshoppers (people who shop outside the area in which they live) have higher incomes, and are mobile. This factor may be product-specific, since outshopping most frequently occurs when buying groceries at an out-of-town shopping centre or buying consumer durables. Outshopping can also occur in the form of a shopping trip to

Marketing in practice

In many parts of the world, differentials exist between prices in one country and prices in another. Sometimes these differences appear as a result of differing taxation and duty regimes between countries, sometimes they occur because one country produces the goods more cheaply than the other, and sometimes they occur because of differential pricing by marketers. Frequently, if the countries are close together, the result is a regular traffic across the border – in some cases, goods are illegally smuggled across, but in many cases there are few if any border controls and shoppers can simply switch countries and save money.

Within the European Union, British consumers used to cross the English Channel in their thousands to take advantage of lower prices on alcohol and tobacco in France. The so-called 'booze cruises' were a major source of revenue for the ferry companies, who of course have shops on board selling alcohol and tobacco at French prices. Shoppers could even buy a ticket that allowed them to park their car on the car deck of the ferry and cross to France and back without ever going ashore – the ferry being a cheaper place to park than the multi-storey car park in the Dover ferry port!

In Brazil and Argentina consumers often cross into Paraguay (especially near the Foz do Iguacu waterfalls) to buy cheap consumer electronic equipment, which is often half-price or less due to different customs regulations. A short bus ride, with minimal border checks (no passports needed within the Mercosur region), and consumers can carry back almost any amount of cheap goods. It is even possible to walk across the bridge over the Parana river.

Cross-border shopping is not confined to alcohol, tobacco and luxury goods, either – many Norwegians cross into Sweden to buy groceries, and 15% of Croatians report that they cross into Bosnia-Herzegovina to do their weekly food shopping, according to a survey carried out in 2011 by the newspaper *Vecernji*.

In the United States shoppers in southern states cross into Mexico to buy tequila, cheap clothing, jewellery, blankets and handicrafts. In some cases, prices are 25% of US prices, and again no passport is required – a US driving licence is enough. In northern states the flow is reversed – changes in the 2012 Canadian budget allowed Canadians to buy $200 worth of duty-free goods if they are in the US for less than 24 hours, but if they stay for 48 hours or more they can bring back $800 worth. In Syracuse, New York State, this has prompted the construction of a huge shopping mall aimed at visitors from Quebec and Ontario. Canadian retailers are fighting back by building even bigger and glitzier malls – but the price differential is often huge.

Of course, the cost of crossing the border whether by ferry or by car means that shoppers need to buy in large quantities to make the exercise economically worthwhile. On the other hand, shrewd marketers in the targeted areas recognise that they are dealing with shopping as entertainment – people are enjoying a day out, and justifying it on the basis that they are saving money. United States petrol stations even give out vouchers for the bridge tolls, and since the fuel itself is much cheaper in the US, the cost of crossing the border is tiny.

a major city, or even a day trip to another country to take advantage of lower prices there.

Likewise, people have varying levels of attitudes about the pain of paying for things. Spendthrifts feel relatively little pain in making purchases, whereas careful savers (tightwads) feel a great deal of pain in making purchases. Tightwads outnumber spendthrifts by a ratio of 3 to 2, so it is important for marketers to understand how and why the pain of paying varies across the population (Rick et al. 2008).

Making the choice

Having gone through the procedures of collecting information, whether by a lengthy search or by simply remembering all the necessary facts, people make a choice based on the collected information. The first procedure is to establish a consideration set, which is the group of products from which the final choice is to be made. This consideration set will usually contain only a small subset of all the possible alternatives, so from the marketer's viewpoint it is essential to be included in the consideration set, and this is the role of much of the advertising activity undertaken. Option framing means creating a base model for the decision, then adding or subtracting options from it: in most cases people will limit the number of options under consideration, and will tend to delete more than they add (Biswas 2009).

Consumers construct the consideration set from the knowledge obtained in the information search. They will often use cut-offs, or restrictions on the minimum or maximum acceptable values. Typically consumers will have a clear idea of the price range they are willing to pay, for example, and any product priced outside this zone will not be included. Incidentally, this price range may have a minimum as well as a maximum; price is often used as a surrogate for judging quality. For example, someone buying a car is unlikely to buy the cheapest available – many people are prepared to pay a little more (or even a lot more) in order to drive a more prestigious vehicle. Again, marketers need to know what the consumer's cut-off point is on given specifications; this can be determined by market research.

Signals are important to consumers when judging product quality. A signal could be a brand name, a guarantee and even the retailer the product is bought from. Because it is common for consumers to equate quality with high price, a useful tactic for low-priced manufacturers is to undermine this perception in as many ways as possible. The use of price as a quality signal is somewhat reduced when other signals are present. For example, if the consumer is easily able to judge the quality by inspecting the product, the relationship may not apply.

Finally, consumers will often select a decision rule or heuristic. Consumers develop these rules over a period of time; for example, a rule might be always to buy the best quality one is able to afford at the time. Some consumers have rules about brand names, or shops they know and trust, or people whose preferences they will always respect.

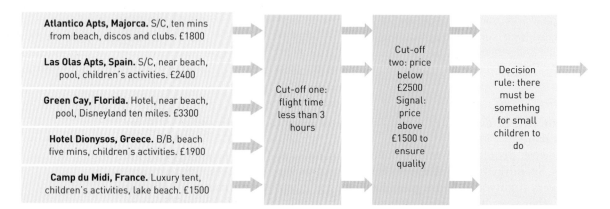

Figure 11.7 An example of a decision-making process for a holiday purchase

Figure 11.7 shows an example of a decision-making process for a holiday purchase. The consumer begins with a choice of five different holidays, which form the consideration set. The relevant information about each holiday has been included, and now the decision rules need to be applied. First of all, the consumer decides that a long flight would be difficult with children so he or she sets a limit of three hours. This cuts out Greece and Florida. Then there is a cut-off on cost (not to go above £2500). This cut-off has no relevance, since none of the remaining holidays costs above £2500, but the consumer also uses price as a signal by which to judge quality, and cuts out the tent in France because it is too cheap. The remaining decision rule is that there must be something for the children to do, and this leaves only the apartment in Spain as the final choice.

Sometimes the consumer will find that applying all the decision rules cuts out all of the alternatives, so that a revision of the rules needs to take place. This can result in establishing a hierarchy of rules according to their relative importance (Bettman 1979). There is also an effect caused by simply thinking about the product group – people often judge the desirability of the options on the basis of their ability to consider the options in advance. In other words, being able to think through and understand the implications of owning a product tends to make the product more desirable (Morewedge and Wegner 2008).

Categorisation of decision rules

Non-compensatory decision rules are absolute; if a product does not meet the decision rule for one attribute, this cannot be compensated for by its strength in other areas. In the holiday example in Figure 11.7, despite the fact that the Florida location is near to Disneyland, and is therefore a very strong candidate as far as entertaining the children is concerned, the cost and the flight time rule it out. In the lexicographic approach the consumer establishes a hierarchy of attributes, comparing products first against the most important attribute, then against the second most important, and so forth. In the holiday example, the consumer might feel that availability of children's activities is the most important attribute, in which case the Florida destination might be the most attractive. Decisions can be made by elimination of aspects whereby the product is examined against other brands according to attributes, but then each attribute is checked against a cut-off; in the above example, this led to Florida being rejected on grounds of flight time and cost.

> **Non-compensatory decision rule** A heuristic that cannot be offset by other factors

The conjunctive rule is the last of the non-compensatory rules. Here each brand is compared in turn against all the cut-offs; only those brands that survive this winnowing-out will be compared with each other.

> **Conjunctive rule** A heuristic by which brands are compared to all cut-offs until only a few surviving brands remain

Compensatory decision rules allow for trade-offs, so that a weakness in one area can be compensated for in another. The simple additive rule involves a straight tally of the product's positive aspects, and a comparison of this tally with the tally for other products. The product with the most positive attributes will be the one chosen. A variation of this is the weighted additive approach, which gives greater weight to some attributes than to others. In each case, though, the products do not necessarily have to have all the attributes in common (or, indeed, any of them).

Phased decision strategies may involve using rules in a sequence. For example, the consumer may use a non-compensatory cut-off to eliminate products from the consideration set, then use a weighted additive rule to decide between the remaining products.

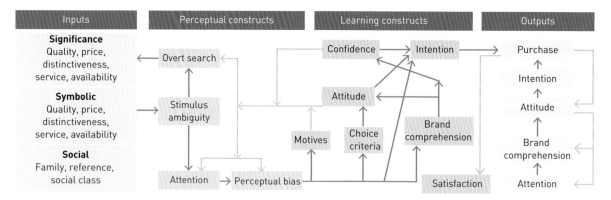

Figure 11.8   Howard–Sheth model. (Adapted from Howard and Sheth 1969)

Two more special categories of decision rule exist. First, the consumer may need to create a constructive decision rule. This means establishing a rule from scratch when faced with a new situation. If the rule thus created works effectively, the consumer will store it in memory until the next time the situation is encountered, and 'recycle' the rule then. Second, affect referral is the process whereby consumers retrieve a 'standard' attitude from memory. For example, a consumer may strongly disapprove of American foreign policy, and this attitude prevents the inclusion of any American products in the consideration set.

For marketers, it is clearly useful to know how consumers are approaching their decision-making. If, for example, consumers are using a weighted additive rule, it would be useful to know which attributes are given the greatest weightings. If, however, consumers are using a conjunctive rule with cut-offs at known levels, the product can be designed to fall within the cut-offs. The initial aim for marketers must be to ensure that the product becomes part of the consideration set for most consumers, and therefore it must pass at least the first hurdles in terms of the cut-offs and signals employed in the decision process.

Several attempts have been made to bring the factors in consumer decision-making together in one model. Most of these models are complex, since there are many factors which interrelate in a number of ways; an example is the Howard–Sheth model shown in Figure 11.8. This is a somewhat simplified version; the original requires one diagram to be superimposed on another. In the diagram the solid arrows show the flow of information; the dotted arrows show the feedback effects. Essentially, the diagram deals with the way the inputs are dealt with by perception and by learning, and eventually become outputs.

Following on from the purchase, there will be an evaluation of both the product itself and the decision process. The learning process will feed back into the internal search, and new heuristics will be developed. There is more on this in Chapter 15.

Involvement

Involvement is the perceived relevance of the object based on the person's inherent needs, values and interests (Zaichowsky 1985). It is about the degree to which the individual feels attached to the product or brand, and the loyalty felt towards it. Involvement has both cognitive and affective elements: it acts on both the mind and on the emotions.

Involvement is sometimes seen as the motivation to process information (Mitchell 1979). Someone who is closely attached to a product will probably tend to process information about the product much more readily than will someone who has no such association. At a low level of involvement, individuals only engage in simple processing of information: at high levels of involvement, people will link incoming information to their pre-existing knowledge system, in a process called elaboration (Otker 1990). The degree of involvement will lie somewhere on a continuum from complete inertia (someone who makes decisions out of habit, lacking the motivation to consider alternatives) through to high involvement where we might expect to find an intensity of feeling that borders on the religious. At the extreme, we would expect to find people who worship celebrities, or who have a brand tattooed onto their skin (Harley-Davidson owners have been known to do this). Such people have often become involved with cult products such as Harley motorcycles, Barbie dolls, sports teams or rock bands.

Inertia Making decisions out of habit rather than from any conscious loyalty

Figure 11.9 shows the continuum in action. Someone who has no real interest in the product category and makes only routine purchases of generic products (or no purchases at all) exhibits inertia. Someone with a mild interest in the product exhibits a willingness to listen to explanations or advice about the product. Someone who is involved at a medium level would take an interest in anything he or she happens to see concerning the product, and someone who is highly committed would actively seek out information. Finally, someone who is totally committed to the brand identifies with it to the point of obsession.

Figure 11.10 summarises categories of involvement. Involvement is not always confined to products. People can experience message–response involvement or advertising involvement in which they become eager to process information obtained from advertising (Batra and Ray 1983). In some cases the messages are passive (as in the case of TV advertising) whereas in other cases messages involve more effort on the part of the observer (for example print advertisements) and some marketing communications require a great deal of interaction (some mail shots and some Internet advertising).

Purchase situation involvement is about the different contexts in which purchase takes place. For example, if one were buying an expensive gift for a new girlfriend or boyfriend, one might be extremely involved in the purchase since there is a high social risk involved if a mistake is made. If, on the other hand, the gift-buying is almost obligatory (e.g. buying a birthday gift for a relative one has little liking for and rarely sees) the involvement level will be considerably lower.

Ego involvement is about the importance of the product to the individual's self-concept. Making a mistake in purchase could lead to a high social risk – the individual's self-concept might be damaged, to embarrassing effect. For example, a committed vegan would be horrified to find that a supposedly vegan product contained animal fat. In some cases, the product purchase is linked to a 'tribe': such

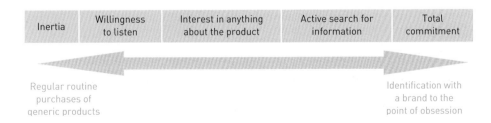

Figure 11.9 Involvement continuum

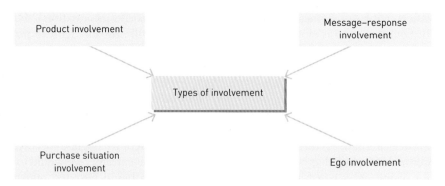

Figure 11.10   Categories of involvement

communities are supported by social networking sites, celebrity affiliations and self-generated communications (Hamilton and Hewer 2010).

High product involvement is driven by the degree to which the individual feels that the product's attributes are linked to end goals or values. Lower levels of involvement occur if the attributes only link to function, and very low levels of involvement occur if the product attributes are irrelevant to consequences.

In other words, high-involvement products are those that figure strongly in the individual's lifestyle. They involve decisions it is important to get right, preferably first time. In most cases these products are ones the consumer knows a lot about, and about which he or she has strong opinions. This means that high-involvement consumers are hard to persuade: they will not easily be swayed by advertising, or even by persuasive sales pitches. For example, an amateur chef might favour using a specific type of oil for cooking. If the oil is unavailable, he or she is unlikely to be persuaded that a different oil is 'just as good'; an attempt by a salesperson to persuade in those circumstances would just make the salesperson appear stupid. The discrepant information is ignored or disparaged, so the source of the information (the salesperson) will lose esteem in the eyes of the consumer.

Levels of involvement are influenced by two sources: personal sources and situational sources. Personal sources (also called intrinsic self-relevance) are derived from the means–end knowledge stored in the individual's memory, and are influenced both by the person and by the product. People who believe that the attributes of the product link to important end goals are likely to be more heavily involved with the product because the importance of the end goal means that it is more

Intrinsic self-relevance
Sources of involvement derived from means–end knowledge stored in the individual's memory

Challenging the status quo

Do we really become that emotionally attached to products? Surely we are not so shallow that the most important thing in our lives is a brand of cooking oil! People might be in the habit of saying, 'I really love my car!' but isn't that just a figure of speech? Saying that we like something a lot is not the same as saying we love it, and saying that we think a product is the best available does not mean that we cannot live effectively without it.

In the course of a long life we fall in love with many people and things – surely we are not so blinded by love that we cannot be aware of the possibility of changing the brand of underwear we buy!

important to be right first time. Even products such as snacks can have personal involvement issues – pre-teen girls have been shown to have very specific requirements for snacks, based on what friends find acceptable (Dibley and Baker 2001). Involvement does not necessarily depend on the outcome being positive; sometimes involvement might be greater if the possible outcomes are negative, since the consumer will take care to choose products which will avoid negative outcomes.

People who are motivated by ethics and social responsibility in their shopping will sometimes (though by no means always) be prepared to forgo aspects such as customer service, product quality and so forth (Megicks et al. 2008). This has led to calls for better labelling, especially for controversial products such as genetically-modified foods (D'Souza et al. 2008). It has also led to the opening of many farmers' markets, where people can buy locally produced food (even when it is less convenient to do so rather than use a supermarket) (McEachern et al. 2010). Consumers will go so far as to 'punish' or 'reward' suppliers by either boycotting their stores or 'buycotting' them. This has been dubbed political consumerism (Neilson 2010).

There is always a risk with any purchase behaviour, but high-involvement goods carry the greatest perceived risk since these are the purchases that are most important to the consumers. This means that consumers are more likely to engage in extended problem-solving behaviour when considering high-involvement goods. People are therefore unlikely to switch brands in the case of high-involvement goods unless forced to (for example, if the product is taken off the market). When brand switching becomes unavoidable, the individual needs to go through the same extended decision-making behaviour as before.

Situational sources of involvement are concerned with aspects of the immediate social or physical surroundings of the individual. Sometimes a change in social circumstances will increase involvement: most people will give considerable thought to how they dress when going on a first date, for example. Physical environment issues are about the circumstances that arise in the surrounding environment rather than those arising from people. For example, a climber might revise her view of the importance of reliability if a climbing rope were to fail half way up a mountain. Likewise, experience of cold weather might cause an individual to become strongly involved with a ski jacket.

Marketers may be able to manipulate some of the environmental aspects in order to increase consumer involvement in some way. For instance, a salesperson might explain the possible consequences of buying the wrong type of double glazing (showing that not all double glazing has the same insulating properties, for example). This may make the customer aware that the end result (having paid out a lot of money for windows that do not keep the heat in) could be highly self-relevant.

In some cases, involvement increases because the individual co-creates the product itself. This has been shown to happen in historical re-creations such as living museums (Chronist and Hampton 2008) and in self-assembly furniture. People who visit a living museum (where actors re-enact historical events or dress, speak and act in the context of the historical period) will be active in creating and maintaining the authenticity of the museum: if the experience is not 'authentic' they feel a strong sense of dissonance (Hede and Thyne 2010). People who assemble furniture themselves often have a feeling of achievement when the project is finished – this has been called the IKEA effect, after the Swedish furniture company (Norton and Ariely 2008).

In some cases, co-creation of value moves away from the firm altogether and is controlled by the consumers themselves. The Internet has dramatically increased the possibilities for doing this, because people can cooperate in modifying the product post-purchase, especially when it is a service rather than a physical product (Harwood and Garry 2010).

Dimensions of involvement

Laurent and Kapferer (1985) developed a five-factor model for assessing the dimensions of involvement. The factors were as follows:

- The personal interest a person has in the product category, its personal meaning or importance. For example, people often become very involved in art galleries or orchestras (Slater and Armstrong 2010).
- The perceived importance of the potential negative consequences associated with a poor choice of product (risk importance).
- The probability of making a bad purchase.
- The pleasure value of the product category.
- The sign value of the product category (how closely it relates to the self).

The researchers found that buying a product such as a vacuum cleaner scored high on the risk dimension (because vacuum cleaners are likely to last for many years) but low on the pleasure and sign value dimensions. On the other hand, chocolate scores high in terms of pleasure, but low on sign value and risk value. The evidence is, therefore, that different products may be high involvement for different reasons.

It is possible to use these dimensions of involvement to segment the market for a given product. For example, for some people an iPod might have a strong sign value, while for others it has a strong pleasure value: the approach to each of these groups would be different in terms of marketing communication. Such factors would also be different between different countries, and this is especially true of food and drink items. A food which is an everyday purchase in one country might be a luxury only available in delicatessens in another country, and therefore the sign value of serving the product to friends or guests is very different.

Involvement with brands

People often develop relationships with brands. Typical examples might be favourite perfumes, jeans, cars, cigarettes and even coffee. Research by Brann Consulting showed that people are more likely to think of their brand of coffee as a friend than they are to think of their bank this way: banks are acquaintances at best, enemies at worst. This

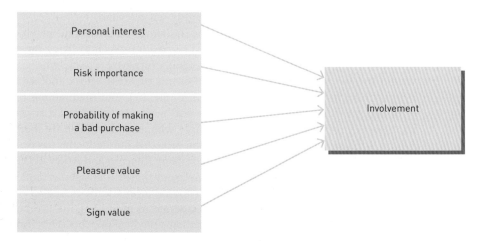

Figure 11.11 Dimensions of involvement

Consumer behaviour in action: Dinner parties

Inviting friends to eat with us is a great pleasure for most people, and it is a particularly human thing to do as well. Although all humans share food with their friends (unlike most other creatures, who will tend to push their fellows aside rather than share), the rules surrounding the process are very different between cultures.

In Britain, few people would serve traditional British food at a dinner party. It would be the norm to provide something foreign. In France the reverse would be the case – even if the host entertained at home, instead of inviting friends to a restaurant, traditional French recipes would be on the menu. What is served reflects on the

host in most countries – in Brazil, it would be regarded as almost insulting to serve bananas for dessert, since bananas are so cheap it would mark the host out as a mean person.

In Hawaii, dinner guests would bring small snacks (puu puus) and in many parts of the United States it would not be unusual for guests to bring substantial quantities of food if invited to dinner. In Britain, this would be seen as a criticism – the sign value of offering interesting and exotic food to one's guests is so important within the culture that many indifferent cooks will either not host dinner parties at all, or will hire caterers to provide the food.

The very fact of hosting a dinner party carries sign values as well as pleasure values. Some people like to be known as good dinner party hosts: keen amateur chefs like to show off their skills, to the extent that there are several TV programmes dedicated to the amateur chef. Cookery programmes are a perennial favourite on British TV, something that would be surprising in some other countries.

Pleasure and sign values are the main elements in dinner parties, but not the only ones. Some hosts spend large amounts of money on ingredients, simply to be sure that the quality of the food will be as high as can be managed. There is a considerable risk, of course, in having an amateur chef dealing with very expensive ingredients. In a sense, it seems crazy that people should be so involved (and anxious) about something which is so straightforward – meeting up with friends and sharing some food!

may seem surprising considering that banks are composed of people, whereas coffee is inanimate, but it is perhaps due to the fact that coffee is consumed at home or with friends whereas bank services are often regarded as an unpleasant necessity.

It is, of course, the brand that the individual has the relationship with, not the product. In blind taste tests most smokers are unable to distinguish their favourite brand from other similar brands, but it would take considerable persuasion to make them switch brands; likewise, drivers often develop affectionate relationships with their cars. Someone's first car is often personalised with stickers and accessories, and not infrequently given a name. Drivers even talk to their cars (sometimes in less than flattering terms). Involvement also has an influence on decision-making styles (Bauer et al. 2006). Even when the product itself might be considered to have few differences, people are prepared to pay more for the branded product – research in the United States showed that people would pay more for branded pork than for unbranded pork (Ubilava et al. 2011).

Involvement can be considered in terms of attachment theory, specifically avoidance and anxiety factors. Avoidance factors are those that make people shun relationships

Table 11.1   Categorising consumers according to involvement

Brand loyalists	Strong affective links to a particular brand. Usually these people tend to link the product category to the provision of personally relevant consequences. These people buy the 'best brand' within the category, but also feel that the product category itself is an important part of their lives
Routine brand buyers	These people have low personal sources of involvement, but have a favourite brand. They are more interested in the types of consequences associated with regular brand purchases, and will not necessarily look for the 'best' brand: a satisfactory brand will do. For these consumers, it is easier to buy the same brand each week, and even if it is not the 'best' it is at least reliable
Information seekers	These consumers have positive means–end information about the product category, but no one brand stands out as superior. This means that they will use a great deal of information to help them find a suitable brand from within the product category
Brand switchers	These people have low brand loyalty and low personal involvement. They do not believe that the choice of brand has any important consequences, even if the product category is interesting. Usually they do not have a strong relationship with the product category either, which means that they are easily affected by environmental factors such as sales promotions

Source: Adapted from Peter, J.P. and Olsen, J.C. (1994) *Understanding Consumer Behaviour*. Burr Ridge, IL: Irwin.

due to a fear of intimacy (or, for brands, read fear of becoming too dependent) while anxiety factors are those that make people fear loss, anxiety or rejection. People who are low or high on both dimensions report high satisfaction with brands, whereas people who are high on one dimension and low on the other report low satisfaction rates (Thompson and Johnson 2002). Presumably this means that people with a fear of becoming dependent, and a fear of loss, will be less likely to form relationships with brands and will therefore have no problems with them, whereas people who have no fear of becoming dependent and also no fear of loss will have many favourite brands. There are gender differences in brand relationship formation: when considering the two propositions 'I understand the brand' and 'The brand understands me' women use both dimensions to judge their closeness to the brand, whereas men judge only by their own actions towards the brand (Monga 2002).

For any given product category, people can be classified according to their level of involvement, as shown in Table 11.1. The relationship between these factors is shown in Figure 11.2. Even when the product has other products associated with it, the involvement may only apply to one of the products: for example, someone might be staunchly loyal to a brand of whisky without caring much which brand of soda goes in it. While it is true that some people may be heavily involved in several brands, there is no evidence that high involvement in one brand will lead to high involvement in another brand from a different product category.

Involvement does not equate to price. A high-involvement product is not necessarily a high-priced one, nor is a low-involvement product always a cheap one. Beer drinkers can be heavily committed to their brand of beer, costing only a few pounds

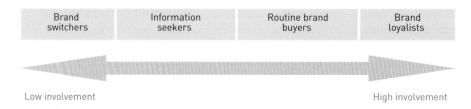

Figure 11.12   Categorising consumers

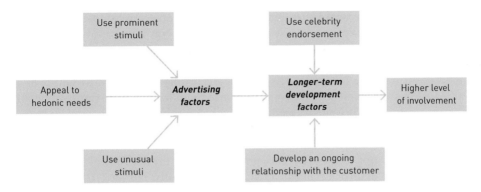

Figure 11.13 Increasing involvement

a pint, whereas other people might not care what make of car they drive as long as it gets them from A to B. Equally, someone might spend a large amount of money on a computer without being a computer enthusiast – such an individual might simply be intending to work from home. In other words, there might be no affective element in the purchase, and hence little involvement except regarding the end result. High involvement always has a strong affective component, and this does not necessarily mean a high cost commitment – people also fall in love with cheap products.

Increasing involvement levels

From a marketer's viewpoint, increasing consumers' involvement levels is clearly a priority. Marketers will try to increase consumer involvement with the products whenever it is possible to do so, since this will make communications easier and loyalty levels higher. As Figure 11.13 summarises, there are various techniques available to marketers for encouraging consumers to process relevant information, as follows (Stewart and Furse 1984):

- Appeal to hedonic needs. Advertising that appeals to the senses generates higher levels of attention (Holbrook and Hirschman 1982). There is evidence that the pleasure of shopping tends to increase involvement with clothing (Michaelidou and Dibb 2006).
- Use unusual stimuli to attract attention.
- Use celebrity endorsement. The viewer's involvement with the celebrity is likely to transfer to the product, although there are dangers with this approach.
- Use prominent stimuli such as fast action or loud music. This will help to capture the viewer's attention.
- Develop an ongoing relationship with consumers. This can often be done by using a well-designed interactive website to generate involvement.

Ultimately, of course, consumers develop their own ideas about involvement, and will only become involved in products which appeal to their innermost selves. Marketers can only facilitate a process which would have happened (at least to some extent) in any case.

Loyalty

Involvement with a brand should, in the vast majority of cases, lead to feelings of loyalty. In recent years, marketers have taken the view that it is better to generate loyalty and therefore retain customers than it is to keep recruiting new customers. This view has been expressed most clearly by Ehrenberg, who proposes the 'leaky bucket' theory. In the past, most companies have operated on a 'leaky bucket' basis, seeking to refill the bucket with new customers while ignoring the ones leaking away through the bottom of the bucket. According to research by Gupta et al. (2004) a 1% improvement in customer retention will lead to a 5% improvement in the firm's value. A 1% improvement in marginal cost or customer acquisition cost only generates a 1% increase in firm value respectively. In other words, according to Gupta et al., customer retention is five times as effective as cutting costs.

Satisfaction is not necessarily enough to generate loyalty, however. East et al. (2006) found no evidence that satisfaction breeds loyalty, but have found evidence that satisfaction leads to personal recommendations and therefore to recruitment of new customers. In fact, in many ways people are not loyal, and their loyalty cannot be bought: only a small percentage of loyalty card holders actually are loyal (Allaway et al. 2006), and the existence of loyalty cards has had minimal impact on market structures because every store issues them now, and most people carry several cards (Meyer-Waarden and Benavent 2006). Loyalty to the store tends to be higher in the case of on-line suppliers, which may be a function of trust (Buttner and Goritz 2008). Since on-line purchases are perceived to be higher risk than buying from a physical bricks-and-mortar store, people will tend to return to the same supplier even when price, brand and size of supplier are less than ideal (Cui and Wang 2010).

The importance of the purchase has an effect on satisfaction and also on loyalty: the more important the purchase, the more disastrous a failure in performance will be and the greater the effect on satisfaction and loyalty. Perhaps surprisingly, if the purchase importance is low, perceived performance has a stronger influence on satisfaction (Tam 2011).

If loyalty can be generated, though, it does increase profitability (Helgesen 2006). Since companies are often not good at acquiring new customers, loyalty becomes important (Ang and Buttle 2006). It also has the effect of reducing the evaluation of brand extensions – people tend to assume that the extension will be as good as the original brand (Hem and Iversen 2003).

Purchasing high-tech consumer durables

Defining what is a high-tech consumer durable is somewhat difficult. In general, the category includes most recent electronic devices such as mobile telephones, digital cameras, computers, DVD recorders and so forth. Such products are frequently high-involvement purchases because there is usually a high level of personal relevance when someone is contemplating buying an expensive and highly visible piece of equipment. This could be because of the social values applied (friends being envious or admiring) or perhaps because of a situational change. Someone contemplating a high-tech purchase is likely to have acquired, or be acquiring, extensive means–end knowledge.

Factors in the decision-making process include the following:

- *Self-image considerations.* The potential buyer needs to ask him- or herself whether the piece of equipment fits into the kind of image the buyer has of him- or herself, or (perhaps more importantly) the kind of image the buyer would like to project to others.
- *Situational sources of involvement.* These are the considerations surrounding the immediate need. For example, a laptop computer purchaser might need to ensure that the machine will run software that is compatible with that used at work.

Figure 11.14 Factors in decision-making for high-tech products

- *Product-related considerations.* Issues such as the reliability and durability of the equipment will come into play here. Consumer durables are usually only purchased every few years, perhaps only once a decade, so there is a strong incentive to buy products that will suit the purpose for a long period.
- *Information considerations.* Purchasers will probably be information-seekers, since frequency of purchase is low, and high-tech products (almost by definition) develop rapidly. Personal sources of information (i.e. information held in memory) are likely to obsolete.
- *Financial risk.* This is fairly high, since high-tech goods are usually fairly expensive. Mobile telephone providers found a way round this by building the cost of the telephone into the cost of the 'line' rental, with the intention of expanding the market rapidly. The thinking was that consumers would be unlikely to commit the true cost of the telephones 'up front'.
- *Social risk.* This can also be high, since the purchaser may have friends who know more about the product category than does the purchaser. A friend may even be a maven (see Chapter 13) and might be contemptuous of a poor purchase decision.
- *Rational approaches to marketing communications.* Marketers will often adopt an informative, rational communications strategy because the consumers are likely to be information-seekers. For example, makers of hi-fi sound equipment often produce very detailed, highly technical brochures and information. Occasionally consumers criticise these for being too complex, but many hi-fi enthusiasts not only understand all the jargon, but welcome it as an indication of their membership of an elite group.

In Figure 11.14 the self-image of the individual leads to rational information processing and an assessment of the financial and social risk. This happens within the context of the product itself, and the overall situation.

Word of mouth plays a strong role in the purchase of high-tech consumer durables, because purchases tend to be infrequent. In this context, mavens may play an important role (see Chapter 13) since they make a hobby out of knowing about such products, and are more than willing to share their knowledge.

Unsought goods

So far, we have looked at consumer behaviour when seeking out goods to meet a specific, recognised need. While most products fall into the category of being sought out as a way of meeting a need, there is a category of unsought goods that consumers do not look for.

Information-seekers
People who enjoy finding out about products

Unsought goods Products that are bought as a result of coercion rather than through desire

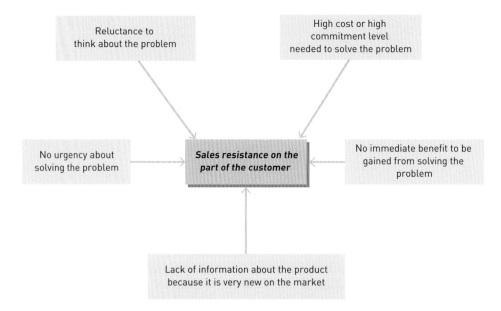

Figure 11.15   Reasons for postponing purchase of unsought goods

Unsought goods are those goods for which consumers will recognise a need, but which they nevertheless tend to avoid buying. Examples are life insurance, wills and funeral plans (because people prefer not to contemplate their own deaths), and home improvements (because major capital expenditures can always be postponed).

If consumers do not seek out these products, two questions arise: first, why do people not seek out these products when they have already recognised a need for them, and second, how are such products marketed?

The possible reasons for not seeking out the products, summarised in Figure 11.15, are as follows:

- People do not like to think about the reasons for needing the products. Because people do not like to think about old age and death, they prefer not to think about pensions and insurance.
- The products are expensive or require a long-term commitment, and people do not like to risk making a mistake.
- There is no urgency about seeking a solution. Retirement may be a long way off, or the roof may last another year or two.
- The consumer may not see any immediate benefit. In the case of life insurance, the insured person never benefits directly, since the policy only pays out on proof of death.
- Some unsought goods are new on the market, so the level of knowledge about them is low and the individual automatically rejects any marketing approach because the benefits are not obvious. Trust in both the product and the brand needs to be established first before information can be transferred.

Marketers can overcome these problems with a series of tactics, but the main one is to use salespeople to explain the benefits of the product and close the sale. These salespeople usually have to overcome an initial resistance to the idea of spending time listening to a presentation, since the consumer of unsought goods is not engaged in an information search and is therefore unlikely to want to spend time and resources on listening to a sales presentation. The salesperson will therefore need to employ a

Table 11.2   Decision-making model for unsought goods

Stage	Techniques for management
Need recognition	Sales representatives activate the need by asking questions about the individual's current circumstances
Information search	The sales representative performs a lengthy presentation, explaining the product's features and benefits. Questions and objections are dealt with as they arise
Evaluation of alternatives	The salesperson 'no-sells' competitors by pointing out ways in which the competitors' products are inferior
Choice decision	The salesperson closes the sale by using a phrase or technique that elicits a yes or no decision
Post-purchase evaluation	The company may follow up on the sale by sending comments forms, the salesperson may call back to elicit feedback, or a sales manager might call back. In the case of buyers' remorse, there will be a return visit by the salesperson or by a sales manager

tactical device to gain the customer's attention for long enough to activate the need for the product. Table 11.2 shows how a salesperson can contribute to each stage of decision-making for this type of purchase.

The selling techniques used for unsought goods have attracted a great deal of adverse publicity, but it is worth bearing in mind that the vast majority of double-glazing owners are perfectly happy with the product, as are the vast majority of timeshare owners. Generally speaking, people are not stupid enough to commit large sums of money to products they do not want and do not see a need for.

Summary

This chapter has been about consumer decision-making processes. The processes often happen largely below the conscious level, and people often fall in love with a product without having much real knowledge of it, but the processes nevertheless occur, even if only at the subconscious level.

Decision-making flows from both needs and from attitudes. People need to be able to justify their decisions, both in terms of cost and of the usefulness of the products they buy; marketers need to be able to influence the decision by influencing attitudes, cost and utility as well as understanding the mental processes people go through both before and after making purchases.

 **Key points**

- Needs become activated when there is a divergence between the actual and the desired states.
- Any information search is likely to be limited, since there is a cost attached as well as a risk reduction aspect.

- The type of problem-solving undertaken will depend in part on whether the consumer is replenishing the assortment or extending it.
- The consideration set doesn't include every possible solution.
- Most decisions involve decision rules, either pre-programmed or invented on the spot.
- Involvement is the motivation to process information.
- High involvement is linked to end goals and values.
- Dimensions of involvement can be used to segment markets.
- Word of mouth is a strong factor in high-tech purchases.
- Unsought goods are those for which people recognise a need, but still avoid buying.

Review questions

1 What type of information search would you expect someone to undertake when buying a new type of television?
2 What might be a suitable marketing communications approach for a shop whose main target market is composed of women?
3 What might be a suitable marketing communications approach for a shop whose main target market is composed of men?
4 Which is likely to be a more powerful motivation – assortment depletion or assortment extension?
5 How might a compensatory decision rule operate when buying an expensive item such as a new car?
6 What factors cause people to become involved in products or brands?
7 How might a marketer increase involvement?
8 How can marketers reconcile the sale of unsought goods with the marketing concept?
9 What causes a product to move from being an unsought good to being a sought good?
10 Why might someone become involved with a brand, rather than with the benefits of the product itself?

Case study revisited: Confused.com

Confused.com plays well to an audience that has become increasingly bewildered by the welter of information available on-line. The company has grown dramatically in its life of just over a decade – more than 30 million visits to its website in a year, which is no small feat from a UK population of only 60 million.

The ability to automate (to some extent) the information search is a big advantage for most people. This is particularly the case for insurance, which is an unsought product – because people only buy insurance when they really have to and they certainly do not want to have to spend long periods sifting through the various offers, rules, qualifications, no-claim bonuses and prices to find a policy that fits their needs. Car insurance is especially prone to this factor, since it is a legal requirement for UK motorists and is something that many of them would not buy if they didn't have to.

Of course, the success of the company has meant that imitators have followed. This may in time erode the effectiveness of Confused.com, but not just because the other companies will take business from them. The problem is rather that a large number of comparison websites will mean that people will become equally confused as to which comparison website to choose.

Perhaps in future there will be a comparison website to help in choosing which comparison website is best.

Case study: Loyalty cards

Loyalty cards are offered by supermarkets and others as a way of encouraging customers to continue to shop at the particular store. They offer customers a system of rewards, according to how much they spend in-store: the rewards work out to around 1% of the customer's spend.

In most cases, loyalty cards are given away free. Some retailers have tried in the past to charge for the card, on the (probably correct) assumption that the individual will use the card at least long enough to regain the initial purchase price. This system is used, for example, by Brittany Ferries, which operates a scheme aimed at holiday-home owners by which they pay an annual subscription (currently £100 for a card which covers all Brittany Ferries services). People who use the ferries regularly may well save back the initial outlay in a single crossing, since the card provides up to 30% discount on published fares, plus discounts in the on-board restaurants, a free breakfast on overnight crossings and a free cabin on some daytime crossings.

Two of the 'Big Four' supermarkets in Britain have loyalty cards. Tesco's card was the first supermarket-only card (the Clubcard), launched in 1995. Sainsbury's followed in 1996 with its Reward card, which was replaced in 2002 by the Nectar card. Each card gives approximately 1% discount, but points earned on the Sainsbury's card can be used to gain discounts from other suppliers (hotels, luxury holidays, some airlines) which can be worth a great deal more than the 1% customers can gain by cashing in the points in Sainsbury's stores. Tesco Clubcard points are redeemed in the form of vouchers which the company sends out four times a year, giving cash off in-store purchases. Tesco also use the information gained from the Clubcard programme to target customers with specific offers: someone who is known to buy mineral water regularly will be given a special offer on mineral water, for example.

Loyalty cards occupy a strange niche in terms of marketing theory. Are they in fact a sales promotion scheme? Perhaps they are a marketing research device – after all, people have to supply their names and addresses, so their entire shopping pattern can be calculated and acted upon by the supermarkets. Perhaps the cards are part of a relationship marketing exercise – making people feel good towards the shop where they buy their groceries. Of course, there is nothing to stop people holding more than one card, so loyalty is far from guaranteed anyway.

Globally, loyalty cards have caught on in a big way. In Hong Kong, the smart card used for accessing public transport now also functions as a loyalty card for various businesses including McDonald's and the Wellcome supermarkets. In Malaysia, the Genting Highlands Resort has its own loyalty card, but it is valid for use in Starbucks, Coffee Bean and Häagen-Dazs outlets in three countries (Malaysia, Singapore and Hong Kong).

It seems that loyalty cards are an important plank in the marketing platform, yet some firms do not use them at all – the ASDA supermarket chain in the UK claims simply to offer lower prices rather than operate a complex loyalty card, with all the administration input such a scheme requires. Other supermarkets have tried loyalty cards and subsequently discontinued them – Safeway discontinued theirs in 2000, for example. Whether that decision contributed to the store's ultimate demise in Britain (it was bought out by Morrison's in 2004 and the brand disappeared in 2005) may never be known.

The abiding fact remains that most adults in Britain carry at least one loyalty card, and some carry several, even for competing firms. This is clearly a testimony to the desirability of the cards.

Questions

1 What type of loyalty does a loyalty card engender?
2 How might loyalty cards work better in an on-line situation?
3 Why would someone pay up-front for a loyalty card?
4 If a membership fee ensures that people are actually more loyal, why don't Tesco and Sainsbury's charge for their loyalty cards?
5 How might a loyalty card help someone in decision-making?

Further reading

For an indication of some of the surrogates people use when deciding on whether to buy a new product, see Roger Bennett and Helen Gabriel's (2000) paper 'Charity affiliation as a determinant of product purchase decisions'. *Journal of Brand and Product Marketing* 9 (4/5): 255–68. It turns out that people's perception of the value for money aspects of products sold by charities affects their view of other products that may be entirely unrelated to the first products.

For a much deeper account of loyalty programmes and involvement, take a look at Wan Jou-Wen's book *The Effect of the Reward Programme Scheme: The Effect of Timing of Reward, Business Longevity and Involvement on Consumers' Perception and Behavioural Intention Toward the Reward Programme* (Saarbrücken: VDM Verlag, 2009). The title is almost as long as the book, but it does offer a very deep (and academic) insight into the interrelationship between loyalty programmes, involvement and timing.

Many models of consumer behaviour seem to assume that people think about what they are doing when making decisions. Gerd Gigerenzer disagrees – and his book *Gut Feelings: Short Cuts to Better Decision Making* (Harmondsworth: Penguin, 2008) outlines the idea that we make our best decisions based on gut instinct rather than conscious thought. This is a book for people who enjoy some controversy!

Involvement, and especially involvement in luxury brands, is alive and well and lives in Japan. *The Cult of the Luxury Brand: Inside Asia's Love Affair with Luxury* by Radha Chadha and Paul Husband (London: Nicholas Brealey International, 2006) tells the whole story of how Asian countries have discovered consumerism – and gone for it in a big way.

An aspect of decision-making which is often ignored is the decision to say 'enough is enough'. John Naish's book *Enough: Breaking Free from the World of Excess* (London: Hodder Paperbacks, 2009) offers as its main premise the idea that human beings are hard-wired to grab as much as they can of anything they like, when in fact there is a point at which further acquisitions simply become tiresome. It's an interesting read for those who have doubts about the consumerist society in which we live.

References

Aggarwal, P. and Vaidyanathan, R. (2003) Eliciting online customers' preferences: conjoint vs. self-explicated and attribute-level measurement. *Journal of Marketing Management* 19 (1/2): 157.

Allaway, A.W., Gooner, R.M., Berkowitz, D. and Davis, L. (2006) Deriving and exploring behaviour segments within a retail loyalty card programme. *European Journal of Marketing* 40 (11/12): 1317–39.

Ang, L. and Buttle, F. (2006) Managing for successful customer acquisition: an exploration. *Journal of Marketing Management* 22 (3/4): 295–317.

Bailey, A.A. (2004) Thiscompanysucks.com: the use of the Internet in negative consumer-to-consumer articulations. *Journal of Marketing Communications* 10 (3): 169–82.

Batra, R. and Ray, M.L. (1983) Operationalising involvement as depth and quality of cognitive responses. In Alice Tybout and Richard Bagozzi (eds), *Advances in Consumer Research*. Ann Arbor, MI: Association for Consumer Research. pp. 309–13.

Bauer, H.H., Sauer, N.E. and Becker, C. (2006) Investigating the relationship between product involvement and consumer decision-making styles. *Journal of Consumer Behaviour* 5 (July–Aug): 342–54.

Baumeister, R.F. (2004) Self-regulation, conscious choice, and consumer decisions. *Advances in Consumer Research*, 31 (1): 48–9.

Bettman, J. R. (1979) *An Information Processing Theory of Consumer Choice.* Reading, MA: Addison–Wesley. Ch. 7.

Bettman, J.R. and Park. C.W. (1980) Effects of prior knowledge and experience and phase of choice processes on consumer decision processes: a protocol analysis. *Journal of Consumer Research* 7 (August): 234–48.

Biswas, D. (2009) The effects of option framing on consumer choices: making decisions in rational versus experiential processing modes. *Journal of Consumer Behaviour* 8 (5): 284–99.

Blackwell, R.D., Miniard, P.W. and Engel, J.F. (2005) *Consumer Behaviour*, 10th edition. Mason, OH: Thomson Southwest.

Bloch, P. H., Sherrell, D.L. and Ridgway, N.M. (1986) Consumer search: an extended framework. *Journal of Consumer Research* 13 (June): 111–26.

Bucklin, L.P. (1963) Retail strategy and the classification of consumer goods. *Journal of Marketing* 27 (January): 50–5.

Buttner, O.B. and Goritz, A.S. (2008) Perceived trustworthiness of online shops. *Journal of Consumer Behaviour* 7 (1): 35–60.

Chronist, A. and Hampton, R.D. (2008) Consuming the authentic Gettysburg: how a tourist landscape becomes an authentic experience. *Journal of Consumer Behaviour* 7 (2): 111–26.

Cleveland, M., Babin, B.J., Laroche, M., Ward, P. and Bergeron, J. (2003) Information search patterns for gift purchases: a cross-national examination of gender differences. *Journal of Consumer Behaviour* 3 (1): 20–47.

Cui, G. and Wang, Y. (2010) Consumers' SKU choices in an online supermarket: a latent class approach. *Journal of Marketing Management* 26 (5&6): 495–514.

D'Souza, C., Rugimbana, R., Quazi, A. and Nanere, M.G. (2008) Investing in consumer confidence through genetically modified labelling: an evaluation of compliance options and their marketing challenges for Australian firms. *Journal of Marketing Management* 24 (5&6): 621–35.

Dewey, J. (1910) *How We Think.* Boston, MA: DC Heath & Co.

Dibley, A. and Baker, S. (2001) Uncovering the links between brand choice and personal values among young British and Spanish girls. *Journal of Consumer Behaviour* 1 (1): 77–93.

East, R., Hammond, K. and Gendall, P. (2006) Fact and fallacy in retention marketing. *Journal of Marketing Management* 22 (1/2): 5–23.

Formisan, R.A., Olshavsky, R.W. and Tapp, S. (1982) Choice strategy in a difficult task environment. *Journal of Consumer Research* 8 (March): 474–9.

Foxall, G.R. (2008) Reward, emotion and consumer choice: from neuroeconomics to neurophilosophy. *Journal of Consumer Behaviour* 7 (4/5): 368–96.

Gupta, S., Lehmann, D.R. and Stuart, J.A. (2004) Valuing customers. *Journal of Market Research* 41 (1): 7–18.

Hamilton, K.L. and Hewer, P.A. (2010) Tribal mattering spaces: social networking sites, celebrity affiliations and tribal innovations. *Journal of Marketing Management* 26 (3/4): 271–89.

Harwood, T. and Garry, T. (2010) It's mine! Participation and ownership within virtual co-creation environments. *Journal of Marketing Management* 26 (3&4): 290–301.

Hawkins, S. (1962) The significance of impulse buying today. *Journal of Marketing* 26 (April): 59–62.

Hede, A. and Thyne, M. (2010) A journey to the authentic: museum visitors and their negotiation of the inauthentic. *Journal of Marketing Management* 26 (7&8): 686–705.

Helgesen, O. (2006) Are loyal customers profitable? Customer satisfaction, customer (action) loyalty and customer profitability at the individual level. *Journal of Marketing Management* 22 (3/4): 245–66.

Hem, L. and Iversen, N.M. (2003) Transfer of brand equity in brand extensions: the importance of brand loyalty. *Advances in Consumer Research* 30: 72–9.

Hogue, A.Y. and Lohse, G.I. (1999) An information search cost perspective for designing interface for electronic commerce. *Journal of Marketing* 6 (3): 387–94.

Holbrook, M.B. and Hirschman, E.C. (1982) The experiential aspects of consumption: consumer fantasies, feelings and fun. *Journal of Consumer Research* 9 (Sept): 132–40.

Howard, J.A. and Sheth, J.N. (1969) *The Theory of Buyer Behaviour.* New York: John Wiley.

Hoyer, W.D. and Ridgway, N.M. (1984) Variety seeking as an explanation for exploratory purchase behaviour: a theoretical model. *Advances in Consumer Research* 11: 114–19.

Kiel, G.C. and Layton, R. A. (1981) Dimensions of consumer information seeking behaviour. *Journal of Marketing Research* 18 (May): 233–9.

Laurent, G. and Kapferer, J. (1985) Measuring consumer involvement profiles. *Journal of Marketing Research* 22 (Feb): 41–53.

McEachern, M., Warnaby, G., Carrigan, M. and Szmigin, I. (2010) Thinking locally, acting locally? Conscious consumers and farmers' markets. *Journal of Marketing Management* 26 (5&6): 395–412.

Megicks, P., Memery, J. and Williams, J. (2008) Influences on ethical and socially responsible shopping: evidence from the UK grocery sector. *Journal of Marketing Management* 24 (5&6): 637–59.

Meyer-Waarden, L. and Benavent, C. (2006) The impact of loyalty programmes on repeat purchase behaviour. *Journal of Marketing Management* 22 (1/2): 61–88.

Michaelidou, N. and Dibb, S. (2006) Product involvement: an application in clothing. *Journal of Consumer Behaviour* 5 (Sep–Oct): 442–53.

Mitchell, A. (1979) Involvement: a potentially important mediator of consumer behaviour. In William L. Wilkie (ed.), *Advances in Consumer Research* 6: 191–6.

Monga, A.B. (2002) Brand as a relationship partner: gender differences in perspectives. *Advances in Consumer Research* 29 (1): 41.

Morewedge, C. and Wegner, D. (2008) Effects of merely thinking about what one might acquire. *Advances in Consumer Research* 35: 153.

Muylle, S., Moenart, R. and Despontin, M. (1998) *World-wide web search behaviour: a multiple case-study research.* Proceedings of the 3rd Annual Conference of the Global Institute for Corporate and Marketing Communications, Glasgow. Strathchlyde Business School.

Neal, D., Wood, W. and Pascoe, A.M. (2008) Triggers of real-world habits: implications for consumer behavior. *Advances in Consumer Research* 35: 145.

Neilson, L.A. (2010) Boycott or buycott? Understanding political consumerism. *Journal of Consumer Behaviour* 9 (3): 214–27.

Norton, M.I. and Ariely, D. (2008) The IKEA effect: why labour leads to love. *Advances in Consumer Research* 35: 153.

Onkvisit, S. and Shaw, J.J. (1994) *Consumer Behaviour, Strategy and Analysis.* New York: Macmillan.

Otker, T. (1990) The highly involved consumer: a marketing myth? *Marketing and Research Today* Feb: 30–6.

Rick, S., Knutson, B., Wimmer, E., Prelec, D. and Loewenstein, G. (2008) Neural predictors of purchases. *Advances in Consumer Research* 35: 139.

Shankar, A., Cherrier, H. and Canniford, R. (2006) Consumer empowerment: a Foucauldian interpretation. *European Journal of Marketing* 40 (9/10): 1013–30.

Sharma, P., Sivakumaran, B. and Marshall, R. (2010) Exploring impulse buying and variety seeking by retail shoppers: towards a common conceptual framework. *Journal of Marketing Management* 26 (5&6): 473–94.

NEW AND REPEAT BUYING BEHAVIOUR

Slater, A. and Armstrong, K. (2010) Involvement, Tate, and me. *Journal of Marketing Management* 26 (7&8): 727–48.

Stewart, D.W. and Furse, D.H. (1984) Analysis of executional factors in advertising performance. *Journal of Advertising Research* 24: 23–6.

Tam, J.L.M. (2011) The moderating effect of purchase importance in customer satisfaction process: an empirical investigation. *Journal of Consumer Behaviour* 10 (4): 205–15.

Thompson, M. and Johnson, A.R. (2002) Investigating the role of attachment dimensions as predictors of satisfaction in consumer–brand relationships. *Advances in Consumer Research* 29: 42.

Ubilava, D., Foster, K.A., Lusk, J.L. and Nilsson, T. (2011) Differences in consumer preferences when facing branded versus non-branded choices. *Journal of Consumer Behaviour* 10 (2): 61–70.

Urbany, J.E. (1986) An experimental investigation of the economics of information. *Journal of Consumer Research* 13 (Sep).

Zaichowsky, J.L. (1985) Measuring the involvement construct in marketing. *Journal of Consumer Research* 12 (Dec): 341–52.

More online

To gain free access to additional online resources to support this chapter please visit: **www.sagepub.co.uk/blythe**

CHAPTER 12

Innovation

LEARNING OBJECTIVES

After reading this chapter you should be able to:

- Explain how the product life cycle drives innovation.

- Describe some of the characteristics of innovators.

- Show how innovators are not necessarily innovators under all circumstances.

- Describe different types of innovation.

- Explain the role of mavens in the adoption of innovation.

- Explain how resistance to innovation can happen, and formulate some ideas for dealing with this problem.

Introduction

Innovation is said to be the lifeblood of successful companies. Firms that fail to innovate are thought to become moribund very quickly, and eventually to disappear altogether because competitors introduce new products that supersede the old ones.

However, this constant stream of innovation does create problems from a consumer behaviour viewpoint. Decision-making and information-gathering are at their most complex when consumers are considering an innovative product. Thousands of new products are launched onto the market every year, with varying success rates; the vast majority never recoup their development costs. (Estimates of new-product success rates vary, largely due to the difficulty of defining what constitutes success.)

Case study: Trunki

When Rob Law first designed the Trunki in 1997 he little knew how big it might be. Trunki is ride-on luggage for children: in effect, it is a plastic suitcase with wheels underneath and a seat on top. It can be towed, using a nylon strap, or the child can propel it along by using his or her feet. Rob was a student at the time, studying design, and as an assignment he was told to design some new luggage. After looking at luggage in department stores he realised how awkward children's luggage was – mainly consisting of backpacks, so that the child would be carrying his or her own luggage and no doubt complaining after a while. The Trunki has the advantage that it is the luggage that carries the child, not the other way round.

In 2006 Rob appeared on TV reality show *Dragons' Den*. The show involves inventors and businesspeople making a pitch to investors with a view to getting funding for their products. One of the investors broke the strap on the luggage, which of course put him off the idea: one of the other Dragons offered £100,000 for 50% of the business, but Rob turned it down as being inadequate. Rob hawked his idea around retailers, toy manufacturers, luggage manufacturers and indeed anyone who might be prepared to take on the product, initially without success. Eventually he secured a deal with John Lewis, the UK department store chain – on the proviso that he make the strap a lot stronger.

Rob has the Trunkis made in China and the United States, but recently he has opened a factory in the UK. Despite costs (especially wages) being much higher in the UK than in China, he feels more in control – one of the company's setbacks occurred when the Chinese government seized the company's tooling when the factory there closed.

The company now produces several other products aimed at children who travel – a car booster seat that doubles as a backpack, a waterproof pack for taking things to the beach, a travelling toy box and several other items.

How to impress your examiner

You may be asked about the influences on new product adoption. There is a difference between influencer and mavens – influencers are people who are looked up to and emulated, whereas mavens (although very respectable, of course) are simply friends who have a deeper knowledge of the product category, and enjoy sharing that knowledge. You should also be clear about the limitations of adoption models: in particular, Rogers' model involves circular reasoning, and does not actually define what makes an innovator.

The product life cycle

Products are constantly being superseded by newer, more effective products. For this reason firms seek to develop new products; those firms that fail to innovate will, eventually, only be producing products that are obsolescent. The product life cycle illustrates the process of introduction, growth, maturity and obsolescence in products.

Products tend to lose money when they are first introduced, because the amount of marketing support they need is not justified by the initial sales as the product tries to become established in the market. As the product moves into a growth phase, profits begin to come in, and when the product becomes well-established (i.e. mature) the profits are also at a peak. Eventually, the product will go into decline as competing products enter the market, or fashions change, or the market becomes saturated.

In fact, the situation is often much more complex than this, so the basic product life cycle (as shown in Figure 12.1) does not always describe what actually happens in practice. The product life cycle is a useful concept for explaining what happens to products, but it suffers from a number of weaknesses. First, the model is no use for making predictions, because there is no good way of knowing what the length of the maturity phase will be: for a fashion item, the maturity phase might only last a few months, whereas for a product such as pitta bread the maturity phase has already lasted several thousand years and shows no sign of changing. Second, the model ignores the effects of marketing activities. If a product's sales are declining, marketers might decide to reposition the product in another market, or might run a major promotional campaign, or might decide to drop the product altogether and concentrate resources on another product in the portfolio. These alternatives are shown in Figures 12.2 and 12.3.

Third, the model does not account for those products that come back into fashion after a few years in the doldrums. Recent examples include the Mini Cooper, the Volkswagen Beetle and the yo-yo (which seems to undergo revivals every ten to fifteen years).

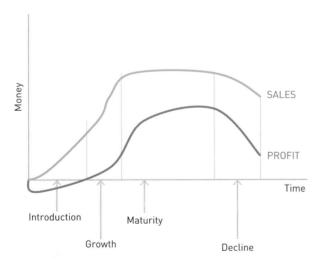

Figure 12.1 The product life cycle

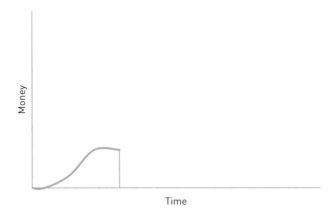

Figure 12.2   Product dropped shortly after introduction

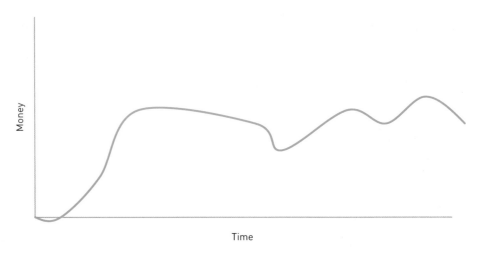

Figure 12.3   Effects of marketing activities on the product life cycle

 Challenging the status quo

It is not unusual for products to disappear almost as soon as they are launched: test marketing sometimes shows disappointing results, so the product is taken off the shelves. But the product life cycle tells us that products often lose money at first – and some products are 'sleepers', which do nothing for several years and then suddenly take off for no apparent reason.

There are also products that appear to be eminently sensible and yet do not find a market, possibly through a lack of professionalism on the part of the marketers. So should there be a marketer's life cycle instead? If the product doesn't perform, should we keep the product and fire the managers?

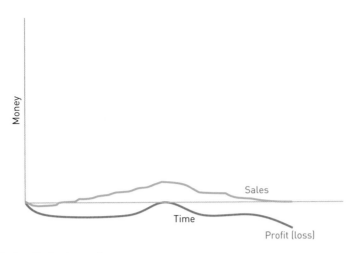

Figure 12.4   Failed product

Fourth, the model does not take account of the fact that the vast majority of new products fail. This would give a life cycle such as that shown in Figure 12.4, where the product never moves into profit.

Finally, the product life cycle looks at only one product, whereas most marketing managers have to balance the demands of many different products, and decide which of them is likely to yield the best return on investment (or perhaps which one will take the company nearest to achieving its strategic objectives).

The product life cycle can be explained in terms of consumer behaviour. In the introduction and growth stage, innovative consumers are adopting the product. In the maturity phase, more cautious consumers buy the product, until finally another product comes along which has more benefits or which does a better job, and people switch to the new product. The basic problem for marketers lies in knowing how long the maturity phase will last; the product life cycle does tell us, though, that all products eventually fade and die, and marketers should therefore develop new products to replace the old ones as these products fall out of favour with consumers.

Although we can be reasonably sure that all old products will eventually fail, we cannot by any means be sure that a new product will succeed. The lack of a good predictive system for forecasting product success wastes resources since producers will spend time and effort making things that consumers do not want to buy. The ideal outcome for a producer is to develop products that become culturally anchored – that become part of modern life. Recent examples are the mobile telephone, cable television and the personal computer – none of which would have been part of the average household thirty years ago, but which now would be difficult to manage without. In practice such breakthroughs are hard to achieve. Understandably, with so much at stake for firms, there has been a great deal of research interest in innovation, with many researchers trying to determine what are the critical factors in new product success.

Cultural anchoring The process by which an innovation becomes part of everyday life

Adoption of innovation

The process of adoption of innovation is much more to do with communication throughout the population than with individual decision-making. Each individual

Challenging the status quo

It's all very well to talk about making products that will become culturally anchored – but how do we do this in practice? It's easy to think that something will come along which will become essential to daily life, but in fact most such 'whizzo ideas' fail dismally.

Even when there is a clear advantage people might not be ready for it. What happened to the video telephones of the 1960s? Why have they suddenly made a comeback in the voice-over Internet protocol of Skype? What happened to the Philips laserdisc system, and why did it flop in the 1980s but re-appear as DVDs in the 1990s?

So how can it be useful to talk about getting our products to be culturally anchored? It's pure luck if it happens, surely!

will make decisions by the processes already outlined for existing products; the main difference is that there will be many fewer sources of information about an innovative product, since few people will have any experience of it as yet.

Everett M. Rogers (1983) postulated that products would be adopted if they possessed most of the attributes shown in Table 12.1.

Table 12.1   Attributes necessary for adoption

Attribute	Explanation	Examples
Relative advantage	The product must have some advantage over the products already on the market. It must offer the consumer a better range of benefits than the existing solution, in other words	Before the Sony Walkman was launched, the only way to listen to stereo-quality music was to carry a 'ghetto-blaster' on your shoulder. The Walkman replaced this cumbersome and anti-social device within a few years – and iPods have replaced the Walkman equally effectively
Compatibility	The product must fit in with the consumer's lifestyle	Video on demand has become a popular service offered by cable TV companies, allowing people to watch TV shows or movies at times that suit them, rather than the broadcaster
Complexity	The product must not be too complex for the consumer to understand	Amazon's Kindle device was designed around the concept of being so simple to use that people would forget the device and simply enjoy reading the book. Kindle was designed to be as easy-to-use and intuitive as a paper book
Trialability	Products that can be tried out are more likely to succeed	Whenever a motor manufacturer launches a new vehicle people are invited to test drive it
Observability	The more observable the product, the quicker the diffusion process. If other potential consumers are able to see the product in use, this is bound to raise interest in it	Part of the reason for Kindle's worldwide success is that it can clearly be observed in use. Likewise, new fashion ideas seem to catch on very quickly; this is due to the high level of observability

There have been several models of the adoption process, most of which assume a somewhat complex process of assessing the new product. In the case of radically new products (those that will alter the user's lifestyle) this may well be the case, but since most products that are classified as new are, in fact, adaptations of existing products, it might be safe to assume that consumers do not necessarily carry out a lengthy evaluation of the type assumed by most researchers. Five adoption models are shown in Figure 12.5.

The AIDA model is probably among the oldest models in marketing. It is commonly quoted when considering promotions, but it applies equally well to adoption of innovation. The model is somewhat too simplistic, however; it implies that the process is mechanical, without any conscious thought on the part of the individual who adopts the product. There is also the view that the model implies something being done *to* consumers (leading them through a process) rather than something that is done *for* them (meeting a need).

The Adoption Process model includes some thought on the part of the customer. In this case, becoming interested in the product leads to some serious evaluation before trial and adoption. This model portrays adoption as a sequence which the individual follows, using conscious thought and interaction with the product to come to the adoption decision.

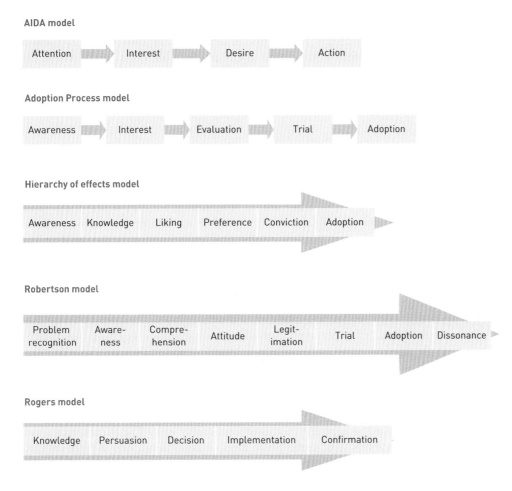

Figure 12.5 Models of the adoption and diffusion process

The Hierarchy of Effects model suggests that each stage of the process leads the customer closer to the decision – as each stage is passed, the individual is further up the hierarchy and therefore becoming more committed. Obviously an individual might drop out of the model at any stage, and thus the sale will not happen, but the model implies that people must normally pass through each stage in the correct order if a sale is to result. This is a suspect proposition, since people are likely to skip stages or even buy the product on impulse without any real evaluation at all.

Robertson's (1967) model is by far the most complex, seeking to break down the process into more stages. Robertson shows how the attitude is formed rather than simply subsuming it into a category of 'liking'. This model provides more of an insight into the internal workings of the adopter's mind, rather than simply describing behaviour.

Rogers (1983) includes the concept of persuasion in his model. Persuasion does not necessarily come from outside, however – it may just as easily come from within the individual. Persuasion is clearly of interest to marketers, whether it is marketing-generated or whether it is produced socially via peer pressure (normative compliance).

The main feature that all these models have in common is that they imply that adoption of innovation is a linear process, following logical steps. This may or may not be true – individuals may follow a straight line, or they may be diverted by circumstances. The models also show that innovations take a long time to be adopted. This means that it may be a year or more before a new product begins to show a return; this is implicit also in the shape of the product life cycle curve, where the introduction phase shows a slow start. Often firms decide too early that a product is not succeeding and take it off the market before consumers have completed the evaluation process.

Consumers as innovators

A second focus in the research has been on the consumers most likely to buy new products – the **innovators**, in other words. The reason for this is that there is an assumption that innovation is diffused by word of mouth, or that innovators are likely to influence others to buy the products. This is implicit in the product life cycle, and in Rogers' observability criterion (Rogers 1983).

It is perfectly feasible to classify consumers in terms of their attitude to new products; the problem with identifying innovators is that they are not usually innovative in all their buying habits. That is to say, an innovator for hi-fi equipment is not necessarily an innovator for breakfast cereals, and although there is some evidence that there may be a kind of super-innovator who likes virtually everything that is new, these people are difficult to find, and it is debatable whether they are likely to influence other buyers anyway.

Everett Rogers classified consumers as innovators (2.5% of the population), early adopters (13.5%), early majority (34%), late majority (34%) and laggards (16%). These classifications were originally devised from agricultural product adoptions, but have been widely accepted as applying to consumers equally well. The percentages given are arbitrary; everybody is at some point along a continuum, and Rogers decided that those whose scores lay more than two standard deviations from the mean would be classed as innovators, those whose scores lay between one and two standard deviations would be early adopters, and those whose scores lay within

Early adopters Those who, although not the first to buy a new product, do so very shortly after its introduction

Early majority Those who adopt a new product after it has been on the market for a while, but before most people have adopted it

Late majority People who only adopt a new product after most people have already done so

Laggards People who are the last to adopt a new product

Consumer behaviour in action: Optical Recording Systems

In 1973 the giant Dutch Philips corporation announced a radical new system for recording and playing back movies. It was the Videodisc system, which used laser technology to burn information onto a disc that was about the size of a vinyl LP.

The system was at prototype stage then, but by 1978 the Videodisc was up and running, and in collaboration with MCA and Pioneer Electronics Philips appeared ready to take the world by storm. At about the same time, the first home video recorders were also appearing on the market – heavy and clunky to use, and with relatively poor picture quality, the new VCRs were expensive. However, they had one major advantage over the videodisc system – they could record programmes from the TV for later replay. Consumers rejected the videodisc system in favour of the VCR, and eventually the JVC VHS system became the standard means of watching movies at home.

By 1981, technical teething problems and consumer apathy about the videodisc system had combined to kill the project almost entirely. Philips continued to market machines produced by MCA and Pioneer, but essentially the whole idea of selling laser-recorded movies for home viewing was regarded as a complete flop. Even IBM's vast resources could not keep the project afloat.

In 1989, Pioneer bought up all the Philips patents on the technology and went into business producing DVDs. Although these were hardly a roaring success initially, eventually they became the format of choice – especially when systems for burning DVDs at home became available.

Now DVD systems, based on the original videodisc technology, have taken over from VHS entirely. It is hard to explain why the videodisc system failed in 1980, and yet 30 years later has proved to be the innovation success story of the decade. Perhaps it is due to consumer fickleness, or perhaps it is due to the existence in 1980 of several competing systems – people were hardly likely to adopt all the available systems, and VHS won at that time. Now, of course, BluRay is gradually taking over from DVD, for reasons of picture and sound quality. Whatever the reason, executives at Philips must feel frustrated at the outcome.

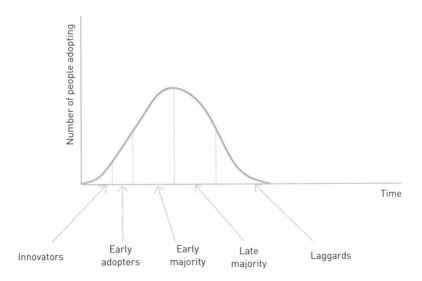

Figure 12.6   Classification of innovators

one standard deviation from the mean would be the early majority. Scores below the mean were classified in the same way: those within one standard deviation of the mean were classified as the late majority, and everyone else as laggards. This means that Rogers' classifications involve circular reasoning: people are innovators because they innovate, and laggards because they are slow to innovate. The classification tells us nothing about the characteristics of the people involved.

Innovativeness **The degree to which an individual or firm creates or adopts new products**

Innovativeness is the degree to which a person tends to adopt innovations earlier than other people. It can be measured very simply using the Goldsmith–Hofacker Innovativeness Scale, which uses six questions to determine an individual's innovativeness in respect to a particular product category (Goldsmith and Hofacker 1991). The Goldsmith–Hofacker Scale is, in a sense, too simplistic because it merely asks what the individual's behaviour is, without finding out what it is about people that makes them into innovators. In order to try to discover what it is that makes somebody an innovator, studies have been carried out into known innovators to find out what they have in common.

Three main groups of variable have been identified thus far: socio-economic factors, personality factors and communication behaviour. It should be noted, again, that all these studies are based on limited product categories, and are therefore not necessarily generally applicable.

Socio-economic variables **Those factors that derive from an individual's class and income**

Socio-economic variables that are positively related to innovativeness are as follows:

- Education
- Literacy
- Higher social status
- Upward social mobility
- Larger-sized units
- Commercial rather than subsistence orientation
- More favourable attitude towards credit
- More specialised operations.

Clearly, higher-income people are in a much better position to take the risk of buying new products. Those who are educated and literate are also more likely to hear about new products before other people do.

Personality and attitude variables associated with innovativeness are as follows:

- Empathy
- Ability to deal with abstractions
- Rationality
- Intelligence
- Favourable attitude towards change
- Ability to cope with uncertainty
- Favourable attitude towards education
- Favourable attitude toward science
- Achievement motivation
- High aspirations.

There are some personality traits that militate against innovativeness, however:

- Dogmatism
- Fatalism.

One personality trait that appears to have a strong influence is the degree to which someone likes to be different from other people. All of us have a need to be assimilated into the group, and also an opposing need to be distinct from the group, i.e. an individual. Someone's position on that continuum will influence their attitude to innovation (Timmor and Katz-Navon 2008).

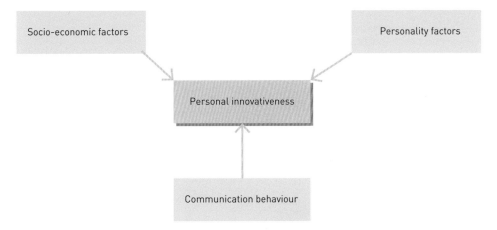

Figure 12.7 Variables that affect innovativeness

M.J. Kirton (1986) showed that consumers can be classified as either adapters or innovators. Adapters tend to take existing solutions and adjust them as necessary to fit the current need problem; innovators tend to look for radical solutions. Kirton's Adaption–Innovation Index has proved to be a very reliable measure of innovativeness.

Cognitive innovators tend to be those who seek out new intellectual experiences, whereas sensory innovators are those who seek new sensory experiences. In both cases the innovators are seeking something new for its own sake; and there is ample research to indicate that novelty is an attractive feature of a product in its own right.

Communication variables that are positively associated with innovativeness are as follows:

- Social participation
- Interconnectiveness with the social system
- Cosmopolitanism
- Change agent contact
- Mass media exposure
- Exposure to interpersonal communication channels
- Knowledge of innovations
- Opinion leadership
- Belonging to highly interconnected systems.

Although innovators for one product group are not necessarily innovators for other groups, there are some correlations. For example, technophiles are people who like technology for its own sake, and who are prepared to take an interest in (and even buy) new computers, electronic gadgets, GPS equipment and so forth, whereas technophobes have a loathing for such devices. In general, the level of involvement with the product category will go a long way towards explaining an individual's innovativeness: research has shown that people who are very environmentally aware are also likely to adopt new environment-friendly products. This is due to a favourable configuration of values, beliefs and norms (Jansson et al. 2011).

Feick and Price (1987) identified a group of influencers they called market mavens. A market maven is someone who has an intense interest in, and a high level of knowledge about, a specific category of product. Mavens are able to provide price and availability information to others, as well as information about the products themselves: in effect, they act as an extension of the gatekeeper role in disseminating information about new products. Mavens are usually motivated by the desire to share information, to show off their knowledge and to help others in reaching the right decisions (Walsh

Cognitive innovators Those who seek new intellectual experiences

Sensory innovators Those who seek new sensory experiences

Technophiles People who like new technology for its own sake

Technophobes People who are fearful of new technology

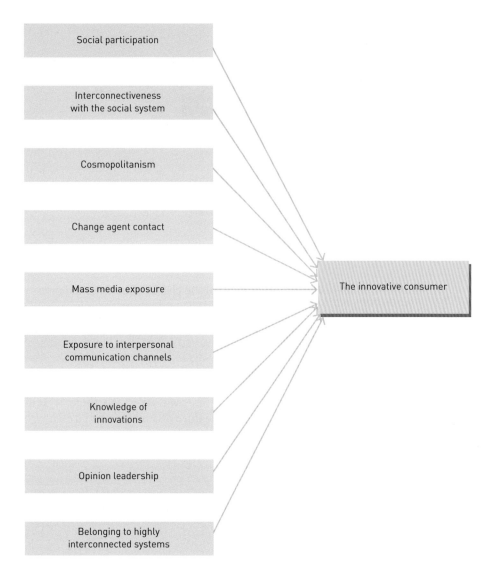

Figure 12.8   Communication variables associated with innovativeness

et al. 2004). Mavens are also sometimes known as infomediaries, particularly when they operate predominantly on-line: many chatrooms and weblogs are inhabited by such experts, who enjoy helping others with purchasing decisions.

Innovative products

From the viewpoint of a marketer, it would appear that there is a demand for newness *per se*. In other words, as a general rule people like new things and like to feel that the product they buy now is better than the one they bought ten years ago. On the other hand, people are not necessarily prepared to take the risk of buying products that are radically different from their existing purchases.

In terms of the effect on the consumer's lifestyle (and consequently the risk to the consumer), innovations can be classified under three headings (Robertson 1967):

1 Continuous innovation: a relatively minor change in the product, for example the packaging or the styling.
2 Dynamically continuous innovation: changes which materially affect the core functioning of the product. An example might be a coupe version of a family saloon.
3 Discontinuous innovation: a product that is new to the world, and changes the lifestyles of those who adopt it. In recent years the Kindle electronic book and the i-Phone have revolutionised people's approach to reading, and to communications respectively.

For someone to take the risk of adopting a technologically advanced product (i.e. a discontinuous innovation) there must be a corresponding advantage. The technology acceptance model (Bagozzi and Warshaw 1992; Davis 1989) states that new technology adoption relies on two factors: ease of use and usefulness. If a product is too difficult to use in practice it will not be adopted readily, even if it is really useful; likewise, a product that is easy to use but fulfils no useful function will not be adopted. It is for this reason that both the Kindle and the i-Phone were designed to be simple to use: both are intuitive in use, with little need for an instruction manual.

The technology acceptance model has been criticised on the grounds that it has limited heuristic value, and very little predictive value – in other words, it doesn't help much with decision-making or with predictions of the potential success of a new technology (Chuttur 2009). Having said that, it is still widely used as an explanatory tool for understanding new product success (and failure) when considering discontinuous innovation.

A study by Calentone and Cooper (1981) found that the most successful new products were, in fact, only incremental improvements on existing products, rather than radically new products; this study also emphasised the need for the product to have a marketing synergy rather than be simply a wonderful idea that the engineering department thought might succeed.

In this connection, the trend towards benchmarking is likely to lead to even more 'me-too' or incremental product offerings. Benchmarking is the process by which firms compare their activities with the best in the industry, and try to match the best practice of their competitors in each area. The aim is to become the best of the best. To this end, motor manufacturers buy their competitors' cars and strip them down to see how they are made and what their features are, then try to emulate the best

Continuous innovation A new product that follows closely on from a previous product and has a clear relationship to the previous product

Dynamically continuous innovation The development of a new product that differs radically from its predecessors while still retaining some commonality

Discontinuous innovation Developing a new product that relates only distantly, or does not relate at all, to previous products

Benchmarking Measuring the firm's performance against that of other firms across a wide range of factors

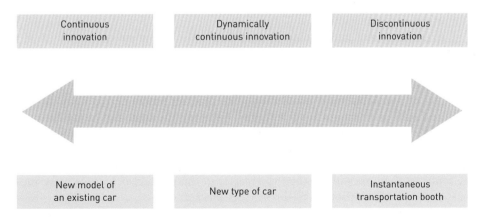

Figure 12.9 Degrees of innovation

Challenging the status quo

If the most successful products are me-toos, and the easiest and cheapest way of refreshing the product range is to copy someone else's designs, why does any firm bother to take the risk to innovate at all? Why do we have people like Akio Morita developing the Walkman in the face of opposition from his marketing people? Why do we have loopy inventors banging on manufacturers' doors demanding to be allowed to show their latest gadget?

Is it perhaps because we just get carried away with the fun of inventing something new, and then we have to find a market for it? Or is it that being first to market with a radical, life-changing new product could mean making millions, instead of just rubbing along showing a decent profit?

of them in their own product offerings. This is called reverse engineering. Inevitably this will lead to more copying of competitors' products if the philosophy is applied to new product development.

Part of the problem for manufacturers is that there is no generally agreed upon definition of newness. For the purposes of marketing, manufacturers really have to rely on the consumer's perception of what is new and what is not. Since this is very much a subjective and individualistic perception, the manufacturer frequently finds himself in a marketing minefield.

Marketing approaches to new product launches

Relative advantage The degree to which a new product is superior to the one it replaces altering them in any way

Compatibility The degree to which a new product matches the individual's existing lifestyle, attitudes and possessions

Complexity The degree to which a new product requires extensive learning before it can be used effectively

Trialability The degree to which a product can be tested before the customer needs to commit to its adoption

Observability The degree to which the purchase of a new product can be seen by others

Combining decision-making theory and diffusion theory, it is possible to come up with some broad recommendations for launching new products:

1 *Need recognition.* Marketers should activate needs by mentioning them in advertising. The advertising needs to make people aware of what's new, and how it will have a relative advantage over current competitors.

2 *Pre-purchase activities* or *search.* Information sources are strongly linked to marketing strategy; brochures, product information adverts, leaflets, PR activities and salespeople all contribute to the process. Marketers should ensure that there is an emphasis on the product's compatibility with the target market's lifestyles and aspirations.

3 *Evaluation and purchase decision.* Salespeople have a strong contribution to make to this part of the process; marketers must ensure a high quality of presentation of information materials, and the salesforce must be able to guide consumers through the complexity of the product.

4 *Act of purchase and consumption.* The product has to be right for the task, and fulfil the manufacturer's claims. Allowing the customer to try the product out is a good means of reducing the risk, so trialability is a key issue in this context.

5 *Post-purchase evaluation.* After-sales service has a strong role to play here, and ideally there should be some observability in the product if there is to be rapid diffusion of the product to the broader market.

Some new products have greater potential than others for consumer acceptance. Sometimes it is difficult to analyse exactly what it is that makes one new product more acceptable than another – if marketers knew this, there would be fewer failures of new products. There is, after all, no point in trying to market a product for which consumer acceptance will be limited.

One route around the acceptance problem is mass customisation. Here customers are able to design the product themselves from a range of possible options: the application of this concept ranges from Subway sandwiches through to Dell computers. The advantage is that customers are able to design something that meets their own needs very closely indeed, and do not have to accept (or pay for) features which are only present because most people want them. At first sight, it would seem that a driver for mass customisation would be that customers can save money by paying only for features they actually need, but in fact research shows that such customers are actually prepared to pay a substantial premium, in some cases more than double the ordinary price, in order to design something to their own specification (Schreier 2006). This may be due to a better perceived fit, it may be due to perceived uniqueness of the product or it may be simply pride of authorship – the pleasure of knowing that one has created something unique.

> **Customisation** Redesigning a product to make it fit a customer's needs more exactly

Resistance to innovation can come from several sources, as can facilitation of innovation. First, channels of communication might create a barrier: as we saw in Chapter 10, communications received from respected opinion leaders will be taken seriously and often acted upon, whereas communications from a member of a dissociative group will be ignored or will tend to militate against action. Poorly executed advertising can create negative attitudes about the product, as can other poorly executed approaches such as insensitive salespeople, over-persuasive direct mail shots, or negative press coverage. On the other hand, some forms of communication have greatly aided the adoption of innovation – the Internet has provided a wide variety of on-line forums which have enabled people to exchange information rapidly about new products. Likewise, mobile telephones have provided people with rapid interpersonal communication (as opposed to landlines, which provide communication only from one place to another). Text messages, and in particular commercial permission-based text messages, have greatly increased the rate at which information about new products is disseminated. Although the rate at which bad news travels will also increase, the net result is that those who are likely to adopt the product hear about it much faster than they might have done a few years ago.

The social system can also create a barrier. The social system is the physical, cultural and social environment within which decisions are made: for marketers, it usually corresponds to the market segment (or target market). For example, there is a social system that functions in most jobs or professions: lawyers discuss cases, Young Farmers Societies organise social events, academics have conferences and students have Student Unions. Social systems might have traditional values, in which case innovation is likely to be stifled, or they may have modern values, in which case innovation

Figure 12.10 Barriers to innovation

Consumer behaviour in action: Effects of new technology on society

So far we have looked at ways in which consumer behaviour affects adoption of new technology. However, technology also affects consumer behaviour, creating new possibilities for social interaction, new possibilities for entertainment and new possibilities for improving one's standard of living. These improvements are, of course, the motivation for adopting new products, but in many cases marketers are taken by surprise by consumer responses to new products.

For example, take the telephone. In the late 19th century, when the telephone was first introduced, suppliers assumed that the main customers would be sophisticated, relatively wealthy city dwellers.

From a telephone company's viewpoint, these would be easier to connect than would rural dwellers – the length of cable required would clearly be a great deal shorter, apart from any other considerations. However, it transpired that farmers were the most keen to acquire the new technology, because they were so isolated otherwise. Before the telephone, the only way a farmer could hear a voice other than that of his immediate family and a few farmhands was to saddle up a horse and ride to the nearest town. The telephone also provided a lifeline in case of emergencies. In the cities, on the other hand, most people could not see an immediate use for a telephone, and the telephone companies had to spend considerable sums of money on persuading people that they would find a telephone useful.

Other uses for the telephone disappeared almost without trace. In 1895 the Electraphone was introduced in London. This used the telephone lines to 'broadcast' live concerts and even church services to subscribers. After twelve years of operation there were only 600 subscribers, so the system was abandoned; interestingly, a similar system introduced in Budapest was a runaway success, perhaps because it also broadcast the news.

Consider also the trend towards text messages. The result of this is that younger people now have stronger, more agile thumbs than the older generation, but they also report to doctors with repetitive strain injury due to excessive texting. The fear of radiation from mobile phones still worries some people, in the same way that Victorians feared catching tuberculosis from telephone mouthpieces. Texting is having an effect on the language as well – children commonly use the shorter 'text' forms of words in their school essays.

Other innovations have wrought even greater social changes. The development of cheap commercial flights has contributed to an explosion in holiday home purchases, which has had a dramatic effect on the culture in some countries: in France there are whole villages which are now British, and in coastal Spain the local culture has (in some places) been overwhelmed by an influx of foreign holiday-home owners and retirees. Likewise, the Internet has further reduced the number of people who use reference libraries, and the invention of weblogs has increased possibilities for people to contact complete strangers, for good or ill.

Each new technological advance carries with it the possibility of social change. This is what science fiction is concerned with. In the long run, a society is defined by its technology as much as by its members – the available tools will determine how people behave, what resources become available to them and how much time they have to act out and develop their lives.

is likely to be stimulated. Modern social systems have the following characteristics (Rogers and Shoemaker 1971):

- A positive attitude towards change.
- An advanced technology and skilled labour force.
- A general respect for education and science.
- An emphasis on rational and ordered social relationships rather than on emotional ones.
- An outreach perspective, in which members of the system frequently interact with outsiders.
- A system in which members can easily see themselves in different roles.

Social systems can be of any size, up to and including entire countries. The prevailing social climate has already been discussed in Chapter 9, but it clearly has relevance for innovation, as it does for any other consumer behaviour.

Finally, adoption may be blocked because the individuals concerned object to the product and its use: for example, an environmentalist would not respond favourably to a new low-cost airline or a new model of four-wheel drive car. Nor would a vegetarian be likely to adopt a new type of sausage snack. Such people may well be innovative in adopting the stances they do, but not be innovative in terms of product purchases.

Summary

Adoption of new products is a somewhat hit-and-miss affair. Companies need to introduce new products regularly in order to avoid being left with an obsolete product portfolio, but on the other hand it is extremely difficult to predict consumers' responses to innovative products. Many firms therefore simply make minor incremental changes to their products rather than make radical innovations.

On the other hand, most people like some novelty in their lives, and many people like a lot of novelty. This means that at least some people will be open to the idea of buying a new product, or of trading in an existing product for something different. The problem for marketers lies in knowing which new products would be acceptable to which target market segments.

 **Key points**

- The product life cycle shows that all products eventually become obsolete and must be replaced.
- Innovators are usually educated and relatively well-off, as well as being well-connected socially.
- Innovators for one product category are not necessarily innovators for any other product category.
- The most successful products are often me-toos or continuous innovations.
- Mavens have a high level of interest in specific product categories, and enjoy airing their knowledge.
- Innovation can be continuous, dynamically continuous or discontinuous.
- Resistance to innovation can come from many sources.

Review questions

1   What is the role of mavens in word of mouth communication?
2   What barriers to adoption might there be for a new type of alcoholic drink?
3   How does trickle-down theory relate to adoption of new products?
4   What is the key difference between a dynamically continuous innovation and a discontinuous innovation?
5   Why is the product life cycle difficult to use as a predictor?
6   How might a marketer speed up the adoption process?
7   Why do most new products fail?
8   Why do most new products lose money at first?
9   What can marketers do to help overcome barriers to adoption?
10 What are the main criticisms of Everett Rogers' classification of consumers?

Case study revisited: Trunki

The Trunki was something of a slow burn in terms of reaching market: nine years after the initial design was produced, it finally went into production. However, the publicity from the *Dragons' Den* appearance meant that the product was already familiar to people. In fact, one of the Dragons famously said that the Trunki was 'the one that got away' and was the only product he regretted not having backed.

The basis of the Trunki's success is that it has obvious advantages over the alternatives. Children like the bright colours and the faces on the luggage (Trunkis now come in several designs, from animal-based designs to the Princess Carriage) and parents like the idea of the child riding on the luggage. Airports are big, bustling places and often there are long distances to walk: small legs get tired, and of course if the child has to carry a backpack as well there will be tears before bedtime. The Trunki is also big enough to carry a substantial amount of luggage, far more than a child could comfortably carry, so taking into account airline baggage restrictions it means that much more can be carried.

The Trunki has been designed to fit airline hand-luggage regulations. It only weighs 1.7 kilos, and it has all the features children like – it has secret compartments, teddy bear seat-belts, a towing strap that can be used as a carrying strap, and comes with stickers so that it can be customised. It sells for a very competitive £40, too.

Essentially, Trunki ticks all the boxes for a successful new product. It meets a known need, it has definite advantages over existing solutions, it is innovative and interesting, it is easy to use and understand, and it is inexpensive so there is a low financial risk for the purchaser.

Trunkis are now a familiar sight at airports throughout the world. They are sold in 62 countries, and as of June 2012 1,300,000 Trunkis have been sold worldwide. The product has won over 50 design awards, and Rob Law has been awarded an MBE. The company showed profits of over £1m in 2011 – not bad for a company founded only five years previously, to sell an idea created by a student.

Case study: Failed inventions

In 2010 *Time Magazine* published a list of the 50 worst inventions ever. These included the Segway, a two-wheeled platform stabilised by some very sophisticated (and expensive) gyroscopes. The Segway should have revolutionised city transport – it is small, easy to store, easy to park, ridiculously cheap to run and easy to drive. Yet for some reason it has never fulfilled its potential, and has become the vehicle of choice for shopping mall security guards and lazy tourists.

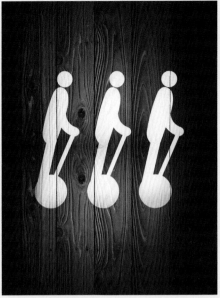

Then there are the downright dangerous inventions. Agent Orange was a herbicide used for over a decade during the Vietnam War: it was intended to destroy the jungle foliage so that Viet Cong troops would have nowhere to hide from aerial reconnaissance, but it didn't kill the foliage and did kill a lot of human beings, as well as causing birth defects and other long-term health hazards. US troops exposed to Agent Orange had to be paid $180 million in compensation. And how about hydrogenated oils – trans fats – originally developed to increase the shelf life of foods, but actually a major cause of heart attacks and now banned in several countries.

A further dangerous invention was the 1971 Ford Pinto, a car that had a habit of bursting into flames if it was involved in a rear-end collision.

From Victorian times, *Time* singled out the crinoline. A voluminous petticoat sometimes as much as six feet across, the crinoline effectively prevented women from doing pretty much anything, even walking through a doorway. Yet it was the must-have fashion item of the mid-19th century. Another irritating and pointless invention was Microsoft's Clippy, a cartoon paperclip that used to jump up on the screen offering 'helpful' suggestions about one's word processing (for example – 'I see you're writing a letter. Do you need help?'). Clippy prompted a number of responses to that question, none of which are fit to print.

From the lunatic fringe (no pun intended) came hair in a can. An aerosol product, hair in a can is supposed to cover up bald spots, which it does, but with a fine powder rather than actual hair. Better to go bald gracefully, perhaps. Another lunatic-fringe invention was actually very successful for a while – the Tamagotchi. A Tamagotchi was an electronic pet you could keep in your pocket. It needed to be fed, exercised and cleaned, and if you forgot to look after it, it would die. The egg-shaped device sold in its millions, but presumably once they had all died people grew tired of the concept and (possibly) bought a real pet instead.

The Baby Cage perhaps crosses categories between the lunatic and the dangerous – it was a device, popular in the 1930s, which could be hung out of an apartment window and was in fact a cage in which the baby could be placed, thus freeing up floor space indoors.

The Ford Pinto had another life as a flying car. In 1973, an inventor named Henry Smolinski added the wings and tail from a Cessna aircraft to a Pinto and took to the air. Unfortunately the hybrid car-o-plane crashed on a test flight, killing the inventor.

The world is full of inventions, and of course some are crazier than others. *Time*'s list is obviously a personal one dreamed up by the journalist, but every invention listed above was bought or used by someone, and often by a lot of someones.

Questions

1 Why might the Segway not have caught on as a mainstream product?
2 What would be the driving force behind the adoption of the crinoline?
3 Why are dangerous products sometimes successful?
4 What would be the appeal of the Tamagotchi?
5 What would be the appeal of a flying car?

Further reading

Innovations can easily disrupt industries, and sometimes even very large companies fall victim to someone else's innovation. *The Innovator's Dilemma: When New Products Cause Great Firms to Fail* by Clayton Christensen (Boston, MA: Harvard Business School Press, 1997) shows how new ideas create big problems.

Following on from this book, Christensen co-authored another with Jeff Dyer and Hal Gregerson. This book, *The Innovator's DNA: Mastering the Five Skills of Disruptive Innovators* (Boston, MA: Harvard Business School Press, 2011), outlines the traits and behaviours that innovators exhibit – in particular those who come up with the radical ideas that disrupt business for their competitors.

Websites are notorious for disappearing, but this one is great fun provided it is still around when you buy this book: http://www.dailyfinance.com/photos/top-25-biggest-product-flops-of-all-time/#photo-1 Although it is mainly concerned with brand extensions, it does highlight some fairly appalling new product launches – and although we shouldn't gloat over someone else's failure, there are certainly lessons to be learned here.

The Art of Innovation: Success Through Innovation the IDEO Way by Tom Kelley (with Jonathan Littman) (London: Profile Books, 2001) describes techniques for becoming more innovative. It is written entirely from a practitioner's viewpoint: Kelley is the co-founder of an innovation and design company, and outlines how the firm brainstorms for ideas (including how NOT to manage a brainstorming session).

The Effect of Negative Ties on the Innovative Consumer's Creativity: An Empirical Study of New Service Idea Generation in a Social Networking Environment by Phillippe Duverger (Cambridge: Proquest/UMI Dissertation Publishing, 2011) is a PhD thesis that explores the relationship between social networking and the empowerment of consumers as innovators for the firms they buy from. Although the thesis is very academic in style, and therefore hard going at times, the author offers some very good insights into ways in which consumer creativity can be fostered, and ways in which it can be damaged.

References

Bagozzi, R.P. and Warshaw, P.R. (1992) Development and test of a theory of technological learning and usage. *Human Relations* 45 (7): 660–86.

Calentone, R.J. and Cooper, R.G. (1981) New product scenarios: prospects for success. *American Journal of Marketing* 45: 48–60.

Chuttur, M.Y. (2009). Overview of the technology acceptance model: origins, developments and future directions. Indiana University, USA . Sprouts: Working Papers on Information Systems, 9 (37). http://sprouts.aisnet.org/9-37.

Davis, F.D. (1989) Perceived usefulness, perceived ease of use, and user acceptance of information technology. *MIS Quarterly* 13 (3): 319–40.

Feick, L.F. and Price, L.L. (1987) The market maven: a diffuser of marketplace information. *Journal of Marketing* 51: 83–97.

Goldsmith, R.E. and Hofacker, C.F. (1991) Measuring consumer innovativeness. *Journal of the Academy of Marketing Science* 19 (3): 209–22.

Jansson, J., Marell, A. and Nordlund, A. (2011) Exploring consumer adoption of a high involvement eco-innovation using value-belief-norm theory. *Journal of Consumer Behaviour* 10 (1): 51–60.

Kirton, M.J. (1986) Adapters and innovators: a theory of cognitive style. In K. Gronhaugh and M. Kauffman (eds), *Innovation: A Crossdisciplinary Perspective.* New York: John Wiley.

Robertson, T.S. (1967) The process of innovation and the diffusion of innovation. *Journal of Marketing* January: 14–19.

Rogers, E.M. (1983) *Diffusion of Innovation.* New York: Free Press.

Rogers, E.M. and Shoemaker, F. (1971) *Communication of Innovation.* New York: Macmillan.

Schreier, M. (2006) The value increment of mass-customised products: an empirical assessment. *Journal of Consumer Behaviour* 5: 317–27.

Timmor, Y. and Katz-Navon, T. (2008) Being the same and different: a model explaining new product adoption. *Journal of Consumer Behaviour* 7 (3): 249–62.

Walsh, G., Gwinner, K.P. and Swanson, S.R. (2004) What makes mavens tick? Exploring the motives of market mavens' initiation of information diffusion. *Journal of Consumer Marketing* 21 (2): 109–22.

More online

To gain free access to additional online resources to support this chapter please visit: **www.sagepub.co.uk/blythe**

CHAPTER (13)
Post-purchase behaviour

CHAPTER CONTENTS

LEARNING OBJECTIVES

After reading this chapter you should be able to:

- Explain how the attributes of a product and the relationship between supplier and consumer contribute to the perception of quality.

- Explain how satisfaction and dissatisfaction are generated.

- Show how complaints develop.

- Explain the advantages and disadvantages of various supplier approaches to complaint handling.

- Show how consumers might reduce dissonance.

- Explain the different routes open to consumers when disposing of used or unwanted products.

- Describe how lateral recycling works.

Introduction

For some marketers, the job appears to be finished once the sale is made. For consumers, the purchase is only the beginning of the consumption experience. The post-purchase behaviour of consumers determines (ultimately) whether they will buy again, whether they will come back and complain or (in the worst case) whether they will tell their friends, family and even consumer protection organisations about their bad experience with the product.

Post-purchase evaluation and behaviour are therefore key issues for marketers, particularly in a relationship marketing context. Within this evaluation, expected and actual quality of the products plays a role in leading to a decision as to whether the product represents value for money; a product that falls below the expected quality will create dissatisfaction, but the problem for marketers lies in deciding what consumers believe quality actually is.

Disposal of used products (and even of products that still have some useful life left in them) has become central to the cause of environmentalism

Case study: Gumtree

Gumtree is the brainchild of two Londoners, Simon Crookall and Michael Pennington. In March 2000, they had the idea of setting up a website to host classified ads, originally just for people living in the London area. The ads helped people to find 'somewhere to live, someone to live with, or something for the home', in the words of the company's website.

Within months the site had become a hugely popular way to dispose of almost anything. This is recycling in action – because it's free to advertise, and Gumtree doesn't take a slice of the selling price (unlike eBay), the site became extremely popular and went national. Of course, Gumtree doesn't provide the safeguards eBay does – it is simply an advertising medium for people who want to recycle.

The site currently allows people to specify what they want to buy, and where they want to buy it: the site will then list the nearest examples of the item. Although it is perfectly possible to see ads from anywhere and everywhere in the UK, Gumtree has the country broken down into separate pages, each for a specific region or city. That way, people do not have to wade through ads from all over the country in order to find the item they want in a convenient location for collection. For example, somebody looking for a piano in the Cardiff area would see ads for pianos anywhere within a thirty-mile or so radius. In all, Gumtree covers 43 cities in the UK, but those covered can be broken down into areas of the city – suburbs and districts can be searched if the individual is looking for something really close to home.

Of course, all this has to be paid for. Gumtree operates by charging for sponsored links, so that commercial organisations can attract potential customers for new products. Because Gumtree is able to direct people to exactly the products they are looking for, commercial organisations can target very accurately and have their ad in front of someone who has already indicated that he or she is interested in the product.

From the viewpoint of consumers, Gumtree offers an opportunity to dispose of no-longer-needed items without adding to landfill, and with the added bonus of bringing in some money.

How to impress your examiner

Post-purchase behaviour seems to focus heavily on complaining behaviour – you may be asked to explain the various theories around post-purchase dissonance and complaining. However, post-purchase consonance is equally important and much more common, so you will gain marks if you bring in references to word of mouth recommendation and mavenism.

It always helps to think outside the box a little – post-purchase behaviour is also part of the learning process and information search for pre-purchase (repeat purchase) behaviour. Referring to this kind of area will show you understand the whole picture.

in recent years. Recycling, using products to the full, and care in disposal into the environment have been near the top of the agenda, and consumer behaviour in these areas has come under considerable scrutiny.

Quality

Following on from a purchase, people will evaluate whether the purchase has worked out well or not. This is a process of comparing the outcome with the previous expectation of the product: the result is an estimate of the quality of the product.

Quality is a complex construct subject to varying definitions. In many cases marketers use the term as a substitute for the word 'good' – high quality means very good; poor quality means bad. In fact this is an over-simplification. Here are some definitions of quality in current use:

> *Quality is defined as fully satisfying agreed customer requirements at the lowest internal price. (Bank 1992)*

> *Quality means conforming to requirements. (Crosby 1984)*

> *Quality is about fitness for use. (Juran 1982)*

> *Quality can only be defined by customers and occurs where an organisation supplies goods or services to a specification that satisfies their needs. (Palmer 1998)*

There have been attempts to distinguish between subjective and objective measures of quality. Swan and Combs (1976) defined two elements of service quality. First, they referred to instrumental quality, which describes the physical aspects of the product or service, and second they referred to the expressive dimension, which is about the intangible or psychological aspects. Although the authors were talking about services in particular, there appears to be no reason why the same dimensions should not apply to physical products. Gronroos (1984) identified technical quality and functional quality as the components of overall quality, with technical quality being the quantifiable aspects of the quality construct, and functional quality being those aspects that arise through the interaction between consumer and supplier.

Figure 13.1 shows how the interaction between supplier and customer leads to functional quality, which then combines with technical quality to generate the overall quality.

Because technical quality can be easily measured it is something that both the supplier and the consumer can agree on. For example, the reliability of delivery of mail is a technical aspect of the Post Office service: the percentage of letters that arrive on time can be calculated, and (provided the statistics are honest) both parties can agree that this is, in fact, the technical quality of what is happening. What cannot be agreed is the degree to which individual consumers regard reliable delivery as important. For some, a next-day delivery is of lesser importance than a convenient delivery time in the morning, or perhaps a lower cost of postage.

People are also influenced by how the benefits are delivered to them. This is what Gronroos calls the functional quality, and it cannot be measured objectively because it is a function of the individual's needs and expectations. This problem of assessing quality is much harder in services markets, because the functional quality forms a much greater proportion of the total product experience. This means that effective communication with consumers becomes more important as we move towards the 'service' end of the product continuum.

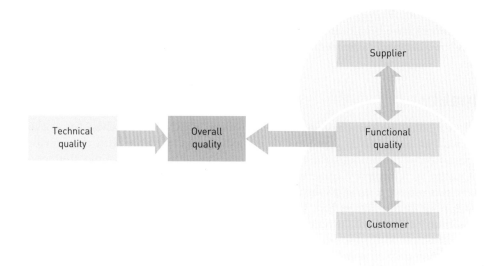

Figure 13.1 Components of quality

In summary, quality seems to relate to the extent to which a product's performance meets customers' expectations and requirements, so it would appear to be a construct between what the marketers provide and what the customer receives. This is, of course, subjective: there is therefore no absolute measure of quality.

 ## Challenging the status quo

In recent years, especially in the UK, we have heard a great deal about offering people choice. This has been particularly the case in public services such as schools and hospitals, where formerly people were simply sent to the nearest school or hospital whatever their personal preferences or, indeed, needs.

Now we have league tables for schools and universities, published statistics for hospitals, and choices about where and when we receive these services. Yet is that actually improving the situation for consumers? If there is a league table, doesn't that simply place added burdens on already-overstretched teachers and administrators?

Wouldn't it be better if we just ensured that all local services worked efficiently and effectively? If we get the technical quality right, surely for most people the functional quality will not lag far behind!

Post-purchase evaluation

An evaluation of the product's performance against the consumer's pre-purchase expectation will result in several possible outcomes. In most cases, people are satisfied with their purchases to a greater or lesser extent. In some cases, people may be dissatisfied to a greater or lesser extent, and in a few cases they will be extremely dissatisfied. Equally, in a few cases the individual will be more than satisfied, perhaps even delighted, with the product. The process of post-purchase evaluation is shown in Figure 13.2.

Satisfaction has been described as the full meeting of one's expectations (Oliver 1980), but there are probably degrees of satisfaction, i.e. points at which the

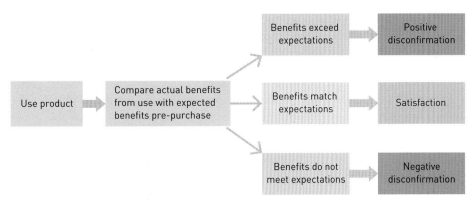

Figure 13.2   Post-purchase evaluation

individual feels less than completely satisfied, but would still feel that reasonable expectations have been met. From a marketing viewpoint, customer satisfaction is regarded as the most important factor in developing the business and meeting corporate goals: satisfied customers are more likely to generate positive word of mouth, they are more likely to return and buy again and they are more likely to increase the quantities purchased. Satisfaction does not necessarily mean that the customer will always return; dissatisfaction almost certainly means that the customer will not return, however, provided there are other options available. Therefore satisfaction is necessary but not sufficient for developing loyalty in customers.

In choosing between products, customers are likely to anticipate the level of satisfaction they will obtain from making a particular purchase. In anticipating satisfaction, people are more likely to pay attention to product attributes that are 'vivid' in nature (i.e. are easy to visualise, and easy to imagine as experiences) than they are to less vivid attributes (Shiv and Huber 2000). For example, someone who is thinking about buying a new outfit is likely to concentrate more on how it will look when worn, and possibly on how easy it is to keep clean, than on what materials it is made of or even what it costs to buy. After owning the clothes for a while, the individual might find that the material wears out quickly or stretches out of shape. Anticipated satisfaction is therefore related to how the individual thinks the product will function rather than to the actual performance of the product in use.

Measuring satisfaction and dissatisfaction relies on what is called the disconfirmation paradigm. The two variables in this paradigm are pre-purchase expectations and post-purchase disconfirmation. Expectations are matched by either positive disconfirmation (the product performs better than expected) or negative disconfirmation (the product performs worse than expected). The greater the positive disconfirmation, the greater the satisfaction (Churchill and Surprenant 1982), and if the difference between the two is large enough the consumer feels delighted (Oliver 1997). Managing expectations is therefore a key factor in managing overall satisfaction – raising unrealistic expectations will lead to negative disconfirmation, even though low expectations may well mean that the initial purchase is less likely.

Santos and Boote (2003) describe four post-purchase affective states, as follows:

1 *Delight.* This occurs when either performance of the product falls between the individual's ideal and desired level of performance (a disconfirmed experience of delight) or when the consumer expected to be delighted (a confirmed experience of delight).

Positive disconfirmation An unexpectedly good outcome of a purchase

Negative disconfirmation A state of affairs in which the expected outcome is disappointing or fails in some way to satisfy

Affective state The physical or psychological condition of an individual which may lead to an interruption in planned behaviour

2 *Satisfaction* (or positive indifference). This occurs when product performance falls between desired and predicted level (a disconfirmed experience of satisfaction) or when the person expected to be satisfied (a confirmed experience of satisfaction). This is probably a fairly common experience.

3 *Acceptance* (or negative indifference). Acceptance occurs when product performance falls between the person's predicted and minimum tolerable level of expectation (a disconfirmed experience of acceptance) or when the person expected the performance to be no more than satisfactory (a confirmed experience of acceptance).

4 *Dissatisfaction*. When product performance falls between the minimum tolerable and the worst imaginable levels of expectation, there will be a disconfirmed experience of dissatisfaction. If the consumer expected to be dissatisfied, there will be a confirmed experience of dissatisfaction. For example, if a holidaymaker is setting off on a pre-booked package holiday and the weather forecast is extremely bad, he or she is expecting not to enjoy the holiday – the thunderstorms and gales will come as no surprise, but will still lead to dissatisfaction.

The psychological impact of loss is often greater than the impact of a comparable gain (Hankuk and Agarwal 2003). Interestingly, these researchers found that loss of quality takes precedence over loss of price – in other words, if people feel that they have overpaid for something this is less important than if they feel that they have bought something which is of poor quality. This implies that firms need to make a large reduction in price if people are to be happy with a poor-quality product.

People often evaluate other people's purchases, and often take pleasure from seeing other people's purchases fail (Sundie et al. 2006). Pleasure at the downfall of another is called schadenfreude and may not be the noblest of human emotions, but it does exist. According to Sundie et al., schadenfreude is greater when a high-status product fails than when a low-status product fails: in other words, when your friend's new Porsche breaks down you will feel a certain secret delight, whereas when his new yard brush snaps you simply feel sorry for him.

Schadenfreude Pleasure felt at the downfall of another

Consequences of post-purchase evaluation

How people act following on from their evaluation of the consequences of their purchases is of course of intense interest for marketers. Typically, post-purchase behaviour falls into the following categories:

- Repurchase
- Complaint
- Word of mouth recommendation
- No change of behaviour at all.

Repurchase is almost always a clear indicator that the customer was satisfied with the product. Repurchase is perhaps best explained by the operant conditioning model discussed in Chapter 6: an action that has a positive outcome (consuming the product) is likely to be repeated (buying another of the same). Repeat buying behaviour has already been discussed in more detail in Chapter 12.

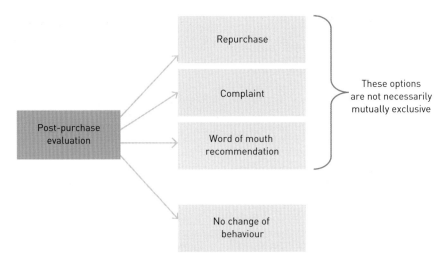

Figure 13.3   Consequences of post-purchase evaluation

Figure 13.3 shows the possible consequences of post-purchase evaluation, in other words how evaluation might translate into behaviour. Note that the first three options are not mutually exclusive – it is perfectly possible for someone to complain, but still repurchase (for example, if the complaint is handled to the individual's satisfaction). This might in turn lead to positive word of mouth recommendation. Clearly no change of behaviour rules out the other three since they are behaviours.

Complaining behaviour may take one of three forms (Singh 1988). These are as follows:

1   *Voiced complaints*. These are complaints made directly to the supplier, and are probably the best outcome from the supplier's viewpoint (apart, of course, from complete satisfaction with the product) since they provide an opportunity for the supplier to redress the problem. Such complaints should be dealt with promptly and effectively, since there is some evidence to indicate that customers whose complaints are dealt with to their complete satisfaction may become more loyal than customers who did not have a complaint in the first place. Some people (older people, for example) are often reluctant to voice complaints, so may need extra encouragement (Grougiou and Pettigrew 2009).
2   *Third-party complaints*. In this case, the complainer goes to a lawyer, a consumer rights champion or even the news media to make the complaint. This can create serious problems for the supplier, although to be fair most third parties would check with the supplier first, and give them a chance to make amends, before taking further action.
3   *Private complaints*. Here the complainer tells friends, family, work colleagues and anyone else who will listen about the failure on the part of the supplier. This negative word of mouth can be destructive for the supplier, depending on how far it reaches and whether it is passed on further. In recent years, there have been examples of negative word of mouse (Internet or e-mailed complaining behaviour).

Shadow websites
Websites that offer an
opportunity to post negative
stories about specific
companies or brands

Consumer behaviour in action:
Shadow websites

In 1996, partly in response to the longest-running libel case in British legal history, a new website started up. Called McSpotlight, the website was started by the McInformation Network, a group of anti-McDonald's, anti-globalisation, possibly anti-capitalist activists based in 16 countries. McSpotlight is dedicated to attacking McDonald's on every front – providing information about McDonald's 'exploitation' of meat animals, about the company's low wages, about dubious marketing practices, about the endless stream of litigation which McDonald's has engaged in, and about the health hazards of fast foods. The website owners say that they are not especially against McDonald's, but are rather against what McDonald's represents in terms of globalisation, environmental damage and exploitation of consumers.

The Anti-Nuclear Alliance of Western Australia also runs a website on which it attacks Rio Tinto (the mining corporation) among others. In particular, the site attacks Rio Tinto's Namibian uranium mining operations, attacking exploitation of workers and environmentally damaging mining methods.

In New York, the Killer Coke campaign uses a website to allege that Coca-Cola uses strong-arm tactics to break up union activities in Colombia and elsewhere. The website is detailed in its allegations – and the authors of the website have no problem revealing their address.

Toys R Us fell victim (or put themselves in a bad position, depending on your viewpoint) to a website calling itself Roadkills R Us. This was a spoof website, founded by one Miles O'Neal in 1988: it existed merely to exercise O'Neal's chaotic sense of humour, and had no products, no finances, no premises and in fact no existence outside cyberspace. Toys R Us threatened O'Neal with legal action unless he closed down his 'company', but under US law (and that of most other countries) running an obviously satirical website is not against the law. The result? O'Neal started a counter-campaign, publicising Toys R Us and their 'sledgehammer' approach. The Roadkills site still exists, but now it has a great deal to say about Toys R Us.

McSpotlight also have a website dedicated to Shell Oil, offering similar opportunities for people to attack the company. There is little that Shell can do about this – the website operates from several countries, and therefore it is difficult or even impossible for Shell to locate the perpetrators, let alone sue them (bearing in mind that different countries have different rules about libel and freedom of speech).

Many large companies have attracted the attention of people who are Net-literate enough to create a counter-website. As a way of complaining about a company it certainly puts the customer in charge – if the website is named carefully, and the right keywords are chosen, it should come up within the first ten or so sites and therefore will be seen by anyone accessing the corporation's legitimate site. From the corporation's viewpoint, this is probably not good, but of course most people are aware that the Internet is not a reliable source of information – after all, anyone can say anything on there without much fear of reprisals.

The companies that do respond do so at their peril – being seen as humourless, bullying or just plain stupid probably does more to damage the corporate image than being pilloried by a small group of people with very limited resources.

People do not always complain, even when dissatisfied. Complainers are more likely to be involved with the product, and also have impulsive personalities (Sharma et al. 2010). Complaining behaviour will only occur when some or all of the following conditions apply:

1 The consumer blames someone else for the problem. If the individual attributes blame to themselves (perhaps knowing that the purchase decision was a mistake) there is no one to complain to.
2 The experience was particularly negative. A minor problem is likely to be overlooked, for example poor service in a restaurant might not be worth complaining about: the customer simply does not eat at that restaurant again.
3 There is a reasonable chance of some kind of redress being forthcoming. There is no point in complaining if the customer believes that the supplier either will not, or cannot, make amends: if people do not think that their complaint will be taken seriously, they are more likely simply to switch brands than to complain (Richins 1987). For example, if the product was purchased in a closing-down sale and the shop has since gone out of business there is really no point in complaining. Note that this behaviour is likely to extend to private complaints as well as voiced or third-party complaints. The complaining activity will be possible within the level of the individual's time and money resources. There is no point in complaining about a product bought in a duty-free shop at Istanbul Airport if one is now at home in Manchester. At a less obvious level, a packet of biscuits that turn out to be almost all broken is unlikely to be worth complaining about, even if the grocery shop is a few hundred yards away.

The factors are summarised in Figure 13.4.

Customers who are dissatisfied but also powerless (perhaps because the company has high exit barriers) are likely to hold a grudge, avoid further dealings with the company if possible, and will want to retaliate if opportunity presents itself (Bunker and Ball 2009). For example, if someone has a bad experience with their broadband supplier, it may be very difficult to switch providers – having to have a new e-mail address, perhaps having a contract to complete, or having to lose favourite TV channels might make it very complex to move. The customer will then avoid taking up any further services, and may well give negative word of mouth to friends and family. Some people go so far as to make spurious telephone calls or complaints as a means of retaliation.

The current thinking is that marketers should actively encourage people to complain: people who are dissatisfied are more likely to spread the bad news to friends and family in private responses than they are to spread good news if they are satisfied (Schibrowsky and Lapidus 1994). Also, it turns out that people whose

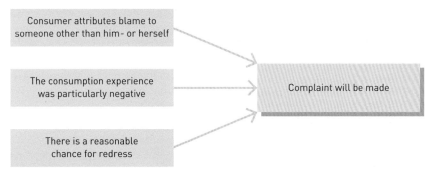

Figure 13.4   Factors in complaining behaviour

complaints are completely satisfied feel even better about the supplier than they would if nothing had gone wrong in the first place (Speer 1996). This may seem surprising, but actually it makes sense: consumers know that we do not live in a perfect world, and things will occasionally go wrong, so knowing that a supplier will put things right promptly is reassuring and helps build the relationship between supplier and consumer (Alvarez et al. 2011). Another supplier represents an unknown quantity on this dimension. Of course, good complaint handling is no substitute for providing a good service in the first place (Liljander 1999).

The rapid growth in on-line purchasing has created a further problem in that people often find that what is delivered is not exactly what they wanted. There is an additional risk in making purchases on-line, because it is much harder to inspect the product: obviously this does not matter if the product in question is something that has been bought before – ordering a printer cartridge or a DVD on-line is not very risky – but in other cases the product may well not come up to standard. This means that on-line retailers need to have a no-quibble return policy in order to reduce the perceived risk. This in turn means that people may abuse the system by using a product once or twice and then returning it. This abuse is not different in kind from someone buying a dinner suit or evening dress, wearing it for one special occasion, and then returning it to the shop: it is part of the risk for the retailer, but in the on-line environment it is almost entirely unavoidable if business is to be done at all.

However, there is a downside to encouraging complaint behaviour. First, it can lead people to believe that there are likely to be problems, and consequently the initial purchase becomes less likely. Second, it can lead to a 'complaining culture' in which people complain at the slightest excuse. At the extreme, it can lead to the 'professional complainer' who deliberately searches out something to complain about in order to obtain a price reduction or a free gift of some sort. Professional complainers are known to exist in the package holiday industry, for example (see the Consumer Behaviour in Action box).

Obviously the existence of professional complainers creates a problem for suppliers, in that they need to judge whether a complaint is genuine, frivolous or fraudulent. Making a mistake could lead to serious consequences, so (at present at least) most suppliers would rather pay out the occasional fraudulent or frivolous claim rather than risk annoying a genuine customer or being sued for a genuine claim.

Challenging the status quo

There was once a cartoon in which a very large man with a cudgel was shown standing underneath a sign saying 'Complaints Department'. Like most jokes, this was funny because it stated a real truth in many companies – complaining will only result in verbal abuse, and being tossed onto the street.

Nowadays we expect our complaints to be taken seriously, because the law is on our side and anyway it's only fair. So if we take a new suit or dress back to the shop, we expect a refund of our money, even if there is nothing wrong with the item except that we changed our minds. We expect the shop to change it even if we wore it to go out for an evening. Because that's what's right, right?

No, it isn't right. People who complain are adding to the cost of products that other people buy. If our complaints department is a large man with a cudgel, our costs will drop – and they would drop even further if we didn't have a complaints department at all, as is the case with some cheap airlines. Those savings can be passed on to customers who do not complain, who accept that the world is not perfect and who accept that life is risky!

Consumer behaviour in action

Tour operators used to say that Brits were the least likely to complain. If it turned out that the hotel was overbooked, the Swedes and Germans would bang on the counter and demand to be accommodated, while the Brits would shrug meekly and get back on the tour bus. In recent years, though, consumer protection organisations have been plugging the idea of complaining if things are not entirely satisfactory – with the result that some people seem to think that complaining is compulsory.

Airtours, a major UK holiday tour operator, deals with 17,000 complaints a year: the company now provides its reps with a catalogue of the more bizarre complaints so that they can prepare themselves for dealing with the lunatic fringe of complainers. Some examples follow:

No one told us there would be fish in the sea. The children were startled …

My fiancé and I booked a twin-bedded room and we were placed in a double-bedded room. We now hold you responsible for the fact I find myself pregnant. This would not have happened if you had put us in the rooms that we booked …

The brochure stated: 'No hairdressers at the accommodation'. We're trainee hairdressers, will we be OK staying here …?

It took us nine hours to fly to Jamaica from England – it only took the Americans three hours …

It is your duty as a tour operator to advise us of noisy or unruly guests before we travel …

I compared the size of our one-bedroom apartment to our friends' three-bedroom apartment and ours was significantly smaller …

I was bitten by a mosquito – no one said they could bite …

Some people apparently did not realise that there would be foreigners abroad:

There were too many Spanish people. The receptionist spoke Spanish. The food is Spanish. Too many foreigners.

Since this person was, technically, holidaying in Spain this situation was scarcely surprising.

The issue for the tour operator is, of course, planning how to deal with the ridiculous, stupid or even malicious complaint. It is hard to believe that someone would seriously complain that the sand on the beach was white rather than the yellow depicted in the brochure, or that there was no air conditioning outside their hotel, but the holiday reps on site have had to deal with exactly those complaints. The rep has to decide whether the customer is being merely stupid, in which case the response needs to be extremely tactful, or whether the customer is trying to gain a refund or other advantage unfairly. In some cases it must be difficult not to laugh, but each complaint must be dealt with as if it were serious – the world has become much more ready to rush off to the lawyers. For example, one couple cancelled a two-week holiday in Majorca because of the SARS epidemic. The tour operator pointed out there was no SARS epidemic within 7000 miles of Majorca, and charged a cancellation fee: the couple are now suing for compensation.

Airtours do not say whether the above complaints ever resulted in compensation being paid, but they are warning holidaymakers not to waste their reps' time with frivolous or vexatious complaints. The problem here is that it might discourage the person with a genuine problem from complaining – but this might be a small price to pay for not having to deal with bizarre complaints from obvious crackpots.

Sometimes the staff in retail stores can feel threatened by customers' complaining behaviour. If the complainant becomes aggressive, staff will sometimes become angry themselves: if they are unable to release the anger, considerable stress may result. In some cases, staff members have organised their own ways of relieving their feelings – there is a website for staff called 'Customers Suck', for example, where staff can post stories about unpleasant, aggressive or even violent customers. The webmasters make it clear that the vast majority of customers present no problems – but the site still provides a valuable safety valve for staff who deal with the problem cases. Staff will also sometimes sabotage the customer in some way – especially if the employee has a poor job performance rating (Skarlicki et al. 2008).

Figure 13.5 offers some ideas for dealing with complaints. In the case of a genuine complaint, the supplier should put matters right, but should perhaps also offer some extra compensation as a reward for bringing the problem to the firm's attention. In the case of frivolous complaints, the supplier should explain why the complaint is not going to be addressed, and should reject it. In the case of attempted fraud, the complaint should be rejected and also the firm should consider blacklisting the customer, since this is clearly someone that the firm should not be doing business with in future.

The type of compensation makes a difference to the customer's perceptions. For example, in the event of a service failure a branded form of compensation is better received than a generic form. In other words, if a customer complains about service in a coffee shop, a mug with the coffee shop's name on it is better received than a mug with 'coffee' on it (Mogilner and Aaker 2008).

Complaining behaviour is a way of relieving one's feelings, releasing the anger and frustration that is often felt when a purchase does not go according to plan. This is a way of reducing cognitive dissonance, which will be discussed in the next section.

Cognitive dissonance
The tension caused by holding two conflicting pieces of information at once

Word of mouth recommendation often occurs when people are satisfied, either because friends or family ask about the product, or because the individual is sufficiently delighted to want to share the positive experience. Research from Germany indicates that people who have recently switched to a new energy supplier exhibit higher levels of word of mouth activity than people who have been loyal to the energy supplier for a long time, in other words recent 'converts' like to tell people about their new supplier. This is perhaps not surprising – people who have been with the company for a while have probably already told anybody who might be interested all about their experiences. However, people who have switched as the result of a recommendation from someone else (referral switchers) have higher satisfaction levels, are more loyal and give more positive word of mouth than any other group (Wangenheim and Bayon 2004).

From this it would seem that, if we want to be satisfied with the things we buy, we should listen to our friends' recommendations.

Cognitive dissonance

Cognitive dissonance is the psychological tension that results from holding two conflicting ideas at the same time. The term came originally from work by Carl Festinger in the late 1950s, in which he experimented on people's motivation to lie. Festinger recruited students to perform a tedious task (specifically, putting pegs into holes, rotating the pegs a quarter-turn, then removing the pegs). He then told the students that he needed more recruits for the tests, and asked them to 'sell' their friends on the idea of helping with the tests by telling them that the

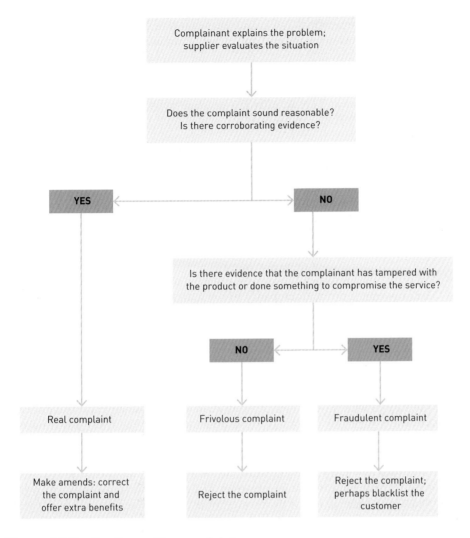

Figure 13.5   Dealing with complaints

experiment was really interesting and good fun. He offered some students a dollar for telling this lie, and others $25 (a considerable sum in 1957). Interestingly, the ones who were only paid a dollar actually began to believe the lie themselves: Festinger's explanation for this was that they could not justify their statements on the basis that they were being paid to make them, so therefore the statements had to be true (Festinger 1957).

The mechanism by which dissonance arises is simple. When working through the goal hierarchy, the consumer will form a view of what it will be like to own the product, and will develop a perceptual map of the anticipated benefits (see Chapter 5 for more on perception). The perceptual map is a mental picture of what life will be like with the product included. The expectancy disconfirmation model (Oliver 1980) says that satisfaction and/or dissatisfaction is the result of comparing pre-purchase expectations and post-purchase outcomes.

In the realm of consumer behaviour, post-purchase dissonance arises when the idea that a product was going to be a good purchase turns out to be wrong. The new information (that the product was not a good purchase) conflicts with the existing information, and the individual needs to resolve the dissonance. Pre-purchase expectations fall into three categories, as follows:

1 **Equitable performance**, which is a judgement regarding the performance one could reasonably expect given the cost and effort of obtaining the product (Woodruff et al. 1983).
2 **Ideal performance**. This is what the individual really hoped the product would do, if the world were a perfect place (Holbrook 1984).
3 **Expected performance**. This is what the product probably will do (Leichty and Churchill 1979).

If later experience shows that the product actually has different attributes, and the expected benefits do not materialise, the purchaser experiences a discord (or dissonance) since there is a clash between anticipation and actuality. Of course, post-purchase consonance is equally important: if the individual is happy with the product, he or she will experience post-purchase consonance, which may lead to recommendations and repeat purchases (see Figure 13.6).

The level of dissonance depends on the following factors:

- The degree of divergence between the expected outcome and the actual outcome.
- The importance of the discrepancy to the individual.
- The degree to which the discrepancy can be corrected.
- The cost of the purchase (in terms of time, money and risk).

For example, if someone buys a DVD player that turns out to have a scratch on the case, this is probably only a minor fault that does not affect the working of the equipment and is, in any case, easily corrected. In many cases, the customer would simply accept the scratch without bothering to seek redress from the supplier: if the scratch is a small one, it probably is not worth the effort of taking the DVD player back to the retailer for replacement, especially as the retailer might claim that the customer could have scratched the case while unpacking it or installing it. Some studies have shown that only one-third of dissatisfied customers will complain or seek redress: the remainder will boycott the products in future or simply complain to others (Day 1984). In the case of minor dissonance, or in cases where there is a high cost of complaint (for instance, returning goods to the duty-free shop at a foreign airport), the reluctance to complain is perfectly understandable.

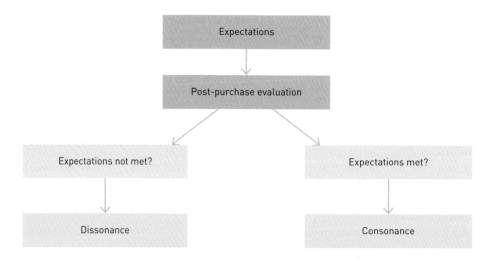

Figure 13.6 Dissonance and consonance

On the other hand, if the DVD player has a major fault (failing to play DVDs effectively being the main one) there is a major discrepancy between the expected outcome and the actual outcome. The biggest problems arise when the product does not live up to expectations but there is no available redress (for example, it breaks down after the warranty has expired). In these circumstances, the dissonance is likely to be considerable since the original goal has been frustrated.

Dissonance reduction is not always straightforward. Essentially, there are four basic strategies, as follows:

1 Ignore the dissonant information and seek consonant information. For example, if one has just made a major purchase and a friend says that the supplier has a bad reputation, one could ignore the new information altogether (perhaps rationalising this by thinking that the friend is just jealous) and one could perhaps search on-line for reports to confirm the good reputation of the supplier.
2 Distort the dissonant information. Here one might agree with the friend's statement, but rationalise it by thinking that the supplier's bad reputation arises from things which would not affect the product's performance (for example, a reputation for treating its workers badly).
3 Minimise the importance of the issue. One might agree that the supplier has a bad reputation, but also believe that this is not important in the context of the product itself, which is manifestly perfectly all right.
4 Change one's behaviour. In this case, one might take the product back for a refund, or not make further purchases in future.

Cognitive dissonance is a motivator to process information or to act, because the individual is driven to reduce dissonance wherever possible. Dissonance can occur at any point in the purchase cycle: when considering a major purchase, pre-purchase dissonance can easily affect the way decisions are arrived at, and in particular can easily delay the final purchase as the individual spends time reducing dissonance. Inevitably some doubt will remain, of course.

In Figure 13.7, the gap between the expected outcome and the actual outcome is what causes the post-purchase dissonance. The actual outcome is used as the benchmark for choosing which route to go down in reducing the dissonance, and the end result of the dissonance-reducing activity is fed back into the dissonance itself to cause the reduction.

From a marketer's point of view, it is important to reduce post-purchase dissonance. The evidence is that people will try to do so themselves, often by complaining about the product. If they do not win redress from the supplier, they will complain about the product to their friends and family. If people experience dissonance, there are four general approaches they take to minimise the problem. These are as follows:

1 Ignore the dissonant information and look for positive (consonant) information about the product. For example, a newly purchased car may be slower than expected, but on the plus side it is solidly built and reliable.
2 Distort the dissonant information. The car may be slow, but at least it's faster than taking a bus.
3 Play down the importance of the issue. The car is slow, but it goes from A to B eventually.
4 Change one's behaviour. Perhaps the consumer will sell the car, trade it in for something else, or buy a bicycle.

Marketers are able to back up these general approaches. Some car manufacturers, aware that their cars are reliable rather than exciting, will make use of this in their

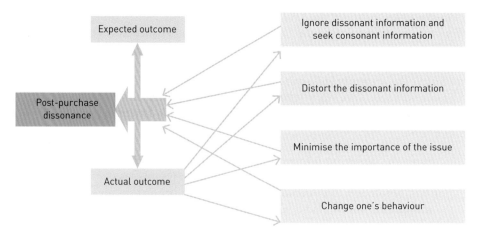

Figure 13.7 Dissonance reduction strategies

advertising. For example, Volkswagen used the slogan, 'If only everything in life was as reliable as a Volkswagen' for several years. In general, it is better to avoid the occurrence of post-purchase dissonance by ensuring that the purchaser has accurate information about the product and its performance: in other words, ensuring that the customer's perceptual map conforms as closely as possible with later experiences of using the product.

Complaining behaviour

If post-purchase dissonance does occur, the consumer may take action against the producer to redress the situation. For this reason it would be foolish to assume that the marketing job has finished once the sale is completed. Consumers' actions tend to fall into one of three general categories: voice responses, where the consumer comes back to the supplier to complain; private responses, where the consumer generates negative word of mouth by complaining to family and friends; and third-party responses, where the consumer takes legal action or complains to a consumer rights organisation (Singh 1988).

Figure 13.8 shows the outcomes that may arise when a consumer feels dissonance as a result of a purchase. Voice responses are the only ones with any chance of a positive outcome for the supplier.

When faced with a voiced response, the supplier and the consumer may have differing views on the legitimacy of the complaint. Managers may sometimes feel that the consumer wants something for nothing, or may feel that there is an implied criticism in the complaint (this is not unreasonable, of course – any complaint means that the customer thinks that the supplier has done a bad job). Consumers will always feel that there should be some response to the complaint, and the way in which the complaint is handled affects satisfaction and dissatisfaction (Cobb et al. 1987). One study has shown that, as the level of complaints increases, the willingness of managers to listen decreases (Smart and Martin 1991). This naturally tends to lead to an increase in the number of complaints, since managers are less likely to put right whatever is going wrong, and a vicious circle develops.

Third-party responses can range from a complaint to a regulatory body such as the UK's Trading Standards Office, through legal action in the courts, to a complaint

Third-party response In complaining, the act of involving someone other than the complainer or the supplier, for example a lawyer or consumer rights campaigner

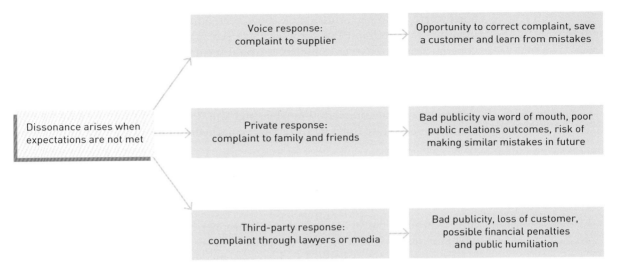

Figure 13.8 Complaining behaviour and its outcomes

to a consumer rights TV programme or newspaper column. In virtually all such cases the consumer will already have tried a voice response, and if he or she has not done so the third party will urge him or her to do so: a court case is unlikely to succeed if the supplier has not been given an opportunity to make amends.

From a marketer's viewpoint, it is better to cooperate with the third party than to be obstructive. For example, using a blanket 'no comment' response to a consumer affairs reporter is likely to be construed as an admission of guilt.

The following factors appear to affect whether or not a complaint will be made (Day 1984):

- The significance of the consumption event. This is likely to be a combination of product importance, cost, social visibility and time required in consumption. Consumers will be unlikely to complain if the product is cheap and unimportant, and was not expected to last long anyway.
- The consumer's knowledge and experience. The number of previous purchases, level of product knowledge, self-perception of one's ability as a consumer, and previous complaining experience are all factors in consumer experience. People who have successfully complained in the past are more likely to do so in the future, and people who have a high level of knowledge about the product category are more likely to complain, presumably because they have much better-defined expectations of the product.
- The difficulty of seeking redress, in terms of time, cost and nuisance. People are unlikely to complain if the product was purchased a long way away, or if complaining would result in a disproportionate amount of time and trouble.
- The perceived probability that a complaint will lead to a positive outcome (Halstead and Droge 1991). Complaints are far more likely if the consumer has a guarantee or feels that he or she is dealing with a reputable supplier who will resolve the problem. Also, consumers are less likely to complain if the problem is perceived as being incapable of being put right or compensated for. For example, someone staying in a hotel where other guests have gone out for the evening, leaving a noisy dog in their room, might feel that there is little the hotel management can do about the problem until the dog owners return.

Since there is ample evidence to show that putting a complaint right actually increases the likelihood of the consumer remaining loyal to the producer, and consequently purchasing in future, it would seem sensible to encourage people to voice their complaints rather than use private responses or (worse still) third-party responses.

Complainers appear to be members of higher socio-economic groups than those who do not complain (Francken and Van Raaij 1985), and the more people blame someone else for their dissatisfaction, the more likely they are to complain (Richins 1983).

Disposal

After a product has been used up, the consumer has the problem of disposing of whatever remains. In some cases, what is left still has value – the second-hand car market is an obvious example. In other cases, the product has been so totally used up that virtually nothing remains, as is the case with most food products.

In some cases, people form strong attachments to products (see Chapter 14 for a description of high-involvement products) and find it difficult to 'let go'. Favourite clothing, a much-loved car and even now-obsolete vinyl records may be kept until there is really no further possibility of using them any longer. Such possessions are our links with our past, and giving them up removes one of the anchors of our identities (Belk 1989). People who retain possessions have been defined as packrats, whereas people who regularly dispose of their possessions have been defined as purgers (Coulter and Ligas 2003). Packrats attach more meaning to their possessions, and see themselves as thrifty: they usually do not mind giving possessions away to other people or to charities, but they hate waste. Purgers, on the other hand, think packrats are messy and disorganised, and do not attach much significance to their possessions. Motivations for either of these behaviours are not clear-cut: hoarding in particular is an ambiguous concept (Maycroft 2009). One motivation may be the sentimental value attached to the objects: mothers sometimes keep children's toys as mementos, for example, although they will throw away broken toys (Sego 2010). Certainly if people are temporarily separated from some possessions (for example, leave a laptop in a taxi, or even have to fly economy when one normally flies business class) there is a loss of self-identity (Black 2011).

No matter how assiduously some of us might try to hoard our possessions, sooner or later everything must go. When the object is no longer of any use the individual has a choice of three options, summarised in Figure 13.9:

1 *Keep the item.* This may mean putting the item away in a safe place – a loft or a garage – or it may mean re-using the product in some way. For example, an old bath might be recycled as a garden pond, or a broken radio might be incorporated into an artwork.
2 *Temporarily dispose of the item.* Christmas decorations might be put away for use the following year, for example. Equally, products might be lent to someone else, or even rented to someone. For example, someone who will be working abroad for a year might rent out his or her house rather than sell it.
3 *Permanently dispose of the item.* This could be achieved by selling the item, giving it away, putting it into the refuse disposal system, or by some other permanent means such as burning it. Trade-in can also be used – exchanging the used product as part-payment for a new one greatly increases the buyer's willingness to buy (Zhu et al. 2008).

Packrats Individuals who tend to keep their possessions for a long time

Purgers People who regularly discard their possessions

In recent years, there has been an increasing emphasis on recycling items that are no longer of any use. In some cases the recycled article can be renovated, cleaned or donated as itself: for example, used spectacles can be collected and sent to developing countries to be worn by people who otherwise could not afford glasses. Since individuals' eyes deteriorate over time, everyone needs new spectacles with a different strength from time to time, so glasses that are still perfectly usable need to be disposed of. Equally, bottles can be cleaned and re-used as bottles rather than being smashed in a bottle bank and re-melted. Before the 1970s virtually all bottles were re-used in this way.

Clothing, books and used household items are often contributed to charity shops where they are sold to new users. Customers of charity shops are not necessarily short of money – some are anti-corporatist, some are looking for vintage clothing, some seek to transform their purchases into new clothing or objects. Charity shops effectively re-commoditise clothing for these buyers (Brace-Govan and Binay 2010). This is a necessary function, because it distances the new owner from the previous wearer of the clothes – most people feel slightly uncomfortable wearing clothes of unknown provenance, but rationalise this by imagining the previous owner as being much like themselves (Roux 2010). Clothing that is completely beyond re-use can be processed for paper-making: high-quality writing paper uses recycled fabric fibres (known in the trade as 'tramp's trousers') to strengthen the paper.

Some countries place a greater emphasis on recycling than do others, and there is also some debate over which recycling options are worthwhile and which are not.

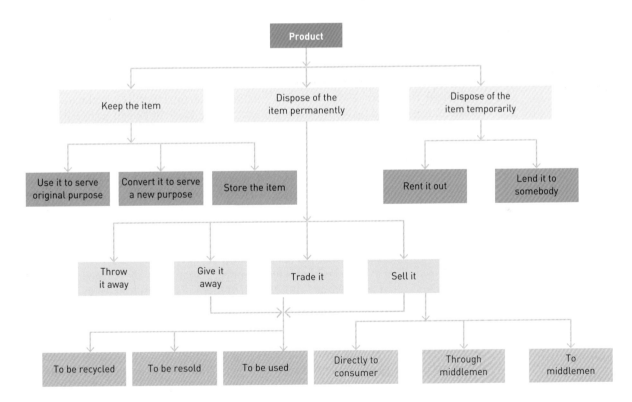

Figure 13.9 Disposal options

Source: Adapted from Jacob Jacoby, Carol K. Berning and Thomas F. Dietvorst (1977) What about disposition? *Journal of Marketing* 41 (Apr): 23.

Challenging the status quo

In the 1950s everything was recycled. People took bottles back to the shop and were refunded a small deposit, milk bottles were given back to the milkman (and he would get pretty nasty if he didn't get his bottles back), and food scraps were collected by pig-keepers. Ashes were spread on gardens or made into building blocks, paper and scrap wood were burned in household boilers to heat water, clothes were repaired, darned and eventually re-cut or unpicked and re-knitted to make new clothes. Newspapers were used to wrap food (notably in the UK, fish and chips), and in some households were used as toilet paper.

So what right do our 21st-century consumers have to tell us to recycle? Sending newspapers away to be re-pulped instead of simply using them as packaging? Breaking bottles and re-melting them instead of re-using them as bottles? Packing milk in one-way, irreplaceable plastic containers instead of in multi-use glass bottles?

Since the environmental movement started, we seem to have become LESS environmentally responsible than we were before!

In some cases, the cost of collecting and recycling used items (including the energy used) may mean that it is less environmentally damaging to use new materials rather than attempt to recycle. One study showed how specific instrumental goals were linked to abstract terminal values, and thus to recycling behaviour. Lower-order goals that were identified were 'avoid filling up landfills', 'reduce waste', 're-use materials' and 'save the environment'. These were linked to terminal values of 'promote health and avoid sickness', 'achieve life-sustaining ends' and 'provide for future generations'. The perceived effort of recycling turns out to be the best predictor of whether people will actually take the trouble at all. In other words, even when people are sold on the idea of recycling and believe it to be important, difficulty in actually recycling will often outweigh their motivation to do so (Bagozzi and Dabholkar 1994).

There is some evidence that the eagerness to recycle is levelling off somewhat and is certainly far from embedded in people's consciousnesses. Much depends on culture and on the availability of recycling schemes – Germans appear to be far more recycling-conscious than, for example, Spaniards or Britons. There is some evidence that women are more environmentally conscious than men, but this is based on American research and may not be true for other countries (Iyer and Kashyap 2007). These authors conclude that recycling will not succeed unless people are offered incentives and are reminded regularly about the need to recycle. Interestingly, they also found that recycling attitudes and behaviours correlate weakly with environmental attitudes and behaviours – in other words, having environmentally friendly attitudes in some areas (cycling rather than driving, using eco-friendly products) does not necessarily mean that one also believes in recycling.

As some consumers become more environmentally friendly, they may seek to distance themselves from the materialism of modern life and take a more minimalist approach to consumption. These people experience a transformation as they dispose of their goods, deciding what to keep and what to get rid of, and move away from the profane marketplace and towards a more sacred type of consumption in which they consume only goods that fit into their new lifestyle (Cherrier 2009). Often this disposal process helps develop a sense of community – for example, people who join clothing exchanges participate in the life of the goods by passing them on to friends (Albinsson and Perera 2009).

Lateral recycling is the term given to selling goods on, donating them to others, or exchanging them for other items. Car boot sales (also called flea markets) exist to facilitate this process, as do charity shops. A more recent arrival in the lateral recycling market is eBay and similar websites, on which people can sell almost anything. eBay has become an international institution of its own, with people selling and buying in an almost compulsive manner – the website has rules about what can and cannot be sold, but even so some very dubious items have appeared from time to time. The existence of eBay has meant that previously worthless goods have become transformed into valuable stock-in-trade for many people (Denegri-Knott and Molesworth 2009). On-line trading of this sort creates a self-sufficient, self-regulating and self-sustaining community (Arsel 2010).

Selling used products has become a lucrative business for some people – clearly antique dealers and the like can make their livings from selling off previously unwanted products, but even dedicated car boot sale attendees and eBayers can make substantial amounts of money from buying and selling. Reclaimed architectural products such as Victorian fireplaces, antique tiles, decorative roofing features, stained glass windows and so forth are often traded both on- and off-line. When goods are auctioned off, their previous cultural worth becomes commoditised – in other words, the history of an object becomes eroded by the fact that it is being sold, although some history still travels with the object. For many buyers, it is the history rather than the object that is important (Cheetham 2009).

Given the huge increase in wealth in developed countries over the past thirty years or so, and the correspondingly dramatic increase both in number of possessions per household and in quantities of rubbish produced, disposal is becoming one of the hot issues of the 21st century. People can no longer simply throw things away – in the words of one researcher, there is no longer an 'away' to throw things to (Sherry 1990). Marketers are likely to find that, if they do not address the issue of disposal and find ways to tap the potential of recycling in all its forms, they will be forced to do so by legislation. Already the European Union (largely at the instigation of Germany) is moving towards legislation that will require companies to take cradle-to-grave responsibility for their products.

Lateral recycling
Donating goods to others, selling them on, or otherwise transferring ownership to someone who will obtain further use of the goods

Summary

Especially in recent years, what happens after the purchase has been made has become of increased importance. First, from the viewpoint of suppliers it is important to know that customers are satisfied with their purchases, and if they are not satisfied it is important to know that they are able to come back and explain the problem so that it can be dealt with at source in future, thus reducing the potential for further dissatisfaction.

Disposal of used-up products, packaging, accessories and so forth has become a key issue in the environmental movement. There simply are not enough landfill sites to absorb the quantities of materials being thrown away, and at the same time the world's supply of raw materials cannot keep up with the demands of producers. Recycling has therefore become an essential part of the 21st century consumer behaviour repertoire.

Key points

- Technical quality refers to quantifiable aspects of the product; functional quality refers to the interaction between consumer and supplier.
- Satisfaction and dissatisfaction are measured by disconfirmation, which may be positive or negative.
- Complaints will only occur if the consumer blames someone else, the experience was particularly negative and there is a good chance of redress.
- Encouraging complaints helps prevents bad word of mouth, but may encourage frivolous complaints.
- Dissatisfied customers will act to reduce dissonance.
- There are three options for disposal: keep and store the article, dispose of it temporarily, or dispose of it permanently.
- Lateral recycling (passing the product on to someone else for re-use) is a growing phenomenon.

Review questions

1   How might a company minimise the number of fraudulent or false complaints, without discouraging genuine complaints?
2   Why might a company encourage environmentally friendly disposal of its products?
3   What methods exist for customers to reduce dissonance?
4   How does disconfirmation theory affect complaining behaviour?
5   What are the basic routes for disposal of used products?
6   What are the drivers for lateral recycling?
7   How might a company encourage positive word of mouth from people whose complaints have been satisfactorily dealt with?
8   Why would someone only complain if he or she can blame someone else for the problem?
9   Why is quality not an absolute?
10 How can firms improve the customer's perception of the quality of their products?

Case study revisited: Gumtree

Gumtree has over 2 million ads on its website at any one time. The need for the website is clear – people can no longer justify throwing away articles that have years of life left in them, nor can they continue to store such products indefinitely 'just in case'.

Of course, there is a downside – scams are also popular on Gumtree. Fake 'landlords' who accept deposits for houses they don't own, sellers who ask for up-front cash and then disappear, sellers who switch the product and then disappear, and even 'lonely hearts' who ask for the train fare to come and meet up (at least, this happened until Gumtree closed down their 'dating and encounters' category). Gumtree are well aware of the scam problem, and ask site users to report anything suspicious. Gumtree can, and do, block unsuitable or fraudulent users of the site, and they have advice on the site telling people how to avoid being ripped off.

Gumtree aficionados could be purgers or packrats: packrats don't mind disposing of stuff, they just don't like to feel it has been wasted. On the purchase side, packrats like to have stuff, and are easily tempted to buy. Purgers like to clear out their cupboards now and then, so they are also a good source of advertising since they might as well have some money for their unwanted items.

Given the current emphasis on safeguarding the environment, and of course the economic crisis, Gumtree and similar sites should see an even bigger increase in visits in the coming months and years.

Case study: TripAdvisor

Much is made of people who complain after they have been on holiday. It is perhaps natural not to comment unless one has a complaint – but there are still many people who would like the opportunity to praise a hotelier or restaurant when praise is deserved.

TripAdvisor exists to publish reviews from the general public – whether positive or negative. The site was founded in February 2000 by Stephen Kaufer, and has been the subject of various mergers and acquisitions since then. In 2011 it was once again launched as an independent company, and has operated as a stand-alone corporation ever since.

The site itself shows details of hotels with reviews posted by former guests. People can rate the hotel, and can also advise whether it is suited to honeymoon couples, business travellers, singles, families and so forth; people can post lengthy descriptions of the hotels, their facilities, staff attitudes and so forth. Perhaps surprisingly, TripAdvisor has managed to avoid being simply a clearing-house for complainers – many, perhaps even most, of the comments posted are positive, or at least even-handed. Most people who post reviews seem to be fair-minded and accept (for example) that a budget hotel will not have the facilities or comfort level of a five-star hotel.

The site doesn't confine itself to hotels, either. Prospective visitors to a city can look up reviews of local attractions, restaurants, museums, parks, theatres and even airlines flying in and out of the city. TripAdvisor aims to provide the prospective traveller with user reviews of everything about the destination – and also provides some useful articles about etiquette, language, money and so forth. Someone who makes full use of everything TripAdvisor has to offer will have a trouble-free trip.

Of course, as with anything else on the Internet, there are problems. There have been cases of hoteliers bribing people to post positive comments (or even posting their own, although it's usually fairly obvious from the writing style that the review is a fake one). There have also been cases of malicious negative reviews being posted – posts are anonymous, so would be untraceable. To counter this, TripAdvisor does not allow posts to go through without being checked, and the firm has developed some excellent systems for spotting faked posts. Among many other controls, TripAdvisor checks the e-mail addresses and IP sources for posts in order to detect any suspicious patterns. Hoteliers and others are given the opportunity to respond to negative posts, and many take up the offer; TripAdvisor is very keen to maintain the website's reputation for integrity and honesty throughout, but of course must allow people to express their true feelings about their experiences. The company has blacklisted around 30 hotels in the UK for breaking the rules, including one hotel that was caught bribing guests to post positive reviews.

Despite these minor problems, there is little doubt that TripAdvisor is one of the most reliable sites on the Internet. People's capacity for complaint is certainly very large, so it is something of a relief to find a website that celebrates the positives in travel experiences.

Questions

1 Why would someone want to post a review on TripAdvisor?
2 Most reviews are positive – why would this be the case?
3 How might someone respond to the offer of a bribe from a hotel to post a positive review?
4 Why are hoteliers and restaurateurs given the right to reply?
5 How does post-purchase consonance affect the quality of postings?

Further reading

There has been quite a lot published about consumer complaining behaviour, but Gruber, T., Szmigin, I. and Voss, R. (2009) Handling customer complaints effectively: a comparison of the value maps of female and male complainants. *Managing Service Quality* 19 (6): 636–56 gives some useful ideas on how to handle complaints effectively.

If you liked that paper, this next one might also be of interest: Gruber, T., Abosag, I., Reppel, A. and Szmigin, I. (2011) Analysing the preferred characteristics of frontline employees dealing with customer complaints: a cross national Kano study. *The TQM Journal* 23 (2): 128–44. By some of the same authors, it examines the type of people needed as frontline employees (who are the ones who have to deal with complaints, of course).

For a somewhat academic discourse on complaints and the people who make them, you might like *The Relationship Between Psychological Types, Demographics, and Post-Purchase Buyers' Remorse* by Trevor A. Fried (Charleston, SC: Bibliobazaar, 2011). The author outlines the effects of different demographics and personality types on complaint behaviour, and then goes on to suggest ways of dealing with complainers.

For more on how to handle complaints, and more importantly how to keep your sanity while you do so, read *A Complaint is a Gift: Using Customer Feedback as a Strategic Tool* by Janelle Barlow (San Francisco: Berrett-Koehler, 1996). It's a book full of ideas, and gives plenty of insight into what makes complainers tick.

Word of mouth is an important post-purchase activity. People like to talk about their purchases: for a brief treatise on how this works in post-purchase scenarios, read *Word of Mouth: Influences on the Choice of Recommendation Sources* by Klaus Schofer (Hamburg: Diplomarbeiten Agentur diplom.de, 1998).

References

Albinsson, P.A. and Perera, B.Y. (2009) From trash to treasure and beyond: the meaning of voluntary disposition. *Journal of Consumer Behaviour* 8 (6): 340–53.

Alvarez, L.S., Casielles, R.V. and Martin, A.M.D. (2011) Analysis of the role of complaint management in the context of relationship marketing. *Journal of Marketing Management* 27 (1&2): 143–64.

Arsel, Z. (2010) Exploring the social dynamics of online bartering. *Advances in Consumer Research* 37: 67–8.

Bagozzi, R.P. and Dabholkar, P.A. (1994) Consumer recycling goals and their effect on decisions to recycle: a means–end chain analysis. *Psychology and Marketing* 11 (July/Aug): 313–40.

Bank, J. (1992) *The Essence of Total Quality Management.* Harlow: Prentice Hall.

Belk, R.W. (1989) The role of possessions in constructing and maintaining a sense of past. *Advances in Consumer Research* 17: 669–76.

Black, I.R. (2011) Sorry not today: self and temporary consumption denial. *Journal of Consumer Behaviour* 10 (5): 267–78.

Brace-Govan, J. and Binay, I. (2010) Consumption of disposed goods for moral identities: a nexus of organisation, place, things and consumers. *Journal of Consumer Behaviour* 9 (1): 69–82.

Bunker, M. and Ball, A.D. (2009) Consequences of customer powerlessness: secondary control. *Journal of Consumer Behaviour* 8 (5): 268–83.

Cheetham, F. (2009) Out of control? An ethnographic analysis of the disposal of collectable objects through auction. *Journal of Consumer Behaviour* 8 (6): 316–26.

Cherrier, H. (2009) Disposal and simple living: exploring the circulation of goods and the development of sacred consumption. *Journal of Consumer Behaviour* 8 (6): 327–39.

Churchill, G.A. and Surprenant, C. (1982) An investigation into the determinants of customer satisfaction. *Journal of Marketing Research* 19: 491–504.

Cobb, K.J., Walgren, G.C. and Hollowed, M. (1987) Differences in organizational responses to consumer letters of satisfaction and dissatisfaction. *Advances in Consumer Research* 14: 227-31.

Coulter, R.A. and Ligas, M. (2003) To retain or to relinquish: exploring the disposition practices of packrats and purgers. *Advances in Consumer Research* 30: 38.

Crosby P.B. (1984) *Quality Without Tears.* New York: New American Library.

Day, R.L. (1984) Modeling choices among alternative responses to dissatisfaction. In T.C. Kinnear (ed.), *Advances in Consumer Research*, Vol. 11. Duluth, MN: Association for Consumer Research. pp. 496–9.

Denegri-Knott, J. and Molesworth, M. (2009) I'll sell this and I'll buy them that: eBay and the management of possessions as stock. *Journal of Consumer Behaviour* 8 (6): 305–15.

Festinger, L. (1957) *A Theory of Cognitive Dissonance*. Stanford, CA: Stanford University Press.

Festinger, L. and Carlsmith, J.M. (1959) Cognitive consequences of forced compliance. *Journal of Abnormal and Social Psychology* 58: 203–10.

Francken, D.A. and Van Raaij, F. (1985) Socio-economic and demographic determinants of consumer problem perception. *Journal of Consumer Policy* 8 (3): 303–14.

Gronroos, C. (1984) A service quality model and its marketing implications. *European Journal of Marketing* 18 (4): 36–43.

Grougiou, V. and Pettigrew, S. (2009) Seniors' attitudes to voicing complaints: a qualitative study. *Journal of Marketing Management* 25 (9&10): 987–1001.

Halstead, D. and Droge, C. (1991) Consumer attitudes toward complaining and the prediction of multiple complaint responses. *Advances in Consumer Research*, 18: 210–16.

Hankuk, T.C. and Agarwal, P. (2003) When gains exceed losses: attribute trade-offs and prospect theory. *Advances in Consumer Research* 30: 118–24.

Holbrook, M.P. (1984) Situation-specific ideal points and usage of multiple dissimilar brands. In Jagdish N. Sheth, *Research and Marketing*, Vol. 7. Greenwich, CT: JAI Press. pp. 93–131.

Iyer, E.S. and Kashyap, R.K. (2007) Consumer recycling: role of incentives, information and social class. *Journal of Consumer Behaviour* 6: 32–47.

Juran, J.M. (1982) *Upper Management and Quality*. New York: Juran Institute.

Leichty, M. and Churchill, G.A. Jr (1979) Conceptual insights into consumer satisfaction and services. In Neil Beck et al. (eds), *Educators' Conference Proceedings*. Chicago, IL: American Marketing Association.

Liljander, V. (1999) Consumer satisfaction with complaint handling following a dissatisfactory experience with car repair. *European Advances in Consumer Research* 4: 270–5.

Maycroft, N. (2009) Moving things along: hoarding, clutter and other ambiguous matter. *Journal of Consumer Behaviour* 8 (6): 354–64.

Mogilner, C. and Aaker, J. (2008) Forgiving by not forgetting: the effect of compensations following brand transgressions. *Advances in Consumer Research* 35: 149.

Oliver, R.L. (1997) *Satisfaction: A Behavioural Perspective on the Consumer*. New York: McGraw-Hill.

Oliver, R.L. (1980) A cognitive model of the antecedents and consequences of satisfaction decisions. *Journal of Marketing Research* 17: 460–9.

Palmer, A. (1998) *Principles of Services Marketing*, 2nd edn. Maidenhead: McGraw–Hill.

Richins, M. (1983) Negative word of mouth by dissatisfied consumers: a pilot study. *Journal of Marketing* 47 (1): 68–78.

Richins, M.L. (1987) A multivariate analysis of responses to dissatisfaction. *Journal of the Academy of Marketing Science* 15 (Fall): 24–31.

Roux, D. (2010) Identity and self-territory in second-hand clothing transfers. *Advances in Consumer Research* 37: 65–6.

Santos, J. and Boote, J. (2003) A theoretical exploration and model of consumer affective expectations, post-purchase affective states, and affective behaviour. *Journal of Consumer Behaviour* 3 (2): 142–56.

Schibrowsky, J.A. and Lapidus, R.S. (1994) Gaining a competitive advantage by analyzing aggregate complaints. *Journal of Consumer Marketing* 11 (1): 15–26.

Sego, T. (2010) Mothers' experience related to the disposal of children's clothing and gear: keeping Mister Clatters but tossing Broken Barbie. *Journal of Consumer Behaviour* 9 (1): 57–68.

Sharma, P., Marshall, R., Reday, P.A. and Na, W. (2010) Complainers vs non-complainers: a multinational investigation of individual and situational influences on customer complaint behaviour. *Journal of Marketing Management* 26 (1&2): 163–80.

Sherry, J.F. (1990) A sociocultural analysis of a Midwestern American flea market. *Journal of Consumer Research* 17 (June): 13–30.

Shiv, B. and Huber, J. (2000) The impact of anticipating satisfaction on consumer choice. *Journal of Consumer Research* 27 (2): 202–17.

Singh, J. (1988) Consumer complaint intentions and behavior: definitions and taxonomical issues. *Journal of Marketing* 52 (Jan): 93–107.

Skarlicki, D.P., Van Jaarsfeld, D.D. and Walker, D.D. (2008) Getting even for customer mistreatment: the role of moral identity in the relationship between customer interpersonal injustice and employee sabotage. *Journal of Applied Psychology* 93 (6): 1335–47.

Smart, D.T. and Martin, C.L. (1991) Manufacturer responses to consumer correspondence: an empirical investigation of consumer perceptions. *Journal of Consumer Affairs* 26 (Summer): 104–28.

Speer, T.L. (1996) They complain because they care. *American Demographics* May: 13–14.

Sundie, J.M., Ward, J., Chin, W.W. and Geiger-Oneto, S. (2006) Schadenfreude as a consumption-related emotion: feeling happiness at the downfall of another's product. *Advances in Consumer Research* 33: 96–7.

Swan, J.E. and Combs L.J. (1976) Product performance and consumer satisfaction: a new concept. *Journal of Marketing* 40 (April): 25–33.

Wangenheim, F. and Bayon, T. (2004) Satisfaction, loyalty and word of mouth within the customer base of a utility provider: differences between stayers, switchers, and referral switchers. *Journal of Consumer Behaviour* 3 (3): 211–20.

Woodruff, R.B., Cadotte, E.R. and Jenkins, R.L. (1983) Modelling consumer satisfaction using experience-based norms. *Journal of Marketing Research* 20: 296–304.

Zhu, J., Chen, J. and Dasgupta, S. (2008) Exploring the effect of a trade-in on consumers' willingness to pay for a new product. *Advances in Consumer Research* 35: 157–8.

More online

To gain free access to additional online resources to support this chapter please visit: **www.sagepub.co.uk/blythe**

CHAPTER (14)
Services markets

LEARNING OBJECTIVES

After reading this chapter you should be able to:

- Explain the differences between services and physical products from a purchasing perspective.

- Explain the role of word of mouth in both purchase decisions and in post-purchase behaviour.

- Describe ways in which consumers reduce their risk when buying services.

- Describe the role of involvement in service purchases.

- Explain sales promotion in a service context.

- Describe the role of service levels.

- Describe ways of minimising dissatisfaction, and ways of handling it when it does occur.

Introduction

Services are a major part of the developed world's economies. In Western Europe we manufacture relatively little compared with 100 years ago, and we earn our living through providing services such as finance, tourism, insurance, education and (of course) marketing.

Even our consumption patterns are heavily skewed towards services. We eat out more than we did fifty years ago, we enjoy travel, we play more sports, we enjoy more entertainment and most of us work in service industries. Even our gift-giving is moving more towards the service sector, with the giving and receiving of 'experience' gifts such as weekend breaks, trial flights in light aircraft, motor-racing days and so forth (Clarke 2006). Marketing literature is gradually catching up to this reality, and emphasising service products more and more, but the focus still remains firmly on the marketing of physical products. This chapter is intended to redress the balance somewhat by discussing some differences in people's behaviour when choosing services.

Case study: Steiner salons

In 1901 Henry Steiner created a range of apothecary products for the hair and skin. These were used and sold in the family business, a hairdressing salon in London. Following Henry's death in 1926, Herman Steiner joined his mother in running the business, and embarked on a programme of expansion.

The first Steiner salon in upmarket Mayfair opened in 1937: Herman knew that success in the hairdressing business would only come from prestige, so despite having salons throughout England he needed the Mayfair address. His shrewdness paid off – in 1947 he was granted the Royal Warrant, becoming hairdresser to HM Queen Mary, followed in 1970 by becoming Cosmetician to HM Queen Elizabeth, the Queen Mother.

In 1960 Herman added facials and massages to the range of services on offer in his salons. This was a major breakthrough, taking the business from simple haircare towards a total beauty experience – and it was in the same year that he got his first contract to operate a salon on a cruise liner.

Cruise liners were to prove Steiner's route to fame and fortune. He gained contracts with Cunard, P&O, Union Pacific, Royal Mail Line and Union Castle lines. The company's experience in operating ocean-going beauty salons led to them being asked to build and operate the beauty salon on the liner Queen Elizabeth 2 (QE2), which was built in 1968.

Steiner expanded the Suites at Sea concept and now offers full-service beauty salons on 158 cruise liners. Some of these include acupuncture, Chinese herbal medicine, skin-filler treatments and even botox treatments on board. The company has come a long way from one salon in London.

How to impress your examiner

You may be asked to explain the differences between marketing services and marketing physical products. If so, you need to point out that some schools of thought say there is no difference, because there is no differentiating line between products and services.

Service-dominant logic is the current exciting new idea in marketing. If you can explain how this is affecting our view of not only services but also physical products, you will impress any examiner.

Services – products or not?

From the consumer's viewpoint a service is as much a bundle of benefits as is a physical product. The consumer is paying money for the purpose of getting something back; the fact that the product is not actually something that can be held in the hand is irrelevant.

For example, consider the difference between a pizza bought from a supermarket and one bought in a pizza restaurant. The supermarket pizza will be pretty much identical to the one next to it in the freezer, and may have been produced weeks beforehand; the purchaser may not consume it for several more weeks, if he or she is stocking up the freezer. The individual is buying the pizza in order to have a convenient meal at some later date.

In a pizza restaurant, though, the benefits go far beyond merely satisfying hunger. Often the individual will be with friends (or on a date), thus satisfying social needs as well. The restaurant provides a pleasant atmosphere, and does the washing up, and even panders to esteem needs by waiting on customers. The actual pizza will vary from one customer to another – partly because the pizzas are made to order, and partly because the chef may not use exactly the same quantities of the various ingredients each time, or it may be a different chef each night. Clearly, though, the bulk of what the customer is paying for in a restaurant is the intangible part of the transaction: the atmosphere, the socialising, the attention of the waiter. The pizza is certainly part of it, but it probably represents less than 20% of the final bill.

Challenging the status quo

Isn't the difference between a pizza bought in a supermarket and a pizza bought in a restaurant a somewhat artificial distinction? After all, someone had to assemble the supermarket pizza, probably by hand, and probably for a minimum wage. Likewise, the average fast-pizza place operates the same way – the staff manufacture the pizzas by hand, probably also for minimum wage.

Surely there is still a big services component in each pizza? Even the fact that it is sold in a supermarket contributes to the service element! So how do we draw the line between a product with a little bit of service and one with a large amount of service?

Usually services cannot be tested before the individual agrees to purchase them, because the only way to test is to actually use the service. For instance, someone who bought the pizza from a supermarket could take a good look at it first, read the ingredients list and see if it looked like an appealing brand; in a restaurant, the pizza will have been ordered, cooked and served before the individual has a chance to examine it. Likewise, some of the peripheral aspects of the restaurant pizza (such as the ambience of the restaurant itself, the quality of the waiters and waitresses, and even the attitude of the other diners) can affect the overall experience. Unfortunately, if a diner does not like the waitress in the restaurant, this is difficult to complain about (unless there is something seriously wrong with the way the meal has been served). The customer in these circumstances can only pay up and smile, perhaps leaving a smaller tip than he or she had intended to. Refusal to pay afterwards only works if the service is very seriously poor. The differences between services and physical products are shown in Figure 14.1.

From the supplier's viewpoint, a further problem is apparent. Services cannot be stockpiled in the same way as physical products. If the restaurant has a quiet night, the waiters and chefs still have to be paid; the service they would have provided has not been sold, but the cost of employing them remains. Conversely, if the supermarket

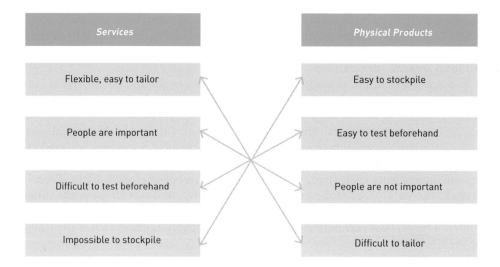

Figure 14.1   Services vs. physical products

does not sell the frozen pizza today, it can be sold tomorrow. Services are, therefore, highly perishable compared with physical products.

We can see, then, that services are distinguished from physical products by the following characteristics:

1 They are intangible.
2 Production and consumption usually happen at the same time.
3 There is a lack of trialability.
4 Services are variable, even from the same supplier.
5 Services are perishable.

This naturally leads to problems for the consumer, since buying a service will inevitably look like buying a pig in a poke. In effect, consumers are buying a promise; the service provider is offering certain benefits that may or may not appear, and the consumer has little redress if the service does not come up to expectation. This means that the decision-making process is affected considerably when someone is buying a product with a high service component.

In practice, of course, very few products are either entirely physical or entirely service-based. Most products appear at some point along a continuum, having characteristics of service and of physical products in varying degrees. The further towards the service end of the spectrum a product is, the greater it will show the characteristics of intangibility, perishability and so forth; equally, the greater the uncertainty for the consumer, and therefore the greater the tendency for the consumer to exhibit behaviours associated with choosing service products.

There is a school of thought that holds that all products are in fact services. The thinking is that a customer is not buying a drill, nor even is he or she buying holes, but is in fact buying a hole-drilling service, part of which is supplied by the customer. This way of looking at marketing is called service-dominant logic, and it has a number of implications. Service-dominant logic has ten foundational premises, as follows (Vargo and Lusch 2004, 2008):

1 Service is the fundamental basis of exchange. This is because people want the benefits, not the physical product; the benefits are always a service.

2 Indirect exchange masks the fundamental basis of exchange. This is because any service outcome involves a very large number of inputs, from finance to transport to manufacture.

3 Goods are a distribution method for service provision. An electric drill is only a vehicle for creating a hole-drilling service.

4 Operant resources are the fundamental source of competitive advantage. Operant resources act upon other resources to create wealth.

5 All economies are service economies. This is because all products are services.

6 The customer is always a co-creator of value. Value can only exist when a customer benefits, so even the most passive customer participates in its creation.

7 The enterprise cannot deliver value, it can only offer value propositions. This is because value cannot be created without a customer – a car is worthless unless someone drives it.

8 A service-centred view is inherently customer-orientated and relational. Customers are seen as co-creators, so there must be a relationship between customers and the firm.

9 All social and economic actors are resource integrators. Resources need to be integrated if value is to be created.

10 Value is always uniquely and phenomenologically determined by the beneficiary. If something is not of value to an individual, then it cannot have value in any absolute sense.

Service-dominant logic brings together a lot of previous ideas and provides a single conceptual platform for them. While it may not create a radical change in what marketers do on Monday morning, it does provide a new perspective for considering marketing problems, and especially for recognising the role consumers play in creating value.

Consumer approaches to information-gathering

In services markets consumers rely much more on word of mouth than is the case with physical products. Because of the intangibility of the product, the consumer is unable to carry out many of the usual processes of information-gathering; advertising is less verifiable, the suppliers are often unable to be specific about the service and the quality thereof, and most services are less subject to close regulation by government or trade bodies. Prospective consumers of a service are therefore likely to rely heavily on personal recommendations by friends and colleagues. This is particularly true for services such as hairdressing and restaurants.

For professional services the consumer may also ask questions about the qualifications and credentials of the service provider. For example, someone who is looking for a solicitor to handle a divorce case will naturally want to seek out a specialist in family law, and will look into this aspect of the solicitor's experience. Professional services rely heavily on referrals from other professionals; estate agents recommend solicitors, who recommend accountants, and so forth.

Because the service is hard to assess, prospective customers are likely to use surrogates when choosing a service provider. For example, solicitors might be judged on the quality of their office accommodation, hairdressers on the location of their salons and restaurants on their prices. People often spend more time on the information search for a service than would be the case for a physical product, simply because of the greater risks involved.

Figure 14. 2 shows some of the effects of good sources of communication. The individual will obtain reassurance that the decision is the right one, will reduce risk,

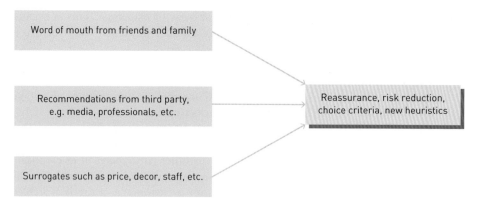

Figure 14.2   Sources of information

will develop new criteria for choosing and may develop useful long-term heuristics for making similar decisions in future.

Risk and uncertainty

Consumers will naturally want to minimise risk. Risk involves not only the possible loss of the purchase price of the product, but also some consequential losses. In the case of purchase of services, these consequential losses can be quite substantial; for example, poor legal advice could conceivably result in the loss of a large amount of money, or even one's liberty. Even the injudicious purchase of a restaurant meal could result in food poisoning.

Table 14. 1 illustrates some of the risks and the possible remedies.

Of course, there is a risk attached to the purchase of physical products as well, but usually the risk is confined to the purchase price (no doubt there are many exceptions to this general rule) and in the event of buying a faulty product, it is possible to obtain a replacement or a refund. Consumers therefore need to weigh up the purchase decision for both value for money (assuming the service the consumer expects when agreeing to the purchase is what is actually obtained) and also the possible consequential loss if the service offering goes wrong. Because of the risk of consequential loss, consumers will frequently avoid the cheapest services, on the assumption that there 'must be something wrong with it'. Though this phenomenon is also noticeable for purchases of physical products, it is far more common with the purchase of services. For example, ladies' hairdressing is not price-sensitive, and consumers often show perverse price sensitivity (deliberately going to a more expensive salon, all other aspects being equal). Naturally consumers will still expect to see value for money, having made the decision to opt for the higher-price alternative. Consumer responses to risk are diagrammed in Figure 14.3.

Consumers are faced with a greater degree of uncertainty when purchasing services, in that the service is (a) intangible and (b) variable. Even the supplier of the service cannot always guarantee that the outcome will be to the consumer's satisfaction: this is particularly true of professional services, such as lawyers and accountants. Lawyers still expect to be paid even if they lose the case, and likewise an accountant will still expect a fee even if the profit-and-loss account isn't as healthy as the client would like, or the tax authorities do not allow all the deductions. Equally, if

Table 14.1   Risks and remedies in services

Type of risk	Possible consumer response	Possible supplier remedy	Explanation
Consequential loss	Law suit	Ensure that risks are explained beforehand; use disclaimers in contracts; carry public or professional liability insurance	Consequential losses arise when a service goes wrong and causes damage to the customer. For example, if a train is late and the customer misses a vital business meeting, there may be a big consequential loss. Rail companies have disclaimers on the back of the ticket for this type of loss
Purchase price risk	Refusal to pay	Correct the fault; check with the customer during the service provision that everything is all right	It is too late afterwards to ask if everything's all right (although this should be done). Checking during the service (a) makes it less likely that things will go wrong and (b) makes it harder for the consumer to claim that the service went wrong in order to avoid paying
Misunderstanding about what was wanted	Complaint, perhaps a refusal to pay	Before providing the service go through everything carefully and explain exactly what's going to be done, when, and why. Perhaps even explain why the job can't be done the way the consumer would like it to be done	One of the commonest problems in service provision is lack of real communication. This is particularly true in professional services, where the professional perhaps rightly feels that the customer wouldn't understand the finer technical details of the job. It is worthwhile providing an explanation, however, since there is otherwise a potential for post-purchase dissonance

Figure 14.3   Consumer responses to risk

the restaurant is not as romantic as the customer expected and his or her date is displeased, the waiter will still expect the customer to pay for the meal.

This is, of course, outside the scope of errors or misunderstandings. If someone ordered a mild curry and got a spicy one instead, he or she would have cause to complain; the problem arises when what is described in good faith turns out differently from what was

Challenging the status quo

Life is risky – for sure, nobody gets out of it alive. So are we perhaps blinded by our fear of loss so much that we cannot see where our best interests lie? Are we really prepared to pay well above the going rate for a service, in the hope that in some way there will be a relationship between a high price and good service?

After all, there is no rational reason to suppose that a high price has anything whatever to do with a good product. There are plenty of products around that are both expensive and no good – and there are certainly plenty of lawyers, accountants, mechanics, financial advisers and so forth who are hopelessly incompetent but also expensive. Why do we assume that expensive equals good, when we have overwhelming evidence to show that the relationship between high prices and good quality is the same as that between chalk and Wednesday – i.e. there is no relationship at all!

expected. The uncertainty usually arises from the gap between what the consumer is expecting in the way of benefits, and what the service provider can actually provide.

For example, it is well known in ladies' hairdressing that some clients expect to come out looking like their favourite movie star or pop singer. While it is sometimes (though by no means always) possible to recreate the appropriate hairstyle, it is not possible to carry out plastic surgery, and the particular hairstyle may not suit the customer's facial or physical features. Not unnaturally this causes post-purchase dissonance: either the stylist must explain to the customer why the hairstyle will not work, or the stylist has to reproduce the hairstyle and handle the customer's disappointment.

Consumers may seek to reduce uncertainty by looking for guarantees from the service provider; unfortunately, since services are perishable and not reclaimable, the supplier is rarely able to recoup anything from a 'returned' service. This makes suppliers reluctant to offer money-back guarantees, and therefore the consumer would normally be faced with a greater level of uncertainty.

Purchase of a service differs slightly from purchase of a physical good. Figure 14. 4 illustrates the differences between the two.

The fact that the service is frequently not paid for until after it has been delivered and consumed means that the consumer is offered a considerable degree of reassurance. Also, because the service is being consumed as it is being produced, the supplier and the consumer have ample opportunity to confirm that what is being supplied is meeting the consumer's expectations.

This is why waiters will typically check with diners that their meals are OK; this reduces the risk that people will complain after the meal has been eaten.

Reducing the risk for the consumer will, of course, increase it for the supplier. Suppliers often have problems with customers who do not pay up on time, and it can be difficult for the supplier to recoup the loss; it is not possible to repossess a dinner for two or a haircut, and suing clients for non-payment of professional services such as accountancy can prove problematic, since the client can easily claim that the service was inadequate in some respect. Service industries tend to lose more money this way than physical product suppliers lose through pilfering.

Involvement

Involvement is the perceived importance or personal relevance of an object or event (see Chapter 11). Because of the greater risks and uncertainty attached to purchase

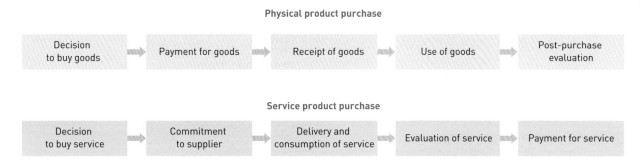

Figure 14.4   Comparison of purchase of physical products vs. services

of services, consumers are likely to become more involved with the service provider, and therefore more brand-loyal. In other words, having found a restaurant that provides a reliable meal in the right atmosphere, the individual will tend to keep returning there rather than risk going somewhere new.

This is particularly true in the case of personal services, such as hairdressing. Loyalty to the service provider is extremely strong, because of the personal contact necessary for carrying out the service, and typically extends beyond loyalty to the salon. The loyalty is usually extended to the actual hairstylist providing the service. In many cases, the relationship between the hairstylist and the customer becomes a lifetime one, only breaking down when the hairstylist retires. Figure 14.5 shows how involvement affects service purchase.

For comparison, consider how loyal the average motorist is to a car manufacturer. Despite car purchase being used by textbook authors as a prime example of a high-involvement purchase, most motorists will have tried several different manufacturers, and certainly many different models, over a lifetime's driving. It would be difficult for car manufacturers to find customers who always buy their brand, yet it has been fairly straightforward for Frizzell Insurance to find a group of customers who have always insured their cars through them. Frizzell has successfully used these customers in advertising campaigns.

This is true of most services, from restaurants to banking. Consumers are reluctant to switch bank accounts, even when problems become apparent with their current bankers; likewise people will tend to use the same lawyer rather than switch. For this reason, lawyers tend to operate from practices large enough to accommodate the various specialist functions (family law, criminal law, conveyancing, etc.) because the client who originally came to the firm for a house purchase is likely to return when he needs to be defended on a drunk-driving charge, or needs to sue somebody for a debt.

Likewise, although people will readily switch brands of baked beans in order to take advantage of sales promotions, they will buy the beans from their usual supermarket. This is because the consumer knows where everything is in the supermarket, knows what the store's policy is on returned goods, knows which credit cards are acceptable, knows what the store's own brands are like, and so forth. Supermarkets worldwide encourage this by the use of loyalty cards.

Figure 14.5   Services and involvement

Consumer behaviour in action: Endsleigh Insurance

Anybody who has ever been a student in the UK is familiar with Endsleigh Insurance. The company specialises in the specific needs of students, who are often living away from home for the first time, in shared accommodation, surrounded by strangers who may have less than honest backgrounds. Generations of students have had good reason to be grateful to Endsleigh when their rooms have been burgled, or their stereo equipment, guitar, laptop or mobile phone has mysteriously disappeared. Endsleigh also offer travel insurance for backpacking, car insurance for old bangers, cover for studying abroad and bicycle insurance.

What many people are less aware of is that Endsleigh will continue to look after their customers long after the graduation ceremony. Endsleigh look to establish a lifetime relationship with their customers – a sensible move in view of the fact that graduates earn more than people without degrees, and will therefore typically drive more expensive cars, live in more valuable houses and own more possessions – especially the portable possessions beloved by thieves.

Endsleigh therefore offer winter sports insurance, multi-trip travel insurance including business travel, very high-value home and contents insurance, and extreme activities cover. In fact, everything the rising young executive needs in terms of insurance.

Endsleigh retain a high proportion of their former student customers: after all, if the service has been good and the costs reasonable, why go elsewhere? Starting by servicing the student community has proved to be a very successful strategy: Endsleigh now employs over 1000 people throughout the UK and is one of Britain's best-known insurers. Additionally, the company has carved out a market among people who are not only well-off, but are also less likely to make a claim – which is insurance heaven!

EPOS Electronic point of sale

The reason for this is not that the supermarkets have suddenly become aware of the involvement phenomenon, but rather that the technology of EPOS (electronic point-of-sale) equipment has become sophisticated enough to handle the amount of data involved. Supermarkets are able to keep complete records of each customer's buying pattern and act accordingly; for example, it would be quite feasible in future to remind customers at the checkout that they are running low on, say, tomato ketchup – and to know the brand and size that the customer usually buys (Evans 1994). In fact, although the technology to do this already exists, it is unlikely to happen because consumers are likely to regard it as an unwarranted invasion of privacy (Patterson et al. 1997).

Sales promotion

Promotion schemes for services are therefore somewhat problematic; customers are less likely to switch merely because of a temporary price reduction or 'special offer'. It is possible, as we have seen, to encourage existing customers to stay (and in fact this is likely to be the most cost-effective way of doing business, as it is in the case of physical products) but it is harder to bring in new customers.

Typically, service providers focus on problems they have identified with the competition. For example, some bank customers feel strongly about banks who invest in countries with oppressive regimes; the Co-Operative Bank has been able to capitalise on this by promising that they will never do so. In this case the bank is playing off one involvement (with the customer's existing bank) against another (the customer's involvement with a social cause).

Likewise, First Direct (a subsidiary of HSBC) has based its entire existence on the fact that most working people cannot get to a bank during normal banking hours; the bank has made deep inroads into the personal banking sector by offering 24-hour telephone and Internet banking.

Many service providers make good use of the consumer's need to belong by offering 'club' membership. This ranges from the 'exclusive flight deals' offered by RCI, the timeshare exchange company, through to the 'Friends of the Theatre' benefits offered by some theatres and theatrical companies. Museums and galleries often offer season tickets, as (of course) do transport services such as trains and buses.

Perhaps the biggest phenomenon in loyalty schemes for regular customers is the frequent-flyer programmes, which began in the USA during the late 1970s and early 1980s. Following the deregulation of US airspace, many companies sprang up to compete with the majors; routes were no longer the exclusive province of the big airlines, and government-sanctioned monopolies no longer applied, with the result that fierce price wars broke out. Airlines that had previously not had to compete at all in any real sense suddenly found themselves scrambling for business; the result was a burgeoning frequent-flyer programme, by which airlines gave free flights to loyal customers.

This type of programme now exists among all the world's major airlines, and usually also covers 'associate' airlines; for example, 26 airlines have formed the Star Alliance, which now operates almost 17,000 flights every day. The member airlines do not compete on the same routes, but they do operate a single frequent-flyer programme so that flights on one airline can contribute to free flights on another. This ensures that customers flying with any of those airlines can still obtain frequent-flyer points for the entire journey, so that the airline prevents competitors from offering a more comprehensive route coverage and thus luring customers away. Each airline benefits, since they don't compete directly with each other; also the small airlines have a better chance of surviving in an industry dominated by the big players.

This type of loyalty programme should be distinguished from promotions such as Avios (formerly Airmiles). Since Avios can be collected from a large number of outlets and suppliers, they cannot be considered as a loyalty programme; the Avios scheme is intended as a sales promotion exercise, to persuade customers to use one supplier rather than another.

Service levels

The service level refers to the degree to which the customer's needs are met. For example, an airline might aim for a service-level criterion of ensuring that 95% of flights arrive within ten minutes of the scheduled time. Or perhaps a pizza delivery service might guarantee that pizzas will be delivered within thirty minutes, or the pizza is free. (This particular type of guarantee was outlawed in Dublin because it resulted in too many road accidents caused by over-hasty pizza delivery drivers.)

The UK government's efforts to establish Citizen's Charters for various government departments is an example of trying to improve service levels. In effect, there has been a recognition that taxpayers are actually paying for a service, and Her Majesty's Revenue and Customs, DSS, National Health and other departments are there to provide that service. Clearly it cannot always be the case that the service is provided to the complete satisfaction of the client (nobody is happy to pay the revenue department) but at least the service can be run in a sympathetic way that minimises inconvenience to the customer.

Here are some examples of firms seeking to raise service levels:

- Aurora Energy of Tasmania will pay $80 to anyone who experiences more than 12 power cuts in a year, or whose power stays off for more than 12 hours.
- Tesco supermarkets guarantee that if there is one other person in front of you they will open another checkout, unless all the checkouts are open already.

Service level The target a firm sets for providing customer satisfaction through intangible benefits

- Virgin Trains will provide vouchers to the value of 25% of the fare if the train is delayed for more than an hour, and will refund the fare in full if the train is delayed for more than two hours.
- Post Office Counters guarantee that 95% of clients will be dealt with within five minutes.

The decision about service levels will depend mainly on economic factors and the value-for-money perception of the clients. This reverts back to the problem examined earlier, that clients will often pay more for a service because they believe that this will mean, in itself, that they will get a better service; disappointment may creep in afterwards. Put another way, someone who is paying £250 a night to stay in a five-star hotel will expect the room service to be comprehensive, polite and prompt. The same person staying in Mrs Boggins' Bed and Breakfast for £50 a night will not expect any room service at all. Conversely, small B&B guest houses have a reputation for providing a good, filling, old-fashioned British breakfast, and guests will be expecting this as part of the service.

The service level must relate to something that the customer feels is important. A supermarket that ensures that shopping trolleys are returned to the pick-up point within ten minutes of the previous customer abandoning them at the other end of the car park is unlikely to be of much help to the customer. Guaranteeing never to be out of stock of certain essential items is probably far more relevant.

Likewise, the service level set must be within the firm's powers to achieve. Guaranteeing sunshine for a holidaymaker clearly is beyond the control of a tour operator (but a cash rebate for every day when the sun doesn't shine is within the supplier's control, and might be highly relevant). Factors in setting service levels are shown in Figure 14.6.

It is important to understand here that the service level must be appropriate to meet expectations, not at the maximum. A consumer paying a low price will be expecting drawbacks: people who are prepared to pay only the lowest prices for

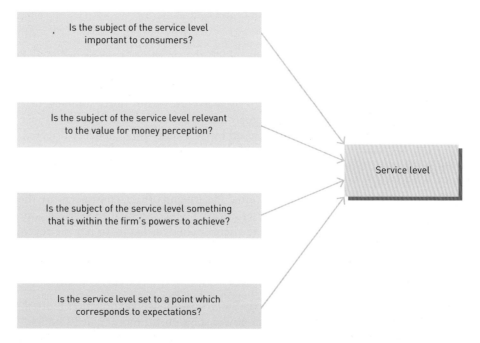

Figure 14.6   Factors in setting service levels

services do not expect to be looked after very well, and may become suspicious if the service is too good. In other words, it is possible to make your customers think that there must be a catch somewhere.

The early experience of Safeway Supermarkets in the UK markets bore this out. In the USA, Safeway (in common with most other supermarkets) employ packers to pack customers' purchases into carrier bags, and even carry the bags to the customer's car (usually in the expectation of a tip). There is no charge for this service. When Safeway entered the UK market, the company followed the same practice, but UK shoppers (who are not used to this level of service) became suspicious and assumed that the shop's prices must be higher in order to pay for the higher service level. Safeway was sold to Morrison's in 2004 and the brand no longer exists in the UK – needless to say, Morrisons do not employ packers.

Likewise, customers shopping at discount stores such as Lidl expect that the goods will be less attractively displayed and that the checkout queues will be longer. The store management deliberately keep the surroundings less attractive than the mainstream supermarkets so that the customer's perception is that the prices must be much lower. Aldi, on the other hand, maintain a pleasant shopping environment while still keeping prices extra-low; this may, in the long run, prove counter-productive as it runs counter to the common perception.

To sum up this section, the main decision criteria regarding service levels are as follows:

1 The service level must relate to a benefit the customer feels is important.
2 The service level must be achievable.
3 The service level must be appropriate rather than optimal.

Handling dissonance

Of course, sometimes things go wrong and the customer is not happy with what has been provided. In other words, what was delivered is not what was expected, and the service provider has to attempt to make amends in some way. Following on from a service failure, people adopt coping strategies: service recovery (which means going back to the supplier and trying to obtain redress), re-evaluation of the brand's trust-worthiness, apportioning blame or re-interpreting the brand in terms of stereotypes (Chung and Beverland 2006). For example, someone who has had a disappointing service from a builder might ask the builder to come back and do the work again, might decide that the builder is not very good or reliable, might blame the poor work on the pre-existing state of the building or might simply decide that modern builders are not the craftsmen their fathers and grandfathers were.

As we have seen in Chapter 13, consumers will tend to express their dissatisfaction in one of three ways (Singh 1988):

1 Voice responses, in which the customer comes back and complains.
2 Private responses, which would include telling friends about the poor service.
3 **Third-party** responses, such as taking legal action.

The majority of service providers try to ensure that this does not happen, by using the following methods:

1 Explaining the service in great detail beforehand and explaining what the possible drawbacks might be.
2 Checking with the client during the provision of the service that everything is satisfactory.

Voice response **A type** of complaint in which the complainer returns to the supplier to seek redress

Private response Complaining behaviour directed at friends or acquaintances rather than at the perpetrator of the problem

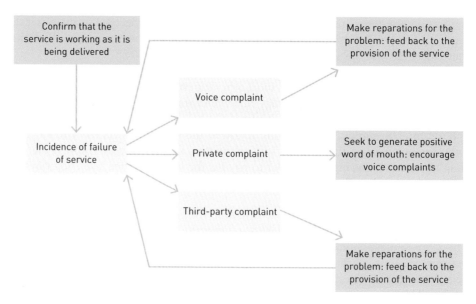

Figure 14.7   Complaint routes and damage limitation

An example of the first type of dissonance-reduction technique would be the initial consultation with a lawyer regarding a court case; the lawyer will typically warn the client that the outcome of any court case cannot be guaranteed, that the client may incur substantial court (and lawyer) costs without actually winning the case, that the opposition may come up with some line of defence (or attack, as the case may be) which is unanticipated, and so forth.

An example of the second approach would be in an aircraft first-class cabin, where the flight attendants check regularly with the passengers to ensure that all is well. This approach is often used where the service is carried out over a period of time where the client is present throughout the service provision: medical procedures, air travel, hairdressing, beauty treatments, etc.

It is always worthwhile checking that the client fully understands what is being provided, whether the supplier is a doctor explaining the prognosis for a surgical operation or a waiter explaining that the dish being ordered is extra-spicy. This is why detailed descriptions of ingredients, and even the cooking instructions, are usually given on restaurant menus. All these approaches are shown diagrammatically in Figure 14.7.

Even so, things can go wrong, sometimes because the variability of the service leads to a failure to provide the service at the level expected. Even the service provider can be surprised at the outcome in these cases.

The remedy has, of course, to fit the circumstances. Because the customer's loss falls into two categories, loss of the service and consequential loss, it may be necessary to lay down specific rules beforehand to limit the supplier's liability. For example, transport companies such as bus companies limit their liability to the price of the ticket to avoid being asked for compensation for missed meetings and lost theatre tickets.

Services fall into the following categories, for the purpose of correcting complaints:

1 Services where it is appropriate to offer a repeat service or a voucher. Examples are dry cleaners, domestic appliance repairers and takeaway food outlets.
2 Services where giving the money back will usually be sufficient. Examples here would be retail shops, cinemas and theatres, and film rental companies.
3 Services where consequential losses (those that go beyond the fees paid) may have to be compensated for. Examples would be medical services, solicitors and hairdressers.

Challenging the status quo

Obviously no company can guarantee that things will never go wrong. The question is, where do we draw the line and decide on liability? Naturally the customer will tend to think that liability lies with the supplier – but in the case of services, the product is so variable it would be almost impossible for a supplier to be able to guarantee anything.

Hence the small print. But who ever reads the small print? Who among us actually reads the Terms and Conditions before we tick the box saying that we have read the Terms and Conditions? Any of us? And even if we did read them, how much sense would they make, given that they are usually written in obscure legal language?

The bottom line is whether the supplier and the customer can agree between them whose fault it is when something goes pear-shaped: standing on the strict letter of the small print might be legal, but it isn't necessarily good business! So we're back to finding some way of drawing a line, of negotiating an agreement about liability and of (ultimately) dumping the small print!

The above categorisations are not necessarily exclusive, in the sense that (in most cases) giving disappointed theatre-goers their money back is sufficient, but sometimes they may sue for travelling costs (or even for injury, in the event of an accident during a performance). For this reason, service providers usually carry public-liability insurance, and the third category of service providers usually also have professional liability insurance which covers for consequential losses.

Unlike compensation for the failure of a physical product, it is often difficult to quantify an appropriate level of compensation for a failed service. For example, if a new iPod breaks down in the first week it can be replaced with an identical model or the customer's money can be returned. If, however, a perm is not quite tight enough for the client, a repeat service may not be possible (due to the risk of over-processing the hair) and clearly the service is only a partial failure. In this case, returning the money may be an over-compensation, but still something needs to be done. In an extreme case, where (for example) a hairdressing client's scalp is damaged permanently by chemicals, substantial compensation might be ordered by a court, or (more likely) paid out by the hairdresser's insurers. These situations require careful judgement as to the degree of the client's dissatisfaction, and the best way of compensating the client; this will often require some skilful negotiation, and will be best carried out by somebody with a high level of authority.

Because service provision relies heavily on word of mouth, it is even more important that complaints are dealt with to the complete satisfaction of the customer than would be the case with physical products. As with physical products, consumers tend to be more prone to use negative word of mouth than positive word of mouth, but complaints correctly handled will generate more positive word of mouth than will a good service in itself. This means that a dissatisfied customer who is pleased with the compensation offered will be more likely to speak positively of the service provider than would a customer whose expectations had been met in the first place. (See Chapter 13 for a more complete discussion of post-purchase dissonance.)

For this reason it is important to ensure that dissatisfied customers voice their dissatisfaction, and the service provider answers the problem effectively. Airlines, tour operators and theatres frequently ask consumers to fill in market research questionnaires to determine satisfaction levels for various aspects of the service provision, but this is somewhat harder to do for restaurants and personal services; here it is more usual to rely on discussion between the service provider and the customer, rather than formal research.

Summary

This chapter has been about consumer attitudes towards service provision. Although there is some debate in academic circles about the differences between physical products and services, and whether the differences are real enough to alter marketing strategy, there are distinct differences in approach as far as consumers are concerned. Products that have a high service component will almost always engender a different approach in terms of customer behaviour, if only because the risk element is higher: this necessitates a different approach from suppliers.

Key points

- A service is as much a product as is a physical item, even though it can't be handled; this is because a service provides a bundle of benefits to the consumer, in exchange for payment.
- Services may be the only products in existence, with customers co-creating service value through the use of physical products.
- Consumers rely much more on word of mouth when choosing services, and will be more prone to using word of mouth after purchasing a service – whether to praise or condemn.
- Consumer risk is greater when buying a service than when buying a physical product, particularly as regards consequential losses.
- Some of this risk is reduced because consumers usually pay for services after consuming them.
- Consumers tend to be more loyal to service providers than to physical product suppliers, because there is often greater involvement.
- Sales promotion schemes tend to focus on comparisons with the competition, rather than on 'money off' deals.
- Service levels need to be appropriate, not optimal.
- Dissonance can be reduced by careful prior explanation of the service, and by monitoring during consumption.
- It is worthwhile encouraging customers to express dissatisfaction, rather than waiting for them to use word of mouth to damage your business.

Review questions

1   What are the main problems in establishing appropriate service levels?
2   What is the basis of service-dominant logic?
3   Why is purchasing a service more risky than purchasing a physical product?
4   How can service providers reduce risk for customers?
5   What is the role of involvement in service purchases?
6   What is the role of word of mouth in service purchases?
7   How can a professional service provider such as a lawyer or accountant improve customers' perception of service quality?
8   Why has services marketing become more important in recent years?
9   Why are people important to the service experience?
10 How can service providers minimise post-purchase dissonance?

Case study revisited: Steiner salons

For many people, going on a cruise represents the ultimate in luxury. The food is excellent, there are staff available to wait on passengers and supply their every need, and it is an opportunity (all too rare for most of us) to feel pampered and cosseted. For most women, and not a few men, having a spa treatment, a hairdo and a make-up session is the ultimate in pampering, not to mention that cruise ships are often very elegant – one is expected to dress for dinner and look one's best, so having one's face made up and one's hair done is an essential before dining at the captain's table.

Training is the basis of all quality services, and Steiner operates its own beauty schools across the United States. This enables them to spot talent early, and to ensure that the beauticians and hairdressers aboard Steiner ships and in Steiner salons are the best available. The schools also train beauticians for other salons – Steiner is not afraid of competition.

Steiner's own staff training programme includes training for specific salon themes on board the ships. For example, Princess Cruises has an Asian-themed spa brand, Lotus, and staff will need to be trained to understand the brand (and will wear the appropriate uniform). Because cruise ships vary in size, some will have a wider range of facilities than others, so staff need to be trained for specific ships since they may need to deal with different equipment or treatments. Because the company is global, staff also need to be qualified according to local licensing regulations.

From the viewpoint of the clients of Steiner salons on board, there is reassurance in knowing that the brand is global, and also land-based. This means that complaints (if any) can be taken to a shore spa if necessary. Most women remain fiercely loyal to their hairdresser, so knowing that one is dealing with a global, very professional company is important if one is submitting to some very personal, even invasive treatments.

Ultimately, Steiner is in the business of making women feel good. This is a must-have service for a cruise liner, and Steiner has carved out a niche for itself in the business: women trust the company, and the cruise line companies know that Steiner will provide a top-class service to their passengers. As in all services, trust and confidence are everything, and Steiner has that with both customers and cruise lines.

Case study: Barclays' Premier Account

Barclays is a worldwide bank headquartered in the UK. During the 1970s and 1980s banks in Britain began to offer free current accounts – customers would not be charged for any banking services provided their accounts remained in credit. This concept quickly caught on, and all banks were forced (through competition) to offer free banking.

This, of course, created a problem because banks do have to show a profit, and most people do not keep enough in their current accounts to enable the banks to lend it out for enough to cover the costs of operating banking services. This meant that borrowers would have to pay more for credit, and at the same time the banks would need to make money from selling other financial services products such as insurance, credit cards, pension plans, capital management services and so forth. Naturally, this placed pressure on bank staff to meet targets, which in turn led to competitive pressures and sometimes to mis-selling of products, where staff sold unsuitable products to some customers in order to make their sales quotas. Eventually this led to investigations by regulatory bodies – pretty much all banks were criticised for mis-selling, and ordered to pay compensation to customers.

Barclays has always considered itself to be an ethical bank, so a new approach needed to be found. The bank has always been at the sharp end of new ideas: Barclays introduced the UK's first credit card in 1966, and the world's first ATM in 1967. In 1987 Barclays introduced Connect, the UK's first debit card, and in 2004 the bank took over sponsorship of the Premier League football competition. The next new idea was the establishment of the Premier bank account.

The Premier Account is a paid-for bank account which bundles a large number of benefits together. Premier Account holders pay a subscription which covers all bank charges, plus benefits such as worldwide travel insurance, UK and European car breakdown cover, 'gadget' insurance for mobile telephones, computers etc., access to executive lounges at airports, extended warranties for household appliances, and many more financial service products. For some people, the package contains items that will never be of any use; for others, the package represents a substantial saving on paying for the individual products separately. For example, a subscription of £17 a month which contains breakdown cover provided by the Royal Automobile Club (normally around £100 a year), worldwide travel insurance (around £120 a year) and European breakdown cover (around £60 a year) works out as a bargain, without taking account of all the other benefits that are available.

Of course, not all the benefits are worthwhile for everyone. Someone who rarely travels will not need the travel insurance, someone who doesn't drive outside the UK will not need Continental breakdown cover, and so forth. This was seen as opening the door to potential accusations of mis-selling: signing someone up for a lot of benefits that are of no use would sound suspiciously like some of the unethical practices banks had been accused of in the past. So in 2012 Barclays introduced the Features Store, which allowed people to bundle only those services which they really needed. Now, customers pay a basic £10 a month for the Premier Account (which already has built-in features such as a Premier Account bank manager, priority treatment in bank branches, a special debit card and loans at preferential rates) and add on just the extras they want, for an extra fee.

Other banks also have their own equivalents of premier banking, but so far no one has gone as far as Barclays in customising the packages. In August 2012, the new chairman of Barclays, Sir David Walker, said that he agreed 'in principle' with the idea that banks should return to charging for operating current accounts. This provoked an angry backlash from the public – message forums were scathing in their rebuke of Sir David, presumably because most of them could not remember a time before so-called 'free' banking. The problem is, of course, that no bank wants to make the first move towards charging their customers. At least premier banking is a voluntary option that might provide a way forward.

Questions

1 Why would someone prefer to buy worldwide travel insurance from the bank rather than direct from the insurer?
2 What prevents banks from charging for current accounts?
3 What are the main benefits of the Features Store?
4 How might other banks respond to Barclays' initiative?
5 What is the effect of the mis-selling scandal on Barclays' strategy?

Further reading

For a textbook on services marketing, you could do a lot worse than Valerie A. Zeithaml, Mary Jo Bitner and Dwayne D. Gremler's *Services Marketing* (New York: McGraw-Hill, 2008). Zeithaml and Bitner have researched and written about services marketing for over thirty years, and are undoubtedly among the world's experts on the subject.

Music consumption has become a hot topic in marketing lately. For a starter (or should that be an overture?), try Larsen, G., Lawson, R. and Todd, S. (2010) The symbolic consumption of music. *Journal of Marketing Management* 26 (7/8): 671–85.

For a look at how organisational culture affects service quality, you might like Ifie, K., Jayawardhena, C. and Cadogan, J.W. (2010) The organisational culture antecedents of service delivery. European Marketing Academy Annual Conference, Copenhagen, June. This is a conference paper, so you may have to hunt around a bit to find it, but it gives a concise account of culture and service delivery.

For an interesting view of how service-dominant logic affects strategic planning components, see Rondell, Jimmie and Sorhammer, David (2010) Functional identities, resource integrators and the service-dominant logic. *Journal of Customer Behaviour* 9 (1): 19–36.

If you would like to know more about service-dominant logic, you need to go to the source. Robert Lusch and Stephen Vargo have co-edited *The Service Dominant Logic of Marketing: Dialogue, Debate and Directions* (New York: M.E. Sharpe, 2006). Although it is probably due for a new edition, this book provides an excellent overview of the issues surrounding service-dominant logic, and shows how the academic debate is developing.

References

Chung, E. and Beverland, M. (2006) An exploration of consumer forgiveness following marketer transgressions. *Advances in Consumer Research* 33: 98–9.

Clarke, J.R. (2006) Different to 'dust collectors'? The giving and receiving of experience gifts. *Journal of Consumer Behaviour* 5 (Nov–Dec): 533–49.

Evans, M. (1994) Domesday marketing? *Journal of Marketing Management* 10 (5): 409–31.

Patterson, M., O'Malley, L. and Evans, M.J. (1997) Database marketing: investigating privacy concerns. *Journal of Marketing Communications* 3 (3): 151–74.

Singh, J. (1988) Consumer complaint intentions and behavior: definitions and taxonomical issues. *Journal of Marketing* 52: 93–107.

Vargo, S.L. and Lusch, R.F. (2004) Evolving to a new dominant logic for marketing. *Journal of Marketing* 68 (Jan): 1–17.

Vargo, S.L. and Lusch, R.F. (2008) Service-dominant logic: continuing the evolution. *Journal of the Academy of Marketing Science* 36: 1–10.

More online

To gain free access to additional online resources to support this chapter please visit: **www.sagepub.co.uk/blythe**

CHAPTER 15

Organisational buying behaviour

LEARNING OBJECTIVES

After reading this chapter you should be able to:

- Explain the pressures that influence industrial buyers.

- Explain the role of the decision-making unit.

- Describe the main factors that influence industrial buyers.

- Explain the role of customers in driving the reseller market.

- Describe approaches to government markets.

- Explain how to approach institutional markets.

- Show how industrial markets can be divided.

- Describe the different types of buying situation, and the factors that are involved for making buying decisions within those situations.

- Understand the role of team selling in industrial markets.

Introduction

Organisational buyers are often supposed to be more rational and less emotional than when they are buying items for consumption by their friends and family. However, it would be wrong to assume that organisational buying is always entirely rational: those responsible for making buying decisions within organisations are still human beings, and do not leave their emotions at the door when they come to work, so it seems unrealistic to suppose that they do not have some emotional or irrational input in their decision-making.

Businesses, government departments, charities and other organisational purchasers actually represent the bulk of marketing activities, yet much of the attention in marketing is focused on business-to-consumer markets rather than on business-to-business markets. The reasons for this are obscure, but may have much to do with the fact that we are all consumers and can therefore relate more easily to consumer marketing issues.

This chapter looks at the ways organisational buyers make decisions, and also at some of the influences buyers are subject to.

Case study: Moda

Every year, the National Exhibition Centre in Birmingham hosts the UK's biggest fashion show, Moda. It is open to trade visitors only – no curious members of the public allowed – and it encompasses the five main branches of the fashion industry: menswear, women's fashions, lingerie and swimwear, footwear, and accessories.

Exhibitors display over 1400 brands during the three days of the show, and there are regular catwalk shows from major labels and new brands. What's more, Moda organises seminars from leading industry experts so that buyers can update their knowledge of the business as a whole.

In 2012 the exhibition ran while the Olympic Games were being held in London. This was an excellent time for many of the buyers, since travelling in and out of London was made much more difficult by the huge numbers of visitors to the Games. As a result, many Londoners tried to find ways of avoiding working in the city wherever possible: for a fashion buyer from a West End store, Moda provided the perfect excuse.

For exhibitors, Moda is almost a must-do. It would certainly look odd if a supplier did not have a stand at Moda – and there are advantages to be had in terms of meeting buyers from all over the UK and indeed the rest of the world. With 1400 exhibitors attending, it would be easy to get lost in the crowd, so the Moda website has a system built in for visitors to research exhibitors before attending the exhibitions. Visitors are able to click through quickly to exhibitors' websites and contact them beforehand to make an appointment to visit the stand. This is a major time-saver for buyers, who typically only have one day at the exhibition and may want to see perhaps a dozen potential suppliers.

Since exhibitions are always funded by the exhibitors (even though they are presumably of great benefit to buyers as well) the exhibitors need to feel confident that their money is being well spent. Moda, like all other exhibition organisers, seeks to reassure potential exhibitors by using phrases such as 'meet the best buyers' and 'buyers flocking to Birmingham'. Research shows that it isn't quite as simple as that – many buyers are just on information-gathering expeditions, or have sent the office junior to collect brochures. Having said that, exhibitors really have little choice – not being there would send entirely the wrong signals.

How to impress your examiner

Industrial buyer behaviour is not always included in consumer behaviour courses, but there are parallels between the ways consumers meet their needs and the ways buyers make decisions. If you are asked about industrial buying behaviour, it is worth remembering that buyers are also human beings – they are as affected by emotion and 'gut feeling' as anyone else, but need to keep this in control in the working environment. Using parallels from family decision-making will show that you understand the issues.

The decision-making unit

It is rare for a business purchasing decision to be made by only one person. Even in a small business it is likely that several people would have some input into the buying process at some stage or another. Because of this, the decision-making process often becomes formalised, with specific parts of the process being carried out by members of the decision-making unit (DMU), so that roles and responsibilities are shared. The DMU, also called the buying centre, often cannot be identified on the company organisation chart because it varies in make-up from one buying situation to another. Individuals may participate for only a brief time, for a specific buying decision, or alternatively may be part of the group right through the process from beginning to end.

The decision-making unit is generally thought to contain the following categories of member (Webster and Wind, 1972):

- Initiators. These are the individuals who first recognise the problem.
- Gatekeepers. These individuals control the flow of knowledge, either by being proactive in collecting information, or by filtering it. They could be junior staff members who are perhaps given the task to research potential suppliers of a particular component, or a receptionist or personal assistant who sees his or her role as being to prevent salespeople from 'wasting' the decision-maker's time.
- Buyers. These individuals are given the task of making the actual purchase. Often this is merely a case of completing the administrative tasks necessary for buying, but it is likely to involve finding suitable suppliers and negotiating the final deal. Buyers usually work to a specific brief, and may have very little autonomy, even though they may be the only contact a supplier's salespeople have at the purchasing organisation.
- Deciders. These are the people who make the final decisions, and may be senior managers or specialists. They may never meet any representatives of the supplying companies. Deciders generally rely on advice from other members of the DMU, so they are influenced strongly by gatekeepers.
- Users. These are people who will be using the products that are being purchased: they may be engineers or technicians, or even the cleaning staff who use cleaning products. Their opinions may well be sought by the deciders, and in many cases the users are also the initiators.
- Influentials. These people have direct contact with the deciders, and are often asked for advice. They are trusted advisers, but from the supplying company's viewpoint they are extremely difficult to identify. Influentials may be employees of the purchasing firm (for example, engineers, information systems managers or research managers) or they may be consultants (for example, architects, health and safety consultants, or business advisers such as lawyers and accountants). An influential might even be the decider's best friend, tennis partner or favourite uncle.

The relationships are summarised in Figure 15.1.

These categories are not, of course, mutually exclusive. A user might also be an influential, or a gatekeeper might also be an initiator. The categories were originally developed to explain purchasing within families – which may be an example of the apparent similarities between business-to-business marketing and consumer marketing.

Members of the decision-making unit are, of course, human beings so they are affected both by rational and emotional motivations. Buyers are affected by their liking or dislike for the suppliers' sales representatives, and often buyers have their own work agendas, for example seeking a promotion, or feeling threatened in terms of job security, or even conducting a vendetta with a colleague. Any of these influences

Decision-making unit A group of people who influence, control or carry out purchasing activities

Buying centre See *Decision-making unit*

Initiators The members of a decision-making unit who first identify a need

Gatekeepers People who control the flow of information to a decision-making unit

Buyers Those with the responsibility of making the actual purchase of a product, often (in the industrial context) working to a specific brief

Deciders Members of a decision-making unit who have responsibility for making a final purchase decision

Users Those members of a buying group who will actually make use of a product (not necessarily consumers)

Influentials People who are respected for their opinions and lifestyles, and who therefore inform purchase behaviour

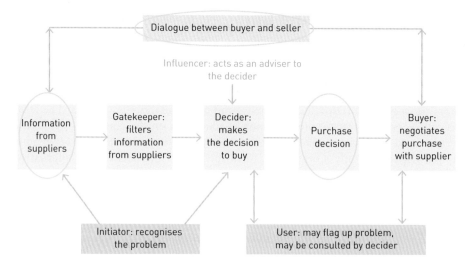

Figure 15.1   Relationships in the DMU

might affect the buyers' behaviour, but all of them would be difficult or impossible for a supplier's salesperson to identify correctly and act upon.

Members of a decision-making unit are likely to be more risk-averse than consumers because they have more to lose in the event of a wrong decision: for a consumer, the main risk is financial, but even that is limited since most retailers will replace or refund goods purchased in error. For industrial purchasers a serious mistake can result in major negative consequences for the business as well as embarrassment in front of colleagues, loss of possible promotion, or even losing one's job if the mistake is a big enough one. The professional persona of the industrial buyer is liable to be compromised by purchasing errors, which in turn means that the buyer will feel a loss of self-esteem.

Depending on the purchasing situation, the relative power of each member of the DMU will be different. This makes it hard to know what each member's influence will be on any specific decision. Ronchetto et al. (1989) identify the following characteristics of individuals who will probably exert the most influence in a DMU:

- important in the corporate and departmental hierarchy
- close to the organisational boundary
- central to the workflow
- active in cross-departmental communications
- directly linked to senior management.

Fairly obviously, buyers are most important in repetitive purchases while the managing director and other senior management will only become involved in unique, expensive or very risky buying decisions.

Because industrial buyers are likely to suffer from risk more than would be the case for consumers, they use a variety of risk-reducing tactics (Hawes and Barnhouse 1987). These are as follows, and are presented in order of importance:

1 Visit the premises of the potential supplier to observe its viability.
2 Talk to existing customers of the supplier about their experience with the supplier.

3 Multisource the order (buy the same component or materials from several suppliers) to ensure a backup source of supply.
4 Insert penalty clauses in the supplier's contract.
5 Ask colleagues about the potential supplier.
6 In choosing a supplier, favour firms that your company has done business with in the past.
7 Confirm that senior management are in favour of using the supplier.
8 Limit the search for, and ultimate choice of, a potential supplier to well-known firms only.
9 Obtain the opinion of a majority of your colleagues that the chosen supplier is satisfactory.

Influences on buyers

Buyers are affected by individual, personal factors as well as environmental and organisational factors. Personally they are subject to many of the same influences on the buying decision that consumers have: the desire to play a role, for example, may cause a buyer to be difficult to negotiate with as he or she tries to drive a hard bargain. The desire for respect and liking may cause a buyer to want to give the order to a salesperson who is exceptionally pleasant or helpful, and to deny the order to a salesperson who is regarded as being unpleasant or pushy. Business buyers are likely to be affected by some or all of the following environmental influences (Loudon and Della Bitta 1993) which are summarised in Figure 15.2:

- *Physical influences.* The location of the purchasing firm relative to its suppliers may be decisive, since many firms prefer to source supplies locally. This is especially true in global markets, where a purchasing company may wish to support local suppliers, or may prefer to deal with people from the same cultural background. In many cases, buyers seem reluctant to source from outside their own national boundaries, even when cost and quality considerations mean that the foreign supplier would be better.
- *Technological influences.* The level of technological development available among local suppliers will affect what the buyer is able to obtain, but also the

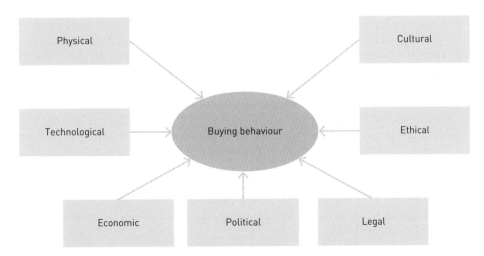

Figure 15.2 Environmental influences on buyer behaviour

technology of the buyer and the seller must be compatible. International technical standards remain very different for most products, which means that cross-border sourcing can be complex. Despite efforts within the European Union to harmonise technical standards, Europe still does not have standardised electrical fittings, plumbing fittings or even computer keyboards. For this reason, European firms often find it easy to trade with former colonies thousands of miles away simply because the technical standards are identical.

- *Economic influences.* These divide into the macro-economic environment (which is concerned with the level of demand in the economy, and with the current taxation regime within the buyer's country) and the micro-economic environment, which is about the firm's current financial health. Obviously the state of the company finances dictates buyers' budgets for good or ill. Macro-economic conditions can affect buyers' ability to buy goods as well as the firm's need for raw materials: if demand is low, demand for raw materials will also be low. On a more subtle level, the macro-economic climate affects the buyer's confidence in the same way as it affects consumer confidence. For example, a widespread belief that the national economy is booming will encourage buyers to commit to major investments in stock, equipment and machinery. In a global context, the fact that countries enter and leave recessions at different times will affect the timing of marketing efforts on the part of vendors.

- *Political influences.* Governments frequently pass laws to regulate businesses, particularly in international trade. Trade sanctions, trade barriers (both tariff and non-tariff), preferred-nation status and so forth all affect the ways in which buyers are permitted or encouraged to buy. In some cases, governments help businesses as part of an economic growth package; in other cases, international agreements prevent them from doing so. The political stability of countries also affects the risk level of doing business with suppliers – a revolution in a supplying country can disrupt business for a long period.

- *Legal influences.* Laws may lay down specific technical standards that affect buyer decisions. Buyers may be compelled to incorporate safety features into products, or may be subject to legal restrictions in buying some raw materials. Often, suppliers can obtain competitive advantage by anticipating changes in the law. For example, in May 2007 a scandal regarding food additives broke when a Chinese company supplied animal feed containing melamine, a compound used in the manufacture of plastics. American pet food manufacturers incorporated the feed in their products, causing thousands of pets to die from kidney failure and other diseases. In fact, adding melamine to food products was banned in China only a few weeks after the supply had been made.

- *Ethical influences.* In general, buyers are expected to act at all times for the benefit of the organisation, not for personal gain. This means that, in most cultures, buyers are not allowed to accept bribes, for example. However, in some cultures bribery is built into normal business life, which leaves the vendor with a major ethical problem – refusing to give a bribe is likely to lose the business, but giving a bribe is probably unethical or illegal in the company's home country. The OECD Anti-Bribery Convention has now been widely adopted, so most companies would be breaking the law if they offer or accept bribes. As a general rule, buyers are likely to be highly suspicious of doing business with a salesperson who appears to be acting unethically – after all, if the salesperson is prepared to cheat his or her employer, he or she might be even more prepared to cheat the buyer.

- *Cultural influences.* When dealing internationally, cultural influences come to the forefront: in the UK it might be customary to offer a visitor a cup of tea or coffee, whereas in China it might be customary to offer food. Dim Sum originated as a way for Chinese businessmen to offer their visitors a symbolic meal, as a way of establishing rapport. There is evidence that national culture is less important than it once was, however; other barriers to international trade such as political issues, geographic distance and even time zone differences are often more important (Pressey and Selassie 2003). Within the national culture is the corporate culture, sometimes defined as 'the way we do things round here'. Corporate culture encompasses the strategic vision of the organisation, its ethical stance and its attitudes towards suppliers among other things. In addition, many businesspeople act in accordance with their professional culture (Terpstra and David 1991). Each of these will affect the way business is done.

Organisational factors derive from corporate culture, as well as from strategic decisions made by senior management within the firm. Organisational policies, procedures, structure, systems of rewards, authority, status and communication systems will all affect the ways buyers relate to salespeople. Figure 15.3 shows the main categories of organisational influence on buyers' behaviour.

Consumer behaviour in action: Lockheed

Lockheed is one of the world's largest aircraft manufacturers, conducting business throughout the world. Though primarily a military aircraft manufacturer (producing the F1-11 fighter and the Galaxy transport plane) Lockheed also produced the TriStar commercial aircraft until 1983, when the company left the commercial aircraft business permanently.

In 1976 Lockheed revealed that it had paid over $22 million in 'sales commissions' to foreign government officials, including $1 million to Prince Bernhard of the Netherlands, in exchange for placing orders with Lockheed. Although there was

some doubt at the time as to whether these were bribes or were payments extorted by officials under threat of cancelling orders, several senior Lockheed executives were forced to resign and a shocked US government passed legislation outlawing such practices even when they occurred outside the United States.

Unfortunately the legislation seems to have done little to prevent bribery from happening. Lockheed were fined in 1995 for bribing the Egyptian government, General Electric were fined for diverting funds from the Military Aid Program to finance the sale of aircraft engines to Israel, and in 2000 Boeing were fined for exporting arms to Turkey. It seems that the only way to do business in some countries is to pay 'commissions' or to 'grease the wheels' even if this does violate the law. In fact, the US government ignores even its own policies on the issue of corruption by continuing to give contracts to these companies – but of course they have little choice in practice, unless they took the bizarre step of placing defence contracts with foreign suppliers rather than with their own companies.

Ultimately, the morality of bribery is not in question, even in countries where it is rife. Bribery is immoral and in most cases illegal. It is damaging to business, to the countries where it happens, and to the people who give and accept the bribes. Yet it still goes on, because immediate gain often outweighs long-term disadvantages – especially when the stakes are as high as they are in the aircraft industry.

Challenging the status quo

The expansion of the European Union in 2004 was hailed (rightly) as a historic event, reuniting Europe peacefully for the first time in its long and bloody history. For business, the expansion was expected to bring great rewards in terms of bigger markets and greater choice of suppliers.

Yet many firms still preferred to deal with countries thousands of miles away, where the technical standards are the same. So why not create closer links with these countries? Why did Britain, for example, join the EU and reject its former empire just at the time when transportation costs had fallen dramatically? Surely the wider range of climate, availability of raw materials and greater diversity of the Commonwealth made it a better bet?

Or perhaps the Commonwealth countries (for the most part) are so poor that they have no choice but to sell to us anyway – and we need to ally ourselves with the rich rather than with the poor!

Figure 15.3   Organisational influences on buyer behaviour

Buying tasks differ greatly between firms, but may also differ significantly within firms. For example, the buying task for a supermarket clearly differs from that for a manufacturing company, since the supermarket intends to sell the vast majority of its purchases unchanged, whereas the manufacturer is largely concerned with sourcing components and raw materials. The supermarket has other, internal, variations in the buying task: buying canned goods will be totally different from buying fresh produce such as vegetables or fresh fish. Equally, the manufacturer will have a different approach when buying basic raw materials compared with buying components, and yet another set of approaches when buying lubricating oil or business services or new factory premises. The different purchasing tasks affect the buyer's thinking and negotiating approach, so firms will usually have separate buyers for each type of buying task.

Structure of the organisation falls into two categories: the formal structure is what shows on the organisation chart; the informal structure is the network of personal relationships that dictates staff behaviour in most cases. The formal organisation structure determines such issues as the degree of centralisation in purchasing decision-making, the degree to which buying decisions follow a formal procedure (i.e. how constrained by the rules the buyers are) and the degree of specialisation in buying for different purposes or different departments in the organisation.

The informal structure dictates such issues as rivalry between buyers, recognition by management, cooperation between buyers in maintaining each other's status in the eyes of the boss, and so forth. The maze of informal relationships can be extremely complex, especially for a salesperson observing it from the outside, and this complexity is likely to be crucial in the success or failure of key-account selling. In the global context, the informal structure is subject to many cultural influences – the Oriental concern with gaining or losing face, for example, can be a crucial factor in doing business. The informal structure is also the major factor in determining who will be the most important influentials in the decision-making unit; some colleagues' opinions may be regarded as more trustworthy than others, for example.

The organisation's technology base also affects the buyer's level of control over purchasing. For example, computer-controlled stock purchasing, particularly in a just-in-time purchasing environment, can limit the buyer's ability to negotiate deals and in many cases removes the buyer from the process altogether. Models for inventory control and price forecasting are also widely used by buyers, so that in many cases the negotiating process is virtually automated with little room for manoeuvre on the part of the buyer. If this is the case, the selling organisation needs to go beyond the buyer to the other members of the DMU in order to change the rules or find creative ways round them. Technology-minded companies are likely to use electronic communications systems (e-mail being only one example) to a greater extent than other firms; research shows that technology-mediated communications have a positive, direct effect on future intentions to buy, but of course this is still affected considerably by factors of trust and commitment (McDonald and Smith 2004). E-commerce in business-to-business marketing relies on the following factors (Claycomb et al. 2005):

- Compatibility with existing systems.
- Co-operative norms with customers.
- Lateral integration within the firm.
- Technocratic specialisation.
- Decentralisation of information technology.

The characteristics of the people involved in the organisation will determine the organisation culture, but will in any event control the interpretation of the rules under which the purchasing department operates. At senior management level, the character of the organisation is likely to be a function of the senior management, and in many cases the organisation's founder will have set his or her personality firmly on the

Challenging the status quo

We frequently hear about the global village, and about the convergence of cultures, and about a new world order in which we accept and understand each other's cultures. So why is it necessary to consider cultural issues when we are marketing products and services? Surely the goods themselves speak for themselves – does crude oil have a cultural value, or does a stamp mill have a cultural connotation?

Shouldn't buyers be prepared to accept and understand cultural differences? Otherwise how are we to do business? Or perhaps the buyers arrogantly believe that the sellers should adapt their approach to meet the buyers' culture – thus possibly missing out on getting the best deals for their organisations.

If we get clashes between corporate cultures within the same country, how much worse will the clashes be in globalised markets?

organisation's culture. Virgin is clearly an offshoot of Richard Branson's personality, as Bodyshop is an offshoot of Anita Roddick's.

Classifying business customers

A business customer is one who is buying on behalf of an organisation rather than buying for personal or family consumption. In everyday speech, we usually talk about organisations as the purchasers of goods, but of course this is not the case: business customers, in practice, are human beings who buy on behalf of organisations.

Organisations might be classified according to the types of buying and end-use they have for the products. Table 15.1 shows the commonly accepted classifications.

Table 15.1   Classification of buying organisations

Type of organisation	Description
Business and commercial organisations	These organisations buy goods that are used to make other goods, and also those items that are consumed in the course of running the organisation's business. These organisations buy foundation goods and services (goods used to make other products), facilitating goods and services (those that help an organisation achieve its objectives) and entering goods and services (those that become part of another product)
Reseller organisations	Resellers buy goods in order to sell them on to other organisations or to final consumers. Typically, resellers will be wholesalers or retailers, but they may also be agents for services, for example travel agents or webmasters who act as facilitators for other firms
Governmental organisations	Governments buy everything from paperclips to submarines through their various departments. Because national and local government departments operate under specific rules that are often rigid, negotiations can be difficult to conduct: buyers are often severely constrained in what they can do. Contracts are often put out to tender, with the lowest bidder being awarded the contract
Institutional organisations	Institutional organisations include charities, educational establishments, hospitals and other organisations that do not fit into the business, reseller or government categories. These organisations may be in the market for almost any kind of product, but they are used to achieve institutional goals that probably do not include profit

Business and commercial organisations

Business and commercial organisations can be segmented as original-equipment manufacturers, users and aftermarket customers. Original-equipment manufacturers (OEMs) buy foundation, entering and facilitating goods including machinery and equipment used to make products, and products that are incorporated directly into the final product. For example, computer manufacturers may buy machine tools to make computer cases and also buy silicon chips from specialist producers: the chips are incorporated into the final product, but the same type of chip might be incorporated in computers from several different OEMs. The Intel Pentium chip is an example.

OEM Original-equipment manufacturer

For OEM buyers, the key issue will be the quality of the products or services. Such buyers are usually operating to fairly exact specifications laid down by their own production engineers and designers; it is unlikely that the supplying firm will be able to do very much to have the specification changed, except by approaching the designers during the design process. This means that introducing a new product to an OEM will be a lengthy process, since the supplying company will need to establish a long-term relationship with the customer in order to become involved at the design stage for new products.

Consumer behaviour in action

2001 Electronic Components Ltd is an electronic components supplier based in Stevenage, Herts. The company supplies all types of components direct to industry, and acts as a wholesaler for many of the world's leading manufacturers. For this small company in a specialised market, reaching the decision-makers is a real problem – so the company uses press releases as an effective tool for reaching users.

Using press releases is, of course, cheaper than advertising since the journals print the releases free, as news. Credibility is greater, and the target audience is more likely to read the releases. The company has a sophisticated website that potential buyers are directed to, and offers high-speed on-line ordering. Everything is geared to making it easy for buyers to buy – but it is the press releases that bring in the buyers in the first place!

User customers buy products that are used up within the organisation, either as components in their own equipment or to make the equipment perform properly, for example lubricating oils or cleaning products. These products are not re-sold, but may be bought in considerable quantities. Many of these user products are services – accountancy or legal services, cleaning services, and maintenance or building services are all contained within the firm and not resold.

Aftermarket customers are those involved in the maintaining, repairing and overhauling (MRO) of products after they have been sold. For example, central heating systems are likely to be maintained by independent contractors rather than the original manufacturers or installers. The reason for this is that maintenance requires an investment in expensive testing equipment and different training from that required for installation or manufacture. These contractors buy the components, supplies and services they need from the most convenient supplier.

MRO A company that carries out maintenance, repair and overhaul

The classification split between OEM, users and aftermarket customers is only relevant to the supplier. OEMs can also be user customers for some suppliers. For example, a plastic moulding company may sell components to an OEM and plastic tools to a user as well as plastic replacement parts to an aftermarket organisation: in some cases these may even be the same organisation. Buying motivations for each type of purchase are clearly very different, and the supplying firm is likely to be dealing with different buyers for each category of product, if the customer company is a large one. In Figure 15.4, the same suppliers sometimes provide goods or services for several firms in the supply chain. In some cases there will be considerable crossover between firms.

Reseller organisations

The majority of manufactured goods are sold through reseller organisations such as retailers and wholesalers. Intermediaries provide useful services such

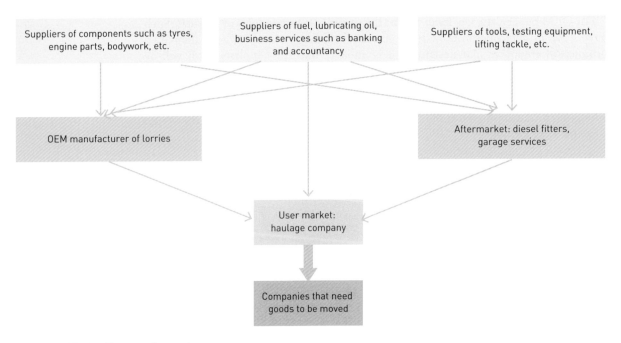

Figure 15.4   Types of purchase

as bulk breaking, assortment of goods and accumulation of associated product types: due to increased efficiencies resulting from these services, intermediaries tend to reduce overall prices for the final consumer. Cutting out the middle-man usually reduces efficiency and tends to increase prices; if this were not so, intermediaries would be unable to justify their existence and firms would simply bypass them.

Reseller organisations are driven almost entirely by their customers. This means that they will buy only those products they believe will sell easily; there is therefore a premium on employing buyers who have a clear understanding of customer needs. Unlike the OEM buyers, there is little need for resellers to understand the technical aspects of the products they buy – they merely need to feel confident that the ultimate consumers will want the products.

Reseller organisations carry out the following basic functions:

- Negotiation with suppliers.
- Promotional activities such as advertising, sales promotion, providing a sales-force, etc.
- Warehousing, storage and product handling.
- Transportation of local and (occasionally) long-distance shipments.
- Inventory control.
- Credit checking and credit control.
- Pricing and collection of price information, particularly about competitors.
- Collection of market information about consumers and competitors.

For manufacturers, this places a premium on establishing close long-term relationships with resellers. Shared information, as part of an integrated channel management strategy, becomes crucial to forward planning.

Consumer behaviour in action: B&W Speakers

B&W Speakers is a company well-known to hi-fi enthusiasts. The company produces state-of-the-art loudspeakers which are sold worldwide: technical excellence is maintained by its research and development facility in the south of England.

The challenge for B&W is maintaining close relationships with manufacturers, retailers and the hi-fi media in the 70 countries in which it operates. The company is relatively small, and operates in a specialist area where maintaining contact by the traditional method of sending sales representatives to customers regularly is difficult or impossible.

B&W has therefore developed a sophisticated extranet which enables customers and others to log onto a special website. Each customer has a password, so the system can offer each one a personalised greeting and can also record the interactions for marketing research purposes. Distributors have access to all areas of the extranet, but retailers have less access and the media have their own section on the site. This helps to maintain confidentiality and protect corporate secrets. The extranet is multi-lingual so that each customer, no matter what their native language, is able to access information much more easily than would be the case by using (for example) the telephone.

The result of using the extranet is increased service levels for all parties, and enhanced communication with all relevant stakeholders. The extranet offers added value for distributors and retailers because the services provided are relevant to them and they have access to all relevant information instantly. B&W benefit because they have much more accurate and timely information about their distributors and retailers, and also have a more loyal group of customers.

Government organisations

Government and quasi-government organisations are major buyers of almost every-thing. In some markets, the government is heavily involved in industry. For instance, all insurance in India is a government monopoly and the oil industry in Mexico is controlled by PEMEX, a quasi-government entity. Governments are thought to be the largest category of market in the world, if all levels of government are included in the equation. The structure of government varies from one country to another: for example, in Spain there is the national government based in Madrid, the regional governments (e.g. the Junta de Andalucia), the provincial governments (e.g. Provincia de Granada) and the local town halls (e.g. Ayuntamiento de Ugijar). Sometimes these local town halls group together to form an alliance that carries out mutually beneficial activities such as tourism marketing or funding a local swimming pool, but frequently they act independently of one another within the frameworks of their own jurisdictions. Figure 15.5 summarises the types of purchase that might be made by each of the tiers of government.

Because of the strict rules under which most government organisations operate, special measures are often needed to negotiate deals. In particular, government organisations almost always put contracts out for tender, so that firms are asked to bid for contracts. The contract is usually offered to the lowest bidder, unless there are overwhelming reasons to do otherwise. From a supplier's viewpoint, this is likely to be problematic, since the lowest price is likely to be the least profitable price, so selling firms will often try to circumvent the process by ensuring that they become involved before the tender is finalised. In this way it may be possible to ensure that the tender is drawn up in a way that favours the proactive firm over its competitors (for example, by including features that competitors cannot offer) thus ensuring that competitors either do not bid at all, or bid at too high a price.

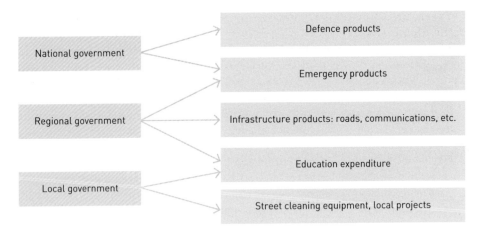

Figure 15.5 Tiers of government and their typical purchases

In some cases, governments need to purchase items that are not available to the general public or to other businesses. Military hardware is an obvious example; clearly ordinary businesses are not allowed to buy submarines or nuclear bombers. On a more subtle level, goods such as handguns are not permitted for private organisations in the UK, but can be sold to the Army or the police force. Some types of computer software are only appropriate for use by the tax authorities, and academic research is paid for largely by the government in the UK. From a marketing viewpoint, these specialist markets present an interesting challenge, since in some cases the products need to be tailored to a specific government or a specific government department. This may mean that there is considerable scope for negotiation, but since the contract might still have to go out to tender, the company may find that it has spent a lot of time developing a specification for a contract that is then awarded to another firm.

Consumer behaviour in action: The European Union

The European Union is intended to provide a 'level playing field' for companies within its borders. This has extended to tendering for government (and even local government) buying. In the past, orders for such items as desks, computers, office supplies and so forth were commonly given to local companies within the government's own country. This was seen as a way of supporting local firms, reducing imports and securing jobs. Under EU rules, though, this type of selective purchasing is anti-competitive and is now banned.

Currently, any government organisation within the EU must offer all contracts for tender throughout the EU, if the contract is above a specific value (currently around £100,000 for services and supplies, and £4m for works). Contracts are advertised in the *Journal of the European Communities*, and also on-line at http://ted.publications. eu.int/. Local business organisations such as chambers of commerce also monitor tenders and pass them on to interested parties.

The end result of this process is that **end users** (the taxpayers, in the last analysis) get better value for money, and the most efficient companies have wider opportunities to expand their businesses.

End user The person or organisation that finally obtains the benefits of the product

In some circumstances governments may issue a 'cost-plus' contract, in which the organisation is given a specific task to carry out and charges according to the cost of the contract plus an agreed profit margin. In the early days of space exploration this type of contract was common, since it was impossible to predict what the costs might be when dealing with an unknown set of circumstances. More recently these contracts have fallen into disrepute since they reward inefficiency and waste.

Institutional organisations

Institutions include charities, universities, hospital trusts and non-profit organisations of all types, schools, and so forth. In some cases these are government-owned but independent for the purposes of purchase and supply (for example, secondary schools); in other cases they are totally independent (for example, registered charities). The traditional view of these organisations is that they are chronically underfunded and therefore do not represent a particularly wealthy market, but in practice the organisations actually have a very substantial aggregate spending power. Figure 15.6 summarises the factors that have to be taken into account in marketing to institutions.

Because budgets are almost always very tight, the marketing organisation may need to be creative in helping the institution to raise the money to buy its products. For example, a firm that produces drilling equipment may find that it has a substantial market at Oxfam, since Oxfam drills wells in many arid regions within

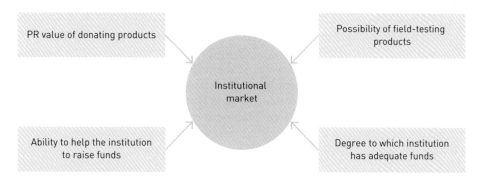

Figure 15.6 Factors in institutional marketing

Challenging the status quo

We are often told that marketing is about managing the exchange process, yet government departments and many institutions seem to lay down the ground rules from the start. Marketers have to play by the buyer's rules to be in the game at all – so how can they possibly be managing the process? Pushed from one set of constraints to the next, it would seem that the average marketer is just a pawn in the buyers' hands!

Yet maybe that is how it should be, if customers are at the centre of everything we do. Not to mention that the management process itself could be construed as a clearing-house for pressures rather than as a directive force – in a sense, no manager is actually in control, so why should marketers be any different?

developing countries. Oxfam relies on public generosity to raise the money to buy the equipment, so the manufacturer may find it necessary to part-fund or even manage a fundraising campaign in order to make the sale.

Suppliers are often asked to contribute to charities, in cash or in products. This may not always be possible, since the supplier's only market might be the charities, but in some cases firms may find it worthwhile to supply free products to charities in order to gain PR value, or sometimes in order to open the door to lucrative deals with other organisations. For example, a charity working in a developing country might be prepared to field-test equipment that could then be sold to a government department in the same country.

Buyers' techniques

Buyers use a wide variety of techniques according to the buying situation they are faced with. Buying situations are generally divided into three types:

Straight rebuy A situation in which a previous order is simply repeated in its entirety

1 **Straight rebuy.** Most organisational buying is routine: for example, a car manufacturer needs to buy much the same number of wheel nuts each month. A straight rebuy is a situation where the buyer is buying the same product in very much the same quantities from the same supplier. In these circumstances the buyer needs no new information, and does not need to engage in much negotiation either. Prudent buyers may occasionally look at other possible sources of components in order to ensure that no new technology is available or that other suppliers are not able to supply the same components more cheaply, but in general the order placement is automatic. In some cases the whole process is automated through an electronic data interchange (EDI) link with a supplier, or there may be an automatic buying procedure facilitated through the Internet without any human involvement. If the product is of minor importance, or represents a low commitment in terms of finance or risk, the buyer will probably not undertake any information search and will simply order the goods. This is called *causal purchasing*, because it results automatically from a cause such as low stock level. For example, a buyer for a large engineering firm probably spends very little time deciding on brands of paper for the photocopier. On the other hand, buying copper cable might be a routine purchase, but the buyer might monitor the market for alternatives occasionally. Such buying is called *routine low-priority buying* because it has a lower priority than would be the case if an entirely new situation were being faced. The company is unlikely to get into serious trouble if it pays 10% more than it should for cable, for example.

Modified re-buy A purchase that, although similar to previous purchases, has been changed in a minor way

2 **Modified rebuy.** In this situation, the buyer re-evaluates the habitual buying patterns of the firm with a view to changing them in some way. The quantities ordered, or the specification of the components, may be changed. Even the supplier may be changed. Sometimes these changes come about because the buyer has become aware of a better alternative than the one currently employed (perhaps through environmental scanning), or sometimes the changes come about because competing suppliers succeed in offering something new. Internal forces (increases or decreases in demand for components) might trigger a renegotiation with suppliers or a search for new suppliers. In such circumstances the buyer is faced with a limited problem-solving scenario in which he or she will need to carry out some

negotiation with existing or new suppliers, and will probably need to seek out new information as well. The buyer may well require potential suppliers to bid against each other for the business: the drawback of this approach is that it often results in damaging a well-established relationship with existing suppliers.

3   **New task**. This type of buying situation comes about when the task is perceived as being entirely new. Past experience is therefore no guide, and present suppliers may not be able to help either. Thus the buyer is faced with a complex decision process. Judgemental new task situations are those in which the buyer must deal with technical complexities of the product, complex evaluation of alternatives and negotiating with new suppliers. Strategic new task situations are those in which the final decision is of strategic importance to the firm – for example, a bank looking for software for on-line banking will be investing (potentially) hundreds of thousands of pounds in retraining staff, and in transferring existing records, not to mention the risks of buying software which lacks the necessary security features or which fails under high demand. In these circumstances, long-range planning at director level drives the buying process, and the relationship with the suppliers is likely to be both long-term and close.

New task A type of purchase for which previous experience does not exist

From the viewpoint of the business marketer, the main chance of winning new customers will come in the new task situation. The risks for buyers involved in switching suppliers are often too great unless there is a very real and clear advantage in doing so; such an advantage is likely to be difficult to prove in practice. In the new task situation, potential suppliers may well find themselves screened out early in the process, and will then find it almost impossible to be reconsidered later.

The various trade-offs in the buying situation are shown in Figure 15.7.

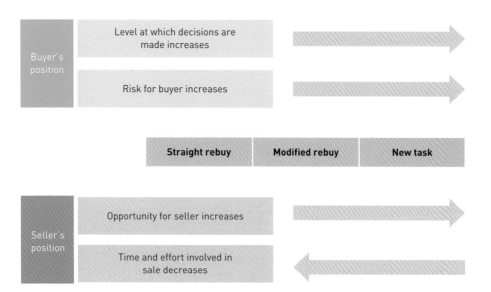

Figure 15.7   Trade-offs in type of buying situation

The buygrid framework

Organisational buying can be seen as a series of decisions, each of which leads to a further problem about which a decision must be made (Cardozo 1983). From the viewpoint of the supplying firm, it would certainly be valuable to be able to diagnose problems by examining the sequence of decisions. The difficulty here is that the decision sequence is probably not known to the marketer unless the firms involved already have a close relationship. If the sequence can be known, marketers can identify the stage at which the firm is currently making decisions, and can tailor the approach accordingly.

The industrial buying process can be mapped against a grid, as shown in Figure 15.8. The most complex buying situations occur in the upper left portion of the framework and involve the largest number of decision makers and buying influences. This is because new tasks require the greatest amount of effort in seeking information and formulating appropriate solutions, but also will require the greatest involvement of individuals at all levels of the organisation. The more people who are involved, the more complex the decision process because each individual will have a personal agenda.

The Buygrid framework has been widely criticised, however. Like most models it tends to oversimplify the case. As in consumer decision-making, the sequence may not be as clear-cut and events may take place in a different order in certain circumstances. For example, a buying firm may not be aware that it has a problem in a particular area until a supplier approaches the firm with a solution, thus cutting out several stages of the process: the firm may well recognise the need and the problem,

Stage	Buying situations		
	New task	Modified rebuy	Straight rebuy
Anticipation or recognition of a problem (need) and a general solution			
Determination of characteristics and quantity of needed item			
Description of characteristics and quantity of needed item			
Search for and qualification of potential sources			
Acquisition and analysis of proposals			
Evaluation of proposals and selection of supplier(s)			
Selection of an order routine			
Performance feedback and evaluation			

Figure 15.8   The Buygrid framework

Source: From the Marketing Science Institute Series *Industrial Buying and Creative Marketing*, by Patrick J. Robinson, Charles W. Faris and Yoram Wind. Copyright 1967 by Allyn and Bacon, Inc., Boston, MA.

but will probably not need to acquire proposals and select a supplier since the supplier is already offering a solution. Second, suppliers go to great lengths to differentiate themselves from competitors as effectively as they can, so that the buyer is unlikely to have any other potential suppliers of the exact product on offer. Third, the model assumes a rational approach to purchasing which is often simply not there. Finally, the boundaries between new task, modified rebuy and straight rebuy are by no means clear-cut.

Because buyers are influenced by both rational and emotional considerations, the potential supplier needs to be aware of the personal agendas of each member of the decision-making unit. Even at a rational level, each member of the DMU will apply different criteria for judging which suppliers should be included and which excluded (Kelly and Coaker 1976): the finance director might emphasise low prices, whereas the chief designer might be concerned with product quality, and the production engineer with reliable delivery. The buyer might be concerned with the relationship with the supplier's sales people. In many cases, brand equity is less important than issues of price and delivery (Bendixen et al. 2004). At the personal, emotional level, office politics, rivalries, jockeying for promotion, liking or disliking the salesperson and many other factors will affect different members of the DMU in different ways.

In the case of key-account management, this problem of dealing with different members of the DMU is often overcome by taking a team approach to the sale. While the key-account manager handles the initial contact and the management of the process, other specialists are brought in to deal with financial aspects, technical aspects and so forth. In this way each member of the DMU is speaking to someone with whom he or she has a common language and a common understanding of the conceptual environment within which each specialty operates. In some cases the number of people working on the account can become large: when IBM were dealing with Lloyds Bank (one of the Big Four UK banks) they had more than 100 people working on the account, and set up a special branch office in the Canary Wharf area to be near Lloyds head office.

> **Key-account manager** A salesperson who has the responsibility of dealing with the most important customers of a firm

There are three types of business net (Moller and Svahn 2004):

- *Stable.* These are networks that are perhaps still growing, but they are following a predictable course.
- *Established.* These networks are fixed and relatively unchanging, and the rules are known by the members.
- *Emerging.* These networks are still growing and changing.

The internal culture of the firm (and the external culture, in an international context) affects the nature of each of these network types.

Managing the network means identifying the key network, developing a strategy for managing the individuals who operate within the network and developing methods at the operational level for managing those actors (Ojasalo 2004). The responsibility for managing the actors is often divided between the members of the selling team.

Value analysis

> **Value analysis** The process of calculating the worth of a purchase in terms of the returns made from its use

Value analysis is a method of evaluating components, raw materials and even manufacturing processes in order to determine ways of cutting costs or improving finished

1. *Annual cost of existing product:*	
250 replacement light bulbs × 45p	£112.50
Cost of electricity: @ 6.7p per kilowatt	
× 60 watts × 150 bulbs × 10 hrs per day × 250 days a year:	£1507.50
Cost of replacing bulbs assuming 10 minutes per bulb @ £10 per hour:	£416.00
TOTAL COST PER ANNUM:	**£2036.00**
2. *Cost of using long-life bulbs:*	
50 replacement bulbs per annum × £3 =	£277.00
Cost of electricity @ 6.7p per kilowatt	
× 11 watts × 150 bulbs × 2500 hrs a year =	£ 277.00
Cost of replacing bulbs assuming 10 minutes per bulb @ £10 per hour =	£ 83.20
TOTAL COST PER ANNUM:	**£637.20**

Figure 15.9   Long-life bulb vs. tungsten-filament bulb

products. Value-in-use is defined as a product's economic value to the user relative to a specific alternative in a particular application (Kijewski and Yoon 1990). Value-in-use is the price that would equate the overall costs and benefits of using one product rather than using another.

For example, consider long-life light bulbs. These bulbs are usually between five and ten times as expensive as ordinary tungsten-filament bulbs to buy, but last five times as long and use only 20% of the electricity. For a domestic consumer, this represents a considerable saving, more than enough to cover the initial outlay for the bulbs, but for a business customer the saving is even greater, since the cost of paying someone to replace blown light bulbs is significant. Assuming the life of a tungsten-filament bulb is 1000 hours on average, compared with 5000 hours for a long-life bulb, the calculation would run as shown in Figure 15.9. Using this calculation, the company can make an immediate saving of just under £1400 a year by switching to long-life bulbs. In fact, the capital cost of changing all the bulbs in the building would be recovered in the first year, although in practice the firm would probably only replace the tungsten-filament bulbs as they fail in use; in this way the labour cost of replacing the bulbs would be no higher than normal.

Table 15.2   Assessing suppliers

Attribute	Assessment method
Technical capability	Visit the supplier to examine production equipment, inspect quality control procedures and meet the engineering staff
Managerial capability	Discuss systems for controlling processes, meet the managerial staff and become involved in planning and scheduling supplies
Financial stability	Check the accounts filed at Companies House or other public record office, run a credit check, examine annual reports if any
Capacity to deliver	Ascertain the status of other customers of the supplier – would any of these take priority? Assess the production capacity of the supplier, warehouse stocks of the product, reputation in the industry

Challenging the status quo

The methods of assessment shown in the table all rely on some kind of judgement on the part of the buyer. Even the financial figures filed at the company record office require interpretation – and may even have been 'massaged' to make the company look more financially viable than it actually is.

So why bother with what is, after all, a somewhat time-consuming exercise? Presumably a rogue supplier would have little difficulty in pulling the wool over the eyes of a buyer who probably lacks the engineering training to understand what is in front of him or her. On the other hand, an honest supplier would probably provide the 'warts and all' picture that might well lose the contract. Maybe buyers would be better advised to go for the supplier who looks the worst – at least we know they are being honest with us!

Because some buyers do use this type of calculation to assess alternative solutions to existing problems, a good salesperson will be prepared with the full arguments in favour of the new solution, including all the relevant factors that make the product more attractive. On the other side of the coin, astute purchasers will involve potential suppliers in the discussions and in the value analysis process (Dowst and Raia 1990).

Evaluating supplier capability

Purchasers also need to assess the capability of potential suppliers to continue to supply successfully. This is a combination of assessing financial stability, technical expertise, reliability, quality assurance processes and production capacity. In simple terms, the purchasing company is trying to ensure that the potential supplier will be in a position to keep the promises it makes. Business customers can gain competitive advantage from tracking the performance of suppliers because they are better able to manage the supply chain (Bharadwaj 2004).

Table 15.2 illustrates some of the ways in which buyers can assess potential suppliers. These methods rely (in most cases) on judgement on the part of the purchaser, who may not in fact have the necessary expertise to understand what the supplier's capability really is.

Evaluating supplier performance

Even after the contract is awarded, the purchasing company will probably re-examine the supplier's performance periodically. In some cases, suppliers have been known to relax and reduce their service level once the contract is awarded, and of course the circumstances of the buying organisation are likely to change over time. If the relationship with the supplier is to continue, then (like all other human relationships) it must adapt to changing circumstances. The basic evaluation methods are as outlined in Table 15.3. All of these methods involve some degree of subjectivity, in other words each method requires buyers to make judgements about the supplier. Expressing the evaluations numerically makes the method appear more credible, but if the basic assumptions are incorrect, no amount of

Table 15.3 Evaluation approaches

Approach	Explanation
Categorical plan	Each department having contact with the supplier is asked to provide a regular rating of suppliers against a list of salient performance factors. This method is extremely subjective, but is easy to administer
Weighted-point plan	Performance factors are graded according to their importance to the organisation: for example, delivery reliability might be more important for some organisations than for others. The supplier's total rating can be calculated and the supplier's offering can be adjusted if necessary to meet the purchasing organisation's needs
Cost-ratio plan	Here the buying organisation evaluates quality, delivery and service in terms of what each one costs. Good performance is assigned a negative score, i.e. the costs of purchase are reduced by good performance; poor performance is assigned a positive score, meaning that the costs are deemed to be greater when dealing with a poor performer

calculation will generate the right answer. Those involved in evaluation exercises of this nature should be aware that the evaluation exercise itself should be evaluated periodically, and the (usually subjective) criteria used by the various individuals involved need to be checked.

In fact, suppliers tend to adapt more often than do purchasers when there is an ongoing relationship (Brennan et al. 2003). This is due to the relative power each has (buyers being more powerful in most circumstances), and managerial preferences. Suppliers that are market-orientated tend to develop a greater customer intimacy, which may also drive suppliers to change (Tuominen et al. 2004). Buyers that are themselves market-orientated tend to become more loyal to their suppliers (Jose Sanzo et al. 2003). Having said that, suppliers do sometimes end unprofitable relationships; many B2B relationships are unprofitable, and often

 Challenging the status quo

Much of the emphasis in the preceding sections has been on the purchaser's evaluation of suppliers. But what about the other way round? Customers are not always plaster saints – some are late payers, some impose unreasonable restrictions, some reject supplies for the flimsiest of reasons, and some are just plain unpleasant to deal with.

So should suppliers have their own systems for assessing purchasers? Should we just grovel at the feet of any organisation willing to buy our goods – or should we stand up and be counted? After all, without supplies no company can survive – so presumably we are equally important to one another.

Maybe this is really the purpose of segmenting our markets – and what is really meant by segmentation.

companies lack the skills to make relationships profitable, so they simply end them (Helm et al. 2006).

Summary

Buyers have a large number of influences on their decision-making. At the very least, buyers have their own personal agendas within the companies they work for; in the broader context, a wide range of political, environmental and technological issues will affect their decision-making. The end result is likely to be a combination of experience, careful calculation and gut feeling.

Although industrial buyers are often assumed to be much more rigorous in their buying, and less swayed by emotion, this is only partly true; consequently, they are as susceptible to good marketing as any other person, and can be influenced by good marketing communications and especially by good sales people.

 **Key points**

- Buyers are subject to many pressures other than the simple commercial ones; emotions, organisational influence, politics and internal structures are also important factors.
- The decision-making unit (DMU) or buying centre is the group of people who will make the buying decision. The roles and composition of DMUs vary widely.
- Business and commercial organisations are likely to be swayed most by past experience with a vendor, product characteristics and quality.
- Resellers are driven by their customers.
- Government markets are large, and almost always use a tendering system.
- Institutional markets may need special techniques to help them afford to buy the products.
- Markets can be divided into those buyers who buy products designed to make other products or who will incorporate the purchase into their own products (original equipment manufacturers); those who consume the product in the course of running their businesses (user markets); and those who serve the aftermarket.
- A purchase may be a straight rebuy, a modified rebuy or a new task. These are given in order of increasing complexity, and do not have discrete boundaries.
- A team approach to buying usually dictates a team approach to selling.

Review questions

1 How would you expect a government department to go about buying a new computer system?
2 How might internal politics affect a buyer's behaviour?

3   What factors might be prominent in the buying decision for cleaning materials?
4   What factors might a supplier take into account when evaluating a purchasing company?
5   How might the directors of a company go about setting standards for evaluating suppliers? What objective criteria are available?
6   What are the main problems with evaluating supplier performance?
7   How should a seller approach a government department?
8   What are the main differences between marketing to commercial organisations and marketing to charities?
9   How might a seller find out who the influentials are in the DMU?
10 How might a seller act to reduce the risk for the buyer?

Case study revisited: Moda

Moda ensures that buyers attend (which of course means exhibitors will attend) by partnering the show with the major trade magazines. This means that buyers will read about the show in advance, will be informed as to which exhibitors are going to attend and will be given the 'post-mortem' after the exhibition ends. For the journals, this is a good way to fill the pages, so they are happy to help.

From a buyer's viewpoint, attending the exhibition ticks a number of boxes. First, they are able to meet potential suppliers on neutral territory, and can see several competing suppliers on the same day if necessary. Second, they can meet up with other companies who may be of help – other retailers, suppliers of professional services and so forth. Third, they can use the exhibition as an information-gathering exercise, as part of the information search that informs the buying process. Finally, going to a trade fair means a day out of the office, seeing new things and meeting new people, which can in itself be a motivation.

Taken all in all, for someone in the fashion industry (which is notoriously fickle and risky) a trip to Moda is likely to be a risk-reducer. Fashion buyers have to be able to predict trends months ahead, because an order might take weeks or months to fulfil. This means that an order placed at the show in August needs to be for spring and summer clothing, and it is impossible to predict what the weather will be doing in April and May. Moda offers the opportunity to see what will be on the market next year, so that even if the weather cannot be predicted that far ahead, the buyer will at least be able to see what the competition will be offering.

Whether the exhibition is about buying, or about information-gathering, or just about getting away from the daily routine, it is certainly a powerful influence on buyers and their decision-making.

Case study: Oxfam and Fair Trade

The concept of ethical business trading is relatively new, and even now, many businesses do not see why they should care about the welfare of their suppliers. Yet at the same time, businesspeople as individuals are as caring about the welfare of their fellow humans as anybody else.

One of the areas in which businesspeople can help is in the field of fair trade. A typical business buyer is likely to be most concerned about obtaining supplies at the highest quality and cheapest price possible, and of course from the viewpoint of creating wealth for the shareholders and good value for consumers this is a perfectly respectable position to take. Unfortunately, the power balance between wealthy, industrialised nations and the developing countries that supply most of our raw materials is such that it is all too easy for big business to take advantage of small producers and unprotected labour forces, even without realising they are doing it.

Oxfam, the charity dedicated to famine relief, has put together a set of documents to help firms source products from developing countries in an ethical and sustainable manner. According to Oxfam, it is often the case that workers have rights, but don't know about them and therefore don't exercise them. In partnership with local civil rights organisations, Oxfam seeks to publicise those rights – in Chile, women workers were given colourful leaflets telling them about their right to a 45-hour working week and a proper employment contract. In Nicaragua, radio station announcements were used to inform domestic workers of their right to a day off and to fixed working hours.

However, none of this will have any lasting effect unless buying companies in the wealthy countries (which of course means buyers themselves) take on board the idea of ethical sourcing. Oxfam therefore makes the point that two-thirds of graduates intend to check out the ethical stance of any company they work for, that 72% of British consumers think that the ethical production of their clothing is important and that 60% of a brand's value is in its reputation. In order to put this into effect, Oxfam offers a unique service – it will provide a consultancy service to check the ethics of a company's supply chain. In other words, Oxfam will advise on an ethical sourcing policy, will provide workshops for buyers (often with buyers from other industries, so that good practice can be shared) and will provide a tailored analysis of the risks involved for a specific firm or industry. It will identify potential problems – whether with child labour, unfair trading terms or environmentally damaging manufacturing processes.

So far the initiative has attracted a wide range of blue-chip companies, including clothing chain Next, supermarket chains Tesco and Asda, department store chain Marks and Spencer, and clothes retailer Gap. From the viewpoint of these companies, help from Oxfam enables them to take the moral high ground, and of course avoid the potential bad publicity that might come from an adversarial confrontation with a pressure group – better to have Oxfam inside the decision-making process than outside creating negative publicity. But apart from those practical, tactical considerations, most of us like to think that we are behaving ethically – it helps us sleep at night.

Questions

1 What might be the conflicts caused for a buyer who is trying to act ethically?
2 Why should companies care about what is happening in another country?
3 How should an intermediary (an importer, for example) respond to an ethical request from a buyer?
4 How does ethics fit into the Buygrid framework?
5 What are the advantages of using Oxfam as a consultant?

Further reading

The following is a small selection from the many available books on business-to-business marketing.

A comprehensive, readable textbook written from a marketing management perspective is Chris Fill and Karen Fill's *Business to Business Marketing: Relationships, Systems and Communications* (Hemel Hempstead: FT Prentice Hall, 2004).

Business to Business Marketing Management (London: Sage, 2013) by Jim Blythe and Alan Zimmerman takes a global perspective on B2B marketing.

Mark Whitehead and Chris Barrat's *Buying for Business: Insights into Purchasing and Supply* (Chichester: John Wiley, 2004) gives the view from the other side. Written as a guide for practitioners, the book takes the buyer's viewpoint.

For an insight into how e-marketing affects business buyers, Shaltoni, Abdel M. and West, Douglas C. (2010) The measurement of e-marketing orientation (EMO) in business-to-business markets. *Industrial Marketing Management* 39 (7): 1097–102 might provide some interesting reading.

For a bit more on ethical marketing, and whether it really matters, Chatzidakis, A., Hibbert, S. and Smith, A. (2006) 'Ethically concerned, yet unethically behaved': towards an updated understanding of consumers' (un)ethical decision making. *Advances in Consumer Research* 32: 693–8 provides an interesting counter-argument. Perhaps consumers are not so ethically conscious as they pretend to be!

References

Bendixen, M., Bukasa, K.A. and Abratt, R.A. (2004) Brand equity in the business to business market. *Industrial Marketing Management* 33 (5): 371–80.

Bharadwaj, N. (2004) Investigating the decision criteria used in electronic components procurement. *Industrial Marketing Management* 33 (4): 317–23.

Brennan, R.D., Turnbull, P.W. and Wilson, D.T. (2003) Dyadic adaptation in business-to-business markets. *European Journal of Marketing* 37 (11): 1636–65.

Cardozo, R.N. (1983) Modelling organisational buying as a sequence of decisions. *Industrial Marketing Management* 12 (Feb): 75.

Claycomb, C., Iyer, K. and Germain, R. (2005) Predicting the level of B2B e-commerce in industrial organisations. *Industrial Marketing Management* 34 (3): 221–34.

Dowst, S. and Raia, E. (1990) Teaming up for the 90s. *Purchasing* 108 (Feb): 54–9.

Hawes, J.M and Barnhouse, S.H. (1987) How purchasing agents handle personal risk. *Industrial Marketing Management* 16 (Nov): 287–93.

Helm, S., Rolfes, L. and Gunther, B. (2006) Suppliers' willingness to end unprofitable customer relationships. *European Journal of Marketing* 40 (3/4): 366–83.

Jose Sanzo, M., Leticia Santos, M., Rodolfo, V. and Alvarez, L.I. (2003) The role of market orientation in business dyadic relationships: testing an integrator model. *Journal of Marketing Management* 19: 73–107.

Kelly, P. and Coaker, J.W. (1976) Can we generalise about choice criteria for industrial purchasing decisions? In Bernhardt K.L. (ed.), *Marketing 1776–1976 and Beyond*. Chicago, IL: American Marketing Association. pp. 330–3.

Kijewski, V. and Yoon, E. (1990) Market-based pricing: beyond price-performance curves. *Industrial Marketing Management* 19 (Feb): 11–19.

Loudon, D.L. and Della Bitta, A.J. (1993) *Consumer behaviour: concepts and application*. New York: McGraw-Hill.

McDonald, J.B. and Smith, K. (2004) The effects of technology-mediated communication on industrial buyer behaviour. *Industrial Marketing Management* 33 (2): 107–16.

Moller, K. and Svahn, S. (2004) Crossing east–west boundaries: knowledge sharing in intercultural business networks. *Industrial Marketing Management* 33 (3): 219–28.

Ojasalo, J. (2004) Key network management. *Industrial Marketing Management* 33 (3): 195–205.

Pressey, A.D. and Selassie, H.G. (2003) Are cultural differences over-rated? Examining the influence of national culture on international buyer–seller relationships. *Journal of Consumer Behaviour* 2 (4): 354–68.

Ronchetto, J.R., Jr, Hutt, M.D. and Reingen, P.H. (1989) Embedded influence patterns in organizational buying systems. *Journal of Marketing* 53 (4): 51–62.

Terpstra, V. and David, K. (1991) *The Cultural Environment of International Business*. Cincinnati, OH: South-Western Publishing Co.

Tuominen, M., Rajala, A. and Moller, K. (2004) Market-driving versus market-driven: divergent roles of market orientation in business relationships. *Industrial Marketing Management* 33 (3): 207–17.

Webster, F.E. and Wind, Y. (1972) *Organisational Buying Behaviour.* Englewood Cliffs, NJ: Prentice-Hall.

More online

To gain free access to additional online resources to support this chapter please visit: **www.sagepub.co.uk/blythe**

CHAPTER (16)

Consumer behaviour and the marketing mix

LEARNING OBJECTIVES

After reading this chapter you should be able to:

- Explain the importance of hedonism as opposed to utilitarianism in consumer behaviour.

- Show how price goes beyond purchase cost.

- Explain how price relates to what people will pay.

- Explain the motivators for shopping behaviour.

- Explain the weak and strong theories of advertising.

- Explain the role of interaction in advertising effectiveness.

- Describe the advantages of radio, cinema and ambient advertising.

- Explain the use and effectiveness of ambient advertising.

- Explain the role of social interaction in evaluating services.

- Describe the importance of getting service levels right.

- Show how physical evidence is used as a surrogate for judging quality of services.

Introduction

Most of this book has been concerned with the theories behind consumer and buyer behaviour, and the influences on their decision-making in purchasing and consumption situations. Eventually, however, marketers need to develop practical tactics for launching new products, expanding existing markets, raising the profile of brands and so forth and must therefore apply their knowledge of how consumers make decisions.

Marketing decision-making areas have for many years been divided according to the 4P model (product, price, place and promotion). During the 1980s this categorisation was expanded to include a further three factors – people, process and physical evidence (Booms and Bitner 1981).

Although the expanded 7P model is probably far from comprehensive in terms of explaining what marketers do, it does provide a degree of structure and is a convenient 'shorthand' device.

Case study: Lucozade

Lucozade is a sports and energy drink produced in the UK by Glaxosmithkline. It is probably the most popular energy drink available, and is used by top athletes as well as amateurs: its distinctive orange colour comes from its high glucose content, which provides instant energy for tired athletes (and indeed anyone else in need of a quick boost). It contains electrolytes and carbohydrates, and is available in a range of flavours and formulations – there is even a low-calorie version which provides instant energy and electrolytes for quick recovery, but which only has 50 calories.

Glaxosmithkline is a major pharmaceutical company, and has gone to some lengths to ensure that the product does what it says it will do – the science is rigorous, and has been verified independently. However, some criticisms have been levelled at Lucozade, notably for the high sugar content of the original formula and even for the trace of alcohol it contains (0.01% per litre) which meant that Muslims were unable to drink it for religious reasons. (Later, in 2004, the Muslim Council of Britain decided that the trace was too small to imperil the soul of a devout Muslim, so the ban was lifted.)

However, it wasn't always like this. Originally, Lucozade was a drink for people who were far from fit – it was targeted at people recovering from serious illnesses. It was originally developed in 1927 by William Owen, a chemist from County Cork in Ireland, and was marketed under the name Glucozade until 1929, when it was rebranded as Lucozade. Originally sold in a glass bottle with a cellophane wrap, it was moved to a PET bottle format in 1983, when the decision was made to reposition the product as an energy drink for athletes.

This decision was made because research showed that the product would sell better if it were not associated with illness, but was instead associated with empowerment. Added to this, improved public health (in particular the advent of the National Health Service) meant that fewer people felt the need to self-medicate at home.

Lucozade needed to be repositioned, even though it was extremely well-established in popular culture.

How to impress your examiner

Questions around how marketers influence consumers could come from almost any aspect of the subject, but something to bear in mind is that consumers are not mere recipients of marketing influences. You will gain marks if you emphasise that marketing is an exchange – consumers co-create value, and often act in ways that marketers would prefer them not to. They are a lot like people in that respect.

Segmentation

Market segmentation is the process of identifying a group of consumers with similar needs and producing a product that will meet those needs at a profit. It has a simple basis in logic: it is that no single product will appeal to all consumers.

Segmentation operates at four levels, as follows:

1 Mass marketing. This is an attempt to produce something that virtually everybody will want, and produce it in such large quantities that the production costs can be minimised and thus the price can be kept low. This approach appeals to production engineers, but is virtually impossible to carry out in the modern world because people prefer a more individual, tailored product that suits their needs more precisely.

2 *Segmented markets*. Here the firm seeks to find groups of people with similar needs. This is a compromise position for both the producer and the customer: for producers, the production runs will be shorter than would be the case for mass marketing, and for the consumer the product is unlikely to be exactly what is wanted.

3 Niche marketing. Niche marketers focus on one subgroup within the larger segments. Some niche marketers concentrate on a product category rather than on a specific type of consumer – Sock Shop and Tie Rack are examples. At first sight this appears to be a product-orientated paradigm, but in fact it is consumer-orientated in that it reduces search time for people looking for the specific product category. This type of niche marketing is the direct opposite to the department-store or supermarket approach to retailing: instead of stocking a few products in a wide range of categories, niche marketers stock a wide range of products in a single category.

4 Micro marketing. This is the practice of tailoring products and marketing programmes to suit specific individuals and circumstances. Even mass-production operations such as motor manufacturers can offer new-car buyers a very wide range of options, but the ultimate in micromarketing is probably Dell Computers. Each computer is built to the customer's specification, using plug-in components. Mass customisation is the ability to produce individual, custom-made products using mass-production techniques, for example producing prescription spectacles on-site, as Vision Express do. Customers are able to have an eye test, choose frames and walk out with the finished spectacles within an hour. In many cases people are not prepared to pay the increased cost of such service, however (Bardacki and Whitelock 2004).

In large markets such as the USA (298 million consumers), the European Union (457 million consumers) or Japan (127 million consumers), there are often enough consumers with a specific need in common for manufacturers to be able to obtain the economies of scale enjoyed by British manufacturers in the mid-19th century. Marketers now are able to treat consumers more as individuals, with individual wants and needs; in most industries we are not yet at the point where we can provide individual attention for individual consumers, so we need to identify groups of people with similar interests and design our approach to fit those groups. This is what segmentation seeks to achieve.

There are many bases for segmenting markets. From a consumer behaviour viewpoint, the ones of interest are those based on psychology, and those based on behaviour.

Mass market A situation in which a standardised product is purchased by a very large number of people

Niche marketing Targeting a small group of customers

Micro marketing Those elements of the environment that affect the individual firm

PSYCHOGRAPHIC SEGMENTATION

Personality characteristics appear, at first sight, to be an extremely useful way of segmenting markets because personality changes relatively slowly. Unfortunately, it is difficult to measure personality traits on a mass scale, so it is difficult to identify groups of people with similar traits. For example, an insurance company might like to target people who are excessively afraid of burglary, but who are also wealthy and have many possessions. Such people might be expected to be careful about locking their houses, would have burglar alarms, and would also invest in security locks. The result would be a group of people who are unlikely to make a claim against their policies – the ideal customers for insurance companies. There is, however, no easy way to target such a group: there is no single advertising medium directed at these people. In practice the only realistic way of approaching these groups is by allowing them to self-select against a mass marketing communications approach, which is expensive and wasteful. Our hypothetical insurance company would need to model the product's use using actors who portray the particular personality traits that are of interest.

A potentially very important segmentation variable has emerged in recent years. Segmentation by environmental attitude may be a good predictor of people's purchasing behaviour, and several attempts have been made to categorise people this way. For example, one study found that 30% of Americans are indifferent to environmental issues, whereas the other 70% have pro-environmental attitudes, of varying strengths (Englis and Bamossy 2010). The degree to which people act on these attitudes is, of course, another story – as we saw in Chapter 7, intended behaviour (conation) does not necessarily result in actual behaviour.

Alternatively, people can be divided into groups according to their lifestyles. Lifestyles are both created by products, and dictate which products will be bought and used; someone who owns a penthouse flat has a different psychology (and lifestyle) from someone who chooses to buy a smallholding and be self-sufficient, but both dwellings are products as well as lifestyle determinants. Incidentally, it is likely that the cost of each type of home will be similar: the choice is about lifestyle, not about financial considerations.

Lifestyle segmentation has the major advantage that it relates directly to purchasing behaviour. It has been said that marketing delivers a lifestyle, so considering consumers on the basis of their chosen lifestyles is certainly logical. The VALS model discussed in Chapter 2 is an example of lifestyle segmentation: consumers are divided into nine lifestyle positions, determined by their attitudes to other people and (to an extent) by their level of wealth.

BEHAVIOURAL SEGMENTATION

Behaviour can be a useful and reliable way of segmenting. At its most obvious, if we are marketing to anglers we are not interested in how old they are, what their views are on strong drink or where they live. All we care about is that they go fishing, and might therefore be customers for our new type of rod. Accessing the segment would be easily undertaken by advertising in the *Angling Times*. At a deeper level we might be interested in such issues as where they buy their fishing tackle, how much they usually spend on a rod, what kind of fish they are after and so forth, but this information is easily obtained through questionnaire-type surveys.

The main behavioural bases for segmentation, summarised in Figure 16.1, are as follows:

- *Benefits sought*. Different people look for different things in each product purchase. Sampson (1992) divided people into three groups: functionality seekers

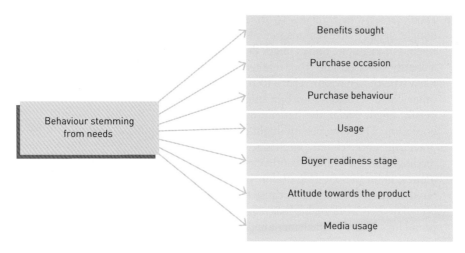

Figure 16.1 Behavioural bases for segmentation

who look for the simple, practical aspects of ownership; image seekers, who look for products which will enhance their self-image in various ways; and pleasure seekers, who look for the hedonic aspects of owning products. For example, someone who buys a car as simple transportation for themselves, their family and their luggage would be classified as a functionality seeker. Someone who buys an upmarket car for its prestige value, to show off to the neighbours, is an image seeker, while someone who simply enjoys driving or looks for a car which has exceptional comfort is a pleasure seeker.

- *Purchase occasion*. Some products are bought on a regular basis, whereas some others are bought as an occasional treat. More importantly, the same product might be a regular purchase for some people, but a treat for others – for example, someone on a strict diet may only buy a chocolate bar very occasionally, whereas someone else might regard a chocolate bar as a normal element in the weekday lunchbox. Likewise, fifty years ago chicken was regarded as an occasional Sunday lunch treat (beef was the usual Sunday lunch roast in the UK) but intensive farming has brought the relative price of chicken down to the point where it is one of the cheapest meats available. Even in the 1950s many people ate chicken regularly, either because they were wealthy enough to do so or because they considered the extra cost to be worthwhile – as is the case with lamb in the 21st century. Another aspect of purchase occasion relates to gift-giving: the vast majority of sales of aftershave are made to women. Relatively little aftershave is bought by men for their own use. Purchase occasion might also relate to situational factors: buying a new car battery may come about because of a growing awareness that the existing battery is getting old, or it might be as a result of a sudden failure of the battery far from home. Different versions of the same product might also be purchased at different times – someone travelling for business purposes may decide to stay in a four-star business-class hotel, but when on holiday might prefer a crumbling old bed-and-breakfast because such places have more character. Going to a restaurant because one is too tired to cook results in a different choice of restaurant from that chosen when celebrating a wedding anniversary or a birthday, and even the choice between a romantic restaurant with cosy corners (for a wedding anniversary or first date) and a lively restaurant with entertainment for celebrating a birthday with friends is an example of purchase occasion differences.

- *Purchase behaviour* relates to time of purchase, place of purchase, quantities bought on each occasion, degree of willingness to buy innovative products and so forth. For example, books might be bought from a bookshop, second-hand from a charity shop, on-line from retailers such as Amazon, or even in a street market. Each type of behaviour relates to the consumer concerned, but may not relate to other characteristics: someone might enjoy shopping on-line, whereas another person might prefer the bargain-hunting aspects of browsing in a second-hand bookshop. The same person might enjoy both ways of buying books – on-line for practical, work-related purchases, second-hand for personal books for leisure reading. The individual's motivation may or may not be concerned with saving money; many people shop on-line because it is more convenient than shopping in retail stores (for example, because the individual lives in a remote area, is house-bound or their working life makes it difficult to get to a bricks-and-mortar retailer). Brand loyalty is also an element in purchase behaviour: high involvement with the brand means that the marketer will try to identify and recruit those customers, whereas brand switchers can only be lured by sales promotions.
- *Usage.* Some customers use the product more frequently and in higher quantities than do others. Users are usually divided into heavy users, medium users, light users, ex-users and non-users. The aim of the marketers is to move people from being non-users to being heavy users if possible. Non-users are not, of course, consumers of the product but they may present an opportunity if the product is appropriate for their needs – clearly there will always be some people who will never buy the product under any circumstances. Light users and medium users can be encouraged to use more of the product, and although this is probably a great deal easier than recruiting new customers most firms still spend the greater part of their effort on recruitment rather than development. A neglected area of marketing has been customer win-back, which is the re-enrolling of former customers. These people represent a good opportunity – they already know the company and its products, and in many cases defected to another company for fairly trivial reasons. In many cases, firms seek to recruit heavy users from their competitors, but this can be a dangerous tactic if it provokes heavy competitive responses.
- *Buyer readiness stage.* Some people may be on the verge of buying the product, whereas others may never have heard of it. Still others may have an interest in the product but do not have any money, others might be aware of the product but are not yet interested, others might be interested but do not at present have a need for the product, and so forth. Marketers need to be aware of these stages and be prepared to act at the appropriate time: for example, a couple who have just bought their first house will not currently be in the market to buy another, but very well might be in five to seven years' time, when perhaps they have started a family or are earning more money. Contacting people at the wrong time (when they are not ready to buy) is irritating for the customer and a waste of resources for the company, whereas contacting people at the right time (when they are considering another purchase) is helpful and productive in terms of generating business.
- *Attitude towards the product.* In some cases, the non-user's attitude towards the product is so hostile that there is really no point in trying to change it. Political parties know that many of their supporters will be loyal no matter what happens, and that the same is true of their opposition; efforts are usually concentrated on the 'floating voters' who might be persuaded one way or the other. Likewise, Disneyland Paris know that about 20% of the population of Europe would never visit the theme park – their values and lifestyles simply would not permit it.
- *Media usage.* The types of media the individual consumes are clearly of interest since (as marketers) we need to communicate with our target audience. Additionally, the quantity of media consumed is relevant – an individual who

reads several newspapers, or who watches a wide range of TV channels, will be exposed to a great deal more advertising than one who rarely opens a newspaper or watches very little TV.

- *Preferences*. Research among Norwegian teenagers found four preference types: food lovers, fish haters, fish lovers, and dislikers. Within these preferences the teenagers chose specific products: the conclusion was that family-related attitude and lifestyle variables explained segment membership much better than demographic variables (Honkanen et al. 2004).

Segmenting markets according to the behaviour of the customers within them makes perfect sense since our interest in customers lies ultimately in how they behave. What people do is a great deal more important than who they are or what they think, at least in terms of marketing. For example, motor vehicle users can be segmented much more effectively in terms of whether they prefer to lease their cars or buy them outright than by demographic characteristics (Trocchia et al. 2006).

Life events can have a profound effect on brand preferences (Mathur et al. 2003). Adjustments to new life situations brought about by moving to a new place, a bereavement, a major conflict with a family member, a change of job or financial status, and so forth may lead to a change of favourite brand. The authors believe that life events and life status changes might prove better predictors of behaviour and hence be a better base for segmentation, but it is hard to see how such a segmentation base could be quantified or the actual segments identified.

Consumer behaviour and products

A product is a bundle of benefits, but those benefits are likely to go far beyond the physical item itself. The overt features and benefits of a product are based on the individual's cognitive faculties, but many aspects of the product will appeal to the individual's affective and conative aspects. The following aspects of products go beyond the rational decision-making process:

- *Branding*. The brand may increase the observability of the product and strengthen the individual's self-image. Wearing the right brand of clothing and driving the right brand of car are both ways of telling the world who one is: getting it wrong can lead to social disaster. The brand of the product appears to be more important than the corporate brand, at least on packaging (Laforet 2011): this may be due to the greater immediacy of the product brand, and the tendency for people to become involved with the brand.
- *Styling*. The appearance of many products adds to the hedonic aspects of the product. For example, a sports car may stand out for its styling rather than for its road performance or brand. Even the appearance of the packaging affects people's perception of the product: since people process positive information differently from the way they process negative information, unattractive packages register in the same part of the brain as unfair offers or disgusting pictures (Stoll et al. 2008).
- *Manufacturer's reputation*. Although reputation is often part of the cognitive aspects of ownership, reputation also colours affective aspects. For example, a manufacturer might have a good reputation for socially responsible business practices, or may have been exceptionally helpful on a previous occasion. People will form a view about a company's ethical credentials based on relatively little information (Brunk 2010). This makes control of corporate reputation rather a challenging proposition.

As we saw in previous chapters, the affective aspects of purchase often outweigh the cognitive. For example, motorcycle manufacturers know that they are largely selling on a self-image platform: the majority of bikers are middle-aged men who can afford the bike and afford the insurance. These men buy the bikes to re-live a dream of youth: this has virtually nothing to do with the practical need for economical transportation which was the motorcycle's original reason for existence.

Being the first to own a new product can be a powerful motivation for an individual. Again, this can be an esteem issue: showing off to one's friends can be powerful. Equally there is a degree of pleasure in just owning something that very few other people have – exclusivity is a powerful factor not only in buying new products, but also in buying expensive ones. Buying a 'tailor-made' product also has a powerful appeal – hence the explosion in mass customisation in recent years, accompanied by a sharp rise in subjectivity (Addis and Holbrook 2001).

From the viewpoint of a supplier, offering a product that appeals to self-image, self-esteem and aesthetic needs is at least as important as offering one that meets practical needs.

As we have seen elsewhere, the brand is an important factor in judging products. Bengtsson (2003) has suggested that the personification of brands by consumers is a result of marketing activities, specifically the discourse from marketers about relationship marketing. This may or may not be true, but it raises interesting issues about how marketers may be able to manipulate opinion. People often conceive a dislike of brands, sometimes because of what the brand symbolises or because of a dislike of the corporation rather than the actual product characteristics (Dalli et al. 2006), so firms would be well advised to avoid manipulative behaviour. During a brand crisis (for example, a major accident on an airline) the news media can amplify the crisis and destroy trust, even when the consumer has direct experience of using the brand (Yannopolou et al. 2011).

Trust has sometimes been engendered by carrying out socially responsible activities such as sponsoring charities. However, companies that carry out socially responsible initiatives that do not appear to have any connection with the firm are often distrusted – perhaps because people perceive it as a 'tick the box' exercise or an attempt to 'whitewash' the firm (Becker-Olsen and Cudmore 2004).

A problem for marketers lies in whether or not to extend a successful brand. In some cases, brand extensions will strengthen the overall brand, but in other cases a brand extension might actually damage the brand. Applying the brand name to a lower-quality product does not always damage the brand (Heath et al. 2006), but the reasons for this are not clear. Other researchers have found that the position of a specific product within the overall brand is more important to consumers than the differences between brands (LeClerc et al. 2002). This may be a function of brand loyalty.

Price That which is given in exchange for receiving the benefits of a product

Price

The price of something is the total cost of adopting the product. This includes the purchase price, the cost of switching from an existing product to the new product and the cost of maintaining and using the product. The balance between these various elements of the total cost will vary from one product to another, of course, but the astute supplier will recognise that (in some cases) prices can be adjusted in one area to take account of costs in another.

Costs to the customer include internal costs (learning to use the product, time spent buying it and getting it to work properly, disposing of the product after use), acquisition costs (purchase price, delivery, installation, etc.) and costs related to risk. The total of these costs will be taken into account when assessing whether the benefits outweigh the price. Note that not all these costs can be expressed in financial terms, and not all of the price asked by the supplier is monetary. For example, a supplier might expect a customer to accept a greater part of the risk in exchange for a lower price, as is the case when someone buys a 'standby' theatre ticket. In exchange for a lower price, the customer accepts that the ticket may not be honoured at the desired time – the supplier has traded off the risk of not being able to sell the seat against getting a lower monetary price.

As can be seen in Figure 16.2, customer benefits fall into functional, operational, financial and personal categories. The functional are those that come to mind most readily, related to the physical aspects of the product – these often relate closely to the individual's cognition of the product. In the longer term, operational benefits such as reliability and durability, financial aspects such as savings made over the period of ownership, and personal benefits such as feelings of well-being and of ownership, will assume greater importance.

Consumers need to balance these factors carefully in order to arrive at a final evaluation of the product's worth. Provided the benefits exceed the costs, the consumer will be happy with the outcome; if the costs exceed the benefits, the consumer will not be happy with the outcome. In the long term, marketers should seek to ensure that benefits always outweigh costs, but either side of the equation can be adjusted: if the marketer can offer greater benefits without increasing the cost to the consumer, this is a valid way of achieving value for money. If benefits cannot be improved, then the only way to improve value for money is to reduce the costs – not necessarily the initial acquisition price, but (possibly) the other costs.

PRICE SENSITIVITY

Establishing the needs of each segment is a precursor to developing appropriate pricing for each segment. In some cases, a product can be customised to meet the specific needs of a segment and priced at a premium because of the customisation. In setting prices for specific segments, the marketing director must estimate the price sensitivity of that particular market segment. Dolan (1995) listed factors that affect customer price sensitivity: these are listed in Table 16.1.

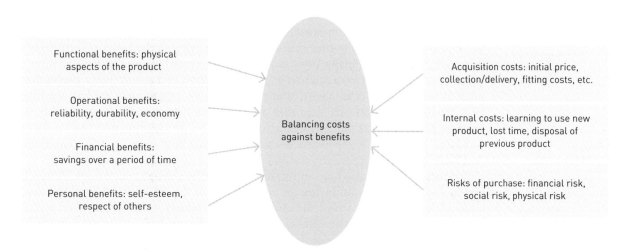

Figure 16.2 Cost–benefit trade-offs

Table 16.1   Factors affecting customer price sensitivity

Economics
• Percentage of total expense
• Type of consumer
• Level of involvement
Search and usage
• Cost of information search
• Ease of comparing competitive alternatives
• Switching costs
Competition
• Differentiation
• Perception of price

The major categories are customer economics, search and usage, and competition. Customers will be more sensitive if the percentage cost of the particular item is large in comparison to the total expense that the customer is making to achieve a particular end. Should the item be of extreme importance to the consumer, price sensitivity will tend to decline because reliability becomes paramount. Of course, some people are simply more frugal than others and therefore sensitive to prices across the board: some students are more frugal in their drinking habits than others, for example (Rose et al. 2010). Equally, even the most loyal customers can be swayed by price promotions (Rajagopal 2008).

Reviewing the search and usage category, customers will be more price-sensitive if information search is easy and cheap, and competitive offerings are easily compared. In addition, the customer's price sensitivity is increased substantially where switching costs are low. Switching costs are all the costs associated with changing from one particular product or service to another. For example, a consumer might become persuaded that Apple Mac software is better than Microsoft, but would find it difficult to change because of the extra time needed to learn the new system, and the time needed to convert existing files. These costs may outweigh the benefits seen from a potential new system. Finally, price sensitivity is decreased where the manufacturer's offering is clearly differentiated from its competition and where price perception gives an aura of quality to a particular product. In general, people are less sensitive to a downsizing in pack size than they are to a price increase: this is presumably an error of perception on the part of the individual, but for routine purchases a slight reduction in quantity is apparently less noticeable than an increase in price (Gourville and Koehler 2003).

Price sensitivity has also been shown to be affected by changing currencies. Research conducted in Germany following the replacement of the deutschmark with the euro showed that people perceived the quality of the products to be higher when priced in deutschmarks because the number of deutschmarks was higher than the number of euros, although the actual price had not changed (Molz and Gielnik 2006).

Price sensitivity can be affected by marketing, and especially selling, approaches. In some cases customers have an unrealistically low expectation of prices. Salespeople will sometimes therefore suggest (in a subtle manner) that the price might be very high indeed so that the real price comes as a pleasant surprise. This technique is also used by some catalogue marketers: by including extremely high-priced articles in the catalogue, marketers can 'price-condition' potential customers into believing that other products in the catalogue represent a bargain (Krishna et al. 2002).

Some pricing methods take no account of customers at all. Cost-plus pricing, in which the total costs of manufacturing the product are totalled up and a profit margin added on, is still commonly used by manufacturers even though it takes no account of what the customers are prepared to pay. The result of this exercise will hardly ever be a price that a consumer would recognise as 'correct': it will almost certainly either be too high or too low. If the price is too high, people will not pay it; if it is too low, people may be suspicious of the quality of the product or at the very least the firm will be forgoing a surplus profit.

CUSTOMER-BASED PRICING METHODS

The various approaches to customer-based pricing do not necessarily mean offering products at the lowest possible price, but they do take account of customer needs and wants.

CUSTOMARY PRICING

Customary pricing is customer-orientated in that it provides the customer with the product for the same price at which it has always been offered. An example is the price of a call from a coin-operated telephone box. Telephone companies need only reduce the time allowed for the call as costs rise. For some countries (e.g. Australia) this is problematical since local calls are allowed unlimited time, but for most European countries this is not the case.

The reason for using customary pricing is to avoid having to reset the call-boxes too often. Similar methods exist for taxis, some children's sweets, and gas or electricity pre-payment meters. If this method were to be used for most products there would be a steady reduction in the firm's profits as the costs catch up with the selling price, so the method is not practical for every firm.

Customary pricing
Retaining the same price for a product over a long period, perhaps by adjusting the quantity provided as a way of maintaining profitability

DEMAND PRICING

Demand pricing is the most market-orientated method of pricing. Here, the marketer begins by assessing what the demand will be for the product at different price levels. This is usually done by asking customers what they might expect to pay for the product, and seeing how many choose each price level. This will lead to the development of the kind of chart shown in Table 16.2

As the price rises, fewer customers are prepared to buy the product, as fewer will still see the product as good value for money. In the example given above, the fall-off is not linear, i.e. the number of units sold falls dramatically once the price goes above £5. This kind of calculation could be used to determine the stages of a skimming policy (see below), or it could be used to calculate the appropriate launch price of a product.

For demand pricing, the next stage is to calculate the costs of producing the product in the above quantities. Usually the cost of producing each item falls as more are made (i.e. if we make 50,000 units, each unit costs less than would be the case if we only make 1000 units). Given the costs of production it is possible to select the price that will lead to a maximisation of profits. This is because there is a trade-off

Demand pricing Calculating the price of a product according to consumer demand at different price levels

Table 16.2 Demand pricing

Price per unit	Number of customers who said they would buy at this price
£3 to £4	30,000
£4 to £5	25,000
£5 to £6	15,000
£6 to £7	5,000

between quantity produced and quantity sold; as the firm lowers the selling price, the amount sold increases but the income generated decreases.

The calculations can become complex, but the end result is that the product is sold at a price that customers will accept, and that will meet the company's profit targets.

PRODUCT-LINE PRICING

Product-line pricing
Pricing that takes account of the price of related products

Product-line pricing means setting prices within linked product groups. Often sales of one product will be directly linked to the sales of another, so that it is possible to sell one item at a low price in order to make a greater profit on the other one.

Consumer behaviour in action: Giving the products away

King C. Gillette, the inventor of the safety razor, was faced with something of a problem in marketing the product. He realised very early on that the revolutionary disposable blades in the razor would be expensive to manufacture unless he could produce them in their millions – but without a large, established market to sell to he would not be able to obtain those economies of scale. The razors themselves were a revolutionary idea, and consequently each prospective purchaser needed to be persuaded to try the new system, but this was simply too time-consuming.

Gillette had, in his youth, been a salesman. He applied his knowledge of customers to the problem and came up with a new idea that is still in use today, over a hundred years later. He simply adjusted the pricing so that the up-front cost of adopting the product was low, and the ongoing maintenance cost relatively higher than it would otherwise have been. He gave away the razors, so that customers could try the new system for free: Gillette knew that hardly any of them would return to using cut-throat razors after using the disposable blades, and he made his money selling the blades.

Safety razors became so well-established in the market that, only a short while later, cut-throat razors are virtually unheard-of. Gillette's company successfully used the same marketing ploy some eighty years later to introduce a multi-blade system, but this was quickly overtaken by disposable razors, which are regarded as the norm nowadays.

Polaroid chose to sell its instant cameras very cheaply (almost for cost price) for the US market and to take their profit from selling the films for a much higher price. For Europe, the firm chose to sell both films and cameras for a medium-level price and profit from sales of both. Eventually this led Kodak to enter the market with its own instant camera, but this was withdrawn from sale in the face of lawsuits from Polaroid for patent infringement.

SKIMMING

Skimming is the practice of starting out with a high price for a product, then reducing it progressively as sales level off. It relies on two main factors: first, that not all customers have the same perception of value for money, and second that the company has a technological lead over the opposition which can be maintained for long enough to satisfy the market.

Skimming is usually carried out by firms that have developed a technically advanced product. Initially the firm will charge a high price for the product, and at this point only those who are prepared to pay a premium price for it will buy. Profit may not be high, because the number of units sold will be low and therefore the cost of production per unit will be high. Once the most innovative customers have bought, and the competition is beginning to enter the market, the firm can drop the price and 'skim' the next layer of the market, at which point profits will begin to rise. Eventually the product will be sold at a price that allows the firm only a minimum profit, at which point only replacement sales or sales to late adopters will be made.

Figure 16.3 shows how skimming works. At each price level, the product shows a standard product life cycle curve. As the curve tops out and begins to fall back, the company lowers the price and the cycle starts again with a new group of consumers. The process continues until either the market is saturated or the company decides that it cannot make any further price reductions.

The advantage of this method is that the cost of developing the product is returned fairly quickly, so that the product can later be sold near the marginal cost of production. This means that competitors have difficulty entering the market at all, since their own development costs will have to be recovered in some other way.

Skimming relies heavily on consumer perceptions and attitudes. In effect, it takes advantage of basic segmentation – people who are prepared to pay a premium price will do so, whereas the laggards and those prepared to pay less will enter the market later.

Skimming Setting price high when a product is launched, then gradually lowering them as competitors enter the market

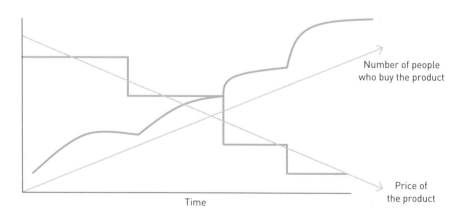

Figure 16.3 Skimming

PSYCHOLOGICAL PRICING

Psychological pricing
Applying prices to goods
based on perceptual
issues such as quality

Psychological pricing relies on emotional responses from the consumer. Higher prices are often used as an indicator of quality, so some firms will use prestige pricing. This applies in many service industries, because consumers are often buying a promise; a service that does not have a high enough quality cannot be exchanged afterwards. Consumers' expectations of high-priced restaurants and hairdressers are clearly higher in terms of the quality of service provision; cutting prices in those industries does not necessarily lead to an increase in business. **Odd–even pricing** is the practice of ending prices with an odd number, for example £3.99 or $5.95 rather than £4 or $6. It appears that consumers tend to categorise these prices as '£3 and a bit' or '$5 and change' and thus perceive the price as being lower. The effect may also be due to an association with discounted or sale prices; researchers report that '99' endings on prices increase sales by around 8% (Schindler and Kirby 1997).

Odd–even pricing The
practice of ending prices with
'99p' or '99c'

Recent research has shown that odd–even pricing does not necessarily work in all cultures (Suri et al. 2004). In Poland, for example, the effects are negligible. Odd–even pricing also has effects on perceptions of discounts during sales. Rounding the price to (say) £5 from £4.99 leads people to overvalue the size of the discount, which increases the perception of value for money (Gueguen and Legoherel 2004). Thus the positive effect on sales of using a 99-ending can be negated when the product is on offer in a sale. There is also evidence that rounding prices up to an even amount encourages trial of products (Bray and Harris 2006).

In China, there is evidence to suggest that prices ending in 8 are more effective than prices ending in 4, because 8 is a lucky number and 4 is unlucky (Simmons and Schindler 2003).

On-line retailers have found that 'bundling' the price and including 'free' shipping and handling appears to work effectively as a purchasing incentive, leading to more favourable memories and fewer product returns (Roggeveen et al. 2006). A similar effect may exist in hire-purchase or credit deals: people relate the benefits they gain from the product to the actual payments they are making at the time. This means that, as the product gets older and the benefits reduce (for example, a car becomes more expensive to maintain and does not run as well), the customer perceives the payments as worse value for money (Seigyoung and Chuang-Foh 2006). This perhaps means that HP companies should reduce the payments over time.

SECOND-MARKET DISCOUNTING

Second-market
discounting Charging a lower
price for one group of people
in order to even out demand

Second-market discounting is common in some service industries and in international markets. The brand is sold at one price in one market, and in a lower price in another; for example, museums offer discounts to students, some restaurants offer discounts to elderly people on week nights, and so forth. Often these discounts are offered to even out the loading on the firm; week-night discounts fill the restaurant on what would otherwise be a quiet night, so making more efficient use of the premises and staff.

Figure 16.4 shows how second-market discounting works. At the bottom of each column is the amount of full-price business a retailer does on each day. Friday and Saturday are the busiest days, so on the other four days of the week the firm offers various discounts. On Monday the retailer offers 10% off to all customers, which boosts business that day to a level higher than that of the weekend trade. Tuesday is senior citizen day, and Wednesday and Thursday are student discount days. These days are aimed at people who are able to shop mid-week.

Obviously these discounts may cannibalise sales on other days: a senior citizen might have been willing to shop on a Saturday and pay the full price (or might even have shopped on a Tuesday anyway, simply because the shop is quieter).

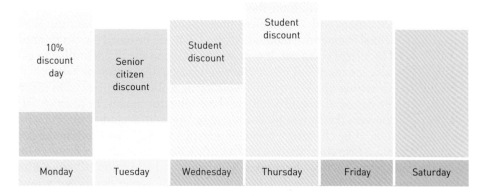

Figure 16.4 Second-market discounting

In international markets products might be discounted to meet local competition. For example, Honda motorcycles are up against strong local competition in India from Royal Enfield, so the price of their basic 50cc scooter is around Rs47,000 (about £570). A similar Honda scooter in the UK costs around £1650. The specifications of the motorcycles do differ somewhat – but it is difficult to see any difference that would account for a £1100 price differential.

PRICING IN BUSINESS MARKETS

In business markets, pricing has a somewhat different role because the purchasing process tends to be more rational, and is often much more price-sensitive. Pricing policies include deciding upon list price and discount levels, allowances, rebates and geographic differences (standardisation vs. differentiation).

The question of list price varies by industry. In some industries, list prices are set in such a way that no customer ever pays that price. The list prices for a product line are set in order to provide various levels of discount. Discounts can be given for volume purchases, whether cumulative or based on individual order, or based on time of order.

Allowances and rebates are simply price reductions given to dealers or distributors to help them promote a particular manufacturer's product. Some firms give advertising allowances to their distributors in order to encourage them to promote their particular product or even for identifying their facilities such as showrooms or service vehicles with a particular brand name. A firm may choose to offer a trade-in allowance for older products in order to replace them with newer versions. A rebate is a fee paid to a purchaser once the product is bought and installed.

COMPETITIVE BIDDING

B2B sales are often completed through competitive bids. This is especially true for government institutions and non-profit organisations such as hospitals. Some non-governmental firms also use competitive bids. In some cases, a firm may require a bid to a particular specification and then reserve the right to negotiate further with the winning bidder. Firms use specification buying especially for large projects. These firms develop detailed specifications either based on the performance or description of a particular product, service or a combination of both. Firms supplying military products or large power factories or other major projects need to develop an expertise not only in the bidding process, but also in the specification process. 'Specmanship' means a firm's sales force is expert at helping a customer develop specifications that will limit the bidders. The most successful sales people can develop specifications with requirements that can be met only by their firm. When faced with a potential competitive bidding situation that will be based on specifications to be developed by a large customer, it is necessary to spend the required time to gain the most favourable specifications possible before bidding documents are released.

The purpose of setting up a competitive bidding or tendering process is, in theory, to ensure that the customer organisation gets best value for money. In practice, suppliers often circumvent the system by encouraging buyers to include specific factors in the specification, or by charging exorbitant amounts for any variations on the contract. For example, a firm contracted to refit an office building might put in a very low bid on the contract, but charge large sums for changing the location of office doors from those specified on the original plans, or for relocating power points. Such minor variations might not actually cost the fitters anything at all, but are simply a way of showing a profit on an otherwise unprofitable low-bid contract.

In some cases, government organisations have become more sophisticated in their dealings with contractors, and take greater care over their specifications to ensure that all external factors are taken into account. For example, the UK Highway Agency now charges road builders a 'rental' for the piece of road they are working on, so that there is an incentive to complete the work more quickly. This was in response to a common practice in the construction industry of agreeing to a large number of contracts at the same time in order to ensure a flow of work for months at a time.

Place

Place The element of the marketing mix concerned with the location where the exchange takes place

Place refers to the location where the exchange takes place. The place element of the marketing mix goes beyond mere convenience: often the place is, in effect, part of the product because it provides hedonic benefits of its own. For example, consider the purchase of antiques. Some antique buyers will scour car boot sales, house clearance sales, auction rooms and so forth in the hope of picking up a bargain. Others will go to antique shops where most of the searching has already been done, while others will visit upmarket antique galleries where the pieces will be artfully displayed and the customer will be offered a glass of wine and a canapé while browsing.

In the course of the antique's passage from car boot sale to gallery the price may well have risen from £5 to £2000, yet at each stage of the process the purchaser has bought a bargain. The reason is that the place element has added value in some way or another. The car boot bargain hunter may have spent weeks or months trawling through junk to find the valuable item, and may also have spent a great deal of money on items that have turned out to be worthless. However, the hedonic aspects of bargain hunting make the search worthwhile. At the other end of the chain, the wealthy collector enjoying a glass of wine at the gallery is enjoying having someone explain the history of the item, and is able to invest a substantial amount of money in something he or she knows is of real value. The reputation of the gallery ensures that the product is the genuine article – something the average boot-sale bargain hunter cannot be sure of.

Buying goods from a catalogue, on-line, from a street market or from a retailer each has its hedonic aspects, and marketers need to balance the place utility (cognitive) aspects against the hedonic (affective) aspects of the point of purchase.

SHOPPING BEHAVIOUR

People have many motives for shopping, going beyond a simple need to obtain goods and services. These can be divided into social motives and personal motives, each of which determine the choice of retailer, the time spent shopping and much of the effort which is expended.

Social motives include the following:

- *Social experience outside the home.* Talking to shop assistants, going shopping with a friend or friends or getting out of the house for a while are included here.
- *Communication with others having a similar interest.* Whether shopping for clothes or computers, people enjoy taking a friend along, especially if the friend has a specific expertise that can be used.
- *Peer group attraction.* Going to specific shops means mingling with people from a similar social background. This is reassuring in terms of self-image.
- *Status and authority.* Being a customer is a pleasant experience – the shop assistants (if they are well-trained) are attentive and interested in the customers' needs, which means that customers enjoy the warm glow of being looked after.
- *Pleasure of bargaining.* In some situations in every country, bargaining is acceptable, and in some countries it is normal practice almost everywhere. The bargaining process is enjoyable because it has the elements of power, of exercising skill and of getting a bargain.

Personal motives include the following:

- *Role playing.* Playing the part of the customer is a pleasant experience: some people even adopt a new persona when shopping, in order to enhance their own self-esteem.
- *Diversion.* Looking at new products is an entertainment in itself, and browsing around the shops can be a relaxing way of spending some time.
- *Self-gratification.* Meeting one's own needs by buying goods relieves the tensions set up by lacking something that is regarded as essential.
- *Learning about new trends.* Learning is, in itself, a pleasurable thing. Being the first to know about new products is important for some people's self-esteem.
- *Physical activity.* Often people have sedentary lives: going for a walk round the shops can relieve this. Often people experience this motivation when on holiday – relaxing on the beach or by the pool quickly becomes boring.
- *Sensory stimulation.* Simply exposing one's senses to new sensations is pleasurable, and shopping fulfils this role admirably.

Choice of retailer is determined by the proximity of the store (the closer, the better), the store design and physical facilities, the merchandise on offer, advertising and sales promotion activities, store personnel, customer service and the other clients. This last is an interesting example of a factor over which the store does not have direct control, but it clearly has an influence on the image of the store and the shopping experience. A store with an upmarket clientele and image will attract people who associate themselves with that image; a store with a downmarket image and a disreputable clientele will repel more upmarket clients.

Promotion

As we saw in Chapter 5, promotion is about creating appropriate perceptions in consumers' minds. However, people also consume marketing messages through the media – they enjoy watching some advertisements, they enjoy watching films which have brands placed in them and they enjoy reading informative articles about product categories with which they are involved.

Promotion The element of the marketing mix concerned with communication

How advertising works (and occasionally whether advertising works) has been a topic for debate in marketing academia for a number of years now. Part of the problem is that there is no way of telling whether something works unless one first defines what it is that one is trying to achieve. Since there are many possible objectives for an advertising campaign, ranging from increasing purchases through to reinforcing attitudes, there can be no single explanation for whether advertising works (Wright and Crimp 2000).

Consumer behaviour in action: Measuring advertising in Australia

The Australian Government, in conjunction with six universities and the state governments of Victoria and Queensland, has established the National Information and Communications Technology of Australia organisation. NICTA, as it is known, has the role of encouraging excellence in research into communications technology.

One of NICTA's inventions is a software system that can recognise faces and determine in which direction they are looking. Linked to a camera, this system allows advertisers to know how many people look at their billboards, and even which area of the billboard has attracted their attention. The software, Targeted Advertising Based on Audience Natural Response or TABANAR, offers advertisers a golden opportunity to fine-tune their billboard ads and also to have a direct measure of audience response. This is likely to be much more accurate than traditional methods of measuring response, which involve, for example, coupon returns, calls made to free telephone numbers or returned text messages.

In some countries there may be issues of privacy involved with putting secret cameras on billboards and recording people without their consent, but the system itself uses remarkable technology to provide information that has been previously unobtainable.

Two general theories about advertising have emerged from the debate, summarised in Figure 16.5. The strong theory suggests that advertising is a powerful force that can change attitudes and make a significant contribution to people's knowledge and understanding. The weak theory of advertising suggests that advertising can only 'nudge' people in the direction in which they are already moving; in other words, it reinforces rather than persuades (Ehrenberg 1992).

The main criticisms of the strong theory of advertising are (first) that there is little evidence to show that consumers develop a strong desire for the brand before trying it, and second the model only considers non-buyers who become buyers. In

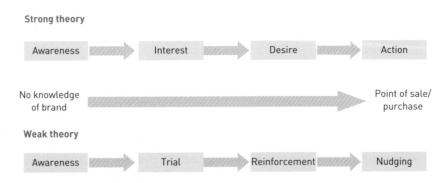

Figure 16.5 Strong and weak theories of advertising

most markets, advertising is intended to affect people who have already tried the product, either with a view to informing them about changes in the product, or to remind them about the product, or to encourage increased purchases of the product. The strong theory tends to be more prevalent in the United States, and it is of course possible that American experience is different from European experience; the weak theory tends to have more adherents in Europe. Research in FMCG (fast-moving consumer goods) markets shows that people are not usually loyal to one brand, and that it is extremely difficult for a new brand to become established in the portfolio of brands people buy. In these circumstances, most advertising is intended to improve brand loyalty and therefore defend the brand: this would tend to support the weak theory, because it implies that the main people to be affected by the advertising are existing customers for the brand.

Challenging the status quo

If advertising is only a weak force, and doesn't persuade anybody, why is so much money spent on it by companies? Surely they wouldn't pay out billions of pounds, dollars, yen and euros every year just on the chance that it might work?

On the other hand, when was the last time you saw an advert and then went rushing out to buy a product? Have you EVER been persuaded by an advertisement? Are advertisements like the bumble bee – in theory too aerodynamically unsound to fly, but in practice it still flies?

Level of involvement has a role to play in determining the effects of advertising, and may also have a bearing on when the strong theory applies, and when the weak theory predominates (Jones 1991). In the case of a high-involvement purchase, consumers are more likely to access sought communications (Blythe 2003; also see Chapter 14), and are likely to be more affected by advertising since they will be actively seeking out advertising messages. In the case of low-involvement purchases, consumers are less likely to seek out advertising and are therefore only likely to be moved slightly by the unsought communications around them.

When there are many competing advertisements for similar products (for example, in specialist magazines such as sport or hobby magazines), varying the context in which the advertisement is seen will increase its memorability (Unnava et al. 2003). In other words, if some method exists for repeating the advertisement in a different context (for example, by putting a copy of the advertisement on a notice board at a sports club), it is more likely to have an impact on the target audience.

> **Unsought communications**
> Messages that have not been looked for by the recipient

ACTIVE MEDIA: TV, RADIO AND CINEMA

TV, radio and cinema are powerful media because they are active (Figure 16.6) – they actually do something. TV and radio are probably the most pervasive media in most countries – in Western Europe, TV ownership is almost 100% and many homes have several television sets. Radio ownership is at least as widespread. People watch TV while eating, doing housework, relaxing or even while entertaining friends. In some homes the set is rarely switched off. Significantly, the biggest-selling consumer magazines in most Western European countries and in the United States are the TV programme guides.

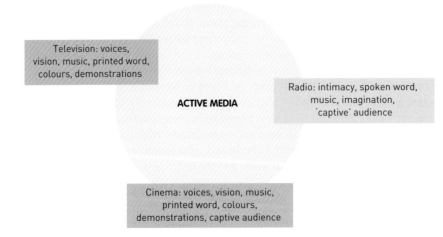

Figure 16.6   Active media

Because television advertising is an unsought communication (people rarely, if ever, switch on the TV in order to see a favourite advertisement) it works best for activating needs or providing information for the internal search. In most cases, advertisers are aiming to build the image of their product or firm, and to a large extent these aims can be met by television (McKechnie and Leather 1998).

Research at the London Business School shows that people do not necessarily watch the advertisements even if they are still in the room when the advertisement airs (Ritson 2003). The researchers identified a total of six behaviours that occur while the advertisement is on-screen: these are shown in Table 16.3 and Figure 16.7. The first three activities are interesting in that the standard method of measuring advertising on TV, which is the people meter, would have shown that people were in the room and would therefore have assumed that they were watching the advertisement. In fact, in each of these three cases, presence in the room does not mean observation of the advertising.

Interestingly, there is research evidence that advertisements that are **zapped** (i.e. the viewer flicks to another channel or turns the sound off) or zipped (fast-forwarded if the viewer is watching a recording) are more likely to have a positive effect on brand purchase than those that are not (Zufryden et al. 1993). This is presumably because the viewer has to watch at least part of the advertisement and process the content before knowing that it is a candidate for zapping.

Fast-paced advertisements appear to have a positive effect on involuntary attention, in other words they are more eye-catching, but have little effect on involuntary attention (they are no more likely to be watched actively) (Bolls et al. 2003). Furthermore, fast-paced advertisements tend to focus people on the style of the advertisement, not on its content: people remember the advertisement, but not the brand. Mood affects people's response to advertisements, so placing the advertisement in an appropriate programme may have a critical effect on its success or otherwise (Bakamitsos and Siomkos 2003).

There is a clear relationship between liking the advertisement and subsequent sales, but this is not always a positive relationship. Liking the advertisement seems to be related to whether the product is meaningful and relevant to the person at the time (Biel 1990), and there is evidence that advertisements relating to food and drink are more likely to be liked than are non-food advertisements (Biel and Bridgwater 1990). Liking is usually linked to a positive view of the product, which in turn is

Zipping Using the TV remote control to fast-forward through advertisements on a recorded programme

Table 16.3 Behaviour in commercial breaks

Behaviour	Explanation
Reading	Many people watch TV with a book or magazine at hand, to read during the breaks. Sometimes the reading will be a TV guide
Social interaction	People often talk about their day, discuss household problems or gossip while the commercial break runs
Tasking	The commercial break often affords an opportunity to load the dishwasher, clean the house, do the ironing, pay bills or make telephone calls
Flicking (zapping)	Jumping from one channel to another appeared to be mainly a male activity. Flicking falls into two categories: almost random surfing across a number of other channels while waiting for the programme to restart, or alternatively going to a 'visit channel' such as a news channel for a specific length of time before returning to the programme
Watching the advertisements	In many cases, advertisements were actually watched, and often commented on by the family members
Advertising interaction	The final behaviour involved not only watching the advertisement, but commenting on it, singing along with the jingles and even playing a game in which family members scored 'points' by being the first to recognise the brand

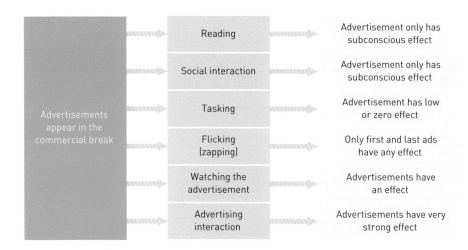

Figure 16.7 Activities in commercial breaks

likely to lead to sales (Biel 1990; Stapel 1991). This situation is sometimes reversed when dealing with, for example, insurance products and the like, where the advertisement might contain shocking imagery as a 'cautionary tale' to show people what can go wrong if they do not have insurance.

It may be difficult to deconstruct all the factors involved, since a truly unpleasant advertisement is likely to be ignored, so that the viewer is less likely to process the information cognitively. Such 'cautionary tale' advertisements are difficult to produce because the affective element is likely to repel the customer, whereas the cognitive element is likely to attract. Products can be placed on an approach–avoidance continuum, with products that are inherently attractive (food and beverages) at one end, and products that are inherently unattractive and are only bought out of dire necessity (pensions, life insurance) at the other (Wells 1980).

Challenging the status quo

If people tend to 'switch off' from unpleasant advertisements, why produce them at all? Why show people scenes of crashed cars and devastated homes in order to frighten them into buying insurance? Maybe the school bully could frighten children into handing over their pocket money – but we're all grown-ups now!

Or maybe people have to be terrorised into buying insurance – otherwise they would just keep putting it off until after they have been burgled or crashed the car! After all, in most countries it is a legal requirement to have car insurance – so doesn't this prove that people won't buy it unless they are threatened with jail?

Off-the-screen commercials (direct-response TV) appear to be a type of television advertising that breaks all the rules. These advertisements have high copy content, are extremely informative and aim to obtain a direct response from viewers by getting them to call an order line and buy the product directly. In the United States, off-the-screen selling has gone a step further with the infomercial, a (typically) half-hour programme consisting of entertainment and news about a specific product. For example, an infomercial about a new type of fishing lure might show anglers using the device, show people catching fish, give tips about the most effective locations for using the lure and so forth. Infomercials are illegal on terrestrial TV in the UK, but they make up approximately 25% of the programming on US cable stations (Steenhuysen 1994). Infomercials provide advertisers with enough time to inform and persuade people about the product's benefits: from the cable TV company's perspective, infomercials fill up air time which would otherwise have to be filled with paid-for programmes.

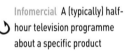

Infomercial A (typically) half-hour television programme about a specific product

RADIO ADVERTISING

Radio is the Cinderella of advertising, often ignored in favour of the higher profile of television. And yet, according to research conducted for Red Dragon Radio, commercial radio has a strong impact on people's lives. According to Red Dragon:

- 44% of radio listeners wake up to a radio alarm.
- 27% of people listen to the radio in the bathroom, and 43% of the 15–24 age group do so.
- 72% of adult listeners listen to the radio in the kitchen.
- 44% of car drivers listen to the radio while driving.
- 44% of employees listen to the radio in the workplace.
- 53% of adults aged 15–24 listen to their radios in the garden.

Radio is a powerful medium because it is intimate: people listen to the radio in private situations, for example in the bathroom or while in bed, and predominantly while driving. Radio acts as a substitute for human company. Radios are cheap and portable, and listening does not require the audience's full attention, so people can do other things (drive, do housework, put on make-up and so forth) while listening.

CINEMA ADVERTISING

For many years the cinema was the only visual advertising medium. Television meant that cinema audiences declined dramatically in the 1950s and 1960s, but in recent years the trend has reversed. A combination of 'blockbuster' movies that have attracted audiences, and the emergence of comfortable, well-equipped cinemas in entertainment complexes has led to a resurgence of cinema attendance as part of a night out.

From the advertiser's viewpoint, cinema has all the advantages of television plus one other: it is impossible to zip, zap or leave the room while the advertisements are on. Consequently, cinemas provide an unrivalled opportunity to speak to a captive audience. British Film Institute statistics show that cinema attendances rose from 34 million per annum in 1988, to 171.6 million visits in 2011: no small audience for advertising. Another factor in rising cinema attendance is the relatively poorer quality of television programming.

Typical cinema audiences are young people in their teens and early twenties: 48% of cinema-goers are aged 7 to 24, although they represent only 22% of the UK population (British Film Institute 2012). The audience in Western countries is also strongly ABC1 in socio-economic profile, while in other less developed countries (notably India) cinema attendance is widespread because of the relatively low level of television ownership.

AMBIENT ADVERTISING

Traditional marketing communications techniques are becoming less effective as markets fragment, costs increase, audiences diminish and clutter worsens (Evans et al. 1996). Therefore, new routes for communicating with customers and consumers are being sought.

Ambient advertising is somewhat difficult to define, although plenty of examples of it are around. In general, it is advertising that becomes part of the environment, where the message is built into the medium. For example, for one campaign an underarm deodorant manufacturer arranged to replace the hanging straps in London Underground carriages with empty bottles of the deodorant. Strap-hanging commuters are acutely aware of underarm odours, and holding onto the bottles instead of the usual straps meant that they had already assumed the position one uses when applying the deodorant. Another development is the invention of a device that converts shop windows into loudspeakers so that the window can 'talk' about the products on display (Grapentine 2003).

Ambient advertising Commercial messages that are designed to become part of the environment

Ambient advertising offers the following advantages:

- It is often cheaper than sales promotions, and when used near the point of purchase gives a good incentive without the loss of profit associated with sales promotion discounts.
- Well-executed ambient campaigns enhance brand image and cut through clutter.
- Novel ambient campaigns often create press coverage: some ambient campaigns are designed with this in mind.
- Ambient advertising is very effective for activating needs.

Ambient advertisers need to consider the relationship between the medium being used, the advertised product or service and the proximity to the point of sale as well as the basic objectives of the campaign. Ambient advertising works best when it is either close to the location of the problem or close to the point of purchase. For example,

Kellogg's Nutrigrain bar was promoted as a snack for commuters who had missed breakfast, so Kellogg's arranged for advertisements for the product to be printed on bus and train tickets. Many travellers were reported to have bought the bars as a result, buying them from station news stands or kiosks near bus stops.

Consumers tend to exhibit little pre-purchase decision-making for low-involvement purchases (Foxall and Goldsmith 1994), and some studies have shown that 70% of all decisions to purchase specific brands are made inside the store (POPAI 1994). Trolley advertising makes around 19% difference to the purchase of specific brands (Shankar 1999a), which demonstrates the power of ambient advertising to nudge consumers. Table 16.4 maps ambient advertising against Ehrenberg's ATRN (Awareness, Trial, Reinforcement, Nudging) model of advertising effects (the weak theory) (Barnard and Ehrenberg 1997; Ehrenberg 1997).

Table 16.4   Mapping of ambient advertising against the ATRN model

Stage	Explanation	Role of ambient advertising
Awareness	Consciousness of a new brand is followed by interest	Consciousness is developed by a high-impact, innovative campaign, e.g. replacing straps with deodorant bottles
Trial	Trial purchase of the brand may occur, perhaps with the consumer in a sceptical frame of mind	Ambient advertising close to the point of sale may be enough to nudge the consumer towards one brand rather than another
Reinforcement	Satisfactory use of the brand will encourage further purchase, or even establish a habitual propensity to buy the brand	Ambient advertising only has a reminder role to play at this stage, and may be no more effective than other advertising
Nudging	Propensity to buy may be enhanced or decreased by the nudging effect of advertising – either the firm's own or that of competitors	Ambient advertising is thought to be better than other advertising for nudging consumers, since it has greater proximity both to the problem and to the point of purchase

Ambient advertising is difficult to measure. First, the creativity of some campaigns is such that no advance predictions can be made. Second, research into the effects of ambient advertising has been relatively small as yet, so suitable test instruments have not been devised. Third, there is no industry-wide evaluation system: there is no estimating system to find out how many people picked up a particular petrol nozzle and therefore saw the advertisement, for example (Shankar 1999b).

In the future, it seems likely that ambient advertising will grow. Although greater creativity is involved in developing a campaign, the impact is high and the cost is relatively low, especially considering the potential spin-off in terms of news coverage. Ambient advertising fits well within an integrated marketing communications approach because it both supports, and is supported by, other communication tools.

INTERNET ADVERTISING

A recent development in Internet advertising has been the use of viral spam programs. Virus writers have been hired by spammers to develop viruses that will propagate spam messages through the address books of infected computers. In 2007 such viral spam programs were used to promote 'penny shares'. Infected computers spread the spam around the world, with some users receiving five to ten copies of the advertisement per day. Clearly such tactics are unethical, and will almost certainly be banned: the difficulty is that the Internet is largely unregulated, messages can originate anywhere in the world, and therefore legislation would need to be ratified by virtually every nation on earth if unethical practices are to be stamped out entirely. It may be possible in the future for ISPs to be forced to develop ways of filtering spam from unregulated countries, but in the current state of the art this is extremely difficult, and many ISPs would regard such measures as being counterproductive since the whole point of the Internet is that it offers worldwide access.

The Internet has empowered consumers to a greater extent than ever before – the ease with which people can research suppliers and are able to switch between them has made suppliers rethink their approach and become much more interactive (Pires et al. 2006). There is evidence that people use various tactics for self-empowerment, as follows (Henry and Caldwell 2006):

- Resignation
- Confrontation
- Withdrawal
- Engagement
- Concealment
- Escapism
- Hedonism
- Spirituality
- Nostalgia
- Creativity.

Trust is sometimes difficult to establish on-line due to the impersonality of the medium. Interpersonal e-trust is important: people respond better if they feel they are dealing with a person rather than a corporation on-line (Pennanen 2011). This may in part account for the observation that pull channels (those approaches that seek to attract end consumers) work better than push channels (those channels that seek to push products down the distribution chain) because they are seen to be more trustworthy (Spilker-Attig and Brettel, 2010).

Regarding Internet tactics, people frequently feel afraid that they will lose control of their inboxes and will be swamped by unsolicited e-mails: this leads them to use tactics such as setting up different e-mail accounts with Internet service providers or giving false details when buying products. The desire to retain control over what is seen as a private medium is strong, and therefore people go to some lengths to avoid becoming victims of clever marketing tactics.

People

As we saw in Chapter 14, some service industries develop strong customer loyalties. These loyalties are almost always based on loyalty to the people working in the industry – whether the business is a hairdressing salon, a butcher's shop or a restaurant, the customer's loyalty is a function of the personal relationship he or she has with the stylist, the butcher or the waiter.

Consumers will tend to use the social interaction as a surrogate measure for judging the quality of the service. A friendly waiter, a confident hairdresser or a knowledgeable butcher will tend to inspire confidence in the overall outcome of the service

People The element of the marketing mix concerned with employees and other consumers

provision, although there is really no guarantee that the actual competence of the supplier relates in any way to these subjective social factors.

Company employees may be divided into four groups (Judd 1987):

Contactors People within an organisation who have daily interaction with customers

1 Contactors. These are the people who have frequent, daily contact with customers. Usually their jobs are marketing-related: salespeople, customer service employees or telesales operators. They are usually trained in customer relations techniques, and are often motivated to deal with customers in an effective and friendly way. Being able to offer a customised recommendation to a consumer is important – people who believe that their preferences are fairly stable appreciate a customised approach (Shen and Ball 2011).

Modifiers People who deal with customers regularly, but who have no specific marketing role

2 Modifiers. These people deal with customers regularly, but have no official marketing role. Receptionists, drivers, telephonists, progress chasers and some warehouse personnel deal with customers on an occasional basis and may need to have some idea of the organisation's marketing policies. It is helpful if modifiers have good people skills, but they may not need special training in this.

Influencers People who exert an advisory role to members of a decision-making unit

3 Influencers. These people have some role within marketing, but have little actual contact with customers. For example, a designer may have the role of styling the product to make it as attractive as possible to consumers, without actually ever dealing with consumers.

Isolateds Employees who have little or no contact with customers

4 Isolateds. These people have no customer contact and little or nothing to do with marketing. Accountants, personnel managers, office cleaners and so forth have important support roles within the organisation but are unlikely ever to do anything which directly impacts on customers. Their role is to help create the right conditions for everyone else to carry out their roles.

A major influence that employees have on customers comes through word of mouth. Employees all go home at the end of the working day, and talk to family and friends about work. This means that each person helps in creating an overall corporate image, which in turn contributes to the customers' perception of the organisation (Maxham and Netemeyer 2003).

The natural variability among human beings will, of course, mean that companies will not always be able to provide optimal service; firms therefore need to be prepared to work to recover from service mistakes when they do occur (Rasmusson 1997). This is often done by empowering contactors and modifiers to make amends immediately. Because the employee is the company (from the viewpoint of the consumer), this approach strengthens the social bonding which is the cornerstone of service provision. In some cases, however, employees may act unethically on behalf of the company; this is especially likely if the employees feel that the company would reciprocate by rewarding them in future, or if they identify strongly with the company (Umphress et al. 2010).

Process The element of the marketing mix concerned with the overall delivery of a service

Process

In services markets, consumers can sometimes be seen as a co-producer of the service. For example, live theatre clearly has serious drawbacks over television: it cannot hope to provide the same level of special effects and scenes, and the actors' performances may not always be perfect (whereas on TV an imperfect performance is simply re-shot). Additionally, going to the theatre involves booking seats, going out in the cold and finding one's way to the theatre, sitting in what are often uncomfortable seats, not being able to have a drink or a snack during the performance, and not being able to press the pause button. The theatre does not allow one to change channels if the play is boring, it does not allow one to turn up the volume if the actors are speaking too quietly and it does not allow one to watch the play wearing a dressing gown. And yet for this experience, people pay for a ticket – so what is the attraction? The main attraction is that there is an atmosphere in the theatre, generated by the presence of an audience – the other consumers. A half-empty theatre seems bleak; a theatre full of people responding to the show helps generate a response in the person watching the play.

As with any other question in marketing, the starting point for developing a service process is the customers' needs. In some cases the needs can be presented as a hierarchy – for example, an aircraft manufacturer may not require new engines to be delivered urgently, but probably would need spare parts to be delivered quickly, as a grounded aircraft is an expensive item. The aero engine manufacturer would therefore see the supply of engines as being less important than the supply of spare parts, and would therefore seek to ensure that the stock of spares is kept up to an appropriate level even if this delayed the completion of new engines.

Service processes fall into three general categories:

1 *Before-sales service processes.* These might include helpful sales staff, readily-available information, availability of samples and availability of supplies.
2 *During-sales processes.* These might include progress-chasing of orders, prompt and reliable delivery, and helpful delivery staff.
3 *After-sales processes.* Courtesy calls, prompt attention to complaints, warranties and service agreements would all be after-sales services.

These processes all involve human interaction, so they all provide opportunities to improve customer loyalty. Unfortunately, they are also easy to copy, and not very difficult to exceed, so it may not be easy to maintain competitive advantage. Also, there is a trade-off between service level and cost: some firms (as we saw in Chapter 14) have been successful by cutting back dramatically on service and reducing prices accordingly. Retailers, low-cost airlines and fast-food restaurants offer minimal service, but have streamlined processes that reduce cost and deliver the core product efficiently. In some cases, the streamlined process might actually be preferable to the more staff-intensive process it replaces – many people find that booking flights on the Internet is a great deal easier than going through a travel agent.

Setting the right level of service can therefore be a source of competitive advantage. The emphasis here is on setting the right level – too high a level of service and the price will have to rise or the profits will have to fall; too low a level and many customers will go elsewhere. Many firms still try to provide a high level of service for a low price – often at the expense of their employees – but this can be done only by shaving profits or otherwise acting in ways that reduce longer-term competitiveness. Note that segmentation still applies – some people are happy to pay for an enhanced service, while others prefer to buy the cheapest. Indeed, individuals often shift between the two levels, depending on the occasion – a couple going out for their 25th wedding anniversary dinner will probably not eat at the same restaurant they might go to for a quick lunch during the working week.

Physical evidence

The intangibility of most of the benefits of a service means that consumers do not have any evidence that the service ever took place. The evidence might be useful to

Physical evidence The element of the marketing mix concerned with the tangible aspects of the products of services

show to other people (a certificate from a training course, a life insurance policy to show to a bank) or it might be simply something to act as a reminder of the pleasure the consumer obtained from the service (a souvenir of a holiday, a menu from a restaurant, a travel kit from an airline). Physical evidence might also be used as a way of assessing the quality of a product before committing to a purchase (the bank branch's decor or the menu in the window of a restaurant).

Challenging the status quo

It's commonly said that you can't judge a book by its cover – yet apparently we are expected to believe that we can judge a bank by its decor. Are we really as naïve as that? Do people seriously think that reading the menu gives any idea of the quality of the food?

There again, what else do we have to go on? We can hardly go into the restaurant and taste the food first! Maybe restaurants should try this as an experiment – let people have a small taste of the food before they commit to buying a meal. This is, after all, what happens in Spain, in many tapas bars.

Some people might think that banks would be better spending their money on reducing their charges or improving their service – but the evidence is that having a smart interior really does affect people's decisions about where to bank. So maybe we really ARE judging the book by the cover!

In some cases the physical element of the product itself is sufficient to act as physical evidence. A meal in a restaurant fulfils this: the food, the surroundings, the quality of the crockery and cutlery all convey evidence about the quality of the experience, even though the greater part of the bill will be absorbed by the chef's time in cooking the food and the waiter's time in delivering it (not to mention the washing up). In other cases, for example life insurance or other financial services, the physical evidence is likely to be much less or lacking altogether, in which case the firm may need to produce something that will provide evidence, for example a glossy brochure or policy document. For practical and legal purposes, most insurance documents could be printed on one or two sheets of paper, but for marketing purposes the document needs to be much more substantial.

There are four generic ways to add value through physical evidence (Figure 16.8):

1 Create physical evidence that increases loyalty.
2 Use physical evidence to enhance brand image.
3 Use physical evidence that has an intrinsic value of its own, e.g. a free gift.
4 Create physical evidence that leads to further sales.

Airlines use their frequent-flyer programmes to increase loyalty; the physical evidence of the flights taken is the regular newsletter that is sent out, and the plastic card the frequent flyer uses to gain access to the executive lounges at airports en route. Some airlines (KLM, for example) also issue special plastic baggage tags which let the baggage handlers know that they are dealing with a very important suitcase: what effect this has on the baggage handlers is debatable, but the effect on the customer is a feeling of importance. At each level of membership of KLM's frequent-flyer programme (Blue Wing, Silver Wing and Gold Wing) the colour of the card changes, as do the benefits to which the holder is entitled. These physical elements of the service are intended to encourage the customer to fly more often with KLM: failure to fly a set number of times a year with the airline will result in a downgrade

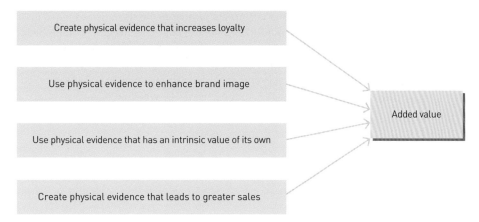

Figure 16.8 Adding value through physical evidence

to a lower level. An intangible benefit of membership for the customer is the occasional free flight – membership points can be exchanged for free flights at a set rate per distance travelled, or for upgrades into business class.

Brand image can be enhanced by using physical evidence that fits in with the brand's essential qualities. For example, an insurance company that wishes to convey a solid, respectable image will produce a glossy policy document full of high-flown legal phrases and reassuring photographs of solid corporate headquarters. A company aiming to convey a more down-to-earth, welcoming image might produce a policy couched in simple language, with photographs of smiling staff and policyholders. Physical evidence need not always be up-market: most low-cost airlines emphasise the cost-cutting aspects of their business by requiring passengers to print off their own tickets on their computers, or by having no tickets at all. This is about as basic as physical evidence can get, but it does emphasise the point that the airline does not waste passengers' money on anything that is not absolutely necessary.

Physical evidence that has an intrinsic value of its own would include free gifts: this is a common ploy in the financial services industry. Clocks, pen sets, DVD players, radio alarm clocks and so forth are often given out to people who take out insurance policies or pension plans. Clearly very few people would take out an insurance policy simply to win a carriage clock, but the existence of the clock on the policyholder's mantelpiece is good evidence of the existence of the policy.

Physical evidence that leads to further business might include reminder cards sent out by garages to let drivers know that their cars are due for a service. Dentists, opticians, hairdressers and some hospitals use reminders like this to tell people they need check-ups: the physical evidence of the previous visit serves to generate more business. Some business gifts fulfil a similar function: a desk calendar, notepad or pen given away at the conclusion of a sale may serve as a reminder when a future need arises.

Summary

The marketing mix offers us a useful 'shorthand' tool for analysing the activities of marketers. Every activity carried out by marketers can only be carried out in cooperation with consumers and customers – customers can end the relationship simply by choosing to spend their money elsewhere, a point that sometimes eludes marketers.

The interplay between marketers and customers is what generates business, and (in the last hundred years or so) has generated the highest standard of living in human history. People's daily needs, from food and shelter through to entertainment and education, are met by marketers eager to please and prepared to go to considerable lengths in serving customers. All the efforts of marketers, and consequently every aspect of the marketing mix, is designed to meet customer needs more effectively, whether those needs are for better information or for better products or even for more convenient delivery.

Key points

- The hedonic aspects of products are often more important than the practical, utilitarian aspects.
- Price has more components than the simple purchase cost.
- Pricing should always take account of what people are prepared to pay.
- Place provides many of the benefits of buying the product; shopping should be a pleasurable experience.
- Advertising is probably only a weak force, nudging people rather than persuading.
- Interaction with advertisements always increases effectiveness, even if the advertisement is 'zapped'.
- Radio is a powerful medium because it is intimate.
- Cinema advertising appeals mainly to younger audiences.
- Ambient advertising works best when it is close to the point of purchase.
- Ambient advertising is particularly good for 'nudging' consumers when they are close to the point of purchase.
- Consumers often use social interactions as a surrogate for judging quality in service situations.
- Service levels should be correct for the target market, not necessarily maximal.
- Physical evidence is often used as a surrogate for judging quality of services.

Review questions

1   Why is cost-plus pricing dangerous?
2   Why is shopping pleasurable?
3   Why might someone ignore an advertisement, even though it is about a product of interest?
4   Why might advertisements that are 'zapped' be more effective than ones that are not?
5   What are the main advantages of radio as an advertising medium?
6   Why do ambient advertisements work well when they are close to the point of purchase?
7   What are the advantages of cinema advertising?
8   How might someone judge the quality of a restaurant they have not visited before?
9   How should service level be decided?
10   What is the difference between skimming and demand pricing?

Case study revisited: Lucozade

In order to reposition the product, Glaxosmithkline needed to carry out a very comprehensive advertising campaign. Lucozade was **iconic** as a drink for sick people; they needed to find something equally iconic with which to replace it.

Ad agency Ogilvy and Mather were brought in to carry out the rebranding. They replaced the original strapline 'Lucozade aids recovery' with the new strapline 'Lucozade replaces lost energy'. At this time there were no other energy drinks on the market, so the field was wide open. Ogilvy and Mather recruited Olympic decathlete Daley Thompson to front the campaign. Thompson was, at the time, a national hero. He had won gold at the 1980 Olympics and would go on to win again in 1984: he is regarded as one of the greatest decathletes of all time, if not the greatest. A natural showman, he was known for being irreverent and for doing things differently from other athletes – so he was a perfect endorsement for Lucozade, since he was clearly far from sick yet he was using the drink to replace lost energy. He also came across well as the sort of man one would enjoy spending an evening at the pub with – he never lost the common touch, despite being awarded an MBE and being a world-class athlete.

The campaign was extremely effective – sales went from around £25 million per annum to over £80 million per annum in only five years. Later, Lucozade used the straplines 'Energising Britain' and 'Get Your Edge Back'. In 2009, the company launched the strapline 'Do More', which has the advantage of being both simple and somewhat vague.

So successful has been the repositioning that most people scarcely remember the original purpose of Lucozade. Sales are now hovering around the £80m mark, having slipped a little during the economic crisis, but Glaxosmithkline have launched some new flavours, and are expecting that the legacy of renewed interest in sport accruing from the London 2012 Olympics will boost sales in the future.

Icon A sign that stands for an object

Case study: Putting on make-up

For most women, putting on make-up is a necessary chore – for many it's a daily one. Converting one's own face into a work of art is a skill little girls aim to acquire from a very early age – but by teenage years it becomes a skill to be agonised over, worked at and prized above many others. It isn't something that is taught in schools (except possibly in expensive finishing schools or drama schools): it is often learned by trial and (painful) error, and it is a skill that requires a lot of advice and assistance from friends.

However, help is at hand. One of the great success stories of YouTube has been the proliferation of on-line make-up tutorials. The professional make-up artist who goes by the on-line alias of makeupbyeman has made

some 170 videos of herself putting on make-up. The results are, needless to say, stunning but more to the point this has become a serious money-making venture. YouTube has a system for kicking back some revenue to their big hitters, and makeupbyeman is currently in line to receive almost $50,000 in royalties for her home-made videos. Not Hollywood, but nice spare-time cash, and of course it hasn't done her main business any harm either – she claims that at least one couple arranged their wedding day around her availability. Eman (her real name) herself is only just past her 30th birthday and lives in Vancouver; her business is thriving, and she has become a wealthy young woman simply through having a passion for make-up.

Of course, Eman is a small-time player compared with the big make-up houses. L'Oréal also has a YouTube presence, offering make-up tutorials that promote their own range of cosmetics. Given that making up is a difficult skill to acquire, it is clearly in the company's interests to ensure that customers get it right when they use L'Oréal products. However, the difference between L'Oréal and Eman is that L'Oréal has the resources of a very large company to put behind the production of their YouTube presence. Their videos are professionally shot, with some of L'Oréal's professional make-up artists applying the cosmetics to models. Attached to the site are links to glamorous events showcasing L'Oréal hair and beauty products, and special 'behind the scenes' shots of Cheryl Cole.

Other cosmetics firms with a YouTube presence include Max Factor and Rimmel. There are, of course, many other one-woman tutorial sites: pixiwoo, sojeanbrodie, CrystallyZed and many others, some of whom are themselves sponsored by make-up manufacturers.

The question is, of course, whether the one-woman shows, with someone (often an amateur) putting make-up on her own face and explaining each stage as she does it, are more effective than the glossy, professional shows where someone is made up by someone else in a slick beauty salon situation. Perhaps each video appeals to a different audience – after all, each woman has her own face, skin, eyes and colouring to contend with when choosing and applying make-up, so it seems likely that different models and different make-up artists will appeal to different women.

Whatever the verdict, women will continue to seek help and advice in putting on cosmetics. Creating a work of art takes time, skill, advice – and a little help from your friends.

Questions

1   Why might someone prefer to watch a woman who is not a make-up professional putting on her make-up and explaining what she's doing, rather than a trained make-up artist working on a model or film star?
2   Why is make-up important?
3   How might a cosmetics company improve the hit rate on a YouTube entry?
4   Why should a major company like L'Oréal invest so much in creating slick videos?
5   What type of influence is being exerted on the YouTube visitors?

Further Reading

There are very few academic texts on pricing, but it is a hot topic for practitioners. For a breezy (and very American) book on practical pricing, try *No B.S. Pricing Strategy – The Ultimate No-Holds-Barred, Kick Butt, Take No Prisoners Approach to Profits, Power and Prosperity* by Dan S. Kennedy and Jason Marrs (New York: Entrepreneur Press, 2011). It might give you something to think about.

For a look at what happens when consumers decide to act for themselves, try Moraes, C., Szmigin, I. and Carrigan, M. (2010) Living production-engaged alternatives: an examination of new consumption communities. *Consumption, Markets and Culture* 13 (3): 273–98. This paper looks at how consumption communities question the current paradigm based on one group of people who produce, versus another group of people who consume.

Another paper that looks at consumer self-empowerment is McCeachern, M., Warnaby, G., Carrigan, M. and Szmigin, I. (2010) Thinking locally, acting locally? Conscious consumers and farmers' markets. *Journal of Marketing Management* 26 (5): 395–412. The authors examine what happens when consumers decide to avoid the big supermarkets and agri-businesses and buy local produce from local producers. It's not quite anti-marketing – but it does show that consumers are not as biddable as some marketers would like to think.

If you want to know more about what motivates people to shop, you might like *The Art of Shopping: How We Shop and Why We Buy* by Seimon Scammel-Katz (London: LID Publishing, 2012). The author aims the book at retailers, explaining what they can do to make shopping easier, more pleasant and more frequent, using insights gained from many years as a consultant.

For a riveting read from a true hero of advertising, try *Ogilvy on Advertising* by David Ogilvy, founder of Ogilvy and Mather (London: Prion Books, 2007). Ogilvy was a real maverick, given to pungent quotes such as, 'The consumer isn't an idiot. She's your wife.' One of the greats of marketing.

References

Addis, M. and Holbrook, M.B. (2001) On the conceptual link between mass customisation and experiential consumption: an explosion of subjectivity. *Journal of Consumer Behaviour* 1 (1): 50–6.

Bakamitsos, G. and Siomkos, G.J. (2003) Context effects in marketing practice: the case of mood. *Journal of Consumer Behaviour* 3 (4): 304–14.

Bardacki, A. and Whitelock, J. (2004) How ready are customers for mass customization? An exploratory investigation. *European Journal of Marketing* 38 (11/12): 1396–496.

Barnard, N. and Ehrenberg, A. (1997) Advertising: strongly persuasive or nudging? *Journal of Advertising Research* 37 (1): 21–31.

Becker-Olsen, K. and Cudmore, B.A. (2004) When good deeds dilute your equity. *Advances in Consumer Research* 31: 78–9.

Bengtsson, A. (2003) Towards a critique of brand relationships. *Advances in Consumer Research* 30: 154–8.

British Film Institute (BFI) (2012) *Statistical Yearbook*. London: British Film Insititute.

Biel, A.L. (1990) Love the ad. Buy the product? *ADMAP* September 299: 21–5.

Biel, A.L. and Bridgwater, C.A. (1990) Attributes of likeable television commercials. *Journal of Advertising Research* 30 (3): 38–44.

Blythe, J. (2003) *Essentials of Marketing Communications*, 2nd edn. Hemel Hempstead: FT Prentice–Hall.

Bolls, P.D., Muehling, D.D. and Yoon, K. (2003) The effects of television commercial pacing on viewers' attention and memory. *Journal of Marketing Communications* 9 (1): 17–28.

Booms, B.H. and Bitner, M.J. (1981) Marketing strategies and organisational structures for service firms. In J.H. Donnelly and W.R. George (eds), *Marketing of Services*. Chicago, IL: American Marketing Association. pp. 47–52.

Bray, J.P. and Harris, C. (2006) The effect of 9-ending prices on retail sales: a quantitative UK based field study. *Journal of Marketing Management* 22 (5/6): 601–17.

Brunk, K. (2010) Reputation building: beyond our control? Inferences in consumers' ethical perception forming. *Journal of Consumer Behaviour* 9 (4): 275–92.

Cinema Advertising Association (1997) UK Cinema Audience Profile. London: Cinema Advertising Association.

Dalli, D., Romani, S. and Gistri, G. (2006) Brand dislike: representing the negative side of consumer preferences. *Advances in Consumer Research* 33: 87–95.

Dolan, R.J. (1995) How do you know when the price is right. *Harvard Business Review* 73 (5): 174–83.

Ehrenberg, A. (1997) How do consumers buy a new brand? *ADMAP* March.

Ehrenberg, A.S.C. (1992) Comments on how advertising works. *Marketing and Research Today* August: 167–9.

Englis, B.G. and Bamossy, G. (2010) Green dilemma: libertarian values trump communal values. *Advances in Consumer Research* 37: 32, 33.

Evans, M., O'Malley, L. and Patterson, M. (1996) Direct marketing communications in the UK: a study of growth, past, present and future. *Journal of Marketing Communications* 2 (March): 51–65.

Foxall, G. and Goldsmith, R.E. (1994) *Consumer Psychology for Marketing*. London: Routledge.

Gourville, J. and Koehler, J. (2003) Downsizing price increases: a differential sensitivity to price over quantity. *Advances in Consumer Research* 30: 106–8.

Grapentine, T. (2003) Window shopping. *Marketing Research* 15 (4): 5.

Gueguen, N. and Legoherel, P. (2004) Numerical encoding and odd-ending prices: the effect of a contrast in discount perception. *European Journal of Marketing* 38 (1): 194–208.

Heath, T., McCarthy, M.S. and Chatterjee, S. (2006) The effect of line extensions up and down in quality on initial choice and subsequent switching tendencies. *Advances in Consumer Research* 33: 75.

Henry, P.C. and Caldwell, M.L. (2006) Self-empowerment and consumption: customer remedies for prolonged stigmatisation. *European Journal of Marketing* 40 (9/10): 1031–48.

Honkanen, P., Olsen, S.O. and Myrland, O. (2004) Preference-based segmentation: a study of meal preferences among Norwegian teenagers. *Journal of Consumer Behaviour* 3 (3): 235–50.

Jones, J.P. (1991) Over-promise and under-delivery. *Marketing and Research Today* November: 195–203.

Judd, V.C. (1987) Differentiate with the fifth P. *Industrial Marketing Management* 16: 241–7.

Krishna, A., Wagner, M. and Yoon, C. (2002) Effects of extreme-priced products on consumer reservation prices. *Advances in Consumer Research* 29: 88.

Laforet, S. (2011) Brand names on packaging and their impact on purchase performance. *Journal of Consumer Behaviour* 10 (1): 18–30.

LeClerc, F., Hsee, C.K. and Nunnes, J.C. (2002) Best of the worst or worst of the best? *Advances in Consumer Research* 29: 59.

Mathur, A., Moschis, G.P. and Lee, E. (2003) Life events and brand preference changes. *Journal of Consumer Behaviour* 3 (2): 129–41.

Maxham III, J.G. and Netemeyer, R.G. (2003) Firms reap what they sow: the effect of shared values and perceived organisational justice on customers' evaluation of complaint handling. *Journal of Marketing* 67 (1): 46–62.

McKechnie, S. and Leather, P. (1998) Likeability as a measure of advertising effectiveness: the case of financial services. *Journal of Marketing Communications* 4: 63–85.

Molz, G. and Gielnik, M. (2006) Does the introduction of the Euro have an effect on subjective hypotheses about the price–quality relationship? *Journal of Consumer Behaviour* 5 (May–Jun): 204–10.

Pennanen, K. (2011) Is interpersonal and institutional e-trustworthiness equally important in consumer e-trust development? Implications for consumers' e-trust building behaviours. *Journal of Consumer Behaviour* 10 (5): 233–44.

Pires, G.D., Stanton, J. and Rita, P. (2006) The Internet, consumers' empowerment, and marketing strategies. *European Journal of Marketing* 40 (9/10): 1013–30.

POPAI (1994) Point of purchase consumer buying habits study. In T.A. Shimp, *Advertising, Promotion and Supplemental Aspects of Integrated Marketing Communications*, 4th edn. Fort Worth, TX: Dryden Press.

Rajagopal, P. (2008) Point-of-sales promotions and buying simulation in retail stores. *Journal of Database Marketing and Customer Strategy Management* 15 (4): 249–66.

Rasmusson, E. (1997) Winning back angry customers. *Sales and Marketing Management* October: 131.

Ritson, M. (2003) *Assessing the Value of Advertising.* London: London Business School.

Roggeveen, A.L., Lan, X. and Monroe, K.B. (2006) How attributions and the product's price impact the effectiveness of price partitioning. *Advances in Consumer Research* 33: 181.

Rose, P., Smith, S.T. and Segrist, D.J. (2010) Too cheap to chug: frugality as a buffer against college-age drinking. *Journal of Consumer Behaviour* 9 (3): 228–38.

Sampson, P. (1992) People are people the world over: the case for psychological market segmentation. *Marketing and Research Today* Nov: 236–45.

Schindler, R.M. and Kirby, P.N. (1997) Patterns of right-most digits used in advertised prices: implications for nine-ending effects. *Journal of Consumer Research* September: 192–201.

Seigyoung, A. and Chuang-Foh, S. (2006) Balancing giving-up vs. taking-in: does the pattern or payments and benefits matter to customers in a financing decision context? *Advances in Consumer Research* 33: 139–45.

Shankar, A. (1999a) Ambient media: advertising's new opportunity? *International Journal of Advertising* 18 (3): 305–22.

Shankar, A. (1999b) Advertising's imbroglio. *Journal of Marketing Communications* 5 (1): 1–17.

Shen, A. and Ball, A.D. (2011) Preference stability belief as a determinant of response to personalised recommendations. *Journal of Consumer Behaviour* 10 (2): 71–9.

Simmons, C.L. and Schindler, R.M. (2003) Cultural superstitions and the price endings used in Chinese advertising. *Journal of International Marketing* 11 (2): 101–11.

Spilker-Attig, A. and Brettel, M. (2010) Effectiveness of on-line advertising channels: a price-level-dependent analysis. *Journal of Marketing Management* 26 (3&4): 343–60.

Stapel, J. (1991) Like the advertisement, but does it interest me? *ADMAP* April.

Steenhuysen, J. (1994) Adland's new billion-dollar baby. *Advertising Age* 11 April.

Stoll, M., Baecke, S. and Kenning, P. (2008) What they see is what they get? An fMRI study on neural correlates of attractive packaging. *Journal of Consumer Behaviour* 7 (4/5): 342–59.

Suri, R., Anderson, R.E. and Kotlov, V. (2004) The use of 9-ending prices: contrasting the USA with Poland. *European Journal of Marketing* 38 (1): 56–72.

Trocchia, P.J., Beatty, S.E. and Hill, W.H. (2006) A typology of motor vehicle consumers using motives for leasing versus financing. *Journal of Consumer Behaviour* 5 (Jul–Aug): 304–16.

Umphress, E.E., Bingham, J.B. and Mitchell, M.S. (2010) Unethical behaviour in the name of the company: the moderating effect of organisational identification and positive reciprocity beliefs on unethical pro-organisational behaviour. *Journal of Applied Psychology* 95 (4): 769–80.

Unnava, H.R., Rajagopal, P. and Raju, S. (2003) Reducing competitive ad interference by varying advertising context: a test of network models of memory. *Advances in Consumer Research* 30: 45–6.

Wells, W.D. (1980) Liking and sales effectiveness: a hypothesis. *Topline* 2 (1).

Wright, L.T. and Crimp, M. (2000) *The Marketing Research Process.* London: Prentice-Hall.

Yannopolou, N., Koronis, E. and Elliott, R. (2011) Media amplification of a brand crisis and its effect on brand trust. *Journal of Marketing Management* 27 (5&6): 530–46.

Zufryden, F.S., Pedrick, J.H. and Sankaralingam, A. (1993) Zapping and its impact on brand purchase behaviour. *Journal of Advertising Research* 33 (Jan/Feb): 58–66.

Interference **Intelligent messages that disrupt communication**

More online

To gain free access to additional online resources to support this chapter please visit: **www.sagepub.co.uk/blythe**

Glossary

Abstraction	The process whereby lower-level goals help to determine what the higher-level goals must be if there is to be overall goal consistency.
Accommodation to the new attitude	Accepting new information and using it to re-form an existing attitude.
Acculturation	The process of adopting a new culture.
ACORN	A Classification of Residential Neighbourhoods.
Actual state	The condition in which the person happens to be at a given time.
Adaptation	The process by which goals are influenced by contextual issues.
Adoption	The process of building an innovating product into one's daily life.
Affect	The emotional element of attitude.
Affective state	The physical or psychological condition of an individual which may lead to an interruption in planned behaviour.
Ambient advertising	Commercial messages that are designed to become part of the environment.
Aspirational group	A group of individuals which one wishes to join
Assortment adjustment	The process of substituting some possessions for others in order to improve one's overall position.
Assortment depletion	The reduction in one's overall quantity of possessions.
Assortment extension	Increasing one's overall quantity of possessions.
Assortment replenishment	Replacing possessions that have been worn out or used up.
Atmospherics	The factors that create the overall ambience in a retail environment.
Attitude splitting	The process of protecting an attitude by accepting only part of a new piece of information that conflicts with the attitude.
Attitudes	A propensity to respond in a consistent manner to a given stimulus of object.
Automatic group	A group of people to which an individual belongs by reason of race, gender or other non-changeable factor.
Autonomic decision-making	A type of decision that is made by the individual without recourse to others.
B2B	Business to business.
B2C	Business to consumer.
Baby Boomer	An individual born between 1945 and 1965, a period of exceptionally high birth rates in Europe and the United States.
Backward conditioning	A situation in which the unconditioned stimulus is presented before the conditioned stimulus.
Behavioural segmentation	Dividing up a potential market according to the behaviour of its members.
Benchmarking	Measuring the firm's performance against that of other firms across a wide range of factors.
Bias	The factor which affects the processing of information as a result of the pre-existing mindset.
Birth rate	The number of babies born per annum, expressed as the number of live births per thousand women.
Buyers	Those with the responsibility of making the actual purchase of a product, often (in the industrial context) working to a specific brief.
Buying centre	See *Decision-making unit*.
Categorisation	The pigeonholing of information in order to prejudge events and products.
Category group	See *Automatic group*.
Cautionary-tale	A story intended to illustrate the possible negative outcomes of a particular course of action.

Central route	A route to attitude change which relies on reasoned argument: an appeal to cognition, in other words.
Chunking	The learning process by which items of information are grouped by the brain.
Class	The social and economic grouping of individuals.
Classical conditioning	The learning process characterised by repeating a stimulus at about the same time as a given behaviour occurs, with the aim of creating a permanent association between the stimulus and the behaviour.
Clutter	Excessive information, especially applied to advertising: a situation in which the recipient is presented with a large number of stimuli at the same time.
Cognition	Thought processes: the element of attitude derived from conscious thought or knowledge.
Cognitive dissonance	The tension caused by holding two conflicting pieces of information at once.
Cognitive effort	The amount of work needed to consider a course of action or understand a set of issues.
Cognitive innovators	Those who seek new intellectual experiences.
Cognitive learning	Acquiring and retaining new information through a conscious effort or thought.
Cognitive structure	The way the individual thinks, and the way new information is fitted into existing knowledge.
Compatibility	The degree to which a new product matches the individual's existing lifestyle, attitudes and possessions.
Complexity	The degree to which a new product requires extensive learning before it can be used effectively.
Conation	The behavioural intentions that arise from attitudes.
Conditioned response	The behaviour that results from classical conditioning.
Conformity	The social pressure to behave in similar ways to other people.
Conjunctive rule	A heuristic by which brands are compared to all cut-offs until only a few surviving brands remain.
Consideration set	The group of brands which a consumer believes will meet his or her need, and which are therefore seriously being considered for purchase.
Consumer	Someone who enjoys the benefit of a product.
Consumer behaviour	Activities undertaken by people in the process of obtaining, using and disposing of goods and services for personal use.
Contactors	People within an organisation who have daily interaction with customers.
Continuous innovation	A new product that follows closely on from a previous product and has a clear relationship to the previous product.
Cue	An external trigger that encourages learning.
Cultural anchoring	The process by which an innovation becomes part of everyday life.
Culture	The set of beliefs, behaviour, customs and attitudes that are common to a large group of people.
Culture shock	The discomfort that arises from being displaced from one's normal cultural milieu.
Customary pricing	Retaining the same price for a product over a long period, perhaps by adjusting the quantity provided as a way of maintaining profitability.
Customer	Someone who makes the decision to buy a product.
Customisation	Redesigning a product to make it fit a customer's needs more exactly.
Deciders	Members of a decision-making unit who have responsibility for making a final purchase decision.
Decision-making unit	A group of people who influence, control or carry out purchasing activities.
Demand pricing	Calculating the price of a product according to consumer demand at different price levels.
Democratic decision-making	See *Syncratic decision-making*.
Demographic segmentation	Dividing up a market according to people's age, income and social standing
Demographic fracture	The disparity between old and new socio-economic structures encountered when moving from one culture to another.
Depth (guided) interview	Open-ended interviews conducted with a small sample of respondents in order to assess their innermost thoughts and feelings.
Desired state	The condition in which the individual would like to be.
Differentiation	Providing a product with features that distinguish it from competing products.

Diffusion	The process of adoption of an innovation throughout the market.
Discontinuous innovation	Developing a new product that relates only distantly, or does not relate at all, to previous products.
Discrimination	The process by which people distinguish between stimuli.
Disinhibition	Removal of the internal inhibitors which constrain behaviour.
Disposal	Divestment of a product when it is worn out or used up.
Disposers	Those who are responsible for divestment of used-up products.
Dissociative group	A social group to which one does not wish to belong.
Dissonance	A mental state that arises when outcomes do not match with expectations.
Drive	The basic force of motivation, which arises when the individual's actual state diverges from the desired state.
Dynamically continuous innovation	The development of a new product that differs radically from its predecessors while still retaining some commonality.
Early adopters	Those who, although not the first to buy a new product, do so very shortly after its introduction.
Early majority	Those who adopt a new product after it has been on the market for a while, but before most people have adopted it.
Economic choice	The choice made when one is unable to afford to buy both alternatives.
Economics	The study of demand.
Ego	The conscious self.
Ego-defensive function	The function of attitude which enables the individual to maintain stability of the conscious self.
Elaboration	The structuring of information within the brain, relating it to existing memory.
Elasticity	The degree to which demand is affected by other factors, for example price changes.
Emotional fracture	The sense of loss of emotional support encountered when moving from one culture to another.
End user	The person or organisation that finally obtains the benefits of the product.
EPOS	Electronic Point of Sale.
Equitable performance	The level of product quality that the consumer would expect, given the price paid and the other circumstances of purchase and use.
Ethnicity	The cultural background of the individual.
Ethnocentrism	The belief that one's own culture is 'correct' and other cultures are derived from it.
Evoked set	The group of brands a consumer can remember spontaneously.
Expectation	The existing information and attitudes that caused people to interpret later information in a specific way.
Expected performance	The level of product quality that the individual anticipates.
Experiment	A controlled activity in which a given stimulus is offered to respondents in order to discover their reactions.
Extinction	The process of forgetting a conditioned reflex.
Extrovert	Someone who demonstrates his or her personality traits in a strongly overt or obvious manner to other people.
Family	A group of people who exhibit shared consumption and who are bound by ties of genetic relationship or adoption.
Fertility rate	The number of children born per thousand women of childbearing age.
Focus groups	A group of people assembled for the purpose of gathering their collective views about a given issue.
Formal group	A group of people with a known, recorded membership and a set of (usually written) rules of membership.
Forward conditioning	A circumstance where the conditioned stimulus comes before the unconditioned stimulus.
Functional fracture	The disparity between old and new systems for daily living encountered when moving from one culture to another.
Gatekeepers	People who control the flow of information to a decision-making unit.
Generalisation	The tendency for a conditioned stimulus to lead to a wider than intended set of conditioned reflexes.
Geographic segmentation	Dividing a market into smaller groups based on location.
Goals	Specific targets towards which consumption behaviour is directed.

Halo effect	The tendency for an individual to believe every aspect of something if good, based on a belief that some aspects are good.
Hedonism	The cult of pleasure.
Heuristic	A decision-making rule.
Homophilous influences	Transmission of ideas between people of similar standing in the community.
Husband-dominant decision-making	A situation in which the male of the household has the most power in consumption decisions.
Hygiene factors	Those aspects of a product which consumers would expect as a basic feature of any product in the category.
Icon	A sign that stands for an object.
Id	The unconscious part of the mind responsible for basic desires.
Ideal performance	The best possible outcome of buying a given product.
Incentives	Reasons for action.
Index	A sign that related to an object by causal connection.
Indifference curve	The graph that shows the points at which one product will be regarded as a suitable substitute for another.
Inertia	Making decisions out of habit rather than from any conscious loyalty.
Inference	Extra detail added to a message by a recipient, based on meta-analysis of the message.
Influencers	People who exert an advisory role to members of a decision-making unit.
Influencers (2)	People who affect the customer experience, but do not have direct contact with customers.
Influentials	People who are respected for their opinions and lifestyles, and who therefore inform purchase behaviour.
Infomercial	A (typically) half-hour television programme about a specific product.
Informal group	A group of people that has no recorded membership and no written rules.
Information-seekers	People who enjoy finding out about products.
Initiators	The members of a decision-making unit who first identify a need.
Innovation	A new product or service; the act of adopting a new product or service.
Innovativeness	The degree to which an individual or firm creates or adopts new products.
Innovators	People who are the first to try a new product.
Instrumental function	The aspect of attitude that enables the individual to obtain the best use from a product.
Interference	Intelligent messages that disrupt communication.
Interrupt	Something that diverts an individual away from a goal, usually temporarily.
Intrinsic self-relevance	Sources of involvement derived from means–end knowledge stored in the individual's memory.
Introvert	Someone who is withdrawn from other people.
Invention	A new product, usually developed by an individual.
Involvement	The degree to which an individual is attracted to, and defined by, a product or brand.
Isolateds	Employees who have little or no contact with customers.
Key-account manager	A salesperson who has the responsibility of dealing with the most important customers of a firm.
Kinesics	The interpretation of non-verbal communications related to body movement.
Laggards	People who are the last to adopt a new product.
Late majority	People who only adopt a new product after most people have already done so.
Lateral recycling	Donating goods to others, selling them on, or otherwise transferring ownership to someone who will obtain further use from the goods.
Law of primacy	First experiences affect the interpretation of later experiences.
Learning	Changes in behaviour that come about through experience.
Least dependent person	The individual within a buying group who has the highest degree of autonomy.
Loyalty	The degree to which an individual will repeat purchase of a product.
Macro-environment	Those environmental elements that are common to all firms in a given industry.
Maintainers	A family member who has the task of ensuring that a shared product is in good condition for the other members to use.
Market maven	Someone who is a self-appointed expert about a particular product category or market.

Marketing mix	The combination of activities which creates an overall approach to the market.
Mass market	A situation in which a standardised product is purchased by a very large number of people.
Message intrigue	The element of a message which revolves around the interest of a recipient.
Micro-environment	Those elements of the environment that affect the individual firm.
Micro marketing	Those elements of the environment that affect the individual firm.
Modelling	The act of demonstrating by example behaviour that which the marketer would like the target audience to imitate.
Modified re-buy	A purchase that, although similar to previous purchases, has been changed in a minor way.
Modifiers	People who deal with customers regularly, but who have no specific marketing role.
Mores	Elements of a culture.
Motivation	The internal force which encourages people to act in a specific way.
MRO	A company that carries out maintenance, repair and overhaul.
Need	A perceived lack of something.
Negative disconfirmation	A state of affairs in which the expected outcome is disappointing or fails in some way to satisfy.
New task	A type of purchase for which previous experience does not exist.
Niche marketing	Targeting a small group of customers.
Non-compensatory decision rule	A heuristic that cannot be offset by other factors.
Normative compliance	The force that compels people towards agreeing with the rest of the group.
Novices	Customers who have purchased the product for the first time within the last 90 days.
Observability	The degree to which the purchase of a new product can be seen by others.
Odd–even pricing	The practice of ending prices with '99p' or '99c'.
OEM	Original-equipment manufacturer.
Operant conditioning	The learning process in which the learner is rewarded for a correct action, and in which the learner plays an active role.
Optimum stimulation level (OSL)	The point at which a need has become strong, but before it has become unpleasantly so.
Packrats	Individuals who tend to keep their possessions for a long time.
Paralanguage	Communication carried out in a manner other than through words.
Peer group	Those people who are near to being one's equals.
People	The element of the marketing mix concerned with employees and other consumers.
Perceived instrumentality	The degree to which an action or product is thought to be useful in a practical way.
Perception	The process of creating a mental 'map' of reality.
Peripheral route	Using emotional appeals in order to change the affective component of attitude.
Personal sources	Sources of involvement derived from means–end knowledge stored in the individual's memory.
Personality	Those factors which make up the individual's mental processes.
Pester power	The ability of children to influence their parents by means of repetitive requests.
Physical evidence	The element of the marketing mix concerned with the tangible aspects of the products or services.
Place	The element of the marketing mix concerned with the location where the exchange takes place.
Positioning	The act of placing a brand in the appropriate place in the consumer's mind relative to competing products.
Positive disconfirmation	An unexpectedly good outcome of a purchase.
Preparers	A family member responsible for transforming a product into a condition suitable for other members to use it.
Price	That which is given in exchange for receiving the benefits of a product.
Price conditioning	Managing the expectations of a potential customer regarding price.
Primary group	The group of people we see daily, and to whom we feel closest.
Private response	Complaining behaviour directed at friends or acquaintances rather than at the perpetrator of the problem.
Process	The element of the marketing mix concerned with the overall delivery of a service.
Product	A bundle of benefits.

Product-line pricing	Pricing that takes account of the price of related products.
Projective test	A research technique whereby respondents are asked to give an opinion of what they think someone else's attitude or feelings might be on a given topic.
Promotion	The element of the marketing mix concerned with communication.
Proxemics	The use of physical space to convey a perceptual stimulus.
Psychographic segmentation	Dividing a market according to the psychological profiles of potential customers.
Psychographics	Using behavioural tendencies to infer personality traits.
Psychological pricing	Applying prices to goods based on perceptual issues such as quality.
Psychology	The science of the mind.
Psychology of complication	The tendency for people to make their lives more complex, and therefore more interesting.
Psychology of simplification	The tendency for people to make their lives less complex and therefore less stressful.
Purchasing agent	Someone who has the task of making purchases on behalf of a group, usually the family.
Purgers	People who regularly discard their possessions.
Reference group	A group of people who act as the yardstick for our behaviour.
Reinforcement	The process of consolidating classical conditioning.
Relationship marketing	Marketing in such a way as to generate a long-term partnership with customers.
Relative advantage	The degree to which a new product is superior to the one it replaces.
Response	The reaction the consumer makes to the interaction between a drive and a cause.
Retention	The stability of learner material over time.
Rite of passage	An event or action which marks a change in an individual's life circumstances.
Role	The place one has within a group.
Role model	An individual who acts as a reference point for judging one's own behaviour.
Routine brand buyers	People who normally buy the same brand every time.
Salient belief	A belief which is key in the formation of an attitude.
Schadenfreude	Pleasure felt at the downfall of another.
Secondary group	A group of people whom we do not necessarily see every day, and who are not our closest friends, but to which we belong nonetheless.
Second-market discounting	Charging a lower price for one group of people in order to even out demand.
Segmentation	The act of dividing up a market into groups of people with similar needs.
Selectivity	The part of perception that deals with rejecting unnecessary stimuli.
Self-actualisation	The need to become the ideal self.
Self-concept	The belief one has about oneself.
Self-enhancement	The practice of airing one's superior knowledge in order to create a better image.
Self-image	The image of oneself that one wishes to present to the world.
Self-monitoring	The regulatory mechanism which controls behaviour, without outside intercession.
Sensory innovators	Those who seek new sensory experiences.
Service-dominant logic	The view that all value is co-created by the consumer and the supplier, and thus that all value can be considered as a service.
Service level	The target a firm sets for providing customer satisfaction through intangible benefits.
Shadow websites	Websites that offer an opportunity to post negative stories about specific companies or brands.
Simultaneous conditioning	In classical conditioning, a state of affairs whereby the conditioned stimulus and the unconditioned stimulus are presented at the same time.
Skimming	Setting prices high when a product is launched, then gradually lowering them as competitors enter the market.
Socialisation	The process of becoming an effective and integrated member of society.
Socio-economic variables	Those factors that derive from an individual's class and income.
Sociology	The study of human behaviour in groups.
Stimulus rejection	The process of protecting an attitude by ignoring information that conflicts with it.
Straight rebuy	A situation in which a previous order is simply repeated in its entirety.
Subculture	A set of beliefs and attitudes which, while part of a main culture, represents a distinctly separate set.
Sub-goal	A target that forms part of a greater aim, and needs to be achieved before the main goal can be achieved.

Subjectivity	Judging everything from a personal viewpoint.
Subliminal perception	Perception that occurs below the conscious level.
Superego	The component of mind that acts as a restraint on behaviour.
Symbol	A method of converting thought into something that can be transmitted as a message.
Symbolic fracture	The disparity between old and new communication paradigms encountered when moving from one culture to another.
Syncratic (democratic) decision-making	In group decision-making, the type of decision that is made on the basis of consultation.
Synthetic	That which is constructed from disparate components. In perception, an overall view derived from grouping together a set of stimuli.
Technophiles	People who like new technology for its own sake.
Technophobes	People who are fearful of new technology.
Third-party response	In complaining, the act of involving someone other than the complainer or the supplier, for example a lawyer or consumer rights campaigner.
Trait	A component of personality.
Transactional marketing	Marketing in which the marketer focuses on the individual sale, not on the long-term relationship with the customer.
Trialability	The degree to which a product can be tested before the customer needs to commit to its adoption.
Trickle-down theory	The belief that innovations are adopted by wealthy, educated people first and eventually 'trickle down' to people in lower socio-economic groups.
Unconditioned response	A natural response to stimulus.
Unconditioned stimulus	A stimulus that occurs without the intervention of an experimenter.
Undifferentiated marketing	Offering one type of product to all possible segments.
Unsought communications	Messages that have not been looked for by the recipient.
Unsought goods	Products that are bought as a result of coercion rather than through desire.
Users	Those members of a buying group who will actually make use of a product (not necessarily consumers).
Utilitarianism	The cult of practicality.
Value analysis	The process of calculating the worth of a purchase in terms of the returns made from its use.
Value importance	The level of satisfaction the individual gains from the achievement of a particular value.
Value-expressive function	The factor in group behaviour that allows the members to display their own beliefs and attitudes.
Value-expressive influence	The factor in normative compliance that causes group members to adopt the values of the group.
Virtual group	A social group mediated by the Internet.
Voice response	A type of complaint in which the complainer returns to the supplier to seek redress.
Want	A specific satisfier for a need.
Weber's Law	The size of the least detectable change will depend on the size of the stimulus.
Wife-dominant decision-making	Decisions that are left to the female adult of the family.
Word of mouse	Electronically mediated personal communications about brands and products.
Zapping	Using the TV remote control to avoid advertisements, often by switching to another channel; also called flicking.
Zipping	Using the TV remote control to fast-forward through advertisements on a recorded programme.

Index